Lecture Notes in Computer Science 15577

Founding Editors

Gerhard Goos
Juris Hartmanis

AF068740

Editorial Board Members

Elisa Bertino, *Purdue University, West Lafayette, IN, USA*
Wen Gao, *Peking University, Beijing, China*
Bernhard Steffen, *TU Dortmund University, Dortmund, Germany*
Moti Yung, *Columbia University, New York, NY, USA*

The series Lecture Notes in Computer Science (LNCS), including its subseries Lecture Notes in Artificial Intelligence (LNAI) and Lecture Notes in Bioinformatics (LNBI), has established itself as a medium for the publication of new developments in computer science and information technology research, teaching, and education.

LNCS enjoys close cooperation with the computer science R & D community, the series counts many renowned academics among its volume editors and paper authors, and collaborates with prestigious societies. Its mission is to serve this international community by providing an invaluable service, mainly focused on the publication of conference and workshop proceedings and postproceedings. LNCS commenced publication in 1973.

Ruben Niederhagen · Markku-Juhani O. Saarinen
Editors

Post-Quantum Cryptography

16th International Workshop, PQCrypto 2025
Taipei, Taiwan, April 8–10, 2025
Proceedings, Part I

Springer

Editors
Ruben Niederhagen
Academia Sinica and University of Southern Denmark
Taipei, Taiwan

Markku-Juhani O. Saarinen
Tampere University
Tampere, Finland

ISSN 0302-9743 ISSN 1611-3349 (electronic)
Lecture Notes in Computer Science
ISBN 978-3-031-86598-5 ISBN 978-3-031-86599-2 (eBook)
https://doi.org/10.1007/978-3-031-86599-2

This Springer imprint is published by the registered company Springer Nature Switzerland AG
The registered company address is: Gewerbestrasse 11, 6330 Cham, Switzerland

Preface

PQCrypto 2025, the 16th International Conference on Post-Quantum Cryptography, was held from April 8–10, 2025, at the Institute of Information Science, Academia Sinica, in Taipei, Taiwan. The PQCrypto conference series serves as a platform for sharing research on cryptography designed to withstand the capabilities of large-scale quantum computers. Over the years, PQCrypto has expanded its focus to encompass not only academic and theoretical work but also applied research, emphasizing practical implementation and deployment of post-quantum cryptographic schemes.

For PQCrypto 2025, a single-blind review process was employed, meaning submissions were not anonymized. 59 papers by 197 authors from 24 countries fulfilled the technical criteria and were accepted for peer review. Each submission was rigorously evaluated by at least three members of the program committee. The committee, comprising 59 members and supported by 38 subreviewers, conducted 209 reviews in total. Following an intensive online discussion phase, 25 high-quality papers were selected for inclusion in the conference program and these proceedings.

The accepted papers showcase a diverse range of topics within the field of post-quantum cryptography, including:

- code-based cryptography,
- multivariate cryptography,
- lattice-based cryptography,
- isogeny-based cryptography,
- cryptanalysis,
- quantum security,
- side-channel attacks, and
- security notions.

The success of PQCrypto 2025 would not have been possible without the contributions of many individuals and organizations. We extend our deepest gratitude to the authors, whose submissions reflect exceptional quality, and to the program committee and external reviewers for their dedicated effort in evaluating and discussing the papers. Their commitment was essential to assembling a strong technical program.

Special thanks go to Academia Sinica for providing outstanding facilities and support for the conference. Our General Chairs, Bo-Yin Yang, Matthias Kannwischer, and Kai-Min Chung, played a key role in organizing this event, along with Hsin-Man Lin, Wei-Ching Chien, and the local organizing team at Academia Sinica and Chelpis. Finally, we express our appreciation to Springer for publishing these proceedings.

April 2025

Ruben Niederhagen
Markku-Juhani O. Saarinen

Organization

General Chairs

Kai-Min Chung	Academia Sinica, Taiwan
Matthias Kannwischer	Chelpis Quantum Corp., Taiwan
Bo-Yin Yang	Academia Sinica, Taiwan

Program Committee Chairs

Ruben Niederhagen	Academia Sinica, Taiwan and University of Southern Denmark, Denmark
Markku-Juhani O. Saarinen	Tampere University, Finland

Program Committee

Sarah Arpin	Virginia Polytechnic Institute and State University, USA
Shi Bai	Florida Atlantic University, USA
Gustavo Banegas	Inria and École Polytechnique, France
Magali Bardet	University of Rouen Normandy, France
Hanno Becker	Amazon Web Services, UK
Daniel J. Bernstein	University of Illinois Chicago, USA
Olivier Blazy	École Polytechnique, France
Daniel Cabarcas	Universidad Nacional de Colombia sede Medellín, Colombia
Fabio Campos	Radboud University, the Netherlands, and RheinMain University of Applied Sciences, Germany
Sanjit Chatterjee	Indian Institute of Science, India
Łukasz Chmielewski	Masaryk University, Czech Republic
Alain Couvreur	École Polytechnique, France
Thomas Decru	Katholieke Universiteit Leuven, Belgium
Martin Ekerå	KTH Royal Institute of Technology, Sweden
Andre Esser	Technology Innovation Institute, UAE
Thibauld Feneuil	CryptoExperts, France
Scott Fluhrer	Cisco Systems, USA

Tako Boris Fouotsa	École Polytechnique Fédérale de Lausanne, Switzerland
Philippe Gaborit	University of Limoges, France
Tommaso Gagliardoni	Kudelski Security, Switzerland
Qian Guo	Lund University, Sweden
Mike Hamburg	Rambus, USA
Julius Hermelink	Max Planck Institute for Security and Privacy, Germany
Andreas Hülsing	Eindhoven University of Technology, the Netherlands, and Sandbox AQ, USA
David Jao	University of Waterloo, Canada
Matthias J. Kannwischer	Chelpis Quantum Corp., Taiwan
Elena Kirshanova	Technology Innovation Institute, UAE
Juliane Krämer	University of Regensburg, Germany
Momonari Kudo	Fukuoka Institute of Technology, Japan
Dustin Moody	National Institute of Standards and Technology, USA
Phong Nguyen	Inria and École Normale Supérieure, France
Elisabeth Oswald	University of Klagenfurt, Austria, and University of Birmingham, UK
Kostas Papagiannopoulos	Radboud University, the Netherlands
Ray Perlner	National Institute of Standards and Technology, USA
Edoardo Persichetti	Florida Atlantic University, USA, and Sapienza University of Rome, Italy
Peter Pessl	Infineon Technologies, Germany
Somindu C. Ramanna	Indian Institute of Technology, India
Angela Robinson	National Institute of Standards and Technology, USA
Mélissa Rossi	Thales, École Normale Supérieure, and French National Cybersecurity Agency, France
Simona Samardjiska	Radboud University, the Netherlands
Palash Sarkar	Indian Statistical Institute, India
Nicolas Sendrier	Inria, France
Benjamin Smith	Inria, France
Rainer Steinwandt	University of Alabama in Huntsville, USA
Gelo Noel Tabia	National Cheng Kung University, Taiwan
Tsuyoshi Takagi	University of Tokyo, Japan
Atsushi Takayasu	University of Tokyo, Japan
Jean-Pierre Tillich	Project Secret and Inria, France
Monika Trimoska	Eindhoven University of Technology, the Netherlands
Alexander Wallet	PQShield, UK

Bow-Yaw Wang	Academia Sinica, Taiwan
Wen Wang	Intel, USA
Thom Wiggers	PQShield, UK
Takashi Yamakawa	NTT Social Informatics Laboratories and Kyoto University, Japan
Bo-Yin Yang	Academia Sinica, Taiwan
Yang Yu	Tsinghua University, China
Yu Yu	Shanghai Jiao Tong University, China
Aaram Yun	Ewha Womans University, South Korea
Rina Zeitoun	IDEMIA, France

Additional Reviewers

Yoshinori Aono
Thomas Aulbach
Henry Bambury
Luís Brandão
Sun Chao
Jean-Sébastien Coron
Anaëlle Le Dévéhat
Max Duparc
Hiroki Furue
Joel Gärtner
Yasufumi Hashimoto
Johan Håstad
Hansraj Jangir
Huiwen Jia
Alexander Karenin
Sabrina Kunzweiler
Péter Kutas
Roch Lescuyer
Simon-Philipp Merz
Antoine Mesnard
Tran Ngo
Masayuki Noro
Hiroki Okada
Shinya Okumura
Tapas Pandit
Lars Ran
Damien Robert
Michael Schaller
Bruno Sterner
Sharwan Kumar Tiwari
Yan Bo Ti
Toi Tomita
Javier Verbel
Yuntao Wang
Maximiliane Weishäupl
Wenwen Xia
Masaya Yasuda
Floyd Zweydinger

Contents – Part I

Code-Based Cryptography

On the Structure of the Schur Squares of Twisted Generalized Reed-Solomon Codes and Application to Cryptanalysis 3
Alain Couvreur, Rakhi Pratihar, Nihan Tanısalı, and Ilaria Zappatore

Quadratic Modelings of Syndrome Decoding 35
Alessio Caminata, Ryann Cartor, Alessio Meneghetti, Rocco Mora, and Alex Pellegrini

An Improved Algorithm for Code Equivalence 71
Julian Nowakowski

An Improved Both-May Information Set Decoding Algorithm: Towards More Efficient Time-Memory Trade-Offs 104
Hiroki Furue and Yusuke Aikawa

Enhancing Threshold Group Action Signature Schemes: Adaptive Security and Scalability Improvements 129
Michele Battagliola, Giacomo Borin, Giovanni Di Crescenzo, Alessio Meneghetti, and Edoardo Persichetti

Multivariate Cryptography

Share the MAYO: Thresholdizing MAYO 165
Sofia Celi, Daniel Escudero, and Guilhem Niot

SoK: On the Physical Security of UOV-Based Signature Schemes 199
Thomas Aulbach, Fabio Campos, and Juliane Krämer

Shifting Our Knowledge of MQ-Sign Security 232
Lars Ran and Monika Trimoska

Lattice-Based Cryptography

Module Learning with Errors with Truncated Matrices 255
Katharina Boudgoust and Hannah Keller

Lattice-Based Sanitizable Signature Schemes: Chameleon Hash Functions and More 278
Sebastian Clermont, Samed Düzlü, Christian Janson, Laurens Porzenheim, and Patrick Struck

Giant Does NOT Mean Strong: Cryptanalysis of BQTRU 312
Ali Raya, Vikas Kumar, Aditi Kar Gangopadhyay, and Sugata Gangopadhyay

Batch Anonymous MAC Tokens from Lattices 349
Yingfei Yan, Sherman S. M. Chow, Lucien K. L. Ng, Harry W. H. Wong, Yongjun Zhao, and Baocang Wang

Author Index 385

Contents – Part II

Isogeny-Based Cryptography

Efficient Theta-Based Algorithms for Computing (ℓ, ℓ)-Isogenies on Kummer Surfaces for Arbitrary Odd ℓ ... 3
Ryo Yoshizumi, Hiroshi Onuki, Ryo Ohashi, Momonari Kudo, and Koji Nuida

Commuting Ramanujan Graphs and the Random Self-reducibility of Isogeny Problems ... 38
Youcef Mokrani and David Jao

Cryptanalysis

Discrete Gaussian Sampling for BKZ-Reduced Basis ... 63
Amaury Pouly and Yixin Shen

An Efficient Collision Attack on Castryck-Decru-Smith's Hash Function ... 89
Ryo Ohashi and Hiroshi Onuki

Heuristic Algorithm for Solving Restricted SVP and Its Applications ... 119
Geng Wang, Wenwen Xia, and Dawu Gu

Cryptanalysis of an Efficient Signature Based on Isotropic Quadratic Forms ... 153
Henry Bambury and Phong Q. Nguyen

Analysis of REDOG: The Pad Thai Attack ... 176
Alex Pellegrini and Marc Vorstermans

Quantum Security

Quantum IND-CPA Security Notions for AEAD ... 195
Mengyuan Zhang, Wenling Wu, and Han Sui

Reducing the Number of Qubits in Solving LWE ... 231
Barbara Jiabao Benedikt

Side-Channel Attacks

Single Trace Side-Channel Attack on the MPC-in-the-Head Framework 267
Julie Godard, Nicolas Aragon, Philippe Gaborit, Antoine Loiseau, and Julien Maillard

Et tu, Brute? Side-Channel Assisted Chosen Ciphertext Attacks Using Valid Ciphertexts on HQC KEM 294
Thales B. Paiva, Prasanna Ravi, Dirmanto Jap, Shivam Bhasin, Sayan Das, and Anupam Chattopadhyay

Security Notions

Treating Dishonest Ciphertexts in Post-quantum KEMs – Explicit vs. Implicit Rejection in the FO Transform 325
Kathrin Hövelmanns and Mikhail Kudinov

IND-CPA^{C}: A New Security Notion for Conditional Decryption in Fully Homomorphic Encryption 351
Bhuvnesh Chaturvedi, Anirban Chakraborty, Nimish Mishra, Ayantika Chatterjee, and Debdeep Mukhopadhyay

Author Index 385

Code-Based Cryptography

On the Structure of the Schur Squares of Twisted Generalized Reed-Solomon Codes and Application to Cryptanalysis

Alain Couvreur[1,2(✉)], Rakhi Pratihar[1,2], Nihan Tanısalı[1,2], and Ilaria Zappatore[3]

[1] Inria, Centre de Saclay, 1 rue Honoré d'Estienne d'Orves, 91120 Palaiseau Cedex, France
{alain.couvreur,rakhi.pratihar,nihan.tanisali}@inria.fr
[2] Laboratoire LIX, CNRS UMR 7161, École Polytechnique, Institut Polytechnique de Paris, 1 rue Honoré d'Estienne d'Orves, 91120 Palaiseau Cedex, France
[3] XLIM, CNRS UMR 7252, Université de Limoges, 123, avenue Albert Thomas, 87060 Limoges Cedex, France
ilaria.zappatore@unilim.fr

Abstract. Twisted generalized Reed-Solomon (TGRS) codes constitute an interesting family of evaluation codes, containing a large class of maximum distance separable codes non-equivalent to generalized Reed-Solomon (GRS) ones. Moreover, the Schur squares of TGRS codes may be much larger than those of GRS codes with same dimension. Exploiting these structural differences, in 2018, Beelen, Bossert, Puchinger and Rosenkilde proposed a subfamily of Maximum Distance Separable (MDS) Twisted Reed–Solomon (TRS) codes over $\mathbb{F}_q$ with ℓ twists $q \approx n^{2^\ell}$ for McEliece encryption, claiming their resistance to both Sidelnikov Shestakov attack and Schur products–based attacks. In short, they claimed these codes to resist to classical key recovery attacks on McEliece encryption scheme instantiated with Reed-Solomon (RS) or GRS codes. In 2020, Lavauzelle and Renner presented an original attack on this system based on the computation of the subfield subcode of the public TRS code.

In this paper, we show that the original claim on the resistance of TRS and TGRS codes to Schur products based–attacks is wrong. We identify a broad class of codes including TRS and TGRS ones that is distinguishable from random by computing the Schur square of some shortening of the code. Then, we focus on the case of single twist (*i.e.*, $\ell = 1$), which is the most efficient one in terms of decryption complexity, to derive an attack. The technique is similar to the distinguisher-based attacks of RS code-based systems given by Couvreur, Gaborit, Gauthier-Umaña, Otmani, Tillich in 2014.

This work is partially funded by the French Agence Nationale de la Recherche project ANR-21-CE39-0009-BARRACUDA, by Plan France 2030 ANR-22-PETQ-0008 and by Horizon-Europe MSCA-DN project ENCODE.

R. Niederhagen and M.-J. O. Saarinen (Eds.): PQCrypto 2025, LNCS 15577, pp. 3–34, 2025.
https://doi.org/10.1007/978-3-031-86599-2_1

Keywords: Twisted generalised Reed-Solomon codes · Schur products · Code-based Cryptography · McEliece encryption scheme · Cryptanalysis

1 Introduction

McEliece's encryption scheme dates back to the early ages of public key cryptography. For a long time it has been considered unusable because of the significant size of the public key. However, with the recent and growing interest of post-quantum cryptographic primitives, Classic McEliece [1] could be standardized in the near future. Besides the seminal proposal by McEliece himself based on classical Goppa codes, there have been many attempts to replace Goppa codes by other families of codes with more efficient decoding algorithms in order to reduce the key size. In 1986, Niederreiter [23] suggested generalized Reed-Solomon codes (GRS) to replace Goppa codes, but it was shown to be insecure by Sidelnikov and Shestakov in [27]. Thereafter, several instantiations using codes "close to GRS" codes appeared. Berger and Loidreau replaced the GRS code by a subcode of low codimension [7]; Wieschebrink [33] included some random columns in a generator matrix of a GRS code; this approach was further enhanced in [30,31] by additionally "mixing" the random columns with the original ones via specific linear transformations; finally, in [2] Baldi, Bianchi, Chiaraluce, Rosenthal, and Schipani proposed to mask the structure of a GRS code by right multiplying it by a "partially weight-preserving" matrix. All these proposals have been partially or fully broken using attacks derived from a square code distinguisher [9,11,15,34].

Twisted Reed-Solomon codes (TRS) are evaluation codes in the Hamming metric. These codes were introduced in [5], adapting to the Hamming setting Sheekey's construction of *twisted Gabidulin codes* [25] in rank metric. Unlike Reed-Solomon codes, TRS codes are not always maximum distance separable (MDS) codes, but this family of codes contains MDS codes that are not equivalent to generalized Reed-Solomon (GRS) codes. Recently, in [3], TRS codes have been proposed as an alternative to Goppa codes for McEliece cryptosystem, and example parameters are given that provide shorter keys compared to the original McEliece cryptosystem for the same security level. The authors also singled out a subfamily of twisted Reed-Solomon codes, which they "provably" claimed to be resistant against several known structural attacks on the McEliece cryptosystem based on RS-like codes: Sidenlikov-Shestakov [27], Wieschebrink [32,34], Schur square-distinguishing [9].

More recently, Lavauzelle and Renner [20] gave an efficient key-recovery attack on the TRS variant proposed in [3] based on identifying some specific structure of the *subfield subcode*. Lavauzelle and Renner assumed the security claims of [3] on the resistance of TRS codes to Schur squares to be true and identified another weakness that was very specific to the chosen public keys (*i.e.* the underlying TRS code is MDS) coming from some tower of extensions of finite fields. It is worth mentioning that their attack restricts to a limited subfamily of TRS codes.

In this paper, *our contributions* are threefold. First, we show the claims of [3] on the resistance of TRS codes to Schur square distinguishing are wrong. This holds even for their generalized version : TGRS codes. Hence we are able to prove that such codes are distinguishable from random as soon as their number ℓ of twists is in $O(1)$. The latter assumption is reasonable since the decoding of such codes is exponential in ℓ. In short, we prove that any TGRS codes that could be proposed for the McEliece scheme are actually distinguishable from random.

Second, for the case of TGRS codes with a single twist ($\ell = 1$) we show how to derive a polynomial time attack from the Schur square distinguisher. This attack is in the very same flavour as the attack of [9,15] on BBCRS scheme [2] and runs in $O(q^3n^4)$ operations in $\mathbb{F}_q$. Note that the family of codes for which such an attack applies is much larger than the family broken by [20], which was restricted to a restricted family of TRS codes.

Third, the attacks in [9,15] involved a heuristic argument that was claimed to hold "with a high probability". In the present article, we provide a detailed analysis of the success probability of the algorithm, providing a proven attack of the scheme. Note that we are able to estimate this success probability for a range of parameters that is **strictly included** in the range of parameters we can actually attack. In short: this attack works on a broad range of parameters and we can prove its success without involving any heuristic arguments in some subrange of parameters.

Outline of the Article

Section 2 provides the basic notation and the necessary prerequisites on GRS codes, TGRS codes, Schur products, and McEliece encryption scheme. In Sect. 3, we introduce a new class of codes called *quasi–GRS codes* which strictly includes TGRS codes, which turns out to be the class of codes we succeed distinguishing from random by computing the Schur square of some of their shortening. In Sect. 4, we show how to distinguish quasi–GRS codes from random. Section 5 is dedicated to the presentation of an attack on the McEliece instantiated with TGRS codes with a single twist and a *SageMath* implementation of the attack together with timing results are given in Sect. 6. Finally, Sect. 7 is dedicated to a probability analysis yielding the proof of a crucial theorem for the attack.

2 Preliminaries

Let q be a prime power, $\mathbb{F}_q$ be a finite field of order q, and $\mathbb{F}_q^n$ the $\mathbb{F}_q$ vector space of dimension n. In this article, vectors are represented by lowercase bold letters: $\boldsymbol{a}, \boldsymbol{b}, \boldsymbol{c}$ and matrices by uppercase bold letters $\mathbf{G}, \mathbf{H}$. Given a positive integer n, we denote $[n]$ to be the set $[n] \stackrel{\text{def}}{=} \{1, \dots, n\}$. We denote by $\mathbb{F}_q[x]_{<k}$ the space of polynomials over $\mathbb{F}_q$ of degree strictly less than k. Finally, given elements $a_1, \dots, a_s$ of a given vector space V, we denote by $\langle a_1, \dots, a_s \rangle$ the vector space spanned by these elements. Note that all the considered vector spaces in this

paper are over $\mathbb{F}_q$, hence the field is not specified when mentioning dimension or vector span.

Sometimes, since we work with *Twisted Generalized Reed Solomon codes*, it would be useful to remove one monomial x^h (for a certain $0 \leqslant h \leqslant k-1$) from the previously defined subspace $\mathbb{F}_q[x]_{<k}$. In that case, we denote:

$$\mathrm{Mon}_{<k,\hat{h}} \stackrel{\text{def}}{=} \left\langle x^0, \dots, \widehat{x^h}, \dots, x^{k-1} \right\rangle, \tag{1}$$

where the hat notation means that the monomial x^h is removed. In a more general situation, when we remove more than one monomial, for instance $x^{h_1}, \dots, x^{h_\ell}$ for $\ell \geqslant 1$, we denote,

$$\mathrm{Mon}_{<k,\hat{\boldsymbol{h}}} \stackrel{\text{def}}{=} \langle x^i : i \in [n] \setminus \{h_1, \dots, h_\ell\} \rangle \quad \text{where} \quad \boldsymbol{h} \stackrel{\text{def}}{=} (h_1, \dots, h_\ell). \tag{2}$$

Finally, the present article crucially uses the notion of *shortening* of codes:

Definition 1. *Given a code $\mathcal{C} \subseteq \mathbb{F}_q^n$ and a subset $I = \{i_1, \dots, i_{|I|}\} \subseteq [n]$, the* shortening *of $\mathcal{C}$ at I, denoted as $\mathcal{C}_I$, is defined as*

$$\mathcal{C}_I \stackrel{\text{def}}{=} \{(x_i)_{i \in [n] \setminus I} \ : \ \boldsymbol{x} = (x_1, \dots, x_n) \in \mathcal{C} \text{ such that } \forall i \in I,\ x_i = 0\}.$$

Remark 1. In short, the shortened code is the subcode of vectors whose entries indexed by I are zero and whose prescribed zero entries are removed. Then at some places in the paper – we will mention it when needed – we will not remove the prescribed zero entries from the shortening and hence take as a definition:

$$\{\boldsymbol{x} \in \mathcal{C} \ : \ \forall i \in I,\ x_i = 0\}.$$

2.1 Schur Products of Linear Spaces and Evaluation Codes

One of the most important tools in the cryptanalysis of the McEliece encryption scheme and its variants is the Schur product of codes. For this reason, we introduce the following definitions.

Definition 2 (Componentwise product). *Given $\boldsymbol{a} = (a_1, \dots, a_n)$ and $\boldsymbol{b} = (b_1, \dots, b_n)$ in $\mathbb{F}_q^n$, we denote by $\boldsymbol{a} \star \boldsymbol{b}$ the* componentwise *or* Schur *product as*

$$a \star b \stackrel{\text{def}}{=} (a_1 b_1, \dots, a_n b_n).$$

Definition 3 (Schur product of linear codes and square code). *The* Schur product *of two linear codes $\mathcal{A}$, $\mathcal{B} \subset \mathbb{F}_q^n$ is defined as,*

$$\mathcal{A} \star \mathcal{B} \stackrel{\text{def}}{=} \langle \{\boldsymbol{a} \star \boldsymbol{b} : \boldsymbol{a} \in \mathcal{A}, \boldsymbol{b} \in \mathcal{B}\} \rangle$$

When $\mathcal{A} = \mathcal{B}$ then $\mathcal{A} \star \mathcal{A}$ is called square *of $\mathcal{A}$ and is denoted by $\mathcal{A}^2$.*

We can easily derive an upper bound on the dimension of the Schur product of two codes and of the square product code : if we consider a basis of $\mathcal{A}$ and $\mathcal{B}$, the product space is generated by the componentwise products of their elements.

Proposition 1. *If $\mathcal{A}$ and $\mathcal{B}$ two linear codes of length n. Then,*

1. $\dim(\mathcal{A} \star \mathcal{B}) \leqslant \dim(\mathcal{A}) \dim(\mathcal{B})$,
2. $\dim(\mathcal{A}^2) \leqslant \binom{\dim(\mathcal{A})+1}{2}$

In particular, for a random code of dimension k and length n, it can be shown that the dimension of the square is $\min\left\{\frac{k(k+1)}{2}, n\right\}$ with high probability. Such a statement is proved in [8, Thm. 2.3] for binary codes and in [16, Thm. 2] for q-ary ones.

Proposition 2. *Let $k, n \geqslant 0$ such that $\binom{k+1}{2} < n$ and $\mathcal{A}$ be a random $[n, k]$ code. We have*

$$Prob\left[\dim \mathcal{A}^2 < \binom{k+1}{2}\right] = o(1).$$

2.2 Generalized Reed-Solomon Codes and the Square Code Construction

Given a vector $\boldsymbol{\alpha} = (\alpha_1, \ldots, \alpha_n) \in \mathbb{F}_q^n$ for distinct α_i's and $\boldsymbol{v} = (v_1, \ldots, v_n)$ a nonzero vector in $\mathbb{F}_q^n$, we consider the following *evaluation map* associated to $\boldsymbol{\alpha}$ and $\boldsymbol{v}$,

$$\mathrm{ev}_{\boldsymbol{\alpha},\boldsymbol{v}} : \begin{cases} \mathbb{F}_q[x] \longrightarrow & \mathbb{F}_q^n \\ f(x) \longmapsto (v_1 f(\alpha_1), \ldots, v_n f(\alpha_n)). \end{cases} \tag{3}$$

Definition 4 (Generalized Reed-Solomon Code). *Let k, n be positive integers, $k < n \leqslant q$. The $[n, k]_q$* generalized Reed-Solomon (GRS) *code associated with $\boldsymbol{\alpha}, \boldsymbol{v}$ is defined as*

$$\mathbf{GRS}_k(\boldsymbol{\alpha}, \boldsymbol{v}) \stackrel{def}{=} \{(\mathrm{ev}_{\boldsymbol{\alpha},\boldsymbol{v}}(f) \ : \ f \in \mathbb{F}_q[x]_{<k})\}.$$

If $\boldsymbol{v} = (1, \ldots, 1)$, then the code is a Reed–Solomon code *denoted as $\mathbf{RS}_k(\boldsymbol{\alpha})$.*

GRS codes lie at the core of algebraic coding theory. Many other algebraic constructions of codes, such as Alternant codes, BCH codes, Goppa codes, Srivastava codes, and so on, are derived from GRS ones. GRS codes are famous because of their optimal parameters: they are known to be *Maximum distance Separable* (MDS), *i.e.* they have the best possible minimum distance with respect to their length and dimension. In addition, such codes benefit from efficient decoding algorithms up to half their minimum distance [24, Chapter 6] and even beyond using list decoding [17,29].

The Schur product (see Definition 3) plays a central role in the cryptanalysis of the McEliece cryptosystem and its variants. It indeed permits to distinguish algebraically *structured* codes such as GRS ones from random codes.

Proposition 3. $\mathbf{GRS}_k(\boldsymbol{\alpha}, \boldsymbol{v}) \star \mathbf{GRS}_\ell(\boldsymbol{\alpha}, \boldsymbol{v}) = \mathbf{GRS}_{k+\ell-1}(\boldsymbol{\alpha}, \boldsymbol{v} \star \boldsymbol{v})$.

Proof. See [9]. □

Given a GRS code of dimension k, Proposition 3 entails that the dimension of its square is $2k-1$ while Proposition 2 asserts that it would be $\min\{n, \frac{k(k+1)}{2}\}$ for a random code. Thus, GRS codes of dimension $k < \frac{n}{2}$ can be easily distinguished from random ones by computing their Schur square. For GRS codes of dimension $\geqslant \frac{n}{2}$, they can be distinguished from random by computing the square of their duals which is itself a GRS code.

Sometimes, the sole use of the Schur product is insufficient to provide a distinguisher, it is then useful to consider the square of a shortening of the the code. Shortening then squaring turns out to be very efficient to distinguish codes "close" to GRS codes, as shown in [9–15]. For this reason, we introduce the following Lemma that will be useful later.

Lemma 1. *Shortening of an $[n, k]$ GRS code at $a \leqslant k$ positions gives an $[n - a, k - a]$ GRS code.*

2.3 Twisted Generalized Reed–Solomon Codes

Twisted Reed–Solomon codes (TRS) and *Twisted Generalised Reed–Solomon* (TGRS) codes are slight variants of GRS codes. First inspired by a rank–metric counterpart [25], they have been first introduced in [4,5] as a possible alternative to GRS codes containing some MDS codes. Next, they have been proposed for cryptographic applications in [3] with the argument that their structure was better hidden with respect to classical attacks such as Sidelnikov Shestakov attack or Schur square attack. They are defined as follows.

Definition 5 (Twisted generalized Reed-Solomon Codes). *For positive integers n, k, ℓ with $\ell \leqslant k \leqslant n \leqslant q$, suppose that $\mathbf{h} = (h_1, \ldots, h_\ell) \in \{0, \ldots, k-1\}^\ell$, $\mathbf{t} = (t_1, \ldots, t_\ell) \in \{1, \ldots, n-k\}^\ell$ and $\boldsymbol{\eta} = (\eta_1, \ldots, \eta_\ell) \in \mathbb{F}_q^\ell$. Then*

$$\mathcal{P}^{n,k}_{\mathbf{t},\mathbf{h},\boldsymbol{\eta}} \stackrel{def}{=} \left\{ f = \sum_{i=0}^{k-1} f_i x^i + \sum_{j=1}^{\ell} \eta_j f_{h_j} x^{k-1+t_j} \ : \ f_i \in \mathbb{F}_q \right\} \tag{4}$$

is a k-dimensional $\mathbb{F}_q$-subspace of $\mathbb{F}_q[x]$. Furthermore, let $\boldsymbol{\alpha} = (\alpha_1, \ldots, \alpha_n) \in \mathbb{F}_q^n$ where α_i, for $i = 1, \ldots, n$ are distinct and $\boldsymbol{v} = (v_1, \ldots, v_n) \in (\mathbb{F}_q^\times)^n$. Then the corresponding linear code is defined as

$$\mathcal{C}^{n,k}_{\boldsymbol{\alpha},\boldsymbol{v},\mathbf{t},\mathbf{h},\boldsymbol{\eta}} \stackrel{def}{=} \mathrm{ev}_{\boldsymbol{\alpha},\boldsymbol{v}}(\mathcal{P}^{n,k}_{\mathbf{t},\mathbf{h},\boldsymbol{\eta}}) \subset \mathbb{F}_q^n.$$

is called $(\boldsymbol{\alpha}, \boldsymbol{v}, \mathbf{t}, \mathbf{h}, \boldsymbol{\eta})$-twisted generalized Reed-Solomon *(TGRS) code. For brevity, we will simply use $\mathcal{P}$ and $\mathcal{C}$ to denote the space of twisted polynomials $\mathcal{P}^{n,k}_{\mathbf{t},\mathbf{h},\boldsymbol{\eta}}$ and the TGRS code $\mathcal{C}^{n,k}_{\boldsymbol{\alpha},\boldsymbol{v},\mathbf{t},\mathbf{h},\boldsymbol{\eta}}$.*

The integer ℓ is referred to as the *number of twists*, and we call the vectors $\boldsymbol{t}, \boldsymbol{h}$ and $\boldsymbol{\eta}$ the *twist* vector, *hook* vector, and *coefficient* vector, respectively.

In [3], the authors also proposed a *brute force* technique to decode Twisted Reed–Solomon codes, which can be easily generalized to TGRS. Given a received word $\boldsymbol{y} = \boldsymbol{c} + \boldsymbol{e} \in \mathbb{F}_q^n$, where $\boldsymbol{c} \in \mathcal{C}$, the main idea consists in guessing ℓ elements $g_1, \dots, g_\ell \in \mathbb{F}_q$ and then decoding $\boldsymbol{y} - \mathrm{ev}_{\boldsymbol{\alpha},\boldsymbol{v}} \sum_{j=1}^{\ell} g_j \eta_i x^{k-1+t_j}$ as a received word of a $\mathbf{GRS}_k(\boldsymbol{\alpha})$. This strategy succeeds if $g_j = f_{h_j}$ for all $1 \leqslant j \leqslant \ell$. The complexity of such a decoder is q^ℓ times the complexity of a GRS decoder, and the decoding radius is the same as the GRS one.

In [5], the authors proposed a decoding strategy for TRS codes based on a *key equation* which can eventually achieve a better complexity than the brute force. In particular, they introduced a *partial unique decoder*, which means that there are some error patterns that cannot be corrected. They also provide heuristic estimations of the *failure probability* of the decoder and of the decoding radius, which can be smaller than half of the minimum distance of the code. However, even if this algorithm achieves a better complexity than brute force, it is still exponential in the number of twists.

2.4 Reasoning on the Level of Polynomial Spaces

All the codes involved are derived from polynomial evaluations. Note that, given the evaluation map $\mathrm{ev}_{\boldsymbol{\alpha},\boldsymbol{v}}$, then by interpolation, any element $\boldsymbol{c} \in \mathbb{F}_q^n$ can be seen as $\boldsymbol{c} = \mathrm{ev}_{\boldsymbol{\alpha},\boldsymbol{v}}(f)$ for a unique $f \in \mathbb{F}_q[x]_{<n}$. Consequently, we will often reason either at the level of codewords, or at the level of polynomials. The correspondence is as follows: for any code $\mathcal{C} \subseteq \mathbb{F}_q^n$, there exists a unique subspace $\mathcal{P}_{\mathcal{C}} \subseteq \mathbb{F}_q[x]_{<n}$ such that

$$\mathcal{C} = \mathrm{ev}_{\boldsymbol{\alpha},\boldsymbol{v}}(\mathcal{P}_{\mathcal{C}}). \tag{5}$$

This correspondence will allow us to move between codewords and polynomials as needed. Similarly to codes, we define products of polynomial spaces as follows. Given, $\mathcal{P}, \mathcal{R} \subseteq \mathbb{F}_q[x]$ we define

$$\mathcal{P}\mathcal{R} \stackrel{\mathrm{def}}{=} \langle fg \ : \ f \in \mathcal{P}, g \in \mathcal{R} \rangle .$$

When $\mathcal{P} = \mathcal{R}$ we call this the *square* of $\mathcal{P}$ and denote it $\mathcal{P}^2$. Next, given a polynomial $f \in \mathbb{F}_q[X]$ we use $f\mathcal{P}$ for $\langle f \rangle \mathcal{P}$.

As in the code setting (see Proposition 1), we have natural upper bounds.

Proposition 4. *Let $\mathcal{P}$ and $\mathcal{R}$ be two subspaces of $\mathbb{F}_q[x]$, then*

$$\dim \mathcal{P}\mathcal{R} \leqslant \dim \mathcal{P} \cdot \dim \mathcal{R} \quad \textit{and} \quad \dim \mathcal{P}^2 \leqslant \binom{\dim \mathcal{P} + 1}{2}.$$

When considering space of polynomials of bounded degree, as in the case of GRS codes, we also have an explicit description of the product.

Proposition 5. $(\mathbb{F}_q[x]_{<k})(\mathbb{F}_q[x]_{<\ell}) = \mathbb{F}_q[x]_{<k+\ell-1}$.

2.4.1 Relation with Schur Squares

The previously introduced map

$$\mathrm{ev}_{\boldsymbol{\alpha},\boldsymbol{v}} : \begin{cases} \mathbb{F}_q[x] \longrightarrow & \mathbb{F}_q^n \\ f \longmapsto (f(\alpha_1), \ldots, f(\alpha_n)) \end{cases}$$

is a surjective ring morphism when $\mathbb{F}_q^n$ is equipped with the Schur product $\star$. Consequently, from the setup in (5), we obtain a surjective map $\mathcal{P}_{\mathcal{C}}^2 \to \mathcal{C}^2$ which yields:

Proposition 6. *Let* $\mathcal{C} = \mathrm{ev}_{\boldsymbol{\alpha},\boldsymbol{v}}(\mathcal{P}_{\mathcal{C}})$ *for* $\mathcal{P}_{\mathcal{C}} \subseteq \mathbb{F}_q[x]_{<n}$. *Then*

$$\dim \mathcal{C}^2 \leqslant \dim \mathcal{P}_{\mathcal{C}}^2.$$

2.4.2 Relations with Shortenings

Given a code $\mathcal{C} = \mathrm{ev}_{\boldsymbol{\alpha},\boldsymbol{v}}(\mathcal{P})$ for some $\mathrm{P} \subseteq \mathbb{F}_q[x]$ and $I \subseteq [n]$, the shortening $\mathcal{C}_I$ of $\mathcal{C}$ at I corresponds to the evaluation of $\mathcal{P} \cap (p_I)$ where (p_I) is the ideal spanned by

$$p_I(x) \stackrel{\text{def}}{=} \prod_{i \in I} (x - \alpha_i).$$

In the sequel, we denote

$$\mathcal{P}_{p_I} \stackrel{\text{def}}{=} \mathcal{P} \cap (p_I).$$

2.5 The McEliece Cryptosystem and Its Variants

McEliece code-based original cryptosystem was introduced in 1978 by McEliece [21] and it used binary Goppa codes. However, it corresponds to very general framework that can be instantiated with many possible codes.

Consider a family of codes $\mathcal{F}$ parameterized by a set $\mathcal{S}$. Hence, we are given a map

$$\mathcal{C} : \begin{cases} \mathcal{S} \longrightarrow \mathcal{F} \\ s \longmapsto \mathcal{C}(s). \end{cases}$$

The above map is the trapdoor: $\mathcal{C}(s)$ should be easy to compute from the knowledge of s but given $\mathcal{C} \in \mathcal{F}$, recovering $s \in \mathcal{S}$ such that $\mathcal{C} = \mathcal{C}(s)$ should be hard. Moreover, suppose that for any $s \in S$ we are given a decoder $D(s)$ that corrects up to t errors for the code $\mathcal{C}(s)$. Here again, decoding should not be possible without the knowledge of s. Then, McEliece encryption scheme can be described as follows:

Key Generation. Draw $s \in \mathcal{S}$ at random. The secret key is s.
The public key is a pair $(\mathbf{G}_{pub}, t)$, where $\mathbf{G}_{pub}$ is a generator matrix of $\mathcal{C}(s)$ and t is the number of errors that the algorithm $D(s)$ can decode.

Encryption. To encrypt a plaintext $\mathbf{m} \in \mathbb{F}_q^k$, choose a random $\mathbf{e} \in \mathbb{F}_q^n$ with Hamming weight $wt_H(\mathbf{e}) = t$. The ciphertext is $\mathbf{c} \stackrel{\text{def}}{=} \mathbf{m}\mathbf{G}_{pub} + \mathbf{e}$.

Decryption. Apply the decoder $D(s)$ to the ciphertext $\mathbf{c}$ to recover $\mathbf{m}$.

Examples of Instantiations. McEliece's original proposal [21] is instantiated with classical Goppa codes, with the secret being the pair (L, g) where L is the so-called *evaluation sequence* and g is the *Goppa Polynomial.* Later on, Niederreiter [23] proposed to instantiate it with GRS codes, where the secret is $(\boldsymbol{x}, \boldsymbol{y})$. This proposal was subsequently broken in [27]. Since then, several alternative instantiations have been suggested (the following list is far from being exhaustive): Reed-Muller codes [26], Algebraic Geometry codes and their subfield subcodes [18], subcodes of GRS codes [7], MDPC codes [22], among others. Several other proposals rely on slightly modified GRS codes; see, for instance, [2,19,30,33]. However, many of the instantiations based on codes "close" to GRS codes have been vulnerable to attacks, with many such attacks involving the Schur product [9–14,34]

Recently, Beelen, Bossert, Puchinger, and Rosenkilde proposed TRS codes in [3] claiming that the corresponding cryptosystem is resistant to the well-known attacks [9,27,32].

2.6 Cryptanalysis of the McEliece System Based on GRS Codes and Their Variants

The TRS variant of the McEliece cryptosystem was already broken in a prior work by Lavauzelle and Renner [20], which examined a setup different from ours. More precisely,

1. they considered a prime power q_0, the integers $k < n \leqslant q_0 - 1$ with $2\sqrt{n}+6 < k \leqslant n/2 - 2$ and a twist ℓ such that,

$$\frac{n+1}{k-\sqrt{n}} < \ell + 2 < \min\{k+3, 2n/k, \sqrt{n}-2\}.$$

   Further, they set $q_i \overset{\text{def}}{=} q_{i-1}^2 = q_0^{2^i}$ for $i = 1, \dots, \ell$, such that $\mathbb{F}_{q_0} \subset \mathbb{F}_{q_1} \subset \cdots \subset \mathbb{F}_{q_\ell} = \mathbb{F}_q$ is a chain of subfields. And finally they take $t_i = (i+1)(r-2) - k + 2$ and $h_i = r - 1 + i$ for $i = 1, \dots, \ell$, where $r \overset{\text{def}}{=} \lceil \frac{n+1}{\ell+2} \rceil + 2$.
   Note that this choice of parameters guarantees the underlying TRS to be MDS [3].
2. They assumed that the integers q_0, n, k, ℓ and the hook and twist vector $\mathbf{h}, \mathbf{t}$ are *public parameters.*

Lavauzelle and Renner's approach **assumes the validity of claims in** [3] **regarding the indistinguishability of such codes** with respect to the Schur square even after shortening. So they use a strategy based on the **recovery of the subfield subcode** to attack the system. The novelty of their approach lies in the fact that, in this case, they use the subfield subcode structure of the TRS to attack the system, whereas usually the subfield subcode operation is used to hide the structure of the code used in encryption to improve the security.

In particular, thanks to the previous choice of parameters, they describe the structure of the subfield subcode (in $\mathbb{F}_{q_0}$) as a subspace of low codimension of a classical RS code, and they exploit this code to recover the hidden TRS code.

In contrast, our work considers a **general TGRS family** without specific parameter assumptions, and we demonstrate that these codes, like GRS codes, can indeed be distinguished from random codes. Then, we extend the distinguisher-based attack of [9] to such a code family.

3 ℓ–Quasi–GRS Codes

In this section, we introduce a broader class of codes called *quasi–GRS* codes, which contains TGRS codes. Notably, the distinguisher we describe further, along with most of the cryptanalysis techniques presented, applies to quasi–GRS codes. The interest of this class is that it is closed under duality and "most of the times", closed under shortening.

Definition 6. *Let $\boldsymbol{\alpha} \in \mathbb{F}_q^n$ be a sequence of distinct elements and $\boldsymbol{v} \in (\mathbb{F}_q^\times)^n$. An ℓ–quasi–GRS (ℓ–qGRS) code is defined as a code $\mathcal{C}$ such that*

$$\mathcal{C} = \mathcal{C}_0 \oplus \mathcal{C}_1,$$

where $\mathcal{C}_0$ is a subcode of codimension ℓ of $\mathbf{GRS}_k(\boldsymbol{\alpha}, \boldsymbol{v})$ and $\mathcal{C}_1$ has dimension ℓ and satisfies $\mathcal{C}_1 \cap \mathbf{GRS}_k(\boldsymbol{\alpha}, \boldsymbol{v}) = 0$.

Proposition 7. *A TGRS code with ℓ twists is an ℓ–qGRS code.*

Proof. Using notation from Definition 5, define

$$\begin{aligned} \mathcal{C}_0 &\stackrel{\text{def}}{=} \text{ev}(\langle x^i \ : \ i \in [n] \setminus \{h_1, \dots, h_\ell\}\rangle) = \text{ev}(\text{Mon}_{<k,\hat{h}}) \\ \text{and} \quad \mathcal{C}_1 &\stackrel{\text{def}}{=} \text{ev}(\langle x^{h_1} + \eta_1 x^{k-1+t_1}, \dots, x^{h_\ell} + \eta_\ell x^{k-1+t_\ell}\rangle). \end{aligned}$$

This yields the result. □

Proposition 8. *The dual of an ℓ–qGRS code is an ℓ–qGRS code.*

Proof. Let $\mathcal{C} = \mathcal{C}_0 \oplus \mathcal{C}_1$ be an ℓ–qGRS code with $\mathcal{C}_0 \subseteq \mathbf{GRS}_k(\boldsymbol{\alpha}, \boldsymbol{v})$ and $\mathcal{C}_1 \cap \mathbf{GRS}_k(\boldsymbol{\alpha}, \boldsymbol{v}) = 0$. Then, $\mathcal{C}$ has codimension ℓ in $\mathbf{GRS}_k(\boldsymbol{\alpha}, \boldsymbol{v}) \oplus \mathcal{C}_1$. Therefore, $\mathbf{GRS}_k(\boldsymbol{\alpha}, \boldsymbol{v})^\perp \cap \mathcal{C}_1^\perp$ has codimension ℓ in $\mathcal{C}^\perp$. Denote by $\mathcal{C}_0' \stackrel{\text{def}}{=} \mathbf{GRS}_k(\boldsymbol{\alpha}, \boldsymbol{v})^\perp \cap \mathcal{C}_1^\perp$ and let $\mathcal{C}_1'$ be a complement subspace of $\mathcal{C}_0'$ in $\mathcal{C}^\perp$. Therefore, it is clear that $\mathcal{C}_0' \oplus \mathcal{C}_1' = \mathcal{C}^\perp$ and $\dim(\mathcal{C}_1') = \ell$. Note that $\mathcal{C}_1' \cap \mathbf{GRS}_k(\boldsymbol{\alpha}, \boldsymbol{v})^\perp = \{0\}$, as otherwise, $\mathbf{GRS}_k(\boldsymbol{\alpha}, \boldsymbol{v})^\perp \cap \mathcal{C}_1' \subseteq \mathbf{GRS}_k(\boldsymbol{\alpha}, \boldsymbol{v})^\perp \cap \mathcal{C}^\perp = \mathcal{C}_0'$ will lead to a contradiction. Now, since $\mathbf{GRS}_k(\boldsymbol{\alpha}, \boldsymbol{v})^\perp$ is again a GRS code and $\mathcal{C}_0'$ has codimension ℓ in $\mathbf{GRS}_k(\boldsymbol{\alpha}, \boldsymbol{v})^\perp$, we can conclude that $\mathcal{C}^\perp$ is an ℓ–qGRS code. □

Proposition 9. *Let $\mathcal{C}$ be an ℓ–qGRS code of dimension k and $I \subseteq [n]$ with $|I| \leqslant k - \ell$. If $\dim \mathcal{C}_I = k - |I|$, then $\mathcal{C}_I$ is an ℓ'–qGRS code for some $\ell' \leqslant \ell$.*

The proof of Proposition 9 rests on the following lemma.

Lemma 2. *Let* $\mathcal{D} = \mathbf{GRS}_k(\boldsymbol{\alpha}, \boldsymbol{v}) \oplus \mathcal{D}_1$ *for some code* $\mathcal{D}_1$ *of dimension* ℓ. *Let* $I \subseteq [n]$ *such that* $|I| < k$. *Denote* $s \stackrel{def}{=} |I|$. *Then,* $\dim \mathcal{D}_I = \dim \mathcal{D} - s$ *and is of the form* $\mathcal{D}_I = \mathbf{GRS}_{k-s}(\boldsymbol{\alpha}', \boldsymbol{v}') \oplus \mathcal{D}'_1$ *for some* $\boldsymbol{\alpha}', \boldsymbol{v}' \in \mathbb{F}_q^{n-s}$ *and some code* $\mathcal{D}'_1 \in \mathbb{F}_q^{n-s}$ *of dimension* ℓ.

Proof. Without loss of generality, by possibly permuting the entries of codewords, one can assume that $I = \{1, \ldots, s\}$. Since $\mathbf{GRS}_k(\boldsymbol{\alpha}, \boldsymbol{v})$ is MDS, it has a systematic generator matrix: $\left(\mathbf{I}_k \mid \mathbf{A}\right)$ for some $\mathbf{A} \in \mathbb{F}_q^{k\times(n-k)}$. Then, by elimination, $\mathcal{D}$ has a generator matrix of the form

$$\begin{pmatrix} \mathbf{I}_k & \mathbf{A} \\ (0) & \mathbf{B} \end{pmatrix}$$

for some matrix $\mathbf{B} \in \mathbb{F}_q^{\ell\times(n-k)}$ in row echelon form. Let $\mathbf{G}$ be the matrix obtained by removing the first s rows and columns of the above matrix. The matrix $\mathbf{G}$ is nothing but a generator matrix of $\mathcal{D}_I$. Since $\mathbf{B}$ is in row echelon form, we have the result on the dimension of $\mathcal{D}_I$. Finally, the $k - s$ first rows of $\mathbf{G}$ give a generator matrix of the shortened GRS code, which is itself a GRS code. This yields the result on the structure of $\mathcal{D}_I$. □

Proof of Proposition 9. By definition, $\mathcal{C}$ has codimension ℓ in a code

$$\mathcal{D} \stackrel{\text{def}}{=} \mathbf{GRS}_k(\boldsymbol{\alpha}, \boldsymbol{v}) \oplus \mathcal{C}_1$$

for some code $\mathcal{C}_1$ of dimension ℓ. By Lemma 2, $\mathcal{D}_I$ has dimension $k + \ell - |I|$. Since by assumption, $\dim \mathcal{C}_I = \dim \mathcal{C} - |I|$, then $\mathcal{C}_I$ has codimension ℓ in $\mathcal{D}_I$. By Lemma 2 again, $\mathcal{D}_I = \mathbf{GRS}_{k-s}(\boldsymbol{\alpha}', \boldsymbol{v}') \oplus \mathcal{C}'_1$ for some $\boldsymbol{\alpha}', \boldsymbol{v}' \in \mathbb{F}_q^{n-s}$ and some code $\mathcal{C}'_1 \subseteq \mathbb{F}_q^{n-s}$. Let $\mathcal{C}'_0 \stackrel{\text{def}}{=} \mathcal{C}_I \cap \mathbf{GRS}_{k-s}(\boldsymbol{\alpha}', \boldsymbol{v}')$. The code $\mathcal{C}'_0$ has codimension $\ell' \leqslant \ell$ in $\mathbf{GRS}_{k-s}(\boldsymbol{\alpha}', \boldsymbol{v}')$ and since $\dim \mathcal{C}_I = k-s$, we deduce that $\mathcal{C}_I$ is the direct sum of a codimension ℓ' subspace of $\mathbf{GRS}_{k-s}(\boldsymbol{\alpha}', \boldsymbol{v}')$ and a code of dimension ℓ'. Hence it is an ℓ'-qGRS code. □

Remark 2. Note that the typical scenario is that the shortening of an ℓ-qGRS code remains an ℓ–qGRS. Cases where ℓ decreases are sporadic. For $\ell = 1$, we can observe the following.

Lemma 3. *Let* $\mathcal{E}$ *be a subspace of codimension* 1 *of* $\mathbb{F}_q[x]_{<k}$ *and assume that*

$$p(x) = \prod_{\alpha_i, i\in I} (x - \alpha_i) \quad \textit{for} \quad I \subsetneq [n] \quad \textit{with} \quad |I| = a.$$

Then $\mathcal{E}_{p(x)}$ *has codimension* 0 *or* 1 *in* $p(x)\mathbb{F}_q[x]_{<k-a}$.

Proof. By definition, $\mathcal{E}_{p(x)} \subseteq p(x)\mathbb{F}_q[x]_{<k-a}$ and $\dim p(x)\mathbb{F}_q[x]_{<k-a} = k - a$. Thus $\dim \mathcal{E}_{p(x)} \leqslant k - a$. On the other hand, note that

$$\mathcal{E}_{p(x)} = \bigcap_{i=1}^{a} \ker \begin{pmatrix} \mathcal{E} \to \mathbb{F}_q \\ f \mapsto f(\alpha_i) \end{pmatrix}. \tag{6}$$

This implies $\dim(\mathcal{E}_{p(x)}) \geqslant \dim(\mathcal{E}) - a = k - 1 - a$, and the result follows. □

Remark 3. It turns out that, in general, the shortening of a TGRS code is not a TGRS one. Therefore, Proposition 9 highlights an important interest of the notion of qGRS codes compared to TGRS codes. This will be particularly useful in the sequel, as the shortening operation plays a crucial role in the distinguishers and attacks to be discussed.

4 TGRS Codes and a Distinguisher Based on Schur Product

In this section, we show how shortening and squaring can be exploited to distinguish qGRS codes from random ones for suitable parameters. From Proposition 9, this straightforwardly leads a distinguisher on TGRS codes for suitable parameters. We start by discussing the general setting, *i.e.* an arbitrary number of ℓ twists. We then focus specifically on the case where $\ell = 1$, for which we will derive an attack in the subsequent section.

4.1 A Distinguisher for General ℓ

4.1.1 Polynomial Setting

Let $(\boldsymbol{\alpha}, \boldsymbol{v})$ such that $\boldsymbol{\alpha}$ is a sequence of distinct elements and $\boldsymbol{v}$ is a sequence of nonzero elements both in $\mathbb{F}_q$. We have the corresponding evaluation map $\mathrm{ev}_{\boldsymbol{\alpha},\boldsymbol{v}} : \mathbb{F}_q[x] \to \mathbb{F}_q^n$.

In what follows, we consider a qGRS code $\mathcal{C}$ (see Definition 6) such that

$$\mathcal{C} = \mathcal{C}_0 \oplus \mathcal{C}_1$$

where $\mathcal{C}_0$ has codimension ℓ in $\mathbf{GRS}_k(\boldsymbol{\alpha}, \boldsymbol{v})$ (thus $\mathcal{C}_0$ is a subcode of $\mathbf{GRS}_k(\boldsymbol{\alpha}, \boldsymbol{v})$), $\mathcal{C}_1$ has dimension ℓ and $\mathcal{C}_1 \cap \mathbf{GRS}_k(\boldsymbol{\alpha}, \boldsymbol{v}) = 0$. In particular, $\mathcal{C}$ has dimension k.

Via the correspondence discussed in § 2.4, $\mathcal{C} = \mathrm{ev}_{\boldsymbol{\alpha},\boldsymbol{v}}(\mathcal{P})$ such that $\mathcal{P} \subseteq \mathbb{F}_q[x]_{<n}$ and

$$\mathcal{P} = \mathcal{P}_0 \oplus \mathcal{P}_1,$$

where $\mathcal{P}_0$ has codimension ℓ in $\mathbb{F}_q[x]_{<k}$ and $\mathcal{P}_1 \cap \mathbb{F}_q[x]_{<k} = 0$. Denote $v_1, \dots, v_\ell$ a basis of $\mathcal{P}_1$ whose elements have strictly increasing degrees and denote by

$$d_\ell \stackrel{\text{def}}{=} \deg(v_\ell) \tag{7}$$

which is the maximal possible degree for an element of $\mathcal{P}$.

4.1.2 Inequalities for Distinguishing

For distinguishing $\mathcal{C}$ from a random code, we examine the dimension of $\mathcal{C}^2$ or $\mathcal{C}_I^2$ for some $I \subseteq [n]$. For $\mathcal{C}$ to be distinguishable from random codes, we need

$$\dim \mathcal{C}_I^2 \leqslant \min \left\{ n - |I|, \binom{\dim \mathcal{C}_I + 1}{2} \right\}.$$

Remark 4. For $|I| < k$, the typical situation is that $\dim \mathcal{C}_I = k - |I|$ and we will assume this situation throughout this section. Note that if this condition does not hold for almost any such I, such an observation would yield a distinguisher on the code.

Proposition 10. *Let $\mathcal{C}$ be an ℓ-qGRS code of dimension k obtained by evaluation of $\mathcal{P} \subseteq \mathbb{F}_q[x]$ with maximal degree d_ℓ. Then,*

$$\dim \mathcal{C}^2 \leqslant \min \left\{ (\ell+2)k - 1 - \frac{\ell(\ell-1)}{2},\ k + d_\ell + \frac{\ell(\ell+1)}{2},\ 2d_\ell + 1 \right\}.$$

Proof. Consider the notation introduced in Sect. 4.1.1. Proposition 6 asserts that

$$\dim \mathcal{C}^2 \leqslant \dim \mathcal{P}^2.$$

Thus we will estimate $\dim \mathcal{P}^2$. Note that

$$\mathcal{P}^2 = \mathcal{P}_0^2 + \mathcal{P}_0\mathcal{P}_1 + \mathcal{P}_1^2. \tag{8}$$

Since $\mathcal{P}_0 \subseteq \mathbb{F}_q[x]_{<k}$, Proposition 5 asserts that $\dim \mathcal{P}_0^2 \leqslant 2k - 1$. Then, by Proposition 4,

$$\dim \mathcal{P}_0\mathcal{P}_1 \leqslant \ell(k-\ell) \quad \text{and} \quad \dim \mathcal{P}_1^2 \leqslant \frac{\ell(\ell+1)}{2}.$$

Including the last estimates in (8) yields:

$$\dim \mathcal{P}^2 \leqslant 2k - 1 + \ell(k-\ell) + \frac{\ell(\ell+1)}{2} = (\ell+2)k - 1 - \frac{\ell(\ell-1)}{2},$$

from which we can deduce the first upper bound.

Next observe that, from the definition of d_ℓ, $\mathcal{P} \subseteq \mathbb{F}_q[x]_{<d_\ell+1}$. Therefore, rewriting (8) as

$$\mathcal{P}^2 \subseteq \mathcal{P}_0\mathbb{F}_q[x]_{<d_\ell+1} + \mathcal{P}_1^2,$$

then, since $\mathcal{P}_0 \subseteq \mathbb{F}_q[x]_{<k}$, from Proposition 5 we get,

$$\mathcal{P}^2 \subseteq \mathbb{F}_q[x]_{<k+d_\ell} + \mathcal{P}_1^2$$

which yields the second upper bound:

$$\dim \mathcal{C}^2 \leqslant k + d_\ell + \frac{\ell(\ell+1)}{2}.$$

Finally, from the inclusion $\mathcal{P} \subseteq \mathbb{F}_q[x]_{<d_\ell+1}$ together with Proposition 5, we can deduce that $\mathcal{P}^2 \subseteq \mathbb{F}_q[x]_{<2d_\ell+1}$ yielding the third inequality:

$$\dim \mathcal{C}^2 \leqslant 2d_\ell + 1.$$

□

Remark 5. The third upper bound $\dim \mathcal{C}^2 \leqslant 2d_\ell + 1$ corresponds to the dimension of the square of the code referred to as the *outer code* in [3].

Theorem 1. *Let $\mathcal{C}$ be an ℓ–qGRS of dimension k and $I \subseteq [n]$ be a set such that $|I| < k$ such that* $\dim \mathcal{C}_I = k - |I|$, *then,*

$$\dim \mathcal{C}_I^2 \leqslant \min \Big\{ (\ell+2)(k-|I|) - 1 - \frac{\ell(\ell-1)}{2}, \\ k + d_\ell - 2|I| + \frac{\ell(\ell+1)}{2},\ 2(d_\ell - |I|) + 1 \Big\}.$$

Proof. According to Proposition 9, the shortening of $\mathcal{C}$ is still an ℓ'–qGRS code for $\ell' \leqslant \ell$. Thus, the result is a direct consequence of Proposition 10 where the following changes of variables, are applied:

$$\ell \leftarrow \ell' \quad k \leftarrow k - |I| \quad d_\ell \leftarrow d_\ell - |I|.$$

Two things may require clarifications. First, according to this change of variables the result should involve ℓ' and not ℓ. However, since the upper bounds of Proposition 10 are increasing functions in ℓ, if they hold for $\ell' \leqslant \ell$ they still hold for ℓ. Thus ℓ' can be replaced by ℓ in the final bounds.

Second, the change of variable $d_\ell \leftarrow d_\ell - |I|$ requires further details. From Sect. 2.4.2, the shortened code $\mathcal{C}_I$ corresponds to the polynomial space $\mathcal{P}_{p_I}$ where $p_I(x) \stackrel{\text{def}}{=} \prod_{i \in I}(x - \alpha_i)$. Since $\mathcal{P} \subseteq \mathbb{F}_q[x]_{<d_\ell+1}$, then $\mathcal{P}_{p_I} \subseteq p_I \mathbb{F}_q[x]_{<d_\ell - |I|+1}$. Therefore, when shortening by forgetting the common factor p_I, we effectively deal with polynomials of degree $\leqslant d_\ell - |I|$. This concludes the proof. □

Corollary 1. *Let $\mathcal{C}$ be a $(\boldsymbol{\alpha}, \boldsymbol{v}, \mathbf{t}, \mathbf{h}, \eta)$ TGRS code of dimension k. Denote by t_{max} the largest entry of $\mathbf{t}$. Let $I \subseteq [n]$ with $|I| < k$. Then*

$$\dim \mathcal{C}_I^2 \leqslant \min \Big\{ (\ell+2)(k-|I|) - 1 - \frac{\ell(\ell-1)}{2}, \\ 2k + t_{max} - 1 - 2|I| + \frac{\ell(\ell+1)}{2},\ 2(k + t_{max} - |I|) - 1 \Big\}.$$

Proof. This is a straightforward consequence of Theorem 1 after observing that $d_\ell = k + t_{max} - 1$. □

4.1.3 The Range of the Distinguisher

There remains to analyze for which parameters qGRS codes can be distinguished from random ones. Since the class of qGRS codes is closed under duality, one can assume that $k \leqslant \frac{n}{2}$ to estimate the range of the distinguisher.

Now our objective is to identify for which parameters (n, k, ℓ) there exists $a < k$ such that for $I \subseteq [n]$ with $|I| = a$ we have

$$\dim \mathcal{C}_I^2 < \min \left\{ n - a, \frac{(k-a)(k-a+1)}{2} \right\}. \tag{9}$$

Theorem 1 yields 3 distinct bounds on $\dim \mathcal{C}_I^2$. The first one is that which decreases the fastest in a, thus, we will only consider this one, which permits a simpler analysis. Later on, when focusing on $\ell = 1$, the other bounds will be useful.

Now, we have to prove the existence of $0 \leqslant a < k$ such that

$$(\ell+2)(k-a) - 1 - \frac{\ell(\ell-1)}{2} < \min\left\{n-a, \frac{(k-a)(k-a+1)}{2}\right\}.$$

A calculation proves that the upper bound $< n - a$ holds for any a satisfying

$$a > \left(\frac{\ell+2}{\ell+1}\right)k - \frac{\ell(\ell-1)}{2(\ell+1)} - \frac{n}{\ell+1}. \tag{10}$$

For the second inequality, we consider a stronger and simpler one:

$$(\ell+2)(k-a) \leqslant \frac{(k-a)^2}{2},$$

which yields

$$a \leqslant k - 2(\ell+2). \tag{11}$$

Now, putting (10) and (11) together, we can conclude that if there exists an a where $a = |I|$ and such that

$$\left(\frac{\ell+2}{\ell+1}\right)k - \frac{\ell(\ell-1)}{2(\ell+1)} - \frac{n}{\ell+1} < a \leqslant k - 2(\ell+2)$$

then dimension of the shortened square code $\mathcal{C}_I^2$ satisfies (9) and so we can distinguishable these kind of codes from random ones.

Theorem 2. *An ℓ–qGRS code of dimension k is distinguishable from random as soon as:*

$$n - k \geqslant \frac{3}{2}\ell^2 + \frac{5}{2}\ell + 4.$$

Recall here that we supposed $k \leqslant \frac{n}{2}$, the left–hand side is then larger than $\frac{n}{2}$ while the right–hand side is in $O(\ell^2)$. For TGRS codes proposed for McEliece encryption, ℓ is supposed to be $O(1)$ since the decoding is exponential in ℓ. So we can conclude that: **TGRS codes proposed for McEliece encryption are distinguishable from random.**

4.2 The Case $\ell = 1$

Let us apply the previous results to a single twisted TGRS code, *i.e.* in the case $\ell = 1$. Recall that $\mathcal{C} = \mathrm{ev}(\mathcal{P})$ where $\mathcal{P} = \mathrm{Mon}_{<k,\hat{h}} + \langle x^h + \eta x^{k-1+t} \rangle$. The previous analysis provides.

Lemma 4. *Let $\mathcal{C}$ be an $(\boldsymbol{\alpha}, \boldsymbol{v}, \mathbf{t}, \mathbf{h}, \eta)$ 1–TGRS code of dimension k with $\mathbf{t} = (t)$ for some positive integer t. Let $I \subseteq [n]$ such that $|I| < k$ and $\dim \mathcal{C}_I = k - |I|$. Then,*

$$\dim \mathcal{C}^2 \leqslant \begin{cases} 3k-1 & \text{for } t \geqslant k, \\ 2k+t & \text{for } t < k. \end{cases}, \quad \dim \mathcal{C}_I^2 \leqslant \begin{cases} 3(k-|I|)-1 & \text{for } t \geqslant k-|I|, \\ 2(k-|I|)+t & \text{for } t < k-|I|. \end{cases}$$

Proof. From Corollary 1, applied with $\ell = 1$ and $t_{max} = t$, we get

$$\dim \mathcal{C}_I^2 \leqslant \min\{3(k-|I|)-1,\ 2k+t-2|I|\}.$$

This yields the proof. □

Next, we can redo the previous analysis in this case while making fewer approximations. We prove that the shortened code $\mathcal{C}_I$ has a square whose dimension differs from the typical one as soon as

$$\frac{3k-n}{2} \leqslant |I| \leqslant k-5. \tag{12}$$

Thus, such a code is distinguishable from random as soon as

$$n-k \geqslant 10.$$

Since we supposed $k \leqslant \frac{n}{2}$, any 1–qGRS code of length > 20 is distinguishable from random.

5 A Key-Recovery Attack on McEliece Scheme with TGRS Codes Using Schur Squares

In this section we present a key recovery attack for the McEliece cryptosystem instantiated with a TGRS code (see Sect. 2.5). Following the previous notations, let $\mathcal{C}$ be the public code generated by $\mathbf{G}_{pub}$, a generator matrix of a q-ary single-twisted TGRS code $\mathcal{C}^{n,k}_{\boldsymbol{\alpha},\boldsymbol{v},\mathbf{t},\mathbf{h},\eta} \subset \mathbb{F}_q^n$ of dimension k.

Note that, unlike [20], we do not impose any restriction on the parameters of the secret TGRS code.

5.1 Context and Notation

Let $\mathcal{C}$ or equivalently, the q-ary single-twisted TGRS code $\mathcal{C}^{n,k}_{\boldsymbol{\alpha},\boldsymbol{v},\mathbf{t},\mathbf{h},\eta}$ have dimension $k \leqslant \frac{n}{2}$ (otherwise, one can work with the dual code of $\mathcal{C}$).

Notation 3. *As $\mathcal{C}$ has a single twist, we let t, h, and η to be the twist, the hook, and the coefficient of $\mathcal{C}$, respectively. Let $\mathcal{P} = \mathcal{M} \oplus \langle x^h + \eta x^{k-1+t} \rangle$, where $\mathcal{M} = Mon_{<k,\hat{h}}$. For a subset $I \subseteq [n]$, we define $p_I(x) = \prod_{i \in I}(x - \alpha_i)$.*

Recall that the injectivity of $\mathrm{ev}_{\alpha,v}$ when restricted to $\mathbb{F}_q[x]_{<n}$ implies $\mathcal{C} = \mathrm{ev}_{\alpha,v}(\mathcal{P})$ and the shortening of $\mathcal{C}$ at I is $\mathcal{C}_I = \mathrm{ev}_{\alpha,v}(\mathcal{P}_{p_I(x)})$. Note that, $\mathcal{M}$ is a codimension 1 subspace of $\mathbb{F}_q[x]_{<k}$. By Lemma 3, $\mathcal{M}_{p(x)}$ is a subspace of $p(x)\mathbb{F}_q[x]_{<k-a}$ of codimension at most 1. Here is an inclusion diagram for the involved polynomial spaces, which are isomorphic to involved codes via the map $\mathrm{ev}_{\alpha,v}$.

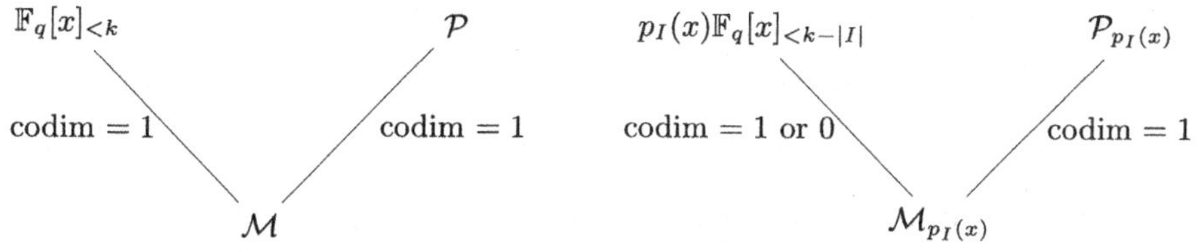

5.2 Key-Recovery Algorithm

We brief the main steps of our key recovery algorithm, which are given in detail in the following sections.

Step 1 Compute a basis of $\mathrm{ev}_{\alpha,v}(\mathcal{M})$ or $\mathrm{ev}_{\alpha,v}(\mathcal{M}_{p_I(x)})$ using a distinguisher-based method (Sect. 5.2.1).

Step 2 Use a Sidelnikov-Shestakov-like method given in [9, § 6.3] to recover the secret evaluation vectors and multipliers for $\mathcal{C}$ (Sect. 5.2.2).

Step 3 Compute the other secret parameters which are the twist t, the hook h, and the coefficient η (Sect. 5.2.3).

5.2.1 Step 1: Recovery of a Codimension One Subcode of the Public (shortened) Code

Following Lemma 4, we know that $\mathcal{C}$ can be distinguished by considering its Schur square for the case $3k < n$ and otherwise by taking the Schur square of a shortened code $\mathcal{C}_I$ with $(3k-n)/2 < |I| < k-5$ (according to (12)). Now, depending on t, we consider the following two cases.

1. If $2k-2+t < n$, then we compute a basis of the subcode $\mathrm{ev}_{\alpha,v}(\mathcal{M})$ of $\mathcal{C}$.
2. Otherwise, we compute a basis of the subcode $\mathrm{ev}_{\alpha,v}(\mathcal{M}_{p_I(x)})$ of the shortened code $\mathcal{C}_I$ for I such that $2k-2+t-n < |I|$.

Note that in Sect. 7, we work with polynomial spaces and to apply those results to the corresponding evaluation codes, we need $\mathrm{ev}_{\alpha,v}$ to be injective. Therefore, the choice of parameters in Case 1 has been made so that $\mathrm{ev}_{\alpha,v}$ is injective on the product space $\mathcal{MP}$. In Case 2, to make sure the injectivity of $\mathrm{ev}_{\alpha,v}$ on $\mathcal{M}_{p_I(x)}\mathcal{P}_{p_I(x)}$, I should be chosen such that $2(k-|I|)-2+t < n-|I|$, or equivalently, $2k+\ t-2-n < |I|$. Injectivity of $\mathrm{ev}_{\alpha,v}$ is crucial to apply the results on polynomial spaces, for instance, Proposition 11 and Theorem 4 to the corresponding codes.

First, we observe that, in Case 1, for a basis $\mathrm{ev}_{\alpha,v}(e_1), \ldots, \mathrm{ev}_{\alpha,v}(e_k)$ of $\mathcal{C}$, if we take three random elements $\mathrm{ev}_{\alpha,v}(f_1), \mathrm{ev}_{\alpha,v}(f_2), \mathrm{ev}_{\alpha,v}(f_3)$ from its monomial subcode $\mathrm{ev}_{\alpha,v}(\mathcal{M})$, then the linear space spanned by

$$\{\mathrm{ev}_{\alpha,v}(f_i) \star \mathrm{ev}_{\alpha,v}(e_j) : i = 1, 2, 3,\ 1 \leqslant j \leqslant k\}$$

has low dimension, more precisely bounded by $2k+2$. This is due to the following statement.

Proposition 11. *Let $f_1, f_2, f_3 \in \mathcal{M}$, then*

$$\dim(\langle f_1, f_2, f_3 \rangle \, \mathcal{P}) \leqslant 2k + 2. \tag{13}$$

Proof. The result follows from the fact that $\mathcal{M} \subset \mathbb{F}_q[x]_{<k}$ and $\mathcal{P} \subseteq \mathcal{M} \oplus \langle c \rangle$ for $c(x) = x^h + \eta x^{k-1+t}$. Thus,

$$\langle f_1, f_2, f_3 \rangle \, \mathcal{P} \subseteq \langle f_1, f_2, f_3 \rangle \, \mathcal{M} + \langle f_1 c, f_2 c, f_3 c \rangle \, .$$

Since $f_1, f_2, f_3 \in \mathcal{M}$ and $\mathcal{M} \subseteq \mathbb{F}_q[x]_{<k}$, the first term of the right–hand side is contained in $\mathbb{F}_q[x]_{<2k-1}$, which yields the result. □

It is important to note that Proposition 11 also holds in Case 2 if we replace $\mathcal{M}$ by $\mathcal{M}_{p_I(x)}$ and $\mathcal{P}$ by $\mathcal{P}_{p_I(x)}$. More importantly, if we consider f_1, f_2, f_3 randomly from $\mathcal{P}$, then due to the higher degree term x^{k-1+t}, the space $\langle f_1, f_2, f_3 \rangle \, \mathcal{P}$ is very likely to have a much larger dimension than $2k + 2$. This is indeed the case, as we prove the following result in Sect. 7. Note that in Sect. 7, we consider the case where $\mathcal{M}_{p(x)}$ has codimension 1 in $p(x)\mathbb{F}_q[x]_{<k-a}$. For the case $\mathcal{M}_{p(x)} = p(x)\mathbb{F}_q[x]_{<k-a}$, the probabilistic estimates actually become even more favorable.

Theorem 4. *Let n, k, t be integers such that $17 \leqslant k < n$ and $17 \leqslant t \leqslant n - k$. Suppose $\mathcal{R} = \mathcal{E}' \oplus \langle c(x) \rangle \subseteq \mathbb{F}_q[x]$, where $\mathcal{E}' \underset{codim\ 1}{\subseteq} \mathbb{F}_q[x]_{<k}$ and $c(x)$ has degree $k - 1 + t$. If $f_1, f_2, f_3 \in \mathcal{R}$ and satisfy*

$$\dim(\langle f_1, f_2, f_3 \rangle \, \mathcal{R}) \leqslant 2k + 2,$$

then $f_1, f_2, f_3 \in \mathcal{E}'$ with probability $\geqslant 1 - \frac{1}{q^2}$. Furthermore, a basis of $\mathcal{E}'$ is recovered with probability $\geqslant (1 - \frac{(k-3)}{q^2})$.

Remark 6. Let us explain why exactly three functions are chosen in Theorem 4 and in Algorithm 1. If we draw s elements of the public at random code, the probability that each one lies in some fixed codimension one subcode is q^{-s}. Hence, in average, we will have $O(q^s)$ trials to perform before succeeding. Thus, the larger the s the larger the complexity of the attack. Next, observe that with $s = 2$ we cannot distinguish elements of the subcodes since for any code $\mathcal{D}$

$$\dim \langle f_1, f_2 \rangle * \mathcal{D} \leqslant 2 \dim \mathcal{D} - 1 < 2 \dim \mathcal{D} + 2.$$

Thus $s = 3$ is the least number of elements that yields a successful attack. Because of the aforementioned complexity issues there is no interest in considering a higher s.

Now, we apply Theorem 4 by taking $\mathcal{R} = \mathcal{P}$ and $\mathcal{E}' = \mathcal{M}$ (Case 1) or $\mathcal{R} = \mathcal{P}_{p_I(x)}$ and $\mathcal{E}' = \mathcal{M}_{p_I(x)}$ (Case 2) to ensure the isomorphism between the polynomial spaces and the corresponding codes via the evaluation map $\mathrm{ev}_{\boldsymbol{\alpha},\boldsymbol{v}}$. Based on the above theorem, which is proved in Sect. 7, we recover the codimension 1 subcode $\mathrm{ev}_{\boldsymbol{\alpha},\boldsymbol{v}}(\mathcal{M})$ of $\mathcal{C}$ (in Case 1) or $\mathrm{ev}_{\boldsymbol{\alpha},\boldsymbol{v}}(\mathcal{M}_{p(x)})$ of $\mathcal{C}_I$ (in Case 2) with probability at least $1-\frac{k-3}{q^2}$ using a distinguisher based method explained in Algorithm 1. This algorithm was introduced in [9, Algorithm 1] in a quite different version: we adapted it to the framework of our attack. Note that the parameter k in Algorithm 1 refers to the dimension of $\mathcal{R}$. Therefore, when we apply the algorithm, it will be for k in Case 1 and for $k - |I|$ in Case 2.

The recovery algorithm (Algorithm 1) proceeds as follows.

In Case 1: 1. Draw random triples $(\boldsymbol{c}_1, \boldsymbol{c}_2, \boldsymbol{c}_3) \in \mathcal{C}^3$ until we find one such that

$$\dim(\langle \boldsymbol{c}_1, \boldsymbol{c}_2, \boldsymbol{c}_3 \rangle \mathcal{C}) \leqslant 2k + 2.$$

According to Theorem 4 such a triple is likely to be in $\mathrm{ev}_{\boldsymbol{\alpha},\boldsymbol{v}}(\mathcal{M})$. Since $\mathcal{M}$ has codimension 1 in $\mathcal{C}$, the probaility of finding such a triple is $\frac{1}{q^3}$ and hence in $O(q^3)$ trials, we should find such a triple.
We collect other elements of $\mathrm{ev}_{\boldsymbol{\alpha},\boldsymbol{v}}(\mathcal{M})$ until we get a basis of this monomial subcode. For this sake, draw $\boldsymbol{c} \in \mathcal{C}$ and keep it if

$$\dim(\langle \boldsymbol{c}_1, \boldsymbol{c}_2, \boldsymbol{c} \rangle \mathcal{C}) \leqslant 2k + 2.$$

Such a $\boldsymbol{c}$ is found in $O(q)$ trials.
In Case 2: We do the same while replacing $\mathcal{C}$ by $\mathcal{C}_I$ and $\mathcal{M}$ by $\mathcal{M}_{p_I}$. Next, we iterate this process by choosing subsets $I_1, \ldots, I_s \subset [n]$ satisfying $\bigcap_{i=1}^{s} I_i = \emptyset$ and $(3k - n)/2 < |I_i| < k - 5$ for all $i = 1, \ldots, s$. The last condition being taken to recover the codimension 1 subcodes $\mathrm{ev}_{\boldsymbol{\alpha},\boldsymbol{v}}(\mathcal{M}_{p_{I_i}})$ of $\mathcal{C}_{I_i}$. We collect shortenings $\mathrm{ev}_{\boldsymbol{\alpha},\boldsymbol{v}}(\mathcal{M}_{p_{I_i}})$ and sum them up until the sum has dimension $k-1$. This permits to recover the monomial subcode $\mathrm{ev}_{\boldsymbol{\alpha},\boldsymbol{v}}(\mathcal{M})$.
This recovery of a subcode by summing up shortenings is already used and discussed in [14, § IV.F].

In summary, whatever the parameters k, t, in the end of this step we have a basis of $\mathrm{ev}_{\boldsymbol{\alpha},\boldsymbol{v}}(\mathcal{M})$.

5.2.2 Step 2: Recovery of the Secret Evaluation Vector and the Multipliers

Now we have access to the space $\mathrm{ev}_{\boldsymbol{\alpha},\boldsymbol{v}}(\mathcal{M})$. Since $\mathcal{M} \subseteq \mathbb{F}_q[x]_{<k}$ and we assumed $k \leqslant \frac{n}{2}$, we see that $\mathcal{M}^2 \subseteq \mathbb{F}_q[x]_{<2k-1}$ and hence $\mathrm{ev}_{\boldsymbol{\alpha},\boldsymbol{v}}(\mathcal{M}) \subsetneq \mathbb{F}_q^n$. Moreover, $\mathcal{M} = \left\langle 1, x, \ldots, \widehat{x^h}, \ldots, x^{k-1} \right\rangle$. A classical argument from combinatorics permits to prove that if $h \neq 1$ or $k-2$, then $\mathcal{M}^2 = \mathbb{F}_q[x]_{<2k-1}$. In such a situation, $\mathrm{ev}_{\boldsymbol{\alpha},\boldsymbol{v}}(\mathcal{M})^2$ is a GRS code, and then the Sidelnikov–Shestakov attack can be applied to it as it is done in [34].

This permits to recover a candidate for the pair $(\boldsymbol{\alpha}, \boldsymbol{v})$.

Algorithm 1. Recovering $\mathcal{C}_0$.

Input : A basis $\{\boldsymbol{c}_1, \ldots, \boldsymbol{c}_k\}$ of $\mathcal{C}$
Output : A basis $\mathcal{B}$ of $\mathcal{C}_0$.

repeat
  for $1 \leqslant i \leqslant 3$ **do**
    Randomly choose $\boldsymbol{b}_i$ in $\mathcal{C}$
  end for
  $\mathscr{D} \leftarrow \langle \{\boldsymbol{b}_i \star \boldsymbol{c}_j \mid 1 \leqslant i \leqslant 3 \text{ and } 1 \leqslant j \leqslant k\} \rangle$
until $\dim(\mathscr{D}) \leqslant 2k+2$ **and** $\dim(\langle \boldsymbol{b}_1, \boldsymbol{b}_2, \boldsymbol{b}_3 \rangle) = 3$
$\mathcal{B} \leftarrow \{\boldsymbol{b}_1, \boldsymbol{b}_2, \boldsymbol{b}_3\}$
$s \leftarrow 4$
while $s \leqslant k-1$ **do**
  repeat
    Randomly choose $\boldsymbol{b}_s$ in $\mathcal{C}$
    $\mathcal{E} \leftarrow \langle \{\boldsymbol{b}_i \star \boldsymbol{c}_j \mid i \in \{1,2,s\} \text{ and } 1 \leqslant j \leqslant k\} \rangle$
  until $\dim(\mathcal{E}) \leqslant 2k+2$ **and** $\dim(\langle \mathcal{B} \cup \{\boldsymbol{b}_s\} \rangle) = s$
  $\mathcal{B} \leftarrow \mathcal{B} \cup \{\boldsymbol{b}_s\}$
  $s \leftarrow s+1$
end while
return $\mathcal{B}$;

Remark 7. We did not consider here the pathological cases $h = 1$ or $k-2$. They should be subject to a separate development that we do not treat in this article.

5.2.3 Step 3: Recovery of the Hook h, the Twist t, and the Coefficient η of the Secret Key

The previous steps provide $\boldsymbol{\alpha}$ and $\boldsymbol{v}$ which we use to recover the hook h, the twist t and the coefficient η.

Recovering h. For $0 \leqslant i \leqslant k-1$, we check if $\boldsymbol{v} \star \boldsymbol{\alpha}^i \in \mathcal{C}$ or not. Our assumption on $\mathbf{G}_{pub}$ implies that there is exactly one i for which $\boldsymbol{v} \star \boldsymbol{\alpha}^i \notin \mathcal{C}$, and that integer would be the hook h.
Recovering t. Take a codeword $\boldsymbol{c} \in \mathcal{C} \setminus \mathrm{ev}_{\boldsymbol{\alpha},\boldsymbol{v}}(\mathcal{M})$. By interpolation we get $f \in \mathbb{F}_q[x]_{<n}$ such that $c = \mathrm{ev}_{\boldsymbol{\alpha},\boldsymbol{v}}(f)$ and $\deg(f) = k-1+t$ for some positive t. Which yields t.
Recovering η. Still considering the same f and denoting by f_i its coefficient of degree i then η satisfies $f_{k-1+t} = \eta f_h$, which permits to deduce η.

5.2.4 Attacked Parameters (with a Proof)

We provide the sets of parameters in Table 1, which includes the TRS codes considered in [20] for the single twist case (labeled as [LR]) as well as the parameters for the provable attack discussed in this article (labeled as [CPTZ]).

We emphasize that,

- In the table, we consider only parameters for which Theorem 4 holds. Note that, in Case 2 (as mentioned in the beginning of Subsect. 5.2.1), we can apply

Theorem 4 if $k - |I| < 17$. Thus considering the conditions $2k + t - 2 - n < |I| \leqslant k - 17$, we get $t < n - k - 15$.

- [20] restricts to a limited subclass of TRS codes while we consider the much broader class of TGRS codes (the attack can be extended to qGRS codes with no difficulty).
  - $q = q_0^2$ and $k < n \leqslant q_0 - 1$ where q_0 is a prime power,
  - $\frac{n}{3} + \sqrt{n} + \frac{1}{3} < k \leqslant \frac{n}{2} - 2$ (the left hand side inequality comes from the lower bound for ℓ in the proposed set of parameters),
  - $r = \lceil \frac{n+1}{3} \rceil + 2$,
  - $t = 2\lceil \frac{n+1}{3} \rceil - k + 2$ and thus $t \geqslant \frac{2n}{3} - \frac{n}{2} + 4 = \frac{n}{6} + 4$.
  - $h = r$ which implies that $h \neq 1, k - 2$.

Table 1. The parameters for provable attacks in the case of single twist

	[LR]	[CPTZ]
q	n^2	n
$k \in$	$\left[\frac{n}{3} + \sqrt{n} + \frac{1}{3}, \frac{n}{2} - 2\right]$	$[\sqrt{2n}, n - 14]$
t	$2\lceil \frac{n+1}{3} \rceil - k + 2$	$[17, n - k - 16]$
h	$\lceil \frac{n+1}{3} \rceil + 2$	$\neq 1, k - 2$

We mention that in [3], $t \geqslant \frac{2n}{3} - \frac{n}{2} + 4 = \frac{n}{6} + 4$. Thus, $t < 17$ will imply $n < 78$, which is really small compared to the practical parameters.

5.3 Complexity

According to [15, Prop. 2], the complexity of computing a Schur square is $O(n^4)$. Next, the bottelneck of the attack is the first step with the recovery of the first triple $(\mathbf{c}_1, \mathbf{c}_2, \mathbf{c}_3) \in \mathrm{ev}_{\boldsymbol{\alpha},\boldsymbol{v}}(\mathcal{M})^3$. We claim that this step is the dominant one in the running of the attack. Since, this step requires $O(q^3)$ trials this yields an overall complexity of $O(q^3 n^4)$ operations in $\mathbb{F}_q$.

5.4 Some Comments About the Non Covered Cases

We observe the cases where the key-recovery attack might fail:

- if $h = 1$ or $k - 2$, the square of the codimension 1 subcode we recover in Step 1, might not have Schur square equal to $\mathbf{GRS}_{2k-1}$.
- for $k, t < 17$, Theorem 4 is no longer valid.

Here we give some ideas on alternative ways to recover a valid secret key without going into detailed description.

5.4.1 When t is Small

We consider in particular the case where $t < k$ and that we still assume that $k < \frac{n}{2}$. Recall that $\mathcal{C} = \mathrm{ev}_{\alpha,v}(\mathcal{P})$, where $\mathcal{P} = \mathcal{M} \oplus \langle c(x) \rangle$ with

$$\mathcal{M} = \left\langle 1, x, \ldots, \widehat{x^h}, \ldots, x^{k-1} \right\rangle$$

for some $h \leqslant k-1$ and $\deg(c) = k-1+t$.

Suppose first that $2k+t < n-2$. In this situation, observe that:

$$\mathcal{P}^2 = \mathcal{M}^2 + \mathcal{C}\mathcal{M} + \left\langle c^2 \right\rangle.$$

Since $\deg(c) < k+t < 2k$ then $\mathcal{M}^2 + \mathcal{C}\mathcal{M} \subseteq \mathbb{F}_q[x]_{2k+t}$ and it is very likely that this inclusion is an equality. In this case, $\mathcal{C}^2$ is the direct sum of a GRS code and the one-dimensional space $\mathrm{ev}_{\alpha,v}(\langle c^2 \rangle)$. In this situation, taking the dual of $\mathcal{C}^2$ yields a codimension 1 subcode of a GRS code whose structure can be recovered using Wieschebrink's attack [34].

When $2k+t > n$, a similar approach can be applied to shortenings of the code.

6 Implementation

The first part of the attack, that is to say the computation of the monomial subcode (Step 1, Subsect. 5.2.1) is implemented in the computer algebra system SageMath v9.5 [28]. It is available on https://github.com/nihantanisali/TGRS. Since the rest of the attack consists in applying Sidelnikov Shestakov attack together with other classical routines we considered that checking the validity of Step 1 was sufficient. Note that our implementation is a proof of concept that is far from being optimized. Hence, due to time and resource constraints we chose smaller q and k. The results are summarized in Table 2. Even though these small-scale instances do not fully capture the computational challenges posed by larger, standard parameters, they demonstrate that our method works in practice.

Table 2. Experimental results obtained by averaging several runtimes of Algorithm 1 on a 13th Gen Intel® Core™ i7-13800H × 20.

q_0	n	k	t	l	h	$a = \lvert I \rvert$	Runtime (s)
53	51	17	17	1	8	–	240
53	51	19	8	1	8	–	261
61	51	25	17	1	19	8	3834

7 A Result on the Polynomial Space

The aim of this section is to provide a proof of Theorem 4. We will consider a polynomial subspace

$$\mathcal{R} = \mathcal{E}' \oplus \langle c(x) \rangle \subseteq \mathbb{F}_q[x],$$

where $\mathcal{E}' \underset{\text{codim } 1}{\subseteq} \mathbb{F}_q[x]_{<k}$, and $c(x) \in \mathbb{F}_q[x]$ such that $\deg(c) = k - 1 + t$ with $t > 0$. We will determine the quantity

$$\dim \langle f_1, f_2, f_3 \rangle \mathcal{R}$$

for different choices of $f_1, f_2, f_3 \in \mathcal{R}$ depending on admissible values of t and k, which will be specified later.

First, recall that Proposition 11 yields an upper bound on $\dim \langle f_1, f_2, f_3 \rangle \mathcal{R}$ for $f_1, f_2, f_3 \in \mathcal{E}'$:

$$\dim \langle f_1, f_2, f_3 \rangle \mathcal{R} \leqslant 2k + 2.$$

Then, we study the general case of $f_1, f_2, f_3 \in \mathcal{R}$ in order to prove Theorem 4. First we define the following sets.

$$\Psi \overset{\text{def}}{=} \{(f_1, f_2, f_3) \in \mathcal{R}^3 : \dim \langle f_1, f_2, f_3 \rangle \mathcal{R} > 2k + 2\}; \tag{14}$$

$$\Gamma \overset{\text{def}}{=} \{(f_1, f_2, f_3) \in \mathcal{R}^3 \setminus \mathcal{E}'^3 : \dim \langle f_1, f_2, f_3 \rangle \mathcal{R} \leqslant 2k + 2\}. \tag{15}$$

We get a partition of $\mathcal{R}^3 = \mathcal{E}'^3 \sqcup \Gamma \sqcup \Psi$ as illustrated in Fig. 1.

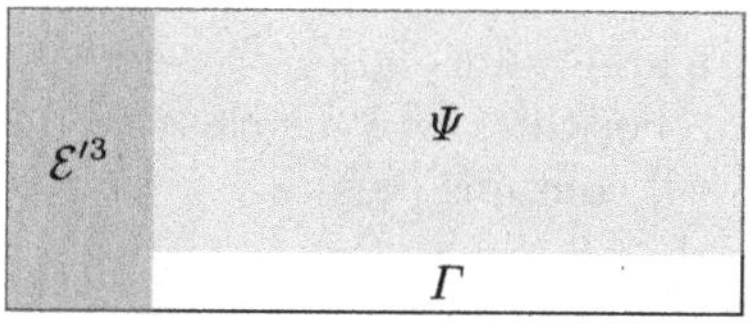

Fig. 1. Illustrates the partition $\mathcal{E}'^3 \sqcup \Psi \sqcup \Gamma$ of $\mathcal{R}^3$

Our main goal in this section is to prove that if $(f_1, f_2, f_3) \in \mathcal{R}^3$ with $\dim \langle f_1, f_2, f_3 \rangle \mathcal{R} \leqslant 2k + 2$, then $(f_1, f_2, f_3) \in \mathcal{E}'^3$ with probability $\geqslant 1 - \frac{1}{q^2}$. This probability corresponds to showing that

$$\frac{|\mathcal{E}'^3|}{|\mathcal{E}'^3 \sqcup \Gamma|} \geqslant 1 - \frac{1}{q^2}. \tag{16}$$

Let $f_1, f_2, f_3 \in \mathcal{R}$. If $f_i \notin \mathcal{E}'$ for some $1 \leqslant i \leqslant 3$, then w.l.o.g. (after taking linear combinations), we can assume that the polynomials are of the form

$$\begin{aligned}
f_1(x) &:= a_0 + a_1 x + \cdots + a_{k-1} x^{k-1} + a_{k-1+t} c(x), \quad a_{k-1+t} \neq 0, \\
f_2(x) &:= b_0 + b_1 x + \cdots + b_{k-1} x^{k-1}, \\
f_3(x) &:= c_0 + c_1 x + \cdots + c_{k-1} x^{k-1}.
\end{aligned}$$

First, note that $\dim \langle f_1, f_2, f_3 \rangle \mathcal{R} \geqslant \dim \langle f_1, f_2, f_3 \rangle \mathcal{E}'$. We now focus on $\dim \langle f_1, f_2, f_3 \rangle \mathcal{E}'$. Clearly, the dimension of the space $f_1\mathcal{E}'$ is $k-1$. We now fix a basis $\{e_1(x), \dots, e_{k-1}(x)\}$ of $\mathcal{E}'$ such that $\deg(e_1) < \cdots < \deg(e_{k-1})$.

For all polynomials $e_i(x) \in \mathcal{E}'$, we have that

$$k - 1 + t \leqslant \deg(e_i(x) f_1(x)) \leqslant 2k - 2 + t.$$

We define the subspace of $f_1\mathcal{E}'$ generated by e_i's of *large degrees*, denoted by $(f_1\mathcal{E}')_l$, as follows:

$$(f_1\mathcal{E}')_l \stackrel{\text{def}}{=} \langle f_1 e_i \; : \; \deg(f_1) + \deg(e_i) \geqslant 2k - 1 \rangle \, .$$

We have

$$\dim((f_1\mathcal{E}')_l) = \begin{cases} k - 1 & \text{if } t \geqslant k, \\ t - 1 \text{ or } t & \text{if } t < k. \end{cases} \tag{17}$$

For $t < k$ in the above (17), $\dim((f_1\mathcal{E}')_l)$ has two possibilities depending on the missing integer $t_1 \in \{0, \dots, k-1\} \setminus \{\deg(e_i) \; : \; i = 1, \dots, k-1\}$. Indeed, if $k - 1 + t + t_1 \geqslant 2k - 1$, then $\dim((f_1\mathcal{E}')_l) = t - 1$ or t, otherwise. Using the fact that the space $f_2\mathcal{E}' + f_3\mathcal{E}'$ contains polynomials up to degree $2k - 2$ (as $\deg(f_2), \deg(f_3) \leqslant k - 1$), we get the equalities

$$\dim \langle f_1, f_2, f_3 \rangle \mathcal{E}' = \begin{cases} k - 1 + \dim \langle f_2, f_3 \rangle \mathcal{E}' & \text{if } t \geqslant k, \\ \left. \begin{array}{l} t - 1 + \dim \langle f_2, f_3 \rangle \mathcal{E}' \\ \text{or,} \quad t + \dim \langle f_2, f_3 \rangle \mathcal{E}' \end{array} \right\} & \text{if } t < \text{ k} \end{cases} \tag{18}$$

We now focus on estimating $\dim \langle f_2, f_3 \rangle \mathcal{E}'$ where f_2 and f_3 are chosen uniformly at random from $\mathcal{E}'$. For this, we use a classical result on polynomials that we prove for the sake of self containedness.

Lemma 5. *Let $f, g \in \mathbb{F}_q[x]_{<k}$ be two polynomials. Then*

$$\dim(f\mathbb{F}_q[x]_{<k} + g\mathbb{F}_q[x]_{<k}) = k + \max\{\deg f, \deg g\} - \deg(\gcd(f, g)).$$

Proof. Set $s = \deg f$, $u = \deg g$, $h = \gcd(f, g)$ and $d = \deg h$. W.l.o.g. one can assume $s = \max\{s, u\}$ and we set $f_1(x) = f(x)/h(x)$ and $g_1(x) = g(x)/h(x)$. Consider the linear map

$$\phi : \begin{cases} \mathbb{F}_q[x]_{<k} \times \mathbb{F}_q[x]_{<k} \longrightarrow f\mathbb{F}_q[x]_{<k} + g\mathbb{F}_q[x]_{<k} \\ \qquad (a, b) \qquad\qquad \longmapsto \qquad af + bg. \end{cases}$$

Any $(a, b) \in \ker \phi$ satisfies $af = -bg$. By dividing both sides by h we get $af_1 = -bg_1$ and since f_1, g_1 are coprime, we deduce that there exists $p \in \mathbb{F}_q[x]$ such that $a = g_1 p$ and $b = -f_1 p$. Since a, b have degrees $< k$, we deduce that $\deg f_1 + \deg p = s - d + \deg p < k$. Therefore,

$$\ker \phi = \{(g_1 p, -f_1 p) \; : \; p \in \mathbb{F}_q[x]_{<k-s+d}\}.$$

Thus, $\dim \ker \phi = k - s + d$ and the rank–nullity theorem permits to conclude. $\square$

Observe that $\dim \langle f_2, f_3 \rangle \mathcal{E}' \geqslant \dim(f_2\mathbb{F}_q[x]_{<k} + f_3\mathbb{F}_q[x]_{<k}) - 2$. Now, (18) implies that in order to get $\dim \langle f_1, f_2, f_3 \rangle \mathcal{E}' > 2k + 2$ it suffices to have

$$\dim \langle f_2, f_3 \rangle \mathcal{E}' > \begin{cases} k+3 & \text{if } t \geqslant k, \\ 2k - t + 3 & \text{if } t < k. \end{cases} \tag{19}$$

As a straightforward consequence of Lemma 5, we reduce the dimension conditions to a condition on the degree of $\gcd(f_2, f_3)$. We give the condition more generally for any pair of polynomials $(f, g) \in \mathbb{F}_q[x]_{<k} \times \mathbb{F}_q[x]_{<k}$ and we call it the *gcd condition* as defined below.

Definition 7. *We say that a polynomial pair $(f, g) \in \mathbb{F}_q[x]_{<k} \times \mathbb{F}_q[x]_{<k}$ with degrees s and u* satisfies the gcd condition *if*

$$\deg(\gcd(f, g)) < \begin{cases} \max\{s, u\} - 5 & \textit{if } t > k \\ \max\{s, u\} - (k - t) - 5 & \textit{if } t \leqslant k. \end{cases} \tag{20}$$

Remark 8. Note that the bounds on the degree of the gcd in (20) are taken so that, if a pair $(f_2, f_3) \in \mathcal{E}' \times \mathcal{E}'$ satisfies the gcd condition in Definition 7, then $(f_1, f_2, f_3) \in \Psi$ for $f_1 \in \mathcal{R} \setminus \mathcal{E}'$ (see (14) for the definition of Ψ). Therefore, it helps to obtain a bound on the size of Ψ, that we determine in the subsequent part.

We aim to find the number of pairs $(f_2, f_3) \in \mathbb{F}_q[x]_{<k} \times \mathbb{F}_q[x]_{<k}$ that satisfy the gcd condition given in Definition 7. For that, we introduce the required notations and notions.

Definition 8. *Let i, j, s, u be non-negative integers such that $s, u < k$. Define*

1. $\mathcal{G} := \{(f, g) \in \mathbb{F}_q[x]_{<k} \times \mathbb{F}_q[x]_{<k} : (f, g)$ *satisfies the gcd condition*$\}$;
2. $\mathcal{G}_{\mathcal{E}'} := \{(f, g) \in \mathcal{E}' \times \mathcal{E}' : (f, g)$ *satisfies the gcd condition*$\}$;
3. $\mathcal{A}(s, u) := \{(f, g) : \deg(f) = s, \;\; \deg(g) = u\}$;
4. $\mathcal{B}(s, u, i) := \{(f, g) : \deg(f) = s, \;\; \deg(g) = u, \;\; \deg(\gcd(f, g)) = i\}$;
5. $\mathcal{B}_j(s, u) := \{(f, g) : \deg(f) = s, \;\; \deg(g) = u, \;\; \deg(\gcd(f, g)) \leqslant j\}$.

In the rest of this section, we will make use of the following result in our counting arguments.

Theorem 5 (**[6, Theorem 3]**). *Let f and g be randomly chosen from the set of polynomials in $\mathbb{F}_q[x]$ of degree s and u respectively, where s and u are not both zero. Then the probability of f and g being coprime is $1 - \frac{1}{q}$.*

We start counting the number of polynomials in $\mathbb{F}_q[x]$ of fixed degrees.

Lemma 6. *Let s, u, i be nonnegative integers such that $s, u < k$. Then $|\mathcal{A}(s, u)| = (q-1)^2 q^{s+u}$ and moreover, among the polynomials in $\mathcal{A}(s, u)$,*

1. *$(q-1)^3 q^{s+u-1}$ many of them are coprime, i.e. $|\mathcal{B}(s, u, 0)| = (q-1)^3 q^{s+u-1}$;*

2. $(q-1)^2 q^{s+u-1}$ *many of them are not coprime;*
3. *For* $i \leqslant \min\{s,u\}$, $|\mathcal{B}(s,u,i)| = (q-1)^3 q^{s+u-i-1}$.

Proof. The first two items follow directly from Theorem 5. The number of monic polynomials h of degree i is q^i. Observe that the number of polynomial pairs (f,g) with $\gcd(f,g) = h$ is equal to the number of polynomial pairs (f',g') with $\deg f' = s-i$, $\deg g' = u-i$ and $\deg(\gcd(f',g')) = 0$. By the first item, there are $(q-1)^3 q^{s+u-2i-1}$ such pairs. Since it is the same number for any $\gcd(f,g) = h$, and we have q^i many choices for h, there are $(q-1)^3 q^{s+u-2i-1} q^i = (q-1)^3 q^{s+u-i-1}$ many polynomial pairs with $\deg(\gcd(f,g)) = i$ where $i \leqslant \min(s,u)$. □

To count the sets of polynomials $\mathcal{G}$ and $\mathcal{G}_{\mathcal{E}'}$, we first count the number of polynomial pairs in $\mathcal{A}(s,u)$ having gcd less than or equal to j where $j \leqslant \min\{s,u\}$.

Lemma 7. *For any positive integers* s,u *and* $j \leqslant s,u < k$, *we have*

$$\frac{|\mathcal{B}_j(s,u)|}{|\mathcal{A}(s,u)|} = 1 - \frac{1}{q^{j+1}}.$$

Proof. Note that $\mathcal{B}(s,u,i)$'s are non intersecting for distinct i and thus $\mathcal{B}_j(s,u) = \bigsqcup_{i\leqslant j} \mathcal{B}(s,u,i)$. Following Lemma 6, we have $|\mathcal{B}(s,u,i)| = (q-1)^3 q^{s+u-i-1}$. Hence,

$$\begin{aligned}\sum_{i\leqslant j} |\mathcal{B}(s,u,i)| &= \sum_{i\leqslant j} (q-1)^3 q^{s+u-i-1} \\ &= (q-1)^3 q^{s+u-j-1} \left(1+\cdots+q^j\right) \\ &= (q-1)^3 q^{s+u-j-1} \frac{(q^{j+1}-1)}{(q-1)} \\ &= (q-1)^2 q^{s+u-j-1} (q^{j+1}-1).\end{aligned}$$

Note that $|\mathcal{A}(s,u)| = (q-1)^2 q^{s+u}$, and therefore,

$$\frac{|\mathcal{B}_j(s,u)|}{|\mathcal{A}(s,u)|} = \frac{(q-1)^2 q^{s+u-j-1}(q^{j+1}-1)}{(q-1)^2 q^{s+u}} = \frac{q^{s+u} - q^{s+u-j-1}}{q^{s+u}} = 1 - \frac{1}{q^{j+1}}.$$

□

Now, we are ready to count the polynomials in $\mathcal{G}$. The lemma to follow yields a density estimate for $\mathcal{G}$ for k,t large enough. The lower bound on k,t are chosen to further obtain a reasonable estimate for the density of $\mathcal{E}'$.

Lemma 8. *For integers* $k,t \geqslant 17$, *we have*

$$\frac{|\mathcal{G}|}{|\mathbb{F}_q[x]_{<k} \times \mathbb{F}_q[x]_{<k}|} \geqslant 1 - \frac{1}{q^7}.$$

Proof. Note that $\mathcal{G} = \bigcup_{s,u<k} \mathcal{B}_j(s,u)$. Let $j_{s,u}$ be the greatest possible degree for $\gcd(f,g)$ such that (f,g) satisfies the gcd condition where $\deg f = s$ and $\deg g = u$. Using this, we get

$$\frac{|\mathcal{G}|}{|\mathbb{F}_q[x]_{<k} \times \mathbb{F}_q[x]_{<k}|} = \sum_{s,u<k} \frac{|\mathcal{A}(s,u)|}{|\mathbb{F}_q[x]_{<k}|^2} \frac{|\mathcal{B}_{j_{s,u}}(s,u)|}{|\mathcal{A}(s,u)|} \tag{21}$$

Observe that if we consider only the pairs (s,u) such that $s+u = r \in \{2k-10,\ldots,2k-2\}$, we get the following lower bound of the sum in (21),

$$\sum_{s,u} \frac{|\mathcal{A}(s,u)|}{|\mathbb{F}_q[x]_{<k}|^2} \frac{|\mathcal{B}_{j_{s,u}}(s,u)|}{|\mathcal{A}(s,u)|} \geqslant \sum_{\substack{r \\ r\geqslant 2k-10}} \sum_{\substack{s,u \\ s+u=r}} \frac{|\mathcal{A}(s,u)|}{|\mathbb{F}_q[x]_{<k}|^2} \frac{|\mathcal{B}_{j_{s,u}}(s,u)|}{|\mathcal{A}(s,u)|}. \tag{22}$$

We replace r by $r' := (2k-2) - r$ in the limits of the summation in the above equation (22). Note that for a fixed r', there are exactly $(r'+1)$-choices for the pairs (s,u) such that $s+u=r$, and following the value of $|\mathcal{A}(s,u)|$ in Lemma 6, we have

$$\frac{|\mathcal{A}(s,u)|}{|\mathbb{F}_q[x]_{<k}|^2} = \left(\frac{q-1}{q}\right)^2 \frac{1}{q^{r'}}. \tag{23}$$

For $r' = (2k-2) - r \leqslant 8$, and $s+u=r$, $\max\{s,u\} \geqslant k-5$. For any pair (s,u) such that $(2k-2) - r' = r = s+u \geqslant 2k-10$, this implies

$$\begin{cases} k-10 \leqslant j_{s,u} < k-6 & \text{if } t > k, \\ t-10 \leqslant j_{s,u} < t-6 & \text{if } t \leqslant k. \end{cases}$$

Since $k,t \geqslant 17$, then $j_{s,u}+1 \geqslant 8$ in both cases. Therefore, following Lemma 7, we get

$$\frac{|\mathcal{B}_{j_{s,u}}(s,u)|}{|\mathcal{A}(s,u)|} = 1 - \frac{1}{q^{j_{s,u}+1}} \geqslant 1 - \frac{1}{q^8}. \tag{24}$$

Combining (21), (22), (23) and (24) all together, we get

$$\frac{|\mathcal{G}|}{|\mathbb{F}_q[x]_{<k}|^2} \geqslant \left(\frac{q-1}{q}\right)^2 \left(1 - \frac{1}{q^8}\right) \sum_{r'=0}^{8} (r'+1) \frac{1}{q^{r'}}.$$

The leftmost term is the truncated Taylor expansion of the function $F = (x-1)^{-2}$ evaluated at $1/q$. Let us write this the Taylor expansion as

$$(x-1)^{-2} = 1 + 2x + 3x^2 + \cdots + 8x^7 + 9x^8 + R_8(x).$$

Moreover, for any $x \in (0, 1/5)$, we have

$$R_8(x) = \frac{F^{(9)}(z)x^9}{9!}$$

for some $z \in (0, 1/5)$ and one can prove that for any such x, we have $|R_8(x)| < 121x^9$. Taking $x = 1/q$ (since we are dealing with GRS codes, one can reasonably assume that $q \geqslant 11$), we finally get

$$\frac{|\mathcal{G}|}{|\mathbb{F}_q[x]_{<k}|^2} \geqslant \left(\frac{q-1}{q}\right)^2 \left(1 - \frac{1}{q^8}\right) \left(\left(\frac{q-1}{q}\right)^{-2} + O\left(\frac{1}{q^9}\right)\right) \geqslant 1 - \frac{1}{q^7}.$$

□

Remark 9. Note that in Lemma 8, the lower bound $1 - \frac{1}{q^7}$ can be improved for larger t, k such that $k, t \gg 17$. As we can condider more r's in (22) for those cases, the error term in the Taylor expansion gets smaller.

The following Lemma will be useful to count polynomials in $\mathcal{G}_{\mathcal{E}'}$.

Lemma 9. *We have that,*

$$\frac{|\mathcal{G}|}{|\mathbb{F}_q[x]_{<k} \times \mathbb{F}_q[x]_{<k}|} \geqslant 1 - \frac{1}{q^w} \implies \frac{|\mathcal{G}_{\mathcal{E}'}|}{|\mathcal{E}' \times \mathcal{E}'|} \geqslant 1 - \frac{1}{q^{w-2}}.$$

for some $w \in \mathbb{Z}_{>0}$.

Proof. Note that,

$$\begin{aligned} |(\mathcal{E}' \times \mathcal{E}') \cup \mathcal{G}| &= |\mathcal{E}' \times \mathcal{E}'| + |\mathcal{G}| - |\mathcal{G} \cap (\mathcal{E}' \times \mathcal{E}')| \\ &\leqslant |\mathbb{F}_q[x]_{<k} \times \mathbb{F}_q[x]_{<k}| = q^2|\mathcal{E}' \times \mathcal{E}'|. \end{aligned}$$

Now, since $\mathcal{G}_{\mathcal{E}'} = \mathcal{G} \cap (\mathcal{E}' \times \mathcal{E}')$, from the previous inequality we can deduce that,

$$|\mathcal{G}_{\mathcal{E}'}| \geqslant (1 - q^2)|\mathcal{E}' \times \mathcal{E}'| + |\mathcal{G}|.$$

From the hypothesis of the lemma,

$$|\mathcal{G}| \geqslant q^2|\mathcal{E}' \times \mathcal{E}'| \left(1 - \frac{1}{q^w}\right),$$

and so, putting all together, we can conclude the desired result (Fig. 2),

$$|\mathcal{G}_{\mathcal{E}'}| \geqslant \left((1 - q^2) + \left(q^2 - \frac{1}{q^{w-2}}\right)\right) |\mathcal{E}' \times \mathcal{E}'| = \left(1 - \frac{1}{q^{w-2}}\right) |\mathcal{E}' \times \mathcal{E}'|.$$

□

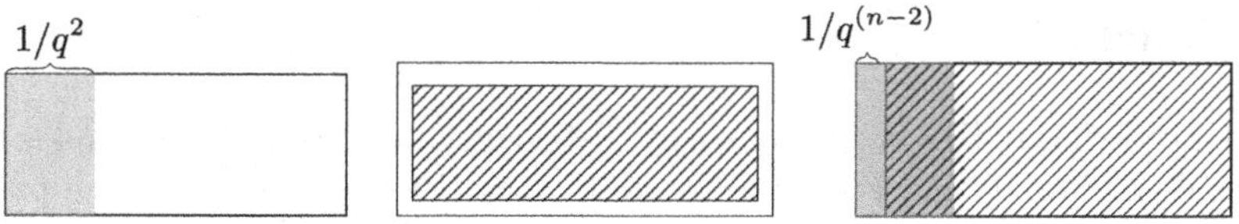

Fig. 2. The first image illustrates the ratio of $\mathcal{E}' \times \mathcal{E}'$ in $\mathbb{F}_q[x]_{<k} \times \mathbb{F}_q[x]_{<k}$, the second one is for the ratio of $\mathcal{G}$ in $\mathbb{F}_q[x]_{<k} \times \mathbb{F}_q[x]_{<k}$ and the third one represents the *worst case* intersection of the first two.

Proof of Theorem 4. We made the observation that the inequality

$$\dim \langle f_1, f_2, f_3 \rangle \mathcal{E}' > 2k + 2 \tag{25}$$

holds true if (f_2, f_3) satisfies the *gcd condition* as given in (20). Using Lemma 8, and then taking $w = 7$ in Lemma 9, this probability is $\frac{|\mathcal{G}_{\mathcal{E}'}|}{|\mathcal{E}' \times \mathcal{E}'|} \geqslant 1 - \frac{1}{q^5}$. Following Remark 8, it means that $\frac{|\Psi|}{|\Psi \cup \Gamma|} \geqslant 1 - \frac{1}{q^5}$. Thus, if a triple $(f_1, f_2, f_3) \in \Psi \cup \Gamma$, then $(f_1, f_2, f_3) \in \Gamma$ with probability $\leqslant \frac{1}{q^5}$. For a triple $(f_1, f_2, f_3) \in \mathcal{R}^3$, the probability of $(f_1, f_2, f_3) \in \Psi \cup \Gamma$ is $1 - \frac{1}{q^3}$. Hence we get:

$$\frac{|\mathcal{E}'^3|}{|\mathcal{E}'^3 \cup \Gamma|} \geqslant \frac{\frac{1}{q^3}}{\left(1 - \frac{1}{q^3}\right)\frac{1}{q^5} + \frac{1}{q^3}} \geqslant 1 - \frac{1}{q^2}.$$

This, together with the subsequent statement complete the proof of the theorem. □

Corollary 2. *Let $f_1, f_2, f_3 \in \mathcal{R}$ are three polynomials chosen uniformly at random. If $f_1, f_2 \in \mathcal{E}'$ and $(f_1, f_2, f_3) \in \mathcal{E}'^3 \cup \Gamma$, then probability of $(f_1, f_2, f_3) \in \mathcal{E}'^3$ is $\geqslant 1 - \frac{1}{q^2}$.*

Proof. Defining

$$\Gamma_0 := \{(f_1, f_2, f_3) \in \Gamma : \dim \langle f_1, f_2, f_3 \rangle \mathcal{R} \leqslant 2k + 2 \text{ and } f_1, f_2 \in \mathcal{E}'\},$$

and using $\Gamma_0 \subseteq \Gamma$ the conditional probability described in the proposition can be lower bounded by

$$\frac{|\mathcal{E}'|}{|\mathcal{E}' \cup \Gamma_0|} \geqslant \frac{|\mathcal{E}'|}{|\mathcal{E}' \cup \Gamma|} \geqslant 1 - \frac{1}{q^2}.$$

□

Remark 10. After iterating the process of appending a polynomial to primarily found $(f_1, f_2, f_3) \in \mathcal{E}'^3 \sqcup \Gamma$ $k - 3$ times, we get a basis of the codimension 1 subspace $\mathcal{E}'$ with probability $(1 - \frac{(k-3)}{q^2})$.

8 Conclusion

We showed that qGRS codes are easily distinguishable from random codes using classical cryptanalysis techniques on algebraic codes. Moreover, we proposed a complete key-recovery attack on TGRS and actually qGRS codes with $\ell = 1$. We left some questions open. First, our proof of the validity of the attack rests on a probability analysis which does not permit us to treat some cases where the attack still probably works. Second, for some very specific cases such as $h = 1$ or $k - 2$, despite being able to distinguish the codes, we cannot conclude the attack. We hope such cases to be attacked but this would require an ad hoc manner to finish the attack. Finally the major remaining question is the case of $\ell > 1$ twists. It is clear that a too high number of twist is not practical for cryptography since the decryption complexity is exponential in the number of twists. Still, the question of small $\ell \geqslant 2$ remains open, since the codes are distinguishable from random ones, one can be optimistic on the possibility to extend the attack to larger ℓ's but this probably requires many technical adaptations both in the attack itself and in the probability analysis to prove the validity of the attack.

References

1. Albrecht, M., et al.: Classic McEliece (merger of Classic McEliece and NTS-KEM) (2022). https://classic.mceliece.org
2. Baldi, M., Bianchi, M., Chiaraluce, F., Rosenthal, J., Schipani, D.: Enhanced public key security for the McEliece cryptosystem. J. Cryptol. **29**, 1–27 (2016)
3. Beelen, P., Bossert, M., Puchinger, S., Rosenkilde, J.: Structural properties of twisted Reed-Solomon codes with applications to cryptography. In: Proceedings of IEEE International Symposium on Information Theory - ISIT 2018, pp. 946–950. IEEE (2018)
4. Beelen, P., Puchinger, S., né Nielsen, J.R.: Twisted Reed-Solomon codes. In: Proceedings of IEEE International Symposium on Information Theory - ISIT 2017, pp. 336–340. IEEE (2017)
5. Beelen, P., Puchinger, S., Rosenkilde, J.: Twisted Reed-Solomon codes. IEEE Trans. Inf. Theory **68**(5), 3047–3061 (2022)
6. Benjamin, A.T., Bennett, C.D.: The probability of relatively prime polynomials. Math. Mag. **80**(3), 196–202 (2007). https://doi.org/10.1080/0025570X.2007.11953481
7. Berger, T., Loidreau, P.: How to mask the structure of codes for a cryptographic use. Des. Codes Cryptogr. **35**, 63–79 (2005)
8. Cascudo, I., Cramer, R., Mirandola, D., Zémor, G.: Squares of random linear codes. IEEE Trans. Inf. Theory **61**(3), 1159–1173 (2015). https://doi.org/10.1109/TIT.2015.2393251
9. Couvreur, A., Gaborit, P., Gauthier-Umaña, V., Otmani, A., Tillich, J.P.: Distinguisher-based attacks on public-key cryptosystems using Reed-Solomon codes. Des. Codes Cryptogr. **73**, 641–666 (2014)
10. Couvreur, A., Lequesne, M.: On the security of subspace subcodes of Reed-Solomon codes for public key encryption. IEEE Trans. Inf. Theory **68**(1), 632–648 (2022). https://doi.org/10.1109/TIT.2021.3120440

11. Couvreur, A., Lequesne, M., Tillich, J.P.: Recovering short secret keys of RLCE in polynomial time. In: Ding, J., Steinwandt, R. (eds.) Post-Quantum Cryptography 2019. LNCS, vol. 11505, pp. 133–152. Springer, Chongquing (2019). https://doi.org/10.1007/978-3-030-25510-7_8
12. Couvreur, A., Márquez-Corbella, I., Pellikaan, R.: Cryptanalysis of McEliece cryptosystem based on algebraic geometry codes and their subcodes. IEEE Trans. Inf. Theory **63**(8), 5404–5418 (2017)
13. Couvreur, A., Otmani, A., Tillich, J.P.: Polynomial time attack on wild McEliece over quadratic extensions. In: Nguyen, P.Q., Oswald, E. (eds.) Advances in Cryptology - EUROCRYPT 2014. LNCS, vol. 8441, pp. 17–39. Springer, Heidelberg (2014). https://doi.org/10.1007/978-3-642-55220-5_2
14. Couvreur, A., Otmani, A., Tillich, J.P.: Polynomial time attack on wild McEliece over quadratic extensions. IEEE Trans. Inf. Theory **63**(1), 404–427 (2017)
15. Couvreur, A., Otmani, A., Tillich, J.-P., Gauthier–Umaña, V.: A polynomial-time attack on the BBCRS scheme. In: Katz, J. (ed.) PKC 2015. LNCS, vol. 9020, pp. 175–193. Springer, Heidelberg (2015). https://doi.org/10.1007/978-3-662-46447-2_8
16. Faugère, J.C., Gauthier-Umaña, V., Otmani, A., Perret, L., Tillich, J.P.: A distinguisher for high-rate McEliece cryptosystems. IEEE Trans. Inf. Theory **59**(10), 6830–6844 (2013). https://doi.org/10.1109/TIT.2013.2272036
17. Guruswami, V., Sudan, M.: Improved decoding of reed-solomon and algebraic-geometric codes. In: Proceedings 39th Annual Symposium on Foundations of Computer Science (Cat. No. 98CB36280), pp. 28–37 (1998). https://doi.org/10.1109/SFCS.1998.743426
18. Janwa, H., Moreno, O.: McEliece public key cryptosystems using algebraic-geometric codes. Des. Codes Cryptogr. **8**(3), 293–307 (1996)
19. Khathuria, K., Rosenthal, J., Weger, V.: Encryption scheme based on expanded Reed-Solomon codes. Adv. Math. Commun. **15**(2), 207–218 (2021). https://doi.org/10.3934/amc.2020053. http://aimsciences.org//article/id/0f055199-6fe4-404f-b206-517ce7d02a58
20. Lavauzelle, J., Renner, J.: Cryptanalysis of a system based on twisted Reed-Solomon codes. Des. Codes Cryptogr. **88**(7), 1285–1300 (2020)
21. McEliece, R.: A public-key system based on algebraic coding theory. Jet Propul. Lab. California Inst. Technol. **3**, 85–86 (1978)
22. Misoczki, R., Tillich, J.P., Sendrier, N., Barreto, P.S.L.M.: MDPC-McEliece: new McEliece variants from moderate density parity-check codes. In: Proceedings of IEEE International Symposium on Information Theory - ISIT, pp. 2069–2073 (2013). https://doi.org/10.1109/ISIT.2013.6620590
23. Niederreiter, H.: Knapsack-type cryptosystems and algebraic coding theory. Prob. Contr. Inf. Theory **15**(2), 157–166 (1986)
24. Roth, R.: Introduction to Coding Theory. Cambridge University Press, New York (2006)
25. Sheekey, J.: A new family of linear maximum rank distance codes. Adv. Math. Commun. **10**(3), 475–488 (2016). https://doi.org/10.3934/amc.2016019. https://www.aimsciences.org/article/id/3ff311ae-18e0-47d8-8edc-ab169dbbd975
26. Sidelnikov, V.M.: A public-key cryptosytem based on Reed-Muller codes. Disc. Math. Appl. **4**(3), 191–207 (1994)
27. Sidelnikov, V.M., Shestakov, S.: On the insecurity of cryptosystems based on generalized Reed-Solomon codes. Disc. Math. Appl. **1**(4), 439–444 (1992)
28. Stein, W., et al.: Sage Mathematics Software (Version 9.5). The Sage Development Team (2022). http://www.sagemath.org

29. Sudan, M.: Decoding of Reed-Solomon codes beyond the error-correction bound. J. Complex. **13**(1), 180–193 (1997). https://doi.org/10.1006/jcom.1997.0439. https://www.sciencedirect.com/science/article/pii/S0885064X97904398
30. Wang, Y.: Quantum resistant random linear code based public key encryption scheme RLCE. In: Proceedings of IEEE International Symposium on Information Theory - ISIT 2016, pp. 2519–2523. IEEE, Barcelona (2016). https://doi.org/10.1109/ISIT.2016.7541753
31. Wang, Y.: RLCE–KEM (2017). http://quantumca.org
32. Wieschebrink, C.: An attack on a modified niederreiter encryption scheme. In: Yung, M., Dodis, Y., Kiayias, A., Malkin, T. (eds.) PKC 2006. LNCS, vol. 3958, pp. 14–26. Springer, Heidelberg (2006). https://doi.org/10.1007/11745853_2
33. Wieschebrink, C.: Two NP-complete problems in coding theory with an application in code based cryptography. In: Proceedings of IEEE International Symposium on Information Theory - ISIT 2006, pp. 1733–1737. IEEE (2006)
34. Wieschebrink, C.: Cryptanalysis of the niederreiter public key scheme based on GRS subcodes. In: Sendrier, N. (ed.) PQCrypto 2010. LNCS, vol. 6061, pp. 61–72. Springer, Heidelberg (2010). https://doi.org/10.1007/978-3-642-12929-2_5

Quadratic Modelings of Syndrome Decoding

Alessio Caminata[1], Ryann Cartor[2(✉)], Alessio Meneghetti[3], Rocco Mora[4], and Alex Pellegrini[5]

[1] Università di Genova, Genoa, Italy
[2] Clemson University, Clemson, USA
rcartor@clemson.edu
[3] Università di Trento, Trento, Italy
[4] CISPA Helmholtz Center for Information Security, Saarbrücken, Germany
[5] Eindhoven University of Technology, Eindhoven, The Netherlands

Abstract. This paper presents enhanced reductions of the bounded-weight and exact-weight Syndrome Decoding Problem (SDP) to a system of quadratic equations. Over $\mathbb{F}_2$, we improve on a previous work and study the degree of regularity of the modeling of the exact weight SDP. Additionally, we introduce a novel technique that transforms SDP instances over $\mathbb{F}_q$ into systems of polynomial equations and thoroughly investigate the dimension of their varieties. Experimental results are provided to evaluate the complexity of solving SDP instances using our models through Gröbner bases techniques.

Keywords: Syndrome Decoding · Gröbner Basis · Cryptanalysis · Code-Based Cryptography · Multivariate Cryptography

1 Introduction

As widespread quantum computing becomes closer to reality, accurate cryptanalysis of post-quantum cryptosystems is of the utmost importance. Code-based cryptography is one of the main areas of focus in the search for quantum-secure cryptosystems. This is well represented by the NIST Post-Quantum Standardization Process, where as many as three finalists, namely Classic McEliece [9] (an IND-CCA2 secure variation of McEliece's very first code-based scheme [32]), HQC [33] and BIKE [2], belong to this family. Similarly, NIST's additional call for digital signatures has numerous proposals that make use of linear codes. Many of the proposed schemes are based on the hardness of (sometimes structured variants of) the syndrome decoding problem.

The parameters of many code-based schemes are carefully chosen to align with the latest advancements with respect to this computational problem. Despite decades of intensive research in this direction, all the algorithms developed so far exhibit exponential complexity. This is not surprising, since the problem has been shown to be NP-hard [8]. In particular, after more than

R. Niederhagen and M.-J. O. Saarinen (Eds.): PQCrypto 2025, LNCS 15577, pp. 35–70, 2025.
https://doi.org/10.1007/978-3-031-86599-2_2

60 years of investigation since the groundbreaking paper of Prange [35], the reduction in the exponent for most parameters of interest has been minimal [7,10,12,23,28,30,31,38]. All the works mentioned fall into the family of Information Set Decoding (ISD) algorithms, whose basic observation is that it is easier to guess error-free positions, and guessing enough of them is sufficient to decode. This resistance to ISD algorithms makes the syndrome decoding problem a reliable foundation for code-based cryptosystems.

To comprehensively assess security, it is imperative to consider attacks stemming from various other realms of post-quantum cryptography. For instance, attacks typically associated with multivariate or lattice-based schemes should also be taken into account for code-based schemes, when applicable. A remarkable example is offered by dual attacks, originally introduced in lattice-based cryptography, where, however, they have been strongly questioned. In contrast, their code-based counterpart [17,18] has recently outperformed ISD techniques for a non-negligible regime of parameters, by reducing the decoding problem to the closely related Learning Parity with Noise problem. Concerning polynomial system solving strategies, another notable illustration of this is the algebraic MinRank attack, which broke the rank-metric code-based schemes RQC and Rollo [4,5] and now represents the state-of-the-art for MinRank cryptanalysis, beating combinatorial approaches.

In the Hamming metric, a reduction that transforms an instance of the syndrome decoding problem into a system of quadratic equations over $\mathbb{F}_2$ was introduced in [34]. The most expensive step of the transformation, in terms of numbers of new variables and new equations introduced, is the so-called *Hamming-weight computation encoding*. Indeed, for a binary linear code of length n, the procedure dominates the overall complexity of the reduction with a complexity of $\mathcal{O}(n \log_2(n)^2)$.

Despite the considerable theoretical interest in this transformation, the latter is too inefficient to be of practical interest in solving the syndrome decoding problem. Thus, the problem of improving the reduction in order to obtain a more effectively solvable system remains open. Moreover, [34] covers only the binary case, leaving unanswered the challenge of modeling through algebraic equations the decoding problem for codes defined over finite fields with more than two elements.

Our Contribution. In this work, we improve on the reduction presented in [34] by a factor of $\log_2(n)$, thereby reducing the number of introduced variables and equations and achieving an overall reduction cost of $\mathcal{O}(n \log_2(n))$. This improvement is achieved by leveraging the recursive structure of the equations generated by the Hamming-weight computation encoding and by transforming the equations similarly to the reduction procedure in Buchberger's algorithm [14] for Gröbner basis computation. When considering a version of the syndrome decoding problem that requires an error vector with a specified Hamming weight, we derive a further improved modeling, for which we study the degree of regularity.

As a second contribution, we present a novel approach that transforms an instance of the syndrome decoding problem over $\mathbb{F}_q$ for $q \geq 2$ into a system of polynomial equations. This significantly broadens the applicability of our methods to a wider range of code-based cryptosystems. A common feature of our algebraic modelings is that if the decoding problem admits multiple solutions, the Gröbner basis naturally determines all of them.

We also provide theoretical and experimental data to analyze the complexity of solving syndrome decoding instances using our modelings, demonstrating that, at least for small parameters, our new strategy is practical and successful. Software (MAGMA scripts) supporting this work can be found here.

Structure of the Paper. The next section recalls the background and notions necessary for this work. In Sect. 3, we review the reduction described in [34] from the syndrome decoding problem to that of finding the zeroes of a set of polynomials. In Sect. 4, we describe two modelings that improve upon [34]. We study the degree of regularity of the modeling for the exact weight syndrome decoding problem, along with experimental results, in Sect. 5. Finally, in Sect. 6, we present a novel modeling of the syndrome decoding problem over $\mathbb{F}_q$ with $q \geq 2$, for which we provide a theoretical study of the variety and experimental analysis of the solving complexity with Gröbner bases techniques.

2 Preliminaries

This paper investigates the reduction of the Syndrome Decoding Problem (SDP) into a Polynomial System Solving Problem (PoSSo). In this section, we briefly recall the definitions of both problems, as well as the notions of solving degree and degree of regularity, which are commonly used to estimate the computational complexity of the PoSSo problem.

2.1 The Syndrome Decoding Problem

An $[n, k]$-linear code $\mathcal{C}$ is a k-dimensional subspace of $\mathbb{F}_q^n$. We call n the length of the code, and k its dimension. An element $\mathbf{x} \in \mathbb{F}_q^n$ is called a codeword if $\mathbf{x} \in \mathcal{C}$. The number of nonzero entries in $\mathbf{x}$ is called the Hamming weight of $\mathbf{x}$ and we denote it as $\mathsf{wt}(\mathbf{x})$. Given a code $\mathcal{C}$ we define a parity check matrix of $\mathcal{C}$ as $\mathbf{H} \in \mathbb{F}_q^{(n-k)\times n}$ such that the right kernel of $\mathbf{H}$ is the code $\mathcal{C}$. The subspace spanned by the rows of $\mathbf{H}$ is called the dual code of $\mathcal{C}$. Many code-based cryptosystems rely on the hardness of solving the Syndrome Decoding Problem (SDP), see Problems 1 and 2 described below.

Problem 1 (SDP: Syndrome Decoding Problem). Given integers n, k, t such that $k \leq n$ and $t \leq n$, an instance of the problem $\mathrm{SD}(\mathbf{H}, \mathbf{s}, t)$ consists of a parity check matrix $\mathbf{H} \in \mathbb{F}_q^{(n-k)\times n}$ and a vector $\mathbf{s} \in \mathbb{F}_q^{n-k}$ (called the syndrome). A solution to the problem is a vector $\mathbf{e} \in \mathbb{F}_q^n$ such that $\mathbf{He}^\top = \mathbf{s}^\top$ and $\mathsf{wt}(\mathbf{e}) \leq t$.

In later sections, we will also refer to Problem 1 as the "Bounded Syndrome Decoding" Problem. We will also consider the following variant of SDP.

Problem 2 (ESDP: Exact Weight Syndrome Decoding Problem). Given integers n, k, t such that $k \leq n$ and $t \leq n$, an instance of the problem $\mathrm{ESD}(\mathbf{H}, \mathbf{s}, t)$ consists of a parity check matrix $\mathbf{H} \in \mathbb{F}_q^{(n-k)\times n}$ and a vector $\mathbf{s} \in \mathbb{F}_q^{n-k}$ (called the syndrome). A solution to the problem is a vector $\mathbf{e} \in \mathbb{F}_q^n$ such that $\mathbf{He}^\top = \mathbf{s}^\top$ and $\mathsf{wt}(\mathbf{e}) = t$.

Additionally, a close variant of the Syndrome Decoding Problem is the *Codeword Finding Problem*, where the syndrome $\mathbf{s}$ is the zero vector $\mathbf{0}$. Since the null vector is always a solution of the parity-check equations $\mathbf{He}^\top = \mathbf{0}^\top$, a nonzero $\mathbf{e}$ of weight at most (or exactly) t is sought. The name of the problem refers to the fact that any element in the right kernel of $\mathbf{H}$ belongs to the code $\mathcal{C}$ having $\mathbf{H}$ as parity-check matrix. We will later need to distinguish this variant in the analysis of one of our modelings.

In addition to length and dimension, a fundamental notion in coding theory and consequently in code-based cryptography is the minimum distance d of an $\mathbb{F}_q$-linear code, i.e. the Hamming weight of the smallest nonzero codeword in the code. Such a quantity is strictly related to the number of solutions to the syndrome decoding problem.

Knowing the expected number of solutions from given parameters is extremely important in cryptography, in order to assess the security correctly. It is guaranteed that the problem does not admit more than one solution as long as the number of errors is upper bounded by $\frac{d-1}{2}$. However, in practice, much better can be done for randomly generated codes. Indeed, it turns out that random codes achieve the so-called Gilbert-Varshamov (GV) distance d_{GV}, defined as the largest integer such that

$$\sum_{i=0}^{d_{GV}-1} \binom{n}{i} (q-1)^i \leq q^{n-k}.$$

It can be shown that, as long as the number of errors is below the Gilbert-Varshamov distance, the Syndrome Decoding problem *typically* has a unique solution. Moreover, the instances where the number of errors attains the GV distance are those supposed to be the most difficult.

2.2 The Polynomial System Solving Problem

The Polynomial System Solving Problem (PoSSo) is the following. We define it over a finite field $\mathbb{F}_q$, athough it can be more generally considered over any field.

Problem 3 (PoSSo: Polynomial System Solving). Given integers $N, r \geq 2$, an instance of the PoSSo problem consists of a system of polynomials $\mathcal{F} = \{f_1, \dots, f_r\}$ in $R = \mathbb{F}_q[x_1, \dots, x_N]$ with N variables and coefficients in $\mathbb{F}_q$. A solution to the problem is a vector $\mathbf{a} \in \mathbb{F}_q^N$ such that $f_1(\mathbf{a}) = \cdots = f_r(\mathbf{a}) = 0$.

Remark 1. A special case of PoSSo when $\deg(f_i) = 2$ for $1 \leq i \leq r$ is called MQ (Multivariate Quadratic) and is the basis for multivaritate cryptography.

The following outlines a standard strategy for finding the solutions of a polynomial system $\mathcal{F}$ by means of Gröbner bases.

1. Find a degree reverse lexicographic (degrevlex) Gröbner basis of the ideal $\langle \mathcal{F} \rangle$;
2. Convert the obtained degrevlex Gröbner basis into a lexicographic (lex) Gröbner basis, where the solutions of the system can be easily read from the ideal in this form.

The second step can be done by FGLM [25], or a similar algorithm, whose complexity depends on the degree of the ideal. This is usually faster than the first step, especially when the system $\mathcal{F}$ has few solutions. Therefore, we focus on the first step.

The fastest known algorithms to compute a degrevlex Gröbner basis are the linear algebra based algorithms such as F4 [26], F5 [27], or XL [20]. These transform the problem of computing a Gröbner basis into one or more instances of Gaussian elimination of the Macaulay matrices. The complexity of these algorithms is dominated by the Gaussian elimination on the largest Macaulay matrix encountered during the process. The size of a Macaulay matrix depends on the degrees of the input polynomials $f_1, \dots, f_r$, on the number of variables N, and on a degree d. In a nutshell, the *Macaulay matrix* $M_{\leq d}$ of degree d of $\mathcal{F}$ has columns indexed by the monic monomials of degree $\leq d$, sorted in decreasing order from left to right (with respect to the chosen degrevlex term order). The rows of $M_{\leq d}$ are indexed by the polynomials $m_{i,j} f_j$, where $m_{i,j}$ is a monic monomial such that $\deg(m_{i,j} f_j) \leq d$. The entry (i, j) of $M_{\leq d}$ is the coefficient of the monomial of column j in the polynomial corresponding to the i-th row.

The *solving degree* of $\mathcal{F}$ is defined as the least degree d such that Gaussian elimination on the Macaulay matrix $M_{\leq d}$ produces a degrevlex Gröbner basis of $\mathcal{F}$. We denote the solving degree of $\mathcal{F}$ by $d_{\mathrm{sol}}(\mathcal{F})$. We have to compute Macaulay matrices up to degree $d_{\mathrm{sol}} = d_{\mathrm{sol}}(\mathcal{F})$, and the largest one we encounter has $a = \sum_{i=1}^{r} \binom{N+d_{\mathrm{sol}}-d_i}{d_{\mathrm{sol}}-d_i}$ many rows and $b = \binom{N+d_{\mathrm{sol}}}{d_{\mathrm{sol}}}$ many columns, where $d_i = \deg f_i$. Therefore, taking into account the complexity of Gaussian elimination of this matrix, an upper bound on the complexity of solving the system $\mathcal{F}$ with this method is

$$\mathcal{O}\left(\binom{N + d_{\mathrm{sol}}}{d_{\mathrm{sol}}}^{\omega}\right), \tag{1}$$

with $2 \leq \omega \leq 3$.

Remark 2. If $\mathcal{F}$ is not homogeneous, Gaussian elimination on $M_{\leq d}$ may produce a row corresponding to a polynomial f with $\deg f < d$, where the leading term of f was not the leading term of any row in $M_{\leq d}$. Some algorithms, for example $F4$, address this by adding rows for polynomials mf ($\deg(mf) \leq d$) for some monomial m and recomputing the reduced row echelon form. If no Gröbner basis is found in degree $\leq d$, they proceed to higher degrees, potentially enlarging the span of $M_{\leq d}$ and reducing the solving degree. Throughout this paper, we consider only the case where no extra rows are added. Note that the solving degree as defined above is an upper bound on the degree at which algorithms using this variation terminate.

Since the solving degree of a polynomial system may be difficult to estimate, several invariants related to the solving degree (that are hopefully easier to compute) have been introduced. One of the most important is the *degree of regularity* introduced by Bardet, Faugère, and Salvy [6]. We briefly recall its definition and connection with the solving degree.

Let $\langle \mathcal{F}^{\text{top}} \rangle = \langle f_1^{\text{top}}, \dots, f_r^{\text{top}} \rangle$ be the ideal of the polynomial ring R generated by the homogeneous part of highest degree of the polynomial system $\mathcal{F}$. Assume that $\langle \mathcal{F}^{\text{top}} \rangle_d = R_d$ for $d \gg 0$. The *degree of regularity* of $\mathcal{F}$ is

$$d_{\text{reg}}(\mathcal{F}) = \min\{d \in \mathbb{N} \mid \langle \mathcal{F}^{\text{top}} \rangle_e = R_e \ \forall e \geq d\}.$$

The degree of regularity can be read off from the Hilbert series of $\langle \mathcal{F}^{\text{top}} \rangle$. Let I be a homogeneous ideal of R, and let $A = R/I$. For an integer $d \geq 0$, we denote by A_d the homogeneous component of degree d of A. The function $\text{HF}_A(-) : \mathbb{N} \to \mathbb{N}$, $\text{HF}_A(d) = \dim_{\mathbb{F}_q} A_d$ is called *Hilbert function* of A.

The generating series of HF_A is called *Hilbert series* of A. We denote it by $\text{HS}_A(z) = \sum_{d \in \mathbb{N}} \text{HF}_A(d) z^d$.

Remark 3. Under the assumption that $\langle \mathcal{F}^{\text{top}} \rangle_d = R_d$ for $d \gg 0$, the Hilbert series of $A = R/\langle \mathcal{F}^{\text{top}} \rangle$ is a polynomial. Then, the degree of regularity of $\mathcal{F}$ is given by $d_{\text{reg}}(\mathcal{F}) = \deg \text{HS}_A(z) + 1$ (see [15, Theorem 12]).

Under suitable assumptions, the degree of regularity provides an upper bound for the solving degree [16,36,37]. Moreover, it is often assumed that the two values are close. Although this occurs in many relevant situations, there are examples where these two invariants can be arbitrarily far apart (see [11,15,22]). We will see in Sect. 5 that the degree of regularity of the system presented in Sect. 4.2 seems to yield a much higher value than the solving degree achieved during the Gröbner basis algorithm.

3 The MPS Modeling

This section is devoted to an overview of the algebraic modeling of the syndrome decoding problem proposed in [34] (referred to as the MPS modeling). We fix the following notation for this section.

Notation 1. *Let $n \geq 2$ and let $\mathcal{C} \subseteq \mathbb{F}_2^n$ be a $[n, k, d]$-linear code having a parity check matrix $\mathbf{H} \in \mathbb{F}_2^{(n-k) \times n}$. We define $\ell = \lfloor \log_2(n) \rfloor + 1$. Let $\mathbf{s} \in \mathbb{F}_2^{n-k}$ play the role of the syndrome and let $0 \leq t \leq \lfloor (d-1)/2 \rfloor$ be the target error weight. Let $X = (x_1, \dots, x_n)$ and $Y = (Y_1, \dots, Y_n)$ with $Y_j = (y_{j,1}, \dots, y_{j,\ell})$ be two sets of variables and we consider the polynomial ring $\mathbb{F}_2[X, Y]$.*

We define the following maps π_i for $i = 1, \dots, n$,

$$\begin{aligned} \pi_i : \mathbb{F}_2^n &\to \mathbb{F}_2^i \\ (v_1, \dots, v_n) &\mapsto (v_1, \dots, v_i). \end{aligned}$$

The construction of the proposed algebraic modeling consists of four steps and uses the variables contained in X and Y to express relations and dependencies. Each of these steps produces a set of polynomials in $\mathbb{F}_2[X, Y]$. An extra step of the construction reduces the aforementioned polynomials to quadratic polynomials.

The idea is to construct an algebraic system having a variety containing elements $(\mathbf{x} \mid \mathbf{y}_1 \mid \cdots \mid \mathbf{y}_n) \in \mathbb{F}_2^{n(\ell+1)}$ whose first n entries represent an element $\mathbf{x}$ of $\mathbb{F}_2^n$ such that $\mathbf{H}\mathbf{x}^\top = \mathbf{s}^\top$. The remaining $n\ell$ entries are considered to be the concatenation of n elements $\mathbf{y}_i \in \mathbb{F}_2^\ell$ where the elements of $\mathbf{y}_i$ represent the binary expansion of $\mathsf{wt}(\pi_i(\mathbf{x}))$ for every $i = 1, \ldots, n$, with $\pi_i(\mathbf{x}) = (x_1, \ldots, x_i)$. By this definition, the list $\mathbf{y}_n$ represents the binary expansion of $\mathsf{wt}(\mathbf{x})$. The system finally enforces that $\mathbf{y}_n$ represents the binary expansion of an integer t' such that $t' \leq t$. The elements of the variety of solutions of this algebraic modeling are finally projected onto their first n coordinates, revealing the solutions to the original syndrome decoding problem.

Here is a description of the four steps of reduction of the MPS modeling. We describe the set obtained in each step as a set of polynomials in $\mathbb{F}_2[X, Y]$.

- *Parity check encoding.* This step ensures that the solution of the algebraic system satisfies the parity check equations imposed by the parity check matrix $\mathbf{H}$ and the syndrome vector $\mathbf{s}$. Here, we compute the set of $n - k$ linear polynomials

$$\left\{ \sum_{i=1}^{n} h_{i,j} x_i + s_j \mid j \in \{1, \ldots, n-k\} \right\}. \tag{2}$$

- *Hamming weight computation encoding.* This part of the modeling provides a set of polynomials that describes the binary encoding of $\mathsf{wt}(\pi_i(\mathbf{x}))$ for every $i = 1, \ldots, n$ described above. The set of polynomials achieving this goal, is given by the union of the three following sets consisting of the $\ell + n - 1$ polynomials in the sets

$$\begin{aligned} &\{f_{1,1} = x_1 + y_{1,1}, f_{1,2} = y_{1,2}, \ldots, f_{1,\ell} = y_{1,\ell}\}, \\ &\{f_{i,1} = x_i + y_{i,1} + y_{i-1,1} \mid i = 2, \ldots, n\} \end{aligned} \tag{3}$$

and the $(n-1)(\ell-1)$ polynomials

$$\left\{ f_{i,j} = \left(\prod_{h=1}^{j-1} y_{i-1,h} \right) x_i + y_{i,j} + y_{i-1,j} \mid i = 2, \ldots, n, \ j = 2, \ldots, \ell \right\}. \tag{4}$$

We labeled the polynomials of the sets in (3) and in (4) because the improvements in the next sections will mainly involve them.

- *Weight constraint encoding.* This part produces a set consisting of a single polynomial that enforces the constraint $\mathsf{wt}(\mathbf{x}) \leq t$ by dealing with the variables in Y_n. Let $\mathbf{v} \in \mathbb{F}_2^\ell$ represent the binary expansion of t. Consider the ℓ polynomials in $\mathbb{F}_2[X, Y]$ defined as

$$f_j = (y_{n,j} + v_j) \prod_{h=j+1}^{\ell} (y_{n,h} + v_h + 1)$$

for $j = 1, \ldots, \ell$. The set is the singleton

$$\left\{ \sum_{j=1}^{\ell} (v_j + 1) f_j \right\}. \tag{5}$$

– *Finite field equations.* The set of $n + n\ell$ finite field polynomials of $\mathbb{F}_2[X, Y]$ is

$$\{x_i^2 - x_i \mid i = 1, \ldots, n\} \cup \{y_{i,j}^2 - y_{i,j} \mid i = 1, \ldots, n,\ j = 1, \ldots, \ell\}, \tag{6}$$

and ensures that the elements of the variety are restricted to elements of $\mathbb{F}_2^{n(\ell+1)}$.

The algebraic system corresponding to an instance of the syndrome decoding problem is then the union of the four sets described above. Clearly, this is not a quadratic system; thus the authors apply a linearization strategy that introduces a number of auxiliary variables used to label monomials of degree 2. This eventually results in a large quadratic system in many more than just $n(\ell + 1)$ variables. In fact, the final quadratic system ends up having equations and variables bounded by $\mathcal{O}(n \log_2(n)^2)$.

4 Improving the MPS Modeling

In this section, we provide improvements of the MPS modeling that reduce the number of equations and variables in the final algebraic system. We keep the same notation as in Notation 1. First, we consider the case of the syndrome decoding problem, i.e. with a bounded weight error. We then consider the case of the exact weight syndrome decoding problem. We observe that one can avoid the linearization step as the resulting system is already quadratic.

4.1 Improved Modeling for the Case of SDP

We consider the degrevlex monomial ordering on $\mathbb{F}_2[X, Y]$ with the X variables greater than the Y variables, and denote by $\mathsf{lm}(p)$ the leading monomial of a polynomial p. Notice that since we are in the binary case, the notions of leading monomial and that of leading term coincide.

Denote by $F = \{f_{i,j} \mid i = 1, \ldots, n,\ j = 1, \ldots, \ell\} \subset \mathbb{F}_2[X, Y]$ the set of polynomials of cardinality $n\ell$ given by (3) and (4) for a code of length n. We aim at building a set $G = \{g_{i,j} \mid i = 1, \ldots, n,\ j = 1, \ldots, \ell\} \subset \mathbb{F}_2[X, Y]$ consisting of polynomials of degree at most 2 such that $\langle G \rangle = \langle F \rangle$. Denote with $F[i, j]$ the polynomial $f_{i,j}$, similarly for G. We first give a description of the set G and then formally describe the new modeling.

Construct G as follows:

– Put $G[1, 1] = x_1 + y_{1,1}$ and $G[1, h] = y_{1,h}$ for $h = 2, \ldots, \ell$;
– Set $G[i, 1] = F[i, 1] = x_i + y_{i,1} + y_{i-1,1}$ for every $i = 2, \ldots, n$;

– Compute

$$\begin{aligned}G[i,j] &= F[i,j] + y_{i-1,j-1}F[i,j-1]\\ &= F[i,j] + \mathsf{lm}(F[i,j]) + y_{i-1,j-1}(y_{i,j-1} + y_{i-1,j-1})\\ &= y_{i,j} + y_{i-1,j} + y_{i-1,j-1}^2 + y_{i,j-1}y_{i-1,j-1}.\end{aligned}$$

for every $i = 2,\dots,n$ and $j = 2,\dots,\ell$, where equality holds because $\mathsf{lm}(F[i,j]) = y_{i-1,j-1}\mathsf{lm}(F[i,j-1])$.

Remark 4. The algebraic system we are going to construct contains the field polynomials $x_i^2 - x_i$ for each $i = 1,\dots,n$ and $y_{i,j}^2 - y_{i,j}$ for every $i = 1,\dots,n$ and $j = 1,\dots,\ell$. Therefore, in terms of generating elements of the ideal, any squared term in $G[i,j]$ can be reduced to a linear term.

The set $G \subset \mathbb{F}_2[X,Y]$ contains $n\ell$ polynomials of degree at most two. The following proposition proves that the set $G \subset \mathbb{F}_2[X,Y]$ computed as above and F generate the same ideal of $\mathbb{F}_2[X,Y]$.

Proposition 1. *We have* $\langle G\rangle = \langle F\rangle$.

Proof. The inclusion $\langle G\rangle \subseteq \langle F\rangle$ is trivial. To prove the other inclusion, we show that we can write any element of the basis F as an $\mathbb{F}_2[X,Y]$-linear combination of elements of the basis G. By construction, $G[1,j] = F[1,j]$ for every $j = 1,\dots,\ell$. For every $i = 2,\dots,n$ we prove $F[i,j] \in \langle G\rangle$ by induction on j.
For $j = 1$ we have $F[i,1] = G[i,1]$.

Assume that $F[i,j] = \sum_{h=1}^{j} p_{i,j,h}G[i,h]$ with $p_{i,j,h} \in \mathbb{F}_2[X,Y]$. Then by construction we have

$$\begin{aligned}F[i,j+1] &= G[i,j+1] - y_{i-1,j}F[i,j]\\ &= G[i,j+1] - y_{i-1,j}\sum_{h=1}^{j} p_{i,j,h}G[i,h]\end{aligned}$$

proving the claim. □

We thus redefine the Hamming weight computation encoding as follows:

– *Hamming weight computation encoding.* Compute the following union of subsets of $\mathbb{F}_2[X,Y]$:

$$\begin{aligned}&\{x_1 + y_{1,1}, y_{1,2},\dots,y_{1,\ell}\} \cup \{x_i + y_{i,1} + y_{i-1,1} \mid i = 2,\dots,n\}\\ &\cup \big\{y_{i,j-1}y_{i-1,j-1} + y_{i,j} + y_{i-1,j-1} + y_{i-1,j}\\ &\quad \mid i = 2,\dots,n,\ j = 2,\dots,\ell\big\},\end{aligned}$$

Further Improvement. Set now $\ell_t = \lfloor \log_2(t) \rfloor + 1$. A further improvement to the MPS modeling (described in Eq. (7)) follows by observing that in the non-trivial case where $t < n$, we can impose that the last $\ell - \ell_t$ entries of $\mathbf{y}_i$ must be 0 for every $i = 1, \dots, n$. This means that we can add the linear equations $y_{i,j} = 0$ for every $i = 1, \dots, n$ and $j = \ell_t + 1, \dots, \ell$. By inspection, setting the aforementioned variables to 0 will make part of the equations of the Hamming weight computation encoding vanish. We can equivalently simply consider the equations that remain, and get rid of the variables which have been set to 0. Consider the following updated notation.

Notation 2. *Let $n \geq 2$ and let $\mathcal{C} \subseteq \mathbb{F}_2^n$ be a $[n, k, d]$-linear code having a parity check matrix $\mathbf{H} \in \mathbb{F}_2^{(n-k)\times n}$. Let $\mathbf{s} \in \mathbb{F}_2^{n-k}$ play the role of the syndrome and let $0 \leq t \leq \lfloor (d-1)/2 \rfloor$ be the target error weight. We define $\ell_t = \lfloor \log_2(t) \rfloor + 1$. Let $X = (x_1, \dots, x_n)$ and $Y = (Y_1, \dots, Y_n)$ with $Y_j = (y_{j,1}, \dots, y_{j,\ell_t})$ be two sets of variables and consider the polynomial ring $\mathbb{F}_2[X, Y]$.*

Under Notation 2, the effect of our improvement on the set of polynomials produced by the Hamming weight computation encoding is the following.

Hamming weight computation encoding. Compute the following union of subsets of $\mathbb{F}_2[X, Y]$:

$$\begin{aligned} &\{x_1 + y_{1,1}, y_{1,2}, \dots, y_{1,\ell_t}\} \cup \{x_i + y_{i,1} + y_{i-1,1} \mid i = 2, \dots, n\} \\ &\cup \big\{y_{i,j-1}y_{i-1,j-1} + y_{i,j} + y_{i-1,j-1} + y_{i-1,j} \\ &\quad \mid i = 2, \dots, n,\ j = 2, \dots, \ell_t\big\} \cup \{y_{i,\ell_t}y_{i-1,\ell_t} + y_{i-1,\ell_t} \mid i = 2, \dots, n\}. \end{aligned} \tag{7}$$

The effect on the weight constraint encoding is simply the decrease in the degree from ℓ to ℓ_t of the produced polynomial. This is the only non-quadratic polynomial left in the modeling. We can turn this polynomial into a set of $\mathcal{O}(t\ell_t)$ polynomials of degree up to 2 in $\mathcal{O}(t\ell_t)$ variables with the same linearization techniques described in [34, Fact 1 and Lemma 11].

To summarize, our modeling is defined in the following way.

Modeling 1 (Improved Modeling for the SDP over $\mathbb{F}_2$). *Given an instance $(\mathbf{H}, \mathbf{s}, t)$ of Problem 1 over $\mathbb{F}_2$, Modeling 1 is the union of the sets of polynomials* (2),(5), (6) *and* (7).

The improved modeling is an algebraic system of $\mathcal{O}(n(\ell_t + 2) - k + t\ell_t)$ polynomials of degree at most 2 in $\mathcal{O}(n(\ell_t + 1) + t\ell_t)$ variables. Note that most applications of the SDP to code-based cryptography, for instance in the McEliece scheme, choose $t \ll n$, hence the asymptotic bounds on the number of polynomials and variables in the improved modeling are both $\mathcal{O}(n\ell_t)$. As shown in Table 1, our modeling improves over MPS by a factor of $\log_2(n)\log_t(n)$.

4.2 Improved Modeling for the Case of ESDP

It is possible to obtain an algebraic modeling for the ESDP by tweaking the modeling described in the previous section. In fact, it is enough to redefine the

Table 1. Comparison with the asymptotic size of the polynomial system in [34, Theorem 13], where n is the length of the code and t the bound on the weight of the target vector, that is $\mathsf{wt}(\mathbf{e}) \leq t$.

	# Polynomials	# Variables
[34]	$\mathcal{O}(n\log_2(n)^2)$	$\mathcal{O}(n\log_2(n)^2)$
Modeling 1	$\mathcal{O}(n\log_2(t))$	$\mathcal{O}(n\log_2(t))$

weight constraint encoding to enforce that $\mathbf{y}_n$ represents the binary expansion of an integer t' such that $t' = t$ exactly. To this end, let $\mathbf{v} \in \mathbb{F}_2^{\ell_t}$ represent the binary expansion of an integer t. Under the same notation as in Notation 2, the following version of the weight constraint encoding describes the ESDP modeling with $\mathsf{wt}(\mathbf{e}) = t$.

– *Weight constraint encoding.* Compute the following set of linear polynomials:

$$\{y_{n,j} + v_j \mid j = 1, \ldots, \ell_t\}. \tag{8}$$

Using these polynomials leads to Modeling

Modeling 2 (Improved Modeling for the ESDP over $\mathbb{F}_2$). *Given an instance* $(\mathbf{H}, \mathbf{s}, t)$ *of Problem 2 over* $\mathbb{F}_2$*, Modeling 2 is the union of the sets of polynomials* (2), (6), (7) *and* (8).

Observe that, replacing the original Hamming weight computation encoding with that in (7) and the weight constraint encoding with that in (8), we obtain an algebraic system of polynomials of degree at most 2 for ESDP. Hence, linearization is not needed, moreover, we can give the exact number of equations and variables of this system. We report these values in Table 2.

Table 2. Number of equations and variables of the algebraic modeling of ESDP with $\mathsf{wt}(\mathbf{e}) = t$. The value of ℓ_t is $\lfloor \log_2(t) \rfloor + 1$.

	# Polynomials	# Variables
Modeling 2	$2n\ell_t + 3n + \ell_t - k - 1$	$n(\ell_t + 1)$

5 Complexity Analysis of Modeling 2

In this section, we investigate the complexity of solving the algebraic system for the ESDP given in Modeling 2 using standard Gröbner basis methods. An upper bound on the complexity is given by the formula (1) which depends on both the number of variables and the solving degree. Typically, the solving degree of the system is estimated by assessing its degree of regularity. However, in our analysis, we experimentally show that the degree of regularity often significantly exceeds the solving degree for systems given in Sect. 4.2 (see the results in Table 3). This distinction is crucial in cryptography, where these concepts are frequently used interchangeably. Our findings underscore the importance of thoroughly verifying such claims to ensure accurate security assessments and parameter selection.

Remark 5. We point out that the study in [13] investigates a particular case of the problem that this paper deals with, that is the *regular* syndrome decoding problem. The regular syndrome decoding problem considers error vectors having a regular distribution of non-zero entries. The algebraic modeling proposed in [13] is conjectured to exhibit semi-regular behavior when the linear parity-check constraints and the fixed, structured quadratic polynomials are considered separately. This suggests that, to some extent, their model behaves like a random polynomial system. Despite the fact that the problem tackled in [13] is a particular case of the problem we consider, our modeling has not been devised as a generalization of their modeling. Furthermore, we show that for the more general case, our modeling yields different results.

For the rest of this section, we retain the notation defined in Notation 2. We consider the polynomial ring $\mathbb{F}_2[X, Y]$ with the degrevlex term order with the X variables greater than the Y variables. Let $S \subset \mathbb{F}_2[X, Y]$ be the set of polynomials of Modeling 2 as described in Sect. 4.2. Let L and Q denote the sets of linear and quadratic polynomials, respectively. Clearly $S = L \cup Q$. Write also $L = L_{\mathbf{H}} \cup P$, where $L_{\mathbf{H}}$ denotes the set of linear polynomials in (2) introduced with the parity check matrix $\mathbf{H}$, and P denotes the remaining linear polynomials in S. In other words, P is the following set

$$\begin{aligned} P = &\{x_1 + y_{1,1}, y_{1,2}, \ldots, y_{1,\ell_t}\} \cup \{x_i + y_{i,1} + y_{i-1,1} \mid i = 2, \ldots, n\} \\ &\cup \{y_{n,j} + v_j \mid j = 1, \ldots, \ell_t\}. \end{aligned}$$

We want to estimate the degree of regularity of S. Since we do not know $L_{\mathbf{H}}$ a priori, we consider the set $S \setminus L_{\mathbf{H}} = Q \cup P$ and compute its degree of regularity. Indeed, we found that analyzing the degree of regularity or solving degree of the system with the linear equations (2) of $L_{\mathbf{H}}$ included was too challenging and unpredictable, as it heavily depends on the specific instance of the parity check matrix $\mathbf{H}$. For this reason, we chose to establish mathematical results for the system without $L_{\mathbf{H}}$, with the aim of providing a clearer foundation. Notice that the degree of regularity of $S \setminus L_{\mathbf{H}} = Q \cup P$ gives an upper bound to the degree of regularity of the whole system S (see Remark 8).

We break down the problem by first computing the degree of regularity of Q and then that of $Q \cup P$. We take advantage of the fact that the Hilbert series of Q and of $Q \cup P$ are polynomials and compute their degree, i.e. for instance, $d_{\mathrm{reg}}(Q) = \deg \mathrm{HS}_{\mathbb{F}_2[X,Y]/\langle Q^{\mathrm{top}}\rangle}(z) + 1$ as per Remark 3, similarly for $Q \cup P$. To this end, we are going to compute the maximum degree of a monomial in $\mathbb{F}_2[X, Y]/\langle Q^{\mathrm{top}}\rangle$, similarly we do for $Q \cup P$.

The Quadratic Polynomials. We begin by studying the degree of regularity of the quadratic part Q of the system S of Modeling 2. The highest degree part of Q has a very nice structure, as explained in the following remark.

Remark 6. The set Q^{top} is the union of the following three sets

$$\{x_i^2 \mid i = 1, \ldots, n\}, \{y_{i,j}^2 \mid i = 1, \ldots, n, \ j = 1, \ldots, \ell_t\}$$

and

$$\{y_{i-1,j}y_{i,j} \mid i = 2, \ldots, n, \ j = 1, \ldots, \ell_t\}.$$

The ideal $\langle Q^{\text{top}} \rangle \subseteq \mathbb{F}_2[X, Y]$ is thus a monomial ideal.

The following lemma gives the structure of the quotient ring $\mathbb{F}_2[X, Y]/\langle Q^{\text{top}} \rangle$.

Lemma 1. *The set Q^{top} is a Gröbner basis of the ideal $\langle Q^{\text{top}} \rangle$.*

Proof. As observed in Remark 6, Q^{top} is a monomial ideal. Given any two elements of $m_1, m_2 \in Q^{\text{top}}$ it is clear that for $a = \text{lcm}(m_1, m_2)/m_1 \in \mathbb{F}_2[X, Y]$ and $b = \text{lcm}(m_1, m_2)/m_2 \in \mathbb{F}_2[X, Y]$ we have that $am_1 - bm_2 = 0$. □

Example 1. Let $n = 4$ be the length of a code, then $\ell_t = 2$. A Gröbner basis of $\langle Q^{\text{top}} \rangle$ is the union of

$$\{y_{1,1}y_{2,1}, y_{1,2}y_{2,2}, y_{2,1}y_{3,1}, y_{2,2}y_{3,2}, y_{3,1}y_{4,1}, y_{3,2}y_{4,2}\}$$

and

$$\{x_1^2, x_2^2, x_3^2, x_4^2, y_{1,1}^2, y_{1,2}^2, y_{2,1}^2, y_{2,2}^2, y_{3,1}^2, y_{3,2}^2, y_{4,1}^2, y_{4,2}^2\}.$$

The following simple lemma is crucial for computing the degree of regularity of Q. For the sake of simplicity, we state it in terms of sets, and it ultimately provides a method to construct maximal monomials in the quotient ring $\mathbb{F}_2[X, Y]/\langle Q^{\text{top}} \rangle$.

Lemma 2. *Let $\mathcal{N} = \{1, 2, 3, \ldots, n\}$ and $\mathcal{P} = \{\{1, 2\}, \{2, 3\}, \ldots, \{n-1, n\}\}$, where $\mathcal{P}$ consists of consecutive pairs of elements from $\mathcal{N}$. Then:*

- *If n is even, there are exactly two sets of maximal cardinality $\mathcal{S}_1, \mathcal{S}_2 \subseteq \mathcal{N}$ such that no set in $\mathcal{P}$ is a subset of $\mathcal{S}$.*
- *If n is odd, there is exactly one set of maximal cardinality $\mathcal{S} \subseteq \mathcal{N}$ such that no set in $\mathcal{P}$ is a subset of $\mathcal{S}$.*

Proof. We aim to find the number of sets of maximal cardinality $\mathcal{S} \subseteq \mathcal{N}$ such that no pair from $\mathcal{P}$ (i.e., no two consecutive elements) appears in $\mathcal{S}$. In order to avoid pairs of consecutive elements, we can only select non-consecutive elements from $\mathcal{N}$. To maximize the size of $\mathcal{S}$, we select every other element from $\mathcal{N}$. The size of such a set of maximal cardinality $\mathcal{S}$ is: $\lceil \frac{n}{2} \rceil$. Thus:

- If n is even, a set of maximal cardinality contains $\frac{n}{2}$ elements.
- If n is odd, a set of maximal cardinality contains $\frac{n+1}{2}$ elements.

Case 1: n is even. Let $n = 2k$. The largest possible set $\mathcal{S}$ will contain $k = \frac{n}{2}$ elements. There are exactly two ways to construct such a set:

1. Start with 1 and select every other element: $\mathcal{S}_1 = \{1, 3, 5, \ldots, n-1\}$. This set contains all the odd-numbered elements of $\mathcal{N}$, and its size is k.
2. Start with 2 and select every other element: $\mathcal{S}_2 = \{2, 4, 6, \ldots, n\}$. This set contains all the even-numbered elements of $\mathcal{N}$, and its size is also k.

Since there are no other ways to select k elements without picking consecutive elements, these are the only two sets of maximal cardinality for n even.
Case 2: n is odd. Let $n = 2k+1$. The largest possible set $\mathcal{S}$ contains $k+1 = \frac{n+1}{2}$ elements. In this case, there is only one way to construct a set of size $k+1$ that avoids consecutive elements, i.e. start with 1 and select every other element: $\mathcal{S}_1 = \{1, 3, 5, \ldots, n\}$. This set contains $k+1$ elements and avoids consecutive pairs. If we were to start with 2 and select every other element, we would only get k elements: $\mathcal{S}_2 = \{2, 4, 6, \ldots, n-1\}$. This is not maximal, as it contains fewer than $k+1$ elements. Thus, for n odd, there is exactly one maximal set. □

Lemma 2 can be used to prove the following corollary, which we will use to construct a maximal degree monomial in $\mathbb{F}_2[X, Y]/\langle Q^{\text{top}}\rangle$. The idea behind the construction lies in the observation that a Gröbner basis of Q^{top} can be written as the union of disjoint subsets $Q^{\text{top}}_{j,n}$ for $j = 1, \ldots, \ell_t$, see Theorem 1, which we describe in the next corollary. Also, the next corollary computes a maximal degree monomial with respect to $Q^{\text{top}}_{j,n}$ for every $j = 1, \ldots, \ell_t$. Given these monomials, computing a maximal degree monomial in $\mathbb{F}_2[X, Y]/\langle Q^{\text{top}} \cup P^{\text{top}}\rangle$, or equivalently, the degree of its Hilbert series, becomes feasible with a slight modification of the subsets due to the presence of linear polynomials in P^{top}.

Corollary 1. *Let $n \in \mathbb{N}$ with $n \geq 2$, and define*

$$Q^{\text{top}}_{j,n} := \{y_{1,j}y_{2,j}, y_{2,j}y_{3,j}, \ldots, y_{n-1,j}y_{n,j}\} \cup \{y_{i,j}^2 \mid i = 1, \ldots, n\} \subset \mathbb{F}_2[y_{1,j}, \ldots, y_{n,j}],$$

for some $j \in \mathbb{N}$. If n is even then there exists two monomials of maximal degree $\lceil \frac{n}{2} \rceil$ in $\mathbb{F}_2[y_{1,j}, \ldots, y_{n,j}]/\langle Q^{\text{top}}_{j,n}\rangle$, namely

$$m_1 = \prod_{\substack{i=1,\ldots,n-1,\\ i \text{ odd}}} y_{i,j} \quad \text{and} \quad m_2 = \prod_{\substack{i=2,\ldots,n,\\ i \text{ even}}} y_{i,j}.$$

If n is odd, then there exists a unique monomial of maximal degree $\lceil \frac{n}{2} \rceil$ in $\mathbb{F}_2[y_{1,j}, \ldots, y_{n,j}]/\langle Q^{\text{top}}_{j,n}\rangle$, namely

$$m = \prod_{\substack{i=1,\ldots,n,\\ i \text{ odd}}} y_{i,j}.$$

We are ready to prove the following theorem, which provides the degree of regularity of Q.

Theorem 1.

$$d_{\text{reg}}(Q) = \begin{cases} n + \ell_t n/2 + 1 & \textit{if } n \equiv 0 \bmod 2 \\ n + \ell_t (n+1)/2 + 1 & \textit{if } n \equiv 1 \bmod 2 \end{cases}.$$

Equivalently,

$$d_{\text{reg}}(Q) = n + \ell_t \lceil n/2 \rceil + 1.$$

Proof. Let $Q_{j,n}^{\text{top}} \subset \mathbb{F}_2[y_{1,j}, \ldots, y_{n,j}]$ as in Corollary 1, for every $j = 1, \ldots, \ell_t$. Observe that

$$Q^{\text{top}} = \bigcup_{j=1}^{\ell_t} Q_{j,n}^{\text{top}} \cup \left\{x_i^2 \mid i = 1, \ldots, n\right\}. \tag{9}$$

Corollary 1 computes a monomial $m_j \in \mathbb{F}_2[y_{1,j}, \ldots, y_{n,j}]$ of maximal degree $\lceil n/2 \rceil$ such that $m_j \notin \langle Q_h^{\text{top}} \rangle$ for every $j = 1, \ldots, \ell_t$ and every $h = 1, \ldots, \ell_t$. This implies that $m_j \notin \langle Q^{\text{top}} \rangle$ for every j. It is now clear that the monomial

$$m := \prod_{i=1}^{n} x_i \prod_{j=1}^{\ell_t} m_j \in \mathbb{F}_2[X, Y]$$

is such that $m \notin \langle Q^{\text{top}} \rangle$. Note that the the set $\left\{x_i^2 \mid i = 1, \ldots, n\right\}$ in (9) enforces that m must be squarefree in the variables $x_1, \ldots, x_n$. By the maximality of each m_j and that of $\prod_{i=1}^{n} x_i$, any multiple of m by a non-constant term would trivially be in $\langle Q^{\text{top}} \rangle$. Since

$$d := \deg m = n + \ell_t \lceil n/2 \rceil,$$

we have that the $(d+1)$-th coefficient of the Hilbert series of $\mathbb{F}_2[X, Y]/\langle Q^{\text{top}} \rangle$ is 0. The result on the degree of regularity $d_{\text{reg}}(Q)$ follows. □

Example 2. Let $n = 8$ and $\ell_t = 3$. According to Theorem 1 the degree of regularity of Q is 21. Using MAGMA, we compute and report the Hilbert series of the quotient ring $\mathbb{F}_2[X, Y]/\langle Q^{\text{top}} \rangle$, i.e.

$$\begin{aligned} \text{HS}_{\mathbb{F}_2[X,Y]/\langle Q^{\text{top}} \rangle}(z) = {} & 125z^{20} + 2500z^{19} + 23075z^{18} + 130800z^{17} + \\ & 511140z^{16} + 1465020z^{15} + 3198081z^{14} + \\ & 5448312z^{13} + 7360635z^{12} + 7966528z^{11} + \\ & 6946904z^{10} + 4889800z^{9} + 2773415z^{8} + \\ & 1260580z^{7} + 454625z^{6} + 128080z^{5} + 27524z^{4} + \\ & 4348z^{3} + 475z^{2} + 32z + 1, \end{aligned}$$

thus $d_{\text{reg}}(Q) = \deg \text{HS}_{\mathbb{F}_2[X,Y]/\langle Q^{\text{top}} \rangle} + 1 = 21$, matching our results.

The Linear Polynomials. In this section, we study how the degree of regularity computed in Theorem 1 changes when we add to the quadratic equations Q also the fixed linear equations of P, which do not depend on the specific instance of the problem. Specifically, we compute the degree of regularity of $Q \cup P$. For this, we need to consider the ideal $\langle Q^{\text{top}} \cup P^{\text{top}} \rangle$. Note that this ideal contains $\langle Q^{\text{top}} \rangle$, which means that the variety of the former is a subset of the variety of the latter. In particular, the ideal $\langle Q^{\text{top}} \cup P^{\text{top}} \rangle$ is also zero-dimensional, so its degree of regularity is well-defined. We will use similar arguments to those applied to $\langle Q^{\text{top}} \rangle$ to study it.

Remark 7. The set $Q^{\text{top}} \cup P^{\text{top}}$ is the union of the following sets

$$\{x_i^2 \mid i=1,\dots,n\}, \{x_i \mid i=1,\dots,n\}, \{y_{i,j}^2 \mid i=1,\dots,n,\ j=1,\dots,\ell_t\},$$
$$\{y_{1,j} \mid j=2,\dots,\ell_t\}, \{y_{n,j} \mid j=1,\dots,\ell_t\}$$

and

$$\{y_{i-1,j}y_{i,j} \mid i=2,\dots,n,\ j=1,\dots,\ell_t\}.$$

and the ideal $\langle Q^{\text{top}} \cup P^{\text{top}} \rangle \subseteq \mathbb{F}_2[X,Y]$ is thus a monomial ideal.

Next lemma provides a Gröbner basis of the ideal $\langle Q^{\text{top}} \cup P^{\text{top}} \rangle \subseteq \mathbb{F}_2[X,Y]$.

Lemma 3. *A Gröbner basis G for $\langle Q^{\text{top}} \cup P^{\text{top}} \rangle \subseteq \mathbb{F}_2[X,Y]$ is*

$$G = \{x_i \mid i=1,\dots,n\} \cup \{y_{i-1,j}y_{i,j} \mid i=3,\dots,n-1,\ j=1,\dots,\ell_t\} \cup$$
$$\{y_{1,1}y_{2,1}\} \cup \{y_{1,j} \mid j=2,\dots,\ell_t\} \cup \{y_{n,j} \mid j=1,\dots,\ell_t\} \cup$$
$$\{y_{i,j}^2 \mid i=2,\dots,n-1,\ j=1,\dots,\ell_t\} \cup \{y_{1,1}^2\}.$$

Proof. The proof of this statements follows directly from inspecting Remark 7 and the same observations as in proof of Lemma 1. □

The next theorem gives the exact value of the degree of regularity of the system $Q \cup P$. The proof uses similar arguments to those used for the proof of Theorem 1.

Theorem 2. *The degree of regularity of $Q \cup P$ is*

$$d_{\text{reg}}(Q \cup P) = \left\lceil \frac{n-1}{2} \right\rceil + (\ell_t - 1)\left\lceil \frac{n-2}{2} \right\rceil + 1.$$

Proof. Define the set

$$\tilde{Q}_{j,n}^{\text{top}} := Q_{j,n-1}^{\text{top}} \setminus \{y_{1,j}y_{2,j}\} \subset \mathbb{F}_2[y_{2,j},\dots,y_{n-1,j}],$$

for every $j=1,\dots,\ell_t$. Let G be a Gröbner basis of $\langle Q^{\text{top}} \cup P^{\text{top}} \rangle$ as in Lemma 3. Due to the presence of the linear monomials contributed by P^{top}, we observe

$$G = Q_{1,n-1}^{\text{top}} \cup \bigcup_{j=2}^{\ell_t} \tilde{Q}_{j,n-1}^{\text{top}} \cup \{x_i^2 \mid i=1,\dots,n\}. \tag{10}$$

Applying Corollary 1, we can get a monomial $m_1 \in \mathbb{F}_2[y_{1,1}, \dots, y_{n-1,1}]$ of maximal degree $\deg m_1 = \lceil (n-1)/2 \rceil$ such that $m_1 \notin \mathbb{F}_2[y_{1,1}, \dots, y_{n-1,1}]/\langle Q^{\text{top}}_{1,n-1} \rangle$. We can obtain other $\ell_t - 1$ monomials m_j of maximal degree $d = \lceil (n-2)/2 \rceil$, such that $m_j \notin \langle \tilde{Q}^{\text{top}}_{h,n-1} \rangle$ for every $h = 1, \dots, \ell_t$ and every $j = 2, \dots, \ell_t$. Let now

$$m := \prod_{j=1}^{\ell_t} m_j \in \mathbb{F}_2[X,Y]/\langle G \rangle$$

then

$$d := \deg m = \left\lceil \frac{n-1}{2} \right\rceil + (\ell_t - 1) \left\lceil \frac{n-2}{2} \right\rceil,$$

meaning that the $(d+1)$-th coefficient of the Hilbert series of $\mathbb{F}_2[X,Y]/\langle G \rangle$ is 0. The result on the degree of regularity $d_{\text{reg}}(Q \cup P)$ follows. □

Example 3. Let $n = 8$ and $\ell_t = 3$. According to Theorem 2 the degree of regularity of $Q \cup P$ is 11. Using MAGMA, we compute and report the Hilbert series of the quotient ring $\mathbb{F}_2[X,Y]/\langle Q^{\text{top}} \cup P^{\text{top}} \rangle$, i.e.

$$\begin{aligned} \mathrm{HS}_{\mathbb{F}_2[X,Y]/\langle Q^{\text{top}} \cup P^{\text{top}} \rangle}(z) = {} & 16z^{10} + 240z^9 + 1188z^8 + 2920z^7 + 4132z^6 + 3608z^5 + \\ & 2005z^4 + 710z^3 + 155z^2 + 19z + 1, \end{aligned}$$

thus $d_{\text{reg}}(Q \cup P) = \deg \mathrm{HS}_{\mathbb{F}_2[X,Y]/\langle Q^{\text{top}} \cup P^{\text{top}} \rangle} + 1 = 11$, matching our results.

Remark 8. Since Theorem 2 considers the set $Q^{\text{top}} \cup P^{\text{top}} = S^{\text{top}} \setminus L^{\text{top}}_{\mathbf{H}}$, it only gives an upper bound to the degree of regularity of S, that is

$$d_{\text{reg}}(S) \le \left\lceil \frac{n-1}{2} \right\rceil + (\ell_t - 1) \left\lceil \frac{n-2}{2} \right\rceil + 1.$$

In the next section, we provide some experimental data showing the gap between the value computed in Theorem 2 and that of the actual solving degree.

5.1 Experimental Results

We performed several experiments for Modeling 2 taking as input both random and Goppa codes, and we obtained a solving degree which is much smaller than the upper bound for the degree of regularity computed in Theorem 2. This results in a much lower complexity estimate. We provide a selection of our experiments in Table 3. The MAGMA code used for our experiments can be found here.

Table 3. This table shows experimental results for $\mathbb{F}_2$-linear codes using Modeling 2 for the ESDP. The number of equations is given in the format (#linear equations, #quadratic equations). The values in the d_{M} column represent the smallest degree D such that MAGMA function GroebnerBasis(F,D) gives the Gröbner basis, i.e. highest step degree achieved when directly computing the Gröbner basis of the system in MAGMA, but ignoring the unnecessary steps in high degree that MAGMA F4 algorithm may do to insure termination. The SR d_{reg} column gives the degree of regularity of a semi-regular system of equations with the associated number of linear equations, quadratic equations, and variables, using [3, Corollary 3.3.8]. The values in d_{reg} column are upper bounds for the degree of regularity of the system as provided by Theorem 2 and Remark 8. Random codes with "*" are decoding challenges from https://decodingchallenge.org/syndrome, with a number of errors slightly above Gilbert-Varshamov distance. The other random code instances are below GV distance instead. Instances with "Goppa" Code Type are random full-length binary Goppa codes with a number of errors equal to the Goppa polynomial degree. The Prange and Modeling 2 columns state the $\log_2$ of the complexities of the Prange algorithm (Esser-Bellini estimator [24]) and Gröbner basis computations (1) with d_{M}, respectively.

n	k	t	Code Type	# Eqs	# Vars	d_{reg}	SR d_{reg}	d_{M}	Prange	Modeling 2
8	2	2	Goppa	(17,38)	24	≤ 8	3	2	9	23
10	5	4	Random*	(20,67)	40	≤ 14	5	3	10	38
16	8	2	Goppa	(27,78)	48	≤ 16	5	3	12	40
20	10	5	Random*	(35,137)	80	≤ 29	7	3	12	46
30	15	7	Random*	(50,207)	120	≤ 44	10	4	15	65
32	12	4	Goppa	(57,221)	128	≤ 47	10	3	16	52
32	17	3	Goppa	(50,158)	96	≤ 32	5	4	16	61
32	22	2	Goppa	(45,158)	96	≤ 32	7	3	15	48
40	20	8	Random*	(67,356)	160	≤ 78	16	5	17	88
50	30	5	Random	(75,347)	200	≤ 74	15	4	20	73
50	40	4	Random	(65,347)	200	≤ 74	17	4	14	73
64	52	2	Goppa	(79,318)	192	≤ 64	14	4	18	72
64	40	4	Goppa	(93,445)	256	≤ 95	19	4	21	77
64	16	8	Goppa	(119,572)	320	≤ 126	21	4	19	81

Comparison with Combinatorial Attacks. We also compare the complexity of solving ESDP using Gröbner basis techniques with the more traditional combinatorial attack proposed by Prange. The latter is widely regarded as a reference algorithm for decoding linear codes in the Hamming metric, and forms the basis of many state-of-the-art attacks on code-based cryptosystems.

However, Gröbner basis computations are known to be computationally expensive, particularly as the number of variables and the degree of the polynomials grow. In contrast, combinatorial methods like Prange exploit structured randomization and search to solve the problem more efficiently, albeit with large memory requirements.

In Table 3, the complexity of the Prange algorithm has been computed using the Esser-Bellini cryptographic estimator [24], see also this link. On the other hand, the complexity of solving the polynomial system of Modeling 2 with Gröbner bases methods has been computed using formula (1) with $N = n(\lfloor \log_2(t) \rfloor + 2)$, the highest step degree d_M achieved in the MAGMA experiments as a proxy for the solving degree d_{sol} and the conservative matrix multiplication constant $\omega = 2.807$.

These results confirm that direct combinatorial attacks like Prange outperform algebraic methods when solving the syndrome decoding problem, particularly for parameters of practical interest in code-based cryptography. Despite this, algebraic approaches remain valuable from a theoretical perspective and may offer insights into alternative solution strategies that could be leveraged in other contexts. We include this comparison to emphasize that the purpose of our Gröbner basis approach is not to compete with combinatorial attacks in efficiency, but rather to provide an alternative algebraic perspective on the syndrome decoding problem. Such perspectives can contribute to understanding the hardness of related problems in post-quantum cryptography.

6 Modelings over $\mathbb{F}_q$

Each of the modelings we have discussed thus far (MPS, Modeling 1, and Modeling 2) are limited to the binary case. To the best of our knowledge, there is no modeling of the general syndrome decoding problem over $\mathbb{F}_q$ for $q > 2$ in the literature. In this section, we adapt the previous modelings to a generic finite field $\mathbb{F}_q$, for some prime power $q \geq 2$, and explain how to efficiently (i.e. in polynomial time) obtain a polynomial system encoding an instance of the Syndrome Decoding Problem.

We will adopt the following notation throughout this section.

Notation 3. *Let $n \geq 2$ and let $\mathcal{C} \subseteq \mathbb{F}_q^n$ be a $[n, k, d]$-linear code having a parity check matrix $\mathbf{H} \in \mathbb{F}_q^{(n-k)\times n}$. The vector $\mathbf{s} \in \mathbb{F}_q^{n-k}$ denotes the syndrome and $0 \leq t \leq \lfloor (d-1)/2 \rfloor$ is the target error weight. Let $r_1, r_2 > 0$ be two integers. We will work over the polynomial ring $\mathbb{F}_{q^{r_1}}[X, Y, Z]$, where $X = (x_1, \dots, x_n)$, $Y = (Y_1, \dots, Y_n)$, $Y_j = (y_{j,1}, \dots, y_{j,r_2})$, and $Z = (z_1, \dots, z_n)$ are variables.*

As in the previous sections, $\mathbf{x} = (x_1, \dots, x_n)$ is the vector of variables corresponding to the solution of the syndrome decoding problem. On the other hand, the role of the integers r_1, r_2 and of the variables Y and Z will be illustrated later.

We separately describe and explain the sets of polynomials that, together, model Problems 1 and 2. Then we provide an analysis of the correctness of our modelings.

6.1 Construction of the Equations

Identifying the Support of a Vector of $\mathbb{F}_q^n$. Unlike the Boolean case, the value of an element in the support of $\mathbf{x}$ is not uniquely determined when $q \geq 3$. In order to count the number of nonzero coordinates with algebraic equations, we first need to map all nonzero elements to a unique element of $\mathbb{F}_q^*$, say 1. Thus, in addition to the Y's variables encoding the partial Hamming weights, we introduce here another length-n vector of variables $Z = (z_1, \dots, z_n)$, each of which can only assume two values, 0 or 1, depending on whether the corresponding X coordinate is nonzero. First, we tackle the problem of describing the relation between X and Z through algebraic equations. We distinguish two cases, depending on the target version of the problem, and then prove the sets of polynomials correctly describe our target.

- *Support constraint encoding for Problem* 1. Compute the following set of $2n$ quadratic polynomials

$$\{x_j(z_j - 1) \mid j = 1, \dots, n\} \cup \{z_j^2 - z_j \mid j = 1, \dots, n\}. \tag{11}$$

- *Support constraint encoding for Problem* 2. Compute the following set of n polynomials of degree $q - 1$

$$\{z_j - x_j^{q-1} \mid j = 1, \dots, n\}. \tag{12}$$

In the first case, the condition $z_j = 1$ if $x_j \neq 0$ is given from the first set of polynomials. Otherwise, the second set implies $z_j \in \{0, 1\}$. Therefore, the support of $(z_1, \dots, z_n)$ contains the support of $(x_1, \dots, x_n)$ and thus $\mathsf{wt}((z_1, \dots, z_n)) \geq \mathsf{wt}((x_1, \dots, x_n))$. In the second case, in order for the corresponding equations to be satisfied, $z_j = 1$ if and only if $x_j \neq 0$, and $z_j = 0$ otherwise. Hence $\mathsf{wt}((z_1, \dots, z_n)) = \mathsf{wt}((x_1, \dots, x_n))$.

From a computational point of view, the support constraint encoding for Problem 2 has a strong limitation, that is the high degree of the polynomials. A Gröbner basis computation would need to reach at least degree $q-1$ before taking into account such polynomials, leading to infeasible calculations unless q is very small. This is reminiscent of the problem of including field equations in modelings over large fields. Yet, this issue does not appear in the support constraint encoding for Problem 1: the polynomials have constant degree 2 regardless of the field size q, making a modeling for Problem 1 more realistic and valuable for effective computations.

Hamming Weight Computation Encoding. A difficulty arising from a direct generalization to large fields of the previous approach is the update of the weight registers, i.e. of the vectors $\mathbf{y}_i$'s. In order to overcome this limitation, we introduce a different strategy for encoding the partial weights. More precisely, we substitute their binary expansion with vectors from a linear recurring sequence over an extension of $\mathbb{F}_q$. As we will see, this approach naturally allows for the choice of different trade-offs between the number of variables and finite field size.

We first recall some known results about (univariate) polynomials over finite fields, companion matrices, and linear recurring sequences. We mainly refer to [29] for this part.

Definition 1 (Companion matrix, Chap. 2, § 5 [29]). *Let* $f(x) = x^d + f_{d-1}x^{d-1} + \cdots + f_0 \in \mathbb{F}_q[x]$ *be a monic polynomial. Its companion matrix is*

$$\mathbf{C}_f = \begin{bmatrix} 0\,0 \cdots 0 & -f_0 \\ 1\,0 \cdots 0 & -f_1 \\ 0\,1 \cdots 0 & -f_2 \\ \vdots\;\vdots\;\ddots\;\vdots & \vdots \\ 0\,0 \cdots 1 & -f_{d-1} \end{bmatrix}. \tag{13}$$

It is well known that the equation $f(\mathbf{C}_f) = 0$ is satisfied, hence, if f is a monic irreducible polynomial over $\mathbb{F}_q$, then its companion matrix $\mathbf{C}_f$ plays the role of a root of f. It follows that the elements of the extension field $\mathbb{F}_{q^d}$ can be written, according to this representation, as polynomials in $\mathbf{C}_f$ of degree strictly less than d.

We also recall that the order of a non-constant polynomial f with $f_0 \neq 0$ is the least positive integer e such that $f(x) \mid x^e - 1$. A polynomial in $\mathbb{F}_q[x]$ of degree d is said primitive if it is monic, $f(0) \neq 0$, and $\mathsf{ord}(f) = q^d - 1$. Such polynomials can be found from the factorization of $x^{q^d-1} - 1$.

The theory of linear recurring sequences says that the sequence of vectors $\mathbf{y}_0, \mathbf{C}_f\mathbf{y}_0, \mathbf{C}_f^2\mathbf{y}_0, \ldots$, for some nonzero $\mathbf{y}_0$ and companion matrix with $f_0 \neq 0$, is periodic with least period equal to the order of f, when the latter is irreducible (cf. [29, Theorem 6.28]). Therefore, by choosing f primitive, we obtain a sequence of vectors $\mathbf{y}_0, \mathbf{C}_f\mathbf{y}_0, \mathbf{C}_f^2\mathbf{y}_0, \ldots$ of maximal order $q^d - 1$. On the other hand, the choice of $\mathbf{y}_0$ does not seem to affect any property of our modeling. Without loss of generality, from now on we fix the initial state vector

$$\mathbf{y}_0 = \begin{pmatrix} 1\,0 \cdots 0 \end{pmatrix}^\top. \tag{14}$$

By tuning the values r_1 and r_2 we can choose the number of variables used for the Hamming weight computation encoding, at the cost of working over more or less large field extensions. More precisely, take

$$m := \min\{i \in \mathbb{N} \mid q^i > \max(t, n-t) + 1\},$$

and let r_1, r_2 be two positive integers such that $m \leq r_1 r_2$. Then, let $f \in \mathbb{F}_{q^{r_1}}[x]$ be a primitive polynomial of degree r_2 and $\mathbf{C}_f \in \mathbb{F}_{q^{r_1}}^{r_2 \times r_2}$ its companion matrix. For convenience sake, we will use the column vector notation for the Y_j's blocks of variables, i.e.

$$Y_j = \begin{pmatrix} y_{j,1} \cdots y_{j,r_2} \end{pmatrix}^\top.$$

The polynomial encoding the partial Hamming weight is the following.

– *Hamming weight computation encoding.* Compute the nr_2 affine bilinear (in Y and Z) polynomials from the expansion of

$$Y_1 - (1 - z_1) \cdot \mathbf{y}_0 - z_1 \cdot \mathbf{C}_f \cdot \mathbf{y}_0 \tag{15}$$

and

$$\{Y_j - (1 - z_j) \cdot Y_{j-1} - z_j \cdot \mathbf{C}_f \cdot Y_{j-1}\,, \qquad \text{for } j \in \{2, \dots, n\}\}. \tag{16}$$

Remark 9. Using this approach, r_1 determines the finite field over which we define the resulting polynomial system (and thus the Multivariate Quadratic Problem instance), while r_2 determines the number of variables required for the weight computation encoding (which is strictly linked to the computational complexity). Observe that, together, Eqs. (15) and (16) correspond to nr_2 polynomial equations over $\mathbb{F}_{q^{r_1}}$ in $nr_2 + n$ variables. In several cases, working with a small amount of variables (namely, r_1 large and r_2 small) is preferable, but there are some instances in which working over small finite fields with a large number of variables (i.e. r_1 small and r_2 large) is advantageous.

The next result shows that the Hamming weight of $\mathbf{z}$ is correctly computed.

Proposition 2. *Consider the system given by* (15) *and* (16) *over* $\mathbb{F}_{q^{r_1}}[Y, Z]$. *Any solution* $(\mathbf{y}, \mathbf{z}) = (\mathbf{y}_1, \dots, \mathbf{y}_n, \mathbf{z}) \in \mathbb{F}_{q^{r_1}}^{r_2 n} \times \{0,1\}^n$ *of the system satisfies*

$$\mathbf{y}_j = \mathbf{C}_f^{\mathsf{wt}(\pi_j(\mathbf{z}))} \mathbf{y}_0.$$

In particular, $\mathbf{y}_n = \mathbf{C}_f^{\mathsf{wt}(\mathbf{z})} \mathbf{y}_0$.

Proof. It follows directly from the hypotheses by an inductive argument.
The first step is considering $\mathbf{y}_1 := (y_{1,1}, \dots, y_{1,r_2})^\top$, which by definition is

$$\mathbf{y}_1 = (1 - z_1)\mathbf{y}_0 + z_1 \mathbf{C}_f \mathbf{y}_0 = \begin{cases} \mathbf{y}_0 \text{ if } z_1 = 0 \\ \mathbf{C}_f \mathbf{y}_0 \text{ if } z_1 \neq 0 \end{cases},$$

namely, $\mathbf{y}_1 = \mathbf{C}_f^{\mathsf{wt}(z_1)} \mathbf{y}_0 = \mathbf{C}_f^{\mathsf{wt}(\pi_1(\mathbf{z}))} \mathbf{y}_0$.
For the inductive step, we consider $\mathbf{y}_{j-1} := (y_{j-1,1}, \dots, y_{j-1,r_2})^\top$ to be equal to $\mathbf{C}_f^{\mathsf{wt}(\pi_{j-1}(\mathbf{z}))} \mathbf{y}_0$, and we look at the definition of $\mathbf{y}_j$. We have

$$\mathbf{y}_j = (1 - z_j)\mathbf{y}_{j-1} + z_j \mathbf{C}_f \mathbf{y}_{j-1} = \begin{cases} \mathbf{y}_{j-1} & \text{if } z_j = 0 \\ \mathbf{C}_f \mathbf{y}_{j-1} & \text{if } z_j \neq 0 \end{cases},$$

and either way, we obtain

$$\mathbf{y}_j = \mathbf{C}_f^{z_j} \cdot \mathbf{y}_{j-1} = \mathbf{C}_f^{z_j} \mathbf{C}_f^{\mathsf{wt}(\pi_{j-1}(\mathbf{z}))} \mathbf{y}_0 = \mathbf{C}_f^{\mathsf{wt}(z_j) + \mathsf{wt}(\pi_{j-1}(\mathbf{z}))} \mathbf{y}_0 = \mathbf{C}_f^{\mathsf{wt}(\pi_j(\mathbf{z}))} \mathbf{y}_0.$$

□

Weight Constraint Encoding. As for the previous modelings, the weight constraint encoding simply ensures that the representation of the last partial Hamming weight coincides with the representation of the total Hamming weight.

- *Weight constraint encoding.* Compute the r_2 affine linear polynomials in Y from the expansion of

$$\mathbf{y}_n - \mathbf{C}_f^t \mathbf{y}_0. \tag{17}$$

Corollary 2. *Consider the system given by (15), (16) and (17) over $\mathbb{F}_{q^{r_1}}[Y, Z]$ and let $z_1, \ldots, z_n$ be either 0 or 1. Then*

1. *The number of solutions $(\mathbf{y}, \mathbf{z}) \in \mathbb{F}_{q^{r_1}}^{r_2 n} \times \{0,1\}^n$ of the system is equal to the number of binary vectors of Hamming weight equal to t, i.e. $\binom{n}{t}$;*
2. *If $(\bar{\mathbf{y}}, \bar{\mathbf{z}})$ and $(\tilde{\mathbf{y}}, \tilde{\mathbf{z}})$ are two distinct solutions, then $\bar{\mathbf{z}} \neq \tilde{\mathbf{z}}$.*

Proof. From Proposition 2 and (17), it follows that any solution $(\mathbf{y}, \mathbf{z})$ satisfies

$$\mathbf{C}_f^t \mathbf{y}_0 = \begin{pmatrix} y_{n,1} \\ \vdots \\ y_{n,r_2} \end{pmatrix} = \mathbf{C}_f^{\mathsf{wt}(\mathbf{z})} \mathbf{y}_0,$$

which implies $\mathsf{ord}(f) \mid |t - \mathsf{wt}(\mathbf{z})|$. Since f is primitive, we obtain

$$\mathsf{ord}(f) = (q^{r_1})^{r_2} - 1 \geq q^m - 1 > \max(t, n-t).$$

On the other hand, $0 \leq \mathsf{wt}(\mathbf{z}) \leq n$, hence $|t - \mathsf{wt}(\mathbf{z})| \leq \min(t, n-t)$. Therefore, the only way $\mathsf{ord}(f)$ can divide $|t - \mathsf{wt}(\mathbf{z})|$, is that $|t - \mathsf{wt}(\mathbf{z})| = 0$, i.e. $\mathsf{wt}(\mathbf{z}) = t$.

Substituting $\mathbf{z}$ in (15) uniquely determines all the values $y_{1,1}, \ldots, y_{1,r_2}$ by linear equations of the form $y_{1,i} = c_i$. Moreover, substituting $y_{j-1,1}, \ldots, y_{j-1,r_2}$ in (16) recursively determines all the values $y_{j,1}, \ldots, y_{j,r_2}$ in a similar manner. Therefore, if $\bar{\mathbf{z}} = \tilde{\mathbf{z}}$ are the projections over the last n coordinates of two solutions, then also $(\bar{\mathbf{y}}, \bar{\mathbf{z}}) = (\tilde{\mathbf{y}}, \tilde{\mathbf{z}})$, which concludes the proof. □

Field Equations. The field equations concern only the X part of the variables.

- *Field equations.* The equations are obtained from the n polynomials

$$\{x_j^q - x_j \mid j = 1, \ldots, n\}. \tag{18}$$

Indeed, $\mathbf{z}$ already lies over $\{0,1\}^n$ because of the support constraint equations (and (18)), while (15) and (16) force Y to lie over $\mathbb{F}_{q^{r_1}}$.

6.2 The Modelings

We are finally ready to describe the algebraic systems over $\mathbb{F}_{q^{r_1}}[X, Y, Z]$ for Problems 2 and 1 and prove their correctness.

Modeling 3 (Modeling for the SDP over $\mathbb{F}_q$). *Given an instance* $(\mathbf{H}, \mathbf{s}, t)$ *of Problem 1 over* $\mathbb{F}_q$*, Modeling 3 is the union of the sets of polynomials* (2), (11), (15), (16), (17) *and* (18).

Modeling 4 (Modeling for the ESDP over $\mathbb{F}_q$). *Given an instance* $(\mathbf{H}, \mathbf{s}, t)$ *of Problem 2 over* $\mathbb{F}_q$*, Modeling 4 is the union of the sets of polynomials* (2), (12), (15), (16), (17) *and* (18).

As already said, finite field equations cannot be efficiently taken into account when dealing with large fields. In the exact weight syndrome decoding modeling, the support constraint equations are high-degree as well, so the problem would persist. On the other hand, it becomes convenient to remove the field equations in the bounded syndrome decoding problem. This leads to a new quadratic modeling.

Modeling 5 (Quadratic Modeling for the SDP over $\mathbb{F}_q$). *Given an instance* $(\mathbf{H}, \mathbf{s}, t)$ *of Problem 1 over* $\mathbb{F}_q$*, Modeling 5 is the union of the sets of polynomials* (2), (11), (15), (16), (17).

In the next section we thoroughly investigate the effect of removing the field equations from Modeling 4. We find, that at least for the parameter choices interesting for cryptography, the solutions of our modeling without field equations still lie over $\mathbb{F}_q$ with high probability.

Table 4 provides the number of variables and equations for the three modelings over $\mathbb{F}_q$.

Table 4. Number of equations, number of variables and maximum degree of the algebraic modelings over $\mathbb{F}_{q^{r_1}}$.

	# Polynomials	# Variables	Degree
Modeling 3	$4n - k + nr_2 + r_2$	$n(r_2 + 2)$	q
Modeling 4	$3n - k + nr_2 + r_2$	$n(r_2 + 2)$	q
Modeling 5	$3n - k + nr_2 + r_2$	$n(r_2 + 2)$	2

Remark 10. Since r_2 can be chosen as at most $m = \mathcal{O}(\log_q(n))$, both the number of polynomials and variables are quasi-linear in the code-length n in all the three modelings, namely they are $\mathcal{O}(\log_2(n))$. At the cost of defining the system over $\mathbb{F}_{q^{r_1}} = \mathbb{F}_{q^m}$, these quantities become linear in n, as the choice $r_2 = 1$ is possible.

The modelings above capture exactly the corresponding syndrome decoding problem variants.

Theorem 3. *Given an instance* $(\mathbf{H}, \mathbf{s}, t)$,

1. *The vector* $(\mathbf{x}, \mathbf{y}, \mathbf{z})$ *is a solution of Modeling 3 if and only if* $\mathbf{x}$ *is a solution of Problem 1 and* $\mathbf{x} \in \mathbb{F}_q$*;*

2. *The vector* $(\mathbf{x}, \mathbf{y}, \mathbf{z})$ *is a solution of Modeling 4 if and only if* $\mathbf{x}$ *is a solution of Problem 2 and* $\mathbf{x} \in \mathbb{F}_q$*;*
3. *The vector* $(\mathbf{x}, \mathbf{y}, \mathbf{z})$ *is a solution of Modeling 5 if and only if* $\mathbf{x}$ *is a solution of Problem 1 and* $\mathbf{x} \in \overline{\mathbb{F}_q}$*, where* $\overline{\mathbb{F}_q}$ *denotes the algebraic closure of* $\mathbb{F}_q$*.*

Proof. Since the parity-check Eq. (2) belong to all three modelings, it remains to prove the conditions on the weight of $\mathbf{x}$ and to determine the base field over the vector can lie.

Proof of 1. Modeling 3 contains the field equations, therefore $\mathbf{x} \in \mathbb{F}_q^n$. It has already been proved that (11) implies $\mathsf{wt}(\mathbf{x}) \leq \mathsf{wt}(\mathbf{z})$. By Corollary 2, (15), (16) and (17) imply that $\mathsf{wt}(\mathbf{z}) = t$, hence $\mathsf{wt}(\mathbf{x}) \leq t$.

Proof of 2. Modeling 4 contains the field equations, therefore $\mathbf{x} \in \mathbb{F}_q^n$. It has already been proved that (12) implies $\mathsf{wt}(\mathbf{x}) = \mathsf{wt}(\mathbf{z})$. By Corollary 2, (15), (16) and (17) imply that $\mathsf{wt}(\mathbf{z}) = t$, hence $\mathsf{wt}(\mathbf{x}) = t$.

Proof of 3. The proof is analogous to the proof of *1.*, with the only exception that Modeling 5 does not contain the field equations. Hence, the solutions of the system are all the vectors defined over the algebraic closure $\overline{\mathbb{F}_q}$ that satisfy the parity-check equations and have weight at most t. □

6.3 The Dimension of the Variety Associated with Modeling 5

Unlike the modelings that include the field equations, Modeling 5 is not a priori associated with a zero-dimensional ideal. This represents the main drawback of Modeling 5 compared to Modeling 3. The zero-dimensional property is desirable because it is necessary for defining the degree of regularity and for applying the FGLM algorithm to convert the degrevlex Gröbner basis into a lex basis. While it is possible to convert non-zero dimensional ideals using methods such as Gröbner walk or others, the process may not be as straightforward [1,19].

In this subsection, we analyze the dimension of the variety associated with the ideal corresponding to Modeling 5. We will explore the conditions under which the variety is zero-dimensional, as well as the probability of this occurring. We begin with the following reduction.

Proposition 3. *Let* $\mathbf{x} \in \mathbb{F}_q^n$ *be a vector which is a solution of Problem 1 for a given instance* $(\mathbf{H}, \mathbf{s}, t)$*. In other words,* $\mathbf{x}$ *satisfies* $\mathbf{H}\mathbf{x}^\top = \mathbf{s}^\top$ *and* $\mathsf{wt}(\mathbf{x}) \leq t$*. Then, there exist finitely many* $(\mathbf{y}, \mathbf{z})$ *such that* $(\mathbf{x}, \mathbf{y}, \mathbf{z})$ *is a solution of Modeling 5.*

Proof. Let us first consider a vector $\mathbf{x}$ satisfying the parity-check equations and such that $\mathsf{wt}(\mathbf{x}) = t$. Then, in Modeling 5, the z_i must detect exactly the support of $\mathbf{x}$, and $\mathbf{x}$ uniquely determines a solution $(\mathbf{x}, \mathbf{y}, \mathbf{z})$ of the system. If instead $\mathsf{wt}(\mathbf{x}) = \bar{t} < t$, then there exist $t - \bar{t}$ indexes where the Z variables can have value 1 while $\mathbf{x}_i = 0$. Thus, for any solution $\bar{\mathbf{x}} \in \mathbb{F}_q^n$ of the parity check matrix of weight $\bar{t}$, there exist

$$\binom{n-\bar{t}}{t-\bar{t}}$$

different solutions $(\bar{\mathbf{x}}, \mathbf{y}, \mathbf{z})$.

A special case is given by the codeword finding problem, i.e. where the syndrome $\mathbf{s}$ is the zero vector. Here the null vector is a solution of Problem 1 and leads to $\binom{n}{t}$ solutions, thus likely increasing a lot the solving degree and the cost of a Gröbner basis computation. We can get rid of all these solutions by fixing one variable $z_i = 1$, thus forcing any solution to have weight at least 1 and removing the null vector. If the target solution has weight t, then the guess has success with probability t/n. We will discuss this strategy in more detail at the end of this subsection. □

Proposition 3 implies that each solution to the decoding problem (Problem 1) corresponds to a finite number of solutions for Modeling 5. This allows us to conduct an analysis that is independent of the specific modeling, as long as it accurately encodes the decoding problem in the sense of Theorem 3. Therefore, we will focus on the Krull dimension of the solution set of Problem 1 and provide a probability estimate for this dimension being zero.

First, in the following remark we briefly collect the definition of Krull dimension and some important properties we will use in the sequel. Expanded details and proofs can be found e.g. in [21, §4, Chap. 9] or other standard references in commutative algebra and algebraic geometry.

Remark 11 (Krull Dimension). Let $\mathbb{K}$ be an algebraically closed field (we will apply the following definitions and results to $\mathbb{K} = \overline{\mathbb{F}_q}$). An affine variety V is the zero locus in $\mathbb{K}^m$ of a proper ideal I of the polynomial ring $\mathbb{K}[x_1, \dots, x_m]$. We say that V is irreducible if it is not possible to write $V = V_1 \cup V_2$ where $V_1, V_2 \subsetneq V$ are two proper subvarieties. Irreducibility of V is equivalent to the corresponding ideal I being prime. The *Krull dimension* or simply the dimension of a variety V is defined as the maximal length d of the chains $V_0 \subsetneq V_1 \subsetneq \cdots \subsetneq V_d$, of distinct nonempty irreducible subvarieties of V. This is also equivalent to the supremum of the lengths of all chains of prime ideals containing the defining ideal I of V. For example, the Krull dimension of an affine linear space $\mathcal{L}$ generated by a linearly independent affine linear polynomials $L_1, \dots, L_a$ is precisely $m - a$, that is its dimension as an affine space. This can be seen by completing the polynomials to a maximal linearly independent system of m equations (in m variables) $L_1, \dots, L_a, L_{a+1}, \dots, L_m$ and then considering the following maximal chain of prime ideals

$$\mathcal{L} = \langle L_1, \dots L_a \rangle \subsetneq \langle L_1, \dots L_a, L_{a+1} \rangle \subsetneq \cdots \subsetneq \langle L_1, \dots L_m \rangle.$$

Notice that each ideal in this chain is prime, being generated by linearly independent polynomials of degree 1. Finally, we mention that, thanks to the Noetherian property of the polynomial ring, a variety V can be written uniquely as the union of irreducible varieties, which are called the irreducible components of V. Thus, the dimension of V coincides with the largest of the dimensions of its irreducible components (see [21, §4, Chapter 9, Corollary 9]).

Let $S \subseteq [n]$. Given a matrix $\mathbf{H}$ with n columns and a vector $\mathbf{x} \in \mathbb{F}_q^n$, we denote by $\mathbf{H}_S$ the submatrix of $\mathbf{H}$ of columns indexed by S and by $\mathbf{x}_S \in \mathbb{F}_q^{|S|}$

the vector obtained by deleting the coordinates corresponding to $[n] \setminus S$ from $\mathbf{x} \in \mathbb{F}_q^n$. On the contrary, let $\mathsf{pad}_S(\mathbf{x}) \in \mathbb{F}_q^n$ be the vector obtained from $\mathbf{x} \in \mathbb{F}_q^{|S|}$ by padding with 0's the positions corresponding to $[n] \setminus S$.

Proposition 4. *Let $\mathcal{C}$ be an $[n,k]$ code with parity-check matrix $\mathbf{H} \in \mathbb{F}_q^{(n-k)\times n}$. Then the set of solutions of Problem 1 with target weight t and syndrome $\mathbf{s}$ for the code $\mathcal{C}$ is the finite union of irreducible components, namely*

$$\bigcup_{S\subset[n],|S|=t} \{\mathsf{pad}_S(\mathbf{x}) \in \mathbb{F}_q^n \mid \mathbf{H}_S\mathbf{x} = \mathbf{s}\}.$$

Proof. For any S of cardinality t, $\mathsf{wt}(\mathsf{pad}_S(\mathbf{x})) = \mathsf{wt}(\mathbf{x}) \leq t$ and $\mathbf{H} \cdot \mathsf{pad}_S(\mathbf{x}) = \mathbf{H}_S\mathbf{x} = \mathbf{s}$. Thus, the set of solutions of the decoding problem contains

$$\bigcup_{S\subset[n],|S|=t} \{\mathsf{pad}_S(\mathbf{x}) \in \mathbb{F}_q^n \mid \mathbf{H}_S\mathbf{x} = \mathbf{s}\}.$$

On the other hand, for any solution $\mathbf{x} \in \mathbb{F}_q^n$ to the decoding problem, let S be a set of cardinality t containing the support of $\mathbf{x}$. Then, $\mathbf{x} \in \{\mathsf{pad}_S(\mathbf{x}) \in \mathbb{F}_q^n \mid \mathbf{H}_S\mathbf{x} = \mathbf{s}\}$. Finally, all the sets $\{\mathsf{pad}_S(\mathbf{x}) \in \mathbb{F}_q^n \mid \mathbf{H}_S\mathbf{x} = \mathbf{s}\}$ are irreducible being affine linear spaces. □

The next proposition characterizes the dimension of the irreducible components of the set of solutions of the decoding problem and the finite field extension over which solutions are defined.

Proposition 5. *The Krull dimension of the solution set of Problem 1 with target weight t and syndrome $\mathbf{s}$ for the linear code with parity-check matrix $\mathbf{H}$ is*

$$t - \min\{\mathsf{rk}(\mathbf{H}_S) \mid S \subseteq [n], |S| = t, \mathsf{rk}((\mathbf{H}_S \mid \mathbf{s})) = \mathsf{rk}(\mathbf{H}_S)\}. \tag{19}$$

Moreover, if the dimension is 0, then all solutions lie over $\mathbb{F}_q$.

Proof. Let us fix the support S of t possible error positions. By Remark 11, the Krull dimension of the irreducible components coincides with their dimensions as affine linear spaces. The case study of the set of solutions of

$$\mathbf{H}_S\mathbf{x} = \mathbf{s},$$

seen as a variety, thus becomes the following:

- if $\mathsf{rk}((\mathbf{H}_S \mid \mathbf{s})) > \mathsf{rk}(\mathbf{H}_S) \Rightarrow$ the variety is empty;
- if $\mathsf{rk}((\mathbf{H}_S \mid \mathbf{s})) = \mathsf{rk}(\mathbf{H}_S) \Rightarrow$ the variety has dimension $t - \mathsf{rk}(\mathbf{H}_S)$. In particular, if the variety has dimension 0, i.e. $\mathsf{rk}(\mathbf{H}_S) = t$, then it has a unique element, which belongs to $\mathbb{F}_q$.

By Remark 11, the dimension of the solutions set is obtained as the maximum dimension over all the irreducible components corresponding to some S for which $\mathsf{rk}((\mathbf{H}_S \mid \mathbf{s})) = \mathsf{rk}(\mathbf{H}_S)$:

$$\begin{aligned}&\max\{t - \mathsf{rk}(\mathbf{H}_S) \mid S \subseteq [n], |S| = t, \mathsf{rk}((\mathbf{H}_S \mid \mathbf{s})) = \mathsf{rk}(\mathbf{H}_S)\}\\ =&t - \min\{\mathsf{rk}(\mathbf{H}_S) \mid S \subseteq [n], |S| = t, \mathsf{rk}((\mathbf{H}_S \mid \mathbf{s})) = \mathsf{rk}(\mathbf{H}_S)\}.\end{aligned}$$

Let us now consider the case of a zero-dimensional variety. Then for any choice of S, there is at most a solution and it must belong to $\mathbb{F}_q^n$. Hence, all solutions belong to $\mathbb{F}_q^n$. □

Corollary 3. *The dimension of the variety associated with Modeling 5 is*

$$t - \min\{\mathsf{rk}(\mathbf{H}_S) \mid S \subseteq [n], |S| = t, \mathsf{rk}((\mathbf{H}_S \mid \mathbf{s})) = \mathsf{rk}(\mathbf{H}_S)\}. \quad (20)$$

Proof. It readily follows from Propositions 11 and 5 and the fact that each solution of Problem 1 corresponds to a finite number of solutions of Modeling 5, thus it does not increase the dimension of the variety. □

For relevant and not too-small parameters, we usually have $t \ll n-k$. Assuming the weight distribution of a linear code follows closely the Bernoulli one, we can estimate the probability that the ideal is zero-dimensional, and thus, by exploiting the proof of Proposition 5, that all the solutions $\mathbf{x}$ lie over $\mathbb{F}_q$.

Proposition 6. *Let $\mathcal{C}$ be an $\mathbb{F}_q$-linear code and let $W_i(\mathcal{C})$ the number of codewords of weight exactly i in $\mathcal{C}$. Then the probability that Modeling 5 provides a variety of strictly positive dimension when $t < n - k$ is upper bounded by*

$$\sum_{i=1}^{t} W_i(\mathcal{C}) \left(\frac{1}{q^{n-k-i+1}} + \binom{n-i}{t-i} \left(\frac{1}{q^{n-k-t+1}} - \frac{1}{q^{n-k-i+1}} \right) \right)$$

for a randomly sampled syndrome. For the codeword finding problem, the same probability is upper bounded by

$$\sum_{i=1}^{t} W_i(\mathcal{C}) \binom{n-i}{t-i}.$$

Proof. It follows from Corollary 3 that the variety has positive dimension if and only if there exists a set $S \subseteq [n]$, $|S| = t$, such that $\mathbf{H}_S$ is not full-rank and the syndrome $\mathbf{s}$ belongs to the column space of $\mathbf{H}_S$.

The parity-check matrix $\mathbf{H}$ has i linearly dependent columns indexed by the set S if and only if the corresponding code $\mathcal{C}$ has a codeword of weight $\leq i$ with support contained in S. Hence any codeword of positive weight $i \leq t$ with support S' identifies a set of $\binom{n-i}{t-i}$ supersets $S \supseteq S'$. On the other hand, each set S of t dependent columns is associated with *at least* one codeword of weight $\leq t$, hence iterating over such codewords is enough to guarantee an upper bound.

Let $W_i(\mathcal{C})$ be the number of codewords in $\mathcal{C}$ of weight exactly i. By splitting the event $\{\mathbf{s} \in \mathsf{ColSpace}(\mathbf{H}_S)\}$ into the union of the two disjoint events $\{\mathbf{s} \in \mathsf{ColSpace}(\mathbf{H}_{\mathsf{supp}(\mathbf{c})})\}$ and $\{\mathbf{s} \in \mathsf{ColSpace}(\mathbf{H}_S) \setminus \mathsf{ColSpace}(\mathbf{H}_{\mathsf{supp}(\mathbf{c})})\}$ and using that $\mathsf{rk}(\mathbf{H}_{\mathsf{supp}(\mathbf{c})}) \leq i-1$ and $\mathsf{rk}(\mathbf{H}_S) \leq \mathsf{rk}(\mathbf{H}_{\mathsf{supp}(\mathbf{c})}) + (t-i)$, we thus obtain an upper bound on the sought probability:

$$\mathbb{P}\left(\bigcup_{\substack{S \subseteq [n] \\ |S|=t \wedge \mathsf{rk}(\mathbf{H}_S)<t}} \{\mathbf{s} \in \mathsf{ColSpace}(\mathbf{H}_S)\} \right)$$

$$\leq \sum_{\substack{S\subseteq[n]\\|S|=t\wedge\mathsf{rk}(\mathbf{H}_S)<t}} \mathbb{P}(\{\mathbf{s}\in\mathsf{ColSpace}(\mathbf{H}_S)\})$$

$$\leq \sum_{\substack{\mathbf{c}\in\mathcal{C}\\\mathsf{wt}(\mathbf{c})\leq t}} \left(\mathbb{P}(\{\mathbf{s}\in\mathsf{ColSpace}(\mathbf{H}_{\mathsf{supp}(\mathbf{c})})\}) + \sum_{\substack{\mathsf{supp}(\mathbf{c})\subseteq S\subseteq[n]\\|S|=t}} \mathbb{P}(\{\mathbf{s}\in\mathsf{ColSpace}(\mathbf{H}_S)\setminus\mathsf{ColSpace}(\mathbf{H}_{\mathsf{supp}(\mathbf{c})})\})\right)$$

$$=\sum_{i=1}^{t} W_i(\mathcal{C}) \left(\frac{q^{\dim_{\mathbb{F}_q}\mathsf{ColSpace}(\mathbf{H}_{\mathsf{supp}(\mathbf{c})})}}{q^{n-k}} + \binom{n-i}{t-i}\frac{q^{\dim_{\mathbb{F}_q}\mathsf{ColSpace}(\mathbf{H}_S)}-q^{\dim_{\mathbb{F}_q}\mathsf{ColSpace}(\mathbf{H}_{\mathsf{supp}(\mathbf{c})})}}{q^{n-k}}\right)$$

$$=\sum_{i=1}^{t} W_i(\mathcal{C}) \left(\frac{q^{\mathsf{rk}(\mathbf{H}_{\mathsf{supp}(\mathbf{c})})}}{q^{n-k}} + \binom{n-i}{t-i}\frac{q^{\mathsf{rk}(\mathbf{H}_S)}-q^{\mathsf{rk}(\mathbf{H}_{\mathsf{supp}(\mathbf{c})})}}{q^{n-k}}\right)$$

$$\leq\sum_{i=1}^{t} W_i(\mathcal{C}) \left(\frac{q^{\mathsf{rk}(\mathbf{H}_{\mathsf{supp}(\mathbf{c})})}}{q^{n-k}} + \binom{n-i}{t-i}\frac{q^{\mathsf{rk}(\mathbf{H}_{\mathsf{supp}(\mathbf{c})})}}{q^{n-k}}(q^{t-i}-1)\right)$$

$$\leq\sum_{i=1}^{t} W_i(\mathcal{C}) \left(\frac{1}{q^{n-k-i+1}} + \binom{n-i}{t-i}\left(\frac{1}{q^{n-k-t+1}}-\frac{1}{q^{n-k-i+1}}\right)\right).$$

Finally, in the case of the codeword finding problem, i.e. if the syndrome is the zero vector, the condition on the positive dimension of the variety boils down to the existence of the set S, $|S|=t$, such that the rank $\mathbf{H}_S$ is defective, as the zero vector belongs to any linear subspace. Therefore, in this case, the calculations are simplified into:

$$\mathbb{P}\left(\bigcup_{\substack{S\subseteq[n]\\|S|=t\wedge\mathsf{rk}(\mathbf{H}_S)<t}} \{0\in\mathsf{ColSpace}(\mathbf{H}_S)\}\right) \leq \sum_{\substack{S\subseteq[n]\\|S|=t\wedge\mathsf{rk}(\mathbf{H}_S)<t}} 1 \leq \sum_{i=1}^{t} W_i(\mathcal{C})\binom{n-i}{t-i}.$$

□

Remark 12. For random codes, the weight distribution follows closely the Bernoulli one, i.e. $W_i(\mathcal{C}) \approx \frac{\binom{n}{i}(q-1)^i}{q^{n-k}}$. Under this assumption, the probability of having a zero-dimensional ideal for the decoding modeling with a random syndrome can be estimated as

$$\frac{1}{q^{n-k}}\sum_{i=1}^{t}\binom{n}{i}(q-1)^i\left(\frac{1}{q^{n-k-i+1}}+\binom{n-i}{t-i}\left(\frac{1}{q^{n-k-t+1}}-\frac{1}{q^{n-k-i+1}}\right)\right),$$

while for the codeword finding problem as

$$\frac{1}{q^{n-k}}\sum_{i=1}^{t}\binom{n}{i}\binom{n-i}{t-i}(q-1)^i.$$

We remark in particular that the bound is independent from the choice of (r_1, r_2). Different admissible pairs provide of course different solutions, but the projections of the varieties with respect to the x_i's variables are the same over the field closure, which is what determines the dimension of the associated ideals.

Table 5. This table gives information from experiments using random $\mathbb{F}_q$-linear codes using Modeling 5. The values in the d_{M} column represent the highest step degree achieved when directly computing the Gröbner basis of the system in MAGMA. The column "#lin" denotes the number of linear equations, i.e. of parity-check equations, which is independent from the field size. The columns "#quad" and "#vars" stand for the number of quadratic equations and the number of variables, which depend on the value r_2 instead. The integer r_1 is the extension field degree over which the equations are defined. We recall that the value m leads to different possible choices of (r_1, r_2) and we give all minima with respect to the standard partial order on pairs.

				$q = 7$					$q = 16, 17$					$q = 127$				
n	k	t	#lin	r_1	r_2	#quad	#vars	d_{M}	r_1	r_2	#quad	#vars	d_{M}	r_1	r_2	#quad	#vars	d_{M}
10	5	2	5	$m = 2$					$m = 1$					$m = 1$				
				2	1	30	30	4	1	1	30	30	4	1	1	30	30	4
				1	2	40	40	3										
15	9	3	6	$m = 2$					$m = 1$					$m = 1$				
				2	1	45	45	4	1	1	45	45	4	1	1	45	45	4
				1	2	60	60	4										
19	10	5	9	$m = 2$					$m = 1$					$m = 1$				
				2	1	57	57	5	1	1	57	57	5	1	1	57	57	5
				1	2	76	76	4										
22	14	4	8	$m = 2$					$m = 2$					$m = 1$				
				2	1	66	66	5	2	1	66	66	5	1	1	66	66	4
				1	2	88	88	4	1	2	88	88	4					
30	20	4	10	$m = 3$					$m = 2$					$m = 1$				
				3	1	90	90	≥ 6	2	1	90	90	≥ 6	1	1	90	90	≥ 6
				2	2	120	120	4	1	2	120	120	5					
				1	3	150	150	4										

In Appendix A, Tables 6 and 7, we provide examples of such bounds for concrete parameters. In the case of syndrome decoding, these probabilities are very small even at Gilbert-Varshamov distance and the issue of having ideals of positive dimension is thus absolutely negligible for the purpose of cryptanalysis. On the opposite, the bound on the probability of the same event for the codeword finding problem becomes completely useless when approaching the Gilbert-Varshamov distance. Indeed, the trivial upper bound "$\mathbb{P} \leq 1$" entries from the two tables mean that the bound given by Proposition 6 gives a number larger than 1. A possible workaround for the described issue with the codeword finding version is to make use of hybrid methods. Indeed, it is enough to guess a number of nonzero positions equal or greater than the ideal dimension to decrease the latter to 0 with high probability. Recalling that the solution space is projective and one the value of one nonzero entry can be chosen arbitrarily, specializing l

coordinates has a success probability of $\frac{\binom{n-l}{t-l}}{\binom{n}{t}(q-1)^{l-1}}$. In cryptanalysis, however, it is usually assumed to know the minimal weight of a (nonzero) solution. This is because, if there exists a solution of weight smaller than the target, then the challenge is actually easier.

A simple strategy to obtain a zero-dimensional ideal in this setting is thus the following. If we suppose to know a lower bound d' the minimum distance $d(C)$ of the code, then it means that any $d' - 1$ columns of the parity-check matrix $\mathbf{H}$ are linearly independent. Therefore, Eq. (19) implies that the dimension of the ideal for the bounded weight modeling with target weight d' is exactly 1 and thus it is enough to specialize one variable x_i to any element in $\mathbb{F}_q$ to obtain a zero-dimensional ideal.

6.4 Experimental Results

We solved the quadratic system associated with Modeling 5 for several random codes. We show in Table 5 that, similarly to the case over $\mathbb{F}_2$, the solving degree is surprisingly small. MAGMA code used for our experiments with Modeling 5 can be found at this link.

7 Conclusion and Future Directions

We have presented a new algebraic cryptanalysis for both the bounded and the exact versions of the Syndrome Decoding problem.

In the binary case, our modelings significantly improved the previous attempt of [34], by capturing the weight condition on the solution vector with quadratic polynomials. We have also experimentally shown that the behavior of the associated Gröbner basis is very different from that of a random system with the same number of variables and equations, *leading to a much better complexity*. We have thus taken an important step towards making algebraic algorithms potentially competitive for the decoding problem.

We introduced algebraic modelings for the first time in the case of the general syndrome decoding problem over larger finite fields. Notably, one of them is quadratic with a number of variables and equations that is linear or quasi-linear in the code length, *independently from the field size*. We have analyzed that, despite the constant degree of the equations involved, the system correctly solves the decoding problem and with high probability does not have spurious solutions for all parameters that are relevant to the problem.

An open question to this work is to understand more clearly the behavior of the Gröbner basis computation both in the binary and in the general finite field cases and to get a theoretical estimate of the complexity that better matches with the one obtained from the experiments. This is a difficult task, as it is often the case for very structured algebraic systems, and probably requires to develop dedicated tools to analyze such behavior.

Another interesting and natural follow-up to this work can be to analyze the impact of hybrid strategies on solving the proposed systems. Since the weight of the solution sought is relatively low, a convenient choice is to set most of the variables of X to 0. It is not difficult to see that this approach is reminiscent of the guess part in Prange or later ISD algorithms.

In the case of binary systems, we have verified experimentally that the best hybrid trade-off actually boils down to the Prange algorithm, the best complexity being indeed obtained when enough zeros to linearize the system are guessed.

However, the system hides a lot of structure and offers many different ways to specialize variables. For example, the auxiliary variables from the vector $\mathbf{y}$ can also be fixed and they too have different probabilities of taking a value equal to 0 or 1. It is therefore not at all unrealistic to speculate that an ad-hoc and smart hybridization technique may lead to a better trade-off than a fully combinatorial approach.

Acknowledgments. We would like to thank the reviewers for their detailed and valuable feedback. Additionally, special thanks to Magali Bardet, Tanja Lange and Alberto Ravagnani for the fruitful discussions and insights.

This publication was created with the co-financing of the European Union FSE-REACT-EU, PON Research and Innovation 2014–2020 DM1062/2021. A. Caminata is supported by the PRIN 2020 grant 2020355B8Y "Squarefree Gröbner degenerations, special varieties and related topics", by the PRIN PNRR 2022 grant P2022J4HRR "Mathematical Primitives for Post Quantum Digital Signatures", by the MUR Excellence Department Project awarded to Dipartimento di Matematica, Università di Genova, CUP D33C23001110001, and by the European Union within the program NextGenerationEU. A. Meneghetti acknowledges support from Ripple's University Blockchain Research Initiative. A. Caminata and A. Meneghetti are members of the INdAM Research Group GNSAGA.

A Section 6.3 Bounds on the Zero-Dimensionality

Table 6. Bound on the probability $\mathbb{P}$ that the ideal associated with the system has a strictly positive dimension for the decoding problem with a randomly sampled syndrome.

$[n,k]_q$	$t = \lfloor (d_{GV}-1)/2 \rfloor$	$t = \lfloor (n-k)/2 \rfloor$	$t = d_{GV}$	$t = d_{GV}+1$
$[100,50]_2$	$t=5$, $\mathbb{P} \leq 2.32 \cdot 10^{-20}$	$t=25$, $\mathbb{P} \leq 1$	$t=12$, $\mathbb{P} \leq 6.73 \cdot 10^{-9}$	$t=13$, $\mathbb{P} \leq 1.84 \cdot 10^{-7}$
$[100,50]_7$	$t=12$, $\mathbb{P} \leq 8.44 \cdot 10^{-51}$	$t=25$, $\mathbb{P} \leq 1.89 \cdot 10^{-20}$	$t=25$, $\mathbb{P} \leq 1.89 \cdot 10^{-20}$	$t=26$, $\mathbb{P} \leq 2.68 \cdot 10^{-18}$
$[100,50]_{127}$	$t=18$, $\mathbb{P} \leq 5.48 \cdot 10^{-118}$	$t=25$, $\mathbb{P} \leq 1.23 \cdot 10^{-84}$	$t=37$, $\mathbb{P} \leq 5.38 \cdot 10^{-30}$	$t=38$, $\mathbb{P} \leq 1.44 \cdot 10^{-25}$
$[100,80]_2$	$t=1$, $\mathbb{P} \leq 9.09 \cdot 10^{-11}$	$t=10$, $\mathbb{P} \leq 1$	$t=4$, $\mathbb{P} \leq 3.14 \cdot 10^{-4}$	$t=5$, $\mathbb{P} \leq 0.0268$
$[100,80]_7$	$t=3$, $\mathbb{P} \leq 4.06 \cdot 10^{-25}$	$t=10$, $\mathbb{P} \leq 2.92 \cdot 10^{-5}$	$t=8$, $\mathbb{P} \leq 1.30 \cdot 10^{-10}$	$t=9$, $\mathbb{P} \leq 6.55 \cdot 10^{-8}$
$[100,80]_{127}$	$t=6$, $\mathbb{P} \leq 1.16 \cdot 10^{-52}$	$t=10$, $\mathbb{P} \leq 1.14 \cdot 10^{-31}$	$t=13$, $\mathbb{P} \leq 1.97 \cdot 10^{-16}$	$t=14$, $\mathbb{P} \leq 1.97 \cdot 10^{-11}$

Table 7. Bound on the probability $\mathbb{P}$ that the ideal associated with the system has strictly positive dimension for the codeword finding problem (i.e. with null syndrome).

$[n,k]_q$	$t = \lfloor (d_{GV}-1)/2 \rfloor$	$t = \lfloor (n-k)/2 \rfloor$	$t = d_{GV}-2$	$t = d_{GV}-1$	$t = d_{GV}$
$[100,50]_2$	$t=5$, $\mathbb{P} \le 2.07 \cdot 10^{-6}$	$t=25$, $\mathbb{P} \le 1$	$t=10$, $\mathbb{P} \le 1$	$t=11$, $\mathbb{P} \le 1$	$t=12$, $\mathbb{P} \le 1$
$[100,50]_7$	$t=12$, $\mathbb{P} \le 8.08 \cdot 10^{-18}$	$t=25$, $\mathbb{P} \le 1$	$t=23$, $\mathbb{P} \le 0.378$	$t=24$, $\mathbb{P} \le 1$	$t=25$, $\mathbb{P} \le 1$
$[100,50]_{127}$	$t=18$, $\mathbb{P} \le 1.46 \cdot 10^{-48}$	$t=25$, $\mathbb{P} \le 6.16 \cdot 10^{-30}$	$t=35$, $\mathbb{P} \le 3.04 \cdot 10^{-5}$	$t=36$, $\mathbb{P} \le 0.00696$	$t=37$, $\mathbb{P} \le 1$
$[100,80]_2$	$t=1$, $\mathbb{P} \le 9.54 \cdot 10^{-5}$	$t=10$, $\mathbb{P} \le 1$	$t=2$, $\mathbb{P} \le 0.0142$	$t=3$, $\mathbb{P} \le 1$	$t=4$, $\mathbb{P} \le 1$
$[100,80]_7$	$t=3$, $\mathbb{P} \le 6.93 \cdot 10^{-10}$	$t=10$, $\mathbb{P} \le 1$	$t=6$, $\mathbb{P} \le 0.00176$	$t=7$, $\mathbb{P} \le 0.165$	$t=8$, $\mathbb{P} \le 1$
$[100,80]_{127}$	$t=6$, $\mathbb{P} \le 4.20 \cdot 10^{-21}$	$t=10$, $\mathbb{P} \le 1.59 \cdot 10^{-8}$	$t=11$, $\mathbb{P} \le 1.65 \cdot 10^{-5}$	$t=12$, $\mathbb{P} \le 0.0155$	$t=13$, $\mathbb{P} \le 1$

References

1. Amrhein, B., Gloor, O., Küchlin, W.: On the walk. Theor. Comput. Sci. **187**(1), 179–202 (1997)
2. Aragon, N., et al.: BIKE: bit flipping key encapsulation (2022)
3. Bardet, M.: Étude des systèmes algébriques surdéterminés. Applications aux codes correcteurs et à la cryptographie. Ph.D. thesis, Université Pierre et Marie Curie-Paris VI (2004)
4. Bardet, M., et al.: An algebraic attack on rank metric code-based cryptosystems. In: Canteaut, A., Ishai, Y. (eds.) EUROCRYPT 2020. LNCS, vol. 12107, pp. 64–93. Springer, Cham (2020). https://doi.org/10.1007/978-3-030-45727-3_3
5. Bardet, M., et al.: Improvements of algebraic attacks for solving the rank decoding and minrank problems. In: Moriai, S., Wang, H. (eds.) ASIACRYPT 2020. LNCS, vol. 12491, pp. 507–536. Springer, Cham (2020). https://doi.org/10.1007/978-3-030-64837-4_17
6. Bardet, M., Faugere, J.C., Salvy, B.: On the complexity of Gröbner basis computation of semi-regular overdetermined algebraic equations. In: Proceedings of the International Conference on Polynomial System Solving, pp. 71–74 (2004)
7. Becker, A., Joux, A., May, A., Meurer, A.: Decoding random binary linear codes in $2^{n/20}$: how 1+1=0 improves information set decoding. In: Pointcheval, D., Johansson, T. (eds.) EUROCRYPT 2012. LNCS, vol. 7237, pp. 520–536. Springer, Heidelberg (2012). https://doi.org/10.1007/978-3-642-29011-4_31

8. Berlekamp, E., McEliece, R., Van Tilborg, H.: On the inherent intractability of certain coding problems (corresp.). IEEE Trans. Info. Theory **24**(3), 384–386 (1978)
9. Bernstein, D.J., et al.: Classic McEliece: conservative code-based cryptography. ffhal-04288769 (2017)
10. Bernstein, D.J., Lange, T., Peters, C.: Smaller decoding exponents: ball-collision decoding. In: Rogaway, P. (ed.) CRYPTO 2011. LNCS, vol. 6841, pp. 743–760. Springer, Heidelberg (2011). https://doi.org/10.1007/978-3-642-22792-9_42
11. Bigdeli, M., De Negri, E., Dizdarevic, M.M., Gorla, E., Minko, R., Tsakou, S.: Semi-regular sequences and other random systems of equations. Assoc. Women Math. Ser. **24**, 75–114 (2021)
12. Both, L., May, A.: Decoding linear codes with high error rate and its impact for LPN security. In: Lange, T., Steinwandt, R. (eds.) PQCrypto 2018. LNCS, vol. 10786, pp. 25–46. Springer, Cham (2018). https://doi.org/10.1007/978-3-319-79063-3_2
13. Briaud, P., Øygarden, M.: A new algebraic approach to the regular syndrome decoding problem and implications for PCG constructions. In: EUROCRYPT (5). Lecture Notes in Computer Science, vol. 14008, pp. 391–422. Springer, Heidelberg (2023). https://doi.org/10.1007/978-3-031-30589-4_14
14. Buchberger, B.: Bruno Buchberger's PhD thesis 1965: an algorithm for finding the basis elements of the residue class ring of a zero dimensional polynomial ideal. J. Symb. Comput. **41**(3-4), 475–511 (2006)
15. Caminata, A., Gorla, E.: Solving multivariate polynomial systems and an invariant from commutative algebra. In: Bajard, J.C., Topuzoğlu, A. (eds.) WAIFI 2020. LNCS, vol. 12542, pp. 3–36. Springer, Cham (2021). https://doi.org/10.1007/978-3-030-68869-1_1
16. Caminata, A., Gorla, E.: Solving degree, last fall degree, and related invariants. J. Symb. Comput. **114**, 322–335 (2023)
17. Carrier, K., Debris-Alazard, T., Meyer-Hilfiger, C., Tillich, J.P.: Statistical decoding 2.0: reducing decoding to LPN. In: International Conference on the Theory and Application of Cryptology and Information Security, pp. 477–507. Springer, Heidelberg (2022). https://doi.org/10.1007/978-3-031-22972-5_17
18. Carrier, K., Debris-Alazard, T., Meyer-Hilfiger, C., Tillich, J.P.: Reduction from sparse LPN to LPN, dual attack 3.0. In: Annual International Conference on the Theory and Applications of Cryptographic Techniques, pp. 286–315. Springer, Heidelberg (2024). https://doi.org/10.1007/978-3-031-58754-2_11
19. Collart, S., Kalkbrener, M., Mall, D.: Converting bases with the Gröbner walk. J. Symb. Comput. **24**(3), 465–469 (1997)
20. Courtois, N., Klimov, A., Patarin, J., Shamir, A.: Efficient algorithms for solving overdefined systems of multivariate polynomial equations. In: Preneel, B. (ed.) EUROCRYPT 2000. LNCS, vol. 1807, pp. 392–407. Springer, Heidelberg (2000). https://doi.org/10.1007/3-540-45539-6_27
21. Cox, D., Little, J., O'shea, D., Sweedler, M.: Ideals, Varieties, and Algorithms, vol. 3. Springer, Heidelberg (1997)

22. Ding, J., Schmidt, D.: Solving degree and degree of regularity for polynomial systems over a finite fields. In: Fischlin, M., Katzenbeisser, S. (eds.) Number Theory and Cryptography. LNCS, vol. 8260, pp. 34–49. Springer, Heidelberg (2013). https://doi.org/10.1007/978-3-642-42001-6_4
23. Dumer, I.: Two decoding algorithms for linear codes. Problemy Peredachi Informatsii **25**(1), 17–23 (1989)
24. Esser, A., Bellini, E.: Syndrome decoding estimator. In: Hanaoka, G., Shikata, J., Watanabe, Y. (eds.) PKC 2022: 25th International Conference on Theory and Practice of Public Key Cryptography, Part I. Lecture Notes in Computer Science, vol. 13177, pp. 112–141. Springer, Cham (2022). https://doi.org/10.1007/978-3-030-97121-2_5
25. Faugère, J.C., Gianni, P., Lazard, D., Mora, T.: Efficient computation of zero-dimensional Gröbner bases by change of ordering. J. Symb. Comput. **16**(4), 329–344 (1993)
26. Faugère, J.C.: A new efficient algorithm for computing Gröbner bases (F_4). J. Pure Appl. Algebra **139**, 61–88 (1999)
27. Faugère, J.C.: A new efficient algorithm for computing Gröbner bases without reduction to zero (F5), pp. 75–83 (2002)
28. Finiasz, M., Sendrier, N.: Security bounds for the design of code-based cryptosystems. In: Matsui, M. (ed.) ASIACRYPT 2009. LNCS, vol. 5912, pp. 88–105. Springer, Heidelberg (2009). https://doi.org/10.1007/978-3-642-10366-7_6
29. Lidl, R., Niederreiter, H.: Introduction to Finite Fields and their Applications, 2nd edn. Cambridge University Press, Cambridge (1994)
30. May, A., Meurer, A., Thomae, E.: Decoding random linear codes in $O(2^{0.054n})$. In: Lee, D.H., Wang, X. (eds.) 2011, vol. 7073, pp. 107–124. Springer, Heidelberg (2011)
31. May, A., Ozerov, I.: On computing nearest neighbors with applications to decoding of binary linear codes. In: Oswald, E., Fischlin, M. (eds.) EUROCRYPT 2015. LNCS, vol. 9056, pp. 203–228. Springer, Heidelberg (2015). https://doi.org/10.1007/978-3-662-46800-5_9
32. McEliece, R.J.: A public-key cryptosystem based on algebraic coding theory. Coding Thv **4244**, 114–116 (1978)
33. Melchor, C.A., et al.: Hamming quasi-cyclic (HQC). NIST PQC Round **2**(4), 13 (2018)
34. Meneghetti, A., Pellegrini, A., Sala, M.: On the equivalence of two post-quantum cryptographic families. Annali di Matematica Pura ed Applicata (1923 -) **202**, 967–991 (2023)
35. Prange, E.: The use of information sets in decoding cyclic codes. IRE Trans. Inf. Theory **8**(5), 5–9 (1962)
36. Salizzoni, F.: An upper bound for the solving degree in terms of the degree of regularity. arXiv:2304.13485 (2023)

37. Semaev, I., Tenti, A.: Probabilistic analysis on Macaulay matrices over finite fields and complexity of constructing Gröbner bases. J. Algebra **565**, 651–674 (2021)
38. Stern, J.: A method for finding codewords of small weight. In: Cohen, G., Wolfmann, J. (eds.) Coding Theory 1988. LNCS, vol. 388, pp. 106–113. Springer, Heidelberg (1989). https://doi.org/10.1007/BFb0019850

An Improved Algorithm for Code Equivalence

Julian Nowakowski(✉)

Ruhr University Bochum, Bochum, Germany
julian.nowakowski@rub.de

Abstract. We study the linear code equivalence problem (LEP) for linear $[n,k]$-codes over finite fields $\mathbb{F}_q$. Recently, Chou, Persichetti and Santini gave an elegant algorithm that solves LEP over *large* finite fields (with $q = \Omega(n)$) in time $2^{\frac{1}{2}\,\mathrm{H}(\frac{k}{n})n}$, where $\mathrm{H}(\cdot)$ denotes the binary entropy function. However, for *small* finite fields, their algorithm can be significantly slower. In particular, for fields of constant size $q = \mathcal{O}(1)$, its runtime increases by an exponential factor in n.

We present an improved version of their algorithm, which achieves the desired runtime of $2^{\frac{1}{2}\,\mathrm{H}(\frac{k}{n})n}$ for *all* finite fields of size $q \geq 7$. For a wide range of parameters, this improves over the runtime of all previously known algorithms by an exponential factor.

Keywords: Linear Code Equivalence Problem · Canonical Form Functions · Cryptanalysis

1 Introduction

Digital signatures schemes based on *equivalence problems* have recently emerged as promising candidates for post-quantum security. Examples of such schemes include LESS [BMPS20], HAWK [DPPv22] and MEDS [CNP+23], which are based on the *linear code equivalence problem*, the *lattice isomorphism problem*, and the *matrix code equivalence problem*, respectively. In this work, we focus on the linear code equivalence problem (LEP).

LEP is an important problem in coding theory. With the recent introduction of LESS, LEP has gained significant interest in cryptography [Beu20, BBN+22, PS23, BBPS23, CPS23]. In a nutshell, the problem is defined as follows: Given generator matrices $\mathbf{G}_1, \mathbf{G}_2 \in \mathbb{F}_q^{k \times n}$ of two linear $[n,k]$-codes $\mathcal{C}_1, \mathcal{C}_2 \subseteq \mathbb{F}_q^n$, one is asked to compute a linear, Hamming weight preserving map $\mathbf{Q}$ that bijectively maps $\mathcal{C}_1$ to $\mathcal{C}_2$ (provided such a map exists). Such maps $\mathbf{Q}$ are precisely those linear maps, that permute the coordinates of the codewords $\mathbf{c} \in \mathcal{C}_1$, and additionally multiply them by units from the underlying field $\mathbb{F}_q$. These maps are called *monomials*.

R. Niederhagen and M.-J. O. Saarinen (Eds.): PQCrypto 2025, LNCS 15577, pp. 71–103, 2025.
https://doi.org/10.1007/978-3-031-86599-2_3

1.1 Previous Work

Support Splitting. The *permutation equivalence problem* (PEP) is a variant of LEP, in which one is asked to find a permutation, mapping $\mathcal{C}_1$ to $\mathcal{C}_2$ (again, provided it exists). Curiously, PEP is easy on average, but seems to be hard in the worst case. Indeed, Sendrier's famous *support splitting algorithm* (SSA) [Sen00] solves random PEP instances with high probability in polynomial time. However, there are worst-case instances (in which $\mathcal{C}_1$ and $\mathcal{C}_2$ are *weakly self-dual codes*), for which SSA requires exponential time.

Since there is a reduction from LEP to PEP [SS13], one can try solving LEP by first reducing it to PEP and then using SSA. For fields of size $q \leq 4$ this approach works just fine. Hence, random LEP instances over $\mathbb{F}_2$ $\mathbb{F}_3$ and $\mathbb{F}_4$ are easy. However, for fields of size $q \geq 5$, the reduction results in weakly self-dual codes, and thus in an exponential runtime for SSA. It is conjectured that this state-of-the-art of SSA cannot be improved, and that random LEP instances over fields of size $q \geq 5$ are hard.

Finding Low-Weight Codewords. An alternative approach for solving LEP is based on computing low-weight codewords. It was first suggested by Leon [Leo82], and is based on the following simple observation: Let us fix some parameter w, and let $L_1(w) \subset \mathcal{C}_1$ and $L_2(w) \subset \mathcal{C}_2$ denote the sets of all codewords in $\mathcal{C}_1$ and $\mathcal{C}_2$ of weight at most w. Since monomials preserve Hamming weight, any monomial that maps $\mathcal{C}_1$ to $\mathcal{C}_2$ has to map $L_1(w)$ to $L_2(w)$. Conversely, if w is only slightly larger than the weight of a minimal-weight codeword in $\mathcal{C}_1$, then any monomial that maps $L_1(w)$ to $L_2(w)$ will – with decent probability – map $\mathcal{C}_1$ to $\mathcal{C}_2$. To solve LEP, Leon thus suggests the following simple two step approach: First compute the sets $L_1(w)$ and $L_2(w)$. Then compute a monomial $\mathbf{Q}$, mapping $L_1(w)$ to $L_2(w)$. Computing $L_1(w)$ and $L_2(w)$ takes time exponential in n, computing $\mathbf{Q}$ can be done in time polynomial in $|L_1(w)| = |L_2(w)|$.

Recently, first Beullens [Beu20], and afterwards Barenghi, Biasse, Persichetti and Santini (BBPS) [BBPS23] have introduced significantly improved variants of Leon's algorithm, following a similar two-step, low-weight codeword finding based approach. In many parameter regimes, Beullens and BBPS improve over Leon's runtime by an exponential factor. As a result, up until very recently, BBPS was in most parameter regimes the fastest algorithm for solving LEP.

Canonical Form Functions. A very recent work by Chou, Persichetti and Santini (CPS) [CPS23] introduced a completely different approach for solving LEP, based on *canonical form functions*. In their work, CPS define a novel equivalence relation for linear codes, which we denote by $\overset{\mathsf{LRL}}{\sim}$. Suppose we have two linear codes $\mathcal{C}_1$ and $\mathcal{C}_2$ with generator matrices $\mathbf{G}_1 = [\mathbf{I}_k \mid \mathbf{A}_1]$, $\mathbf{G}_2 = [\mathbf{I}_k \mid \mathbf{A}_2] \in \mathbb{F}_q^{k \times n}$, where $\mathbf{I}_k$ denotes the k-dimensional identity matrix. We call $\mathcal{C}_1$ and $\mathcal{C}_2$ equivalent with respect to $\overset{\mathsf{LRL}}{\sim}$, if there exist monomials $\mathbf{Q}_r$, $\mathbf{Q}_c$ such that $\mathbf{A}_2 = \mathbf{Q}_r \cdot \mathbf{A}_1 \cdot \mathbf{Q}_c$.[1]

[1] Here, we identify the monomials with their corresponding transformation matrices.

In a nutshell, a canonical form function for $\overset{\mathsf{LRL}}{\sim}$ is an efficient algorithm that takes a generator matrix $\mathbf{G} = [\mathbf{I}_k \mid \mathbf{A}]$ of some code $\mathcal{C}$ as input, and outputs a generator matrix $\mathbf{G}^* = [\mathbf{I}_k \mid \mathbf{A}^*]$ of a *canonical representative* $\mathcal{C}^*$ of the equivalence class of $\mathcal{C}$ (with respect to $\overset{\mathsf{LRL}}{\sim}$). Importantly, CPS allow canonical form functions to *fail*. That is, instead of *always* outputting a canonical representative, a canonical form function may (with some failure probability) also output an error symbol $\perp$.

Initially, CPS introduced canonical form functions to improve signature size in the LESS signature scheme: Suppose we have a canonical form function CF for $\overset{\mathsf{LRL}}{\sim}$ with *success probability* γ. That is, γ denotes the probability that, on input $\mathbf{G} = [\mathbf{I}_k \mid \mathbf{A}] \in \mathbb{F}_q^{k \times n}$ with uniformly random $\mathbf{A} \in \mathbb{F}_q^{k \times (n-k)}$, CF does not output $\perp$. CPS showed that, at the expense of increasing signing time in LESS by a factor roughly γ^{-1}, the canonical form function CF can be used to obtain signatures of essentially optimal size.

However, CPS not only showed that canonical form functions can be used *constructively* to improve the LESS signature scheme, but also *destructively* to attack the underlying linear code equivalence problem: CPS give a transformation, that turns any canonical form function CF into an LEP algorithm with runtime $\gamma^{-1/2} \cdot 2^{\frac{1}{2}\mathrm{H}(\frac{k}{n})n}$, where $\mathrm{H}(\cdot)$ denotes the binary entropy function. In particular, for canonical form functions with (at least) constant success probability $\gamma = \Omega(1)$, the CPS transformation yields a LEP algorithm with runtime $2^{\frac{1}{2}\mathrm{H}(\frac{k}{n})n}$.

As Fig. 1 shows, if such a canonical form function with (at least) constant success probability exists, then the resulting LEP algorithm would – for sufficiently large q – improve over the previously best algorithms by an exponential factor.[2]

Unfortunately, finding canonical form functions with (at least) constant success probability is challenging: CPS give a canonical form function that achieves constant success probability only for large $q = \Omega(n)$. However, for constant $q = \mathcal{O}(1)$, its success probability γ is exponentially small in n: For all inputs $\mathbf{G} = [\mathbf{I}_k \mid \mathbf{A}] \in \mathbb{F}_q^{k \times n}$, in which every row of $\mathbf{A} \in \mathbb{F}_q^{k \times (n-k)}$ contains at least one zero entry, the canonical form function of CPS fails. Hence, its success probability is at most

$$\gamma \leq \min\left\{k \cdot \left(1 - \frac{1}{q}\right)^{n-k}, 1\right\} =: p_{\mathsf{CPS}}.$$

For constant $q = \mathcal{O}(1)$, this is exponentially small in n.

As a consequence, the runtime of the resulting LEP algorithm is

$$\gamma^{-1/2} \cdot 2^{\frac{1}{2}\mathrm{H}(\frac{k}{n})n} \geq 2^{\frac{1}{2}\mathrm{H}(\frac{k}{n})n - \frac{1}{2}\log_2(p_{\mathsf{CPS}})}.$$

As Fig. 2 illustrates, for constant $q = \mathcal{O}(1)$, this is exponentially higher than $2^{\frac{1}{2}\mathrm{H}(\frac{k}{n})n}$. (Of course, for large q, this only becomes visible when also n is large.)

[2] We computed the runtime $T_{\mathsf{lowWeight}}$ in Fig. 1 using the estimator from https://github.com/paolo-santini/LESS_project/blob/main/attacks/LEP/cost.sage.

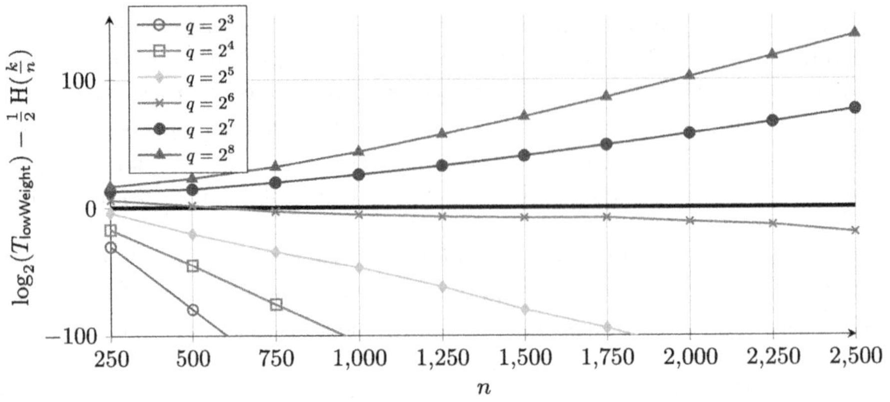

Fig. 1. Comparison between runtime $T_{\text{lowWeight}}$ of low-weight codeword finding based algorithms and the canonical form function based algorithm – assuming the underlying canonical form function has (at least) constant success probability. Results are for codes of rate $\frac{k}{n} = \frac{1}{2}$ over various finite fields $\mathbb{F}_q$.

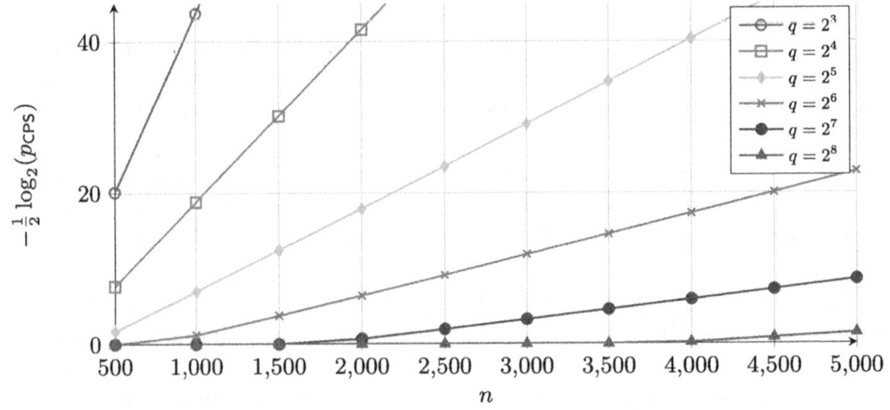

Fig. 2. Lower bound $2^{\frac{1}{2}\,\mathrm{H}(\frac{k}{n})n - \frac{1}{2}\log_2(p_{\text{CPS}})}$ for the runtime of CPS' LEP algorithm compared to $2^{\frac{1}{2}\,\mathrm{H}(\frac{k}{n})n}$. Results are for codes of rate $\frac{k}{n} = \frac{1}{2}$ over various finite fields $\mathbb{F}_q$.

1.2 Our Contributions

New Canonical Form Function, Improved LEP Algorithm. We introduce a novel canonical form function that – for all finite fields of size $q \geq 7$ and codes of constant rate[3] – has success probability $1 - \mathcal{O}(n^{-1})$. Together with the seminal results of CPS, this immediately results in a $2^{\frac{1}{2}\,\mathrm{H}(\frac{k}{n})n}$-time algorithm

[3] An $[n, k]$-code $\mathcal{C}$ has constant rate, if the *code dimension* k grows as $k = R \cdot n$, where n is the *code length* and R is a constant with $0 < R < 1$. In other words, $\mathcal{C}$ has constant rate if $\frac{k}{n} \neq o(1)$, and $\frac{k}{n} \neq 1 - o(1)$. This is the most important setting in practice.

for LEP. As shown in Figs. 1 and 2, we thus improve over the previously fastest known LEP algorithms by an exponential factor.

On the technical side, our novel canonical form function re-uses many of ideas of the original canonical form function by CPS. However, we enhance their ideas via novel techniques, which allow us to circumvent the failure conditions of CPS' algorithm. Thereby, we significantly increase its success probability to $1 - \mathcal{O}(n^{-1})$.

Impact for LESS. The suggested LESS parameters use $q = \Omega(n)$. Hence, for these parameters, the original canonical form function by CPS already has constant success probability. Thus, for the LESS parameters, our novel algorithm does not improve substantially over the LEP algorithm introduced by CPS in [CPS23]. In particular, our novel results do not invalidate the security analysis of LESS.

On a more constructive note, our novel canonical form function might nevertheless impact the LESS signature scheme, and LEP-based cryptography in general: By combining our new results and CPS's ideas for improving LESS via canonical form functions, one might be able to obtain highly efficient LEP-based crypto systems over fields $\mathbb{F}_q$ with q as small as $q = 7$. (In contrast, the proposed LESS parameter sets use rather large $q = 127$.) However, since the focus of our work is cryptanalysis of LEP, and not constructive cryptography, we leave exploring such ideas to future work.

Experimental Results. As discussed above, LEP over $\mathbb{F}_2$, $\mathbb{F}_3$ and $\mathbb{F}_4$ is easy due to support splitting. Our novel algorithm, that provably works for all field sizes $q \geq 7$, thus covers all cryptographically interesting settings, except $q = 5$.

Interestingly, the constraint $q \geq 7$, however, seems to be a mere artifact of our proof technique: We implemented our novel canonical form function in SageMath and ran a series of experiments. Our results suggests that our canonical form function has decent success probability, even for $q = 5$. Hence, in practice, our algorithm applies to *all* cryptographically interesting settings.

Our implementation is publicly available at

https://github.com/juliannowakowski/lep-cf

1.3 Organization of the Paper

In Sect. 2, we introduce notations and provide some background on coding theory and LEP. After that, we formally define canonical form functions in Sect. 3, and revisit the CPS transformation for turning any canonical form function into a LEP algorithm. Building upon Sect. 3, we introduce our novel canonical form function in Sect. 4, which then directly leads to our main result: the improved LEP algorithm. Finally, we end in Sect. 5 with some experimental results, which show that our algorithm performs well in practice.

2 Preliminaries

2.1 Notations

We frequently use soft-$\mathcal{O}$ and soft-Θ notations, i.e., $\widetilde{\mathcal{O}}(\cdot)$ and $\widetilde{\Theta}(\cdot)$, which suppress polynomial factors. For a (finite) set A, we denote by $a \leftarrow A$ that a is sampled uniformly at random from A. The finite field with q elements is denoted by $\mathbb{F}_q$. Its unit group is $\mathbb{F}_q^* := \mathbb{F}_q \setminus \{0\}$. The group of invertible $(k \times k)$-dimensional matrices over $\mathbb{F}_q$ is denoted by $\mathrm{GL}(\mathbb{F}_q^k)$. We denote the set of positive integers by $\mathbb{N}$ and define $\mathbb{N}_0 := \mathbb{N} \cup \{0\}$. For $n \in \mathbb{N}$, we define $[n] := \{1, 2, \ldots, n\}$. For a subset $J \subseteq [n]$, we denote its complement by $\overline{J} := [n] \setminus J$.

All vectors $\mathbf{v} \in \mathbb{F}_q^n$ are row vectors. The i-th unit vector is denoted by $\mathbf{e}_i$, e.g., $\mathbf{e}_1 = (1, 0, \ldots, 0)$. The n-dimensional all-zero and all-one vectors are denoted $\mathbf{0}^n$ and $\mathbf{1}^n$, respectively. Let $\mathbf{G} \in \mathbb{F}_q^{k \times n}$ be a matrix. The transpose of $\mathbf{G}$ is denoted by $\mathbf{G}^T$. For $J \subseteq [n]$, we denote by $\mathbf{G}^J$ the submatrix of $\mathbf{G}$ formed by the columns indexed by J. We call J with $|J| = k$ an *information set* of $\mathbf{G}$, if the matrix $\mathbf{G}^J \in \mathbb{F}_q^{k \times k}$ is invertible. We denote by $\mathsf{RREF}(\mathbf{G})$ the row-reduced echelon form of $\mathbf{G}$. If $\mathbf{G}$ is of the form $\mathbf{G} = [\mathbf{I}_k \mid \mathbf{A}]$, then we say that $\mathbf{G}$ is in *systematic form*. A linear $[n, k]$-code $\mathcal{C}$ over $\mathbb{F}_q$ is a k-dimensional subspace of $\mathbb{F}_q^n$, i.e.,

$$\mathcal{C} = \{\mathbf{x}\mathbf{G} \mid \mathbf{x} \in \mathbb{F}_q^k\},$$

for some full-rank *generator matrix* $\mathbf{G} \in \mathbb{F}_q^{k \times n}$. The corresponding dual code $\mathcal{C}^\perp$ of $\mathcal{C}$ is (the transpose of) the right-kernel of $\mathbf{G}$. By elementary linear algebra, the dual code $\mathcal{C}^\perp$ is a linear $[n, n-k]$-code. The *rate* of an $[n, k]$-code is $\frac{k}{n}$. For $x \in (0, 1)$, the binary entropy function is defined as

$$\mathrm{H}(x) := -x \log_2(x) - (1 - x) \log_2(1 - x).$$

We frequently make use of the approximation $\binom{n}{k} = \widetilde{\Theta}(2^{\mathrm{H}(\frac{k}{n})n})$, which is a direct consequence of Stirling's formula.

2.2 Permutations, Diagonal Matrices and Monomials

Permutations. We denote by Σ_n the group of permutations on n letters. For $\mathbf{P} \in \Sigma_n$, the image of $j \in [n]$ under $\mathbf{P}$ is denoted by $\mathbf{P}[j]$. More generally, for a set $J \subseteq [n]$, we define $\mathbf{P}[J] := \{\mathbf{P}[j] \mid j \in J\}$. We identify permutations $\mathbf{P} \in \Sigma_n$ with $(n \times n)$-matrices with columns $\mathbf{e}^T_{\mathbf{P}^{-1}[1]}, \ldots, \mathbf{e}^T_{\mathbf{P}^{-1}[n]}$. As a consequence, multiplying a vector $\mathbf{v} = (v_1, \ldots, v_n) \in \mathbb{F}_q^n$ by $\mathbf{P}$ gives

$$\mathbf{v} \cdot \mathbf{P} = (v_{\mathbf{P}^{-1}[1]}, \ldots, v_{\mathbf{P}^{-1}[n]}).$$

In other words, multiplying $\mathbf{v}$ by $\mathbf{P}$ permutes the entries of $\mathbf{v}$ according to $\mathbf{P}$.

It is easy to see that the inverse of $\mathbf{P}$ is given by the transpose $\mathbf{P}^T$. Hence, if we have a column vector $\mathbf{w}^T = (w_1, \ldots, w_n)^T$, then $\mathbf{P} \cdot \mathbf{w}^T$ is equal to the vector obtained by permuting the entries of $\mathbf{w}^T$ according to $\mathbf{P}^{-1}$, i.e.,

$$\mathbf{P} \cdot \mathbf{w}^T = (w_{\mathbf{P}[1]}, \ldots, w_{\mathbf{P}[n]})^T.$$

For $J \subseteq [n]$ with $|J| = k$, we denote by $\mathbf{P}^J \in \Sigma_n$ a permutation that, for all matrices $\mathbf{G} \in \mathbb{F}_q^{k \times n}$, satisfies $\mathbf{G} \cdot \mathbf{P}^J = [\mathbf{G}^J \mid \mathbf{G}^{\overline{J}}]$. Stated differently, $\mathbf{P}^J$ permutes the columns indexed by J to the left, and the columns indexed by $\overline{J}$ to the right.

Diagonal Matrices. The group of $(n \times n)$ diagonal matrices over $\mathbb{F}_q^*$ is denoted by $\mathcal{D}_{n,q}$. For a diagonal matrix $\mathbf{D} \in \mathcal{D}_{n,q}$ with diagonal entries $d_1, \dots, d_n \in \mathbb{F}_q^*$ and a permutation $\mathbf{P} \in \Sigma_n$, the matrix $\mathbf{P}^{-1} \cdot \mathbf{D} \cdot \mathbf{P}$ is a diagonal matrix with diagonal entries $d_{\mathbf{P}^{-1}[1]}, \dots, d_{\mathbf{P}^{-1}[n]}$.

Monomials. The group of n-dimensional monomials over $\mathbb{F}_q$ is defined as

$$\mathcal{M}_{n,q} := \{\mathbf{P} \cdot \mathbf{D} \mid \mathbf{P} \in \Sigma_n, \mathbf{D} \in \mathcal{D}_{n,q}\} = \{\mathbf{D} \cdot \mathbf{P} \mid \mathbf{P} \in \Sigma_n, \mathbf{D} \in \mathcal{D}_{n,q}\}. \quad (1)$$

The fact that we can swap the order $\mathbf{P}$ and $\mathbf{D}$ in Equation (1) follows from the facts that $\mathbf{D} \cdot \mathbf{P} = \mathbf{P} \cdot (\mathbf{P}^{-1} \cdot \mathbf{D} \cdot \mathbf{P})$, and that $\mathbf{P}^{-1} \cdot \mathbf{D} \cdot \mathbf{P}$ is a diagonal matrix. Let $\mathbf{Q} \in \mathcal{M}_{n,q}$ be a monomial, and let $k \in [n]$. As first noted in [PS23], we can *factor* $\mathbf{Q}$ as

$$\mathbf{Q} = \mathbf{P}^J \cdot \begin{bmatrix} \mathbf{Q}_r & \\ & \mathbf{Q}_c \end{bmatrix},$$

where $J \subseteq [n]$ with $|J| = k$, $\mathbf{Q}_r \in \mathcal{M}_{k,q}$ and $\mathbf{Q}_c \in \mathcal{M}_{n-k,q}$. Considering such factorizations of monomials can be helpful when studying the action of monomials on matrices. Indeed, for every matrix $\mathbf{G} \in \mathbb{F}_q^{k \times n}$, it holds that

$$\mathbf{G} \cdot \mathbf{Q} = [\mathbf{G}^J \cdot \mathbf{Q}_r \mid \mathbf{G}^{\overline{J}} \cdot \mathbf{Q}_c].$$

Moreover, if J is an information set of $\mathbf{G}$, then $\mathbf{G}^J \cdot \mathbf{Q}_r$ is invertible, and it holds that

$$\mathsf{RREF}(\mathbf{G} \cdot \mathbf{Q}) = [\mathbf{I}_k \mid \mathbf{Q}_r^{-1} \cdot (\mathbf{G}^J)^{-1} \cdot \mathbf{G}^{\overline{J}} \cdot \mathbf{Q}_c].$$

2.3 Linear Code Equivalence Problem

Two linear $[n, k]$-codes $\mathcal{C}_1, \mathcal{C}_2 \subseteq \mathbb{F}_q^n$ are called *linearly equivalent*, if there exists a monomial $\mathbf{Q} \in \mathcal{M}_{n,q}$ such that $\mathcal{C}_2 = \mathcal{C}_1 \cdot \mathbf{Q}$, i.e., $\mathcal{C}_2 = \{\mathbf{c}_1 \cdot \mathbf{Q} \mid \mathbf{c}_1 \in \mathcal{C}_1\}$. Equivalently, $\mathcal{C}_1$ and $\mathcal{C}_2$ are linearly equivalent, if generator matrices $\mathbf{G}_1, \mathbf{G}_2$ of $\mathcal{C}_1, \mathcal{C}_2$ satisfy the following equivalence relation:

Definition 2.1 (Linear Equivalence). *Generator matrices* $\mathbf{G}_1, \mathbf{G}_2 \in \mathbb{F}_q^{k \times n}$ *are called* linearly equivalent, *if there exist* $\mathbf{U} \in \mathrm{GL}(\mathbb{F}_q^k)$ *and* $\mathbf{Q} \in \mathcal{M}_{n,q}$, *such that* $\mathbf{G}_2 = \mathbf{U} \cdot \mathbf{G}_1 \cdot \mathbf{Q}$. *In that case, we write* $\mathbf{G}_1 \sim \mathbf{G}_2$.

It is straight-forward to verify that $\sim$ indeed defines an equivalence relation on the set of all $(k \times n)$ matrices over $\mathbb{F}_q$. Definition 2.1 now suggests the following computational problem:

Definition 2.2 (LEP). *The* linear code equivalence problem (LEP) *with parameters* (n, k, q) *is defined as follows:*

- ***Given:*** *Linearly equivalent generator matrices* $\mathbf{G}_1, \mathbf{G}_2 \in \mathbb{F}_q^{k\times n}$.
- ***Find:*** *Matrices* $\mathbf{U} \in \mathrm{GL}(\mathbb{F}_q^k)$ *and* $\mathbf{Q} \in \mathcal{M}_{n,q}$ *such that* $\mathbf{G}_2 = \mathbf{U} \cdot \mathbf{G}_1 \cdot \mathbf{Q}$.

In cryptography, one usually considers an average case variant of LEP, where the matrices $\mathbf{G}_1$ and $\mathbf{G}_2$ are sampled from the following distribution.

Definition 2.3 (Average Case LEP Distribution). *For parameters* n, k, q, *the* average case LEP distribution $D_{n,k,q}^{\mathsf{LEP}}$ *is defined as follows: Sample a uniformly random matrix* $\mathbf{G}_1 \in \mathbb{F}_q^{k\times n}$, *and a uniformly random monomial* $\mathbf{Q} \in \mathcal{M}_{n,q}$. *Compute* $\mathbf{G}_2 := \mathsf{RREF}(\mathbf{G}_1 \cdot \mathbf{Q})$, *and output the tuple* $(\mathbf{G}_1, \mathbf{G}_2)$.

Formally, the average case variant of LEP ($-LEP) is defined as follows.

Definition 2.4 ($-LEP). *The* average case linear code equivalence problem ($-LEP) *with parameters* (n, k, q) *is defined as follows:*

- ***Given:*** *Linearly equivalent generator matrices* $\mathbf{G}_1$, $\mathbf{G}_2$ *sampled from* $D_{n,k,q}^{\mathsf{LEP}}$.
- ***Find:*** *Matrices* $\mathbf{U} \in \mathrm{GL}(\mathbb{F}_q^k)$ *and* $\mathbf{Q} \in \mathcal{M}_{n,q}$ *such that* $\mathbf{G}_2 = \mathbf{U} \cdot \mathbf{G}_1 \cdot \mathbf{Q}$.

Parameters. As discussed in the introduction, support splitting [Sen00] solves $-LEP instances over $\mathbb{F}_2$, $\mathbb{F}_3$ and $\mathbb{F}_4$ with high probability in polynomial time. However, $-LEP over $\mathbb{F}_q$ with $q \geq 5$ is conjectured to be hard.

In cryptographic applications, the field size q and the rate $R := \frac{k}{n}$ are typically constant, and only n grows with the security level. The most important setting in practice is $R = \frac{1}{2}$. Without loss of generality, we may assume $R \leq \frac{1}{2}$. (Via dual codes, one can easily show that ($-)LEP with parameters (n, k, q) is polynomial time equivalent to ($-)LEP with parameters $(n, n-k, q)$.)

2.4 Probabilities

We need the following concentration bound for the sum of (possibly dependent) $\{0,1\}$-valued random variables $X_1, \ldots, X_n$, which can easily be proved via Markov's inequality.

Lemma 2.5. *Let* $X_1, \ldots, X_n \in \{0,1\}$ *denote (possibly dependent) random variables. Let* $p \in [0,1]$, *such that* $\Pr[X_i = 1] \geq p$ *for every* $i \in [n]$. *Then for* $X := \sum_{i=1}^n X_i$ *it holds that*

$$\Pr\left[X > \frac{p}{2} \cdot n\right] \geq \frac{p}{2}.$$

A proof for Lemma 2.5 is given in Appendix A.1. We note that for *independent* random variables $X_1, \ldots, X_n$, Lemma 2.5 is significantly inferior to more standard concentration bounds, such as the Chernoff bound (which states that $\Pr\left[X > \frac{p}{2} \cdot n\right] > 1 - e^{-\Omega(p \cdot n)}$). However, a major advantage of Lemma 2.5 is that it also applies to *dependent* random variables.

Lemma 2.6. *Let* q *be a prime power and let* $k \in \mathbb{N}$. *A uniformly random matrix* $\mathbf{A} \leftarrow \mathbb{F}_q^{k\times k}$ *is invertible with probability greater than* $\frac{1}{4}$.

Lemma 2.6 is well-known, and frequently used in code-based cryptography. For completeness, we give a proof in Appendix A.2.

3 CPS Revisited

In this section, we revisit the original work of Chou, Persichetti and Santini (CPS) [CPS23]. We start by recalling the definition of *canonical form functions* in Sect. 3.1. As discussed in the introduction, CPS initially introduced these functions to improve signature size in the LESS signature scheme. However, they come with a surprising destructive application: CPS showed that any canonical form function can be transformed into a LEP algorithm. We revisit the transformation and its analysis in Sects. 3.2 and 3.3.

3.1 Canonical Form Functions

LRL Equivalence. CPS introduce a novel framework for studying equivalence relations for linear codes. While CPS use their framework to study five different equivalence relations, we need only one out of these five. CPS call this equivalence relation *Case 5*. However, we choose the more descriptive name *left-right linear equivalence*, or *LRL equivalence*, for short.

Definition 3.1 (LRL Equivalence). *Two generator matrices in systematic form* $\mathbf{G}_1 = [\mathbf{I}_k \mid \mathbf{A}_1], \mathbf{G}_2 = [\mathbf{I}_k \mid \mathbf{A}_2] \in \mathbb{F}_q^{k\times n}$ *are called* left-right linearly equivalent *or* LRL equivalent, *if and only if there exist* $\mathbf{Q}_r \in \mathcal{M}_{k,q}$ *and* $\mathbf{Q}_c \in \mathcal{M}_{n-k,q}$ *such that* $\mathbf{A}_2 = \mathbf{Q}_r \cdot \mathbf{A}_1 \cdot \mathbf{Q}_c$. *In that case, we write* $\mathbf{G}_1 \overset{\mathsf{LRL}}{\sim} \mathbf{G}_2$. *The equivalence class of a generator matrix in systematic form* $\mathbf{G} = [\mathbf{I}_k \mid \mathbf{A}]$ *is denoted by* $[\mathbf{G}]_{\overset{\mathsf{LRL}}{\sim}}$.

Notice that $\overset{\mathsf{LRL}}{\sim}$ indeed defines an equivalence relation on the set of $(k \times n)$-matrices over $\mathbb{F}_q$ in systematic form. We point out that the original definition by CPS is slightly more general than ours, as it also considers generator matrices that are not in systematic form. However, for our purposes, the simplified definition above suffices.

Additionally, we like to point out that LRL equivalence is a special case of linear equivalence: If $\mathbf{G}_1 = [\mathbf{I}_k \mid \mathbf{A}_1]$ and $\mathbf{G}_2 = [\mathbf{I}_k \mid \mathbf{A}_2]$ are LRL equivalent, i.e., $\mathbf{A}_2 = \mathbf{Q}_r \cdot \mathbf{A}_1 \cdot \mathbf{Q}_c$ for some monomials $\mathbf{Q}_r$, $\mathbf{Q}_c$, then for

$$\mathbf{Q} := \begin{bmatrix} \mathbf{Q}_r^{-1} & \\ & \mathbf{Q}_c \end{bmatrix} \in \mathcal{M}_{n,q}, \quad \text{and} \quad \mathbf{U} := \mathbf{Q}_r \in \mathcal{M}_{k,q} \subseteq \mathrm{GL}(\mathbb{F}_q^k),$$

it holds that $\mathbf{G}_2 = \mathbf{U} \cdot \mathbf{G}_1 \cdot \mathbf{Q}$. Hence, the codes generated by $\mathbf{G}_1$ and $\mathbf{G}_2$ are linearly equivalent.

Some Background. Definition 3.1 stems from the following scenario arising in the LESS signature scheme: Suppose Alice and Bob know generator matrices $\mathbf{G}_1$, $\mathbf{G}_2$ of linearly equivalent $[n, k]$-codes $\mathcal{C}_1$ and $\mathcal{C}_2$. Additionally, suppose Alice knows a monomial $\mathbf{Q} \in \mathcal{M}_{n,q}$ such that $\mathcal{C}_2 = \mathcal{C}_1 \cdot \mathbf{Q}$. In the identification protocol, that underlies the LESS signature scheme, Alice wants to prove to Bob that $\mathcal{C}_1$

and $\mathcal{C}_2$ are indeed linearly equivalent. A simple way to do this, would be for Alice to simply send $\mathbf{Q}$ to Bob. However, in the LESS setting, Alice would like to make the proof as *memory-efficient* as possible. To this end, CPS suggest the following approach:

Let us factor $\mathbf{Q}$ as

$$\mathbf{Q} = \mathbf{P}^J \cdot \begin{bmatrix} \mathbf{Q}_r & \\ & \mathbf{Q}_c \end{bmatrix},$$

for some $J \subseteq [n]$ with $|J| = k$, $\mathbf{Q}_r \in \mathcal{M}_{k,q}$ and $\mathbf{Q}_c \in \mathcal{M}_{n-k,q}$. Let us define

$$\mathbf{G}_1' := \mathsf{RREF}(\mathbf{G}_1 \cdot \mathbf{P}^J),$$
$$\mathbf{G}_2' := \mathsf{RREF}(\mathbf{G}_2).$$

For simplicity, let us assume that J is an information set of $\mathbf{G}_1$. Then it holds that

$$\mathbf{G}_1' = [\mathbf{I}_k \mid (\mathbf{G}_1^J)^{-1} \cdot \mathbf{G}_1^{\overline{J}}]. \tag{2}$$

Since $\mathcal{C}_2 = \mathcal{C}_1 \cdot \mathbf{Q}$, we have $\mathbf{G}_2 = \mathbf{U} \cdot \mathbf{G}_1 \cdot \mathbf{Q}$ for some $\mathbf{U} \in \mathrm{GL}(\mathbb{F}_q^k)$. Together with the fact that RREF is invariant under invertible transformations from the left, this implies

$$\mathbf{G}_2' = \mathsf{RREF}(\mathbf{U} \cdot \mathbf{G}_1 \cdot \mathbf{Q}) = \mathsf{RREF}(\mathbf{G}_1 \cdot \mathbf{Q}) = [\mathbf{I}_k \mid \mathbf{Q}_r^{-1} \cdot (\mathbf{G}_1^J)^{-1} \cdot \mathbf{G}_1^{\overline{J}} \cdot \mathbf{Q}_c]. \tag{3}$$

The crucial observation is now that by Equations (2) and (3), the matrices $\mathbf{G}_1'$ and $\mathbf{G}_2'$ are LRL equivalent.

Assume for a moment that Bob has an efficient algorithm for deciding whether two matrices are LRL equivalent. In such a scenario, CPS suggest instead of Alice sending $\mathbf{Q}$ to Bob, to send only J. To verify that $\mathcal{C}_1$ and $\mathcal{C}_2$ are linearly equivalent, Bob can then proceed as follows: Bob computes $\mathbf{G}_2'$, and uses J to compute $\mathbf{G}_1'$. After that, he tests whether $\mathbf{G}_1'$ and $\mathbf{G}_2'$ are LRL equivalent. If so, he accepts that $\mathcal{C}_1$ and $\mathcal{C}_2$ are linearly equivalent.

As shown by CPS, this approach is *sound*, i.e., Bob accepts only if $\mathcal{C}_1$ and $\mathcal{C}_2$ are indeed linearly equivalent. Since storing J requires significantly less memory than storing $\mathbf{Q}$, this approach greatly improves the memory-complexity of the proof. However, it requires access to an efficient algorithm for deciding, whether to matrices are LRL equivalent. For certain parameters of n, k and q, CPS can indeed give such an algorithm. It is based on *canonical form functions*, which we formally define below.

Canonical Form Functions. In a nutshell, a canonical form function for $\overset{\mathsf{LRL}}{\sim}$ is an efficient algorithm CF that takes a generator matrix $\mathbf{G} = [\mathbf{I}_k \mid \mathbf{A}]$ as input, and outputs a canonical representative $\mathbf{G}^* = [\mathbf{I}_k \mid \mathbf{A}^*]$ of the equivalence class $[\mathbf{G}]_{\overset{\mathsf{LRL}}{\sim}}$. Additionally, CF outputs monomials $\mathbf{Q}_r$ and $\mathbf{Q}_c$, such that $\mathbf{A}^* = \mathbf{Q}_r \cdot \mathbf{A} \cdot \mathbf{Q}_c$. More precisely, a canonical form function is defined as follows:

Definition 3.2 (Canonical Form Function). *A* canonical form function *(for LRL equivalence) is a polynomial time algorithm* CF, *that on input of a generator matrix in systematic form* $\mathbf{G} = [\mathbf{I}_k \mid \mathbf{A}] \in \mathbb{F}_q^{k \times n}$ *either outputs*

– *a tuple* $(\mathbf{G}^*, \mathbf{Q}_r, \mathbf{Q}_c) \in [\mathbf{G}]_{\overset{\mathsf{LRL}}{\sim}} \times \mathcal{M}_{k,q} \times \mathcal{M}_{n-k,q}$, *where* $\mathbf{G}^* = [\mathbf{I}_k \mid \mathbf{A}^*]$ *is a representative of the equivalence class* $[\mathbf{G}]_{\overset{\mathsf{LRL}}{\sim}}$, *such that* $\mathbf{A}^* = \mathbf{Q}_r \cdot \mathbf{A} \cdot \mathbf{Q}_c$,
– *or an error symbol* $\perp$.

Furthermore, we require the representative $\mathbf{G}^*$ *to be* canonical. *That is, for all* $\mathbf{G}_1 \overset{\mathsf{LRL}}{\sim} \mathbf{G}_2$ *with* $\mathsf{CF}(\mathbf{G}_1) \neq \perp$, *we require* $\mathsf{CF}(\mathbf{G}_1)$ *and* $\mathsf{CF}(\mathbf{G}_2)$ *to output the same representative of the equivalence class* $[\mathbf{G}_1]_{\overset{\mathsf{LRL}}{\sim}} = [\mathbf{G}_2]_{\overset{\mathsf{LRL}}{\sim}}$. *For a canonical form function* CF, *we define its* success probability *as*

$$\gamma_{\mathsf{CF}}(n,k,q) := \Pr_{\mathbf{A} \leftarrow \mathbb{F}_q^{k \times (n-k)}} \Big[\mathsf{CF}([\mathbf{I}_k \mid \mathbf{A}]) \neq \perp \Big].$$

As with our definition of LRL equivalence (Definition 3.1), we point out that the original CPS definition for canonical form functions is more general than ours, as it also considers inputs that are not in systematic form. However, again our simplified definition suffices.

The Dark Side of CF. While CPS introduced canonical form functions with a *constructive* application in mind (improving signature size in LESS), they have a surprising *destructive* application: CPS give an elegant transformation that turns any canonical form function CF into a algorithm for solving LEP in time $\widetilde{\mathcal{O}}\left(\gamma_{\mathsf{CF}}(n,k,q)^{-1/2} \cdot 2^{\frac{1}{2}\mathrm{H}(\frac{k}{n})n}\right)$. In particular, for canonical form functions with (at least) constant success probability, the transformation results in an LEP algorithm with runtime $\widetilde{\mathcal{O}}\left(2^{\frac{1}{2}\mathrm{H}(\frac{k}{n})n}\right)$. Unfortunately, as discussed in the introduction, finding canonical form functions with constant success probability is challenging: CPS give a canonical form function that achieves constant success probability only for large $q = \Omega(n)$. However, for constant $q = \mathcal{O}(1)$, its success probability is exponentially small – leading to an LEP algorithm that requires time exponentially higher than $2^{\frac{1}{2}\mathrm{H}(\frac{k}{n})n}$.

In Sect. 4, we will introduce our novel canonical form function, that has success probability probability $1 - \mathcal{O}(n^{-1})$ for all $q \geq 7$. By combining our canonical function with the CPS transformation, this immediately implies our novel $\widetilde{\mathcal{O}}\left(2^{\frac{1}{2}\mathrm{H}(\frac{k}{n})n}\right)$-time LEP algorithm. Before we introduce our novel canonical form function, let us revisit the analysis of the CPS transformation.

3.2 LEP as a Collision Finding Problem

The main idea behind the CPS transformation for turning a canonical form function into an LEP algorithm is to view LEP as a collision finding problem: The transformation turns any canonical form function into a meet-in-the-middle algorithm, that on input of a LEP instance $\mathbf{G}_1 \sim \mathbf{G}_2$ tries to find CF-*colliding* information sets J_1, J_2, as defined below.

Definition 3.3 (CF-colliding). *Let* $\mathbf{G}_1 \sim \mathbf{G}_2$ *be an LEP instance, and let* CF *be a canonical form function. We call two information sets* J_1, J_2 *of* $\mathbf{G}_1$ *and* $\mathbf{G}_2$ CF-colliding *for* $(\mathbf{G}_1, \mathbf{G}_2)$, *if*

$$\mathsf{RREF}(\mathbf{G}_1 \cdot \mathbf{P}^{J_1}) \overset{\mathsf{LRL}}{\sim} \mathsf{RREF}(\mathbf{G}_2 \cdot \mathbf{P}^{J_2}),$$

and additionally

$$\mathsf{CF}(\mathsf{RREF}(\mathbf{G}_1 \cdot \mathbf{P}^{J_1})) \neq \bot, \quad \mathsf{CF}(\mathsf{RREF}(\mathbf{G}_2 \cdot \mathbf{P}^{J_2})) \neq \bot.$$

As the following lemma shows, once CF-colliding information sets J_1 and J_2 are found, solving LEP becomes easy:

Lemma 3.4 (Adapted from Proposition 11 in *[CPS23]***).** *Let* $\mathbf{G}_1 \sim \mathbf{G}_2$ *be an LEP instance, and let* CF *be a canonical form function. Let* J_1, J_2 *be* CF*-colliding information sets for* $(\mathbf{G}_1, \mathbf{G}_2)$*. On input* $\mathbf{G}_1, \mathbf{G}_2, J_1, J_2$*, algorithm* $\mathsf{RecoverMon}^{\mathsf{CF}(\cdot)}$ *(Algorithm 1) computes a solution* $\mathbf{U} \in \mathrm{GL}(\mathbb{F}_q^k)$*,* $\mathbf{Q} \in \mathcal{M}_{n,q}$ *to the LEP instance defined by* $\mathbf{G}_1$ *and* $\mathbf{G}_2$ *in polynomial time.*

For completeness, we recall the proof of Lemma 3.4 in Appendix A.3.

Algorithm 1: $\mathsf{RecoverMon}^{\mathsf{CF}(\cdot)}$

Input: LEP instance $\mathbf{G}_1 \sim \mathbf{G}_2 \in \mathbb{F}_q^{k \times n}$,
CF-colliding information sets J_1, J_2 for $(\mathbf{G}_1, \mathbf{G}_2)$.
Output: Solution $\mathbf{U} \in \mathrm{GL}(\mathbb{F}_q^k), \mathbf{Q} \in \mathcal{M}_{n,q}$ with $\mathbf{G}_2 = \mathbf{U} \cdot \mathbf{G}_1 \cdot \mathbf{Q}$.

1 Compute $\mathbf{G}_i' := \mathsf{RREF}(\mathbf{G}_i \cdot \mathbf{P}^{J_i})$ for $i \in \{1,2\}$.
2 Compute $\mathsf{CF}(\mathbf{G}_i') = (\mathbf{G}_i^*, \mathbf{Q}_{r,i}, \mathbf{Q}_{c,i})$ for $i \in \{1,2\}$.
3 Compute $\mathbf{U} := \mathbf{G}_2^{J_2} \cdot \mathbf{Q}_{r,2}^{-1} \cdot \mathbf{Q}_{r,1} \cdot (\mathbf{G}_1^{J_1})^{-1}$.
4 Compute

$$\mathbf{Q} := \mathbf{P}^{J_1} \cdot \begin{bmatrix} \mathbf{Q}_{r,1}^{-1} \cdot \mathbf{Q}_{r,2} & \\ & \mathbf{Q}_{c,1} \cdot \mathbf{Q}_{c,2}^{-1} \end{bmatrix} \cdot (\mathbf{P}^{J_2})^{-1}.$$

5 **return** $\mathbf{U}, \mathbf{Q}$

To see that CF-colliding information sets actually exist, we need Lemma 3.5 below. In the original CPS paper, Lemma 3.5 is not stated explicitly, but only hinted at.[4] For completeness, we give a formal proof in Appendix A.4.

---

[4] Lemma 3.5 is essentially the main idea behind the identification protocol introduced in [CPS23, Section 5.2].

Lemma 3.5. *Let* $\mathbf{G}_1 \sim \mathbf{G}_2 \in \mathbb{F}_q^{k\times n}$ *be linearly equivalent matrices, where*

$$\mathbf{G}_2 = \mathbf{U} \cdot \mathbf{G}_1 \cdot \mathbf{P} \cdot \mathbf{D},$$

for some $\mathbf{U} \in \mathrm{GL}(\mathbb{F}_q^k)$*,* $\mathbf{P} \in \Sigma_n$ *and* $\mathbf{D} \in \mathcal{D}_{n,q}$*. Let* J_1 *be an information set of* $\mathbf{G}_1$*. Then* $J_2 := \mathbf{P}[J_1]$ *is an information set of* $\mathbf{G}_2$*, and it holds that*

$$\mathsf{RREF}(\mathbf{G}_1 \cdot \mathbf{P}^{J_1}) \overset{\mathsf{LRL}}{\sim} \mathsf{RREF}(\mathbf{G}_2 \cdot \mathbf{P}^{J_2}).$$

3.3 A Provably Correct Variant of the CPS Transformation

We are now ready to describe the CPS transformation for converting a canonical form function CF into a LEP algorithm. It is depicted in Algorithm 2. For simplicity, we give a variant of CPS' transformation that only works well for canonical form functions CF with (at least) constant success probability $\gamma_{\mathsf{CF}}(n,k,q) = \Omega(1)$. An advantage of this variant is that it can be shown to be provably correct, whereas the original analysis of CPS for *arbitrary success probabilities* $\gamma_{\mathsf{CF}}(n,k,q)$ relied on a heuristic argument.

The Algorithm. In a nutshell, Algorithm 2 samples on input of a LEP instance $\mathbf{G}_1 \sim \mathbf{G}_2$ sufficiently many random information sets J_1, J_2 of $\mathbf{G}_1$ and $\mathbf{G}_2$, with the hope of sampling at least one CF-colliding pair (see Definition 3.3). If it finds such a pair, it uses $\mathsf{RecoverMon}^{\mathsf{CF}(\cdot)}$ (Algorithm 1) as a subroutine to easily solve the LEP instance. More precisely, it works as follows:

On input $\mathbf{G}_1 \sim \mathbf{G}_2$, Algorithm 2 picks $\left\lfloor \sqrt{\frac{1}{2}\binom{n}{k}} \right\rfloor$ random size-k subsets J_1 of $[n]$, and computes $\mathbf{G}_1' := \mathsf{RREF}(\mathbf{G}_1 \cdot \mathbf{P}^{J_1})$, for every J_1. If $\mathbf{G}_1'$ is in systematic form (or equivalently, if J_1 is an information set of $\mathbf{G}_1$), the algorithm runs CF on $\mathbf{G}_1'$. If CF does not return $\perp$, CF returns a canonical representative $\mathbf{G}_1^*$ of the equivalence class $[\mathbf{G}_1']_{\overset{\mathsf{LRL}}{\sim}}$. Algorithm 2 then stores $\mathbf{G}_1^*$ along with J_1 in some list L. Next, the algorithm tries to find an information set J_2 of $\mathbf{G}_2$, that together with some previously sampled information set J_1 of $\mathbf{G}_1$ is CF-colliding for $(\mathbf{G}_1, \mathbf{G}_2)$. The algorithm can easily detect such a J_2 by simply testing if $\mathbf{G}_2' := \mathsf{RREF}(\mathbf{G}_2 \cdot \mathbf{P}^{J_2})$ is in systematic form, and, additionally, if the computation of $\mathsf{CF}(\mathbf{G}_2')$ yields a canonical representative identical to one of the $\mathbf{G}_1^*$'s, that it has stored in L before (see Definitions 3.2 and 3.3). Once it finds such a J_2, it can easily solve the LEP instance via algorithm $\mathsf{RecoverMon}^{\mathsf{CF}(\cdot)}$ (see Lemma 3.4).

Runtime and Success Probability. The first repeat-loop in Algorithm 2 clearly runs in time $T := \widetilde{\Theta}\left(\sqrt{\binom{n}{k}}\right)$. Sorting L in Line 9 can be done in time T as well. After sorting L, testing for membership in L can be done in time $\widetilde{\Theta}(1)$. Thus, also the second repeat-loop runs in time T. Hence, we obtain an overall runtime of $T = \widetilde{\Theta}\left(\sqrt{\binom{n}{k}}\right) = \widetilde{\Theta}\left(2^{\frac{1}{2}\mathrm{H}(\frac{k}{n})n}\right)$ for Algorithm 2.

As we show below, for canonical form functions with (at least) constant success probability, the algorithm solves the average case variant of LEP ($-LEP, see Definition 2.4) with constant success probability:

Algorithm 2: $\mathsf{LEP\text{-}Coll\text{-}Search}^{\mathsf{CF}(\cdot)}$

Input: LEP instance $\mathbf{G}_1 \sim \mathbf{G}_2 \in \mathbb{F}_q^{k \times n}$.

Output: Solution $\mathbf{U} \in \mathrm{GL}(\mathbb{F}_q^k), \mathbf{Q} \in \mathcal{M}_{n,q}$ with $\mathbf{G}_2 = \mathbf{U} \cdot \mathbf{G}_1 \cdot \mathbf{Q}$, or error symbol $\perp$.

Initialize empty list L.
repeat $\left\lfloor \sqrt{\frac{1}{2}\binom{n}{k}} \right\rfloor$ **times**
    Sample uniformly random size-k subset J_1 of $[n]$.
    $\mathbf{G}_1' := \mathsf{RREF}(\mathbf{G}_1 \cdot \mathbf{P}^{J_1})$.
    if $\mathbf{G}_1'$ is in systematic form **then** ▷ Is J_1 information set?
        if $\mathsf{CF}(\mathbf{G}_1') \neq \perp$ **then**
            Parse the first component of $\mathsf{CF}(\mathbf{G}_1')$'s output as $\mathbf{G}_1^* \in [\mathbf{G}_1']_{\underset{\sim}{\mathsf{LRL}}}$.
            Store $(\mathbf{G}_1^*, J_1)$ in L.
Sort L by the second component.
repeat $\left\lfloor \sqrt{\frac{1}{2}\binom{n}{k}} \right\rfloor$ **times**
    Sample uniformly random size-k subset J_2 of $[n]$.
    $\mathbf{G}_2' := \mathsf{RREF}(\mathbf{G}_2 \cdot \mathbf{P}^{J_2})$.
    if $\mathbf{G}_2'$ is in systematic form **then** ▷ Is J_2 information set?
        if $\mathsf{CF}(\mathbf{G}_2') \neq \perp$ **then**
            Parse the first component of $\mathsf{CF}(\mathbf{G}_2')$'s output as $\mathbf{G}_2^* \in [\mathbf{G}_2']_{\underset{\sim}{\mathsf{LRL}}}$.
            if $(\mathbf{G}_2^*, J_1) \in L$ for some J_1 **then** ▷ Are J_1, J_2 CF-colliding?
                return $\mathsf{RecoverMon}^{\mathsf{CF}(\cdot)}(\mathbf{G}_1, \mathbf{G}_2, J_1, J_2)$
return $\perp$

Theorem 3.6 (Correctness CPS Transformation). *Let $\mathbf{G}_1 \sim \mathbf{G}_2 \in \mathbb{F}_q^{k \times n}$ be a \$-LEP instance, and let* CF *be a canonical form function with (at least) constant success probability. On input $\mathbf{G}_1, \mathbf{G}_2$, Algorithm* $\mathsf{LEP\text{-}Coll\text{-}Search}^{\mathsf{CF}(\cdot)}$ *(Algorithm 2) outputs a solution to the \$-LEP instance defined by $\mathbf{G}_1$ and $\mathbf{G}_2$ in time $\widetilde{\Theta}\left(2^{\frac{1}{2}\mathrm{H}\left(\frac{k}{n}\right)n}\right)$, and with constant success probability.*

The proof of Theorem 3.6 is based on the following technical lemma.

Lemma 3.7. *Let $\mathbf{G}_1 \sim \mathbf{G}_2 \in \mathbb{F}_q^{k \times n}$ be a \$-LEP instance, and let* CF *be a canonical form function with (at least) constant success probability. If we run* $\mathsf{LEP\text{-}Coll\text{-}Search}^{\mathsf{CF}(\cdot)}$ *(Algorithm 2) on input $\mathbf{G}_1, \mathbf{G}_2$, then with constant probability, the list L computed by* $\mathsf{LEP\text{-}Coll\text{-}Search}^{\mathsf{CF}(\cdot)}$ *contains more than*

$$\frac{\gamma_{\mathsf{CF}}(n,k,q)}{8} \cdot \left\lfloor \sqrt{\frac{1}{2} \cdot \binom{n}{k}} \right\rfloor$$

distinct elements.

Proof. Let $T := \left\lfloor \sqrt{\frac{1}{2} \cdot \binom{n}{k}} \right\rfloor$, and $\gamma := \gamma_{\mathsf{CF}}(n,k,q)$. We denote by $J_{1,1}, \ldots, J_{1,T}$ the T sets J_1, that algorithm Algorithm 2 samples in its first repeat-loop. For every i, we define an indicator variable $X_i \in \{0,1\}$, that is equal to 1, if and only if $J_{1,i}$ gets stored in L. Let E_i denote the event that $J_{1,i}$ is an information set of $\mathbf{G}_1$. Looking at Lines 5 and 6 of Algorithm 2, it follows that

$$\Pr[X_i = 1] = \Pr[E_i] \cdot \Pr[\mathsf{CF}(\mathsf{RREF}(\mathbf{G}_1 \cdot \mathbf{P}^{J_{1,i}})) \neq \perp \mid E_i].$$

The set $J_{1,i}$ is an information set of $\mathbf{G}_1$, if and only if $\mathbf{G}_1^{J_{1,i}} \in \mathbb{F}_q^{k \times k}$ is invertible. Since in \$-LEP, the matrix $\mathbf{G}_1$ is uniformly random, also $\mathbf{G}_1^{J_{1,i}}$ uniformly random. Hence, by Lemma 2.6, we have $\Pr[E_i] > \frac{1}{4}$, and thus

$$\begin{aligned}\Pr[X_i = 1] &> \frac{1}{4} \cdot \Pr[\mathsf{CF}(\mathsf{RREF}(\mathbf{G}_1 \cdot \mathbf{P}^{J_{1,i}})) \neq \perp \mid E_i] \\ &= \frac{1}{4} \cdot \Pr[\mathsf{CF}([\mathbf{I}_k \mid (\mathbf{G}_1^{J_{1,i}})^{-1} \cdot \mathbf{G}_1^{\overline{J_{1,i}}}]) \neq \perp \mid E_i] = \frac{\gamma}{4},\end{aligned}$$

where the last equality follows from Definition 3.2 and the fact that in \$-LEP, the matrix $\mathbf{G}_1^{\overline{J_{1,i}}}$ is uniformly random.

Applying Lemma 2.5 to the random variable $|L| = \sum_{i=1}^{T} X_{J_{1,i}}$, we obtain

$$\Pr\left[|L| > \frac{\gamma}{8} \cdot T\right] \geq \frac{\gamma}{8} = \Omega(1).$$

This already shows that, with constant probability, the list L contains more than

$$\frac{\gamma_{\mathsf{CF}}(n,k,q)}{8} \cdot \left\lfloor \sqrt{\frac{1}{2} \cdot \binom{n}{k}} \right\rfloor$$

elements. To finish the proof, we have to show that with constant probability these elements are *distinct*. To this end, we simply note that the probability that the i-th sampled set $J_{1,i}$ is equal to a previously sampled set $J_{1,1}, \ldots, J_{1,i-1}$ is $(i-1)/\binom{n}{k}$. Thus, the probability that all sets $J_{1,i}$ are distinct is

$$\prod_{i=1}^{T} \left(1 - \frac{i-1}{\binom{n}{k}}\right) \geq \left(1 - \frac{T}{\binom{n}{k}}\right)^{T} \geq 1 - \frac{T^2}{\binom{n}{k}} \geq 1 - \frac{\frac{1}{2}\binom{n}{k}}{\binom{n}{k}} = \frac{1}{2} = \Omega(1).$$

This shows that with constant probability all elements in L are distinct, and thus concludes the proof. □

Using Lemma 3.7, we now prove Theorem 3.6.

Proof (Theorem 3.6) We have to show that Algorithm 2 samples in its second repeat-loop with constant probability an information set J_2 of $\mathbf{G}_2$, that, together with some information set J_1 stored in the list L, is CF-colliding for $(\mathbf{G}_1, \mathbf{G}_2)$.

Since $\mathbf{G}_1 \sim \mathbf{G}_2$, we can write $\mathbf{G}_2 = \mathbf{U} \cdot \mathbf{G}_1 \cdot \mathbf{P} \cdot \mathbf{D}$, for some $\mathbf{U} \in \mathrm{GL}(\mathbb{F}_q^k)$, $\mathbf{P} \in \Sigma_n$ and $\mathbf{D} \in \mathcal{D}_{n,q}$. Let $\mathcal{I}_1$ denote the set of all information sets J_1 that

Algorithm 2 stores in the list L, and let $\mathcal{I}_2 := \{\mathbf{P}[J_1] \mid J_1 \in \mathcal{I}_1\}$. By Lemma 3.5, every pair $(J_1, \mathbf{P}[J_1]) \in \mathcal{I}_1 \times \mathcal{I}_2$ is CF-colliding for $(\mathbf{G}_1, \mathbf{G}_2)$. Thus, it suffices to show that Algorithm 2 samples at least one set J_2 with $J_2 \in \mathcal{I}_2$.

Let $\gamma := \gamma_{\mathsf{CF}}(n, k, q)$ and $T := \left\lfloor \sqrt{\frac{1}{2}\binom{n}{k}} \right\rfloor$. By Lemma 3.7, we have with constant probability that $|\mathcal{I}_2| = |\mathcal{I}_1| = |L| > \frac{\gamma}{8} \cdot T$. If indeed $|\mathcal{I}_2| > \frac{\gamma}{8} \cdot T$, then Algorithm 2 samples $J_2 \in \mathcal{I}_2$ with probability at least

$$1 - \left(1 - \frac{\frac{\gamma}{8} \cdot T}{\binom{n}{k}}\right)^T \geq 1 - \exp\left(-\frac{\frac{\gamma}{8} \cdot T^2}{\binom{n}{k}}\right) \geq 1 - e^{-\gamma/16} \geq \frac{\gamma}{32}.$$

Hence, the overall success probability of Algorithm 2 is lower bounded by

$$\Omega(1) \cdot \frac{\gamma}{32} = \Omega(1),$$

as desired. □

A Memoryless Variant. We note that the memory consumption of Algorithm 2 is quite excessive, as (by Lemma 3.7) it requires storing a list of size roughly $\sqrt{\binom{n}{k}}$. However, this issue can easily be avoided via a standard Van-Oorschot-Wiener-like collision-finding algorithm [vW99].

A Quantum Variant. For canonical form functions with (at least) constant success probability, Algorithm 2 naturally gives rise to quantum variant with time and memory $\widetilde{\Theta}\left(2^{\frac{1}{3}\mathrm{H}(\frac{k}{n})n}\right)$: Instead of sampling roughly $\sqrt{\binom{n}{k}}$ sets J_1 in the algorithms first repeat-loop, we sample only $\binom{n}{k}^{1/3}$ such sets. By slightly adapting the proofs of Lemma 3.7 and Theorem 3.6, one can easily show that the probability that a single iteration of the second repeat-loop finds a CF-colliding pair J_1, J_2 then drops from roughly $\binom{n}{k}^{-1/2}$ to roughly $\binom{n}{k}^{-2/3}$. Hence, by replacing the second repeat-loop by Grover search / amplitude amplification, we immediately obtain a quantum algorithm with the desired runtime and memory consumption.

Comparison with Original CPS Analysis. The only difference between Algorithm 2 and the original CPS algorithm is that instead of sampling $\left\lfloor \sqrt{\frac{1}{2}\binom{n}{k}} \right\rfloor$ random index sets J_1, J_2, CPS suggest to sample roughly $\sqrt{\frac{1}{\zeta \cdot \gamma_{\mathsf{CF}}(n,k,q)}\binom{n}{k}}$ such sets, where $\zeta > \frac{1}{4}$ denotes the probability that a uniformly random matrix $\mathbf{A} \in \mathbb{F}_q^{k \times k}$ is invertible (see Lemma 2.6). For this variant, CPS claim runtime roughly $\sqrt{\frac{1}{\gamma_{\mathsf{CF}}(n,k,q)}\binom{n}{k}}$, and "constant success probability which is approximately 1/2". Their argument goes as follows: Since each pair J_1, J_2 is CF-colliding with probability at least $\zeta \cdot \gamma_{\mathsf{CF}}(n, k, q) \cdot \binom{n}{k}^{-1}$, CPS sample on expectation at least one

CF-colliding pair. Since Algorithm 2 is successful, if and only if it samples at least one such pair, it follows that *on expectation*, CPS indeed solve LEP.

Unfortunately, sampling one such pair *on expectation* does not necessarily imply that one actually samples one such pair *with decent probability*.[5] To overcome this issue, CPS heuristically assume that, for any pair of index sets J_1, J_1', the events $[\mathsf{CF}(\mathsf{RREF}(\mathbf{G}_1 \cdot \mathbf{P}^{J_1})) \neq \bot]$ and $[\mathsf{CF}(\mathsf{RREF}(\mathbf{G}_1 \cdot \mathbf{P}^{J_1'})) \neq \bot]$ can be treated as independent.[6] Under this assumption, standard concentration bounds (e.g., the Chernoff bound) indeed imply that that the original CPS algorithm solves LEP with constant probability. However, in reality, these events are of course not perfectly independent, and it is unclear how much of an issue this is in practice. In fact, properly measuring the exact impact of these dependencies in practice is challenging, as it might become visible only for cryptographically-sized parameters. (Similar effects have been observed in the context of *dual attacks* on codes and lattices, where the analysis also heuristically assumed independence of some events [DP23, MT23].)

To circumvent these issues, we resort in the proof of Lemma 3.7 to the concentration bound from Lemma 2.5. We use Lemma 2.5 to show that when sampling $T \in \mathbb{N}$ random index sets J_1, then with probability at least $\gamma_{\mathsf{CF}}(n,k,q)/8$ more than $\gamma_{\mathsf{CF}}(n,k,q)/8 \cdot T$ of these sets satisfy $\mathsf{CF}(\mathsf{RREF}(\mathbf{G}_1 \cdot \mathbf{P}^{J_1})) \neq \bot$. For our setting of canonical form functions with (at least) constant success probability $\gamma_{\mathsf{CF}}(n,k,q) = \Omega(1)$, this is good enough to conclude constant success probability for Algorithm 2. However, for canonical form functions with exponentially small success probability, Lemma 2.5 is too weak to make any meaningful conclusion about the success probability of the original CPS algorithm.

4 A Novel Canonical Form Function

Now that we have formally defined canonical form functions in the previous Sect. 3, we are ready to introduce our novel canonical form function, which we denote by $\mathsf{CF}_{\mathsf{New}}$. As we will show below, $\mathsf{CF}_{\mathsf{New}}$ has over all fields of size $q \geq 7$ success probability $1 - \mathcal{O}(n^{-1})$. Together with Theorem 3.6 from the previous section, this immediately yields our novel $\widetilde{\mathcal{O}}\left(2^{\frac{1}{2}\mathrm{H}(\frac{k}{n})n}\right)$-time LEP algorithm.

Road Map. For ease of exposition, we break $\mathsf{CF}_{\mathsf{New}}$ into four steps. While describing these steps, we prove the correctness of $\mathsf{CF}_{\mathsf{New}}$ along the way. Let us briefly outline our road map for our proof of correctness. To this end, let $\mathbf{G}_1 = [\mathbf{I}_k \mid \mathbf{A}_1] \overset{\mathsf{LRL}}{\sim} \mathbf{G}_2 = [\mathbf{I}_k \mid \mathbf{A}_2] \in \mathbb{F}_q^{k \times n}$ be any pair of LRL equivalent matrices. To prove that our novel canonical form function $\mathsf{CF}_{\mathsf{New}}$ is correct, we have to show that running $\mathsf{CF}_{\mathsf{New}}$ on inputs $\mathbf{G}_1$ and $\mathbf{G}_2$, respectively, returns the

[5] Consider a random variable X with $\Pr[X = 2^n] = 2^{-n}$ and $\Pr[X = 0] = 1 - 2^{-n}$. Then $\mathbb{E}[X] = 1$, but $\Pr[X \geq 1] = 2^{-n}$ is negligible.

[6] More precisely, CPS assume that for any given matrix $\mathbf{G}$ with information set J, the matrix $(\mathbf{G}^J)^{-1} \cdot \mathbf{G}^{\overline{J}}$ obtained from $\mathsf{RREF}(\mathbf{G} \cdot \mathbf{P}^J) = [\mathbf{I}_k \mid (\mathbf{G}^J)^{-1} \cdot \mathbf{G}^{\overline{J}}]$ can be treated as a freshly sampled uniformly random matrix, see [CPS23, Heuristic 1].

same representative of the equivalence class $[\mathbf{G}_1]_{\overset{\text{LRL}}{\sim}} = [\mathbf{G}_2]_{\overset{\text{LRL}}{\sim}}$. To this end, we proceed as follows:

On input $\mathbf{G}_1$, $\mathsf{CF}_{\mathsf{New}}$ computes in the i-th of its four steps a matrix $\mathbf{G}_1^{(i)} = [\mathbf{I}_k \mid \mathbf{A}_1^{(i)}] \in [\mathbf{G}_1]_{\overset{\text{LRL}}{\sim}}$. Analogously, on input $\mathbf{G}_2$, $\mathsf{CF}_{\mathsf{New}}$ computes in its i-th step a matrix $\mathbf{G}_2^{(i)} = [\mathbf{I}_k \mid \mathbf{A}_2^{(i)}] \in [\mathbf{G}_2]_{\overset{\text{LRL}}{\sim}} = [\mathbf{G}_1]_{\overset{\text{LRL}}{\sim}}$. We show that as the steps progress, the matrices $\mathbf{A}_1^{(i)}$, $\mathbf{A}_2^{(i)}$ become increasingly *similar*. Ultimately, after the fourth step, we end up with $\mathbf{A}_1^{(4)} = \mathbf{A}_2^{(4)}$. The final matrices $\mathbf{G}_1^{(4)} = \mathbf{G}_2^{(4)}$ then serve as our canonical representative of the equivalence class $[\mathbf{G}_1]_{\overset{\text{LRL}}{\sim}} = [\mathbf{G}_2]_{\overset{\text{LRL}}{\sim}}$.

Comparison with CPS. Before we begin, we would like to give credit and note that our novel canonical form function $\mathsf{CF}_{\mathsf{New}}$ re-uses many of the original ideas by CPS: In Steps 1 to 3, we run essentially an improved variant of the original CPS canonical form function [CPS23] on well-chosen submatrices of our inputs $\mathbf{A}_1$ and $\mathbf{A}_2$. By restricting ourselves to these submatrices, we can circumvent some of the abort conditions of CPS. The process of choosing these submatrices, as well as the fourth step of $\mathsf{CF}_{\mathsf{New}}$ are, however, completely different from the original CPS canonical form function.

4.1 Step 1

Let $\mathbf{G}_1 = [\mathbf{I}_k \mid \mathbf{A}_1] \overset{\text{LRL}}{\sim} \mathbf{G}_2 = [\mathbf{I}_k \mid \mathbf{A}_2] \in \mathbb{F}_q^{k \times n}$ be the inputs to our canonical form function $\mathsf{CF}_{\mathsf{New}}$. By definition of LRL equivalence, we can write

$$\mathbf{A}_2 = \mathbf{P}_r \cdot \mathbf{D}_r \cdot \mathbf{A}_1 \cdot \mathbf{P}_c \cdot \mathbf{D}_c, \tag{4}$$

for some permutations $\mathbf{P}_r \in \Sigma_k$, $\mathbf{P}_c \in \Sigma_{n-k}$ and diagonal matrices $\mathbf{D}_r \in \mathcal{D}_{k,q}$, $\mathbf{D}_c \in \mathcal{D}_{n-k,q}$.

The first step of $\mathsf{CF}_{\mathsf{New}}$ is given in Algorithm $\mathsf{CF}_{\mathsf{New}}^{(1)}$ (Algorithm 3). On inputs $\mathbf{G}_1$ and $\mathbf{G}_2$, respectively, our canonical form function starts by computing $(\mathbf{A}_1^{(1)}, w_1) := \mathsf{CF}_{\mathsf{New}}^{(1)}(\mathbf{A}_1, i_1)$ and $(\mathbf{A}_2^{(1)}, w_2) := \mathsf{CF}_{\mathsf{New}}^{(1)}(\mathbf{A}_2, i_2)$, respectively, where $i_1, i_2 \in [k]$ are some well-chosen parameters. For ease of exposition, we defer the exact description of the selection process for i_1 and i_2 to later. For the moment, it suffices to know that i_1 and i_2 will satisfy $i_2 = \mathbf{P}_r^T[i_1]$, where $\mathbf{P}_r$ is the permutation from Equation (4).

Relating $\mathbf{A}_1^{(1)}$ and $\mathbf{A}_2^{(1)}$. Let us define $w := w_1$. It is straight-forward to verify that the matrix $\mathbf{A}_1^{(1)}$ is of the shape

$$\mathbf{A}_1^{(1)} = \begin{matrix} 1\{ \\ k-1\{ \end{matrix} \begin{bmatrix} \overbrace{1, 1, \ldots, 1}^{w} & \overbrace{0, 0, \ldots, 0}^{n-k-w} \\ \mathbf{A}_{1,1}^{(1)} & \mathbf{A}_{1,2}^{(1)} \end{bmatrix},$$

Algorithm 3: $\mathsf{CF}^{(1)}_{\mathsf{New}}$

Input: $\mathbf{A} \in \mathbb{F}_q^{k\times(n-k)}$, index $i \in [k]$.
Output: $\mathbf{A}^{(1)} \in \mathbb{F}_q^{k\times(n-k)}$, parameter $w \in [n-k]$.
1 $\mathbf{A}^{(1)} := \mathbf{A}$
2 $\mathcal{J} := \emptyset$
3 Parse the i-th row of $\mathbf{A}^{(1)}$ as $(a_{i,1}, \dots, a_{i,n-k})$.
4 **for** $j = 1, \dots, n-k$ **do**
5   **if** $a_{i,j} \neq 0$ **then**
6   Divide all entries in the j-th column of $\mathbf{A}^{(1)}$ by $a_{i,j}$.
7   **else**
8         $\mathcal{J} := \mathcal{J} \cup \{j\}$.
9 $w := n - k - |\mathcal{J}|$ ▷ `Number of non-zero entries in the` i`-th row of` $\mathbf{A}$.
10 Move all columns of $\mathbf{A}^{(1)}$ indexed by $\mathcal{J}$ to the right of the matrix.
11 Swap the first row of $\mathbf{A}^{(1)}$ with the i-th row.
12 **return** $(\mathbf{A}^{(1)}, w)$

where $\mathbf{A}^{(1)}_{1,1}$ and $\mathbf{A}^{(1)}_{1,2}$ are some matrices. Furthermore, for our choice of $i_2 = \mathbf{P}_r^T[i_1]$, it is straight-forward to verify that $w_1 = w_2$, and that

$$\mathbf{A}_2^{(1)} = \begin{matrix} 1\{ \\ k-1\{ \end{matrix} \begin{bmatrix} \overbrace{1, 1, \dots, 1}^{w} & \overbrace{0, 0, \dots, 0}^{n-k-w} \\ \mathbf{Q}_r^{(1)} \cdot \mathbf{A}_{1,1}^{(1)} \cdot \mathbf{P}_c^{(1)} & \mathbf{Q}_r^{(1)} \cdot \mathbf{A}_{1,2}^{(1)} \cdot \mathbf{Q}_c^{(1)} \end{bmatrix}, \tag{5}$$

for some monomials $\mathbf{Q}_r^{(1)}$, $\mathbf{Q}_c^{(1)}$ and a permutation $\mathbf{P}_c^{(1)}$: Indeed, for our choice of $i_2 = \mathbf{P}_r^T[i_1]$, Lines 6, 10 and 11 ensure that the first rows $\mathbf{a}_{1,1}^{(1)}$ and $\mathbf{a}_{2,1}^{(1)}$ of $\mathbf{A}_1^{(1)}$ and $\mathbf{A}_2^{(1)}$, respectively, are equal to

$$\mathbf{a}_{1,1}^{(1)} = \mathbf{a}_{2,1}^{(1)} = (\mathbf{1}^w, \mathbf{0}^{n-k-w}) \in \mathbb{F}_q^{n-k}. \tag{6}$$

Additionally, for our choice of $i_2 = \mathbf{P}_r^T[i_1]$, Lines 10 and 11 ensure that

$$\mathbf{A}_2^{(1)} = \begin{bmatrix} \overbrace{1}^{1} & \overbrace{\phantom{\widetilde{\mathbf{Q}}_r}}^{k-1} \\ & \widetilde{\mathbf{Q}}_r \end{bmatrix} \cdot \mathbf{A}_1^{(1)} \cdot \begin{bmatrix} \overbrace{\widetilde{\mathbf{Q}}_{c,L}}^{w} & \overbrace{\phantom{\widetilde{\mathbf{Q}}_{c,R}}}^{n-k-w} \\ & \widetilde{\mathbf{Q}}_{c,R} \end{bmatrix}, \tag{7}$$

for some monomials $\widetilde{\mathbf{Q}}_r$, $\widetilde{\mathbf{Q}}_{c,L}$ and $\widetilde{\mathbf{Q}}_{c,R}$.

Let us write $\widetilde{\mathbf{Q}}_{c,L} = \widetilde{\mathbf{D}}_{c,L} \cdot \widetilde{\mathbf{P}}_{c,L}$ for some diagonal matrix $\widetilde{\mathbf{D}}_{c,L}$ and a permutation $\widetilde{\mathbf{P}}_{c,L}$. Combining Equations (7) and (6), we obtain

$$\mathbf{1}^w = \mathbf{1}^w \cdot \widetilde{\mathbf{D}}_{c,L} \cdot \widetilde{\mathbf{P}}_{c,L}.$$

This shows that $\widetilde{\mathbf{D}}_{c,L} = \mathbf{I}_w$, and thus

$$\widetilde{\mathbf{Q}}_{c,L} = \widetilde{\mathbf{D}}_{c,L} \cdot \widetilde{\mathbf{P}}_{c,L} = \widetilde{\mathbf{P}}_{c,L} \in \Sigma_w.$$

Now setting $\mathbf{Q}_r^{(1)} := \widetilde{\mathbf{Q}}_r$, $\mathbf{P}_c^{(1)} := \widetilde{\mathbf{Q}}_{c,L} = \widetilde{\mathbf{P}}_{c,L}$ and $\mathbf{Q}_c^{(1)} := \widetilde{\mathbf{Q}}_{c,R}$ it immediately follows from Equation (7) that $\mathbf{A}_2^{(1)}$ indeed has the shape as in Equation (5).

Staying in the Equivalence Class. Since the output matrices $\mathbf{A}_i^{(1)}, i \in \{1, 2\}$, are obtained by simply permuting and scaling rows and columns of the input matrices $\mathbf{A}_i$, it is clear that the corresponding matrices $\mathbf{G}_i^{(1)} := [\mathbf{I}_k \mid \mathbf{A}_i^{(1)}]$ belong to the equivalence class $[\mathbf{G}_1]_{\underset{\sim}{\mathsf{LRL}}} = [\mathbf{G}_2]_{\underset{\sim}{\mathsf{LRL}}}$, as required.

As we will see below, the remaining three steps of $\mathsf{CF}_{\mathsf{New}}$ also work by simply permuting and scaling rows and columns of the corresponding input matrices. Thus, throughout the execution of $\mathsf{CF}_{\mathsf{New}}$, we will only compute matrices $\mathbf{G}_i^{(1)}, \ldots, \mathbf{G}_i^{(4)}$ from the equivalence class $[\mathbf{G}_1]_{\underset{\sim}{\mathsf{LRL}}} = [\mathbf{G}_2]_{\underset{\sim}{\mathsf{LRL}}}$.

The Value of w. As noted in Line 9 of Algorithm 3, the parameter $w = w_1 = w_2$ is equal to the number of non-zero entries in the i-th row of our input matrix $\mathbf{A}_1$. For uniformly random $\mathbf{A}_1$ we thus have $\mathbb{E}[w] = (1 - \frac{1}{q})(n - k)$. By the Chernoff bound, w meets its expected value up to a small $(1 \pm \delta)$-factor with overwhelming probability $1 - e^{-\Omega(n-k)}$. In particular, for all $q > 2$ (and large enough $n - k$), we can safely assume that $w \geq \frac{n-k}{2}$.

4.2 Step 2

Step 2 of $\mathsf{CF}_{\mathsf{New}}$ is described in Algorithm $\mathsf{CF}_{\mathsf{New}}^{(2)}$ (Algorithm 4). After computing in Step 1 the matrix $\mathbf{A}_i^{(1)}$ and the parameter w_i, where $i \in \{1, 2\}$, our canonical form function $\mathsf{CF}_{\mathsf{New}}$ proceeds to compute $(\mathbf{A}_i^{(2)}, h_i) := \mathsf{CF}_{\mathsf{New}}^{(2)}(\mathbf{A}_i^{(1)}, w_i)$.

Relating $\mathbf{A}_1^{(1)}$ and $\mathbf{A}_2^{(1)}$. Let us introduce some notation: Let $s_2, \ldots, s_k$ denote the values computed in Line 5 of Algorithm 4, when running the algorithm on input $(\mathbf{A}_1^{(1)}, w_1)$. Analogously, let $\widetilde{s}_2, \ldots, \widetilde{s}_k$ denote these values, when running the algorithm on input $(\mathbf{A}_2^{(1)}, w_2)$. Let us write the monomial $\mathbf{Q}_r^{(1)}$ from Equation (5) as $\mathbf{Q}_r^{(1)} = \mathbf{P}_r^{(1)} \cdot \mathbf{D}_r^{(1)}$ for some permutation $\mathbf{P}_r^{(1)}$ and a diagonal matrix $\mathbf{D}_r^{(1)}$. Let $d_1, \ldots, d_{k-1}$ denote the diagonal entries of $\mathbf{D}_r^{(1)}$. For $i \in \{2, \ldots, k\}$, let $\mathbf{a}_i := (a_{i,1}, \ldots, a_{i,n-k})$ denote the i-th row $\mathbf{A}_1^{(1)}$. Let $\widetilde{\mathbf{a}}_i$ denote the i-th row of $\mathbf{A}_2^{(1)}$. Let $\pi[i] := (\mathbf{P}_r^{(1)})^T[i]$.

From Equation (5) it follows that

$$\widetilde{\mathbf{a}}_{\pi[i]} = d_{i-1} \cdot \mathbf{a}_i \cdot \begin{bmatrix} \overbrace{\mathbf{P}_c^{(1)}}^{w} & \\ & \overbrace{\mathbf{Q}_c^{(1)}}^{n-k-w} \end{bmatrix} \tag{8}$$

.

Algorithm 4: $\mathsf{CF}^{(2)}_{\mathsf{New}}$

Input: $\mathbf{A}^{(1)} \in \mathbb{F}_q^{k\times(n-k)}$, parameter $w \in [n-k]$.
Output: $\mathbf{A}^{(2)} \in \mathbb{F}_q^{k\times(n-k)}$, parameter $h \in [k-1]$.

1 $\mathbf{A}^{(2)} := \mathbf{A}^{(1)}$
2 $\mathcal{I} := \emptyset$
3 **for** $i = 2, \ldots, k$ **do**
4   Parse the i-th row of $\mathbf{A}^{(2)}$ as $(a_{i,1}, \ldots, a_{i,n-k})$.
5     $s_i := \sum_{j=1}^{w} a_{i,j}$
6   **if** $s_i \neq 0$ **then**
7   Divide all entries in the i-th row of $\mathbf{A}^{(2)}$ by s_i.
8   **else**
9         $\mathcal{I} := \mathcal{I} \cup \{i\}$
10 $h := k - |\mathcal{I}| - 1$ ▷ Number of rows of $\mathbf{A}^{(1)}$, for which $s_i \neq 0$.
11 Move all rows of $\mathbf{A}^{(2)}$ indexed by $\mathcal{I}$ to the bottom of the matrix.
12 **return** $(\mathbf{A}^{(2)}, h)$

Thus,

$$\tilde{s}_{\pi[i]} = \sum_{j=1}^{w} d_{i-1} \cdot a_{i,(\mathbf{P}_c^{(1)})^T[j]} = d_{i-1} \cdot \sum_{j=1}^{w} a_{i,j} = d_{i-1} \cdot s_i. \tag{9}$$

Hence, if $s_i = 0$, then Line 11 of $\mathsf{CF}^{(2)}_{\mathsf{New}}$ moves both the i-th row of $\mathbf{A}_1^{(1)}$ and the $\pi[i]$-th row of $\mathbf{A}_2^{(1)}$ to the bottom of $\mathbf{A}_1^{(2)}$ and $\mathbf{A}_2^{(2)}$, respectively. On the other hand, if $s_i \neq 0$, then from Equations (8) and (9) it follows that Line 7 of $\mathsf{CF}^{(2)}_{\mathsf{New}}$ replaces the $\pi[i]$-th row of $\mathbf{A}_2^{(1)}$ by

$$\frac{1}{\tilde{s}_{\pi[i]}} \cdot \tilde{\mathbf{a}}_{\pi[i]} = \frac{1}{s_i} \cdot \mathbf{a}_i \cdot \begin{bmatrix} \overbrace{\mathbf{P}_c^{(1)}}^{w} & \overbrace{\phantom{\mathbf{Q}_c^{(1)}}}^{n-k-w} \\ & \mathbf{Q}_c^{(1)} \end{bmatrix},$$

whereas the i-th row of $\mathbf{A}_1^{(1)}$ gets replaced by

$$\frac{1}{s_i} \cdot \mathbf{a}_i.$$

This shows that for all i with $s_i \neq 0$ in the resulting matrices $\mathbf{A}_1^{(2)}$ and $\mathbf{A}_2^{(2)}$, the first w entries of the rows obtained from $\mathbf{a}_i$ and $\tilde{\mathbf{a}}_{\pi[i]}$ are *identical up to permutation.*

Let us define $h := h_1$. Since h_1 is the number of rows of $\mathbf{A}^{(1)}$, for which $s_i \neq 0$ (see Line 5 of Algorithm 4), we have by Equation (9) that $h = h_1 = h_2$. Let us write $\mathbf{A}_2^{(2)}$ as

$$\mathbf{A}_1^{(2)} = \begin{matrix} 1 \\ h \\ k-h-1 \end{matrix}\left\{\begin{bmatrix} \overbrace{1,1,\ldots,1}^{w} & \overbrace{0,0,\ldots,0}^{n-k-w} \\ \mathbf{A}_{1,1}^{(2)} & \mathbf{A}_{1,2}^{(2)} \\ \mathbf{A}_{1,3}^{(2)} & \mathbf{A}_{1,4}^{(2)} \end{bmatrix}\right., \tag{10}$$

for some matrices $\mathbf{A}_{1,1}^{(2)}, \ldots, \mathbf{A}_{1,4}^{(2)}$. By the discussion above, we have

$$\mathbf{A}_2^{(2)} = \begin{matrix} 1 \\ h \\ k-h-1 \end{matrix}\left\{\begin{bmatrix} \overbrace{1,1,\ldots,1}^{w} & \overbrace{0,0,\ldots,0}^{n-k-w} \\ \mathbf{P}_r^{(2)} \cdot \mathbf{A}_{1,1}^{(2)} \cdot \mathbf{P}_c^{(2)} & \mathbf{P}_r^{(2)} \cdot \mathbf{A}_{1,2}^{(2)} \cdot \mathbf{Q}_c^{(2)} \\ \mathbf{Q}_r^{(2)} \cdot \mathbf{A}_{1,3}^{(2)} \cdot \mathbf{P}_c^{(2)} & \mathbf{Q}_r^{(2)} \cdot \mathbf{A}_{1,4}^{(2)} \cdot \mathbf{Q}_c^{(2)} \end{bmatrix}\right., \tag{11}$$

for some monomials $\mathbf{Q}_r^{(2)}, \mathbf{Q}_c^{(2)}$ and permutations $\mathbf{P}_r^{(2)}, \mathbf{P}_c^{(2)}$. In other words, the upper left $((h+1) \times w)$-blocks of $\mathbf{A}_1^{(2)}$ and $\mathbf{A}_2^{(2)}$ are identical up to row and column permutation.

The Value of h. As noted in Line 5 of Algorithm 4, the parameter $h = h_1 = h_2$ is equal to the number of rows of $\mathbf{A}^{(1)}$, for which $s_i \neq 0$. It is easy to see that for uniformly random inputs $\mathbf{A}_1$ to $\mathsf{CF}_{\mathsf{New}}^{(1)}$, the second to k-th rows of the outputs $\mathbf{A}_1^{(1)}$ are still uniformly random. Hence, the s_i's computed by $\mathsf{CF}_{\mathsf{New}}^{(2)}$ are uniformly random over $\mathbb{F}_q$, and we have $\mathbb{E}[h] = (1 - \frac{1}{q})(k-1)$. Arguing exactly as for the parameter w in the previous section, it follows that for all $q > 2$ (and large enough k), we can safely assume that $h \geq \frac{k-1}{2}$.

4.3 Step 3

As shown in the previous section, the upper left $((h+1) \times w)$-blocks of the matrices $\mathbf{A}_1^{(2)}$ and $\mathbf{A}_2^{(2)}$ obtained from $\mathsf{CF}_{\mathsf{New}}^{(2)}$ are identical up to row and column permutation. This observation lets us now easily transform $\mathbf{A}_1^{(2)}$ and $\mathbf{A}_2^{(2)}$ via a simple sorting procedure into matrices $\mathbf{A}_1^{(3)}$ and $\mathbf{A}_2^{(3)}$, in which the upper left $((h+1) \times w)$-blocks are *identical*. More precisely, we can easily compute matrices of the forms

$$\mathbf{A}_1^{(3)} = \begin{array}{r} 1\{ \\ h\{ \\ k-h-1\{ \end{array} \begin{bmatrix} \overbrace{1,1,\ldots,1}^{w} & \overbrace{0,0,\ldots,0}^{n-k-w} \\ \mathbf{A}_{1,1}^{(3)} & \mathbf{A}_{1,2}^{(3)} \\ \mathbf{A}_{1,3}^{(3)} & \mathbf{A}_{1,4}^{(3)} \end{bmatrix}, \tag{12}$$

$$\mathbf{A}_2^{(3)} = \begin{array}{r} 1\{ \\ h\{ \\ k-h-1\{ \end{array} \begin{bmatrix} \overbrace{1,1,\ldots,1}^{w} & \overbrace{0,0,\ldots,0}^{n-k-w} \\ \mathbf{A}_{1,1}^{(3)} & \mathbf{A}_{1,2}^{(3)} \cdot \mathbf{Q}_c^{(3)} \\ \mathbf{Q}_r^{(3)} \cdot \mathbf{A}_{1,3}^{(3)} & \mathbf{Q}_r^{(3)} \cdot \mathbf{A}_{1,4}^{(3)} \cdot \mathbf{Q}_c^{(3)} \end{bmatrix}, \tag{13}$$

Our sorting procedure is described in Algorithm $\mathsf{CF}_{\mathsf{New}}^{(3)}$ (Algorithm 5). From Equations (10) and (11), and the fact that multisets are invariant under permutations, it immediately follows that for $\mathbf{A}_i^{(3)} := \mathsf{CF}_{\mathsf{New}}^{(3)}(\mathbf{A}_i^{(2)}, w_i, h_i)$, $i \in \{1, 2\}$ the outputs $\mathbf{A}_i^{(3)}$ indeed have the desired shape as in Equations (12) and (13) – provided, of course, that $\mathsf{CF}_{\mathsf{New}}^{(3)}$ does not return $\perp$ in Line 9 . Fortunately, as we show below, for all fields of size of $q \geq 7$, the probability of $\mathsf{CF}_{\mathsf{New}}^{(3)}$ not returning $\perp$ is close to 1.

Success Probability. Let us call a matrix is *permutation-free*, if it does not contain a pair of two rows or columns that are identical up to permutation. Then the probability that $\mathsf{CF}_{\mathsf{New}}^{(3)}$ does not return $\perp$ on input $\mathbf{A}_i^{(2)}$ is the probability that the matrix $\mathbf{A}_{1,1}^{(2)}$ from Equation (10) is permutation free. To compute this probability, we need the following technical lemma, which is a direct consequence of [RS09, Theorem 4].

Lemma 4.1. *Let $\mathcal{S} \subseteq \mathbb{F}_q^n$ with $|\mathcal{S}| = \Theta(q^n)$. Let P denote the probability that two independent, uniformly random vectors $\mathbf{v}_1, \mathbf{v}_2 \leftarrow \mathcal{S}$ are identical up to permutation. If $q \geq 7$, then $P = \mathcal{O}(n^{-3})$.*

Proof. Clearly, the larger q, the smaller P. Thus, to prove the upper bound of $P = \mathcal{O}(n^{-3})$ for all $q \geq 7$, it suffices to prove it for the special case of $q = 7$.

Let $\mathcal{A}_7(n)$ denote the set of *abelian squares* over $\mathbb{F}_7^n \times \mathbb{F}_7^n$, i.e., let $\mathcal{A}_7(n)$ denote the set of all tuples $(\mathbf{w}_1, \mathbf{w}_2) \in \mathbb{F}_7^n \times \mathbb{F}_7^n$, where $\mathbf{w}_1$ is a permutation of $\mathbf{w}_2$. Then

$$P = \Pr[(\mathbf{v}_1, \mathbf{v}_2) \in \mathcal{A}_7(n)] = \frac{|\mathcal{A}_7(n) \cap (\mathcal{S} \times \mathcal{S})|}{|\mathcal{S} \times \mathcal{S}|} \leq \frac{|\mathcal{A}_7(n)|}{|\mathcal{S} \times \mathcal{S}|} = \frac{|\mathcal{A}_7(n)|}{|\mathcal{S}|^2}.$$

Algorithm 5: $\mathsf{CF}^{(3)}_{\mathsf{New}}$

Input: $\mathbf{A}^{(2)} \in \mathbb{F}_q^{k\times(n-k)}$, parameters $w \in [n-k]$, $h \in [k-1]$.
Output: $\mathbf{A}^{(3)} \in \mathbb{F}_q^{k\times(n-k)}$, or error symbol $\perp$.

$\mathbf{A}^{(3)} := \mathbf{A}^{(2)}$
for $i = 2, \ldots, h+1$ **do**
  Parse the i-th row of $\mathbf{A}^{(3)}$ as $(a_{i,1}, \ldots, a_{i,n-k})$.
  Let R_i denote the multiset $(a_{i,1}, \ldots, a_{i,w})$.
for $j = 1, \ldots, w$ **do**
  Parse the j-th column of $\mathbf{A}^{(3)}$ as $(a_{1,j}, \ldots, a_{k,j})^T$.
  Let C_j denote the multiset $(a_{2,j}, \ldots, a_{h+1,j})$.
if the R_i's or the C_j's are not pairwise distinct **then**
  return $\perp$
Sort the 2nd to $(h+1)$-th rows of $\mathbf{A}^{(3)}$ according to an lexicographic ordering of the multisets $R_2, \ldots, R_{h+1}$.
Sort the 1st to w-th columns of $\mathbf{A}^{(3)}$ according to an lexicographic ordering of the multisets $C_1, \ldots, C_w$.
return $\mathbf{A}^{(3)}$

As shown in [RS09, Theorem 4],

$$|\mathcal{A}_7(n)| \sim 7^{2n+7/2} \cdot (4\pi n)^{(1-7)/2} = \mathcal{O}(7^{2n} \cdot n^{-3}).$$

Hence $P = \mathcal{O}\left(7^{2n} \cdot |\mathcal{S}|^{-2} \cdot n^{-3}\right) = \mathcal{O}(n^{-3})$, as required. □

By Lines 5 and 7 of Algorithm 4, the rows of our matrix $\mathbf{A}^{(2)}_{1,1} \in \mathbb{F}_q^{h\times w}$ are sampled independently and uniformly random from

$$\mathcal{S}_q^{(1)}(w) := \left\{(v_1, \ldots, v_w) \in \mathbb{F}_q^w \mid v_1 + \ldots + v_w = 1\right\}.$$

Using Lemma 4.1, we now show that such a matrix is permutation-free with probability at least $1 - \mathcal{O}\left(h^2 w^{-3} + w^2 h^{-3}\right)$.

Lemma 4.2. *Let $\mathbf{B} \in \mathbb{F}_q^{h\times w}$ be matrix whose rows sampled independently and uniformly random from $\mathcal{S}_q^{(1)}(w)$. If $q \geq 7$, then $\mathbf{B}$ is permutation-free with probability at least $1 - \mathcal{O}\left(h^2 w^{-3} + w^2 h^{-3}\right)$.*

Proof. Let $\mathbf{r}_1, \ldots, \mathbf{r}_h \in \mathbb{F}_q^w$ be the rows of $\mathbf{B}$, and let $\mathbf{c}_1 \ldots, \mathbf{c}_w \in \mathbb{F}_q^h$ be (the transposes of) the columns of $\mathbf{B}$. Using Lemma 4.1, we show below that for any pair $i \neq j$, it holds that

$$\Pr\left[\mathbf{r}_i, \mathbf{r}_j \text{ are identical up to permutation}\right] = \mathcal{O}(w^{-3}), \tag{14}$$

and

$$\Pr\left[\mathbf{c}_i, \mathbf{c}_j \text{ are identical up to permutation}\right] = \mathcal{O}(h^{-3}). \tag{15}$$

By a union bound over the $\mathcal{O}(h^2)$ pairs of rows and $\mathcal{O}(w^2)$ pairs of columns, the lemma then immediately follows.

Proof for Equation (14): Since $|\mathcal{S}_q^{(1)}(w)| = q^{w-1} = \Theta(q^w)$, we can apply Lemma 4.1 to any pair of rows $\mathbf{r}_i, \mathbf{r}_j$, and Equation (14) immediately follows.

Proof for Equation (15): We show that the columns are *pairwise* independent and uniformly random over $\mathbb{F}_q^h$. This allows us to apply Lemma 4.1 to any pair of columns $\mathbf{c}_i, \mathbf{c}_j$, and Equation (14) immediately follows. Since the rows of $\mathbf{B}$ are drawn independently and uniformly random from $\mathcal{S}_q^{(1)}(w)$, the distribution of the columns is as follows:

1. Sample $\mathbf{c}_1, \ldots, \mathbf{c}_{w-1}$ independently and uniformly at random from $\mathbb{F}_q^h$.
2. Set $\mathbf{c}_w := \mathbf{1}^h - \sum_{i=1}^{w-1} \mathbf{c}_i$.

Hence, even though the columns are obviously dependent when viewed *together*, any subset of at most $w-1$ columns consists of *mutually* independent and uniformly distributed random vectors from $\mathbb{F}_q^h$. In particular, if $w > 2$, the columns are *pairwise* independent and uniformly random over $\mathbb{F}_q^h$, as required. □

From Lemma 4.2, we now can easily derive the success probability of $\mathsf{CF}^{(3)}_{\mathsf{New}}$.

Lemma 4.3. *Let* $(\mathbf{A}^{(1)}, w)$ *be obtained by running* $\mathsf{CF}^{(1)}_{\mathsf{New}}$ *on a uniformly random matrix* $\mathbf{A} \leftarrow \mathbb{F}_q^{k\times(n-k)}$, *and let* $(\mathbf{A}^{(2)}, h) := \mathsf{CF}^{(2)}_{\mathsf{New}}(\mathbf{A}^{(1)}, w)$. *For all* $q \geq 7$ *and constant rate* $\frac{k}{n}$, *we have*

$$\Pr\left[\mathsf{CF}^{(3)}_{\mathsf{New}}(\mathbf{A}^{(2)}, w, h) \neq \bot\right] = 1 - \mathcal{O}(n^{-1}).$$

Proof. By construction, we can upper bound w and h by $w \leq n-k$ and $h \leq k-1$. As discussed in the previous two sections, with overwhelming probabilities $1 - e^{-\Omega(n-k)}$ and $1 - e^{-\Omega(k)}$, we can lower bound w and h by $w \geq \frac{n-k}{2}$ and $h \geq \frac{k-1}{2}$. Thus, for constant rate, where $k = \Theta(n)$ and $n - k = \Theta(n)$, we have $w = \Theta(n)$ and $h = \Theta(n)$ with probability $1 - e^{-\Omega(n)}$. Together with Lemma 4.2, this concludes the proof. □

4.4 Step 4

By Equations (12) and (13), the upper left $((h+1)\times w)$-blocks of the matrices $\mathbf{A}_1^{(3)}$ and $\mathbf{A}_2^{(3)}$ obtained from $\mathsf{CF}^{(3)}_{\mathsf{New}}$ are identical. Additionally, the upper right $((h+1)\times(n-k-w))$-blocks are identical up to a monomial transformation *from the right.* The lower left $((k-h-1)\times w)$-blocks are identical up to a monomial transformation *from the left.* Dealing with monomials that act *only on one side* of the matrix is much easier, than dealing with monomials that act on both sides (as we had to in the previous three sections). Indeed, if we now appropriately divide the $(w+1)$-th to $(n-k)$-th columns, and the $(h+2)$-th to k-th rows of our matrices, we can easily turn them into matrices that are identical up to row and column permutation. After that, we simply invoke our algorithm from Step 3 once more to sort our matrices. Thereby, we finally obtain *identical* matrices $\mathbf{A}_2^{(4)} = \mathbf{A}_1^{(1)}$.

Our approach is formally described in Algorithm $\mathsf{CF}_{\mathsf{New}}^{(4)}$ (Algorithm 6). It is easy to see that its output has the desired shape, i.e., for $\mathbf{A}_i^{(4)} := \mathsf{CF}_{\mathsf{New}}^{(4)}(\mathbf{A}_i^{(3)}, w_i, h_i)$ we have $\mathbf{A}_2^{(4)} = \mathbf{A}_1^{(1)}$ – provided that the algorithm does not return $\perp$.

Algorithm 6: $\mathsf{CF}_{\mathsf{New}}^{(4)}$

Input: $\mathbf{A}^{(3)} \in \mathbb{F}_q^{k \times (n-k)}$, parameters $w \in [n-k]$, $h \in [k-1]$.
Output: $\mathbf{A}^{(4)} \in \mathbb{F}_q^{k \times (n-k)}$, or error symbol $\perp$.

1 $\mathbf{A}^{(4)} := \mathbf{A}^{(3)}$
2 $\mathcal{J} := \{w+1, w+2, \ldots, n-k\}$
3 $\mathcal{I} := \{h+2, h+3, \ldots, k\}$
4 **for** $i = 2, \ldots, h+1$ **do**
5   Parse the i-th row of $\mathbf{A}^{(4)}$ as $(a_{i,1}, \ldots, a_{i,n-k})$.
6   **for** $j \in \mathcal{J}$ **do**
7   **if** $a_{i,j} \neq 0$ **then**
8   Divide the j-th column of $\mathbf{A}^{(4)}$ by $a_{i,j}$.
9   Remove j from $\mathcal{J}$.
10 **for** $j = 1, \ldots, w$ **do**
11   Parse the j-th column of $\mathbf{A}^{(4)}$ as $(a_{1,j}, \ldots, a_{k,j})^T$.
12   **for** $i \in \mathcal{I}$ **do**
13   **if** $a_{i,j} \neq 0$ **then**
14   Divide the i-th row of $\mathbf{A}^{(4)}$ by $a_{i,j}$.
15   Remove i from $\mathcal{I}$.
16 **if** $\mathcal{J} \neq \emptyset$ or $\mathcal{I} \neq \emptyset$ **then**
17   **return** $\perp$
18 $\mathbf{A}^{(3)} := \mathsf{CF}_{\mathsf{New}}^{(3)}(\mathbf{A}^{(3)}, n-k, k)$
19 **return** $\mathbf{A}^{(3)}$

Success Probability. The probability that Algorithm 6 aborts in Line 17 is exponentially small. (The algorithm aborts here only if one of the uniformly random matrices $\mathbf{A}_{1,2}^{(3)}$, $\mathbf{A}_{1,3}^{(3)}$ from Equation (12) contains an all-zero row or column.) Furthermore, using arguments analogous to the proofs of Lemmas 4.2 and 4.3, one can easily show that the probability that Algorithm 6 aborts in Line 18 is upper bounded by $\mathcal{O}(n^{-1})$. Hence, with probability $1 - \mathcal{O}(n^{-1})$ the output of $\mathsf{CF}_{\mathsf{New}}^{(4)}$ indeed has the desired shape.

4.5 Putting Everything Together

We are now almost ready to fully describe our novel canonical form function. The only thing left to do, is describing how to pick the inputs i_1 and i_2, in Step 1. (Recall that in Step 1, we want compute $(\mathbf{A}_1^{(1)}, w_1) := \mathsf{CF}^{(1)}_{\mathsf{New}}(\mathbf{A}_1, i_1)$ and $(\mathbf{A}_2^{(1)}, w_2) := \mathsf{CF}^{(1)}_{\mathsf{New}}(\mathbf{A}_2, i_2)$, where $i_2 = \mathbf{P}_r^T[i_1]$, and $\mathbf{P}_r$ is the permutation from Equation (4).) To this end, we re-use an idea by CPS: On input $\mathbf{G}_1 = [\mathbf{I}_k \mid \mathbf{A}_1]$, we iterate over all values $i_1 = 1, 2, \ldots, k$. For each i_1, we run Steps 1 to 4, such that in the end we obtain a list L_1 of (up to) k matrices from the equivalence class $[\mathbf{G}_1]_{\underset{\sim}{\mathsf{LRL}}}$. We sort L_1 lexicographically and then output the first entry. Analogously, on input $\mathbf{G}_2 = [\mathbf{I}_k \mid \mathbf{A}_2]$, we iterate over all values $i_2 = 1, 2, \ldots, k$ to obtain a list of matrices L_2. For any i_1, the i_1-th entry in L_1 is then identical to the $\mathbf{P}_r^T[i_1]$-th entry in L_2. Hence, by lexicographically sorting L_1 and L_2, we output the same representative from the equivalence class $[\mathbf{G}_1]_{\underset{\sim}{\mathsf{LRL}}} = [\mathbf{G}_2]_{\underset{\sim}{\mathsf{LRL}}}$. The full description of $\mathsf{CF}_{\mathsf{New}}$ is given in Algorithm 7.

Algorithm 7: $\mathsf{CF}_{\mathsf{New}}$

Input: $\mathbf{G} = [\mathbf{I}_k \mid \mathbf{A}] \in \mathbb{F}_q^{k \times n}$
Output: Canonical representative $\mathbf{G}^* = [\mathbf{I}_k \mid \mathbf{A}^*]$ of $[\mathbf{G}]_{\underset{\sim}{\mathsf{LRL}}}$, or error symbol $\perp$.

Initialize empty list L.
for $i = 1, \ldots, k$ **do**
  $(\mathbf{A}^{(1)}, w) := \mathsf{CF}^{(1)}_{\mathsf{New}}(\mathbf{A}, i)$
  $(\mathbf{A}^{(2)}, h) := \mathsf{CF}^{(2)}_{\mathsf{New}}(\mathbf{A}^{(1)}, w)$
  $\mathbf{A}^{(3)} := \mathsf{CF}^{(3)}_{\mathsf{New}}(\mathbf{A}^{(2)}, w, h)$
  if $\mathbf{A}^{(3)} \neq \perp$ **then**
    $\mathbf{A}^{(4)} := \mathsf{CF}^{(4)}_{\mathsf{New}}(\mathbf{A}^{(3)}, w, h)$
    if $\mathbf{A}^{(4)} \neq \perp$ **then**
      Add $[\mathbf{I}_k \mid \mathbf{A}^{(4)}]$ to L.
if L is not empty **then**
  return the lexicographically first entry in L.
else
  return $\perp$

We remark that Definition 3.2 technically requires a canonical form function not only to output both a canonoical representative $\mathbf{G}^* = [\mathbf{I}_k \mid \mathbf{A}^*] \in [\mathbf{G}]_{\underset{\sim}{\mathsf{LRL}}}$, but also to output monomials $\mathbf{Q}_r, \mathbf{Q}_c$, satisfying $\mathbf{A}^* = \mathbf{Q}_r \cdot \mathbf{A} \cdot \mathbf{Q}_c$. For ease of notation, we omit these monomials in the description of Algorithm 7. In practice, the monomials can easily be computed. To this end, one simply has to keep track of the monomial transformations made by $\mathsf{CF}^{(1)}_{\mathsf{New}}, \ldots, \mathsf{CF}^{(4)}_{\mathsf{New}}$. (See also our SageMath implementation, available on GitHub.)

Summarizing the above four sections, we finally obtain the following theorem:

Theorem 4.4 (Correctness $\mathsf{CF}_{\mathsf{New}}$). *For all $q \geq 7$ and constant rate $\frac{k}{n}$, the canonical form function $\mathsf{CF}_{\mathsf{New}}$ has success probability*

$$\gamma_{\mathsf{CF}_{\mathsf{New}}}(n,k,q) = \Pr_{\mathbf{A} \leftarrow \mathbb{F}_q^{k\times(n-k)}}\left[\mathsf{CF}_{\mathsf{New}}([\mathbf{I}_k \mid \mathbf{A}]) \neq \perp\right] \geq 1 - \mathcal{O}(n^{-1}).$$

Combining Theorems 3.6 and 4.4, our main result follows:

Theorem 4.5 (Main Result). *For all $q \geq 7$ and constant rate $\frac{k}{n}$, there is an algorithm that solves \$-LEP with parameters (n,k,q) in time $\widetilde{\Theta}\left(2^{\frac{1}{2}\mathrm{H}(\frac{k}{n})n}\right)$, and with constant success probability.*

5 Experiments

In addition to the asymptotic results from Theorem 4.4, we now want to conclude the paper by determining the concrete success probability of our new canonical form function $\mathsf{CF}_{\mathsf{New}}$ (Algorithm 7). To this end, we implemented our canonical form function in SageMath and ran it on various inputs $\mathbf{G} = [\mathbf{I}_k \mid \mathbf{A}] \in \mathbb{F}_q^{k\times n}$ with uniformly random $\mathbf{A}$. Our implementation is publicly available at

https://github.com/juliannowakowski/lep-cf

In our experiments, we used the following parameters:

- $q \in \{5, 7, 8, 9\}$,
- $n \in \{50, 60, 70, 80, 90, 100\}$,
- $k \in \{0.1n, 0.2n, 0.3n, 0.4n, 0.5n\}$.

Results. We ran our implementation for each combination of (q,n,k) on 50 random instances. The results are in shown in Fig. 3. As Fig. 3 shows, our asymptotic success probability $1 - \mathcal{O}(n^{-1})$ from Theorem 4.4 converges quickly to 1. In particular, for the most important setting of code rate $\frac{k}{n} = \frac{1}{2}$, $\mathsf{CF}_{\mathsf{New}}$ even has success probability 1 – showing that our novel canonical form function $\mathsf{CF}_{\mathsf{New}}$ performs very well in practice.

Choice of Parameters. We did not consider field sizes $q \leq 4$, as LEP over such small fields is easy (due to support splitting). Furthermore, we did not include experiments for larger $q > 9$, as the success probability of $\mathsf{CF}_{\mathsf{New}}$ gets better the larger q, and we already achieved high success probabilities for our small q's with $q \leq 9$. As discussed in Sect. 2, restricting ourselves to rates $\frac{k}{n} \leq \frac{1}{2}$ is without loss of generality.

The Case of $q = 5$. In our theoretical analysis, we could prove the asymptotic success probability $1 - \mathcal{O}(n^{-1})$ of $\mathsf{CF}_{\mathsf{New}}$ for all $q \geq 7$. However, as Fig. 3 shows, $\mathsf{CF}_{\mathsf{New}}$ has even for $q = 5$ a decent success probability (provided the code rate is not extremely small). This phenomenon is due to the fact that we had to resort to a somewhat coarse union bound in the proof of Lemma 4.2, which lead to a slight underestimate in success probability.

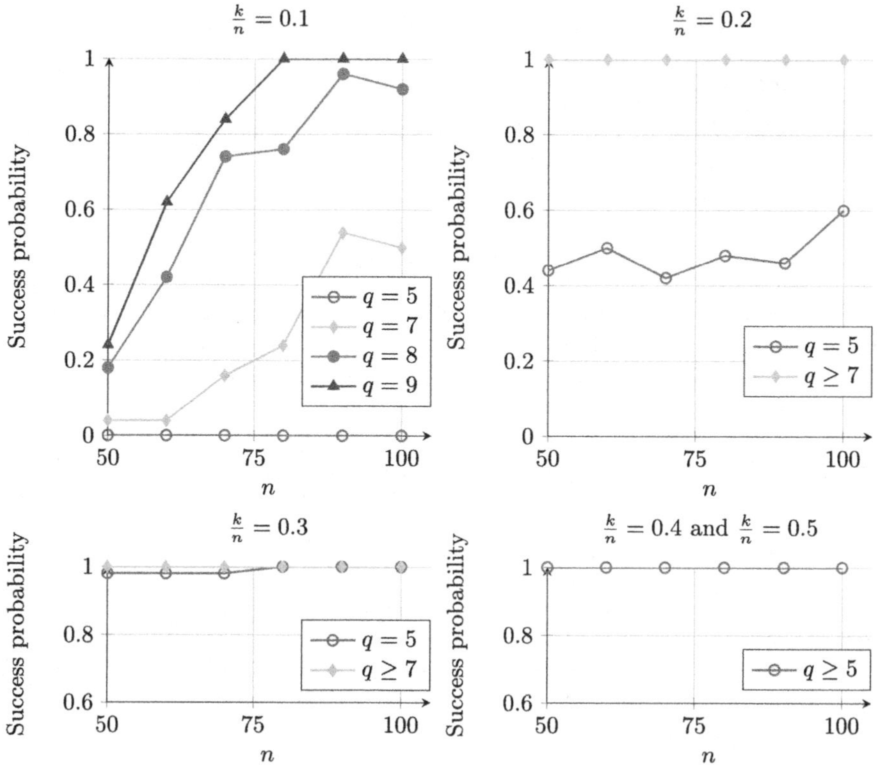

Fig. 3. Performance of $\mathsf{CF}_{\mathsf{New}}$ on 50 random inputs for each combination of (n, k, q).

Convergence Speed. For the extremely small code rate of $\frac{k}{n} = 0.1$, Fig. 3 shows a slightly slower converge speed, than for larger code rates $\frac{k}{n} \geq 0.2$. This phenomenon can be explained as follows: In Sect. 4, we used Lemma 4.2 to show that $\mathsf{CF}_{\mathsf{New}}$ has success probability at least

$$1 - \left(\mathcal{O}\left(\frac{k^2}{(n-k)^3}\right) + \mathcal{O}\left(\frac{(n-k)^2}{k^3}\right)\right) = 1 - \mathcal{O}(n^{-1}),$$

For $k = 0.1n$, we have $\frac{(n-k)^2}{k^3} = 810 \cdot n^{-1}$. Hence, for small code rates, the $\mathcal{O}(n^{-1})$-term hides a rather large constant, thereby leading to slower convergence.

Nevertheless, we like to stress that even for very small $n = 50$ and $q = 7$, we already obtain a non-zero success probability. In particular, it follows that for cryptographically-sized parameters (which use n in the order of a few hundreds), $\mathsf{CF}_{\mathsf{New}}$ works very well in practice.

Acknowledgements. The author is grateful to the anonymous PQCrypto reviewers for catching a mistake in a proof in an earlier version of this paper. The author is funded by Deutsche Forschungsgemeinschaft (DFG, German Research Foundation) grant 465120249.

A Appendix: Additional Proofs

A.1 Lemma 2.5

Lemma 2.3. *Let $X_1, \ldots, X_n \in \{0,1\}$ denote (possibly dependent) random variables. Let $p \in [0,1]$, such that $\Pr[X_i = 1] \geq p$ for every $i \in [n]$. Then for $X := \sum_{i=1}^{n} X_i$ it holds that*

$$\Pr\left[X > \frac{p}{2} \cdot n\right] \geq \frac{p}{2}.$$

Proof. For $p = 1$, the statement is trivial. Thus, without loss of generality, we may assume that $p < 1$. Let us define $Y := n - X$. Using $\mathbb{E}[Y] = n - \mathbb{E}[X] \leq (1-p) \cdot n$, and applying Markov's inequality to the non-negative random variable Y, we obtain

$$\Pr\left[Y \geq \left(1 - \frac{p}{2}\right) \cdot n\right] \leq \Pr\left[Y \geq \frac{1 - \frac{p}{2}}{1-p} \cdot \mathbb{E}[Y]\right] \leq \frac{1-p}{1-\frac{p}{2}} = 1 - \frac{p}{2-p} \leq 1 - \frac{p}{2},$$

and conversely

$$\Pr\left[X > \frac{p}{2} \cdot n\right] = \Pr\left[Y < \left(1 - \frac{p}{2}\right) \cdot n\right] \geq \frac{p}{2},$$

as required. □

A.2 Lemma 2.6

Lemma 2.4. *Let q be a prime power and let $k \in \mathbb{N}$. A uniformly random matrix $\mathbf{A} \leftarrow \mathbb{F}_q^{k \times k}$ is invertible with probability greater than $\frac{1}{4}$.*

Proof. Suppose we sample $m \leq k$ vectors $\mathbf{v}_1, \ldots, \mathbf{v}_m \in \mathbb{F}_q^k$ independently and uniformly at random. Using induction over m, one can easily show that the linear subspace generated by the vectors $\mathbf{v}_1, \ldots, \mathbf{v}_m$ has dimension m with probability exactly $\prod_{i=0}^{m-1}(1 - q^{i-k})$. It follows that a uniformly random matrix $\mathbf{A} \in \mathbb{F}_q^{k \times k}$ is invertible with probability

$$\prod_{i=0}^{k-1}(1 - q^{i-k}) = \prod_{i=1}^{k}(1 - q^{-i}) > \prod_{i=1}^{\infty}(1 - q^{-i}) \geq \prod_{i=1}^{\infty}(1 - 2^{-i}).$$

By Euler's pentagonal number theorem, the product $\prod_{i=1}^{\infty}(1 - 2^{-i})$ is equal to

$$\prod_{i=1}^{\infty}(1 - 2^{-i}) = \sum_{i=-\infty}^{\infty} \frac{(-1)^i}{2^{(3i^2-i)/2}} = 1 - \frac{1}{2} - \frac{1}{2^2} + \frac{1}{2^5} + \frac{1}{2^7} - \ldots,$$

which lets us lower bound it as

$$\prod_{i=1}^{\infty}(1 - 2^{-i}) \geq 1 - \frac{1}{2} - \frac{1}{2^2} + \frac{1}{2^5} + \frac{1}{2^7} - \sum_{n=8}^{\infty} \frac{1}{2^n} = \frac{9}{32} > \frac{1}{4},$$

and thus proves the lemma. □

A.3 Lemma 3.4

Lemma 3.4. (Adapted from Proposition 11 in *[CPS23]***).** *Let* $\mathbf{G}_1 \sim \mathbf{G}_2$ *be an LEP instance, and let* CF *be a canonical form function. Let* J_1, J_2 *be* CF*-colliding information sets for* $(\mathbf{G}_1, \mathbf{G}_2)$*. On input* $\mathbf{G}_1, \mathbf{G}_2, J_1, J_2$*, algorithm* $\mathsf{RecoverMon}^{\mathsf{CF}(\cdot)}$ *(Algorithm 1) computes a solution* $\mathbf{U} \in \mathrm{GL}(\mathbb{F}_q^k)$*,* $\mathbf{Q} \in \mathcal{M}_{n,q}$ *to the LEP instance defined by* $\mathbf{G}_1$ *and* $\mathbf{G}_2$ *in polynomial time.*

Proof. Algorithm 1 starts by computing $\mathbf{G}'_i := \mathsf{RREF}(\mathbf{G}_i \cdot \mathbf{P}^{J_i}) \in \mathbb{F}_q^{k \times (n-k)}$. Since the J_i's are information sets, we have $\mathbf{G}'_i = [\mathbf{I}_k \mid \mathbf{A}_i]$, where

$$\mathbf{A}_i = (\mathbf{G}_i^{J_i})^{-1} \cdot \mathbf{G}_i^{\overline{J_i}} \in \mathbb{F}_q^{k \times (n-k)}. \tag{16}$$

In particular, since the $\mathbf{G}_i$'s are in systematic form, they are valid inputs for CF. (Recall that CF is only defined for inputs in systematic form, see Definition 3.2.) Since the J_i's are CF-colliding, we have $\mathsf{CF}(\mathbf{G}'_i) \neq \perp$. Hence, in Line 2, Algorithm 1 indeed obtains a tuple $(\mathbf{G}^*_i, \mathbf{Q}_{r,i}, \mathbf{Q}_{c,i})$ from the ouptput of CF. By Definition 3.2, we have

$$\mathbf{G}^*_i = [\mathbf{I}_k \mid \mathbf{A}^*_i], \quad \text{for } \mathbf{A}^*_i = \mathbf{Q}_{r,i} \cdot \mathbf{A}_i \cdot \mathbf{Q}_{c,i},$$

Moreover, we have by Definition 3.2 that $\mathbf{A}^*_1 = \mathbf{A}^*_2$, and thus

$$\mathbf{A}_2 = \mathbf{Q}_{r,2}^{-1} \cdot \mathbf{Q}_{r,1} \cdot \mathbf{A}_1 \cdot \mathbf{Q}_{c,1} \cdot \mathbf{Q}_{c,2}^{-1}. \tag{17}$$

Let $\mathbf{U} \in \mathrm{GL}(\mathbb{F}_q^k)$ and $\mathbf{Q} \in \mathcal{M}_{n,q}$ denote the matrices computed by Algorithm 1. (We have $\mathbf{U} \in \mathrm{GL}(\mathbb{F}_q^k)$, since the J_i's are information sets. Furthermore, we have $\mathbf{Q} \in \mathcal{M}_{n,q}$, since the $\mathbf{P}^{J_i} \in \Sigma_n \subseteq \mathcal{M}_{n,q}$'s are monomials.) A tedious but straight-forward computation shows that

$$\mathbf{U} \cdot \mathbf{G}_1 \cdot \mathbf{Q} = \mathbf{G}_2^{J_2} \cdot [\mathbf{I}_k \mid \mathbf{Q}_{r,2}^{-1} \cdot \mathbf{Q}_{r,1} \cdot (\mathbf{G}_1^{J_1})^{-1} \cdot \mathbf{G}_1^{\overline{J_1}} \cdot \mathbf{Q}_{c,1} \cdot \mathbf{Q}_{c,2}^{-1}] \cdot (\mathbf{P}^{J_2})^{-1}.$$

Using Equations (16) and (17), one can simplify the above equation as

$$\mathbf{U} \cdot \mathbf{G}_1 \cdot \mathbf{Q} = \mathbf{G}_2,$$

which shows that $\mathbf{U}$ and $\mathbf{Q}$ form a solution to the LEP instance defined by $\mathbf{G}_1$ and $\mathbf{G}_2$. Since Algorithm 1 clearly runs in polynomial time, this proves the lemma. □

A.4 Lemma 3.5

Lemma 3.5. *Let* $\mathbf{G}_1 \sim \mathbf{G}_2 \in \mathbb{F}_q^{k \times n}$ *be linearly equivalent matrices, where*

$$\mathbf{G}_2 = \mathbf{U} \cdot \mathbf{G}_1 \cdot \mathbf{P} \cdot \mathbf{D},$$

for some $\mathbf{U} \in \mathrm{GL}(\mathbb{F}_q^k)$*,* $\mathbf{P} \in \Sigma_n$ *and* $\mathbf{D} \in \mathcal{D}_{n,q}$*. Let* J_1 *be an information set of* $\mathbf{G}_1$*. Then* $J_2 := \mathbf{P}[J_1]$ *is an information set of* $\mathbf{G}_2$*, and it holds that*

$$\mathsf{RREF}(\mathbf{G}_1 \cdot \mathbf{P}^{J_1}) \overset{\mathsf{LRL}}{\sim} \mathsf{RREF}(\mathbf{G}_2 \cdot \mathbf{P}^{J_2}).$$

Proof. By definition of J_2, we have

$$\mathbf{G}_1 \cdot \mathbf{P} \cdot \mathbf{Q} \cdot \mathbf{P}^{J_2} = \left[\mathbf{G}^{J_1} \cdot \mathbf{Q}_r \mid \mathbf{G}^{\overline{J_1}} \cdot \mathbf{Q}_c\right]$$

for some $\mathbf{Q}_r \in \mathcal{M}_{k,q}$ and $\mathbf{Q}_c \in \mathcal{M}_{n-k,q}$. Since RREF is invariant under invertible transformations from the left, this shows that

$$\begin{aligned}\mathsf{RREF}(\mathbf{G}_2 \cdot \mathbf{P}^{J_2}) &= \mathsf{RREF}(\mathbf{U} \cdot \mathbf{G}_1 \cdot \mathbf{P} \cdot \mathbf{D} \cdot \mathbf{P}^{J_2}) \\ &= \mathsf{RREF}(\mathbf{G}_1 \cdot \mathbf{P} \cdot \mathbf{D} \cdot \mathbf{P}^{J_2}) \\ &= \mathsf{RREF}\left(\left[\mathbf{G}_1^{J_1} \cdot \mathbf{Q}_r \mid \mathbf{G}^{\overline{J_1}} \cdot \mathbf{Q}_c\right]\right) \\ &= \left[\mathbf{I}_k \mid \mathbf{Q}_r^{-1} \cdot (\mathbf{G}_1^{J_1})^{-1} \cdot \mathbf{G}^{\overline{J_1}} \cdot \mathbf{Q}_c\right].\end{aligned}$$

This shows that the matrix $\mathsf{RREF}(\mathbf{G}_2 \cdot \mathbf{P}^{J_2}) = \mathsf{RREF}([\mathbf{G}_2^{J_2} \mid \mathbf{G}_2^{\overline{J_2}}])$ is in systematic form. Hence, J_2 is an information set of $\mathbf{G}_2$. Additionally, this shows that

$$\mathsf{RREF}(\mathbf{G}_2 \cdot \mathbf{P}^{J_2}) \overset{\mathsf{LRL}}{\sim} \left[\mathbf{I}_k \mid (\mathbf{G}_1^{J_1})^{-1} \cdot \mathbf{G}^{\overline{J_1}}\right] = \mathsf{RREF}(\mathbf{G}_1 \cdot \mathbf{P}^{J_1}),$$

and thus proves the lemma. □

References

BBN+22. Barenghi, A., Biasse, J.-F., Ngo, T., Persichetti, E., Santini, P.: Advanced signature functionalities from the code equivalence problem. Int. J. Comput. Math. Comput. Syst. Theory **7**(2), 112–128 (2022)

BBPS23. Barenghi, A., Biasse, J.-F., Persichetti, E., Santini, P.: On the computational hardness of the code equivalence problem in cryptography. Adv. Math. Commun. **17**(1), 23–55 (2023)

Beu20. Beullens, W.: Not enough LESS: an improved algorithm for solving code equivalence problems over $\mathbb{F}_q$. In: Dunkelman, O., Jacobson Jr, M.J., O'Flynn, C. (eds.) SAC 2020: 27th Annual International Workshop on Selected Areas in Cryptography, vol. 12804 of Lecture Notes in Computer Science, pp. 387–403. Springer, Cham (2020)

BMPS20. Biasse, J.-F., Micheli, G., Persichetti, E., Santini, P.: LESS is more: code-based signatures without syndromes. In: Nitaj, A., Youssef, A.M. (eds.) AFRICACRYPT 20: 12th International Conference on Cryptology in Africa. Lecture Notes in Computer Science, vol. 12174, pp. 45–65. Springer, Cham (2020)

CNP+23. Chou, T., et al.: Take your MEDS: digital signatures from matrix code equivalence. In: El Mrabet, N., De Feo, L., Duquesne, S. (eds.) AFRICACRYPT 23: 14th International Conference on Cryptology in Africa. Lecture Notes in Computer Science, vol. 14064, pp. 28–52. Springer, Cham (2023)

CPS23. Chou, T., Persichetti, E., Santini, P.: On linear equivalence, canonical forms, and digital signatures. IACR Cryptol. ePrint Arch., pp. 1533 (2023)

DP23. Ducas, L., Pulles, L.N.: Does the dual-sieve attack on learning with errors even work? In: Handschuh, H., Lysyanskaya, A. (eds.) Advances in Cryptology - CRYPTO 2023. Part III, volume 14083 of Lecture Notes in Computer Science, pp. 37–69. Springer, Cham (2023)

DPPv22. Ducas, L., Postlethwaite, E.W., Pulles, L.N., van Woerden, W.P.J.: Hawk: module LIP makes lattice signatures fast, compact and simple. In: Agrawal, S., Lin, D. (eds.) Advances in Cryptology - ASIACRYPT 2022. Part IV, vol. 13794 of Lecture Notes in Computer Science, pp. 65–94. Springer, Cham (2022)

Leo82. Leon, J.S.: Computing automorphism groups of error-correcting codes. IEEE Trans. Inf. Theory **28**(3), 496–510 (1982)

MT23. Meyer-Hilfiger, C., Tillich, J.-P.: Rigorous foundations for dual attacks in coding theory. In: Rothblum, G.N., Wee, H. (eds.) TCC 2023: 21st Theory of Cryptography Conference, Part IV, vol. 14372 of Lecture Notes in Computer Science, pp. 3–32. Springer, Cham, November / December (2023)

PS23. Persichetti, E., Santini, P.: A new formulation of the linear equivalence problem and shorter LESS signatures. In: Guo, J., Steinfeld, R. (eds.) Advances in Cryptology - ASIACRYPT 2023. Part VII, volume 14444 of Lecture Notes in Computer Science, pp. 351–378. Springer, Singapore (2023)

RS09. Richmond, L.B., Shallit, J.O.: Counting abelian squares. Electron. J. Comb. **16**(1) (2009)

Sen00. Sendrier, N.: Finding the permutation between equivalent linear codes: the support splitting algorithm. IEEE Trans. Inf. Theory **46**(4), 1193–1203 (2000)

SS13. Sendrier, N., Simos, D.E.: The hardness of code equivalence over $\mathbf{F}_q$ and its application to code-based cryptography. In: Gaborit, P. (ed.) Post-Quantum Cryptography, vol. 7932 of LNCS, pp. 203–216. Springer (2013)

vW99. van Oorschot, P.C., Wiener, M.J.: Parallel collision search with cryptanalytic applications. J. Cryptol. **12**(1), 1–28 (1999)

An Improved Both-May Information Set Decoding Algorithm: Towards More Efficient Time-Memory Trade-Offs

Hiroki Furue[1](✉) and Yusuke Aikawa[2]

[1] NTT Social Informatics Laboratories, Tokyo, Japan
hiroki.furue@ntt.com
[2] The University of Tokyo, Tokyo, Japan
aikawa@mist.i.u-tokyo.ac.jp

Abstract. Code-based cryptography is based on the difficulty of the syndrome decoding problem (SDP) and is one of the promising candidates for post-quantum cryptography. Information set decoding (ISD) is known as one of the most efficient frameworks for solving SDP. There has been some work analyzing the time complexity of ISD in the situation where the amount of memory consumption is limited. In this work, we propose a new variant of the Both-May algorithm which is known as the fastest ISD. The proposed algorithm achieves more efficient asymptotic time-memory trade-offs compared with the original Both-May algorithm and existing time-memory trade-off versions of other ISDs.

Keywords: post-quantum cryptography · code-based cryptography · syndrome decoding problem · information set decoding · Both-May algorithm

1 Introduction

Code-based cryptography is a public key cryptosystem based on the difficulty of the decoding problem and is known as one of the promising candidates for post-quantum cryptography (PQC). Indeed, the fourth round of NIST PQC standardization project [21] has selected four encryption schemes, and three of them are code-based schemes, Classic McEliece [1], BIKE [2], and HQC [19]. This situation implies it is likely that one of these code-based schemes will be standardized, and thus analyzing the hardness of the underlying problem is an important task for realizing secure post-quantum schemes.

This paper deals with the syndrome decoding problem (SDP) over the binary field, which is formulated as given the parity check matrix $\mathbf{H}$ of a binary linear code of length n and dimension k and a syndrome $\mathbf{s}$, find a low Hamming weight vector $\mathbf{e}$ such that $\mathbf{He} = \mathbf{s}$. Information set decoding (ISD) is known as one of the most efficient frameworks for solving SDP. ISD was first proposed by Prange [22], and since then there have been many algorithms that improve the asymptotic

R. Niederhagen and M.-J. O. Saarinen (Eds.): PQCrypto 2025, LNCS 15577, pp. 104–128, 2025.
https://doi.org/10.1007/978-3-031-86599-2_4

time complexity with the form of $2^{\alpha n}$ [3,6,7,9,17,18,23]. Indeed, we calculate the time complexities of major ISDs by using the code at https://github.com/Memphisd/Revisiting-NN-ISD and list them in Table 1.

Table 1. Exponents α of asymptotic time complexity $O(2^{\alpha n})$ for major ISD algorithms in full distance setting

Prange [22]	Dumer [9]	MMT [17]	BJMM [3]	MO [18]	BM [7]
0.121	0.116	0.112	0.102	0.0967	0.0951

The Both-May algorithm, which is one of ISDs, was proposed in 2018 [7] and Carrier et al. [8] and Esser [10] revised its complexity estimation. This algorithm uses nearest neighbor search techniques which find all pairs with a small Hamming distance between given two lists of binary vectors. More specifically, the algorithm repeats to construct a depth-d tree and combines lists at each level of the search tree by a nearest neighbor algorithm. As seen in Table 1, the Both-May algorithm is known as the asymptotically fastest algorithm, and it is confirmed in [10] that it also improves the memory complexity compared with some efficient ISDs such as the Becker-Joux-May-Meurer (BJMM) [3] and May-Ozerov [18] algorithms.

Esser, May, and Zweydinger [12] carried out experiments with different list sizes in the May-Meurer-Thomae (MMT) [17] algorithm, and ended up selecting small list sizes to avoid slowdowns arising from memory-access costs. Esser and Zweydinger [14] then proposed better time-memory tradeoffs for the MMT and BJMM algorithms. However, it has been an open problem whether it is possible to construct asymptotic efficient time-memory trade-offs for nearest neighbor based ISDs such as the Both-May algorithm.

Our Contributions. In this work, we propose a new variant of the Both-May algorithm. We show that the proposed algorithm achieves more efficient asymptotic time-memory trade-offs compared with the original Both-May algorithm and the existing time-memory trade-offs of MMT and BJMM. See Fig. 1 in Sect. 5 for the details of our results. Indeed, in the full distance setting with the memory limitation $2^{0.04n}$, although the time complexity of the original Both-May algorithm is given as $2^{0.105n}$, that of the proposed one is given as $2^{0.101n}$.

From a technical point of view, the proposed algorithm utilizes the search tree as in the original one. The original algorithm constructs such a tree from the first level lists in each iteration. On the other hand, in most times of the iterations, the proposed one uses the previous lower level lists and only create the higher level lists for efficiency. This construction incorporates techniques from [14]. In order to compute the time complexity of the proposed algorithm, we need to estimate the number of times we can reuse the same lower level lists. However, there has been no analysis of this number when using a nearest neighbor based algorithm.

A novelty of this work is to introduce a new method to estimate this number, based on the success probability for the nearest neighbor approach used in the Both-May algorithm. As a result, the proposed algorithm achieves a reduction in time complexity compared to the original approach in cases where memory complexity is limited.

Organization of the Paper. The rest of this paper is organized as follows: Sect. 2 gives some notations and recalls SDP, ISD, and nearest neighbor algorithms. Section 3 is devoted to describing the original Both-May algorithm. We describe the proposed algorithm in Sect. 4 and analyze its performance in Sect. 5. Finally, Sect. 6 is devoted to the conclusion, where we summarize the key points and suggest possible future works.

2 Preliminaries

Subsection 2.1 gives some notations. Subsection 2.2 recalls the syndrome decoding problem and Subsect. 2.3 explains the information set decoding algorithms solving this problem. Subsection 2.4 roughly describes a nearest neighbor algorithms used in the Both-May algorithm.

2.1 Notation

Let $\mathbb{F}_2$ be the finite field with two elements. We denote vectors by bold lower case and matrices by bold upper case letters. In the rest of this paper, we generally use column vectors and represent them without the transposition symbol $\top$ for simplicity. For two column vectors $\mathbf{a} \in \mathbb{F}_2^m$ and $\mathbf{b} \in \mathbb{F}_2^n$, we write the concatenation column vector of the two vectors as $(\mathbf{a}, \mathbf{b}) \in \mathbb{F}_2^{m+n}$. Further, for a vector $\mathbf{a}$ and subsets C and D of vector space over $\mathbb{F}_2$, we also set $(\mathbf{a}, C) = \{(\mathbf{a}, \mathbf{c}) \mid \mathbf{c} \in C\}$ and $(C, D) = \{(\mathbf{c}, \mathbf{d}) \mid \mathbf{c} \in C, \mathbf{d} \in D\}$. For a vector $\mathbf{a} \in \mathbb{F}_2^m$, a_i denotes the i-th coordinate of $\mathbf{a}$, and we let $\mathrm{wt}(\mathbf{a}) = |\{i \mid a_i = 1\}|$ be its Hamming weight. We refer to the subset of $\mathbb{F}_2^n$ including elements with Hamming weight ω as $\mathcal{B}(n, \omega)$. The n-dimensional zero vector is represented as $\mathbf{0}_n$. The matrix space with size n-by-m over $\mathbb{F}_2$ is denoted by $\mathbb{F}_2^{n \times m}$. We also denote the n-by-n identity matrix and the n-by-m zero matrix by $\mathbf{I}_n$ and $\mathbf{O}_{n \times m}$, respectively. For $x \in [0, 1]$, we denote by $H(x) = -x\log(x) - (1 - x)\log(1 - x)$ the binary entropy function.

2.2 Syndrome Decoding Problem

A binary linear code $\mathcal{C}$ of length n and dimension k with $k < n$ is defined as a k-dimensional vector subspace of $\mathbb{F}_2^n$. For such a code, we can define a parity-check matrix $\mathbf{H} \in \mathbb{F}_2^{(n-k) \times n}$ whose kernel space is equal to $\mathcal{C}$. In the decoding process, we recover a code word $\mathbf{c} \in \mathcal{C}$ from a given message $\mathbf{c}' = \mathbf{c} + \mathbf{e}$ with a fault $\mathbf{e}$. Syndrome decoding is one of efficient methods of recovering the error term $\mathbf{e}$ from $\mathbf{H}\mathbf{c}' = \mathbf{H}(\mathbf{c} + \mathbf{e}) = \mathbf{H}\mathbf{e}$.

Definition 1 (Syndrome Decoding Problem (SDP)). *For three integers* (n, k, ω) *with* $k < n$ *and* $\omega < n$*, given an* $(n-k) \times k$ *matrix* $\mathbf{H}$ *over* $\mathbb{F}_2$ *and* $\mathbf{s} \in \mathbb{F}_2^{n-k}$*, the syndrome decoding problem asks to find a vector* $\mathbf{e} \in \mathbb{F}_2^n$ *such that* $\mathbf{H} \cdot \mathbf{e} = \mathbf{s}$ *and the Hamming weight* $\mathrm{wt}(\mathbf{e})$ *is equal to* ω*.*

This problem is proven to be NP-complete [4], and we consider that cryptosystems based on this problem have resistance to quantum computing attacks.

2.3 Information Set Decoding

This subsection roughly describes a common framework for information set decoding (ISD) algorithm solving SDP, which was first proposed by Prange [22].

Let (n, k, ω) be a parameter set of SDP as mentioned in Definition 1. For inputs $\mathbf{H}$ and $\mathbf{s}$ and an integer p with $0 \leq p \leq \omega$, the ISD algorithm can be described as follows:

(1) Pick a permutation matrix $\mathbf{P} \in \mathbb{F}_2^{n \times n}$ randomly.
(2) Multiply an invertible matrix $\mathbf{Q} \in \mathbb{F}_2^{(n-k)\times(n-k)}$ such that $\mathbf{QHP}$ has the form of $(\mathbf{I}_{n-k} \mid \mathbf{H}_1)$ with $\mathbf{H}_1 \in \mathbb{F}_2^{(n-k)\times k}$ and let $\mathbf{s}' = \mathbf{Q}\mathbf{s}$.
(3) Find an $\mathbf{e}_2 \in \mathbb{F}_2^k$ such that $\mathrm{wt}(\mathbf{e}_2) = p$ and $\mathrm{wt}(\mathbf{e}_1) = \omega - p$ where $\mathbf{e}_1 = \mathbf{H}_1\mathbf{e}_2 + \mathbf{s}'$.

If we can find a vector $\mathbf{e}_2$ satisfying the above conditions in the third step, then $\mathbf{P} \cdot (\mathbf{e}_1, \mathbf{e}_2)$ is clearly a solution for the given SDP. Otherwise, we return to the first step and repeat these operations until we find a solution. Note that, in some ISDs such as the Dumer [9], MMT [17], and BJMM [3] algorithms, the step (2) transforms $\mathbf{H}$ into the form of

$$\begin{pmatrix} \mathbf{O}_{\ell\times(n-k-\ell)} & * \\ \mathbf{I}_{n-k-\ell} & * \end{pmatrix},$$

but we will not deal with this case in this paper. The subroutines to accomplish the step (3) differ among ISD algorithms. Specifically, the Both-May algorithm [7] described in the next section utilizes a nearest neighbor algorithm to perform the step (3).

We assume that there exists one solution $\mathbf{e} \in \mathbb{F}_2^n$ for the given inputs and the step (3) can always find an $\mathbf{e}_2$ correctly if there exists such a vector satisfying the conditions. Then, the conditions which $\mathbf{P}$ has to satisfy to find a solution are that $\mathrm{wt}(\mathbf{e}_1') = \omega - p$ and $\mathrm{wt}(\mathbf{e}_2') = p$ where $\mathbf{P}^{-1}\mathbf{e} = (\mathbf{e}_1', \mathbf{e}_2')$ with $\mathbf{e}_1' \in \mathbb{F}_2^{n-k}$ and $\mathbf{e}_2' \in \mathbb{F}_2^k$. The probability P that we can choose such a $\mathbf{P}$ is given by

$$P = \frac{\binom{n-k}{\omega-p}\binom{k}{p}}{\binom{n}{\omega}}.$$

If we denote by T the time complexity of each iteration from the step (1) to (3), then the whole time complexity can be estimated by $P^{-1} \cdot T$.

2.4 Nearest Neighbor Algorithm

This subsection gives a concept and complexity of nearest neighbor search algorithms. Given two lists of binary vectors and a distance ε, the algorithms find all pairs with the Hamming distance ε between the two lists. In this paper, we use the algorithm by May and Ozerov [18] for solving the problem following the previous results [7,10]. We here only show the complexity of this algorithm.

Lemma 1 (Corollary 2.1 [10]). *Let $n \in \mathbb{N}$, $\varepsilon' \in [0, \frac{1}{2}]$, and $\lambda', \ell \in [0,1]$. Given two lists L_1 and L_2 with size $2^{\lambda' n}$ containing uniformly random elements from $\mathbb{F}_2^{\ell n}$. Then there is an algorithm that returns all pairs $(\mathbf{x}_1, \mathbf{x}_2)$ with $\mathbf{x}_i \in L_i$ $(i = 1, 2)$ and $\mathrm{wt}(\mathbf{x}_1 + \mathbf{x}_2) = \varepsilon' n$ in expected time $2^{v\ell n(1+o(1))}$, where*

$$v = \begin{cases} (1-\varepsilon)\left(1 - H\left(\frac{\delta^* - \frac{\varepsilon}{2}}{1-\varepsilon}\right)\right) & \text{for } \varepsilon \leq \varepsilon^* \\ 2\lambda + H(\varepsilon) - 1 & \text{for } \varepsilon > \varepsilon^* \end{cases},$$

with $\varepsilon = \varepsilon'/\ell$, $\lambda = \lambda'/\ell$, $\delta^* = H^{-1}(1-\lambda)$, and $\varepsilon^* = 2\delta^*(1-\delta^*)$ using memory $|L_i|^{(1+o(1))}$.

In the rest of this paper, we denote by $\mathcal{N}_{\mathcal{L},\ell,\varepsilon}$ the time complexity of solving a nearest neighbor problem to find all ε close pairs on lists of size $\mathcal{L}$ containing length-ℓ vectors.

3 Both-May Algorithm

This section gives the detail of the Both-May algorithm [7] solving the syndrome decoding problem. For a positive integer $d \geq 2$, Subsect. 3.1 describes the depth-d version of the algorithm. Subsection 3.2 and 3.3 discuss its correctness and complexity, respectively, and these conditions for correctness and complexity analysis are based on the results of [10]. In Subsect. 3.4, we provide a comparison of the time and memory complexity of the algorithm among the depth $2 \leq d \leq 4$.

3.1 Description of Algorithm

As mentioned in Subsect. 2.3, for a permutation matrix $\mathbf{P} \in \mathbb{F}_2^{n \times n}$ and an invertible matrix $\mathbf{Q} \in \mathbb{F}_2^{(n-k)\times(n-k)}$, we suppose that $\mathbf{QHP}$ has the form of $(\mathbf{I}_{n-k} \mid \mathbf{H}_1)$ where $\mathbf{H}_1 \in \mathbb{F}_2^{(n-k)\times k}$. We then try to find an $\mathbf{e}_2 \in \mathbb{F}_2^k$ such that $\mathrm{wt}(\mathbf{e}_2) = p_d$ and $\mathrm{wt}(\mathbf{H}_1\mathbf{e}_2 + \mathbf{s}') = \omega - p_d$ where $\mathbf{s}' = \mathbf{Qs}$ for a parameter p_d with depth-d. Note that we slightly change the notation from the description of the original framework of ISD in Subsect. 2.3 for ease of description. In the following, we explain how to obtain such a vector $\mathbf{e}_2$ using a nearest neighbor algorithm.

The depth-$d \geq 2$ version of the Both-May algorithm divides $n-k$ rows of $\mathbf{QHP}$ into d-layers, and the i-th layer with $1 \leq i \leq d$ is composed of ℓ_i rows from the $(\sum_{j=1}^{i-1} \ell_j + 1)$-th row for parameters $\ell_1, \ldots, \ell_{d-1}$ and $\ell_d = n - k -$

$\sum_{j=1}^{d-1} \ell_j$. For these layers, we define the d projections π_i with $1 \leq i \leq d$ used to search $\mathbf{e}_2$:

$$\pi_i : \mathbb{F}_2^{n-k} \to \mathbb{F}_2^{\ell_i},\ \pi_i(x_1, \ldots, x_{n-k}) = \left(x_{\sum_{j=1}^{i-1} \ell_j + 1}, \ldots, x_{\sum_{j=1}^{i} \ell_j}\right).$$

We then impose new constraints on $\mathbf{e}_2$ from the original framework of the ISD algorithm. When we try to find $\mathbf{e}_2$ with the Hamming weight p_d, we assume that $\mathbf{e}_2$ satisfies the following conditions:

$$\mathrm{wt}(\pi_i(\mathbf{H}_1\mathbf{e}_2 + \mathbf{s}')) = \omega_i^{(d)} \quad (1 \leq i \leq d),$$

for parameters $\omega_1^{(d)}, \ldots, \omega_{d-1}^{(d)}$ and $\omega_d^{(d)} = \omega - p_d - \sum_{j=1}^{d-1} \omega_j^{(d)}$. Then, for $\mathbf{e}_2$ satisfying these conditions, we clearly have $\mathrm{wt}(\mathbf{H}_1\mathbf{e}_2 + \mathbf{s}') = \omega - p_d$. In this case, the algorithm can find a solution if we have

$$\mathrm{wt}(\bar{\mathbf{e}}_2) = p_d,\quad \mathrm{wt}(\pi_i(\bar{\mathbf{e}}_1)) = \omega_i^{(d)}\ (1 \leq i \leq d),$$

where $\mathbf{P}^{-1}\mathbf{e} = (\bar{\mathbf{e}}_1, \bar{\mathbf{e}}_2)$ with $\bar{\mathbf{e}}_1 \in \mathbb{F}_2^{n-k}$ and $\bar{\mathbf{e}}_2 \in \mathbb{F}_2^k$ for a solution $\mathbf{e} \in \mathbb{F}_2^n$ and a permutation $\mathbf{P}$. Then, the probability that $\mathbf{P}$ satisfies these conditions is given as

$$\frac{\binom{k}{p_d} \prod_{i=1}^{d} \binom{\ell_i}{\omega_i}}{\binom{n}{\omega}}.$$

We then show a subroutine of the Both-May algorithm to find $\mathbf{e}_2$ corresponding to the step (3) of ISD in Subsect. 2.3. As in other ISD algorithms, the depth-d version of the Both-May algorithm relies on a search tree in depth-d. More specifically, for parameters $p_1, \ldots, p_{d-1}$, it can be described as the following $(d+1)$ steps:

level-0 Generate $(\mathcal{B}(k/2, p_1/2), \mathbf{0}_{k/2})$ and $(\mathbf{0}_{k/2}, \mathcal{B}(k/2, p_1/2))$.
level-i $(1 \leq i \leq d-1)$
Generate 2^{d-i} lists $\bar{L}_1^{(i)}, \ldots, \bar{L}_{2^{d-i}}^{(i)}$ as subsets of $(\mathcal{B}(k/2, p_i/2), \mathcal{B}(k/2, p_i/2))$.
level-d Generate one list $\bar{L}^{(d)}$ as a subset of $(\mathcal{B}(k/2, p_d/2), \mathcal{B}(k/2, p_d/2))$.

For the resulting list $\bar{L}^{(d)}$, we check if there exists a candidate of solution in $\bar{L}^{(d)}$ or not. More specifically, each level-i $(1 \leq i \leq d-1)$ list is composed of k-dimensional vectors $\mathbf{x} \in (\mathcal{B}(k/2, p_i/2), \mathcal{B}(k/2, p_i/2))$ satisfying the following i conditions

$$\mathrm{wt}(\pi_1(\mathbf{H}_1\mathbf{x})) = \omega_1^{(i)} \quad \text{or} \quad \mathrm{wt}(\pi_1(\mathbf{H}_1\mathbf{x} + \mathbf{s}')) = \omega_1^{(i)},$$
$$\vdots$$
$$\mathrm{wt}(\pi_i(\mathbf{H}_1\mathbf{x})) = \omega_i^{(i)} \quad \text{or} \quad \mathrm{wt}(\pi_i(\mathbf{H}_1\mathbf{x} + \mathbf{s}')) = \omega_i^{(i)},$$

for parameters $\omega_j^{(i)}$ with $1 \leq i \leq d-1$ and $1 \leq j \leq i$. We construct these level-i lists with $1 \leq i \leq d-1$ by the following two steps:

(1) Combine two of the level-$(i-1)$ lists by applying a nearest neighbor algorithm with the condition $\mathrm{wt}(\pi_i(\mathbf{H}_1\mathbf{x})) = \omega_i^{(i)}$ or $\mathrm{wt}(\pi_i(\mathbf{H}_1\mathbf{x}+\mathbf{s}')) = \omega_i^{(i)}$ for a combination vector $\mathbf{x}$.
(2) Filter the resulting lists by checking if each element satisfies the remaining $(i-1)$ conditions and belongs to $(\mathcal{B}(k/2, p_i/2), \mathcal{B}(k/2, p_i/2))$ or not.

Note that in the d-the step, we only perform the first nearest neighbor part with the condition $\mathrm{wt}(\pi_d(\mathbf{H}_1\mathbf{x}+\mathbf{s}')) = \omega_d^{(d)}$ for a combination vector $\mathbf{x}$ of the two level-$(d-1)$ lists. This is because the filtering step does not affect the asymptotic efficiency of the algorithm.

We here give a more formal description of level-i lists with $0 \le i \le d$. First, from the definition, level-0 lists $\bar{L}_1^{(0)}, \ldots, \bar{L}_{2^d}^{(0)}$ are set as

$$\begin{aligned}\bar{L}_j^{(0)} &= \{(\mathbf{x}, \mathbf{0}) \mid \mathbf{x} \in \mathcal{B}(k/2, p_1/2)\}, \ (j = 1, 3, \ldots, 2^d - 1), \\ \bar{L}_j^{(0)} &= \{(\mathbf{0}, \mathbf{x}) \mid \mathbf{x} \in \mathcal{B}(k/2, p_1/2)\}, \ (j = 2, 4, \ldots, 2^d).\end{aligned} \tag{1}$$

Then, in the level-i step with $1 \le i \le d-1$, we first generate 2^{d-i} lists $L_1^{(i)}, \ldots, L_{2^{d-i}}^{(i)}$ by performing the nearest neighbor step as follows:

$$\begin{aligned}L_j^{(i)} &= \left\{\mathbf{x}+\mathbf{y} \mid \mathbf{x} \in \bar{L}_{2j-1}^{(i-1)}, \mathbf{y} \in \bar{L}_{2j}^{(i-1)}, \mathrm{wt}(\pi_i(\mathbf{H}_1(\mathbf{x}+\mathbf{y}))) = \omega_i^{(i)}\right\}, \\ &\quad (j = 1, \ldots, 2^{d-i} - 1), \\ L_{2^{d-i}}^{(i)} &= \left\{\mathbf{x}+\mathbf{y} \mid \mathbf{x} \in \bar{L}_{2^{d-i+1}-1}^{(i-1)}, \mathbf{y} \in \bar{L}_{2^{d-i+1}}^{(i-1)}, \right. \\ &\quad \left. \mathrm{wt}(\pi_i(\mathbf{H}_1(\mathbf{x}+\mathbf{y})+\mathbf{s}')) = \omega_i^{(i)}\right\}.\end{aligned} \tag{2}$$

Further, we perform the filtering step and obtain the level-i lists $\bar{L}_1^{(i)}, \ldots, \bar{L}_{2^{d-i}}^{(i)}$ as

$$\begin{aligned}\bar{L}_j^{(i)} &= \left\{\mathbf{x} \mid \mathbf{x} \in L_j^{(i)}, \mathrm{wt}(\mathbf{x}) = p_i, \mathrm{wt}(\pi_1(\mathbf{H}_1\mathbf{x})) = \omega_1^{(i)}, \cdots, \right. \\ &\quad \left. \mathrm{wt}(\pi_{i-1}(\mathbf{H}_1\mathbf{x})) = \omega_{i-1}^{(i)}\right\}, \quad (j = 1, \ldots, 2^{d-i} - 1), \\ \bar{L}_{2^{d-i}}^{(i)} &= \left\{\mathbf{x} \mid \mathbf{x} \in L_{2^{d-i}}^{(i)}, \mathrm{wt}(\mathbf{x}) = p_i, \mathrm{wt}(\pi_1(\mathbf{H}_1\mathbf{x}+\mathbf{s}')) = \omega_1^{(i)}, \ldots, \right. \\ &\quad \left. \mathrm{wt}(\pi_{i-1}(\mathbf{H}_1\mathbf{x}+\mathbf{s}')) = \omega_{i-1}^{(i)}\right\}.\end{aligned} \tag{3}$$

Note that in the level-1 step, $L_i^{(1)}$ corresponds to $\bar{L}_i^{(1)}$, and thus we do not have to perform the filtering step. Finally, we generate the level-d list as

$$\bar{L}^{(d)} = \left\{\mathbf{x}+\mathbf{y} \mid \mathbf{x} \in \bar{L}_1^{(d-1)}, \mathbf{y} \in \bar{L}_2^{(d-1)}, \mathrm{wt}(\pi_d(\mathbf{H}_1(\mathbf{x}+\mathbf{y})+\mathbf{s}')) = \omega_d^{(d)}\right\}. \tag{4}$$

See Algorithm 1 for the details of the algorithm description.

3.2 Correctness

This subsection discusses the correctness of the algorithm described in Subsect. 3.1. Here, this correctness means whether the algorithm can find a solution or not in the case where the permutation $\mathbf{P}$ is chosen as desired. In the rest of this subsection, we assume that for a solution $\mathbf{e} \in \mathbb{F}_2^n$, we have

$$\mathrm{wt}(\mathbf{e}_2) = p_d, \quad \mathrm{wt}(\pi_i(\mathbf{e}_1)) = \omega_i^{(d)} \ (1 \leq i \leq d),$$

where $\mathbf{P}^{-1}\mathbf{e} = (\mathbf{e}_1, \mathbf{e}_2)$ with $\mathbf{e}_1 \in \mathbb{F}_2^{n-k}$ and $\mathbf{e}_2 \in \mathbb{F}_2^k$.

We first give the number $\mathcal{R}_i$ of possible representations of splittings of each level-i element with $2 \leq i \leq d$. Recall that the level-i lists are given as subsets of $(\mathcal{B}(k/2, p_i/2), \mathcal{B}(k/2, p_i/2))$. For an level-$i$ element $\mathbf{y} \in \mathbb{F}_2^k$, this $\mathcal{R}_i$ means the number of pairs of $\mathbf{x}_1, \mathbf{x}_2 \in \mathbb{F}_2^k$ such that $\mathbf{x}_1 + \mathbf{x}_2 = \mathbf{y}$ and $\mathbf{x}_1, \mathbf{x}_2 \in (\mathcal{B}(k/2, p_{i-1}/2), \mathcal{B}(k/2, p_{i-1}/2))$, and then $\mathcal{R}_i$ is given as

$$\mathcal{R}_i = \binom{p_i}{p_i/2}\binom{k - p_i}{p_{i-1} - p_i/2}. \tag{5}$$

Here the first term counts the number of combinations that distribute $p_i/2$ out of the p_i one entries of $\mathbf{y}$ to $\mathbf{x}_1$ and $\mathbf{x}_2$. The second factor then counts how the remaining $p_{i-1} - p_i/2$ one entries of $\mathbf{x}_1$ and $\mathbf{x}_2$ can cancel out. Note that we do not consider the number of representations of the level-1 elements, since any element of $(\mathcal{B}(k/2, p_1/2), \mathcal{B}(k/2, p_1/2))$ clearly has only one representation composed of elements of $(\mathcal{B}(k/2, p_1/2), \mathbf{0}_{k/2})$ and $(\mathbf{0}_{k/2}, \mathcal{B}(k/2, p_1/2))$.

Algorithm 1. Both-May Algorithm with Depth-d ($d \geq 2$)

Input: $\mathbf{H} \in \mathbb{F}_2^{(n-k)\times n}$, $\mathbf{s} \in \mathbb{F}_2^{n-k}$, and $\omega \in \mathbb{N}$
Output: $\mathbf{e} \in \mathbb{F}_2^n$ s.t. $\mathbf{H} \cdot \mathbf{e} = \mathbf{s}$ and $\mathrm{wt}(\mathbf{e}) = \omega$

Choose parameters

$$p_1, \ldots, p_d, \ell_1, \ldots, \ell_{d-1}, \omega_1^{(1)}, \ldots, \omega_1^{(d)}, \omega_2^{(2)}, \ldots, \omega_2^{(d)}, \ldots, \omega_{d-1}^{(d-1)}, \omega_{d-1}^{(d)}.$$

Generate the level-0 lists $\bar{L}_1^{(0)}, \ldots, \bar{L}_{2^d}^{(0)}$ as in (1).
repeat
  Choose a random permutation matrix $\mathbf{P} \in \mathbb{F}_2^{n\times n}$.
  Compute $\mathbf{Q} \in \mathbb{F}_2^{(n-k)\times(n-k)}$ such that $\mathbf{QHP} = (\mathbf{I}_{n-k} \mid \mathbf{H}_1)$, $\mathbf{H}' \leftarrow \mathbf{QHP}$, and $\mathbf{s}' \leftarrow \mathbf{Qs}$.
  for $j = 1, \ldots, d-1$ **do**
    Generate 2^{d-i} lists $L_1^{(i)}, \ldots, L_{2^{d-i}}^{(i)}$ as in (2) by using a nearest neighbor algorithm.
    Generate the level-i lists $\bar{L}_1^{(i)}, \ldots, \bar{L}_{2^{d-i}}^{(i)}$ as in (3).
  end for
  Generate the level-d list $\bar{L}^{(d)}$ as in (4) by using a nearest neighbor algorithm.
until $\exists \mathbf{e}_2 \in \bar{L}^{(d)}$ s.t. $\mathrm{wt}(\mathbf{e}_2) = p_d, \mathrm{wt}(\mathbf{H}_1\mathbf{e}_2 + \mathbf{s}') = \omega - p_d$
return $\mathbf{P}(\mathbf{H}_1\mathbf{e}_2 + \mathbf{s}', \mathbf{e}_2)$

We then consider the probability q_i that representations of the level-i elements survive the level-$(i-1)$ constraints with $2 \le i \le d$. Recall that the level-i elements have to satisfy the conditions of $\mathrm{wt}(\pi_j(\mathbf{H}_1\mathbf{x})) = \omega_j^{(i)}$ (or $\mathrm{wt}(\pi_j(\mathbf{H}_1\mathbf{x}+\mathbf{s}')) = \omega_j^{(i)}$) with $1 \le j \le i$. When we concentrate on the j-th layer's condition with $1 \le j \le i-1$, we have to compute the probability that both of a representation pair $(\mathbf{x}_1, \mathbf{x}_2)$ of a level-i element $\mathbf{y}$ satisfy the j-th layer's condition of the level-$(i-1)$ list, i.e.,

$$\Pr[\mathrm{wt}(\pi_j(\mathbf{H}_1\mathbf{x}_1)) = \mathrm{wt}(\pi_j(\mathbf{H}_1\mathbf{x}_2)) = \omega_j^{(i-1)} \mid \mathbf{y} = \mathbf{x}_1 + \mathbf{x}_2, \mathrm{wt}(\pi_j(\mathbf{H}_1\mathbf{y})) = \omega_j^{(i)}].$$

Similarly to the computation of $\mathcal{R}_i$, this probability can be estimated as

$$\frac{\binom{\omega_j^{(i)}}{\omega_j^{(i)}/2}\binom{\ell_j-\omega_j^{(i)}}{\omega_j^{(i-1)}-\omega_j^{(i)}/2}}{2^{\ell_j}},$$

by assuming the randomness of the matrix $\mathbf{H}_1$. We then can estimate the probability q_i with $2 \le i \le d$ as

$$q_i = \prod_{j=1}^{i-1} \frac{\binom{\omega_j^{(i)}}{\omega_j^{(i)}/2}\binom{\ell_j-\omega_j^{(i)}}{\omega_j^{(i-1)}-\omega_j^{(i)}/2}}{2^{\ell_j}}, \tag{6}$$

by considering the conditions for the first $(i-1)$ layers simultaneously. Note that the condition of the i-th layer is not related to this q_i, since the level-$(i-1)$ lists have no constraint on the i-th layer.

For the number $\mathcal{R}_i$ of representations and the probability q_i given above, we here assume $q_i\mathcal{R}_i \ge 1$ for each level-i with $2 \le i \le d$. We then can expect that for each element of the level-i lists, there exists at least one representation pair such that both of them satisfy the conditions of the level-$(i-1)$ lists. This means that under these conditions we can always find a desired $\mathbf{e}_2$ as an element of the level-d list if the permutation $\mathbf{P}$ distributes the weight properly. Further, to reduce the time complexity and memory consumption as much as possible, we use the constraints $q_i\mathcal{R}_i = 1$ with $2 \le i \le d$ to check the correctness of parameter sets.

3.3 Complexity

This subsection gives the complexity estimation of the degree-$d \ge 2$ Both-May algorithm under the conditions given in Subsect. 3.2.

We first consider the size of each list to estimate the complexity of nearest-neighbor parts. We here denote by $\mathcal{L}_i$ with $0 \le i \le d-1$ the size of the level-i lists. Since we here consider the expected size, we do not care about the difference in the size among the same level lists. From the definition, $\mathcal{L}_0$ is clearly given as

$$\mathcal{L}_0 = \binom{k/2}{p_1/2}.$$

Table 2. Comparison of the Both-May algorithm between the depth-d with $2 \leq d \leq 4$ (the time complexity, memory complexity, and worst-case rate $\hat{k}$)

d	2	3	4
time	0.0982	0.0951	0.0951
memory	0.0717	0.0809	0.0752
$\hat{k}$	0.43	0.43	0.42

Then, from the conditions of $q_i \mathcal{R}_i = 1$ with $2 \leq$ i $\leq d$ given in Subsect. 3.2, the level-i lists include all possible vectors satisfying the constraints, and thus we have

$$\mathcal{L}_i = \binom{k/2}{p_i/2}^2 \prod_{j=1}^{i} \frac{\binom{\ell_j}{\omega_j^{(i)}}}{2^{\ell_j}} \approx \binom{k}{p_i} \prod_{j=1}^{i} \frac{\binom{\ell_j}{\omega_j^{(i)}}}{2^{\ell_j}},$$

from Stirling's approximation. Note that we do not have to consider the size of the level-d list, since its elements can be checked on-the-fly for being a solution or not.

The time complexity T_i for constructing each level-i list with $1 \leq i \leq d$ is given as

$$T_i = \mathcal{N}_{\mathcal{L}_{i-1}, \ell_i, \omega_i^{(i)}},$$

where $\mathcal{N}_{\mathcal{L}_{i-1}, \ell_i, \omega_i^{(i)}}$ denotes the complexity of a nearest neighbor algorithm and see Subsect. 2.4 for the definition. This is because these nearest neighbor parts are dominant in terms of time complexity. Then, the time complexity per iteration of the loop is clearly given as $\text{Max}_i(T_i)$. Recall that the probability P that the permutation matrix $\mathbf{P}$ distributes the weight as desired is

$$P = \frac{\binom{k}{p} \prod_{i=1}^{d} \binom{\ell_i}{\omega_i^{(d)}}}{\binom{n}{\omega}}.$$

Thus, the whole time complexity is given as

$$P^{-1} \cdot \text{Max}_i(T_i) = \frac{\binom{n}{\omega}}{\binom{k}{p} \prod_{i=1}^{d} \binom{\ell_i}{\omega_i^{(d)}}} \cdot \text{Max}_i(T_i).$$

Then, the memory complexity is given as $\text{Max}_i(\mathcal{L}_i)$.

3.4 Performance Analysis

This subsection analyzes the asymptotic complexity of the Both-May algorithm. We compute the time and memory complexity of the algorithm with the depth $2 \leq d \leq 4$ following the results of [10].

We first show a way of computing the time and memory complexity of ISDs in this paper. When the length n of the code word is given, we set the code rate as

$k = \hat{k}n$ for $0 < \hat{k} < 1$. We here define ω as $H^{-1}(1-\frac{k}{n})n = H^{-1}(1-\hat{k})n$, and this setting is called the full distance decoding and expected that for each random choice of inputs there exists one solution. We then compare the time complexity between $0 < \hat{k} < 1$ and take the time and memory complexity at worst-case rate for the time complexity. We here compute the time and memory complexity as the form of $2^{\alpha n + o(1)}$ and take this value α as the complexity. To find the complexity and optimal parameters, we use a numerical tool provided by the Python library spicy. We ran the optimization a thousand times to increase the confidence of the found optimum for each input parameter set.

Table 2 compares the performance of the Both-May algorithm between the depth-d with $2 \leq d \leq 4$. We use the code at https://github.com/Memphisd/Revisiting-NN-ISD for the computation of these complexities. We can see that the algorithm with $d = 3$ is more efficient compared to the case of $d = 2$ in terms of time complexity. Comparing the cases of $d = 3$ and 4, the time complexity has the same value whereas the $d = 4$ case can decrease the memory consumption. We expect that we can further decrease the time and memory complexity by taking the depth d larger than four. However, when we take $d \geq 5$, the amount of change in the complexity will be slight and the algorithms and optimizations will become more complicated. For these reasons, we choose $d = 4$ as the optimal depth in this paper as in the result of [10]. The next section will also apply our new techniques which make the algorithm more efficient to the case of $d = 4$.

4 New Time-Memory Trade-Offs for Both-May Algorithm

This section proposes a new variant of the Both-May algorithm. The difference between the proposed algorithm and the original Both-May algorithm can be seen as the following two points:

(1) At each iteration for a permutation $\mathbf{P}$, we relax the constraints for parameters and reuse the previous lower level lists of the search tree in some iterations (Subsect. 4.1).
(2) We decompose a permutation $\mathbf{P}$ and apply before generating the lists of each level (Subsect. 4.2).

After explaining these differences in Subsect. 4.1 and 4.2, we describe the proposed algorithm with depth-4 in Subsect. 4.3. Our proposed technique can be applied to the depth-d case with $d \geq 2$, but for readability we here only show the case of $d = 4$ which is seen as the optimal depth in Subsect. 3.4.

4.1 Relaxation of Constraints and Efficient Iteration

This subsection introduces new techniques used in each iteration for permutation matrix $\mathbf{P}$. The first part discusses the conditions for the correctness of the algorithm. The second part shows how to iterate the generation of the level-i

lists with $1 \le i \le 4$, and the third part estimates the number we can repeat to construct lists at each level. The techniques explained in the first two parts are based on the result of [14], and we give a new estimation in the third part.

Relaxation of Constraints. Recall that $\mathcal{R}_i$ denotes the number of possible representations of splittings of each level-i element and is computed as (5) in Subsect. 3.2. Also, q_i denotes the probability that representations of level-i elements survive the level-$(i-1)$ constraints and is computed as (6). For these values, in the case of $d = 4$, the original Both-May algorithm imposes three constraints $q_i\mathcal{R}_i = 1$ with $2 \le i \le 4$ for the correctness of the algorithm. These constraints are determined in order to find a solution with sufficiently high probability with a desired permutation $\mathbf{P}$ and to avoid selecting elements duplicately in each level list. We here relax these constraints by only considering the avoidance of duplication. Indeed, this relaxation reduces the probability that the algorithm finds a solution with a suitable $\mathbf{P}$. We compensate for this influence by repeatedly generating the search tree from the level-1 lists multiple times at each iteration for $\mathbf{P}$.

In the case of $d = 4$, to avoid duplication at the level-2, the constraint changes into $q_2\mathcal{R}_2 \le 1$. Further, we consider the condition for avoiding duplication at the level-3. For each level-3 element, the expected number of representations that satisfy the conditions of the level-2 lists is given as $q_3\mathcal{R}_3$. Note that in the case of $q_2\mathcal{R}_2 < 1$ the level-2 lists do not always include a vector satisfying the conditions of the level-2 lists, and they include any possible element with probability $q_2\mathcal{R}_2$. Then, the probability that both of a pair of representation vectors of a level-3 element are included in the level-2 lists simultaneously is $(q_2\mathcal{R}_2)^2$. Thus, the probability that the level-3 lists include any possible vector is given as $(q_2\mathcal{R}_2)^2 \cdot (q_3\mathcal{R}_3)$, and the constraint for avoiding the duplication at the level-3 is given as $(q_2\mathcal{R}_2)^2 \cdot (q_3\mathcal{R}_3) \le 1$. Similarly, we can estimate the condition for the level-4 list as

$$(q_2\mathcal{R}_2)^4 \cdot (q_3\mathcal{R}_3)^2 \cdot (q_4\mathcal{R}_4) \le 1,$$

since the probability that the level-3 lists contain a possible vector is $(q_2\mathcal{R}_2)^2 \cdot (q_3\mathcal{R}_3)$. We then can give our new conditions for the depth-4 case as

$$\begin{aligned} &q_2\mathcal{R}_2 \le 1, \\ &(q_2\mathcal{R}_2)^2 \cdot (q_3\mathcal{R}_3) \le 1, \\ &(q_2\mathcal{R}_2)^4 \cdot (q_3\mathcal{R}_3)^2 \cdot (q_4\mathcal{R}_4) \le 1. \end{aligned} \tag{7}$$

Furthermore, the number we have to repeat the construction of the search tree for each permutation $\mathbf{P}$ is given as

$$\frac{1}{(q_2\mathcal{R}_2)^4 \cdot (q_3\mathcal{R}_3)^2 \cdot (q_4\mathcal{R}_4)}.$$

This is because $(q_2\mathcal{R}_2)^4 \cdot (q_3\mathcal{R}_3)^2 \cdot (q_4\mathcal{R}_4)$ is the probability that level-4 list includes any element satisfying the conditions and is also the probability that we can find a solution when a permutation $\mathbf{P}$ is the desired one.

We then have to reconsider the estimation of the size $\mathcal{L}_i$ of the level-i lists with $i = 2, 3$. This is because we estimate $\mathcal{L}_2$ and $\mathcal{L}_3$ depending on the original conditions of $q_i\mathcal{R}_i = 1$ with $2 \le i \le 4$ in Subsect. 3.3. From the above discussion, each possible vector in the level-2 and 3 lists is included in the lists with probability $q_2\mathcal{R}_2$ and $(q_2\mathcal{R}_2)^2 \cdot (q_3\mathcal{R}_3)$, respectively. Thus, the size of the level-2 and 3 lists is given as

$$\mathcal{L}_2 = \binom{k}{p_2} \frac{\binom{\ell_1}{\omega_1^{(2)}}}{2^{\ell_1}} \frac{\binom{\ell_2}{\omega_2^{(2)}}}{2^{\ell_2}} \cdot (q_2\mathcal{R}_2),$$
$$\mathcal{L}_3 = \binom{k}{p_3} \frac{\binom{\ell_1}{\omega_1^{(3)}}}{2^{\ell_1}} \frac{\binom{\ell_2}{\omega_2^{(3)}}}{2^{\ell_2}} \frac{\binom{\ell_3}{\omega_3^{(3)}}}{2^{\ell_3}} \cdot ((q_2\mathcal{R}_2)^2 \cdot (q_3\mathcal{R}_3)). \tag{8}$$

Efficient Iterations for Target Vectors. In the above technique, we generate the search tree multiple times for each permutation matrix $\mathbf{P}$, and this number of iterations is given as

$$\frac{1}{(q_2\mathcal{R}_2)^4 \cdot (q_3\mathcal{R}_3)^2 \cdot (q_4\mathcal{R}_4)}.$$

We here introduce a way of reducing this number, and more specifically we do not have to fully generate the level-1 to 4 lists in all of these iterations.

We here consider repeating the generation of the level-3 lists from the same level-2 lists. The original algorithm generates the level-3 lists $L_1^{(3)}$ and $L_2^{(3)}$ by considering the Hamming distance from $\mathbf{0} \in \mathbb{F}_2^{\ell_3}$ and $\pi_3(\mathbf{s}')$, respectively, as in (2). We here suppose that we construct $L_1^{(3)}$ by considering the Hamming distance from a randomly chosen vector $\mathbf{a} \in \mathbb{F}_2^{\ell_3}$. From the algorithm, we then have to construct $L_2^{(3)}$ by considering the Hamming distance from $\pi_3(\mathbf{s}') + \mathbf{a}$. When we suppose that we take $\mathbf{a} \in \mathbb{F}_2^{\ell_3}$ as above randomly, the probabilities that the selection of a solution succeeds can be seen as independent and the same between randomly chosen $\mathbf{a}$. Thus, if we iterate the generation of level-3 lists t_3 times for each set of level-2 lists, we can reduce the number of iterations for the generation of the level-1 and 2 lists per each permutation matrix to $1/\left((q_2\mathcal{R}_2)^4 \cdot (q_3\mathcal{R}_3)^2 \cdot (q_4\mathcal{R}_4) \cdot t_3\right)$.

Similarly, we can repeat the generation of the level-2 lists t_2 times for the same level-1 lists. More specifically, for each iteration, we choose three ℓ_2 dimensional vectors $\mathbf{a}_i$ with $1 \le i \le 3$, and we generate the level-2 lists $\bar{L}_1^{(2)}, \ldots, \bar{L}_4^{(2)}$ by considering the Hamming distance from $\mathbf{a}_1, \mathbf{a}_2, \mathbf{a}_3, \pi_2(\mathbf{s}') + \sum_{i=1}^{3} \mathbf{a}_i$, respectively. We here denote by t_1 the number of iterations for the generation of the level-1 lists. Then, from the above techniques, this t_1 is set as the number of remaining iterations and is given as

$$t_1 = \frac{1}{(q_2\mathcal{R}_2)^4 \cdot (q_3\mathcal{R}_3)^2 \cdot (q_4\mathcal{R}_4)} \cdot \frac{1}{t_2 \cdot t_3}. \tag{9}$$

Estimation of Number of Iterations. We then consider the upper bound of the number t_3 we can repeat the generation of the level-3 lists. From the above discussion, we would like to take this t_3 as large as possible, and this t_3 is clearly lower than or equal to 2^{ℓ_3}. We suppose that there exist four level-2 elements $\mathbf{y}_i \in L_i^{(2)}$ with $1 \le i \le 4$, and these four elements satisfy the conditions for the solution except the one for the third layer's conditions of the level-3 lists which is dependent on a randomly chosen vector $\mathbf{a}$. More specifically, when we let $\mathbf{z}_1 = \mathbf{y}_1 + \mathbf{y}_2$, $\mathbf{z}_2 = \mathbf{y}_3 + \mathbf{y}_4$, and $\mathbf{e}_2 = \mathbf{z}_1 + \mathbf{z}_2$, we assume that $\mathbf{e}_2$ satisfies the conditions of the level-4 list, and $\mathbf{z}_1$ and $\mathbf{z}_2$ satisfy the conditions of the level-3 lists except for

$$\mathrm{wt}(\pi_3(\mathbf{H}_1 \cdot \mathbf{z}_1) + \mathbf{a}) = \omega_3^{(3)},$$
$$\mathrm{wt}(\pi_3(\mathbf{H}_1 \cdot \mathbf{z}_2) + (\pi_3(\mathbf{s}') + \mathbf{a})) = \omega_3^{(3)}.$$

We then compute the probability that it holds the above equations for a randomly chosen target vector $\mathbf{a}$. We can estimate this probability as

$$\frac{\binom{\omega_3^{(4)}}{\omega_3^{(4)}/2}\binom{\ell_3-\omega_3^{(4)}}{\omega_3^{(3)}-\omega_3^{(4)}/2}}{2^{\ell_3}},$$

similarly to the estimation of the probability q_i in Subsect. 3.2. This means that, assuming the existence of such vectors $\mathbf{y}_i$ with $1 \le i \le 4$, we can find such an $\mathbf{e}_2$ in the level-4 list by iterating the construction of the level-3 and 4 lists $2^{\ell_3}/\binom{\omega_3^{(4)}}{\omega_3^{(4)}/2}\binom{\ell_3-\omega_3^{(4)}}{\omega_3^{(3)}-\omega_3^{(4)}/2}$ times with high probability. In other words, it is inefficient that we take the t_3 larger than this value, and thus we set the upper bound of this t_3 as

$$t_3 \le \frac{2^{\ell_3}}{\binom{\omega_3^{(4)}}{\omega_3^{(4)}/2}\binom{\ell_3-\omega_3^{(4)}}{\omega_3^{(3)}-\omega_3^{(4)}/2}}.$$

Similarly, we consider the upper bound of t_2. For three randomly chosen ℓ_2 dimensional vectors used to generate the level-2 lists, we here consider the probability that a candidate of solution satisfies the second layer's conditions of the level-2 and 3 lists. As in the above case, this probability is given as

$$\frac{\left(\binom{\omega_2^{(3)}}{\omega_2^{(3)}/2}\binom{\ell_2-\omega_2^{(3)}}{\omega_2^{(2)}-\omega_2^{(3)}/2}\right)^2 \cdot \left(\binom{\omega_2^{(4)}}{\omega_2^{(4)}/2}\binom{\ell_2-\omega_2^{(4)}}{\omega_2^{(3)}-\omega_2^{(4)}/2}\right)}{2^{3\ell_2}},$$

and thus the upper bound of t_2 is given as

$$t_2 \le \frac{2^{3\ell_2}}{\left(\binom{\omega_2^{(3)}}{\omega_2^{(3)}/2}\binom{\ell_2-\omega_2^{(3)}}{\omega_2^{(2)}-\omega_2^{(3)}/2}\right)^2 \cdot \left(\binom{\omega_2^{(4)}}{\omega_2^{(4)}/2}\binom{\ell_2-\omega_2^{(4)}}{\omega_2^{(3)}-\omega_2^{(4)}/2}\right)}.$$

In conclusion, t_2 and t_3 are determined as follows:

$$t_3 = \mathrm{Min}\left\{ \frac{2^{\ell_3}}{\binom{\omega_3^{(4)}}{\omega_3^{(4)}/2}\binom{\ell_3-\omega_3^{(4)}}{\omega_3^{(3)}-\omega_3^{(4)}/2}}, \frac{1}{(q_2\mathcal{R}_2)^4 \cdot (q_3\mathcal{R}_3)^2 \cdot (q_4\mathcal{R}_4)} \right\},$$

$$t_2 = \mathrm{Min}\left\{ \frac{2^{3\ell_2}}{\left(\binom{\omega_2^{(3)}}{\omega_2^{(3)}/2}\binom{\ell_2-\omega_2^{(3)}}{\omega_2^{(2)}-\omega_2^{(3)}/2}\right)^2 \cdot \left(\binom{\omega_2^{(4)}}{\omega_2^{(4)}/2}\binom{\ell_2-\omega_2^{(4)}}{\omega_2^{(3)}-\omega_2^{(4)}/2}\right)}, \frac{1}{(q_2\mathcal{R}_2)^4 \cdot (q_3\mathcal{R}_3)^2 \cdot (q_4\mathcal{R}_4)} \cdot \frac{1}{t_3} \right\}.$$

We here first choose t_3 as large as possible for the efficiency and then choose t_2 considering the above condition and the value of t_3. Finally, we take the value of t_1 as in (9).

4.2 Efficient Technique on Choice of P

This subsection considers the number of iterations for choosing a desired permutation **P**. We propose this technique for the first time to our best knowledge, but note that the complexity estimation that may have used this proposed method is done in the code at https://github.com/Memphisd/Revisiting-NN-ISD.

The original algorithm reselects the permutation matrix $\binom{n}{\omega}/\binom{k}{p}\prod_{i=1}^{4}\binom{\ell_i}{\omega_i^{(4)}}$ times to find a permutation that distributes the weight of a solution vector as desired. We can reduce this number by regenerating the level-i lists multiple times from the same level-$(i-1)$ lists as in the technique proposed in Subsect. 4.1.

We can roughly describe the algorithm with the technique as follows:

(1) Take matrices **P** and **Q** and generate the level-1 lists.
(2) Choose a random permutation $\mathbf{P}'_1$ with size $(\ell_2 + \ell_3 + \ell_4)$, and set

$$\mathbf{P}_1 = \begin{pmatrix} \mathbf{I}_{\ell_1} & & \\ & \mathbf{P}'_1 & \\ & & \mathbf{I}_k \end{pmatrix} \in \mathbb{F}_2^{n\times n}, \quad \bar{\mathbf{P}}_1 = \begin{pmatrix} \mathbf{I}_{\ell_1} & \\ & \mathbf{P'}_1^{-1} \end{pmatrix} \in \mathbb{F}_2^{(n-k)\times(n-k)}. \tag{10}$$

Then, generate the level-2 lists on $\bar{\mathbf{P}}_1\mathbf{QHPP}_1$ and $\bar{\mathbf{P}}_1\mathbf{Qs}$.
(3) Choose a random permutation $\mathbf{P}'_2$ with size $(\ell_3 + \ell_4)$, and set

$$\mathbf{P}_2 = \begin{pmatrix} \mathbf{I}_{\ell_1+\ell_2} & & \\ & \mathbf{P}'_2 & \\ & & \mathbf{I}_k \end{pmatrix} \in \mathbb{F}_2^{n\times n}, \quad \bar{\mathbf{P}}_2 = \begin{pmatrix} \mathbf{I}_{\ell_1+\ell_2} & \\ & \mathbf{P'}_2^{-1} \end{pmatrix} \in \mathbb{F}_2^{(n-k)\times(n-k)}. \tag{11}$$

Then, generate the level-3 lists on $\bar{\mathbf{P}}_2\bar{\mathbf{P}}_1\mathbf{QHPP}_1$ and $\bar{\mathbf{P}}_2\bar{\mathbf{P}}_1\mathbf{Qs}$.
(4) Generate the level-4 list and check the existence of a solution.

From the original description, one can see that the generation of the level-1 lists is only related to the first ℓ_1 and the last k columns of **QHP**. Thus, we can retake a permutation $\mathbf{P}_1$ of the remaining $(n-k-\ell_1)$ columns after the generation of the level-1 lists. We here also multiply $\bar{\mathbf{P}}_1$ to **QHP** from the left side to remain the identity part of **QHP**. Similarly, since the conditions for the level-2 lists are only related to the first $(\ell_1+\ell_2)$ and the last k columns, we can retake a permutation $\mathbf{P}_2$ of the remaining $(n-k-\ell_1-\ell_2)$ columns after the generation of the level-2 lists.

From the above discussions, the probabilities that $\mathbf{P}$, $\mathbf{P}_1$, and $\mathbf{P}_2$ satisfy the required conditions are given as

$$\frac{\binom{\ell_1}{\omega_1^{(4)}}\binom{\ell_2+\ell_3+\ell_4}{\omega_2^{(4)}+\omega_3^{(4)}+\omega_4^{(4)}}\binom{k}{p}}{\binom{n}{\omega}},\ \frac{\binom{\ell_2}{\omega_2^{(4)}}\binom{\ell_3+\ell_4}{\omega_3^{(4)}+\omega_4^{(4)}}}{\binom{\ell_2+\ell_3+\ell_4}{\omega_2^{(4)}+\omega_3^{(4)}+\omega_4^{(4)}}},\ \frac{\binom{\ell_3}{\omega_3^{(4)}}\binom{\ell_4}{\omega_4^{(4)}}}{\binom{\ell_3+\ell_4}{\omega_3^{(4)}+\omega_4^{(4)}}},$$

respectively. Thus, the number of times we can repeat the step (1), (2), and (3) is given as

$$\frac{\binom{n}{\omega}}{\binom{\ell_1}{\omega_1^{(4)}}\binom{\ell_2+\ell_3+\ell_4}{\omega_2^{(4)}+\omega_3^{(4)}+\omega_4^{(4)}}\binom{k}{p}},\ \frac{\binom{\ell_2+\ell_3+\ell_4}{\omega_2^{(4)}+\omega_3^{(4)}+\omega_4^{(4)}}}{\binom{\ell_2}{\omega_2^{(4)}}\binom{\ell_3+\ell_4}{\omega_3^{(4)}+\omega_4^{(4)}}},\ \frac{\binom{\ell_3+\ell_4}{\omega_3^{(4)}+\omega_4^{(4)}}}{\binom{\ell_3}{\omega_3^{(4)}}\binom{\ell_4}{\omega_4^{(4)}}},$$

respectively.

4.3 Resulting Our Algorithm

This subsection describes the proposed variant of the Both-May algorithm combining the techniques given in Subsect. 4.1 and 4.2.

In the proposed algorithm, we first generate level-0 lists $\bar{L}_1^{(0)},\ldots,\bar{L}_{16}^{(0)}$ as

$$\begin{aligned}\bar{L}_j^{(0)} &= \{(\mathbf{x},\mathbf{0}) \mid \mathbf{x}\in\mathcal{B}(k/2,p_1/2)\},\ (j=1,3,\ldots,15),\\ \bar{L}_j^{(0)} &= \{(\mathbf{0},\mathbf{x}) \mid \mathbf{x}\in\mathcal{B}(k/2,p_1/2)\},\ (j=2,4,\ldots,16),\end{aligned} \tag{12}$$

as in the original algorithm. In the level-1 step, we choose random vectors $\mathbf{a}_1^{(1)},\ldots,\mathbf{a}_7^{(1)}\in\mathbb{F}_2^{\ell_1}$ and set $\mathbf{a}_8^{(1)}=\pi_1(\mathbf{s}')+\sum_{j=1}^{7}\mathbf{a}_j^{(1)}$. For these vectors, we generate the level-1 lists $\bar{L}_j^{(1)}$ with $1\le j\le 8$ as

$$\bar{L}_j^{(1)}=\left\{\mathbf{x}+\mathbf{y}\mid \mathbf{x}\in\bar{L}_{2j-1}^{(0)},\mathbf{y}\in\bar{L}_{2j}^{(0)},\mathrm{wt}\left(\pi_1(\mathbf{H}_1(\mathbf{x}+\mathbf{y}))+\mathbf{a}_j^{(1)}\right)=\omega_1^{(1)}\right\}. \tag{13}$$

Then, in the level-2 step, we choose $\mathbf{a}_1^{(2)},\ldots,\mathbf{a}_3^{(2)}\in\mathbb{F}_2^{\ell_2}$ randomly and set $\mathbf{a}_4^{(2)}=\pi_2(\bar{\mathbf{P}}_1\mathbf{s}')+\sum_{j=1}^{3}\mathbf{a}_j^{(2)}$. We then generate $L_j^{(2)}$ with $1\le j\le 4$ as

$$L_j^{(2)}=\left\{\mathbf{x}+\mathbf{y}\mid \mathbf{x}\in\bar{L}_{2j-1}^{(1)},\mathbf{y}\in\bar{L}_{2j}^{(1)},\mathrm{wt}\left(\pi_2(\bar{\mathbf{P}}_1\mathbf{H}_1(\mathbf{x}+\mathbf{y}))+\mathbf{a}_j^{(2)}\right)=\omega_2^{(2)}\right\}, \tag{14}$$

and generate the level-2 lists $\bar{L}_j^{(2)}$ with $1 \leq j \leq 4$ as

$$\bar{L}_j^{(2)} = \left\{\mathbf{x} \mid \mathbf{x} \in L_j^{(2)}, \mathrm{wt}(\mathbf{x}) = p_2, \mathrm{wt}\left(\pi_1(\bar{\mathbf{P}}_1\mathbf{H}_1\mathbf{x}) + a_{2j-1}^{(1)} + a_{2j}^{(1)}\right) = \omega_1^{(2)}\right\}. \tag{15}$$

Similarly, for a randomly chosen vector $\mathbf{a}_1^{(3)} \in \mathbb{F}_2^{\ell_3}$ and $\mathbf{a}_2^{(3)} = \pi_3(\bar{\mathbf{P}}_2\bar{\mathbf{P}}_1\mathbf{s}') + \mathbf{a}_1^{(3)}$, the level-3 step generates some lists $L_j^{(3)}$ with $1 \leq j \leq 2$ as

$$L_j^{(3)} = \left\{\mathbf{x}+\mathbf{y} \mid \mathbf{x} \in \bar{L}_{2j-1}^{(2)}, \mathbf{y} \in \bar{L}_{2j}^{(2)}, \mathrm{wt}\left(\pi_3(\bar{\mathbf{P}}_2\bar{\mathbf{P}}_1\mathbf{H}_1(\mathbf{x}+\mathbf{y})) + \mathbf{a}_j^{(3)}\right) = \omega_3^{(3)}\right\}, \tag{16}$$

and $\bar{L}_j^{(3)}$ with $1 \leq j \leq 2$ as

$$\begin{aligned}\bar{L}_j^{(3)} = \Bigg\{\mathbf{x} \mid \mathbf{x} \in L_j^{(3)}, \mathrm{wt}(\mathbf{x}) = p_3, \mathrm{wt}\left(\pi_1(\bar{\mathbf{P}}_2\bar{\mathbf{P}}_1\mathbf{H}_1\mathbf{x}) + \sum_{i=4j-3}^{4j} \mathbf{a}_i^{(1)}\right) = \omega_1^{(3)}, \\ \mathrm{wt}\left(\pi_2(\bar{\mathbf{P}}_2\bar{\mathbf{P}}_1\mathbf{H}_1\mathbf{x}) + \mathbf{a}_{2j-1}^{(2)} + \mathbf{a}_{2j}^{(2)}\right) = \omega_2^{(3)}\Bigg\}.\end{aligned} \tag{17}$$

Finally, we generate the level-4 list as

$$\begin{aligned}\bar{L}^{(4)} = \Big\{&\mathbf{x}+\mathbf{y} \mid \mathbf{x} \in \bar{L}_1^{(3)}, \mathbf{y} \in \bar{L}_2^{(3)}, \\ &\mathrm{wt}(\pi_4(\bar{\mathbf{P}}_2\bar{\mathbf{P}}_1\mathbf{H}_1(\mathbf{x}+\mathbf{y}) + \bar{\mathbf{P}}_2\bar{\mathbf{P}}_1\mathbf{s}')) = \omega_4^{(4)}\Big\}.\end{aligned} \tag{18}$$

From the first technique, the conditions for the correctness are given as (7). The sizes of the level-0 and 1 lists are the same as those of the original algorithm, but the sizes of the level-2 and 3 lists are given as (8). When we combine the first and second techniques, the numbers $\bar{t}_1, \bar{t}_2, \bar{t}_3$ we repeat the generation of the level-1, 2, and 3 lists are given as

$$\begin{aligned}\bar{t}_1 &= \frac{\binom{n}{\omega}}{\binom{\ell_1}{\omega_1^{(4)}}\binom{\ell_2+\ell_3+\ell_4}{\omega_2^{(4)}+\omega_3^{(4)}+\omega_4^{(4)}}\binom{k}{p}} \cdot t_1, \\ \bar{t}_2 &= \frac{\binom{\ell_2+\ell_3+\ell_4}{\omega_2^{(4)}+\omega_3^{(4)}+\omega_4^{(4)}}}{\binom{\ell_2}{\omega_2^{(4)}}\binom{\ell_3+\ell_4}{\omega_3^{(4)}+\omega_4^{(4)}}} \cdot t_2, \\ \bar{t}_3 &= \frac{\binom{\ell_3+\ell_4}{\omega_3^{(4)}+\omega_4^{(4)}}}{\binom{\ell_3}{\omega_3^{(4)}}\binom{\ell_4}{\omega_4^{(4)}}} \cdot t_3,\end{aligned} \tag{19}$$

respectively. (See Subsect. 4.1 for the values of t_1, t_2, t_3.) Then, the time complexity of the algorithm is estimated by

$$\mathrm{Max}\left\{\bar{t}_1 \cdot T_1,\ \bar{t}_1 \cdot \bar{t}_2 \cdot T_2,\ \bar{t}_1 \cdot \bar{t}_2 \cdot \bar{t}_3 \cdot T_3,\ \bar{t}_1 \cdot \bar{t}_2 \cdot \bar{t}_3 \cdot T_4\right\},$$

where T_i with $1 \leq i \leq 4$ denotes the complexity for constructing the level-i lists and $T_i = \mathcal{N}_{\mathcal{L}_{i-1}, \ell_i, \omega_i^{(i)}}$.

Algorithm 2. Our Proposed Variant of the Both-May Algorithm Depth-4

Input: $\mathbf{H} \in \mathbb{F}_2^{(n-k)\times n}$, $\mathbf{s} \in \mathbb{F}_2^{n-k}$, and $\omega \in \mathbb{N}$
Output: $\mathbf{e} \in \mathbb{F}_2^n$ s.t. $\mathbf{H} \cdot \mathbf{e} = \mathbf{s}$ and $\mathrm{wt}(\mathbf{e}) = \omega$

Choose parameters

$$p_1, p_2, p_3, p_4, \ell_1, \ell_2, \ell_3, \omega_1^{(1)}, \omega_1^{(2)}, \omega_1^{(3)}, \omega_1^{(4)}, \omega_2^{(2)}, \omega_2^{(3)}, \omega_2^{(4)}, \omega_3^{(3)}, \omega_3^{(4)}.$$

Set $\bar{t}_1, \bar{t}_2, \bar{t}_3$ as in (19).
Generate the level-0 lists $\bar{L}_1^{(0)}, \ldots, \bar{L}_{16}^{(0)}$ as in (12).
repeat $\bar{t}_1$ **times**
  Choose a random permutation matrix $\mathbf{P} \in \mathbb{F}_2^{n\times n}$.
  Compute $\mathbf{Q} \in \mathbb{F}_2^{(n-k)\times(n-k)}$ such that $\mathbf{QHP} = (\mathbf{I}_{n-k} \mid \mathbf{H}_1)$, $\mathbf{H}' \leftarrow \mathbf{QHP}$, and $\mathbf{s}' \leftarrow \mathbf{Qs}$.
  Choose $\mathbf{a}_1^{(1)}, \ldots, \mathbf{a}_7^{(1)} \in \mathbb{F}_2^{\ell_1}$ and $\mathbf{a}_8^{(1)} = \pi_1(\mathbf{s}') + \sum_{j=1}^{7} \mathbf{a}_j^{(1)}$.
  Generate the level-1 lists $\bar{L}_1^{(1)}, \ldots, \bar{L}_8^{(1)}$ as in (13) by a nearest neighbor algorithm. ▷ Subsection 4.1
  repeat $\bar{t}_2$ **times**
    Choose two matrices $\mathbf{P}_1$ and $\bar{\mathbf{P}}_1$ with the form of (10). ▷ Subsection 4.2
    Choose $\mathbf{a}_1^{(2)}, \ldots, \mathbf{a}_3^{(2)} \in \mathbb{F}_2^{\ell_2}$ and $\mathbf{a}_4^{(2)} = \pi_2(\bar{\mathbf{P}}_1\mathbf{s}') + \sum_{j=1}^{3} \mathbf{a}_j^{(2)}$.
    Generate four lists $L_1^{(2)}, \ldots, L_4^{(2)}$ as in (14) by a nearest neighbor algorithm. ▷ Subsection 4.1
    Generate the level-2 lists $\bar{L}_1^{(2)}, \ldots, \bar{L}_4^{(2)}$ as in (15).
    repeat $\bar{t}_3$ **times**
      Choose two matrices $\mathbf{P}_2$ and $\bar{\mathbf{P}}_2$ with the form of (11). ▷ Subsection 4.2
      Choose $\mathbf{a}_1^{(3)} \in \mathbb{F}_2^{\ell_3}$ and $\mathbf{a}_2^{(3)} = \pi_3(\mathbf{P}_2\bar{\mathbf{P}}_1\mathbf{s}') + \mathbf{a}_1^{(3)}$.
      Generate two lists $L_1^{(3)}, L_2^{(3)}$ as in (16) by a nearest neighbor algorithm. ▷ Subsection 4.1
      Generate the level-3 lists $\bar{L}_1^{(3)}, \bar{L}_2^{(3)}$ as in (17).
      Generate the level-4 list $\bar{L}^{(4)}$ as in (18) by a nearest neighbor algorithm.
      if $\exists \mathbf{e}_2 \in \bar{L}^{(4)}$ s.t. $\mathrm{wt}(\mathbf{e}_2) = p_4, \mathrm{wt}(\mathbf{H}_1\mathbf{e}_2 + \mathbf{s}') = \omega - p_4$ **then**
        return $\mathbf{P}(\mathbf{H}_1\mathbf{e}_2 + \mathbf{s}', \mathbf{e}_2)$
      end if
    end
  end
end

See Algorithm 2 for the details of the proposed algorithm. Note that in this description, we repeat t_1 times not only the generation of the level-1 lists but also the choice of $\mathbf{P}$ for simplicity, and this does not affect the asymptotic efficiency.

5 Performance Analysis

This section compares the performance of the proposed variant and the original version of the Both-May algorithm [7,10]. We here calculate the exponents of the time and memory complexity at the worst-case rate as in Subsect. 3.4. We estimate the complexity in the full distance setting with $\omega = H^{-1}(1-\hat{k})n$ and the half distance setting with $\omega = H^{-1}(1-\hat{k})n/2$.

Figure 1 first compares the asymptotic complexity of the original and the proposed variant of the Both-May algorithm in the full distance setting. As a result, the proposed algorithm shows more efficient trade-off curves than the original algorithm. For example, the time complexity of the original algorithm and the proposed one at the memory limitation $2^{0.04n}$ is given as $2^{0.105n}$ and $2^{0.101n}$, respectively. Further, we can confirm that the proposed one outperforms the time-memory trade-off version of BJMM proposed in [14]. The optimal parameters for the proposed algorithm in the case of the memory limitation $2^{0.04n}$ are

$p_1 = 0.01073n, \quad p_2 = 0.01380n, \quad p_3 = 0.01932n, \quad p_4 = 0.02768n,$
$\ell_1 = 0.05943n, \quad \ell_2 = 0.00073n, \quad \ell_3 = 0.07177n,$
$\omega_1^{(1)} = 0.05648n, \omega_1^{(2)} = 0.00195n, \omega_1^{(3)} = 0.00272n, \omega_1^{(4)} = 0.00391n,$
$\omega_2^{(2)} = 0.00003n, \omega_2^{(3)} = 0.00004n, \omega_2^{(4)} = 0.00005n,$
$\omega_3^{(3)} = 0.06142n, \omega_3^{(4)} = 0.01035n.$

In the half distance setting, we obtain a similar improvement. Indeed, at the memory limitation $2^{0.01n}$, the time complexity of the time-memory trade-off BJMM, the original Both-May, and the proposed one is given as $2^{0.0528n}$, $2^{0.0525n}$, and $2^{0.0519n}$, respectively.

Remark 1 (Bit Complexity). It is another way of evaluating the efficiency of ISDs to estimate the bit complexity of them, and there have been recently several results on the bit complexity of ISDs [5,14–16,20]. The bit complexity is estimated by substituting specific parameters for the complexity in the big O notations.

Binary Syndrome Decoding Estimator [11,13] is a useful tool to compute the bit complexity of each ISD algorithm for the SDP with given parameter sets. This estimator uses the depth-2 version of the Both-May algorithm to compute the bit complexity, even though the depth-4 version is known as the best one in terms of the asymptotic time complexity as described in Subsect. 3.4. This is probably because when we take the depth d larger, the efficiency of the algorithm does not improve as much as in the case of asymptotic complexity, and the cost of calculating the bit complexity increases.

On the other hand, in the case of $d = 2$, we cannot apply some of the proposed techniques to the Both-May algorithm. More specifically, we can repeat the generation of higher levels of the search tree only when $d \geq 3$.

For these reasons, the proposed scheme would not reduce the bit complexity of the Both-May algorithm compared with the case of the asymptotic complexity, and thus we do not deal with the bit complexity of the proposed scheme in this paper. It is our future work to estimate the bit complexity of the proposed scheme with $d \geq 3$ and make it more efficient.

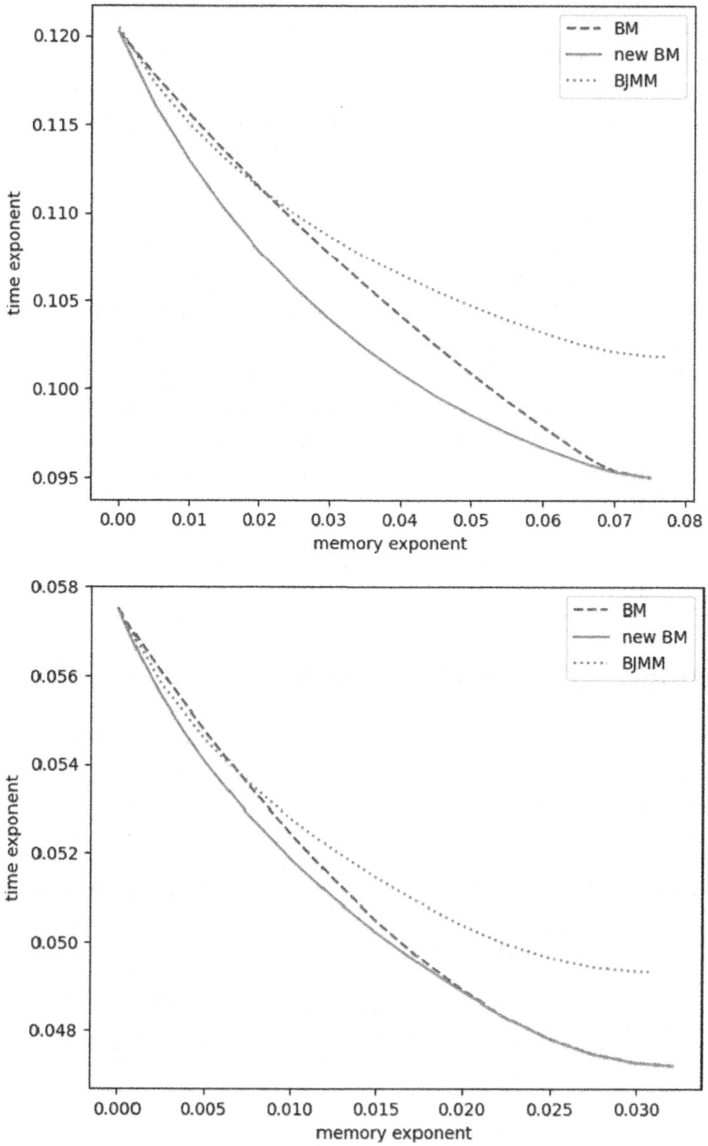

Fig. 1. Comparison between the original and our new trade-off version of the Both-May algorithm, and the time memory trade-off BJMM algorithm in the full distance setting (above) and half distance setting (below)

6 Conclusion

The binary syndrome decoding problem is an important problem upon which code-based cryptosystems rely. The literature sometimes considers the efficiency of algorithms for the problem in the situation where the amount of memory usage is limited. The Both-May algorithm, which is an information set decoding algorithm, is known as the asymptotically fastest algorithm on the decoding problem. However, the efficiency of the Both-May algorithm in the case of limited memory complexity has not been sufficiently studied.

In this work, we proposed a new variant of the Both-May algorithm and analyzed its time-memory trade-offs. The proposed algorithm is constructed by using the previous lower level lists in the search tree and only creating the higher level lists in most times of iterations to reduce the time complexity. More specifically, we provided a novel estimation of the number we can iterate the generation of higher level lists of the tree from the success probability of a nearest neighbor algorithm. As a result, we confirmed that the proposed algorithm can reduce the asymptotic time complexity from the original Both-May algorithm in the situation where the memory consumption is limited. We also showed that the proposed algorithm outperforms the existing time-memory trade-off variants of other ISD algorithms.

Acknowledgements. This work was supported by JSPS KAKENHI Grant Number 24K20771, Japan.

A Complexity Estimation Code

We here provide a code to estimate the time and memory complexity of the proposed algorithm in Python. This code is written based on codes at https://github.com/Memphisd/Revisiting-NN-ISD, and in this framework, we can use the code below.

Listing 1.1. Code to estimate the complexity of the proposed algorithm

```
import collections
from basic_functionalities import *

set_vars = collections.namedtuple('BM', 'p d1 d2 d3 da1 da2 da3 db2
     db3 dc3 la lb lc wa wb wc')

num_vars=16

def inject(f) : return wrap(f, set_vars)

k = lambda x : 0.1
w_=Hi(1-k([0]))
w = lambda x : w_

p3 = lambda x: x.p/2 + x.d3
p2 = lambda x: p3(x)/2 + x.d2
p1 = lambda x: p2(x)/2 + x.d1

wa3 = lambda x: x.wa/2 + x.da3
wa2 = lambda x: wa3(x)/2 + x.da2
```

```
wa1 = lambda x: wa2(x)/2 + x.da1

wb3 = lambda x: x.wb/2 + x.db3
wb2 = lambda x: wb3(x)/2 + x.db2

wc3 = lambda x: x.wc/2 + x.dc3

r1 = lambda x: reps(p2(x), x.d1, k(x))
r2 = lambda x: reps(p3(x), x.d2, k(x))
r3 = lambda x: reps(x.p , x.d3, k(x))

c1 = lambda x: x.la - reps(wa2(x), x.da1, x.la)
c2 = lambda x: x.la - reps(wa3(x), x.da2, x.la) + x.lb - reps(wb3(x), x.db2, x.lb)
c3 = lambda x: x.la - reps(x.wa , x.da3, x.la) + x.lb - reps(x.wb, x.db3, x.lb) + x.lc - reps(x.wc, x.dc3, x.lc)

L1 = lambda x: binomH((k(x))/2, (p1(x))/2.)
L2 = lambda x: binomH( k(x) , p1(x) ) - x.la + binomH(x.la,wa1(x))
L3 = lambda x: binomH( k(x) , p2(x) ) - x.la + binomH(x.la,wa2(x)) - x.lb + binomH(x.lb,wb2(x)) - (c1(x) - r1(x))
L4 = lambda x: binomH( k(x) , p3(x) ) - x.la + binomH(x.la,wa3(x)) - x.lb + binomH(x.lb,wb3(x)) - x.lc + binomH(x.lc,wc3(x)) - (c2(x) + 2 * c1(x) - (r2(x) + 2 * r1(x)))

constraints = [
#representation constraints
{ 'type' : 'ineq', 'fun' : inject(lambda x : c1(x) - r1(x))},
{ 'type' : 'ineq', 'fun' : inject(lambda x : c2(x) + 2 * c1(x) - (r2(x) + 2 * r1(x)))},
{ 'type' : 'ineq', 'fun' : inject(lambda x : c3(x) + 2 * c2(x) + 4 * c1(x) - (r3(x) + 2 * r2(x) + 4 * r1(x)))},

#correctness
{ 'type' : 'ineq', 'fun' : inject(lambda x : (1 - k(x) - x.la ) - (w(x) - x.p - x.wa ))},
{ 'type' : 'ineq', 'fun' : inject(lambda x : (1 - k(x) - x.la - x.lb ) - (w(x) - x.p - x.wa - x.wb ))},
{ 'type' : 'ineq', 'fun' : inject(lambda x : (1 - k(x) - x.la - x.lb - x.lc) - (w(x) - x.p - x.wa - x.wb - x.wc))},
{ 'type' : 'ineq', 'fun' : inject(lambda x : 1 - k(x) - x.la - x.lb - x.lc )},

{ 'type' : 'ineq', 'fun' : inject(lambda x : w(x) - x.p - x.wa - x.wb - x.wc) },

{ 'type' : 'ineq', 'fun' : inject(lambda x : k(x) - x.p - x.d3 )},
{ 'type' : 'ineq', 'fun' : inject(lambda x : k(x) - p3(x) - x.d2)},
{ 'type' : 'ineq', 'fun' : inject(lambda x : k(x) - p2(x) - x.d1)},
{ 'type' : 'ineq', 'fun' : inject(lambda x : k(x) - p1(x) )},
```

```
{ 'type' : 'ineq', 'fun' : inject(lambda x : x.la - x.wa - x.da3)
    },
{ 'type' : 'ineq', 'fun' : inject(lambda x : x.la - wa3(x) - x.da2
    ) },
{ 'type' : 'ineq', 'fun' : inject(lambda x : x.la - wa2(x) - x.da1
    ) },
{ 'type' : 'ineq', 'fun' : inject(lambda x : x.la - wa1(x) ) },

{ 'type' : 'ineq', 'fun' : inject(lambda x : x.lb - x.wb - x.db3)
    },
{ 'type' : 'ineq', 'fun' : inject(lambda x : x.lb - wb3(x) - x.db2
    ) },
{ 'type' : 'ineq', 'fun' : inject(lambda x : x.lb - wb2(x)) },

{ 'type' : 'ineq', 'fun' : inject(lambda x : x.lc - x.wc - x.dc3)
    },
{ 'type' : 'ineq', 'fun' : inject(lambda x : x.lc - wc3(x)) },
]

def memory(x):
    return max(L1(x),L2(x),L3(x),L4(x))

def time_lists(x):
    timeL1=mo_nn(L1(x), x.la, wa1(x))
    timeL2=mo_nn(L2(x), x.lb, wb2(x))
    timeL3=mo_nn(L3(x), x.lc, wc3(x))
    timeL4=mo_nn(L4(x), 1 - k(x) -x.la - x.lb - x.lc, w(x) - x.p
        - x.wa - x.wb - x.wc)

    return timeL1, timeL2, timeL3, timeL4

def time_perms(x):
    perms_p = binomH(1. , w(x) ) - binomH(1 - k(x) , w(x) - x.p )
        - binomH(k(x), x.p )
    perms_a = binomH(1 - k(x) , w(x) - x.p ) - binomH(1 - k(x) -
        x.la , w(x) - x.p - x.wa ) - binomH(x.la, x.wa)
    perms_b = binomH(1 - k(x) - x.la , w(x) - x.p - x.wa ) -
        binomH(1 - k(x) - x.la - x.lb , w(x) - x.p - x.wa - x.wb
        ) - binomH(x.lb, x.wb)
    perms_c = binomH(1 - k(x) - x.la - x.lb, w(x) - x.p - x.wa -
        x.wb) - binomH(1 - k(x) - x.la - x.lb - x.lc, w(x) - x.p
        - x.wa - x.wb - x.wc) - binomH(x.lc, x.wc)

    return perms_p, perms_a, perms_b, perms_c

def time(x):
    x = set_vars(*x)
    perms_p, perms_a, perms_b, perms_c = time_perms(x)
    timeL1, timeL2, timeL3, timeL4 = time_lists(x)

    t3 = lambda x: min(c3(x) + 2 * c2(x) + 4 * c1(x) - (r3(x) + 2
        * r2(x) + 4 * r1(x)), x.lc - reps(x.wc, x.dc3, x.lc))
    t2 = lambda x: min(c3(x) + 2 * c2(x) + 4 * c1(x) - (r3(x) + 2
        * r2(x) + 4 * r1(x)) - t3(x), 3 * x.lb - reps(x.wb , x.
        db3, x.lb) - 2 * reps(wb3(x), x.db2, x.lb))
```

```
    t1 = lambda x: c3(x) + 2 * c2(x) + 4 * c1(x) - (r3(x) + 2 *
        r2(x) + 4 * r1(x)) - t3(x) - t2(x)

    return perms_p + perms_a + t1(x) + max(timeL1, perms_b + t2(x)
        + max(timeL2, perms_c + t3(x) + max(timeL3, timeL4)))
```

References

1. Albrecht, M.R., et al.: Classic McEliece: Conservative code-based cryptography. In: Submission to NIST Post-Quantum Cryptography Standardization Process (2022)
2. Aragon, N., et al.: BIKE: Bit flipping key encapsulation. In: Submission to NIST Post-Quantum Cryptography Standardization Process (2022)
3. Becker, A., Joux, A., May, A., Meurer, A.: Decoding random binary linear codes in $2^{n/20}$: How $1 + 1 = 0$ improves information set decoding. In: Pointcheval, D., Johansson, T. (eds.) EUROCRYPT 2012. LNCS, vol. 7237, pp. 520–536. Springer, Heidelberg (2012). https://doi.org/10.1007/978-3-642-29011-4_31
4. Berlekamp, E., McEliece, R., Tilborg, H.V.: On the inherent intractability of certain coding problems (corresp.). IEEE Trans. Inf. Theory **24**(3), 384–386 (1978)
5. Bhattacharyya, S., Sarkar, P.: Concrete time/memory trade-offs in generalised Stern's ISD algorithm. In: INDOCRYPT 2023. LNCS, vol. 14459, pp. 307–328. Springer, Heidelberg (2024). https://doi.org/10.1007/978-3-031-56232-7_15
6. Both, L., May, A.: Optimizing BJMM with nearest neighbors: full decoding in $2^{2/21n}$ and McEliece security. In: WCC Workshop on Coding and Cryptography, p. 214 (2017)
7. Both, L., May, A.: Decoding linear codes with high error rate and its impact for LPN security. In: Lange, T., Steinwandt, R. (eds.) PQCrypto 2018. LNCS, vol. 10786, pp. 25–46. Springer, Cham (2018). https://doi.org/10.1007/978-3-319-79063-3_2
8. Carrier, K., Debris-Alazard, T., Meyer-Hilfiger, C., Tillich, J.-P.: Statistical decoding 2.0: reducing decoding to LPN. In: ASIACRYPT 2022. LNCS, vol. 13794, pp. 477–507. Springer, Heidelberg (2022). https://doi.org/10.1007/978-3-031-22972-5_17
9. Dumer, I.: On minimum distance decoding of linear codes. In: Proceedings of 5th Joint Soviet-Swedish International Workshop Information Theory, pp. 50–52 (1991)
10. Esser, A.: Revisiting nearest-neighbor-based information set decoding. In: IMACC 2023. LNCS, vol. 14421, pp. 34–54. Springer, Heidelberg (2023). DOI: https://doi.org/10.1007/978-3-031-47818-5_3
11. Esser, A., Bellini, E.: Syndrome decoding estimator. In: PKC 2022. LNCS, vol. 13177, pp. 112–141. Springer, Heidelberg (2022). DOI: https://doi.org/10.1007/978-3-030-97121-2_5
12. Esser, A., May, A., Zweydinger, F.: McEliece needs a break - solving McEliece-1284 and Quasi-Cyclic-2918 with modern ISD. In: EUROCRYPT 2022. LNCS, vol. 13277, pp. 433–457. Springer, Heidelberg (2022). https://doi.org/10.1007/978-3-031-07082-2_16
13. Esser, A., Verbel, J.A., Zweydinger, F., Bellini, E.: SoK: cryptographicestimators - a software library for cryptographic hardness estimation. In: AsiaCCS, pp. 560–574. ACM (2024)
14. Esser, A., Zweydinger, F.: New time-memory trade-offs for subset sum - improving ISD in theory and practice. In: EUROCRYPT 2023. LNCS, vol. 14008, pp. 360–390. Springer, Heidelberg (2023)

15. Hamdaoui, Y., Sendrier, N.: A non asymptotic analysis of information set decoding. Cryptology ePrint Archive, Paper 2013/162 (2013)
16. Li, Y., Wang, L.-P.: Security analysis of the Classic McEliece, HQC and BIKE schemes in low memory. J. Inf. Secur. Appl. **79**, 103651 (2023)
17. May, A., Meurer, A., Thomae, E.: Decoding random linear codes in $\tilde{O}(2^{0.054n})$. In: Lee, D.H., Wang, X. (eds.) ASIACRYPT 2011. LNCS, vol. 7073, pp. 107–124. Springer, Heidelberg (2011). https://doi.org/10.1007/978-3-642-25385-0_6
18. May, A., Ozerov, I.: On computing nearest neighbors with applications to decoding of binary linear codes. In: Oswald, E., Fischlin, M. (eds.) EUROCRYPT 2015. LNCS, vol. 9056, pp. 203–228. Springer, Heidelberg (2015). https://doi.org/10.1007/978-3-662-46800-5_9
19. Melchor, C.A., et al.: HQC: Hamming quasi-cyclic key encapsulation. In: Submission to NIST Post-Quantum Cryptography Standardization Process (2022)
20. Narisada, S., Uemura, S., Okada, H., Furue, H., Aikawa, Y., Fukushima, K.: Solving McEliece-1409 in one day—cryptanalysis with the improved BJMM algorithm. In: ISC 2024. LNCS, vol. 15258, pp. 3–23. Springer, Heidelberg (2024). https://doi.org/10.1007/978-3-031-75764-8_1
21. NIST. Status report on the third round of the NIST post-quantum cryptography standardization process. NIST Internal Report 8413 (2022)
22. Prange, E.: The use of information sets in decoding cyclic codes. IRE Trans. Inf. Theory **8**(5), 5–9 (1962)
23. Stern, J.: A method for finding codewords of small weight. In: Cohen, G., Wolfmann, J. (eds.) Coding Theory 1988. LNCS, vol. 388, pp. 106–113. Springer, Heidelberg (1989). https://doi.org/10.1007/BFb0019850

Enhancing Threshold Group Action Signature Schemes: Adaptive Security and Scalability Improvements

Michele Battagliola[1(✉)], Giacomo Borin[2,3], Giovanni Di Crescenzo[4], Alessio Meneghetti[5], and Edoardo Persichetti[6]

[1] University Polytechnic of Marche, Ancona, Italy
battagliola.michele@proton.me
[2] University of Zurich, Zürich, Switzerland
grass@gbor.in
[3] IBM Research - Zurich, Zürich, Switzerland
[4] Peraton Labs, Barstow, USA
gdicrescenzo@peratonlabs.com
[5] University of Trento, Trento, Italy
alessio.meneghetti@unitn.it
[6] Florida Atlantic University, Boca Raton, USA
epersichetti@fau.edu

Abstract. Designing post-quantum digital signatures is a very active research area at present, with several protocols being developed, based on a variety of mathematical assumptions. Many of these signatures schemes can be used as a basis to define more advanced schemes, such as ring or threshold signatures, where multiple parties are involved in the signing process. Unfortunately, the majority of these protocols only considers a static adversary, that must declare which parties to corrupt at the beginning of the execution. However, a stronger security notion can be achieved, namely security against adaptive adversaries, that can corrupt parties at any times.

In this paper we tackle the challenges of designing a post-quantum adaptively secure threshold signature scheme: starting from the GRASS signature scheme, which is only static secure, we show that it is possible to turn it into an adaptive secure threshold signature that we call GRASS+. In particular, we introduce two variants of the classical GAIP problem and discuss their security. We prove that our protocol is adaptively secure in the Random Oracle Model, if the adversary corrupts only $\frac{t}{2}$ parties. We are also able to prove that GRASS+ achieves full adaptive security, with a corruption threshold of t, in the Black Box Group Action Model with Random Oracle. Finally, we improve the performance of the scheme by exploiting a better secret sharing, inspired from the work of Desmedt, Di Crescenzo, and Burmester from ASIACRYPT'94.

Keywords: Post-Quantum Cryptography · Digital Signature · Threshold Signatures · Group Action

R. Niederhagen and M.-J. O. Saarinen (Eds.): PQCrypto 2025, LNCS 15577, pp. 129–161, 2025.
https://doi.org/10.1007/978-3-031-86599-2_5

1 Introduction

A (t,n)-threshold digital signature scheme is a protocol designed to distribute the privilege to sign messages among n parties, such that any subset of at least t of them is able to sign. Moreover, we require that any subset with t or fewer parties is not able to sign any message. Recently, driven by both the NIST calls for Post-Quantum Standardization [37,38] and the call for Multi-Party Threshold Schemes [15], many researchers have started to investigate post-quantum threshold digital signature schemes. In this regard, we can mention [8,18,24,27] that present threshold signatures from isogeny assumptions, in particular based on the CSi-FiSh group action; a threshold signature based on Raccoon [40]; a framework for hash-based threshold signatures [35] and a group-action-based threshold signature that uses the group action as black box [6]. Unfortunately, all these works only consider static security, and they are not secure against an adaptive adversary.

1.1 Static and Adaptive Security

In the static setting, the adversary decides which parties to corrupt at the beginning of the protocol, before any message exchange. This model places a great restriction on the adversary's power: indeed in realistic protocols, malicious entities may corrupt a party at any time, and often they do so after seeing some messages.

Adaptive security is a strictly stronger notion and captures this second case. A naive idea to transform a statically secure scheme into an adaptively secure one is to guess the corrupted parties and aborting if incorrect. As noted in [19] by Canetti et al., the main problem with this approach is that the resulting proof of security results in a tightness loss of $\binom{n}{t-1}$, that grows exponentially in the value of the threshold. To solve this issue, the authors of [19] proposed a method which revolves around secure erasures of the secret state, which, however, is not easily enforced in practice. Other alternatives, like [20,33] usually rely on heavyweight tools, such as non-committing encryption.

The recent NIST call for multi-party threshold schemes included adaptive security as a main goal, ideally supporting up to 1024 participants. This caused a surge in interest in adaptively secure threshold signature schemes, in particular with regard to threshold Schnorr signatures, with notable examples such as [2,3,26] (whose techniques paved the way for our work), and lattice-based signatures like [30,34].

1.2 Our Contribution

As a first result, we present an improvement of the GRASS key generation algorithm. In particular, GRASS relies on Replicated Secret Sharing, that becomes quite unpractical for large n. We adapt a sharing introduced in [28] and get a new solution that requires a number of rounds only linear in t to perform the signature procedure. We then analyze the performance and security of the sharing scheme, obtaining new and non-asymptotic upper bounds on the number of shares compared to the one introduced in [28]. This new method significantly reduces the number of shares that each party needs to store, even if it still does not achieve the same efficiency as Linear Secret Sharing Schemes.

Next, we present our main result: the design of an adaptively secure post-quantum threshold signature scheme. To do so, we introduce and study two new problems: Chain-GAIP and Graph GAIP (Problems 2 and 3), that translate the classic One More Discrete Logarithm (OMDL) problem in the context of group actions.

We modify the signature algorithm of the GRASS signature scheme [6] to achieve adaptive security, by inserting online-extractable ZKPs[1], and we reduce the adaptive security of the full n-out-of-n threshold scheme to the hardness of n-Chain GAIP, first against $\frac{n-1}{2}$ corruptions in the random oracle model and then against $n-1$ corruptions in the Black Box Group Action Model from [12]. Finally, we discuss when it is possible to extend these results to the more general t-out-of-n schemes and under which assumptions.

1.3 Outline

We begin in Sect. 2, where we provide all the necessary preliminary definitions and notions used in the paper. In Sect. 3 we introduce two new conjectured hard problems, Chain-GAIP and Graph GAIP, that are used to prove the security of our protocol. Then, in Sect. 4 we present and study the new key generation algorithm. In Sect. 5 we present the new signature protocol and next we prove its security in Sect. 6.

2 Preliminaries

In this work we use the symbol $\xleftarrow{\$}$ to denote sampling from uniform distribution, while the symbol $\leftarrow$ denotes that the right value is assigned to the left variable. We use again the symbol $\leftarrow$ to denote that we assign to the left variable the output of a (potentially randomized) algorithm. We denote the security parameter as λ. For any positive integer n we define $[n] := \{0, ..., n-1\}$.

2.1 Cryptographic Group Actions

A *group action* $(G, X, \star)$ can be described as a function, as shown below, where X is a set and G a group.

$$\begin{aligned} \star : G \times X &\to X \\ (g, x) &\mapsto g \star x \end{aligned}$$

[1] ZKP(s) stands for Zero Knowledge Proof(s).

A group action's only requirement is to be *compatible* with the group; using multiplicative notation for G and denoting with e its identity element, this means that for all $x \in X$ we have $e \star x = x$ and that moreover for all $g, h \in G$, it holds that $h \star (g \star x) = (h \cdot g) \star x$. The orbit of a set element is the set $\mathscr{O}(x) := \{g \star x \mid g \in G\}$. We say that two set elements $x', x'' \in X$ are *linked* if we know a group element $g \in G$ such that $x'' = g \star x'$ or $x' = g \star x''$. A group action is also said to be:

- *Transitive*, if for every $x, y \in X$, there exists $g \in G$ such that $y = g \star x$;
- *Faithful*, if there does not exist a $g \in G$ such that $x = g \star x$ for all $x \in X$, other than the identity;
- *Free*, if an element $g \in G$ is equal to identity whenever there exists an $x \in X$ such that $x = g \star x$;
- *Regular*, if it is free and transitive.

The adjective *cryptographic* is added to indicate that the group action in question has additional properties that are relevant to cryptography. For instance, a cryptographic group action should be *one-way*, i.e., given randomly chosen $x, y \in X$, it should be hard to find $g \in G$ such that $g \star x = y$ (if such a g exists). Indeed, the problem of finding such an element is known as the *vectorization* problem, or sometimes *Group Action Inverse Problem (GAIP)*.

Problem 1 (GAIP). Given $x \in X$ and y uniformly distributed in $\mathscr{O}(x)$, compute an element $g \in G$ such that $y = g \star x$.

2.2 Sigma Protocol for GAIP

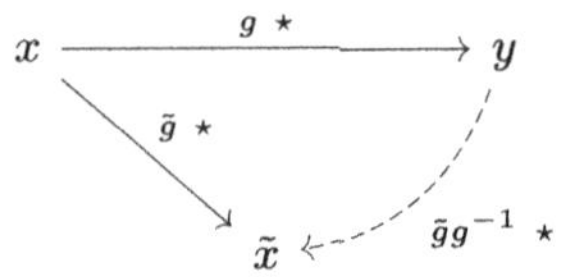

Fig. 1. Sigma protocol for the knowledge of the group action.

Sigma protocols for the knowledge of a solution to the GAIP have been used successfully in many cryptographic protocols and they usually follow the same structure [14]. In this section we summarize the general idea for a generic group action.

Let $(G, X, \star)$ be a group action such that GAIP (Problem 1) is hard and consider $x, y \in X$ and $g \in G$ such that $y = g \star x$. Figure 1 shows how a prover who knows g, can prove its knowledge to a verifier knowing only x, y. The protocol works as follows:

- the prover picks a random $\tilde{g} \in G$ and sends $\tilde{x} = \tilde{g} \star x$ to the verifier,

- the verifier chooses a random bit $b \in \{0, 1\}$ and sends it to the prover,
- the prover sends w to the verifier, where $w = \tilde{g}$ if $b = 0$ or $w = \tilde{g}g^{-1}$ if $b = 1$,
- the verifier accepts if $w \star x = \tilde{x}$ when $b = 0$ or $w \star y = \tilde{x}$ when $b = 1$.

It is easy to see that the above protocol satisfies the classical properties of completeness, special soundness and honest verifier zero-knowledge; thus it is possible to apply the Fiat-Shamir Transform to obtain a secure digital signature. The protocol can then be improved by applying several optimizations, getting different tradeoffs in the signature scheme parameters. More information on the construction of digital signatures from group actions can be found in [14].

Examples of this approach are CSi-Fish [7], MEDS [22], Alteq [11] and LESS [5,9], with the latter being among the fourteen candidates selected for the second round of the NIST call for post quantum digital signature schemes.

2.3 Threshold Signatures

We briefly summarize here the relevant notions for threshold signature schemes. In a nutshell, a (t, n)-threshold signature is a multi-party protocol that allows any t parties out of a total of n to compute a signature that may be verified against a common public key. We assume that each user has access to a secure, reliable and authenticated private channel with each of the other users, without worrying about specific design and peculiarities of the channel.

Usually, threshold signature protocols involve a key-generation protocol that constructs the key pair $(\texttt{pk}, \texttt{sk})$ as well as shares of the private key $\texttt{sk}_i$, and a multiparty signature protocol TSign, such that any set of t parties who agree on a common message $\texttt{mes}$ is able to compute a signature, which is verifiable against the public key via the procedure Ver. KeyGen can be executed by a trusted party or by the n parties alone collaborating. In this "decentralized" case, the parties get access to the additional exchanged information.

Even if it is possible to have a more general definition, we tailor the syntax of our definition to both the inherited Σ-protocol-like and sequential round-robin structures of our protocol, which are the same as the original [6]. By sequential round-robin, we mean that the parties take turns to produce the final output, instead of working simultaneously.

Definition 1. *(Threshold Signatures) A threshold signature scheme* TSign *with two round-robin consists of polynomial time algorithms*

$$\mathsf{TSign} = (\mathsf{Setup}, \mathsf{KeyGen}, (\mathsf{TSign}_1, \mathsf{Fin}_1), (\mathsf{TSign}_2, \mathsf{Fin}_2), \mathsf{Ver}),$$

defined as follows:

- $\mathsf{Setup}(1^\lambda) \to \texttt{par}$: *on input the security parameter* 1^λ, *it outputs the public parameters* $\texttt{par}$.
- $\mathsf{KeyGen}(\texttt{par}, 1^n, 1^t) \to (\texttt{pk}, \{\texttt{sk}_i\}_{[n]})$: *a probabilistic algorithm that takes as input the public parameters, the number of signers and the threshold* t *and outputs the common public key* $\texttt{pk}$ *and a share* $\texttt{sk}_i$ *of the private key for each signer.*

- $(\mathsf{TSign}_1, \mathsf{Fin}_1), (\mathsf{TSign}_2, \mathsf{Fin}_2)$ *are two pairs of algorithms where* TSign_i *represents one round-robin each and* Fin_i *represents a final broadcast that "finalizes" the round-robin. Both* TSign_1 *and* TSign_2 *are done by each party in the signing set* $\mathcal{S}_{\mathsf{sig}}$ *following the round-robin order and are defined as follows:*

$$(\mathtt{pm}_{i,1}, \mathtt{st}_{i,1}) \leftarrow \mathsf{TSign}_1(\mathcal{S}_{\mathsf{sig}}, \mathtt{mes}, \mathtt{sk}_i, \{\mathtt{pm}_{j,1}\}_{j \in \mathcal{S}_{\mathsf{sig}}, j<i})$$
$$\mathtt{dcmt}_i \leftarrow \mathsf{Fin}_1(\mathcal{S}_{\mathsf{sig}}, \mathtt{mes}, \mathtt{sk}_i, \{\mathtt{pm}_{j,1}\}_{j \in \mathcal{S}_{\mathsf{sig}}})$$
$$(\mathtt{pm}_{i,2}, \mathtt{st}_{i,2}) \leftarrow \mathsf{TSign}_2(\mathcal{S}_{\mathsf{sig}}, \mathtt{mes}, \mathtt{sk}_i, \mathtt{st}_{i,1}\{\mathtt{pm}_{j,2}\}_{j \in \mathcal{S}_{\mathsf{sig}}, j<i}, \{\mathtt{pm}_{k,1}, \mathtt{dcmt}_k\}_{k \in \mathcal{S}_{\mathsf{sig}}})$$
$$\sigma_i \leftarrow \mathsf{Fin}_2(\mathcal{S}_{\mathsf{sig}}, \mathtt{mes}, \mathtt{sk}_i, \{\mathtt{pm}_{j,1}\}_{j \in \mathcal{S}_{\mathsf{sig}}}, \{\mathtt{pm}_{j,2}\}_{j \in \mathcal{S}_{\mathsf{sig}}}, \{\mathtt{dcmt}_j\}_{j \in \mathcal{S}_{\mathsf{sig}}})$$

where $\mathtt{pm}_{i,1}, \mathtt{pm}_{i,2}$ *are* public messages *broadcast by party* i, $\mathtt{st}_{i,1}, \mathtt{st}_{i,2}$ *are the states of party* i *at the end of each round and the final signature* σ *can be computed deterministically from all the partial signature* σ_i.
- $\mathsf{Ver}(\mathtt{pk}, \mathtt{mes}, \sigma) \rightarrow 0/1$*: a deterministic algorithm that takes as input the public key* $\mathtt{pk}$*, a message* $\mathtt{mes}$ *and a signature* σ *and outputs* 1 *if* σ *is valid, else it outputs* 0.

We require that the threshold signature scheme is correct, *i.e., for all security parameters* λ*, all* $1 \leq t \leq n$*, all* $\mathcal{S}_{\mathsf{sig}} \subseteq [n]$ *such that* $|\mathcal{S}_{\mathsf{sig}}| \geq t$*, all messages* $\mathtt{mes}$ *if* $\mathsf{KeyGen}(\mathtt{par}, n, t) \rightarrow (\mathtt{pk}, \{(\mathtt{pk}_i, \mathtt{sk}_i)\}_{[n]})$ *then the algorithms* $\mathsf{TSign}_1, \mathsf{Fin}_1, \mathsf{TSign}_2$ *and* Fin_2 *return a valid signature* σ *such that* $\mathsf{Ver}(\mathtt{pk}, \mathtt{mes}, \sigma) = 1$.

Informally speaking, first all the parties engage in a round-robin protocol. Each party i, on input the signing set, its secret key, the message, and all the output from the previous rounds, outputs some public messages $\mathtt{pm}_{i,1}$ and its secret state $\mathtt{st}_{i,1}$. Then a second round-robin is done. There, again, each party i, on input the signing set, its secret key and state, the message, and all the outputs from the first round-robin and from the previous rounds, outputs some public messages $\mathtt{pm}_{i,2}$ and its secret state $\mathtt{st}_{i,2}$. After each round-robin, there is a final broadcast, where each party, on input all the public data, outputs some public data, in particular the second finalization protocol outputs the signature.

Remark 1. The above definition of threshold signature is very complex and notation heavy. The main reason why we need such a definition is to better define security, allowing the adversary maximum freedom in opening parallel sessions. Indeed, when defining the security game for adaptive security, we allow the adversary to freely query the oracle on each of the above four algorithms in any order. Since each algorithm corresponds to one message sent, this simulates the possibility of opening parallel executions.

Adaptive Security. An important notion for threshold signature security is adaptive security, where the adversary is able to corrupt parties dynamically, in contrast to static security, where it is required to declare all the corrupted parties at the beginning of the execution. Here we adapt the definition given in [26] to suit the case of threshold signatures having a round-robin structure.

Definition 2 (Adaptive EUF-CMA). *Let* TSign *be a threshold signature scheme and* $\mathcal{A}$ *be an adversary playing the adaptive EUF-CMA game defined in Fig. 2. Let define the advantage of* $\mathcal{A}$ *as:*

$$\boldsymbol{Adv}_{\mathcal{A}}^{\mathsf{a-euf-cma}}(\lambda, \mathsf{frac}) = \Pr(\mathsf{Exp}_{\mathcal{A}}^{\mathsf{a-euf-cma}}(\lambda, \mathsf{frac}) = 1)$$

We say that TSign *is unforgettable against adaptive chosen message attacks with* frac *corruptions if and only if* $\boldsymbol{Adv}_{\mathcal{A}}^{\mathsf{a-euf-cma}}$ *is negligible for every probabilistic polynomial time adversary* $\mathcal{A}$.

Informally speaking in the adaptive EUF-CMA game the adversary can interact with the following oracles:

- $\mathcal{O}^{\mathsf{Corrupt}}$: if the total number of corruptions is lower than frac, then the $\mathcal{O}^{\mathsf{Corrupt}}$ returns the private key and all the internal states of the chosen party.
- $\mathcal{O}^{\mathsf{TSign}_i}$: the adversary asks the oracle to perform one round of the round-robin. First the oracle checks that all the previous parties in the round-robin have done their turn (in the case of TSign_2 it also checks whether Fin_1 was executed or not); if so, it executes TSign_i, publishes the public data and stores the private data.
- $\mathcal{O}^{\mathsf{Fin}_i}$: the adversary asks the oracle to perform the finalization protocol. First the oracle checks that the previous round-robin is finished; if so, it performs the finalization algorithm Fin_i on behalf of all the honest parties and sends the result to the adversary. In case of Fin_1, if the adversary refuses (or fails) to execute Fin_1, then the oracle will stop the execution during the TSign_2.

2.4 Black Box Group Action Model

As will become clearer later in Sect. 6, to prove the adaptive security of GRASS we need to perform a rewind in order to extract all the secrets we need. Unfortunately, this implies that the adversary can corrupt at most $\frac{t-1}{2}$ parties, otherwise we would incur the risk of needing more queries than allowed to the oracle we use in our security assumption, since the adversary could corrupt different parties after the rewind. In order to extract all the group actions after a single forgery, we need to use the Black Box Group Action Model (BBGAM) introduced in [12], which generalizes the Generic Group Model to consider group actions.[2]

In this model, direct computation over set elements is possible only by querying an oracle to do all the computation. In particular, each party is provided with a starting set of set elements $x_0, ..., x_r \in X$ and three oracles:[3]

- $\mathcal{O}^{\mathsf{Eq}}(x, y)$, with $x, y \in X$ that returns 1 if $x = y$, 0 otherwise.
- $\mathcal{O}^{\mathsf{Act}}(g, x)$ that, on input $g \in G$ and a previously seen set element $x \in X$, returns the set element $g \star x$.

[2] We do not consider [29] since they restrict themselves to the abelian group case.

[3] To be very formal, the parties do not have access directly to set elements but instead have access to handles. For the sake of simplicity, with abuse of notation, we will simply write x instead of $\langle x \rangle$, even when referring to handles.

$\mathsf{Exp}_{\mathcal{A}}^{\mathsf{a-euf-cma}}(\lambda, \mathsf{frac})$

$\mathsf{par} \leftarrow \mathsf{Setup}(1^\lambda)$
$\mathtt{Q_{mes}} \leftarrow \emptyset, \mathtt{Q_{st}} \leftarrow \emptyset$
$(\mathsf{cor}, \mathtt{st}_{\mathcal{A}}) \leftarrow \mathcal{A}(\mathsf{par})$
$\textbf{if } |\mathsf{cor}| > \mathsf{frac} \vee \mathsf{cor} \not\subset [n]$
$\quad \textbf{return } \bot$
$\mathsf{hon} \leftarrow [n] \setminus \mathsf{cor}$
$(\mathsf{pk}, \{(\mathsf{pk}_i, \mathsf{sk}_i)\}) \leftarrow \mathsf{KeyGen}(\mathsf{par}, n, t)$
$\mathtt{st}_{\mathcal{A}} \leftarrow (\mathsf{pk}, \{\mathsf{pk}_i, \mathsf{sk}_i\}_{\mathsf{cor}}, \mathtt{st}_{\mathcal{A}})$
$(\mathtt{mes}^*, \sigma^*) \leftarrow \mathcal{A}^{\mathcal{O}^{\mathsf{TSign}_i}, \mathcal{O}^{\mathsf{Fin}_i}, \mathcal{O}^{\mathsf{Corrupt}}}(\mathtt{st}_{\mathcal{A}})$
$\textbf{return } \mathtt{mes}^* \notin \mathtt{Q_{mes}} \wedge \mathsf{Ver}(\mathsf{pk}, \mathtt{mes}^*, \sigma^*)$

$\mathcal{O}^{\mathsf{TSign}_1}(k, \mathtt{mes}, \mathtt{ssid})$

$\mathtt{Q_{mes}} \leftarrow \mathtt{Q_{mes}} \cup \mathtt{mes}$
$\textbf{if } (k \notin \mathsf{hon}) \vee (\mathtt{Q_{st}}[k, \mathtt{ssid}, 1] \neq \bot)$
$\quad \textbf{return } \bot$
$\textbf{for } j \in \mathcal{S}_{\mathsf{sig}}, j < k$
$\quad \textbf{if } \mathtt{Q_{pm}}[j, \mathtt{ssid}, 1] = \bot$
$\quad\quad \textbf{return } \bot$
$(\mathtt{pm}_{k,1}^{\mathtt{ssid}}, \mathtt{st}_{k,1}^{\mathtt{ssid}}) \leftarrow \mathsf{TSign}_1(\mathcal{S}_{\mathsf{sig}}, \mathtt{mes}, \mathtt{sk}_k, \{\mathtt{pm}_{j,1}^{\mathtt{ssid}}\}_{j \in \mathcal{S}_{\mathsf{sig}}, j<i})$
$\mathtt{Q_{st}}[k, \mathtt{ssid}, 1] \leftarrow \mathtt{st}_{k,1}^{\mathtt{ssid}}$
$\mathtt{Q_{pm}}[k, \mathtt{ssid}, 1] \leftarrow \mathtt{pm}_{k,1}^{\mathtt{ssid}}$
$\textbf{return } \mathtt{pm}_{k,1}^{\mathtt{ssid}}$

$\mathcal{O}^{\mathsf{Corrupt}}(k)$

$\textbf{if } k \notin \mathsf{hon} \vee |\mathsf{cor}| = \mathsf{frac}$
$\quad \textbf{return } \bot$
$\mathsf{cor} \leftarrow \mathsf{cor} \cup \{k\}$
$\mathsf{hon} \leftarrow \mathsf{hon} \setminus \{k\}$
// Retrieve all state for party k
$\mathtt{st}_k \leftarrow \mathtt{Q_{st}}[k, \cdot, \cdot]$
$\textbf{return } (\mathtt{sk}_k, \mathtt{st}_k)$

$\mathcal{O}^{\mathsf{TSign}_2}(k, \mathtt{mes}, \mathtt{ssid}, \{\mathtt{pm}_{j,1}\}_{j \in \mathcal{S}_{\mathsf{sig}}})$

$\textbf{if } (k \notin \mathsf{hon}) \vee (\mathtt{ssid} = \bot)$
$\quad \vee (\mathtt{Q_{Fin}}[\mathtt{ssid}] = \bot) \vee (\mathtt{Q_{pm}}[k, \mathtt{ssid}, 2] \neq \bot)$
$\quad \textbf{return } \bot$
$\textbf{for } j \in \mathcal{S}_{\mathsf{sig}}, j < k$
$\quad \textbf{if } \mathtt{Q_{pm}}[j, \mathtt{ssid}, 2] = \bot$
$\quad\quad \textbf{return } \bot$
$(\mathtt{pm}_{k,2}^{\mathtt{ssid}}, \mathtt{st}_{k,2}^{\mathtt{ssid}}) \leftarrow \mathsf{TSign}_2(\mathcal{S}_{\mathsf{sig}}, \mathtt{mes}, \mathtt{sk}_k, \{\mathtt{pm}_{j,2}^{\mathtt{ssid}}\}_{j<i}, \{\mathtt{pm}_{j,2}^{\mathtt{ssid}}\}_{j \in \mathcal{S}_{\mathsf{sig}}})$
$\mathtt{Q_{pm}}[k, \mathtt{ssid}, 2] \leftarrow \mathtt{pm}_{k,2}^{\mathtt{ssid}}$
$\mathtt{Q_{st}}[k, \mathtt{ssid}, 2] \leftarrow \mathtt{st}_{k,2}^{\mathtt{ssid}}$
$\textbf{return } (\mathtt{pm}_{k,2}^{\mathtt{ssid}})$

$\mathcal{O}^{\mathsf{Fin}_1}(\mathtt{mes}, \mathtt{ssid}, \mathcal{S}_{\mathsf{sig}})$

$\textbf{for } j \in \mathcal{S}_{\mathsf{sig}}$
$\quad \textbf{if } \mathtt{Q_{pm}}[j, \mathtt{ssid}, 1] = \bot$
$\quad\quad \textbf{return } \bot$
$\textbf{for } i \in \mathsf{hon} \cap \mathcal{S}_{\mathsf{sig}}$
$\quad \mathtt{dcmt}_i^{\mathtt{ssid}} \leftarrow \mathsf{Fin}_1(\mathcal{S}_{\mathsf{sig}}, \mathtt{mes}, \mathtt{sk}_i, \{\mathtt{pm}_{j,1}^{\mathtt{ssid}}\}_{j \in \mathcal{S}_{\mathsf{sig}}})$
$\{\mathtt{dcmt}_j^{\mathtt{ssid}}\}_{j \in \mathsf{cor}} \leftarrow \mathcal{A}(\{\mathtt{dcmt}_i^{\mathtt{ssid}}\}_{i \in \mathsf{hon}})$
$\mathtt{Q_{Fin}}[\mathtt{ssid}] = 1$
$\textbf{for } j \in \mathsf{cor}$
$\quad \textbf{if } \mathtt{dcmt}_j^{\mathtt{ssid}} = \bot$
$\quad\quad \mathtt{Q_{Fin}}[\mathtt{ssid}] = \bot$
$\textbf{return}$

$\mathcal{O}^{\mathsf{Fin}_2}(\mathtt{mes}, \mathtt{ssid}, \mathcal{S}_{\mathsf{sig}})$

$\textbf{for } j \in \mathcal{S}_{\mathsf{sig}}$
$\quad \textbf{if } \mathtt{Q_{pm}}[j, \mathtt{ssid}, 2] = \bot$
$\quad\quad \textbf{return } \bot$
$\textbf{for } i \in \mathsf{hon} \cap \mathcal{S}_{\mathsf{sig}}$
$\quad \sigma_i \leftarrow \mathsf{Fin}_1(\mathcal{S}_{\mathsf{sig}}, \mathtt{mes}, \mathtt{sk}_i, \{\mathtt{pm}_{j,1}^{\mathtt{ssid}}, \mathtt{pm}_{j,2}^{\mathtt{ssid}}, \mathtt{dcmt}_i^{\mathtt{ssid}}\}_{j \in \mathcal{S}_{\mathsf{sig}}})$
$\textbf{return } \{\sigma_i\}_{i \in \mathsf{hon}}$

Fig. 2. Security game for adaptive EUF-CMA.

- $\mathcal{O}^{\mathsf{sample}}(s)$ that, on input a seed s, returns a random element $x \in X$, potentially on a different orbit from the previously returned set elements. For some group action we can even not allow this oracle.

The core idea behind the model is that the only way for the adversary to derive additional meaningful set elements is to query the action oracle $\mathcal{O}^{\mathsf{Act}}$, i.e., compute a group action on a defined set element. In this way, given a set element $\bar{x}$ resulted from one of the party computations, we can always look at all the previous oracle queries. Thus, we can find a group element $\bar{g}$ such that $\bar{x} = \bar{g} \star x_i$ for $i = 0, ..., r$ or, if $\mathcal{O}^{\mathsf{sample}}$ is allowed, $\bar{x} = \bar{g} \star x$ for some x uniformly distributed in X, which is obtained from $\mathcal{O}^{\mathsf{sample}}$. Note that for our setting we consider the case in which all the set elements $x_0, ..., x_r$ are in the same orbit.

Moreover, if the adversary tries to cheat by sending elements from a different orbit, the malicious behavior will be caught thanks to the ZKPs used.

The BBGAM in Practice. The reliance of the model clearly depends on the group actions we want to model. To justify it we need to argue that, with respect to a particular group action, the only way to obtain a new set element is by applying a group action on a known set element or (eventually) by random sampling (i.e., using $\mathcal{O}^{\mathsf{sample}}$).

It is well known that this model can safely be applied to the group actions based on isogenies of supersingular elliptic curve, like [21]. In fact, it is a major open problem in isogeny based cryptography to compute a valid supersingular elliptic curve not starting from an isogeny applied on a known one, this is known as the *hashing to the supersingular elliptic curve graph problem* [13], so it may even make sense to not even allow the use of $\mathcal{O}^{\mathsf{sample}}$. More detailed discussion can be found e.g., from [39, Section 4.3].

For the other group actions, like the ones used for LESS [5], MEDS [22] and ALTEQ [11], it is always possible to generate a random set element by sampling a random linear code or tensor, but this lies in the same orbit only with negligible probability, thus giving no advantage to the adversary (moreover, this behavior would be quickly caught by the honest parties, since the protocol uses ZKPs to prevent the usage of set elements that are not linked to other ones). This can be verified with simple computations; e.g., for LESS, the number of monomial maps, i.e., of group elements (that is an upper bound on the orbits sizes), is $(q-1)^n n!$, which for the regime of interest ($n > 200$) is negligible with respect to the number of possible linear codes, $\approx q^{\frac{n^2}{4}}$. We assume this is the case for the group actions considered in this work.

Even if, to the best of our knowledge, it is not possible to use these random elements to get additional information, we must include the possibility of sampling random elements in the set X since there is no efficient way to test if two set elements lie in the same orbit, i.e., to solve the decisional version of GAIP. In the case of LESS, it is even known that GAIP reduces to the problem of deciding if two codes are equivalent [4,10].

Again, as far as we know, starting from a linear code or an alternating tensor in the literature, there are no other meaningful ways to obtain new objects related to them. For example, one could try to flip or reorder some entries, but these would yield set elements which, from a group action point of view, unrelated to the starting ones. We believe that, for now, these observations justify the use of the model for group actions cited above. Note that for $[m \times m, k]$-matrix codes, in principle it would be possible to obtain a new code by transposing the matrices in the code. This new code preserves part of the algebraic relations between group elements and set elements, so, even if we do not know how to exploit this to get a meaningful attack, we have to admit that for the group action used in MEDS, the use of the BBGAM is a stronger assumption than for other group action frameworks.

3 Chain and Graph Versions of GAIP

In this Section we introduce two new problems, to be used in the security proof, that aim to generalize the *One More Discrete Logarithm* Problem [36].

3.1 Chain-GAIP

Problem 2 (n-Chain-GAIP). Consider $x \in X$ and $g_0, ..., g_{n-1} \in G$ chosen uniformly at random. Let $x_{i+1} = g_i \star x_i$ for all $i = 0, ..., n-1$, where we have defined x_0 as x. Given $\{x_i\}_{i=0,...,n}$ and access to an oracle that, on input (x_i, x_{i+1}) returns g_i for at most $n-1$ queries, find g such that $x_n = g \star x_0$.

As we can expect, our reduction incurs a security loss which is proportional to n, the number of elements in the chain.

Proposition 1. *If there exists probabilistic polynomial-time algorithm $\mathcal{A}_{\mathsf{Chain}}$ that solves the n-Chain-GAIP problem with probability ϵ and in time T, then there exists a probabilistic polynomial-time algorithm $\mathcal{A}_{\mathsf{GAIP}}$ that solves GAIP in the same time T and with probability ϵ/n.*

Proof. Given as input a GAIP challenge $(x, y) \in X \times X$ the algorithm $\mathcal{A}_{\mathsf{GAIP}}$:

1. samples $n-1$ group elements $g_0, ..., g_{\ell-1}, g_{\ell+1}, .., g_{n-1} \in G$, with $\ell \in \{0, ..., n-1\}$ chosen uniformly at random,
2. sets $x_0 = x, x_n = y$. Then *completes* the chain by defining

$$\begin{cases} x_{i+1} = g_i \star x_i \text{ for } 0 < i < \ell \\ x_i = g_i^{-1} \star x_{i+1} \text{ for } \ell < i < n \end{cases} . \quad (1)$$

3. $\mathcal{A}_{\mathsf{GAIP}}$ sends the chain to $\mathcal{A}_{\mathsf{Chain}}$ and acts as oracle, returning g_i when queried on (x_i, x_{i+1}) for $i \neq \ell$ and failing otherwise.

It is immediate to see that as long as $\mathcal{A}_{\mathsf{Chain}}$ solves the n-Chain-GAIP instance without querying $(x_{\ell-1}, x_\ell)$, then $\mathcal{A}_{\mathsf{GAIP}}$ can return the n-Chain GAIP solution as a GAIP solution. Under the claim that the chain x_i is a valid n-Chain-GAIP instance, with a probability distribution independent of ℓ, the algorithm solves GAIP with probability ϵ/n. Let idx be the index of the pair that is not queried in an execution of $\mathcal{A}_{\mathsf{Chain}}$[4] interacting with the n-Chain-GAIP oracle, since, under our claim, ℓ is independent of the distribution from item 2 we have

$$\Pr[\mathcal{A}_{\mathsf{Chain}} \text{ succeeds } \wedge \mathsf{idx} = \ell] = \epsilon \cdot \frac{1}{n} .$$

This property is preserved also when interacting with $\mathcal{A}_{\mathsf{GAIP}}$ (item 3) since the distribution of group elements is the same, thus $\mathcal{A}_{\mathsf{GAIP}}$ can extract a valid solution for $(x_{\mathsf{ch}}, y_{\mathsf{ch}})$ with probability ϵ/n.

[4] wlog we can suppose that it always perform $n-1$ queries.

To prove Proposition 1 we only need to prove the above claim on the distributions of the elements from item 2. Since the group elements $g_1, ..., g_{\ell-1}, g_{\ell+1}, .., g_n$ are uniformly distributed in G then also both g_i^{-1} are uniformly distributed on G. Finally, since the GAIP solution g with $y = g \star x$ is uniform on G so it is the secret group element g_ℓ linking $x_\ell, x_{\ell+1}$.

As said, the security loss with respect to GAIP is at most proportional to n. Luckily, since n is the number of parties, it is expected to be polynomial, so this does not cause any major issue with the scheme. Since it is clear that any solver to GAIP is a solver to n-Chain GAIP (just need to directly tackle the instance and discard the chain related information), the cost of solving n-Chain GAIP with respect to the cost of solving GAIP lies somewhat in between 1 and $1/n$.

However, from a heuristic standpoint, it is reasonable to believe that any algorithm able to solve GAIP should not gain any benefit from knowing other group action that are sampled independently. For example, we may argue that a solver could try to solve these n GAIP *intermediate* instances independently, to then stop at the first success, thus linearly increasing the probability of success, and ask the remaining $n - 1$ instances to the oracle. Anyway this does not decrease the overall cost of the attack since it still requires n parallel independent executions.

3.2 Graph-GAIP

To prove the adaptive security of schemes with more complicated sharing mechanisms, we need to introduce a second problem. Instead of having a single chain, we consider a graph, where the vertices are set elements and the edges are the actions that relate them. Formally we have the following:

Problem 3 (N-Graph-GAIP). Let $x \in X$ and $g \in G$ be chosen uniformly and define $y = g \star x$. Consider N set elements $x_1, ..., x_N \in \mathcal{O}(x)$ sampled uniformly at random and the graph $\mathcal{G} = (V, E)$ with vertices $V = \{x, y\} \cup \{x_1, ..., x_N\}$ and no edges $E = \emptyset$. Find g such that $y = g \star x$ having access to a solver oracle $\mathcal{O}^{\mathcal{G}}$ that on input two set elements $x', y' \in V$:

- if x' is linked to x (resp. to y) in the graph $\mathcal{G}$ and y' is linked to y (resp. to x) in the graph $\mathcal{G}$, return $\perp$;
- else add $\{x', y'\}$ to E and return $g' \in G$ such that $y' = g' \star x'$.

What essentially oracle $\mathcal{O}^{\mathcal{G}}$ does is providing links, i.e., solutions to the group action inversion problem, for all the possible pairs of set elements provided at the start, as long as they cannot be composed to get a link between x and y, that is equivalent to get a solution for the GAIP on x, y. It is important that the set elements are fixed from the start, otherwise the adversary could perform a trivial attack by creating two random set element $\tilde{x} = \tilde{g} \star x$ and $\tilde{y} = \tilde{g} \star y$, asking a solution g' for $\tilde{x}, \tilde{y}$ and find a solution $\tilde{g}^{-1} g' \tilde{g}$.

As for n-Chain GAIP we can get reductions to GAIP by trying to generate the set elements ourselves and trying to guess the queries in advance, however in this case the security loss would be exponential in the number N of set elements, compromising the utility of the reduction. This is because, differently from n-Chain GAIP there is no restriction on the allowed queries to the oracle, i.e., no fixed topology of the graph $\mathcal{G}$ but for having two disconnected components[5] containing x and y. However, as before, we have no reason to believe that in practice the additional information provided to a solver can be used meaningfully to solve the GAIP between x and y.

4 Improved Secret Sharing

In this section we extend the secret sharing scheme from [28] to work for group actions, show an improved analysis of the scheme, and discuss its main properties of interest for our threshold signature protocol.

In [28], the authors present a multiplicative secret sharing scheme for the (t, n)-threshold access structure, for any $1 \leq t \leq n$, and any (non-Abelian) group with efficiently computable operation and inverses, and show its application to threshold cryptography (specifically, threshold zero-knowledge proofs of knowledge of secrets encoded as graph isomorphisms). Here, we adapt this scheme to work for any group action, show an improved analysis of the size of the shares. The resulting scheme, denoted as $(\mathsf{RecKeyGen}, \mathsf{Recover})$, is detailed in Fig. 3.

Algorithm $\mathsf{RecKeyGen}$ needs to be run by a Trusted Third Party Dealer, that recursively shares the secret key $\mathtt{sk} = g$ associated to the public key $\mathtt{pk} = (x, y)$, i.e., such that $y = g \star x$, between n users $\mathcal{P}$ with a t-out-of-n sharing. Whenever g', x', LBL are sent to the user P, this party will store g', x' under the label LBL. When a set $\mathcal{T}$ of t users wants to recover the secret, each user runs algorithm $\mathsf{Recover}$ which uses the LBL labels to find the correct share to use.

Informal Idea. The core idea is to use a recursive strategy. To do a 1-out-of-n sharing the dealer just forward g', x to all the n users and for an n-out-of-n sharing, the dealer splits g as $g_{n-1} \cdot \cdots \cdot g_0$, sets $x_0 = x$, computes $x_{i+1} = g_i \star x_i$, then forward g_i, x_i to the i-th party P_i, for $i = 1, .., n$.[6]

Otherwise, to do a t-out-of-n sharing, with $t \neq 1, n$, the user set is split in two sides $\mathcal{P}_{\mathsf{left}}$ and $\mathcal{P}_{\mathsf{right}}$ of approximately the same size $\lfloor \frac{n}{2} \rfloor$ and $\lceil \frac{n}{2} \rceil$. Then for any ℓ such that $\max(0, t - \lceil \frac{n}{2} \rceil) \leq \ell \leq \min(t, \lfloor \frac{n}{2} \rfloor)$, split g as $g_2 \cdot g_1$, then:

- perform recursively an ℓ-out-of-$|\mathcal{P}_{\mathsf{right}}|$ sharing of $g_1, x, g_1 \star x$ on the user set $\mathcal{P}_{\mathsf{right}}$;
- perform recursively a $(t - \ell)$-out-of-$|\mathcal{P}_{\mathsf{left}}|$ sharing of $g_2, g_1 \star x, y$ on the user set $\mathcal{P}_{\mathsf{left}}$.

---

[5] i.e., two disjoint non-empty subsets of the graph such that no vertex in the first set is linked to a vertex in the second one.

[6] This point could technically be avoided and considered a consequence of the latter point.

```
RecKeyGen(g, x, y, 𝒫, t, LBL) → {(g_i, x_i, LBL_i) : i}

n ← |𝒫|
x_0 ← x
parse 𝒫 → {P_0, ..., P_{n-1}}
if t = 1
  for P ∈ 𝒫 :
    Send g, x, LBL to P
if t = n > 1
  g_i ←$ G, i = 1, ..., n − 1
  g_0 ← (g_1 · ... · g_{n-1})^{-1} · g
  for i = 0, ..., n − 1
    x_{i+1} ← g_i ⋆ x_i
    Send g_i, x_i, LBL to P_i
if 1 < t < n
  c ← ⌊n/2⌋
  𝒫_left ← {P_0, ..., P_{c-1}}
  𝒫_right ← {P_c, ..., P_{n-1}}
  for ℓ = max(0, t − ⌈n/2⌉), ..., min(t, ⌊n/2⌋)
    if ℓ = 0
      RecKeyGen(g, x, y, 𝒫_left, t, LBL||(𝒫_left, t))
    elseif ℓ = t
      RecKeyGen(g, x, y, 𝒫_right, t, LBL||(𝒫_right, t))
    else
      g_1 ←$ G
      x_1 ← g_1 ⋆ x_0
      g_2 ← g · g_1^{-1}
      RecKeyGen(g_1, x, x_1, 𝒫_left, t − ℓ, LBL||(𝒫_left, t − ℓ))
      RecKeyGen(g_2, x_1, y, 𝒫_right, ℓ, LBL||(𝒫_right, ℓ))
```

```
Recover(P, 𝒯, 𝒫, LBL) → g_i, x_i

n, t ← |𝒫|, |𝒯|
assert P ∈ 𝒯
parse 𝒫 → {P_0, ..., P_{n-1}}
if t = 1 or t = n
  get share received with LBL
if 1 < t < n
  c ← ⌊n/2⌋
  𝒫_left ← {P_0, ..., P_{c-1}}
  𝒫_right ← {P_c, ..., P_{n-1}}
  ℓ ← 𝒯 ∩ 𝒫_right
  if ℓ = 0
    Recover(P, 𝒯, 𝒫_left, LBL||(𝒫_left, t))
  if ℓ = t
    Recover(P, 𝒯, 𝒫_right, LBL||(𝒫_right, t))
  else
    if P ∈ 𝒫_right
      Recover(P, 𝒯 ∩ 𝒫_right, 𝒫_right, LBL||(𝒫_right, ℓ))
    if P ∈ 𝒫_left
      Recover(P, 𝒯 ∩ 𝒫_left, 𝒫_left, LBL||(𝒫_left, t − ℓ))
```

Fig. 3. Recursive algorithms both for the sharing of the secret g between any subset of t users of $\mathcal{P}$ and the recovery of each individual share, given the set of users $\mathcal{P}$ and the subset of allowed users $\mathcal{T}$ in which P belongs. In the first call to each of the two algorithms, LBL is set as $\emptyset$. The RecKeyGen algorithm is later used as part of the KeyGen algorithm for the signature, while Recover is used as part of the signing algorithm, to retrieve the correct share.

To allow each user to correctly combine their secret shares the dealer also labels each share with a list containing all the recursive steps performed to arrive to the sharing.

If a subset $\mathcal{T}$ of t users want to recover a subset of shares multiplying to g, each user $P \in \mathcal{T}$ essentially repeats the share generation as before to recompute the correct label. The idea is to recover ℓ^* as $|\mathcal{T} \cap \mathcal{P}_{\mathsf{right}}|$; if $P \in \mathcal{P}_{\mathsf{left}}$ then they compute the label of a $(t - \ell^*)$-out-of-$|\mathcal{P}_{\mathsf{left}}|$ sharing on $\mathcal{T} \cap \mathcal{P}_{\mathsf{left}}$ recursively, or, if $P \in \mathcal{P}_{\mathsf{right}}$, then they compute the label of an ℓ^*-out-of-$|\mathcal{P}_{\mathsf{right}}|$ sharing on $\mathcal{T} \cap \mathcal{P}_{\mathsf{right}}$, again recursively. When $t = 1$ or $t = |\mathcal{P}|$ they can recover the share under the computed label.

In the signature, the algorithm RecKeyGen is used by the trusted dealer to perform the KeyGen algorithm. The algorithm Recover is executed by each party at the beginning of every signing session to retrieve the correct share to use in that session.

4.1 Correctness and Secrecy

The above protocol preserves the claim in [28, Theorem 4]; i.e., it is a multiplicative (perfect) secret sharing scheme for the t-out-of-n access structure. Specifically, it satisfies correctness (i.e., any participant subset of cardinality $\geq t$ can recover the secret g), secrecy (i.e., any participant subset of size $\leq t-1$ obtains no information about g), and is multiplicative (i.e., the secret can be reconstructed by a multiplicative expression over a non-Abelian group, to which any t parties can apply one of their shares). All 3 properties are proved by induction over the recursion level.

4.2 Performances

In [28], the authors show how to compute and bound the total number of shares.

Definition 3. *Let t, n be the parameter of the threshold secret sharing defined by Fig. 3. We define as $S(t, n)$ the total number of shares.*

Remark 2. By the recursive nature of the secret sharing scheme, it immediately holds that

$$
\begin{aligned}
S(t,n) &= \sum_{i=0}^{t} S\left(i, \left\lfloor \frac{n}{2} \right\rfloor\right) + S\left(t-i, \left\lceil \frac{n}{2} \right\rceil\right), && \text{for } t \in \left[2, \left\lfloor \frac{n}{2} \right\rfloor\right] \\
S(t,n) &= \sum_{i=t-\lfloor \frac{n}{2} \rfloor}^{\lfloor \frac{n}{2} \rfloor} S\left(i, \left\lfloor \frac{n}{2} \right\rfloor\right) + S\left(t-i, \left\lceil \frac{n}{2} \right\rceil\right), && \text{for } t \in \left[\left\lfloor \frac{n}{2} \right\rfloor + 1, n-1\right] \\
S(t,n) &= n && \text{for } t = 1 \text{ or } t = n \\
S(t,n) &= 0 && \text{for } t \leq 0 \text{ or } t > n.
\end{aligned}
$$

We revisit the analysis of the scheme in [28], looking for an improved upper bound on the number of shares distributed to all participants. The proofs for these bounds are slightly technical and long, hence they are included in the full version of the paper. Our main result is the following:

Theorem 1. *For any $t, n \in \mathbb{N}$ such that $t \in [2, n-1]$, it holds that $S(t,n) \leq 2n \cdot \min\{ub_0, ub_1, ub_2\}$, where*

$$
ub_0 = \left(\frac{e(a+b)}{a}\right)^a, \quad ub_1 = \left(\frac{e(a+b)}{b}\right)^b, \quad ub_2 = \sqrt{\frac{(a+b)}{2\pi \cdot a \cdot b}} \cdot \frac{(a+b)^{a+b}}{a^a b^b},
$$

and where $a = \lceil \log n \rceil$, $b = t-1$, and e is Euler's constant (i.e., $e = 2.781...$).

The total number of shares represents also a bound on the number of group operations during the key generation procedure (Fig. 3). However, for our scenario, it is also relevant to bound on the number of shares each user receive, lets call it $U(t,n)$. Using the same techniques in the proof of Theorem 1, we can bound $U(t,n)$ using the bounds ub_0, ub_1, ub_2, divided by the number of parties n. We can also recursively compute $U(t,n)$ in this way:

$$U(t,n) = 1 \qquad \text{if } t = 1 \text{ or } t = n$$

$$U(t,n) = \sum_{\ell=\max\left(1,t-\left\lfloor\frac{n}{2}\right\rfloor\right)}^{\min\left(t,\left\lfloor\frac{n}{2}\right\rfloor\right)} U\left(\ell,\left\lceil\frac{n}{2}\right\rceil\right) \qquad \text{otherwise.}$$

We remark that the upper bound given in [28] for the total number of shares can be considered an asymptotic-notation version of our upper bound ub_0, focusing on large values of t (e.g., $t = \omega(\log n)$). Thus, our analysis additionally generalizes their bound to any t, and shows that the constant hidden in their asymptotic notation, is small. In Fig. 4 we compared the 3 upper bounds for $n = 100$ and all $t \leq n/2$. We conclude that upper bound ub_1 is lower than ub_0 for small values of t, and upper bound ub_2 is always smaller than both, by a factor of about 10 or more, thus positively answering the first open question from [28] (i.e., on whether their upper bound could be improved). Similar numerical considerations were derived up to $n = 10$K. Now, we analyze the scheme's performance in specific scenarios depending on the relative values of t and n.

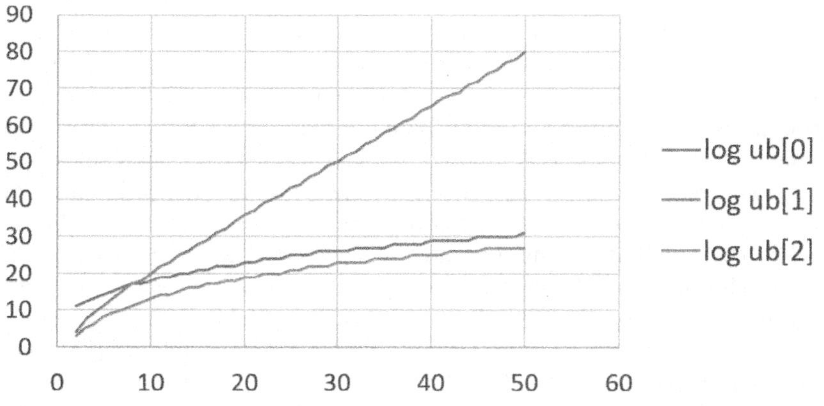

Fig. 4. Comparing (the logarithm of) the 3 upper bounds as a function of $t \leq n/2$, for $n = 100$.

Case t Constant (in n). In this case, upper bound ub_1 shows that every participant is given at most a *polylogarithmic* in n (specifically, $O((\log n)^{t-1})$) number of group elements, thus extending the analogue observation done in [28] for $t = 2$, and improving the upper bound in Replicated Secret Sharing [1,32], which is *polynomial* in n. In Fig. 5 (top), we compare exact values of the number of group elements shared among all participants or to any one participant, for both sharing approaches, when $t = 2$.

Case t Logarithmic (in n). Here, the upper bound ub_0 shows that every participant is given at most a *polynomial* in n number of group elements. Specifically, when $t = c \log n$, for some constant c, we have that $S(t, n) = O(n^d)$, for a related constant $d = \log(e(c+1))$. This improves the upper bound in Replicated Secret Sharing [1,32], which is *super-polynomial* in n. In Fig. 5 (center), we compare exact values of the number of group elements shared among all participants or to any one participant, for both sharing approaches, when $t = \lfloor \log n \rfloor$.

Case Arbitrary t. Here, our upper bounds ub_0 and ub_2 show that participants are given a *slightly super-polynomial* in n number of group elements, thus improving the upper bound in Replicated Secret Sharing [1,32], which is *exponential* in n. In Fig. 5 (bottom), we compare exact values of the number of group elements shared among all participants or to any one participant, for both sharing approaches, when $t = \lfloor n/2 \rfloor$. Sequence Sharing of [16] can be used to produce a multiplicative threshold scheme but would also require an exponential number of group elements to be distributed. The multiplicative threshold scheme in [25] would distribute an (asymptotically) polynomial number of group elements for any t, but the involved constants make it a very impractical scheme. Thus, it still remains of interest to find a multiplicative threshold scheme over arbitrary groups, distributing a practically efficient number of group elements for any t.

Comparison with GRASS key generation. This sharing, with respect to the Replicated Secret Sharing [1,32] used in [6], has the disadvantages of a much more complicated sharing procedure, that was designed with a centralized key generation in mind. In fact, the natural approach to decentralize this key generation procedure requires the participants to agree on $O(S(t, n))$ group values. Moreover, now each share is composed of a group element (even if some of them can be compressed as seed) and a full set element, that for code based group actions are considerably more expensive than single seeds. However, this is balanced by the fact that the number of total shares and individual shares is much lower, as shown by our bounds in Theorem 1 and plots in Fig. 5. More importantly, RecKeyGen has the key advantage that the number of interactive rounds necessary for multiparty computation of g now is only t, instead of $\binom{n}{t}$. This can immediately be applied to the GRASS scheme [6], obtaining a scheme with only $2t + 1$ interaction rounds between the parties (t for the commitment generation and t for the response), independently of n, greatly reducing the latency of the protocol.

4.3 Simulatability

We investigate simulatability properties of the presented Key Generation scheme, which are important when using it in the context of a threshold signature scheme.

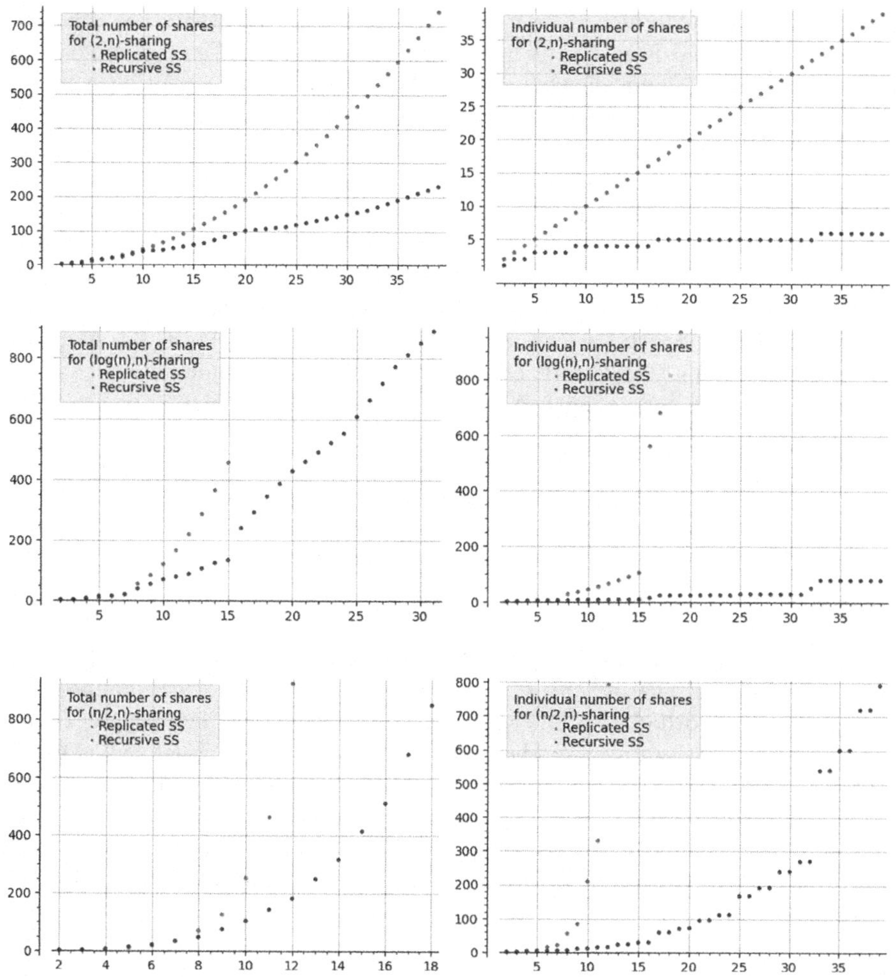

Fig. 5. Total and individual number of shares in the following parameter scenarios: (top) $t = 2$, (center) $t = \lfloor \log(n) \rfloor$, (bottom) $t = \lfloor \frac{n}{2} \rfloor$, when $n \in [2, 35]$

This does not follow immediately from [28] since in our protocol the dealer also needs to publish the set elements corresponding to the group elements; however, they can easily be simulated from the shares of the group elements. Also note that the dealer samples new group elements at every recursion, so (with overwhelming probability) no group element is used twice, thus the attacks from [17] cannot be applied.

Proposition 2. *The procedure* RecKeyGen *is simulatable, i.e., given a valid public key* pk $= (x, y)$*, there exist a simulator* $\mathcal{S}$ *that can simulate the view of* RecKeyGen *applied on* pk *for any corrupted set with cardinality less than the threshold* t*.*

Proof. We prove by induction on n that given x, y set elements in the same orbit we can simulate shards with the same distribution of RecKeyGen (i.e. uniform) in polynomial time without knowledge of a GAIP solution, i.e. g such that $y = g \star x$. For this we exploit the recursive structure of RecKeyGen.

We start the induction from $n = 2$. In $t = 1$ we do not have anything to prove (there are no corrupted parties). If $t = 2$ we sample $g' \in G$ and send it to the corrupted party P_{cor}, then if P_{cor} is the first user we send x to P_{cor}, otherwise we send $x' = g'^{-1} \star y$. Since the other share is implicitly defined as a product of g and g' (or its inverse), as in RecKeyGen, the shares have the same uniform distribution. It is clear that when $t = n$ (for any n) we can repeat the same simulation strategy with longer chains: let i^* be the honest player, the simulator knows all the g_i for $i \neq i^*$, so it can compute all the set elements for $i \leq i^*$ by computing $x_i = g_i \star x_{i-1}$, with $X_0 = x$ and all the set elements for $i > i^*$ by computing $x_i = g_i^{-1} \star x_{i+1}$, with $X_n = y$.

Now we prove this for n assuming that we have a simulation strategy for any $n' < n$. The cases $t = 1, n$ are already solved above, so let's focus on the case $t \neq 1, n$, thus we need to iterate through ℓ as it is done in line 17 of RecKeyGen (Fig. 3). If $\ell = 0, t$ we can just simulate the sharing on a smaller set of users($\mathcal{P}_{\mathsf{left}}$ or $\mathcal{P}_{\mathsf{right}}$) using the simulation strategy that we have by the induction hypothesis since $\lceil \frac{n}{2} \rceil < n$.

Otherwise, we define $\mathtt{cor}_{\mathsf{left}} = \mathtt{cor} \cap \mathcal{P}_{\mathsf{left}}$ and $\mathtt{cor}_{\mathsf{right}} = \mathtt{cor} \cap \mathcal{P}_{\mathsf{right}}$. Now since $\mathtt{cor} < t$ necessarily $\mathtt{cor}_{\mathsf{left}} < t - \ell$ or $\mathtt{cor}_{\mathsf{right}} < \ell$, wlog suppose that $\mathtt{cor}_{\mathsf{right}} < \ell$, the other case follows in the same way. We sample $g_1 \in G$ and define $x_1 = g_1 \star x$. Again, since the other share g_2 is implicitly defined as $g \cdot g_1^{-1}$ all the generated shares are uniformly distributed as in RecKeyGen. Thus, we can simulate the ℓ-out-of-$|\mathcal{P}_{\mathsf{right}}|$ sharing on x_1, y using the simulation strategy, given by the induction hypothesis since $|\mathcal{P}_{\mathsf{right}}| = \lceil \frac{n}{2} \rceil < n$. Then we share g_1, x, x_1 on $\mathcal{P}_{\mathsf{left}}$ using RecKeyGen (here we do not even need to simulate anything since we know g_1).

5 Protocol Description

In this section we present GRASS+, an improved version of GRASS, presented in [6]. The concept of the protocol remains consistent with the original work, while we add ZKP to achieve better security and the key generation of Sect. 4.

Each signing session is uniquely identified by a session identifier `ssid`. Let $\mathcal{S}_{\mathsf{sig}}$ be the signing set for the session. Wlog we consider $\mathcal{S}_{\mathsf{sig}} = \{1, ..., t\}$. All the parties involved have multiplicative shares of g such that $g_1 \cdots g_t = g$. Moreover, let (x, y) be the public key and $\{x_j\}_{j=0,...,t}$ the intermediate set elements satisfying $x_i = g_i \star x_{i-1}$, with $x_0 = x$ and $x_t = y$. These set elements are known to the parties (the i-th party knows both x_i and x_{i-1}).

The signature protocol can be read in Fig. 6. The signing session involves a double round-robin ($\mathsf{TSign}_1, \mathsf{TSign}_2$), each followed by a finalization protocol ($\mathsf{Fin}_1, \mathsf{Fin}_2$). In the Fin_1 protocol, each party i discloses the value r_i committed during TSign_1. These values are subsequently aggregated, and the result is utilized as a salt in the challenge generation. This approach prevents the adversary from predicting the challenge in advance during the simulation, as explained in Remark 3.

In particular, starting from the first party, each party repeat $\mathsf{rps} = \lambda$ times in parallel the following:

- chooses a random group element (line 8),
- apply it to the set element broadcast by the previous party,
- the resulting set element is then broadcast as well as a ZKP about the knowledge of the group action.

The ZKPs need to be online-extractable, for reasons that will be more clear in the proof, as explained in Remark 4. A possible proof Π_{GAK} obtained using the Unruh [41] transform is shown in Appendix B. Unfortunately, this decrease the performance of the protocol, since Unruh transform basically double the size of the transcript: indeed, since the challenge space is binary, during each round the prover needs to send the response to one of the two challenges (as in normal Fiat-Shamir) and the hash of the other one.

Then, after all the first round-robin is finished, the parties engage in a second round-robin to compute the signature. In particular, when the challenge bit is 0 all the parties reveal the random group element chosen, while if the challenge bit is 1 the parties engage in an iterative protocol as follows:

- each party retrieve the group element from the previous player (the first player starts with the identity element 1),
- each player multiplies it by the nonce chosen in TSign_1 (on the left) and by the inverse of its private key (on the right).

In this way the response of each player is the group element that links the player public key to the commitment sent during TSign_1. If this equation does not hold then the next party aborts, otherwise the protocol continue until the last player, which produce the final signature.

The verification protocol is the same of the centralized signature, that we report for completeness in Fig. 7.

6 Adaptive Security

In our protocol we suppose the existence of a broadcast channel, where the messages are published. To avoid the usage of a broadcast channel, when every party sends a message to another one it is required to sign the message. For further information about this technique see [26].

We divide the proof in three steps: first we consider the full threshold case (i.e. all the parties are needed to sign) and we prove the security for $\frac{n-1}{2}$ corruptions (Sect. 6.1) and $n-1$ corruptions (Sect. 6.2). Finally, we show how to generalize (parts of) our proofs to any general t-out-of-n threshold.

$\mathsf{TSign}_1(\mathcal{S}_{\mathsf{sig}}, \mathsf{mes}, \mathsf{sk}_i, \{\mathsf{pm}_{j,1}\}_{j \in \mathcal{S}_{\mathsf{sig}}, j < i})$	$\mathsf{TSign}_2(\mathcal{S}_{\mathsf{sig}}, \mathsf{mes}, \mathsf{sk}_i, \{\mathsf{pm}_{j,1}, r_j\}_{j \in \mathcal{S}_{\mathsf{sig}}}, \{\mathsf{pm}_{j,2}\}_{j \in \mathcal{S}_{\mathsf{sig}}, j < i})$
1: $\tilde{x}_0^k \leftarrow x$ for all $k \in \{1, ..., \mathsf{rps}\}$	1: parse $(\{\tilde{g}_i^k\}_{k=1,...,\mathsf{rps}}) \leftarrow \mathsf{st}_{i,1}[1]$
2: if $i \neq 1$	2: for $j \in \mathcal{S}_{\mathsf{sig}}$
3: for $j \in \mathcal{S}_{\mathsf{sig}}, j < i$	3: parse all $(\{\tilde{x}_j^k\}_{k=1,...,\mathsf{rps}}, \pi_j, \mathsf{cmt}_j) \leftarrow \mathsf{pm}_{j,1}$
4: $\{\tilde{x}_j^k,\}_{k=1,...,\mathsf{rps}}, \pi_i \leftarrow \mathsf{pm}_{j,1}[1,2]$	4: if $\mathsf{V}(\pi_j) = \bot$ or $\mathsf{cmt}_j \neq \mathsf{H}(\mathsf{ssid}, r_j)$
5: if $\mathsf{V}(\pi_i) = \bot$	5: return $\bot$
6: return $\bot$	6: $r \leftarrow \bigoplus_{j \in \mathcal{S}_{\mathsf{sig}}} r_j$
7: $r_i \xleftarrow{\$} \{0,1\}^{\mathsf{rps}}$	7: $\mathsf{ch} \leftarrow \mathsf{H}(r \| \tilde{x}_t^1 \| ... \| \tilde{x}_t^{\mathsf{rps}} \| \mathsf{mes})$
8: $\mathsf{cmt}_i \leftarrow \mathsf{H}(\mathsf{ssid}, r_i)$	8: for $j \in \mathcal{S}_{\mathsf{sig}}, j < i$
9: for $k = 1, ..., \mathsf{rps}$	9: parse all $(\{\mathsf{rsp}_j^k\}_{k=1,...,\mathsf{rps}}) \leftarrow \mathsf{pm}_{j,2}$
10: $\tilde{g}_i^k \xleftarrow{\$} \mathbb{G}$	10: for $k = 1, ..., \mathsf{rps}$
11: $\tilde{x}_i^k \leftarrow \tilde{g}_i^k \star \tilde{x}_{i-1}^k$	11: if $\mathsf{ch}_k = 0$
12: $\pi_i \leftarrow \Pi_{\mathsf{GAK}}(\tilde{g}_i^k, \tilde{x}_i^k, \tilde{x}_{i-1}^k)$	12: if $\mathsf{rsp}_j^k \star \tilde{x}_{j-1}^k \neq \tilde{x}_j^k$ return $\bot$
13: $\mathsf{pm}_{i,1} \leftarrow (\{\tilde{x}_i^k\}_{k=1,...,\mathsf{rps}}, \pi_i, \mathsf{cmt}_i)$	13: if $\mathsf{ch}_k = 1$
14: $\mathsf{st}_{i,1} \leftarrow (\{\tilde{g}_i^k\}_{k=1,...,\mathsf{rps}}, r_i)$	14: if $\mathsf{rsp}_j^k \star x_j \neq \tilde{x}_j^k$ return $\bot$
15: return $(\mathsf{pm}_{i,1}, \mathsf{st}_{i,1})$	15: for $k = 1, ..., \mathsf{rps}$
	16: if $i = 1$
	17: $\mathsf{rsp}_0^k = 1$
	18: if $\mathsf{ch}_k = 0$
	19: $\mathsf{rsp}_i^k \leftarrow \tilde{g}_i^k$
	20: if $\mathsf{ch}_k = 1$
	21: $\mathsf{rsp}_i^k \leftarrow \tilde{g}_i^k \cdot \mathsf{rsp}_{i-1}^k \cdot g_i^{-1}$
	22: $\mathsf{pm}_{i,2} \leftarrow \{\mathsf{rsp}_i^k\}_{k=1,...,\mathsf{rps}}$

$\mathsf{Fin}_1(\mathcal{S}_{\mathsf{sig}}, \mathsf{mes}, \mathsf{sk}_i, \{\mathsf{pm}_{j,1}\}_{j \in \mathcal{S}_{\mathsf{sig}}})$	$\mathsf{Fin}_2(\mathsf{ch}, \mathcal{S}_{\mathsf{sig}}, \mathsf{mes}, \mathsf{sk}_i, \{\mathsf{pm}_{j,1}, \mathsf{pm}_{j,2}, r_j\}_{j \in \mathcal{S}_{\mathsf{sig}}})$
1: $r_i \leftarrow \mathsf{st}_{i,1}[2]$	1: parse all $\{\mathsf{rsp}_i^k\}_{k=1,...,\mathsf{rps}} \leftarrow \mathsf{pm}_{i,2}$
2: return r_i	2: $r \leftarrow \bigoplus_{j \in \mathcal{S}_{\mathsf{sig}}} r_j$
	3: for $k = 1, ..., \mathsf{rps}$
	4: if $\mathsf{ch}_k = 0$
	5: $\mathsf{rsp}^k \leftarrow \prod_{j=1}^t \mathsf{rsp}_j^k$
	6: if $\mathsf{ch} = 1$
	7: $\mathsf{rsp}^k \leftarrow \mathsf{rsp}_{\max(\mathcal{S}_{\mathsf{sig}})}^k$
	8: $\sigma \leftarrow \mathsf{rsp}^1 \| ... \| \mathsf{rsp}^{\mathsf{rps}} \| \mathsf{ch} \| r$
	9: return σ

Fig. 6. Signature protocol for GRASS+.

$\mathsf{Ver}((x, y), \mathtt{mes}, \sigma) \rightarrow 0/1$

$$
\begin{array}{l}
\textbf{parse } (\{\mathtt{rsp}_k\}_{k=1,\dots,\lambda}, \mathtt{ch}, r) \leftarrow \sigma \\
\textbf{for } k = 1, \dots, \lambda \\
\quad \textbf{if } \mathtt{ch}_k = 0 \\
\quad\quad \tilde{x}_t^k \leftarrow \mathtt{rsp}_k \star x \\
\quad \textbf{if } \mathtt{ch} = 1 \\
\quad\quad \tilde{x}_t^k \leftarrow \mathtt{rsp}_k \star y \\
\textbf{return } \mathtt{ch} = \mathsf{H}(r || \tilde{x}_t^1 || \dots || \tilde{x}_t^\lambda || \mathtt{mes})
\end{array}
$$

Fig. 7. Verification algorithm for GRASS+

6.1 $(n-1)/2$ Corruptions

Theorem 2. *Let $(G, X, \star)$ be a group action such that n-Chain-GAIP (Problem 2) is hard, then the digital signature of Fig. 6 is secure against adaptive chosen message attack with up to $\frac{n-1}{2}$ corruptions in the Random Oracle Model.*

Outline of the Proof. The proof follows a standard game-based approach. The goal is to show that if an adversary is able to produce a forgery, then it is possible to build an adversary able to win the n-Chain-GAIP problem (Problem 2). To do so we need to simulate the EUF-CMA game of Fig. 2. The strategy is very similar to the one used to prove the honest-verifier zero-knowledge of the base centralized protocol (see [5] for an example, where the group action used is the code equivalence):

- every time a new session query is started the simulator choose a random challenge $\mathtt{ch}$;
- the simulator then simulates the signature generation using the chosen challenge. Notice that a single round is basically an execution of the centralized protocol, so the same strategy can be exploited.

To avoid inconsistencies when answering the random oracle queries, we need that the simulator knows the input in challenge computation before the adversary. This is done by adding a random salt as additional input of the hash function, that the simulator can extract from the adversary.

Lastly, the simulator needs to answer to the corruption queries. Unfortunately the strategy adopted makes impossible to reconstruct all the private data, so the simulator needs some additional information. In particular, the simulator needs to be able to extract all the secret nonces used by the adversary, this is possible thanks to the online-extractable ZKP introduced during the execution of TSign_1.

Proof. Consider a probabilistic polynomial-time adversary $\mathcal{A}$ that make up to $\frac{n-1}{2}$ corruption queries, q_s sign queries and q_h quantum call to the random oracle $\mathcal{O}^{\mathsf{H}}$. We build a probabilistic polynomial-time algorithm $\mathcal{S}$ for n-Chain-GAIP that use $\mathcal{A}$ as a subroutine. In the proof $\mathcal{S}$ runs $\mathcal{A}$ two times. In this way, $\mathcal{S}$ makes no more than $n-1$ queries to its oracle $\mathcal{O}^{\mathsf{chain}}$ and aims to output the n groups elements that constitute the chain. If the total number of queries is less than $n-1$ then $\mathcal{S}$ performs the additional queries required to extract the solution.

The idea of the proof is that during the two iterations, $\mathcal{S}$ reprograms the random oracle $\mathcal{O}^{\mathsf{H}}$ to output a different random value on a single input, so that it can extract the action from x to y.

We now describe how $\mathcal{S}$ can simulate the game $\mathsf{Exp}_{\mathcal{A}}^{\mathsf{euf-cma}}$. In particular $\mathcal{S}$ is responsible for simulating the key generation and the response to the oracles $\mathcal{O}^{\mathsf{Corrupt}}, \mathcal{O}^{\mathsf{TSign}_1}$ and $\mathcal{O}^{\mathsf{TSign}_2}$ as well as all the random oracle queries $\mathcal{O}^{\mathsf{H}}$. $\mathcal{S}$ initializes two empty tables to save all the oracle queries and the sign queries done by the adversary. Let Q_{H} and Q_{TSign} such tables. At the beginning of the second iteration of $\mathcal{A}$, $\mathcal{S}$ resets Q_{TSign} to the empty set, while it keeps Q_{H}. Lastly $\mathcal{S}$ initialize a corruption counter $\mathtt{cc} = 0$ that will count the number of corruption made by the adversary. If $\mathtt{cc}$ ever surpass $\frac{n-1}{2}$ $\mathcal{S}$ aborts. $\mathcal{S}$ resets such counter to 0 at the beginning of the second iteration.

n-Chain-GAIP challenge. $\mathcal{S}$ takes as input an n-Chain-GAIP challenge in the form of $\{x_i\}_{i=0,\dots,n}$. $\mathcal{S}$ has also access to an oracle $\mathcal{O}^{\mathsf{chain}}$ that can answer to up to $n-1$ queries, $\mathcal{S}$ will use it to answer to the corruption queries made by the adversary. $\mathcal{S}$ sets $(x, y) = (x_0, x_n)$ as the public key of the $\mathsf{Exp}_{\mathcal{A}}^{\mathsf{euf-cma}}$ game, with (x_{i-1}, x_i) being the public key of party i and g_i be the corresponding private key.

Simulating the RO Queries. When $\mathcal{A}$ queries the random oracle $\mathcal{O}^{\mathsf{H}}$ on input X, $\mathcal{S}$ checks whether $X \in Q_{\mathsf{H}}$. If this is the case then $\mathcal{S}$ answers with the same output, otherwise $\mathcal{S}$ samples $c \xleftarrow{\$} \{0,1\}^{\mathsf{rps}}$ randomly, saves (X, c) in the table Q_{H} and returns c.

Simulating Signature. $\mathcal{S}$ needs to simulate both $\mathcal{O}^{\mathsf{TSign}_1}$ and $\mathcal{O}^{\mathsf{TSign}_2}$. The simulation proceeds as follows:

- $\mathcal{O}^{\mathsf{TSign}_1}()$. $\mathcal{S}$ do the checks in at the beginning of the game of Fig. 2. In particular $\mathcal{S}$ checks whether i is an honest party and whether the session id $\mathtt{ssid}$ is correctly defined (in the case $i = 0$, then $\mathcal{S}$ choose a random session id $\mathtt{ssid}$) or not. Lastly, $\mathcal{S}$ checks whether all the previous player correctly sent their data and the corresponding ZKP. During this step $\mathcal{S}$ can also extract all the previous $\tilde{g}_j$ from the adversary. If all the checks are passed then $\mathcal{S}$ checks whether a challenge $\mathsf{ch}^{\mathtt{ssid}}$ is defined or not. In case it is not defined (meaning that this is the first time $\mathcal{S}$ participate in the signing session $\mathtt{ssid}$), $\mathcal{S}$ choose a random string and sets it as $\mathsf{ch}^{\mathtt{ssid}}$. See Remark 3 for more details. For $k = 1, \dots, \mathsf{rps}$ does the following:
  - if $\mathsf{ch}_i^{\mathtt{ssid}} = 0$ then follows the protocol normally,
  - if $\mathsf{ch}_i^{\mathtt{ssid}} = 1$ then $\mathcal{S}$ choose a random $\tilde{g}_i^k \in \mathbb{G}$ and sets $\tilde{x}_i^k = \tilde{g}_i^k \star x_{i-1}$. Then it simulates the ZKPs necessary and compute π_i.

- $\mathcal{O}^{\mathsf{TSign}_2}()$: by construction, the challenge is $\mathsf{ch} = \mathsf{ch}^{\mathtt{ssid}}$, except with negligible probability (see Remark 3). Thanks to the value chosen in the simulation of $\mathcal{O}^{\mathsf{TSign}_1}()$ $\mathcal{S}$ can successfully answer both challenges.

Corruption Query. $\mathcal{S}$ needs to answer the corruption queries made by the adversary. When $\mathcal{A}$ asks for the corruption of party i, $\mathcal{S}$ checks that i is an honest party and if there are less than $\frac{n-1}{2}$ corrupted parties. If both checks are true then $\mathcal{S}$ queries $\mathcal{O}^{\mathsf{chain}}$ on input (x_{i-1}, x_i) to get g_i.

At this point $\mathcal{S}_i$ can successfully retrieve all the $\tilde{g}_i^k$ used in all the active signing session involving i, filling all the $\mathtt{st}_{i,1}$ (excluding those for which i has not yet sent a message). In particular $\mathcal{S}$ needs to reconstruct $\tilde{g}_i^k$ when the challenge is 1, since $\mathcal{S}$ follows the protocol honestly when the challenge is 0. For every session, let $i^* < i$ be the last honest player, controlled by $\mathcal{S}$. In the case where all the player before i are corrupted or i is the first player we set $i^* = 0$. Clearly $\mathcal{S}$ knows all the g_j with $i^* < j < i$, as well as g_i since they are all corrupted parties. Moreover, $\mathcal{S}$ extracted all the $\tilde{g}_j^k$ from the ZKPs (lines 5 and 10 of TSign_1). Thus, $\mathcal{S}$ knows both the action from x_{i^*} to x_i and the action from $\tilde{x}_{i^*}^k$ to $\tilde{x}_{i-1}^k$. Lastly $\mathcal{S}$ knows both the action from x_i to $\tilde{x}_i^k$ and the action from x_{i^*} to $\tilde{x}_{i^*}^k$ by construction (see the simulation of TSign_1 when the challenge bit is 1). In the case $i^* = 0$ $\mathcal{S}$ can simply set $\tilde{x}_{i^*}^k = x_0$ for all k and thus the action is the identity element. In this way $\mathcal{S}$ can compute the actions from $\tilde{x}_{i-1}^k$ to $\tilde{x}_i^k$.

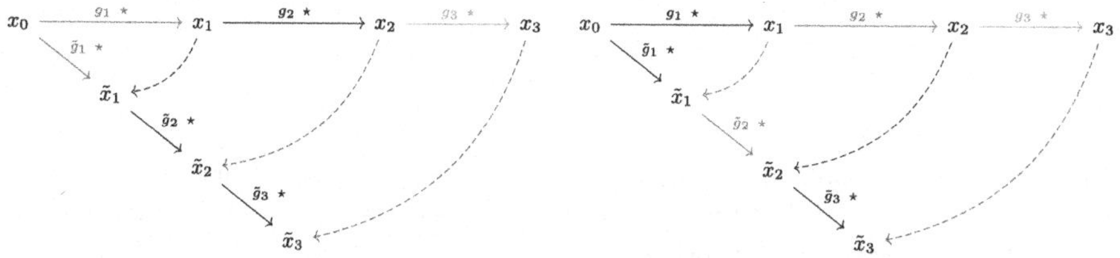

(a) The previous player is honest. (b) The previous player is corrupted.

Fig. 8. Simulation of a corruption query on player P_2 (in green). (Color figure online)

Figure 8a and Fig. 8b show schematically how the corruption queries (on P_2, in green) are simulated, depending on whether the previous player is corrupted (in red) or not.

- Figure 8a since P_1 is honest, the simulator knows both the blued arrows and the green arrow (thanks to the $\mathcal{O}^{\mathsf{Corrupt}}$ made to the n-Chain-GAIP oracle). Thus, it can compute $\tilde{g}_3$ by composing the three actions.
- Figure 8b since P_2 is corrupted, the simulator cannot do the same computation of the previous case. However, the simulator knows both the blued arrows, the green arrow (thanks to the $\mathcal{O}^{\mathsf{Corrupt}}$ made to the n-Chain-GAIP oracle) and both the red arrows (thanks to the online extractable ZKP and a previous corruption query). Hence, it can compute $\tilde{g}_3$ by composing the five actions.

Solving n-Chain-GAIP. After the simulation the adversary outputs a forgery. At this point the simulator rewind and change the challenge corresponding to the forgery made by the adversary, thus extracting the action form x to y. $\mathcal{S}$ the use the same action to win the n-Chain-GAIP game.

Remark 3. The simulator chooses the challenge for each session after receiving a query for it for the first time. Then, for all the session, the simulator continues to use the same challenge chosen. To reprogram the random oracle in such a way $\mathsf{ch}^{\mathtt{ssid}}$ is as expected the Simulator just need to collect the set elements $\tilde{x}_t^k$ for $k = 1, ..., \mathsf{rps}$, sent after the last execution of TSign_1, and all the random salt values r_i. The adversary need to commit on these salt values, so the simulator can extract them from the random oracle queries, but they are all revealed only in Fin_1 after the $\tilde{x}_t^k$ are produced. Thus, the simulator learns them ahead of time and can reprogram the random oracle accordingly.

The only way that the simulation fails is if a query with the same input has already been sent to the random oracle, however this happens with negligible probability since at least one of the salt values is chosen uniformly at random.

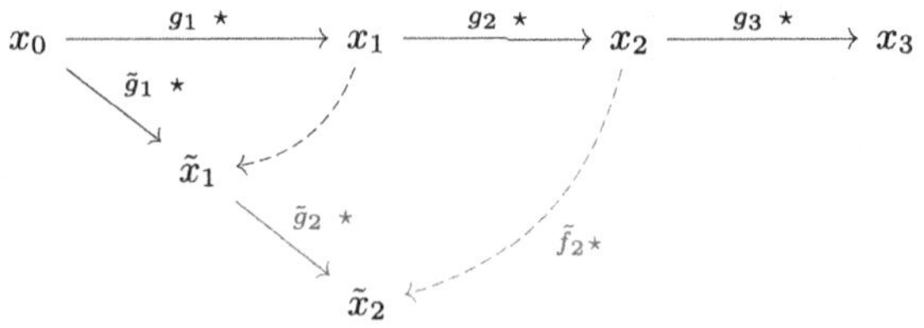

Fig. 9. The simulation failure without the ZKP of TSign_1. If the simulator computes $\tilde{x}_2$ using the red arrow and then the adversary, that controls P_1, corrupts P_2, the simulator is not able to retrieve the blue arrow.

Remark 4. The main difference from the original static secure signature [6] is the non-interactive ZKP in TSign_1. Unfortunately, this is necessary to allow the simulator to correctly answer to the corruption queries. Indeed, let us consider a (3, 3) signature where the adversary controls P_1, while P_2, P_3 are honest (see Fig. 9). Notice that since the threshold is 3, the adversary can perform a second corruption query at any time. Moreover, suppose that the challenge is 1. According to the simulator strategy, the simulator compute $\tilde{x}_2$ starting from x_2 (red arrow) instead of $\tilde{x}_1$ (blue arrow).

Now, suppose that after receiving $\tilde{x}_2$ the adversary perform a corruption query on P_2. The simulator then get g_2 from the n-Chain-GAIP oracle, however it is unable to retrieve $\tilde{g}_2$, and thus the simulation fails. Notice that the simulator knows $\tilde{f}_2$ by construction and g_1, g_2 thanks to the n-Chain-GAIP oracle. In this way, the oracle can compute $\tilde{g}_1 \cdot \tilde{g}_2$, however it cannot compute neither $\tilde{g}_1$ nor $\tilde{g}_2$, otherwise it would be able to break the GAIP problem.

6.2 $n - 1$ Corruptions

Theorem 3. *Let $(G, X, \star)$ be a group action such that n-Chain-GAIP (Problem 2) is hard. Then the digital signature of Fig. 6, with $\mathsf{rps} = \lambda + \log(n)$ is secure against adaptive chosen message attack with up to $n - 1$ corruptions in the Random Oracle and Black Box Group Action Model.*

Proof. The simulation strategy is the same as the previous proofs, the only difference is that the simulator needs to extract the solution for the n-Chain-GAIP after a single forgery.

For this proof we use the same notation of the previous proof, so $x_0 = x$, $x_n = y$, $x_1, ..., x_{n-1}$ are the intermediate set elements and $g_0, .., g_{n-1}$ the secret group elements from n-Chain-GAIP. Let $\mathtt{mes}, \sigma$ the forgery sent by the adversary, from which we can recover the commitment set elements $\tilde{x}^1, ..., \tilde{x}^{\mathsf{rps}}$, the salt r and the responses $\mathtt{resp} = (\mathtt{resp}^1, ..., \mathtt{resp}^{\mathsf{rps}})$. Recall that $\mathtt{ch} \leftarrow \mathsf{H}(r||\tilde{x}_t^1||...||\tilde{x}_t^{\mathsf{rps}}||\mathtt{mes})$. We summarise the input of the random oracle as

$$\mathtt{cmt} = (r, \tilde{x}^1, ..., \tilde{x}^{\mathsf{rps}}, \mathtt{mes}) \; . \tag{2}$$

Since we are in the BBGAM for each $\tilde{x}^i$ we can "follow" the adversary queries and the computations done by the simulator to recursively find a group element $\bar{g}$ and an index j such that $\tilde{x}^i = \bar{g} \star x_j$, i.e. to find a link to one of the known elements $x_0, x_1, ..., x_n = y$, let $\mathsf{idx}(\tilde{x}^i) := j$. Observe that the validity of the transcript implies that the commitment elements $\tilde{x}^i$ are all part of the same orbit $\mathcal{O}(x) \ni x, y$. Thus, it is not possible for the adversary to link one of the commitment elements to a random set element got using $\mathcal{O}^{\mathsf{sample}}$ since the probability that a random set element lies in the same orbit of a given element is negligible (as discussed in Sect. 2.4).

Let IDX be $(\mathsf{idx}(\tilde{x}^1), ..., \mathsf{idx}(\tilde{x}^{\mathsf{rps}}))$. Thanks to our simulation strategy $\mathtt{ch}$ has been sampled uniformly at random and its distribution is independent of the one the adversary used to generate $\mathtt{cmt}$. In fact, thanks to the salt, $\mathcal{A}$ get access to it only *after* querying the random oracle on $\mathtt{cmt}$.

Using this independence we want to show that we extract a solution to n-Chain-GAIP with non-negligible probability. Now, for any $\ell \in \{0, ..., n-1\}$ we can define the vector $\mathsf{split}_\ell(\mathsf{IDX})$ such that its i-th entry is 1 if $\mathsf{idx}(\tilde{x}^i) > \ell$ and 0 otherwise. Now consider the union set of these n vectors derived from :

$$\mathsf{S}(\mathsf{IDX}) = \{\mathsf{split}_\ell(\mathsf{IDX}) \;\text{ for } \ell = 0, .., n-1\} \; .$$

This set is a deterministic function of $\mathtt{cmt}$, thus its distribution is independent of $\mathtt{ch}$, thus

$$\Pr[\mathtt{ch} \in \mathsf{S}(\mathsf{IDX})] = \frac{n}{2^{\mathsf{rps}}} = \frac{n}{2^{\lambda + \log(n)}} = 2^{-\lambda} \; ,$$

i.e. with overwhelming probability $\mathsf{split}_\ell(\mathsf{IDX}) \neq \mathtt{ch}$ for all ℓ.

We can finally use the forgery information to solve the n-Chain-GAIP. To perform the simulation we have queried $n-1$ solutions g_i to the n-Chain-GAIP oracle (if less we perform the missing one at random), define ℓ such that the only missing pair is $(x_\ell, x_{\ell+1})$. We show now how to extract the missing secret g_ℓ.

By the previous discussion $\mathsf{split}_\ell(\mathsf{IDX}) \neq \mathtt{ch}$. Let i be one of the indexes where they differ.

Consider the case in which $\mathtt{ch}_i = 1$. Thus, $\tilde{x}^i$ is linked to both y (thanks to $\mathtt{resp}$) and x_j, with $j = \mathsf{idx}(\tilde{x}^i)$ (thanks to the BBGAM). We can combine this information to get a group element g' such that $y = g' \star x_j$. Also, $\mathtt{ch}_i = 1$ implies that the i-th entry of split_ℓ is 0, i.e. that $j = \mathsf{idx}(\tilde{x}^i) \leq \ell$. Thus, by previous queries to n-Chain-GAIP oracle, we known $g_0, ..., g_{j-1}$ such that $x_j = (g_{j-1} \cdots g_0) \star x_0$ and we can solve n-Chain GAIP since

$$y = g \star x_0 \text{ with } g = g'(g_{j-1} \cdots g_0)^{-1} .$$

If $\mathtt{ch}_i = 0$ we can adapt the same strategy using instead that $\tilde{x}^i$ is linked to both x and x_j for $j > \ell$. Thus, with probability $1 - \frac{1}{2^\lambda}$ we can solve the n-Chain GAIP problem, without rewinding.

6.3 Adapting the Proof for Any Threshold

Replicated Secret Sharing. It is easy to see that the above technique can be easily adapted to any threshold t when the key generation is done via replicated secret sharing, as in the original work [6].

Proof (Sketch). Indeed, it is enough to consider a $\binom{n}{t}$-Chain-GAIP instance having the total number of elements equal to the total number of shards. Then, the simulator can simulate the key distribution by sharing the $\{x_i\}$ among all the parties, according to the replicated secret sharing algorithm (notice that it is not important to know all the action g_i during this step). Then the simulation can be carried out as before, except that when the adversary asks for a corruption query the oracle needs to retrieve all the secret key, by doing multiple query to the oracle. This is not a problem since by doing at most $t - 1$ corruptions the simulator will not ask all the group elements to the oracle.

While the above proof sketch is enough to prove the adaptive security of GRASS against $t - 1$ corruptions, there is a performance issue: indeed using replicated secret sharing implies that the total number of shares is $\binom{n}{t}$, and thus the Chain-GAIP challenge should have $\binom{n}{t}$ actions. It is immediate to see from the proof to Theorem 3, that the security loss is thus $\binom{n}{t}$. This is exactly the same security loss that can be achieved by guessing the corrupted set of parties and abort if the guess is incorrect. However, it is important to notice that, while the "naive" approach inherently incurs in such a security loss, our proof is instead tight with respect to the new Chain-GAIP problem. Thus, if the total number of shares is reduced using a better algorithm, then the security loss can be reduced as well, leading to a tighter security compared to simply guessing the adversary corruptions.

Lastly, note that this performance issue impacts also other aspects of the protocol, thus we need anyway $\binom{n}{t}$ to be small.

New Secret Sharing. Given the considerations of the previous paragraph, the first idea to solve the issue would be to use the newly introduced secret sharing of Sect. 4. However, this is not as straightforward as it could seem. Indeed, the secret sharing of Sect. 4 does not output a single chain of group actions, but many of them, with many intersections. Thus, we cannot reduce the security of the signature to the n-Chain-GAIP. In particular, to prove the security with the improved secret sharing, we reduce it to N-Graph-GAIP, introduced in Problem 3.

Theorem 4. *Let $(G, X, \star)$ be a group action such that N-Graph-GAIP (Problem 3) is hard. Then the digital signature of Fig. 6 with the secret sharing of Sect. 4 is secure against adaptive chosen message attack with up to $\frac{n-1}{2}$ corruptions in the Random Oracle and Black Box Group Action Model.*

Proof. The proof is the same as the full threshold case (Theorem 2), where instead of receiving an n-Chain-GAIP challenge, the simulator receives as input an N-Graph-GAIP (Problem 3) challenge. Then the simulator set the public key according to it, distributing all the shards to the users following the secret sharing of Sect. 4 and start the interaction with the adversary. The number of set elements N involved in N-Graph-GAIP is set in such a way to have enough shares for the sharing in Sect. 4, thus it is bounded by the number of shards $S(t, n)$.

Every time the adversary asks for the corruption of party P_i, the simulator retrieves all the public key of P_i and queries the oracle on them. Notice that since the adversary performs at most t corruptions, then the simulator never asks for an invalid query (i.e., a query that links x, y) by construction, so the simulator can answer all the queries correctly.

The remaining part of the simulation is the same, since the signature algorithm is equal to the full threshold case.

7 Conclusion

In this paper we improved the GRASS signature scheme [6] in two ways: our main result is a post-quantum threshold signature scheme secure against adaptive attacks. This schemes can be instantiated with a variety of cryptographic group actions, in particular [5,7,11,22]. Additionally, as a second result, we were able to improve the key generation protocol.

Even if the asymptotic complexity remains the same, concrete results show a considerable reduction in the number of shares that each party needs to store, allowing a wider choice for the parameters. Improving the secret sharing, possibly reaching a constant number of shares, is still an open problem. In this context, a possible research area is to adapt classical techniques from MPC, like Beaver Triples, to achieve better performance. Another open problem is to define an efficient decentralized version of the new Key Generation procedure.

It is also important to note that improving the secret sharing and the key generation algorithm does not impact only the performance, but also the security of the scheme. As discussed in Sect. 6, the security loss is often proportional to the number of shares used, so a more efficient protocol would lead to a tighter security reduction.

Unfortunately, our protocol still suffers the same performance issues of the original GRASS and other group-based threshold signature schemes like [24], since we require a double round-robin[7], moreover we introduced expensive ZKPs that are necessary for achieving adaptive security. Trying to reduce the computational overhead while still reaching the higher level of security is a very important challenge to tackle, and possible improvements can be obtained both by compressing the ZKPs (since the Unruh transform is very expensive) or by finding a way to reduce the number of ZKPs needed.

Acknowledgements. This collaboration was initiated during the "Post-Quantum Group-Based Cryptography" workshop at the American Institute of Mathematics (AIM), April 29 - May 3, 2024.

This work has been partially supported by project SERICS (PE00000014) under the MUR National Recovery and Resilience Plan funded by the European Union - NextGenerationEU and by the European Union FSE-REACT-EU, PON Research and Innovation 2014–2020 DM1062/2021.

The first author is supported by the Italian Ministry of University's PRIN 2022 program under the "Mathematical Primitives for Post Quantum Digital Signatures" (P2022J4HRR) and "POst quantum Identification and eNcryption primiTives: dEsign and Realization (POINTER)" (2022M2JLF2) projects funded by the European Union - Next Generation EU. The second author is supported by SNSF Consolidator Grant CryptonIs 213766. The third author's work was supported the Defense Advanced Research Projects Agency (DARPA), contract number HR001120C0156. The fourth author acknowledges support from Ripple's University Blockchain Research Initiative.

A Secret Sharing

We briefly recall the definition and main properties of the type of secret sharing scheme that is sufficient for this paper's needs.

Let $\mathcal{P} = \{P_1, \ldots, P_n\}$ denote a set of n participants. The *(t, n)-threshold access structure* over $\mathcal{P}$ is the set of subsets of $\mathcal{P}$ of size at least t. A *secret sharing scheme for the (t, n)-threshold access structure* is a pair of efficient algorithms (Share, Recover) with the following syntax and requirements. On input a value s, called the *secret*, algorithm Share returns n (sets of) values $sh_1, \ldots, sh_n$, called *shares*. On input a subset of shares, algorithm Recover returns a value in s'. The *correctness* requirement says that if an authorized subset of shares (i.e., at least t out of n) is input to Recover, then $s' = s$. The *secrecy* requirement says that the distribution of the secret is independent on the distribution of any unauthorized subset of shares (i.e., at most $t - 1$ out of n).

A secret sharing scheme for the (t, n)-threshold access structure with values in a group G is *multiplicative* (see, e.g., Definition 2 in [28]) if in the reconstruction phase the secret can be written as the group product of t values in G, each of

[7] It is worth noting that the usage of one round-robin is optimal, as shown in [23].

these being locally computed by a different participant, as a function of the share obtained at the end of the distribution phase. A major research question in the area of secret sharing schemes is minimizing the size of the shares.

B Online Extractable Proofs

In this section we provide the online-extractable ZKP used in the signature protocol. Our protocol is essentially the Unruh transform [41] of the standard proof for group action knowledge. Other alternatives are possible, such as using the Fischilin transform [31].

Let g be the secret group action and x, y public set elements, with $y = g \star x$. Let $\mathsf{H}, \mathsf{H}_{\mathsf{ch}}$ two hash functions, with $\mathsf{H}_{\mathsf{ch}} : \{0,1\}^* \to \{0,1\}^\lambda$. Figure 10 shows how the prover, who knows g, can convince the verifier about it.

$\Pi_{\mathsf{GAK}}(g, x, y)$

for $i = 1, ..., \lambda$
    $\tilde{g}_i \xleftarrow{\$} G$
    $\tilde{x}_i = \tilde{g}_i \star x$
    $\mathtt{rsp}_{i,0} = \tilde{g}_i$
    $\mathtt{rsp}_{i,1} = \tilde{g}_i \cdot g^{-1}$
    $\mathtt{cmt}_{i,0} = \mathsf{H}(\mathtt{rsp}_{i,0})$
    $\mathtt{cmt}_{i,1} = \mathsf{H}(\mathtt{rsp}_{i,1})$
$\mathtt{ch} = \mathsf{H}_{\mathsf{ch}}(\tilde{x}_1 || \mathtt{cmt}_{1,0} || \mathtt{cmt}_{1,1} || ... || \tilde{x}_\lambda || \mathtt{cmt}_{\lambda,0} || \mathtt{cmt}_{\lambda,1})$
for $i = 1, ..., \lambda$
    if $\mathtt{ch} = 0$
        $\mathtt{rsp}_i = (\mathtt{rsp}_{i,0}, \mathtt{cmt}_{i,1})$
else
        $\mathtt{rsp}_i = (\mathtt{rsp}_{i,1}, \mathtt{cmt}_{i,0})$
$\pi = (\mathtt{ch}, \{\mathtt{rsp}_i\})$

Fig. 10. Online extractable ZKP for group action knowledge

The verify procedure V consist in computing all the $\tilde{x}_i$ and $\mathtt{cmt}_{i,j}$ for $j = 0, 1$ $i = 1, ..., \lambda$ and then checking the correctness by computing $\mathtt{ch}$. In particular, for each challenge bit $\mathtt{ch}_i$ the verifier compute the following

- if $\mathtt{ch}_i = 0$ then $\tilde{x}_i = \mathtt{rsp}_{i,0} \star x$ and $\mathtt{cmt}_{i,0} = \mathsf{H}(\mathtt{rsp}_{i,0})$,
- if $\mathtt{ch}_i = 1$ then $\tilde{x}_i = \mathtt{rsp}_{i,1} \star y$ and $\mathtt{cmt}_{i,0} = \mathsf{H}(\mathtt{rsp}_{i,1})$,

then check whether $\texttt{ch} = \mathsf{H}_{\texttt{ch}}(\tilde{x}_1||\texttt{cmt}_{1,0}||\texttt{cmt}_{1,1}||...||\tilde{x}_\lambda||\texttt{cmt}_{\lambda,0}||\texttt{cmt}_{\lambda,1})$ or not.

The correctness, honest-verifier zero-knowledge and online-extractability properties follow directly from the security of the base protocol and the properties of the Unruh transform. The protocol efficiency can be improved by using well-known optimizations like seed trees and fixed-weight challenges (see e.g. a survey in [14]) and by storing the commitments $\texttt{cmt}_{i,j}$ in more efficient structures, like Merkle Trees. In the interest of clarity, we omit these optimizations from the description.

References

1. Baccarini, A., Blanton, M., Yuan, C.: Multi-party replicated secret sharing over a ring with applications to privacy-preserving machine learning. Cryptology ePrint Archive (2020)
2. Bacho, R., Loss, J., Stern, G., Wagner, B.: HARTS: High-threshold, adaptively secure, and robust threshold Schnorr signatures. Cryptology ePrint Archive, Paper 2024/280 (2024). https://eprint.iacr.org/2024/280
3. Bacho, R., Loss, J., Tessaro, S., Wagner, B., Zhu, C.: Twinkle: threshold signatures from DDH with full adaptive security. In: Joye, M., Leander, G. (eds.) Advances in Cryptology – EUROCRYPT 2024. LNCS, vol. 14651, pp. 429–459. Springer, Cham (2024). https://doi.org/10.1007/978-3-031-58716-0_15
4. Bardet, M., Otmani, A., Saeed-Taha, M.: Permutation code equivalence is not harder than graph isomorphism when hulls are trivial. In: IEEE International Symposium on Information Theory (ISIT), pp. 2464–2468. IEEE Press (2019). https://doi.org/10.1109/ISIT.2019.8849855
5. Barenghi, A., Biasse, J.-F., Persichetti, E., Santini, P.: LESS-FM: fine-tuning signatures from the code equivalence problem. In: Cheon, J.H., Tillich, J.-P. (eds.) PQCrypto 2021 2021. LNCS, vol. 12841, pp. 23–43. Springer, Cham (2021). https://doi.org/10.1007/978-3-030-81293-5_2
6. Battagliola, M., Borin, G., Meneghetti, A., Persichetti, E.: Cutting the grass: threshold group action signature schemes. In: Topics in Cryptology - CT-RSA 2024: Cryptographers' Track at the RSA Conference 2024, San Francisco, CA, USA, May 6-9, 2024, Proceedings, pp. 460–489. Springer-Verlag, Heidelberg (2024). https://doi.org/10.1007/978-3-031-58868-6_18. ISBN 978-3-031-58867-9
7. Beullens, W., Kleinjung, T., Vercauteren, F.: CSI-FiSh: efficient isogeny based signatures through class group computations. In: Galbraith, S.D., Moriai, S. (eds.) ASIACRYPT 2019. LNCS, vol. 11921, pp. 227–247. Springer, Cham (2019). https://doi.org/10.1007/978-3-030-34578-5_9
8. Beullens, W., Disson, L., Pedersen, R., Vercauteren, F.: CSI-RAShi: distributed key generation for CSIDH. In: Cheon, J.H., Tillich, J.-P. (eds.) PQCrypto 2021 2021. LNCS, vol. 12841, pp. 257–276. Springer, Cham (2021). https://doi.org/10.1007/978-3-030-81293-5_14
9. Biasse, J.-F., Micheli, G., Persichetti, E., Santini, P.: LESS is more: code-based signatures without syndromes. In: Nitaj, A., Youssef, A. (eds.) AFRICACRYPT 2020. LNCS, vol. 12174, pp. 45–65. Springer, Cham (2020). https://doi.org/10.1007/978-3-030-51938-4_3

10. Biasse, J.-F., Micheli, G.: A search-to-decision reduction for the permutation code equivalence problem. In: 2023 IEEE International Symposium on Information Theory (ISIT), pp. 602–607 (2023).https://doi.org/10.1109/ISIT54713.2023.10206940
11. Bläser, M., et al.: The Alteq signature scheme: Algorithm specifications and supporting documentation (2023). https://pqcalteq.github.io/ALTEQ_spec_2023.09.18.pdf
12. Boneh, D., Guan, J., Zhandry, M.: A lower bound on the length of signatures based on group actions and generic isogenies. In: Hazay, C., Stam, M. (eds.) Advances in Cryptology – EUROCRYPT 2023. LNCS, vol. 14008, pp. 507–531. Springer, Cham (2023). https://doi.org/10.1007/978-3-031-30589-4_18
13. Booher, J., et al.: Failing to hash into supersingular isogeny graphs. Comput. J. **67**, 2702–2719 (2024)
14. Borin, G., Persichetti, E., Santini, P., Pintore, F., Reijnders, K.: A Guide to the Design of Digital Signatures Based on Cryptographic Group Actions (2023)
15. Brandao, L., Peralta, R.: NIST first call for multi-party threshold schemes (2023)
16. Brickell, E., Di Crescenzo, G., Frankel, Y.: Sharing block ciphers. In: Dawson, E.P., Clark, A., Boyd, C. (eds.) ACISP 2000. LNCS, vol. 1841, pp. 457–470. Springer, Heidelberg (2000). https://doi.org/10.1007/10718964_37
17. Budroni, A., Chi-Domínguez, J.J., D'Alconzo, G., Di Scala, A.J., Kulkarni, M.: Don't use it twice! Solving relaxed linear equivalence problems. In: Chung, KM., Sasaki, Y. (eds) Advances in Cryptology. ASIACRYPT 2024. LNCS, vol. 15491, pp. 35–65. Springer, Singapore (2025). https://doi.org/10.1007/978-981-96-0944-4_2
18. Campos, F., Muth, P.: On actively secure fine-grained access structures from isogeny assumptions. In: Cheon, J.H., Johansson, T. (eds.) Post-Quantum Cryptography. PQCrypto 2022. LNCS, vol. 13512, pp. 375–398. Springer, Cham (2022). https://doi.org/10.1007/978-3-031-17234-2_18
19. Canetti, R., Gennaro, R., Jarecki, S., Krawczyk, H., Rabin, T.: Adaptive security for threshold cryptosystems. In: Wiener, M. (ed.) CRYPTO 1999. LNCS, vol. 1666, pp. 98–116. Springer, Heidelberg (1999). https://doi.org/10.1007/3-540-48405-1_7
20. Canetti, R., Feige, U., Goldreich, O., Naor, M.: Adaptively secure multi-party computation. In: Proceedings of the Twenty-Eighth Annual ACM Symposium on Theory of Computing, STOC 1996, pp. 639–648, New York, NY, USA, 1996. Association for Computing Machinery. ISBN 0897917855. https://doi.org/10.1145/237814.238015
21. Castryck, W., Lange, T., Martindale, C., Panny, L., Renes, J.: CSIDH: an efficient post-quantum commutative group action. In: Peyrin, T., Galbraith, S. (eds.) ASIACRYPT 2018. LNCS, vol. 11274, pp. 395–427. Springer, Cham (2018). https://doi.org/10.1007/978-3-030-03332-3_15
22. Chou, T., et al.: Take your MEDS: digital signatures from matrix code equivalence. In: El Mrabet, N., De Feo, L., Duquesne, S. (eds.) Progress in Cryptology. AFRICACRYPT 2023. LNCS, vol. 14064, pp. 28–52. Springer, Cham (2023). https://doi.org/10.1007/978-3-031-37679-5_2
23. Cozzo, D., Giunta, E.: Round-robin is optimal: lower bounds for group action based protocols. In: Rothblum, G., Wee, H. (eds.) Theory of Cryptography. TCC 2023. LNCS, vol. 14372, pp. 310–335. Springer, Cham (2023). https://doi.org/10.1007/978-3-031-48624-1_12
24. Cozzo, D., Smart, N.P.: Sashimi: cutting up CSI-FiSh secret keys to produce an actively secure distributed signing protocol. In: Ding, J., Tillich, J.-P. (eds.) PQCrypto 2020. LNCS, vol. 12100, pp. 169–186. Springer, Cham (2020). https://doi.org/10.1007/978-3-030-44223-1_10

25. Di Crescenzo, G., Frankel, Y.: Existence of multiplicative secret sharing schemes with polynomial share expansion. In: Tarjan, R.E., Warnow, T.J. (eds.), Proceedings of the Tenth Annual ACM-SIAM Symposium on Discrete Algorithms, 17-19 January 1999, Baltimore, Maryland, USA, pp. 895–896. ACM/SIAM (1999). http://dl.acm.org/citation.cfm?id=314500.315074
26. Crites, E., Komlo, C., Maller, M.: Fully adaptive Schnorr threshold signatures. In: Advances in Cryptology - CRYPTO 2023: 43rd Annual International Cryptology Conference, CRYPTO 2023, Santa Barbara, CA, USA, August 20-24, 2023, Proceedings, Part I, pp. 678–709, Heidelberg (2023). https://doi.org/10.1007/978-3-031-38557-5_22. ISBN 978-3-031-38556-8
27. De Feo, L., Meyer, M.: Threshold schemes from isogeny assumptions. In: Kiayias, A., Kohlweiss, M., Wallden, P., Zikas, V. (eds.) PKC 2020. LNCS, vol. 12111, pp. 187–212. Springer, Cham (2020). https://doi.org/10.1007/978-3-030-45388-6_7
28. Desmedt, Y., Di Crescenzo, G., Burmester, M.: Multiplicative non-abelian sharing schemes and their application to threshold cryptography. In: Advances in Cryptology-ASIACRYPT 1994: 4th International Conferences on the Theory and Applications of Cryptology Wollongong, Australia, November 28–December 1, 1994 Proceedings 4, pp. 19–32. Springer (1995). https://doi.org/10.1007/bfb0000421
29. Duman, J., Hartmann, D., Kiltz, E., Kunzweiler, S., Lehmann, J., Riepel, D.: Generic models for group actions. In: Boldyreva, A., Kolesnikov, V. (eds.) Public-Key Cryptography – PKC 2023. LNCS, vol. 13940, pp. 406–435. Springer, Cham (2023). https://doi.org/10.1007/978-3-031-31368-4_15
30. Espitau, T., Katsumata, S., Takemure, K.: Two-round threshold signature from algebraic one-more learning with errors. In: Reyzin, L., Stebila, D. (eds.) Advances in Cryptology – CRYPTO 2024. LNCS, vol. 14926, pp. 387–424. Springer, Cham (2024). https://doi.org/10.1007/978-3-031-68394-7_13
31. Fischlin, M.: Communication-efficient non-interactive proofs of knowledge with online extractors. In: Shoup, V. (eds.) Advances in Cryptology – CRYPTO 2005. LNCS, vol. 3621, pp. 152–168. Springer, Heidelberg (2005). https://doi.org/10.1007/11535218_10
32. Ito, M., Saito, A., Nishizeki, T.: Secret sharing scheme realizing general access structure. Electron. Commun. Japan **72**, 56–64 (1989)
33. Jarecki, S., Lysyanskaya, A.: Adaptively secure threshold cryptography: introducing concurrency, removing erasures. In: Preneel, B. (ed.) EUROCRYPT 2000. LNCS, vol. 1807, pp. 221–242. Springer, Heidelberg (2000). https://doi.org/10.1007/3-540-45539-6_16
34. Katsumata, S., Reichle, M., Takemure, K.: Adaptively secure 5 round threshold signatures from MLWE/MSIS and DL with rewinding. In: Reyzin, L., Stebila, D. (eds.) Advances in Cryptology – CRYPTO 2024. LNCS, vol. 14926, pp. 459–491. Springer, Cham (2024). https://doi.org/10.1007/978-3-031-68394-7_15
35. Khaburzaniya, I., Chalkias, K., Lewi, K., Malvai, H.: Aggregating and thresholdizing hash-based signatures using starks. In: Proceedings of the 2022 ACM on Asia Conference on Computer and Communications Security, ASIA CCS 2022, pp. 393–407, New York, NY, USA. Association for Computing Machinery. ISBN 9781450391405 (2022). https://doi.org/10.1145/3488932.3524128
36. Nick, J., Ruffing, T., Seurin, Y.: MuSig2: simple two-round Schnorr multi-signatures. In: Malkin, T., Peikert, C. (eds.) CRYPTO 2021. LNCS, vol. 12825, pp. 189–221. Springer, Cham (2021). https://doi.org/10.1007/978-3-030-84242-0_8
37. NIST: Call for Additional Digital Signature Schemes for the Post-Quantum Cryptography Standardization Process (2023). https://csrc.nist.gov/projects/pqc-dig-sig/standardization/call-for-proposals

38. NIST: Post-Quantum Cryptography Standardization (2017). https://csrc.nist.gov/Projects/Post-Quantum-Cryptography
39. Orsini, E., Zanotto, R.: Simple two-message OT in the explicit isogeny model. IACR Commun. Cryptol. **1**(1), 1-34 (2024). https://doi.org/10.62056/a39qgy4e-
40. del Pino, R., Katsumata, S., Maller, M., Mouhartem, F., Prest, T., Saarinen, M.J.: Threshold raccoon: practical threshold signatures from standard lattice assumptions. In: Joye, M., Leander, G. (eds.) Advances in Cryptology – EUROCRYPT 2024. LNCS, vol. 14652, pp. 219–248. Springer, Cham (2024). https://doi.org/10.1007/978-3-031-58723-8_8
41. Unruh, D.: Non-interactive zero-knowledge proofs in the quantum random oracle model. In: Oswald, E., Fischlin, M. (eds.) EUROCRYPT 2015. LNCS, vol. 9057, pp. 755–784. Springer, Heidelberg (2015). https://doi.org/10.1007/978-3-662-46803-6_25

Multivariate Cryptography

Share the MAYO: Thresholdizing MAYO

Sofia Celi[1(✉)], Daniel Escudero[2], and Guilhem Niot[3]

[1] Brave Software, Lisbon, Portugal
cherenkov@riseup.net
[2] J.P. Morgan AI Research & J.P. Morgan AlgoCRYPT CoE, New York, USA
daniel.escudero@protonmail.com
[3] PQShield, Univ Rennes, CNRS, IRISA, Rennes, France
guilhem@gniot.fr

Abstract. We present the first comprehensive study on thresholdizing practical OV-based signature schemes, specifically focusing on MAYO and UOV. Our approach begins by addressing the challenges associated with thresholdizing algorithms that sample solutions to linear equation systems of the form $\mathbf{A}\mathbf{x} = \mathbf{y}$, which are fundamental to OV-based signature schemes. Previous attempts have introduced levels of leakage that we deem insecure. We propose a novel minimum-leakage solution and assess its practicality. Furthermore, we explore the thresholdization of the entire functionality of these signature schemes, demonstrating their unique applications in networks and cryptographic protocols.

Keywords: Post-quantum · threshold-cryptography

1 Introduction

Nowadays, threshold signatures [Des90, DF90] are an emerging field in cryptography, as they provide many real-world applications by allowing the distribution of signing power to several parties using different access structures. This distribution of signing power is often given to any subset of t parties among a set of n of signers but with the restriction that $t - 1$ cannot sign. While the case for efficient EC-DSA-based or Schnorr-based threshold-signature schemes has gathered renewed interest in the recent years [Sho99, GGN16, Bol03, KG20, Lin24, Ruf+22, Gar+21, Doe+19, Doe+23] (the former for their wide applications and the latter mostly due to their applications in blockchain), they are mostly centered in a classical setting and have not focused on providing security against quantum-adversaries. Moreover, the security of these schemes is nuanced, often requiring additional mechanisms to address potential misbehavior by parties. This misbehavior can stem from parties being either dishonest or *honest but curious*. Furthermore, from a practical setting, some threshold schemes are incompatible with widely-used standardised signature schemes, or, when they are, they tend to be inefficient or reliant upon ad-hoc assumptions.

R. Niederhagen and M.-J. O. Saarinen (Eds.): PQCrypto 2025, LNCS 15577, pp. 165–198, 2025.
https://doi.org/10.1007/978-3-031-86599-2_6

Recently, there has been a renewed interest in providing quantum-security to threshold signatures, as "quantum resistance" is listed as an important criterion on the recent NIST standardization call [PB23, Sections 3.2 and 3.3] for threshold signatures. A starting point in research on this area has focused on actively looking at the proposed submissions for the NIST PQC standardization call [NIS22] and analyzing what it will take to have a threshold variant of them. Due to this, we have seen recently proposals of lattice-based threshold schemes [Bos+24, Pin+24, ENP24, ASY22], isogeny-based threshold schemes [DM20], and hashed-based threshold schemes [Kha+22]. Notably, Cozzo et al. [CS19] explored the viability of applying generic MPC techniques to many of the NIST PQC submissions at the time[1] in order to instantiate threshold signatures schemes.

In this work, we are interested in thresholdising multivariate-based signature schemes, as they seem to arrive at practical communicational and computational measures, and seem to be tailored and feasible for real-world applications [Wes24, Adr24]. Ostensibly, both the MAYO [Beu+23a] and UOV [Beu+23b] signature schemes seem to be highly practical, and their security relies on a well-studied problem that has withstood the test of time despite cryptanalytic efforts.

Our starting point, as noted, will be the work of Cozzo et al. [CS19]. Our goal is to explore what it will take to make threshold variants of both UOV and MAYO, as practical OV-based schemes that are part of Round-2 of the "on-ramp" post-quantum process [Ala+24]. Hence, we prioritize schemes that might be standardized (and, thus, might become widely available), grounded in a well-studied problem, and practical. We push the study further, and do not only focus on constructing threshold signing for OV-based schemes; we propose each functionality in its own: distributed key generation (DKG), multi-party signature generation, and multi-party verification. This modular approach caters to diverse application needs, allowing for tailored solutions.

Contributions. We contribute the following results in our work:

- **Threshold variant of Solving Systems of Linear Equations:** We present a minimum-leakage threshold variant for the solving systems of linear equations algorithm. We provide an in-depth discussion of its leakage characteristics and strategies for minimization.
- **Threshold variants of OV-based schemes:** We propose threshold variants of the MAYO and UOV signature schemes, addressing the demand for quantum-resistant cryptographic solutions that securely operate in multi-party settings. We highlight their "MPC-friendliness" and present a"matrix-only" perspective that facilitates efficient MPC operations.
- **Practical Framework:** Our work outlines a practical framework for constructing these threshold schemes, ensuring that the proposed schemes maintain efficiency and compatibility with existing standardized signature algorithms. We identify optimization opportunities and situate our work within an established MPC framework and model.

[1] At the Round-2 of the NIST post-quantum first standardization process.

- **Modular Functionality:** We introduce a modular approach to threshold schemes by separately addressing critical functionalities to enhance flexibility and usability.

Outline. We start with the needed preliminaries in Sect. 2. Then, we provide a description of OV-based schemes in Sect. 3. In Sect. 4, Sect. 5 and Sect. 6, we present threshold protocols implementing system solving of linear equations, DKG, signing and verification algorithms. In Sect. 7, we discuss the costs and optimization techniques applicable to our protocol.

2 Preliminaries

Sets, functions, and distributions. For an integer $N > 0$, we note $[N] = \{0, \ldots, N-1\}$. To denote the *assign* operation, we use $y := f(x)$ when f is deterministic and $y \leftarrow f(x)$ when randomized. When S is a finite set, we note $\mathcal{U}(S)$ the uniform distribution over S, and shorthand $x \xleftarrow{\$} S$ for $x \leftarrow \mathcal{U}(S)$. We use $||$ to denote concatenation and λ as the security parameter. We use the standard Landau notation $O(\cdot)$ for asymptotics.

Finite fields $\mathbb{F}_q$, and vectors over $\mathbb{F}_q$. Given q, a power of a prime number, we denote $\mathbb{F}_q$ a finite field with q elements. We give an explicit representation for $\mathbb{F}_{16}$ as $\mathbb{Z}_2[x]/(x^4 + x + 1)$. We denote the addition and multiplication of field elements a and b as $a + b$ and ab respectively, and we denote the multiplicative inverse of a as a^{-1}. We denote by $\mathbb{F}_q^n$ the set of column vectors of length n over $\mathbb{F}_q$. Vectors are noted with small bold letters (i.e., $\mathbf{x}$), and we write $(x_0, ..., x_{n-1})$ for the coordinates of $\mathbf{x} \in \mathbb{F}_q^n$.

Matrices. We denote by $\mathbb{F}_q^{m\times n}$ the set of (zero-indexed) matrices over $\mathbb{F}_q$ with m rows and n columns. We denote by $\mathbf{I}_n \in \mathbb{F}_q^{n\times n}$ the identity matrix of size n-by-n. Abusing notation, we see a vector $\mathbf{b} \in \mathbb{F}_q^n$ as a matrix of dimension $n \times 1$. If $\mathbf{A} \in \mathbb{F}_q^{m\times n}$, we denote by $\mathbf{A}[i, j]$ the entry in the i-th row and the j-th column of $\mathbf{A}$, and the j-th column of $\mathbf{A}$ by $\mathbf{A}[:, j] \in \mathbb{F}_q^m$. We say that a matrix $\mathbf{A} \in \mathbb{F}_q^{n\times n}$ is upper triangular if $\mathbf{A}[i, j] = 0$ for all $0 \le j < i < n$.

If $\mathbf{A}, \mathbf{B} \in \mathbb{F}_q^{m\times n}$ are matrices of same size, then we denote their (entry-wise) sum as $\mathbf{A} + \mathbf{B}$. If $\mathbf{A} \in \mathbb{F}_q^{m\times n}$ and $\mathbf{B} \in \mathbb{F}_q^{n\times k}$, then we denote the matrix product by $\mathbf{AB}$, i.e. $\mathbf{AB} \in \mathbb{F}_q^{n\times k}$ is the matrix whose entry in row i and column j is equal to $\sum_{l=0}^{n} \mathbf{A}[i, l]\mathbf{B}[l, j]$. We denote by $\mathbf{A}^\top$ the transpose of $\mathbf{A}$, i.e. the matrix in $\mathbb{F}_q^{n\times m}$ such that $\mathbf{A}^\top[i, j] = \mathbf{A}[j, i]$ for all $0 \le j < m$ and $0 \le i < n$.

We define the function $\mathsf{Upper} : \mathbb{F}_q^{n\times n} \to \mathbb{F}_q^{n\times n}$ that takes a square matrix $\mathbf{M}$ as input, and outputs the upper triangular matrix $\mathsf{Upper}(\mathbf{M})$, defined as $\mathsf{Upper}(\mathbf{M})_{i,i} = \mathbf{M}_{i,i}$ and $\mathsf{Upper}(\mathbf{M})_{i,j} = \mathbf{M}_{i,j} + \mathbf{M}_{j,i}$ for $i < j$.

Network model. We assume a synchronous network, as already assumed and required by modern threshold signature schemes [Kon+21, GG19, LNR18]. We also consider that the adversary can observe any message sent, and choose to deliver or block messages at will on this network.

2.1 The UC Framework: Model and Functionalities

For our ideal functionalities, adversarial model, and proofs, our scheme instantiations rely on the Universal-Composability (UC) framework introduced by Canetti [Can01]. This framework allows for the independent implementation of functionalities and to securely compose them. In the following, we give a brief overview of the framework, where we use the traditional notation to refer to protocols in uppercase and procedures in the lowercase.

UC Protocols. The UC framework is based on *Probabilistic Polynomial-Time* (PPT) *Interactive Turing machines* (ITM) entities that are used to model parties, adversaries, and simulators.

In the *real-world* experiment, we have n ITM-based parties $(P_1, \ldots, P_n)$ that execute a protocol Π, an adversary $\mathcal{A}$ that can corrupt any subset of parties, and an environment $\mathcal{Z}$ that is initialized with an advice string z. All entities are initialized with the security parameter λ and with a random tape. The environment $\mathcal{Z}$ activates the parties involved in Π, selects their inputs, receives their outputs, and communicates with the adversary $\mathcal{A}$, who may instruct the corrupted parties to deviate from Π in any manner. The real-world experiment completes when Z ceases to activate parties and produces a decision bit.

Conversely, the *ideal-world* experiment involves n ITM-based dummy parties $(P_1, \ldots, P_n)$, an ideal functionality $\mathcal{F}$, an ideal-world adversary $\mathcal{S}$ (the simulator), and an environment $\mathcal{Z}$. The dummy parties relay messages from $\mathcal{Z}$ to $\mathcal{F}$. The simulator $\mathcal{S}$ can corrupt any subset of these dummy parties and interact with $\mathcal{F}$ on their behalf communicating directly with $\mathcal{F}$ according to its specification. Throughout the experiment, $\mathcal{Z}$ and $\mathcal{S}$ interact with the simulator, the role of the simulator goal being to convince the environment that it is participating in the real experiment. The ideal-world experiment completes when $\mathcal{Z}$ stops activating parties and outputs a decision bit.

The $\mathcal{F}$-hybrid Model. When a protocol Π operates in a hybrid model of computation where parties can communicate as usual and have access to an unlimited number of instances of the ideal functionality $\mathcal{F}$, it is called the $\mathcal{F}$–hybrid model [Can+02]. In this setting, let P denote a protocol that UC-realizes $\mathcal{F}$, and let Π^{P} be the "composed protocol". Composition here means that Π^{P} is identical to Π, except that each interaction with $\mathcal{F}$ is substituted by an activation of the concrete instance of the protocol, with P's outputs serving as values provided by $\mathcal{F}$. A fundamental theorem states that in such conditions, Π and Π^{P} exhibit the same input/output behavior: P behaves just like the ideal functionality $\mathcal{F}$ even when composed with an arbitrary protocol Π. A special case of this theorem asserts that if Π UC-realizes some ideal functionality $\mathcal{G}$ in the $\mathcal{F}$-hybrid model, then Π^{P} also UC-realizes $\mathcal{G}$.

UC-Security Model. [Can01] defines a notion of security for a protocol Π by comparing it to the ideal functionality $\mathcal{F}$. The core intuition is that any attack on Π would be no more effective than an attack on $\mathcal{F}$. Let $\mathsf{IDEAL}_{\mathcal{F},\mathcal{S},\mathcal{Z}(\lambda,z)}$ denote the random variable representing the output of the *ideal-world* experiment; let

$\mathsf{REAL}_{\Pi,\mathcal{A},\mathcal{Z}(\lambda,z)}$ denote the random variable representing the output of the *real-world* experiment.

Definition 1 (UC-security). *A protocol Π UC-realizes the functionality $\mathcal{F}$, if for every PPT $\mathcal{A}$, there is a simulator $\mathcal{S}$ that for every PPT "admissible" environment $\mathcal{Z}$,*

$$\{\mathsf{REAL}_{\Pi,\mathcal{Z}(\lambda,z)}\}_{\lambda\in\mathbb{N}^+,z\in\{0,1\}^{\mathsf{poly}(\lambda)}} \approx_c \{\mathsf{IDEAL}_{\mathcal{F},\mathcal{S},\mathcal{Z}(\lambda,z)}\}_{\lambda\in\mathbb{N}^+,z\in\{0,1\}^{\mathsf{poly}(\lambda)}}$$

Remark 1 (On the Difference between Procedures and Protocols). Universal Composability (UC) security is crucial not only for ensuring composability but also for facilitating a modular approach to protocol design. It enables the definition of functionalities that can be instantiated and utilized later without the need to focus on their concrete implementations. However, when developing complex protocols, it can be beneficial to create several separate "sub-protocols" that can be invoked within the main protocol, even if the specific functionalities these sub-protocols instantiate are not explicitly defined. To address this, we introduce the concept of a *procedure*. Procedures resemble protocols in that they outline the steps parties must follow, but unlike protocols, they are not intended to instantiate a specific functionality. Instead, they serve as modular blocks that can be integrated into an actual protocol that does instantiate functionality. A useful analogy is to compare procedures to "macros" in programming languages such as C or C++. Like macros, which are expanded in the code before compilation, procedures provide a flexible way to structure protocols. In contrast, functionalities can be likened to "binaries", which can be utilized without needing to understand their internal workings.

2.2 The Arithmetic Black-Box Model

MPC protocols are typically designed using secret-sharing techniques. Secret-sharing is a method that enables a dealer to distribute a secret $x \in \mathbb{F}_q$ among parties in such a way that no subset of $\leq t$ parties learns anything about the secret, while any subset of $\geq t+1$ parties can completely reconstruct it. This is commonly denoted with $[\![x]\!]$. The specific choice of secret-sharing schemes is typically influenced by the concrete security setting (*e.g.* passive vs active security, or honest vs dishonest majority). To remain agnostic to any choice, we use a standard abstraction from the literature known as the *arithmetic black box* (ABB), which precisely models the ability of parties to distribute secrets, perform arithmetic operations on them, and reconstruct secrets. The allowed arithmetic operations include both affine operations such as additions, subtractions, or multiplication by constants—all of which can be typically performed *locally* in an actual instantiation thanks to the linear properties of secret-sharing schemes—and also the multiplication of secrets, which requires an interactive protocol in an actual instantiation.

Remark 2 (Sampling both public and secret random values). For our protocols, we describe a slightly modified version of ABB model which allows for a few extra operations that will be useful for our constructions. These are: (1) the ability to sample random strings known to all parties, and (2) the ability to sample *secret* random values that are unknown to any party. Both of these are common in the literature and can be realized using standard techniques. For instance, sampling secret random values can be generated by having each party distribute a random share and then summing these shares to produce the secret value (for honest majority this can be optimized by using super-invertible matrices [DN07]). For public randomness, the parties can reconstruct a secret random value, and if longer strings are needed, a PRG can be used to expand it.

Given this, our ABB functionality ($\mathcal{F}_{\mathsf{ABB}}$) is given below. We set all of our schemes in this $\mathcal{F}_{\mathsf{ABB}}$-hybrid model.

Functionality 1: $\mathcal{F}_{\mathsf{ABB}}$

The functionality keeps track of an internal dictionary of pairs $(x, \mathtt{id})$ mapping field elements to IDs. Although we do not write this explicitly, the functionality aborts in obvious cases such as if the provided parties' IDs are inconsistent, if the IDs are not populated when the functionality is asked to read them, or if the IDs are populated when the functionality is asked to write them. The functionality supports the following commands:

- On input $(\mathsf{input}, \mathtt{id}, P_i)$ from all parties and $(\mathsf{input}, \mathtt{id}, P_i, x)$ from P_i, the functionality stores $(x, \mathtt{id})$.
- On input $(\mathsf{add}, \mathtt{id}_1, \mathtt{id}_2, \mathtt{id}_3)$ from all parties, the functionality fetches $(x, \mathtt{id}_1)$ and $(y, \mathtt{id}_2)$, and stores $(x + y, \mathtt{id}_3)$.
- On input $(\mathsf{addmult\text{-}cons}, \mathtt{id}_1, \mathtt{id}_2, (a, b))$ from all parties, the functionality fetches $(x, \mathtt{id}_1)$ and stores $(a \cdot x + b, \mathtt{id}_2)$.
- On input $(\mathsf{mult}, \mathtt{id}_1, \mathtt{id}_2, \mathtt{id}_3)$ from all parties, the functionality fetches $(x, \mathtt{id}_1)$ and $(y, \mathtt{id}_2)$, and stores $(x \cdot y, \mathtt{id}_3)$.
- On input $(\mathsf{output}, \mathtt{id}, P_i)$ from all parties, the functionality fetches $(x, \mathtt{id})$ and sends x to P_i.
- On input $(\mathsf{rand}, \mathtt{id})$ from all parties, the functionality samples $r \leftarrow \mathbb{F}_q$ uniformly at random and stores $(r, \mathtt{id})$.
- On input (coin) from all parties, the functionality samples $r \leftarrow \mathbb{F}_q$ uniformly at random and sends r to all parties.

Remark 3 (On optimizations of concrete instantiations). The primary advantage of the ABB model is its generality, which allows for a cleaner description that accommodates multiple adversarial settings. However, actual implementations of our protocols can be significantly *optimized* by leveraging specific characteristics of the underlying adversarial model. This is especially beneficial in scenarios with passive security or an honest majority setting, where multiple efficiency improvements are possible. We discuss some of these specific optimizations in Sect. 7.

Notation and Simplification of the ABB. When applying the ABB model in our constructions, we omit low-level details as noting IDs for simplicity. We denote a value x that is stored $(x, \mathtt{id})$ by $[\![x]\!]$, where, as noted, we ignore the specific ID from the notation. For operations, we write $[\![x+y]\!] \leftarrow [\![x]\!] + [\![y]\!]$ to represent a call to the add command, and similarly for other operations. We also use $\alpha \leftarrow$ coin and $[\![x]\!] \leftarrow$ rand for when the parties call the commands coin and rand, respectively. This notation is typically reserved for secret-sharing schemes and it is deliberate: in a concrete instantiation of the ABB model, $[\![x]\!]$ would mean that x is secret-shared among the parties. Furthermore, it will not be uncommon that we refer to $[\![x]\!]$ as the parties having "shares" of x.

The majority of our constructions work with matrices, and we let notation reflect this by using $[\![\mathbf{X}]\!]$ for matrices $\mathbf{X}$, meaning that each individual entry is stored in the functionality. Sometimes we also use $[\![\mathbf{X}]\!] \leftarrow \mathsf{rand}(\mathbb{F}_q^{a\times b})$ to emphasize the dimensions of the sampled matrix. Matrix operations such as addition and multiplication can be instantiated with the underlying field arithmetic, Note that matrix addition and multiplication can be instantiated with the underlying field arithmetic, though matrix multiplication can be optimized by leveraging its structure rather than naively applying field operations. In some cases, multiplication of $n \times n$ matrices can be reduced from n^3 products to n^2. Additionally, other optimizations can be considered when concretely instantiating the model by exploiting several intricacies of the adversarial model at hand. We discuss some of these specific optimizations in Sect. 7.

2.3 Digital Signature Schemes

We start by introducing a formal definition of signature schemes in the standard model. A signature scheme is a tuple of algorithms (SetUp, KeyGen, Sign, Verify), defined as follows (henceforth, pp will be implicitly given to all functionality):

$\mathsf{SetUp}(1^\lambda) \rightarrow \mathsf{pp}$. Given the security parameter as input 1^λ, the procedure outputs the public parameters pp.

$\mathsf{KeyGen}_{\mathsf{pp}}() \rightarrow (\mathsf{pk}, \mathsf{sk})$. The key generation procedure outputs a verification key pk and a private signing key sk.

$\mathsf{Sign}_{\mathsf{pp}}(\mathsf{pk}, \mathsf{sk}, \mathsf{msg}) \rightarrow \mathsf{Sig}$. The signing procedure takes as input the public and private keys, as well as a message to sign (msg), and it outputs a signature Sig.

$\mathsf{Verify}_{\mathsf{pp}}(\mathsf{pk}, \mathsf{msg}, \mathsf{Sig}) \rightarrow \{0/1\}$. The verification procedure takes as input a verification key pk, a message msg, and a signature Sig, and it outputs 1 if Sig is valid for msg under the verification key pk, and 0 otherwise.

We define threshold signatures as protocols that realize the different features of the signature: key generation, signing, and verification. In this work, we ensure the security of our protocols by proving that they UC-realize ideal functionalities that perform the different algorithms (KeyGen, Sign, Verify). This is a common way to study the soundness of distributed protocols [Doe+18, Cas+19, Ara+21]. In particular, we do not attempt to define threshold signatures in the UC framework as in previous works [ADN06, BKP13, BMP22, Mak22].

3 OV-based Schemes: UOV and MAYO

In this section, we introduce OV-based schemes, and propose a unified description to represent UOV and MAYO as instances of it. OV-based schemes are are type of multivariate-based cryptography, which is based on the Polynomial System Solving (*PoSSo*) problem of solving systems of m multivariate non-linear polynomial equations in n variables over finite fields. The *PoSSo problem* is proven to be NP-hard even sfor the simplest case of quadratic equations over the field with two elements [GJ90] (in its decisional variant). When all polynomials are of the quadratic form, the *PoSSo problem* is called the *MQ-Problem*, and known attacks against the problem are exponential. The first attempt to build a cryptographic scheme based on multivariate quadratic polynomials was done by Ong, Schnorr and Shamir [OSS84], but its security is still based on the difficulty of factoring. Modern multivariate-based schemes are based on 1988's C^* scheme of Matsumoto and Imai [MI88] (broken in [Pat00]), which can be used both for encryption and signatures. More concretely, modern multivariate-based schemes are built upon the *Oil and Vinegar* (OV) scheme [Pat97], a simple and well-studied scheme. While broken in polynomial time by [KS98] for a specific set of parameters ($n = 2m$), a variant of the scheme, called the *Unbalanced Oil and Vinegar scheme* (UOV) has withstood all cryptanalysis since 1999 [KPG99].

Oil and Vinegar-based (OV-based) schemes rely on a trapdoor function constructed using multivariate quadratic equations. Specifically, the function $\mathcal{P} : \mathbb{F}_q^n \to \mathbb{F}_q^m$ consists of m homogeneous quadratic polynomials in n variables over a small finite field $\mathbb{F}_q$. The assumption underlying these schemes is that finding preimages (solving the system of quadratic equations) is computationally hard. However, if one possesses additional structural information, known as the trapdoor, it becomes efficient to find preimages for any output. The trapdoor, or secret key, in these schemes is a linear subspace $\mathcal{O} \subset \mathbb{F}_q^n$ of dimension o, such that for all vectors $\mathbf{o} \in O$, the function $\mathcal{P}$ vanishes: $\mathcal{P}(\mathbf{o}) = 0$. In the case of the Oil and Vinegar (OV) scheme, this subspace $\mathcal{O}$ is structured such that $o = m$, and the quadratic map $\mathcal{P}$ can be used to verify the validity of a signature for a message msg using the public key $\mathcal{P}$. This structural property of the secret subspace $\mathcal{O}$ enables the signer, who knows $\mathcal{O}$, to efficiently solve a system of m linear equations to generate valid signatures. In contrast, for anyone without knowledge of this trapdoor structure, generating such signatures remains infeasible. To mitigate known attacks, the *Unbalanced Oil and Vinegar* (UOV) scheme suggests using an unbalanced parameter set where $n > 2m$. This adjustment helps ensure the security of the scheme by increasing the complexity of solving the associated system of equations without the trapdoor.

3.1 Unbalanced Oil and Vinegar (UOV)

The UOV signature scheme (submitted to the "on-ramp" post-quantum NIST process [Beu+23b]) is a OV-based scheme, created from the described trapdoor function with the *Full Domain Hash* approach (specifically, the *Hash-and-Sign with Retry* approach): a signature on a message msg is simply sampled given a target input $\mathbf{t}$ such that $\mathcal{P}(\mathbf{t}) = \mathcal{H}(\mathsf{msg}||\mathsf{salt})$, where $\mathcal{H}$ is as a cryptographic hash function that outputs elements in the range of $\mathcal{P}$, and salt is a fixed-length bit string chosen uniformly at random for every signature. As noted the linear subspace $\mathcal{O} \subset \mathbb{F}_q^n$ of dimension o ($o = m$) is the trapdoor. To generate the trapdoor function, one picks this subspace $\mathcal{O}$ uniformly at random and then picks $\mathcal{P}$ uniformly at random from the set of multivariate quadratic maps with m components in n variables that vanish on $\mathcal{O}$. Note that on top of the q^m artificial zeros in the subspace $\mathcal{O}$ (guaranteed by the structure of the trapdoor function), we expect roughly q^{n-m} natural zeros that do not lie in $\mathcal{O}$: since $\mathcal{P}$ consists of m equations in n variables, the total number of solutions to $\mathcal{P}(s) = 0$ is roughly q^{n-m}.

Following the description of [Beu20], concretely, when given a target $\mathbf{t}$, one picks a random vector $\mathbf{v} \in \mathbb{F}_q^n$ (a *vinegar* vector) and solves the system $\mathcal{P}(\mathbf{v}+\mathbf{o}) = \mathbf{t}$ for a vector $\mathbf{o} \in \mathcal{O}$ (the *oil* vector). For public quadratic maps $\mathcal{P}$, we can define its differential (or "polar form" [Beu21]) $\mathcal{P}'$ as $\mathcal{P}'(\mathbf{x}, \mathbf{y}) := \mathcal{P}(\mathbf{x}+\mathbf{y}) - \mathcal{P}(\mathbf{x}) - \mathcal{P}(\mathbf{y})$, which is a symmetric bilinear map in $\mathbf{x}$ and $\mathbf{y}$. One can then solve the linear system for $\mathbf{o}$, as:

$$\mathcal{P}(\mathbf{v}+\mathbf{o}) = \underbrace{\mathcal{P}'(\mathbf{v}, \mathbf{o})}_{\text{Linear in } \mathbf{o}} + \underbrace{\cancel{\mathcal{P}(\mathbf{o})}}_{=0} + \underbrace{\mathcal{P}(\mathbf{v})}_{\text{fixed}} = \mathbf{t}$$

With success average probability of roughly $1 - 1/q$ over the choice of $\mathbf{v}$ the linear map $\mathcal{P}'(\mathbf{v}, \cdot)$ will be non-singular, which means that the linear system $\mathcal{P}(\mathbf{v} + \mathbf{o}) = \mathbf{t}$ has a unique solution. If it is not the case, one restarts for a new value of $\mathbf{v}$. It should be noted that there is no formal security proof of the scheme which concretely reduces it to a "hard" mathematical problem(s) (though, there has been efforts on this front [SSH11, CDP22, Cog+24, KX24]). Instead, the security analysis of UOV relies on looking at all the known attacks and analyzing how they influence its concrete hardness.

3.2 MAYO

MAYO is a OV-based signature scheme that has been submitted to the "on-ramp" NIST PQC standardization process [Beu+23a]. As it is OV-based, $\mathcal{P}$ has the same structure as in OV-based schemes with the exception that the dimension of the linear subspace $\mathcal{O}$ on which the trapdoor $\mathcal{P}$ evaluates to zero is "too small", i.e., $\dim(\mathcal{O}) = o$, with o less than m. As the oil subspace is hidden in $\mathbb{F}_q^n$, if its size is smaller, it follows that it is harder to search for it. This, in turn, means that other parameters of the scheme can be reduced without an impact, and that key sizes can be reduced. As in UOV, to generate the trapdoor function, one first picks the subspace $\mathcal{O}$ uniformly at random and then one picks $\mathcal{P}$ uniformly at random from the set of multivariate quadratic maps with m components in n variables that vanish in $\mathcal{O}$. Reducing the dimension of $\mathcal{O}$ drastically shrinks the key sizes, but it also means that the signing algorithm will not work anymore as there are not enough degrees of freedom to always create a signature with high probability. To solve this problem, in MAYO, $\mathcal{P}$ is not used as is in the signature and verification procedures, and instead relies on a "whipping technique"[2]. Both the signer and verifier "whip-up" $\mathcal{P}$ into a k-fold larger map $\mathcal{P}^\star : \mathbb{F}_q^{kn} \to \mathbb{F}_q^m$, with m polynomials in k sets of n variables, where k is a fixed parameter of the scheme. This, in turn, means that if $\mathcal{P}$ vanishes on $\mathcal{O}$, then it follows that $\mathcal{P}^\star$ vanishes on $\mathcal{O}^k$. Formally, $\mathcal{P}^\star$ is defined as:

$$\mathcal{P}^\star(\mathbf{x}_1, \ldots, \mathbf{x}_k) := \sum_{i=1}^{k} \mathbf{E}_{ii}\mathcal{P}(\mathbf{x}_i) + \sum_{i=1}^{k} \sum_{j=i+1}^{k} \mathbf{E}_{ij}\mathcal{P}'(\mathbf{x}_i, \mathbf{x}_j),$$

For all $i \in \{1, \ldots, k\}$ and all $j \in \{i+1, \ldots, k\}$, the matrix $\mathbf{E}_{ij} \in \mathbb{F}_q^{m \times m}$ is fixed and public. These matrices are chosen such that, under the correspondence between vectors in $\mathbb{F}_q^m$ and polynomials in $\mathbb{F}_q[X]$ of degree at most m, multiplication by $\mathbf{E}_{ij}$ corresponds to multiplication by powers of X modulo an irreducible polynomial $f(X) \in \mathbb{F}_q[X]$ of degree m. A MAYO signature, $\mathbf{S} = (\mathbf{s}_1, \ldots, \mathbf{s}_k) \in \mathbb{F}_q^{nk}$, is considered valid if $\mathcal{P}^\star(\mathbf{s}_1, \ldots, \mathbf{s}_k) = \mathcal{H}(\mathsf{msg})$, where $\mathcal{H}(\mathsf{msg})$ is the hash of a message.

To compute $\mathcal{P}^\star(\mathbf{S})$, the verifier (see algorithm 3) begins by calculating $\mathcal{P}(\mathbf{s}_i)$ and $\mathcal{P}'(\mathbf{s}_i, \mathbf{s}_j)$ for all $i \in \{1, \ldots, k\}$ and all $j \in \{i+1, \ldots, k\}$, and then combines them to obtain $\mathcal{P}^\star(\mathbf{S})$. Given that matrices $\mathbf{E}_{ij}$ represent multiplication by powers of X (mod $f(X)$), the verifier can apply the appropriate powers of X to the polynomials for $\mathcal{P}(\mathbf{s}_i)$ and $\mathcal{P}'(\mathbf{s}_i, \mathbf{s}_j)$ and perform a single reduction modulo $f(X)$. Similarly, to sign a message (see algorithm 2), the signer partially evaluates $\mathcal{P}$ and $\mathcal{P}'$ on k vectors $(\mathbf{v}_1, \ldots, \mathbf{v}_k) \in \mathbb{F}_q^{n-o}$, and combines these results to determine the coefficients of a linear system, $\mathbf{A}\mathbf{x} = \mathbf{y}$, whose solution yields the signature. Just as in UOV, MAYO has a restart probability in case that the linear system does not have a solution. It is defined as a probability average-bounded by $\frac{q^{k-(n-o)}}{q-1} + \frac{q^{m-ko}}{q-1}$. As in UOV, the security analysis of MAYO mostly relies on looking at all the known attacks and analyzing how they influence its hardness.

3.3 OV-based Schemes Description

In this section, we present a unified representation for both UOV and MAYO (as OV-based schemes) that allows us to simultaneously thresholdize them. We will refer to them as OV-based henceforth.

Parameters. OV-based schemes are parameterized by the following:

- q the size of a finite field $\mathbb{F}_q$. In MAYO, in all current proposed parameter sets, $q = 16$; in UOV, it varies depending on the security level.
- m, the number of multivariate quadratic polynomials in the public key.

[2] Similar to the "whipping techniques" of the SNOVA algorithm [Wan+23, Beu24, Cab+24].

- n, the number of variables in the multivariate quadratic polynomials in the public key.
- o, the dimension of the oil subspace $\mathcal{O}$.
- k, the whipping parameter, satisfying $(k < n - o)$. This parameter is only present in MAYO.
- $\mathbf{E}_{i,j} \in \mathbb{F}_q^{m \times m}$ for $(0 \le i \le j < k)$, fixed public matrices.

These parameters cover both UOV and MAYO by adopting the following constraints:

- UOV is instantiated with $o = m$, $k = 1$, and $\mathbf{E}_{0,0} = \mathbf{I}_m$.
- MAYO fixes the public matrices $(\mathbf{E}_{i,j})_{i,j}$ such that

$$\begin{bmatrix} \mathbf{E}_{1,1} & \mathbf{E}_{1,2} & \dots & \mathbf{E}_{1,k} \\ \mathbf{E}_{1,2} & \mathbf{E}_{2,2} & \dots & \vdots \\ \vdots & \vdots & \ddots & \vdots \\ \mathbf{E}_{1,k} & \mathbf{E}_{k-1,1} & \dots & \mathbf{E}_{k,k} \end{bmatrix}$$

is non-singular. They correspond to multiplication by $z \mod f(Z)$

Description. In the following, we formally describe the algorithms that constitute an OV-based signature scheme. Contrary to the specifications of both MAYO and UOV, we generalize their description such that operations are only performed over matrices. Note that, for practicality in thresholdizing, we replace the private seed expansion for generating key material with direct sampling of values. Although this modifies the concrete execution of the algorithms from their specifications, it does not impact security, and signature verification remains unchanged. In practice, we can easily revert to seed sampling in the final protocol for the expansion of pseudo-random matrices in the public key.

Key Generation functionality. The functionality is described in Algorithm 1. In the following, we note some details of the functionality. To create the trapdoor, one chooses at random a sequence of m multivariate quadratic polynomials $(\mathcal{P})$ that vanish on the space spanned by rows of $\left(\mathbf{O}^\intercal\ \mathbf{I}_o\right)$, where $\mathbf{O}$ is sampled at random and $\mathbf{I}$ is the identity matrix. Each polynomial $p_i(\mathbf{x})_{i \in m}$ can be uniquely represented by an upper triangular matrix:

$$x^\top \begin{pmatrix} \mathbf{P}_i^{(1)} & \mathbf{P}_i^{(2)} \\ \mathbf{0} & \mathbf{P}_i^{(3)} \end{pmatrix} x$$

so that $p_i(\mathbf{x}) = \mathbf{x}^\top \mathbf{P}_i \mathbf{x}$. Each polynomial p_i vanishes in $\mathbf{O}$ if:

$$\mathbf{O}^\intercal \mathbf{P}_i^{(1)} \mathbf{O} + \mathbf{O}^\intercal \mathbf{P}_i^{(2)} + \mathbf{P}_i^{(3)}$$

is skew-symmetric. Hence, one picks $\mathbf{P}_i^{(1)} \in \mathbb{F}_q^{(n-o)\times(n-o)}$ and $\mathbf{P}_i^{(2)} \in \mathbb{F}_q^{(n-o)\times o}$ uniformly at random, and derives $\mathbf{P}_i^{(3)} = \mathsf{Upper}(-\mathbf{O}^\top \mathbf{P}_i^{(1)} \mathbf{O} - \mathbf{O}^\top \mathbf{P}_i^{(2)})$. As part of the key generation process, we also generate a value, denoted by $\mathbf{L}_i$, designed to improve signing efficiency. We'll delve into its purpose and functionality in the following section.

Algorithm 1. OV-based.KeyGen()

Output: A key pair (pk, sk).

//Derive $\mathbf{O}$ and $(\mathbf{P}^{(1)}, \mathbf{P}^{(2)})$ randomly. Note that this differs from the specification, as we are not deriving them from a fixed seed.

$\mathbf{O} \xleftarrow{\$} \mathbb{F}_q^{(n-o)\times o}$

$\{\mathbf{P}_i^{(1)}, \mathbf{P}_i^{(2)}\}_{i\in[m]} \xleftarrow{\$} (\mathbb{F}_q^{(n-o)\times(n-o)}, \mathbb{F}_q^{(n-o)\times o})$

//Compute $\mathbf{P}_i^{(3)} \in \mathbb{F}_q^{o\times o}$.

for i from 0 to $(m-1)$ **do**

  $\mathbf{P}_i^{(3)} \leftarrow \mathsf{Upper}(-\mathbf{O}^\mathsf{T}(\mathbf{P}_i^{(1)}\mathbf{O} - \mathbf{P}_i^{(2)}))$

  $\mathbf{L}_i \leftarrow ((\mathbf{P}_i^{(1)} + \mathbf{P}_i^{(1)\mathsf{T}})\mathbf{O} + \mathbf{P}_i^{(2)})$

return $(\mathsf{pk} = (\{\mathbf{P}_i^{(1)}, \mathbf{P}_i^{(2)}, \mathbf{P}_i^{(3)}\}_{\{i\in[m]\}}), \mathsf{sk} = (\mathbf{O}, \{\mathbf{L}_i\}_{\{i\in[m]\}}))$.

Signing. The functionality is described in Algorithm 2. To sign a message, $\mathsf{msg} \in \{0,1\}^\star$, the signer first hashes msg together with a salt, $\mathsf{salt} \in \{0,1\}^{\mathsf{saltlen}}$ (whose purpose is to protect against side-channel and fault injection attacks). The result is a target vector $\mathbf{t} = \mathcal{H}(\mathsf{msg}||\mathsf{salt}) \in \mathbb{F}_q^m$. The signature is comprised of salt and a preimage $\mathbf{s} \in \mathbb{F}_q^{kn}$ for $\mathbf{t}$. To compute this preimage $\mathbf{s}$, the signer deterministically generates a "vinegar" vector $\mathbf{v} = \mathsf{Expand}_v(m||\mathsf{salt}||\mathbf{O}||\mathsf{ctr}) \in \mathbb{F}_q^{n-o}$, where ctr is a byte-sized counter, initialized at 0x0. Then, the signer solves a system of linear equations to find a vector $\mathbf{x} \in \mathbf{F}_q^{ko}$ so that $\mathbf{s} = (\mathbf{v}+\mathbf{Ox})||\mathbf{x} \in \mathbf{F}_q^{kn}$ is the preimage of $\mathbf{t}$. If the linear system is singular, ctr is incremented by one, and the signing starts again with the new $\mathbf{v} = \mathsf{Expand}_v(\mathsf{msg}||\mathsf{salt}||\mathbf{O}||\mathsf{ctr})$. It is noteworthy that the signer does not have to keep secret how many attempts were required to find a solution, and it is, thus, not an issue to leak that the attempt failed. After d failed attempts, the signer aborts: in honest executions, this happens with an extremely small probability ($\leq 2^{-786}$ for UOV, for example). For this functionality, we use the values $\mathbf{L}_i$, and, as this value is independent of msg, we pre-compute it once during key generation, and store it as part of the secret key.

Note that for the signing functionality, we call internally the functions: OV-based.Compute_A, OV-based.Compute_y and $\mathbf{x} \leftarrow \mathsf{SampleSolution}(\mathbf{A}, \mathbf{y})$. The first and second are algorithms to compute intermediate values, while the latter is used to find a solution to a system of linear equations of the form $\mathbf{Ax} = \mathbf{y}$ for an unknown $\mathbf{x}$. This can be implemented in two ways as noted by [Beu+23c]: (i) directly computing the solution using constant-time Gaussian elimination, or (ii) first computing the right-inverse and multiplying it by the right side of the equation. The MAYO specification uses the first approach with a random vector $\mathbf{r} \in \mathbb{F}_q^{ko}$ that is used to pick each of the q^{ko-m} solutions with equal probability. If the input matrix $\mathbf{A}$ does not have rank m, then $\mathsf{SampleSolution}(\mathbf{A}, \mathbf{y}, \mathbf{r})$ outputs $\perp$.

Algorithm 2. OV-based.Sign(sk, pk, msg)

Input: Secret key (sk), public key (pk).
Input: Message msg.
Output: Signature Sig = $(\mathbf{S}, \mathsf{salt})$.

1: //Parse $(\mathbf{O}, \{\mathbf{L}_i\}_{\{i\in[m]\}})$ and $(\{\mathbf{P}_i^{(1)}\}_{\{i\in[m]\}}, \{\mathbf{P}_i^{(2)}\}_{\{i\in[m]\}})$ from sk and pk.
2: $(\mathbf{O}, \{\mathbf{L}\}_{\{i\in[m]\}}) \leftarrow \mathsf{sk}$
3: $\{\mathbf{P}_i^{(1)}, \mathbf{P}_i^{(2)}\}_{i\in[m]} \leftarrow \mathsf{pk}$
4: //Hash salted message.
5: $\mathsf{salt} \xleftarrow{\$} \{0,1\}^{\lambda+64}$
6: $\mathbf{t} \leftarrow \mathcal{H}(\mathsf{msg}||\mathsf{salt})$ ▷ $\mathbf{t} \in \mathbb{F}_q^m$
7:
8: $\mathbf{V} \xleftarrow{\$} \mathbb{F}_q^{k\times(n-o)}$
9: **for** i from 1 to m **do**
10: $\quad \mathbf{M}_i \leftarrow \mathbf{V} \cdot \mathbf{L}_i$ ▷ $\mathbf{M}_i \in \mathbb{F}_q^{k\times o}$
11: $\quad \mathbf{Y}_i \leftarrow \mathbf{V} \cdot \mathbf{P}_i^{(1)} \cdot \mathbf{V}^\mathsf{T}$ ▷ $\mathbf{Y}_i \in \mathbb{F}_q^{k\times k}$
12: //Build the linear system $\mathbf{Ax} = \mathbf{y}$.
13: $\mathbf{A} \leftarrow$ OV-based.Compute_A$(\{\mathbf{M}_i\}_{i\in[m]})$
14: $\mathbf{y} \leftarrow \mathbf{t} -$ OV-based.Compute_y$(\{\mathbf{Y}_i\}_{i\in[m]})$
15:
16: //Try to sample a random solution $\mathbf{x}$ to $\mathbf{Ax} = \mathbf{y}$.
17: $\mathbf{x} \leftarrow$ SampleSolution$(\mathbf{A}, \mathbf{y})$ ▷ $\mathbf{x} \in \mathbb{F}_q^{ko} \cup \{\perp\}$
18: **if** $\mathbf{x} = \perp$ **then**
19: $\quad$ **go to** 7
20: //Output the signature.
21: $\mathbf{X} \leftarrow$ Matrixify$(\mathbf{x})$ ▷ $\mathbf{X} \in \mathbb{F}_q^{k\times o}$, s.t. $\mathbf{x}$ is concatenation of rows of $\mathbf{X}$
22: $\mathbf{S} \leftarrow (\mathbf{V} + (\mathbf{O}\mathbf{X}^\mathsf{T})^\mathsf{T}, \mathbf{X})$ ▷ $\mathbf{S} \in \mathbb{F}_q^{k\times n}$
23: **return** Sig = $(\mathbf{S}, \mathsf{salt})$.

Verification. The functionality can be seen in Algorithm 3. The verifier accepts a signature $\mathbf{s} = \mathcal{H}(\mathsf{msg}||\mathsf{salt})$ by first recomputing $\mathbf{t} = \mathcal{H}(\mathsf{msg}||\mathsf{salt})$ and checking that $\mathcal{P}^\star(\mathbf{s}_i) = \mathbf{t}$.

4 Solving Systems of Linear Equations Obliviously

To enable our threshold constructions, we require a core operation: solving a system of linear equations in which both the input matrix and the target vector remain secret (hence, solving in an oblivious manner). This operation, which is the SampleSolution algorithm (which is used in Line 17 of Algorithm 2), must sample a solution uniformly at random from the set of all possible solutions.

A simple protocol for this task was proposed by Cozzo and Smart [CS19] (which we refer to as "One-Sided Masking") in the case where the matrix defining the system is *square*. This simple protocol outputs a solution or $\perp$: the latter occurs in the case that the input matrix has a determinant zero (hence, the matrix is singular) or the "one-side" masking has a determinant zero (which

Algorithm 3. OV-based.Verify(pk, msg, Sig)

Input: Public key (pk).
Input: Message msg.
Input: Signature Sig = (**S**, salt).
Output: A boolean indicating if the signature is valid.

```
//Parse ({P_i^(1)}_{i∈[m]}, {P_i^(2)}_{i∈[m]}, {P_i^(3)}_{i∈[m]}) from pk.
```
$\{\mathbf{P}_i^{(1)}, \mathbf{P}_i^{(2)}, \mathbf{P}_i^{3}\}_{i\in[m]} \leftarrow \mathsf{pk}$
```
//Hash salted message.
```
$\mathbf{t} \leftarrow \mathcal{H}(\mathsf{msg}\|\mathsf{salt})$ ▷ $\mathbf{t} \in \mathbb{F}_q^m$
for i from 1 to m **do**
$$\mathbf{Y}_i \leftarrow \mathbf{S}\begin{pmatrix} \mathbf{P}_i^{(1)} & \mathbf{P}_i^{(2)} \\ \mathbf{0} & \mathbf{P}_i^{(3)} \end{pmatrix}\mathbf{S}^{\mathsf{T}}$$
$\mathbf{y} \leftarrow \mathsf{Compute\_y}(\{\mathbf{Y}_i\}_{i\in[m]})$ ▷ $\mathbf{y} = \mathcal{P}^*(\mathbf{s})$
return $\mathbf{y} == \mathbf{t}$ ▷ Accept signature if $\mathbf{y} = \mathbf{t}$.

happens with probability $1/q$). However, their protocol leaks sensitive information about the input matrix structure if it is rank-deficient, disclosing far more than mere non-invertibility, which we discuss more extensively in the full version.

In this work, we address this limitation by proposing a novel approach that, first, works for general non-square matrices, and, secondly, (and crucial for the security of our threshold schemes), reveals only the rank of the matrix in cases of rank deficiency: this significantly reduces the leakage compared to [CS19].

In Sect. 5.5, we provide explanations as to why this reduced leakage appears secure for our specific threshold setting. Still, we leave as an open problem the design of a protocol for linear system solving that, in cases of rank deficiency, reveals only that the matrix is not full rank without additional leakage. In the following, we begin by defining the target functionality in Sect. 4.1, and, in Sect. 4.2, we follow with the presentation of our concrete protocol.

4.1 Functionality for Solving Systems of Linear Equations in the ABB Model

Recall that our work is set in the ABB model to ensure general applicability. Consequently, we model the task of sampling solutions to linear systems of equations as an extended functionality, denoted $\mathcal{F}_{\mathsf{ABB+Solve}}$, which augments the ABB model by adding one extra instruction that, precisely, samples solutions to systems defined by matrix and target vectors that are *stored in the ABB's dictionary* (representing values that are "secret-shared"). To ensure completeness, we provide a full, detailed description of the functionality, including necessary specifics regarding indexes of the dictionary. However, as mentioned in Sect. 2.2, afterward (and in particular for our protocol) we simplify the notation substantially by working at the level of matrices instead of individual values, and omitting indexes where possible, among other notational simplifications.

The functionality $\mathcal{F}_{\mathsf{ABB+Solve}}$ takes as a parameter a distribution $L(r)$ which models leakage as a function of the rank r of $\mathbf{A}$. In the concrete protocol, when

$\mathbf{A}$ is rank-deficient, the difference $r - r^+$ is revealed (where $r^+ \leftarrow L(r)$) rather than r itself, which potentially provides an extra layer of security.

Functionality 2: $\mathcal{F}_{\mathsf{ABB+Solve}}(L)$

The functionality has the *exact same* operations as $\mathcal{F}_{\mathsf{ABB}}$, with the addition of: On input (solve, $\{\mathtt{id}_{ij}\}_{i,j=1,1}^{s,t}$, $\{\mathtt{id}_i\}_{i=1}^{s}$, $\{\mathtt{id}'_j\}_{j=1}^{t}$) from the parties, where $s \leq t$, the functionality fetches $\{(a_{ij}, \mathtt{id}_{ij})\}_{i,j=1,1}^{s,t}$ and $\{(b_i, \mathtt{id}_i)\}_{i=1}^{s}$ and proceeds as follows:

1. Let $\mathbf{A} \in \mathbb{F}_q^{s\times t}$: the (i,j) entry of $\mathbf{A}$ is a_{ij}. Let $\boldsymbol{b} \in \mathbb{F}_q^s$ so that $\boldsymbol{b}[i] = b_i$. Let $r = \mathsf{rank}(\mathbf{A})$.
2. Sample $r^+ \leftarrow L(r)$. If $r - r^+ < s$, then send $(\mathsf{rank\text{-}defect}, r - r^+)$ to all parties.
3. Else, sample a uniformly random element $\mathbf{x} \in \mathbb{F}_q^t$ constrained to $\mathbf{A} \cdot \mathbf{x} = \mathbf{b}$, and store $(\mathbf{x}[j], \mathtt{id}'_j)$ for $j \in [t]$.

4.2 Concrete Protocol for Solving Systems of Linear Equations

Our protocol to instantiate $\mathcal{F}_{\mathsf{ABB+Solve}}$ is given as Protocol Π_{Solve} below. Let us recall that we write $[\![\mathbf{A}\cdot\mathbf{B}]\!] \leftarrow [\![\mathbf{A}]\!]\cdot[\![\mathbf{B}]\!]$ for when parties use the command mult in $\mathcal{F}_{\mathsf{ABB}}$, and similarly we write $[\![\mathbf{A}+\mathbf{B}]\!] \leftarrow [\![\mathbf{A}]\!] + [\![\mathbf{B}]\!]$ for when they use the command add. Importantly, we remark that, in an actual instantiation of $\mathcal{F}_{\mathsf{ABB}}$, additions will come *for free* in terms of communication costs while multiplications require some form of interaction. To emphasize this, in the functionality, we write "parties compute locally" for additions and other local operations, even though in the ABB model there is no such thing as "local computation".

Protocol 1: Π_{Solve}

The protocol is set in the $\mathcal{F}_{\mathsf{ABB}}$-hybrid. All the commands except for (solve) are forwarded directly to $\mathcal{F}_{\mathsf{ABB}}$.

On input (solve, $[\![\mathbf{A}]\!]$, $[\![\mathbf{b}]\!]$), where $\mathbf{A}$ has dimensions $s \times t$ and $[\![\mathbf{b}]\!]$ has dimension s, the parties proceed as follows:

1. Parties call $[\![\mathbf{R}]\!] \leftarrow \mathsf{rand}(\mathbb{F}_q^{s\times s})$ and $[\![\mathbf{S}]\!] \leftarrow \mathsf{rand}(\mathbb{F}_q^{t\times t})$.
2. Parties call $[\![\mathbf{A}\cdot\mathbf{S}]\!] \leftarrow [\![\mathbf{A}]\!]\cdot[\![\mathbf{S}]\!]$.
3. Parties call $[\![\mathbf{T}]\!] \leftarrow [\![\mathbf{R}]\!]\cdot[\![\mathbf{A}\cdot\mathbf{S}]\!]$.
4. Parties open $\mathbf{T} \leftarrow [\![\mathbf{T}]\!]$. If $r = \mathsf{rank}(\mathbf{T}) < s$ then the parties output $(\mathsf{rank\text{-}defect}, r)$.
5. Otherwise, let $\mathbf{T}^{-1} \in \mathbb{F}_q^{t\times s}$ be a right inverse of $\mathbf{T}$, that is, $\mathbf{T}\mathbf{T}^{-1} = \mathbf{I}_{s\times s}$. The parties call $[\![\mathbf{A}^{-1}]\!] \leftarrow [\![\mathbf{S}]\!]\cdot\mathbf{T}^{-1}\cdot[\![\mathbf{R}]\!]$. It can be checked that $\mathbf{A}^{-1} \in \mathbb{F}_q^{t\times s}$ satisfies $\mathbf{A}\cdot\mathbf{A}^{-1} = \mathbf{I}_{s\times s}$.
6. Let $\beta_1, \ldots, \beta_{t-s} \in \mathbb{F}_q^{t-s}$ be a basis for $\mathsf{ker}(\mathbf{T})$. The parties call $([\![z_1]\!], \ldots, [\![z_{t-s}]\!]) \leftarrow \mathsf{rand}(\mathbb{F}_q^{t-s})$.

7. Parties compute locally $[\![\mathbf{z}]\!] \leftarrow \sum_{i=1}^{t-s} [\![z_i]\!] \cdot \boldsymbol{\beta}_i$.
8. Parties call $[\![\mathbf{x}]\!] \leftarrow [\![\mathbf{A}^{-1}]\!] \cdot [\![\mathbf{b}]\!] + [\![\mathbf{S}]\!] \cdot [\![\mathbf{z}]\!]$
9. Output $[\![\mathbf{x}]\!]$.

Theorem 1. *Protocol Π_{Solve} instantiates functionality $\mathcal{F}_{\mathsf{ABB+Solve}}(L)$ in the $\mathcal{F}_{\mathsf{ABB}}$-hybrid model, where $L(r)$ is such that:*

$$L(r) = \left\{ r - \mathsf{rank}\left(\mathbf{R} \cdot \begin{bmatrix} \mathbf{I}_r & \mathbf{0}_{s\times(t-r)} \\ \mathbf{0}_{(s-r)\times r} & \end{bmatrix} \cdot \mathbf{S} \right) \mid \mathbf{R} \leftarrow \mathbb{F}_q^{s\times s}, \mathbf{S} \leftarrow \mathbb{F}_q^{t\times t} \right\}$$

Proof. To prove Theorem 1, we describe a simulator $\mathcal{S}$ that interacts with the ideal functionality $\mathcal{F}_{\mathsf{ABB+Solve}}(L)$ and with the adversary, emulating internally the arithmetic and coin-sampling functionalities, and emulating virtual honest parties.

Initially, $\mathcal{S}$ calls $\mathcal{F}_{\mathsf{ABB+Solve}}(L)$, receiving either (as output) some sharings $[\![\mathbf{w}]\!]$ of a solution,[3] or $(\mathsf{rankdef}, r - r^+)$ with $r - r^+ < s$ and $r^+ \leftarrow L(r)$. $\mathcal{S}$ proceeds by emulating rand in Item 1 by distributing random shares: this is possible because the adversary's shares are independent of the underlying secret. $\mathcal{S}$ also emulates the shared multiplications in Item 2 and Item 3. To match the real-world distribution in Item 4, $\mathcal{S}$ samples invertible matrices $\mathbf{U}' \leftarrow \mathbb{F}_q^{s\times s}$ and $\mathbf{V}' \leftarrow \mathbb{F}_q^{t\times t}$, adjusting the shares of the honest parties so that the reconstruction yields $\mathbf{T}' = \mathbf{U}' \cdot \mathbf{J} \cdot \mathbf{V}'$, where $\mathbf{J}$ is a matrix with $r - r^+$ ones in its diagonal and zeros elsewhere. We claim this has the same distribution as the real world, where parties reconstruct $\mathbf{T} = \mathbf{R} \cdot \mathbf{A} \cdot \mathbf{S}$ with $\mathbf{R} \in \mathbb{F}_q^{s\times s}$ and $\mathbf{S} \in \mathbb{F}_q^{t\times t}$ as uniform matrices that are unknown to the adversary, conditioned on the event $\mathsf{rank}(\mathbf{T}) = r - r^+$. To see this, as an intermediate step, consider the distribution of matrices $\mathbf{T}'' = \mathbf{X} \cdot (\mathbf{R} \cdot \mathbf{A} \cdot \mathbf{S}) \cdot \mathbf{Y}$, with $(\mathbf{X} \in \mathbb{F}_q^{s\times s}, \mathbf{Y} \in \mathbb{F}_q^{t\times t})$ as random invertible matrices and $(\mathbf{R} \in \mathbb{F}_q^{s\times s}, \mathbf{S} \in \mathbb{F}_q^{t\times t})$ as uniformly distributed matrices, conditioned on $\mathsf{rank}(\mathbf{T}'') = r - r^+$. We can easily see that $\mathbf{X} \cdot \mathbf{R}$ and $\mathbf{S} \cdot \mathbf{Y}$ are uniformly distributed since $\mathbf{X}$ and $\mathbf{Y}$ are invertible. Hence, $\mathbf{T}''$ has the same distribution as $\mathbf{T}$.

Now, let us study in more detail the distribution of $\mathbf{T}''$: remember that we condition on $\mathsf{rank}(\mathbf{T}'') = r - r^+$, and we observe that $\mathsf{rank}(\mathbf{T}'') = \mathsf{rank}(\mathbf{R} \cdot \mathbf{A} \cdot \mathbf{S})$ as $(\mathbf{X}, \mathbf{Y})$ are invertible matrices. We can, hence, write $\mathbf{R} \cdot \mathbf{A} \cdot \mathbf{S} = \mathbf{U} \cdot \mathbf{J} \cdot \mathbf{V}$ for some invertible matrices $(\mathbf{U}, \mathbf{V})$. Thus, it holds that $\mathbf{T}' = \mathbf{R}' \cdot (\mathbf{R} \cdot \mathbf{A} \cdot \mathbf{S}) \cdot \mathbf{S}'$ with $\mathbf{R}' := \mathbf{U}'\mathbf{U}^{-1}$ and $\mathbf{S}' := \mathbf{V}^{-1}\mathbf{V}'$. Since $\mathbf{U}$ and $\mathbf{V}$ are invertible, and $\mathbf{U}'$ and $\mathbf{V}'$ are uniform and invertible matrices unknown to the adversary, it follows that $\mathbf{R}'$ and $\mathbf{S}'$ are also uniform and invertible matrices that are unknown to the adversary. Therefore, $\mathbf{T}'$ follows the same distribution as $\mathbf{T}''$ conditioned on the value of its rank, and consequently holds the same distribution as $\mathbf{T}$. We additionally note that the distribution of $r - r^+$ follows exactly the distribution of ranks of $\mathbf{T}$ by choice of $L(r)$.

[3] We use $\mathbf{w}$ instead of $\mathbf{x}$ to distinguish between the output in the ideal and real worlds.

In case $\mathsf{rank}(\mathbf{T}') < s$, then $\mathcal{S}$ returns its rank as leakage, as in the real world. Now, in the case in which $\mathsf{rank}(\mathbf{T}') = s$ and a solution $[\![\mathbf{w}]\!]$ was distributed by $\mathcal{F}_{\mathsf{ABB+Solve}}(L)$, we proceed as following Let $\mathbf{x}$ be the output in the real world, and note that:

$$\begin{aligned}\mathbf{A} \cdot \mathbf{x} &= \mathbf{A} \cdot (\mathbf{A}^{-1}\mathbf{b} + \mathbf{S}\mathbf{z}) \\ &= \mathbf{A} \cdot (\mathbf{S}\mathbf{T}^{-1}\mathbf{R}\mathbf{b}) + \mathbf{A}\mathbf{S}\mathbf{z} \\ &= \mathbf{R}^{-1} \cdot \left(\mathbf{R}\mathbf{A}\mathbf{S} \cdot \mathbf{T}^{-1} \cdot \mathbf{R}\mathbf{b} + \mathbf{R}\mathbf{A}\mathbf{S} \cdot \mathbf{z}\right) \\ &= \mathbf{R}^{-1} \cdot \left(\mathbf{T} \cdot \mathbf{T}^{-1} \cdot \mathbf{R}\mathbf{b} + \mathbf{T} \cdot \mathbf{z}\right) \\ &= \mathbf{R}^{-1} \cdot (\mathbf{I}_{s \times s} \cdot \mathbf{R}\mathbf{b} + \mathbf{0}) \\ &= \mathbf{b}.\end{aligned}$$

Hence, the output $\mathbf{x}$ produced by Π_{Solve} is indeed a valid solution to the system. Next, we need to establish that $\mathbf{x}$ is uniformly distributed. For this, note that $\mathbf{z}$ is a uniformly random element—and unknown to the adversary—in $\mathsf{ker}(\mathbf{T})$ and hence $\mathbf{S} \cdot \mathbf{z}$ is a uniformly random element in $\mathsf{ker}(\mathbf{R} \cdot \mathbf{A}) = \mathsf{ker}(\mathbf{A})$. This implies that $\mathbf{A}^{-1} \cdot \mathbf{b} + \mathbf{S} \cdot \mathbf{z}$ is a uniformly random element that maps to $\mathbf{b}$ under $\mathbf{A}$, as required.

□

5 Threshold OV-based: UOV and MAYO Signatures

Now we describe our main contribution, which consists of threshold variants of OV-based signatures in the ABB model, as specified by Functionality $\mathcal{F}_{\mathsf{ABB+Solve}}$ in page 15. Recall that this functionality extends the standard ABB model ($\mathcal{F}_{\mathsf{ABB}}$) from Sect. 2.2 by enabling sampling solutions to "secret-shared" systems of equations: an essential component in the OV-based signing algorithm. We begin in Sect. 5.2 by describing our approach to Distributed Key Generation (DKG), a straightforward process due to the inherent "arithmetic-friendliness" of these signature schemes Next, in Sect. 5.3, we introduce our threshold signing protocols that generate signatures for a given public message using a "secret-shared" private key. Before detailing these constructions, we provide an overview of the functionality we aim to implement in Sect. 5.1.

5.1 Threshold OV-based Functionality

The functionality $\mathcal{F}_{\mathsf{ThrSign}}$ described below models the threshold version of OV-based signatures. In an initial "setup phase", the functionality samples a secret key, stores it internally, and announces the corresponding public key. Following this, any public message can be provided jointly by the parties and the functionality will compute a signature for it, returning it to all parties.

As discussed in Sect. 3, the matrix $\mathbf{A}$ may be rank deficient with non-negligible probability. In a local signature computation, a signer can simply sample a new $\mathbf{V}$ and try again (in Line 7 of Algorithm 2). However, in an MPC context, the runtime of the protocol must be public and, hence, as a minimum, we leak the number of attempts until a full rank **A** is obtained and a solution can be found. Our protocol, nevertheless, leaks slightly more than just the number of attempts: for each failed attempt, we leak a random variable depending on the *rank* of the corresponding rank-deficient matrix **A**. This behavior is captured by the set Leaks and by distributions $L(r)$ for $0 \leq r \leq s$. We provide a deeper discussion on this matter in Sect. 5.5.

Functionality 3: $\mathcal{F}_{\mathsf{ThrSign}}(L)$

Setup phase: On input (sample-key) from all the parties for the first time (future calls to this command are ignored), the functionality proceeds as follows:

1. Run $(\mathsf{pk}, \mathsf{sk}) \leftarrow$ OV-based.KeyGen().
2. Internally store the secret key $\mathsf{sk} = (\mathbf{O}, (\mathbf{L}_i)_{i\in[m]})$.
3. Output to all parties the public key $\mathsf{pk} = (\mathbf{P}_i^{(1)}, \mathbf{P}_i^{(2)}, \mathbf{P}_i^{(3)})_{i\in[m]}$.

Signing: On input (sign, msg), where $\mathsf{msg} \in \{0,1\}^*$ is the message to be signed, the functionality proceeds as follows:

1. Sample $\mathsf{salt} \xleftarrow{\$} \{0,1\}^{\lambda+64}$ and let $\mathbf{t} \leftarrow \mathcal{H}(\mathsf{msg}\|\mathsf{salt}) \in \mathbb{F}_q^m$.
2. Initialize Leaks = [ ].
3. Sample a matrix $\mathbf{V} \leftarrow \mathbb{F}_q^{k\times(n-o)}$.
4. For $i \in [m]$: Compute $\mathbf{M}_i = \mathbf{V}\cdot\mathbf{L}_i$, and $\mathbf{Y}_i = \mathbf{V}\cdot\mathbf{P}_i^{(1)}\cdot\mathbf{V}^\intercal$.
5. Compute $\mathbf{A} \leftarrow$ OV-based.Compute_A($\{\mathbf{M}_i\}_{i\in[m]}$) and $\mathbf{y} \leftarrow \mathbf{t} -$ OV-based.Compute_y($\{\mathbf{Y}_i\}_{i\in[m]}$). Let $r = \mathsf{rank}(\mathbf{A})$ and $r^+ \leftarrow L(r)$.
6. If $r - r^+ < m$, append $r - r^+$ to Leaks and **go to** 3.
7. Sample $\mathbf{x} \in \mathbb{F}_q^{ko}$ uniformly at random constrained to $\mathbf{A}\mathbf{x} = \mathbf{y}$ (by calling SampleSolution).
8. Compute the signature $\mathbf{S} \leftarrow (\mathbf{V} + (\mathbf{O}\mathbf{X}^\intercal)^\intercal, \mathbf{X})$, where $\mathbf{X} \leftarrow$ Matrixify($\mathbf{x}$), and output (($\mathbf{S}$, salt), Leaks) to all parties.

5.2 Procedure for Distributed Key Generation

In certain threshold applications, like key management via MPC (cf. [Lin20]), the secret key is held by a single party. This party utilizes a set of additional parties for threshold signing, effectively safeguarding the key similarly to the functionality of a hardware security module[4]. However, several other applications assume that the full view of the secret key is unknown to any single party, for which it is paramount to execute a *Distributed Key Generation* (DKG) protocol to produce "shares" of the secret key while only leaking the corresponding public key.

[4] We note that our construction trivially allows for these use cases, by letting the owner of the secret key call the input command in $\mathcal{F}_{\mathsf{ABB+Solve}}$ (which in practice corresponds to distributing secret-shares of the secret key under certain secret-sharing schemes).

In the classical setting, there are some DKGs for Discrete-Logarithm (DLOG)-based threshold signatures though few of them arrive at a round-optimal [Kat23], fully-secure [Wik05, Gen+07] solution. In the classical setting, a simple solution sees the parties generate random shares of a secret key $\langle s \rangle$, locally use those as exponents to compute $\langle g^s \rangle$, and reconstruct g^s. However, for a post-quantum setting, like lattice-based signatures schemes, there is no simple solution: parties must sample obliviously from Gaussian distributions, for example, which is a much harder problem [ENP24].

In this section, we show that, fortunately, the structure of OV-based public keys allows for very simple and efficient DKG protocols. We describe our DKG for OV-based schemes in Procedure π_{KeyGen} below.

Procedure 2: π_{KeyGen}

Input: No inputs. The procedure is set in the $\mathcal{F}_{\mathsf{ABB+Solve}}$-hybrid model.

Output: A public key $\mathsf{pk} = (\mathbf{P}_i^{(1)}, \mathbf{P}_i^{(2)}, \mathbf{P}_i^{(3)})_{i \in [m]}$, and a secret-shared secret key $([\![\mathbf{O}]\!], [\![\mathbf{L}_1]\!], \ldots, [\![\mathbf{L}_m]\!])$, where $\mathbf{O} \in \mathbb{F}_q^{(n-o)\times o}$ and $\mathbf{L}_i \in \mathbb{F}_q^{(n-o)\times o}$.

1. Parties call $[\![\mathbf{O}]\!] \leftarrow \mathsf{rand}(\mathbb{F}_q^{(n-o)\times o})$.
2. For $i \in [m]$, parties call $\mathbf{P}_i^{(1)} \leftarrow \mathsf{coin}(\mathbb{F}_q^{(n-o)\times(n-o)})$ and $\mathbf{P}_i^{(2)} \leftarrow \mathsf{coin}(\mathbb{F}_q^{(n-o)\times o})$.
3. For $i \in [m]$, parties locally compute $[\![\mathbf{P}_i^{(1)} \cdot \mathbf{O}]\!] \leftarrow \mathbf{P}_i^{(1)} \cdot [\![\mathbf{O}]\!]$.
4. For $i \in [m]$, parties call $[\![\mathbf{O}^\mathsf{T} \cdot (\mathbf{P}_i^{(1)} \cdot \mathbf{O} - \mathbf{P}_i^{(2)})]\!] \leftarrow [\![\mathbf{O}^\mathsf{T}]\!] \cdot ([\![\mathbf{P}_i^{(1)} \cdot \mathbf{O}]\!] - \mathbf{P}_i^{(2)})$.
5. Parties compute locally $[\![\mathbf{P}_i^{(3)}]\!] \leftarrow \mathsf{Upper}([\![-\mathbf{O}^\mathsf{T}(\mathbf{P}_i^{(1)}\mathbf{O} - \mathbf{P}_i^{(2)})]\!])$.
6. Parties reveal $\mathbf{P}_i^{(3)}$.
7. For $i \in [m]$, parties compute locally $[\![(\mathbf{P}_i^{(1)} + \mathbf{P}_i^{(1)\mathsf{T}})\mathbf{O}]\!] \leftarrow (\mathbf{P}_i^{(1)} + \mathbf{P}_i^{(1)\mathsf{T}}) \cdot [\![\mathbf{O}]\!]$.
8. Parties compute locally $[\![\mathbf{L}_i]\!] \leftarrow [\![(\mathbf{P}_i^{(1)} + \mathbf{P}_i^{(1)\mathsf{T}})\mathbf{O}]\!] + \mathbf{P}_i^{(2)}$ for $i \in [m]$.
9. All parties output $(\mathsf{pk} = (\{\mathbf{P}_i^{(1)}, \mathbf{P}_i^{(2)}, \mathbf{P}_i^{(3)}\}_{\{i \in [m]\}})$ as the public key, and they store $([\![\mathbf{O}]\!], \{[\![\mathbf{L}_i]\!]\}_{\{i \in [m]\}}))$ as the "shares" of the secret key.

5.3 Procedure for Threshold Signing

We are now concerned with instantiating the threshold signing procedure of Functionality $\mathcal{F}_{\mathsf{ThrSign}}$. Consider a secret key $\mathsf{sk} = (\mathbf{O}, \{\mathbf{L}_i\}_{i \in [m]})$, where $\mathbf{O} \in \mathbb{F}_q^{(n-o)\times o}$ and $\mathbf{L}_i \in \mathbb{F}_q^{(n-o)\times o}$, and assume it is stored in the ABB as $([\![\mathbf{O}]\!], [\![\mathbf{L}_1]\!], \ldots, [\![\mathbf{L}_m]\!])$. The procedure to securely compute a threshold signature on a public message msg is given below as Procedure π_{Sign}.

Procedure 3: π_{Sign}

Input: Public key and secret key stored in $\mathcal{F}_{\mathsf{ABB+Solve}}$: $\mathsf{pk} = (\mathbf{P}_i^{(1)}, \mathbf{P}_i^{(2)}, \mathbf{P}_i^{(3)})_{i\in[m]}, \mathsf{sk} = ([\![\mathbf{O}]\!], [\![\mathbf{L}_1]\!], \ldots, [\![\mathbf{L}_m]\!])$. A message msg to be signed.

Output: A signature $\mathbf{S} \in \mathbb{F}_q^{k\times n}$ on msg.

1. Parties call $\mathsf{salt} \leftarrow \mathsf{coin}(\{0,1\}^{\lambda+64})$ and let $\mathbf{t} \leftarrow \mathcal{H}(\mathsf{msg}\|\mathsf{salt}) \in \mathbb{F}_q^m$. Let $\mathsf{Leaks} = [\ \ ]$.
2. Parties call $[\![\mathbf{V}]\!] \leftarrow \mathsf{rand}(\mathbb{F}_q^{k\times(n-o)})$
3. For $i \in [m]$: Parties call $[\![\mathbf{M}_i]\!] \leftarrow [\![\mathbf{V}]\!] \cdot [\![\mathbf{L}_i]\!]$.
4. For $i \in [m]$: Parties call $[\![\mathbf{Y}_i]\!] \leftarrow [\![\mathbf{V}]\!] \cdot \mathbf{P}_i^{(1)} \cdot [\![\mathbf{V}^\intercal]\!]$.
5. Compute locally $[\![\mathbf{A}]\!] \leftarrow \mathsf{OV\text{-}based.Compute\_A}(\{[\![\mathbf{M}_i]\!]\}_{i\in[m]})$ and $[\![\mathbf{y}]\!] \leftarrow [\![\mathbf{t}]\!] - \mathsf{OV\text{-}based.Compute\_y}(\{[\![\mathbf{Y}_i]\!]\}_{i\in[m]})$. This is possible since both OV-based.Compute_y and OV-based.Compute_A are *linear* functions of their arguments.
6. Parties call the command solve of $\mathcal{F}_{\mathsf{ABB+Solve}}$ on inputs $[\![\mathbf{A}]\!]$ and $[\![\mathbf{y}]\!]$. If the output is $(\mathsf{rank\text{-}deficient}, r)$, parties append r to Leaks and **go to** 2.. Else, let $[\![\mathbf{x}]\!]$ be the output.
7. Parties compute locally $[\![\mathbf{X}]\!] \leftarrow \mathsf{Matrixify}([\![\mathbf{x}]\!])$ and call $[\![\mathbf{X}\cdot\mathbf{O}^\intercal]\!] \leftarrow [\![\mathbf{X}]\!] \cdot [\![\mathbf{O}^\intercal]\!]$.
8. Parties compute locally $[\![\mathbf{S}']\!] \leftarrow [\![\mathbf{V} + (\mathbf{O}\mathbf{X}^\intercal)^\intercal]\!]$, and they open $\mathbf{S}' \leftarrow [\![\mathbf{S}']\!]$.
9. Parties return as output $(\mathsf{Sig} = (\mathbf{S}, \mathsf{salt}), \mathsf{Leaks})$, where $\mathbf{S} = (\mathbf{S}' \mid \mathbf{X}) \in \mathbb{F}_q^{k\times n}$.

5.4 Protocol for Instantiating $\mathcal{F}_{\mathsf{ThrSign}}$

Finally, we compose the procedures π_{KeyGen} and π_{Sign} to instantiate the Functionality $\mathcal{F}_{\mathsf{ThrSign}}$. This is detailed in the protocol Π_{ThrSign} below, along with the corresponding simulation-based proof in Theorem 2.

Protocol 4: Π_{ThrSign}

The protocol is set in the $\mathcal{F}_{\mathsf{ABB+Solve}}$-hybrid model.

Setup phase: On input $(\mathsf{sample\text{-}key})$, the parties execute π_{KeyGen}. They obtain a stored secret key $[\![\mathsf{sk}]\!]$ and a corresponding public key pk.

Signing: On input $(\mathsf{sign}, \mathsf{msg})$ and, if the setup was previously performed, parties call π_{Sign} on input the key pairs and msg, which results in $(\mathsf{Sig} = (\mathbf{S}, \mathsf{salt}), \mathsf{Leaks})$. The parties return this result as the output of Π_{ThrSign}.

Theorem 2. *Protocol Π_{ThrSign} instantiates $\mathcal{F}_{\mathsf{ThrSign}}(L)$ in the $\mathcal{F}_{\mathsf{ABB+Solve}}(L)$-hybrid model. For the proof, see the full version of the paper.*

5.5 On the Leakage in $\mathcal{F}_{\mathsf{ABB+Solve}}$

Recall that our functionality $\mathcal{F}_{\mathsf{ABB+Solve}}$ (see Sect. 4.2) not only produces a signature, but also a set of positive integers Leaks representing the *rank* of each matrix $\mathbf{A}$ that turned out to be rank-deficient. This arises from the difficulty of determining whether a given secret matrix is full rank without leaking the rank itself. Now, the "most ideal" functionality that models OV-based signing should produce the signature, and *nothing else*. Since our functionality technically leaks more than such an ideal setting, we discuss the potential implications of this in terms of the unforgetability of the underlying scheme.

We first note here that many OV-based schemes (including MAYO and UOV) follow the *Hash and Sign with Retry* paradigm [KX22]. For a given selection of random coins in the inverse trapdoor function, and a given message hash, a preimage of the hash may not necessarily exist. At a high level, the signature algorithm addresses this challenge by resampling the coins used in the inverse of the trapdoor function until a valid preimage is found. The term "retry" reflects this resampling process. Once a preimage is successfully obtained, it is output as the signature for the message, along with the salt if one is used. These retries, in turn, imply a bias in the sampling and that an amount of information leakage is present in these schemes, but there does not seem to be any attack that can take advantage of the information leakage[5]. In the ROM-based security proof for MAYO, for example, (see Sect. 5.2 of [Beu+23a]), an adversary can make at most Q_s signing queries to the random oracle. Given the probability average-bounded by $B = \frac{q^{k-(n-o)}}{q-1} + \frac{q^{m-ko}}{q-1}$ if $Q_s \cdot B \leq 1/2$, this results in only a constant factor reduction in advantage, indicating that security of MAYO is not compromised by much. If $Q_s \cdot B > 1$, the security proof no longer provides guarantees; but, as pointed out in the specification, there does not seem to be any attack that can take advantage of the leakage. The same analysis applies to UOV, but with a bigger leakage due to the larger restarting probability of approximately $B = 1/q$. After decades of cryptanalysis, no attacks are known that can efficiently make use of this leakage. While this leakage is noted in the specifications of OV-based schemes, it should be further formalized in their security proofs, for instance with a Renyi divergence argument.

In our threshold cases, note that nothing else besides the rank of the rank-deficient matrix $\mathbf{A}$ is revealed, and furthermore, such a matrix is entirely discarded, and a freshly new matrix $\mathbf{V}$ is sampled for a new attempt (leading to a new matrix $\mathbf{A}$). While leaking the rank $\mathbf{A}$ during signing appears like non-trivial information on the private material, the security of this tweaked scheme follows rather naturally from the assumptions described and made in OV-based schemes. Leaking the rank of $\mathbf{A}$ slightly increases the information available to an attacker over just leaking the rank deficiency of $\mathbf{A}$. However, as shown in [Cog+24], the

[5] In fact, for many OV-based schemes, including UOV and MAYO, leaking that the matrix is not invertible or how many attempts were tried via a timing side-channel is not an issue as the matrix is discarded anyway [Beu+23c]. Many novel side-channel analyses of these schemes do not take advantage of this information [Aul+23a, Aul+23b].

rank of **A** is concentrated in a small interval with overwhelming probability, and thus we conjecture that leaking it is roughly equivalent to leaking that **A** is rank deficient. In the continuity of previous works on multivariate cryptography, we thus conjecture that the rank leakage of our threshold solution does not significantly increase the probability that an adversary could forge a signature in UOV or MAYO.

6 Verifying OV-based Signatures Obliviously

In Sect. 5, we described the procedures and protocols that allows us to perform threshold signing. In this section, we will focus on the procedure to verify said threshold signatures, but we will go beyond that and explore other types of verification in threshold settings. Normally, the task of threshold signatures schemes is concerned with signing and verifying a public message using secret-shared keys. However, there are some practical applications that involve *verifying* the validity of a *secret-shared signature* on a *secret-shared message*. For instance, in [Ara+21,BJ18], it is noted that general MPC does not put any restriction on what kind of inputs are allowed: one can ensure, for example, that a given secret-shared input provided to some MPC computation is valid in regards to a verification procedure. For example, in the classical millionaire's problem [Yao82] where Alice and Bob want to determine who has the highest net worth without revealing anything else (their input), it may be important for the parties to ensure that the inputs provided are not fabricated but rather that they correspond to the actual net worth. To achieve this, parties supply not only their net worth but also a signature from an authority (like certified banks) as part of the MPC input[6]. Prior to executing the actual protocol, parties run the signature verification algorithm in MPC to confirm that their inputs are correctly signed.

In this section, we will first introduce the functionality (see Sect. 6.1) and protocols needed for threshold verification (see Sect. 6.2), and, later, expand them for secret-shared signatures and secret-shared messages.

6.1 Threshold OV-based Functionality: Verification

The functionality $\mathcal{F}_{\mathsf{ThrVerif}}$ described below models the verification of threshold OV-based signature schemes. The functionality is straightforward as the verification procedure of OV-based schemes simply involves a matrix product.

[6] It is also important to note that the signature must also be in secret-shared form to maintain confidentiality. Traditional signature schemes do not inherently ensure the privacy of the message: appending a message to a given signature results in a signature scheme that lacks privacy.

Functionality 4: $\mathcal{F}_{\mathsf{ThrVerif}}$

The functionality has all the commands as $\mathcal{F}_{\mathsf{ABB}}$.

On input $(\mathsf{verify}, \mathsf{msg}, \mathsf{pk}, \mathsf{Sig})$, where $\mathsf{msg} \in \{0,1\}^*$ is the message to be verified, the functionality proceeds as follows:

1. Parse $(\mathbf{S}, \mathsf{salt})$ from Sig and $(\{\mathbf{P}_i^{(1)}\}_{\{i\in[m]\}}, \{\mathbf{P}_i^{(2)})\}_{\{i\in[m]\}}, \{\mathbf{P}_i^{(3)})\}_{\{i\in[m]\}}$ from pk. Let $\mathbf{t} \leftarrow \mathcal{H}(\mathsf{msg}||\mathsf{salt}) \in \mathbb{F}_q^m$.
2. For i from 1 to m, set: $\mathbf{Y}_i \leftarrow \mathbf{S}\begin{pmatrix}\mathbf{P}_i^{(1)} & \mathbf{P}_i^{(2)} \\ \mathbf{0} & \mathbf{P}_i^{(3)}\end{pmatrix}\mathbf{S}^{\mathsf{T}}$
3. Set: $\mathbf{y} \leftarrow \mathsf{OV\text{-}based.Compute\_y}(\{\mathbf{Y}_i\}_{i\in[m]})$
4. Send $(\mathsf{accept}, \mathsf{Sig})$ to all parties if $\mathbf{y} == \mathbf{t}$. Else, send $(\mathsf{reject}, \mathsf{Sig})$.

6.2 Protocol for Threshold Verification

To securely instantiate $\mathcal{F}_{\mathsf{ThrVerif}}$, the protocol leverages the simplicity of the verification algorithm in OV-based schemes, which reduces to a matrix product. The protocol Π_{ThrVerif} is essentially the same as Algorithm 3, where the last step (the check) leaks no information in case of failure.

6.3 Certifying Inputs in a Threshold Manner

Given the functionality $\mathcal{F}_{\mathsf{ThrVerif}}$ and its instantiation, Π_{ThrVerif}, we consider the possibility of expanding its scope to verify not only a complete view of the signature and message but also their secret-shared representations. This extension would enable the certification of both public values and secret-shared ones, broadening the functionality's applicability. We call this ability "certifying inputs in a threshold manner".

In a classical setting, in [Ara+21], the authors make use of PS signatures [PS15], based on the observation that PS signatures are somewhat "MPC-friendly" and will allow for this certification. OV-based schemes exhibit a limited degree of this MPC-friendliness (in the verification procedure) as they require messages to be hashed prior to signing/verifying, and hashing of secret-shared data is quite costly. However, it is worth mentioning that the verification procedure of OV-based schemes offers opportunities for enhancing other MPC functionalities (as we see in $\mathcal{F}_{\mathsf{ThrVerif}}$). Here, we present a verification procedure that removes the use of the hash function (and of the salt) and assumes that the target $\mathbf{t}$ is already the result of hashing of secret-shared $(\mathsf{msg}||\mathsf{salt})$: $\mathbf{t}$ is, hence, defined over the message space $\mathbb{F}_q^m$ directly. The assumption made here is that a trusted party performs and distributes the hashing of the secret-shared data. Below we define a functionality $\mathcal{F}_{\mathsf{ABB+CertInp}}$ which has the same features as the ABB model from Sect. 2.2 and expands it with the ability for parties to prove that a given (secret) input is "correct". Concretely, we model this by allowing the parties to provide as additional (secret) input a OV-based signature, which the functionality verifies using a public key provided by all parties. Crucially, $\mathcal{F}_{\mathsf{ABB+CertInp}}$ differs from $\mathcal{F}_{\mathsf{ThrVerif}}$ in that fetches the already distributed $\mathbf{t}$, contrary to the hashing performed in Item 1.

Functionality 5: $\mathcal{F}_{\mathsf{ABB+CertInp}}$

The functionality has all the commands as $\mathcal{F}_{\mathsf{ABB}}$.

On input ($\mathsf{cert-verify}, \mathtt{IDs}, \mathsf{pk}$), where $\mathtt{IDs}$ is a set of IDs, the functionality proceeds as follows:

1. Parse $(\{\mathbf{P}_i^{(1)}\}_{\{i\in[m]\}}, \{\mathbf{P}_i^{(2)})\}_{\{i\in[m]\}}, \{\mathbf{P}_i^{(3)})\}_{\{i\in[m]\}}$ from pk.
2. Use $\mathtt{IDs}$ to fetch a stored value $\mathbf{t} \in \mathbb{F}_q^m$ and a stored signature $\mathbf{S} \in \mathbb{F}_q^{k\times n}$ (without the salt).
3. For i from 1 to m, set: $\mathbf{Y}_i \leftarrow \mathbf{S}\begin{pmatrix}\mathbf{P}_i^{(1)} & \mathbf{P}_i^{(2)} \\ \mathbf{0} & \mathbf{P}_i^{(3)}\end{pmatrix}\mathbf{S}^{\mathsf{T}}$
4. Set: $\mathbf{y} \leftarrow \mathsf{OV\text{-}based.Compute\_y}(\{\mathbf{Y}_i\}_{i\in[m]})$
5. Send (accept, S) to all parties if $\mathbf{y} == \mathbf{t}$. Else, send (reject, S).

The protocol ($\Pi_{\mathsf{ABB+CertInp}}$) for securely instantiating $\mathcal{F}_{\mathsf{ABB+CertInp}}$ is relatively straightforward given that the verification algorithm in OV-based schemes simply involves a matrix product. However, a subtlety in this protocol is that, at the end, the functionality performs an equality check, leaking nothing in case the check fails. A standard approach in MPC for such equality checks is to compute the difference between the two values ($\mathbf{y}$ and $\mathbf{t}$), multiply this difference by a secret random value, and then reconstruct the result. If the two original values are equal, the result will be zero; otherwise, it will appear uniformly random due to the non-zero product with a random factor, ensuring no information is leaked. This approach is effective provided the underlying field has size $> 2^\kappa$, where κ is a statistical security parameter. In smaller fields, the secret random value could unintentionally be zero, compromising the reliability of the check.

We adopt a similar approach, tailored to accommodate the relatively small size of the field $\mathbb{F}_q$ (for instance, in MAYO, $\mathbb{F}_q = 16$ for all security levels). First, recall that in $\mathcal{F}_{\mathsf{ABB+CertInp}}$, the final equality check (see Item 5) is performed between two vectors of dimension m over $\mathbb{F}_q$. After subtraction, this becomes a check for equality to $\mathbf{0}$ on a vector $\mathbf{z} \in \mathbb{F}_q^m$, where each entry is"secret-shared." Assume that $q^m \gg 2^\kappa$, which holds in the OV-based setting[7] (in MAYO, for example, $q^m = 2^{256}$ for security level 1). Let τ be chosen so that $q^\tau \approx 2^\kappa$. We first compress the equality check by taking τ linear combinations of the entries in $\mathbf{z}$ with public random coefficients from $\{0, 1\}$. With probability at least $1 - 2^{-\kappa}$, if $\mathbf{z} \neq 0$, then at least one of these linear combinations will be non-zero. Therefore, it suffices to check whether each of these τ combinations is zero. Let $\mathbf{w} \in \mathbb{F}_q^\tau$ represent these τ linear combinations. We then treat $\mathbf{w}$ not as a vector of dimension τ over $\mathbb{F}_q$ but as a single element W in the extension

[7] If $q^m \approx 2^\kappa$ or $q^m \ll 2^\kappa$, the protocol step involving "subset sums" can be omitted.

field $\mathbb{F}_{q^\tau}$. This allows us to perform a single zero-check on W, which is feasible because W now belongs to a sufficiently large field.

Note that for this approach to work, the ABB model must support arithmetic not only over $\mathbb{F}_q$, but also over the extension field $\mathbb{F}_{q^\tau}$. While operations over $\mathbb{F}_{q^\tau}$ can be implemented using arithmetic over $\mathbb{F}_q$, a straightforward approach may lead to an overhead of approximately m^2 for multiplications, as each product in $\mathbb{F}_{q^\tau}$ would require about m^2 multiplications in $\mathbb{F}_q$. Therefore, we assume the ABB model can natively support arithmetic over $\mathbb{F}_{q^\tau}$, which can be instantiated directly for better efficiency, avoiding the overhead associated with "emulating" $\mathbb{F}_{q^\tau}$ arithmetic via $\mathbb{F}_q$.

Remark 4. If $q^\tau \ll 2^\kappa$, we can simply append zeros. Conversely, if $q^\tau \gg 2^\kappa$, we can improve the zero-check by taking $\log(\kappa)$ linear combinations of $\boldsymbol{z}$ with random public 0/1 vectors (sampled using coin). This produces a vector in $\mathbb{F}_q^{\log(\kappa)}$ that is zero if and only if $\boldsymbol{z} = 0$, with overwhelming probability.

Protocol 5: $\Pi_{\mathsf{ABB+CertInp}}$

The protocol is set in the $\mathcal{F}_{\mathsf{ABB}}$-hybrid. All the commands except for (solve) are forwarded directly to $\mathcal{F}_{\mathsf{ABB}}$.
On input (verify, $[\![\mathbf{t}]\!]$, $[\![\mathbf{S}]\!]$, pk), the parties execute:

1. Parse $(\{\mathbf{P}_i^{(1)}\}_{\{i\in[m]\}}, \{\mathbf{P}_i^{(2)}\}_{\{i\in[m]\}}, \{\mathbf{P}_i^{(3)}\}_{\{i\in[m]\}})$ from pk.
2. For i from 1 to m, call: $[\![\mathbf{Y}_i]\!] \leftarrow [\![\mathbf{S}]\!] \begin{pmatrix} \mathbf{P}_i^{(1)} & \mathbf{P}_i^{(2)} \\ \mathbf{0} & \mathbf{P}_i^{(3)} \end{pmatrix} [\![\mathbf{S}^\mathsf{T}]\!]$
3. Locally compute: $[\![\mathbf{y}]\!] \leftarrow [\![\mathsf{OV\text{-}based.Compute\_y}(\{\mathbf{Y}_i\}_{i\in[m]})]\!]$, followed by $[\![\mathbf{z}]\!] \leftarrow [\![\mathbf{y}]\!] - [\![\mathbf{t}]\!]$.
4. For $i \in [\tau]$, call $(\alpha_{1i}, \ldots, \alpha_{mi}) \leftarrow \mathsf{coin}(\{0,1\})$.
5. For $i \in [\tau]$, locally compute: $[\![w_i]\!] \leftarrow \sum_{j=1}^{m} \alpha_{ji} \cdot [\![z_j]\!]$, where $\mathbf{z} = (z_1, \ldots, z_m)$. Let $\boldsymbol{w} = (w_1, \ldots, w_m)$.
6. Interpret $[\![\mathbf{w}]\!]$ as $[\![W]\!]$, where $W \in \mathbb{F}_{q^\tau}$ (a local operation). Call $[\![R]\!] \leftarrow \mathsf{rand}(\mathbb{F}_{q^\tau})$.
7. Call $[\![R \cdot W]\!] \leftarrow [\![R]\!] \cdot [\![W]\!]$.
8. Open $U \leftarrow [\![R \cdot W]\!]$. If $U = 0$, output (accept); else, output (reject).

Theorem 3. *Protocol* $\Pi_{\mathsf{ABB+CertInp}}$ *instantiates* $\mathcal{F}_{\mathsf{ABB+CertInp}}$ *in the* $\mathcal{F}_{\mathsf{ABB}}$*-hybrid model.*

Proof (Sketch). We do not provide a full simulation-based proof but instead, outline the main security arguments. The protocol mirrors the steps of $\mathcal{F}_{\mathsf{ABB+CertInp}}$ within the ABB model, with the main subtlety arising in the final equality check. Security follows from the following observations:

- If there exists any $z_j \neq 0$, then with probability at least $1 - q^{-\tau} \approx 1 - 2^{-\kappa}$, at least one of the linear combinations w_j will also be non-zero.

– If $W = 0$, then $R \cdot W = 0$. Otherwise, when $W \neq 0$, $R \cdot W$ appears uniformly random over $\mathbb{F}_{q^\tau}$ (which can be simulated). This value is zero only if $R = 0$, which occurs with negligible probability, as $q^\tau \approx 2^\kappa$.

7 Instantiation, Costs and Optimizations

Our different protocols and procedures have been described in the ABB model from Sect. 2.2, with the goal of making the presentation general and applicable to many different security settings and concrete constructions. However, once a concrete security scenario is considered, instantiating the ABB and applying it to our protocols lends itself to several optimizations that can noticeably boost the efficiency of the final result. In this section, we discuss concrete instantiations and several optimizations that can be done to our protocols (see Sect. 7.1). Note that our scheme supports adaptive corruption of parties, as long as the instantiation of the ABB model does. We also discuss the approximate costs of our protocols (see Sect. 7.2).

7.1 Optimizations to Our Threshold Signature Protocol

Given a concrete security setting (a dishonest or honest majority setting, for example), we can apply several optimizations to our generic protocol Π_{ThrSign} that exploits certain specific properties. We discuss them in the following.

Dishonest Majority for Π_{ThrSign}. For a dishonest majority setting, the following optimizations/observations can be applied to Π_{Solve}, which is used inside Π_{ThrSign}.

Matrix triples. As observed in [Che+20,MZ17], Beaver's approach [Bea92] can be optimised in the case in which two matrices are being multiplied. In a naive implementation, multiplying two matrices $(\mathbf{A}, \mathbf{B})$ of dimensions $n \times m$ and $m \times \ell$, respectively, requires a total of $nm\ell$ individual multiplications. Since the ABB model provides only field multiplications by default, our protocols and procedures effectively translate matrix products into $nm\ell$ secure multiplications, leading to significant computational overhead. The key insight from the aforementioned works is that by preparing *matrix triples* instead of individual triples, the cost of the online phase can be reduced from $O(nm\ell)$ to $O(nm + m\ell)$.

The technique can be summarized as follows. Let $[\![\cdot]\!]$ denote the secret-sharing scheme used (additive secret-sharing with MACs, for example). To multiply two secret-shared matrices $[\![\mathbf{X}]\!]$ and $[\![\mathbf{Y}]\!]$, the parties first preprocess a triple $([\![\mathbf{A}]\!], [\![\mathbf{B}]\!], [\![\mathbf{C}]\!])$, where $\mathbf{A}$ and $\mathbf{B}$ are random n-by-m and m-by-ℓ matrices, respectively, and $\mathbf{C} = \mathbf{A} \cdot \mathbf{B}$. In the online phase, the parties then locally compute and open the values $\mathbf{D} \leftarrow [\![\mathbf{X}]\!] - [\![\mathbf{A}]\!]$ and $\mathbf{E} \leftarrow [\![\mathbf{Y}]\!] - [\![\mathbf{B}]\!]$. Then, they locally compute the product and output: $[\![\mathbf{X} \cdot \mathbf{Y}]\!] \leftarrow \mathbf{D} \cdot [\![\mathbf{B}]\!] + [\![\mathbf{A}]\!] \cdot \mathbf{E} + \mathbf{D} \cdot \mathbf{E} + [\![\mathbf{C}]\!]$. The cost of these openings is $O(nm + m\ell)$, which is substantially lower than the naive approach $O(nm\ell)$ for meaningful parameter regimes.

The generation of the matrices $(\llbracket \mathbf{A} \rrbracket, \llbracket \mathbf{B} \rrbracket, \llbracket \mathbf{C} \rrbracket)$ can vary in costs depending on the specific instantiation. While a naive approach would still require $O(nm\ell)$ products, [Che+20] presents a more efficient method that leverages the structural properties of these matrix triples, significantly reducing the overall cost compared to a generic set of $nm\ell$ arbitrary products.

Products by a random matrix. In various stages of our protocol and procedures, parties need to compute the product between a given secret-shared matrix $\llbracket \mathbf{X} \rrbracket$ and a newly sampled shared matrix $\llbracket \mathbf{Y} \rrbracket$, which is generated using the ABB command rand. Notably, by leveraging the matrix triple concept discussed earlier, we can reduce the communication overhead in the online phase by half. The procedure is as follows. After obtaining $\llbracket \mathbf{X} \rrbracket$, parties generate a matrix triple $(\llbracket \mathbf{A} \rrbracket, \llbracket \mathbf{B} \rrbracket, \llbracket \mathbf{C} \rrbracket)$ in the offline phase. They then locally compute and open the value $\mathbf{D} \leftarrow \llbracket \mathbf{X} \rrbracket - \llbracket \mathbf{A} \rrbracket$. Next, they locally compute the product $\llbracket \mathbf{X} \cdot \mathbf{B} \rrbracket \leftarrow \mathbf{D} \cdot \llbracket \mathbf{B} \rrbracket + \llbracket \mathbf{C} \rrbracket$. By setting $\llbracket \mathbf{Y} \rrbracket := \llbracket \mathbf{B} \rrbracket$, the parties effectively obtain $\llbracket \mathbf{X} \cdot \mathbf{Y} \rrbracket$ for a random $\mathbf{Y}$, as required. Importantly, this approach only incurs the cost of *one* matrix opening instead of the two that would be necessary for an implementation.

Honest Majority for Π_{ThrSign}. For an honest majority setting, the following optimizations/observations can be applied to Π_{ThrSign}.

Late Degree-Reduction for Matrix Products. While matrix triples can be effectively utilized in the honest majority context, an alternative approach that circumvents the need for preprocessing triples may be more advantageous. As previously mentioned, in an honest majority scenario, it is common to perform local multiplications that increase the polynomial degree from t to $2t$, followed by degree reduction using double sharings to revert to degree t. A significant benefit of this method is that it allows the parties to compute dot products with the same cost as a single product. Specifically, they can locally multiply the terms, raising the degree to $2t$. Instead of individually reducing the degree of each product, they first sum the degree-$2t$ sharings, yielding degree-$2t$ sharings of the desired dot product, which can subsequently be reduced. By applying this strategy to matrix multiplication, the product of an n-by-m with an m-by-ℓ matrix can be computed with communication complexity proportional to $O(n \times \ell)$, significantly improving upon the naive complexity $O(nm\ell)$ (and, in fact, this is better than the matrix triple approach if m is substantially large).

Active Security with Sublinear Overhead. This observation highlights a crucial aspect of our protocols rather than a straightforward optimization. Our construction is fundamentally based on the ABB model, which inherently requires only secure additions and multiplications. Recent advancements in actively secure honest majority MPC leverage techniques known as *distributed zero-knowledge* [Bon+19], which ensure that the overhead compared to passive security is minimal (specifically, *sublinear* in the number of multiplications performed). These techniques are particularly effective for verifying multiplications, aligning well with our objectives. This is significant, as many other threshold signature schemes, such as those based on elliptic curve cryptography (e.g., ECDSA), necessitate additional operations like group exponentiations. The fact that OV-based signatures schemes require only additions and multiplications is a pivotal advantage: it enables the use of novel methodologies in *generic* MPC.

7.2 Concrete Costs of Our Protocols

In the following, we conduct an approximate evaluation of the practicality of our protocols, focusing on both round complexity and computational time. We calculate the number of rounds required for each protocol (specifically, for Π_{ThrSign}), assuming that each depth of multiplication takes one round, coin sampling requires two rounds, and linear and random operations are performed locally. Since the computation time of these protocols is primarily influenced by the secure multiplications, we provide an inventory of the multiplications executed.

Key generation: π_{KeyGen}**.** Looking at the procedure, we see that Item 1 and Item 2 (sampling of random values) take two rounds. The multiplications needed for Item 7 and Item 4 take two additional rounds. A final round is required for Item 6. This results in a total of 5 rounds for key generation

The multiplications performed in this procedure are: m matrix multiplications of dimension $o \times (n - o)$ and $(n - o) \times o$, and m matrix multiplications of dimension $(n - o) \times (n - o)$ and $(n - o) \times o$.

Signature generation: π_{Sign}**.** Looking at the procedure, we see that Item 1 (sample of salt) takes two rounds. In parallel, one depth of multiplication is required for Item 3 and Item 4, which results in an extra round. For the procedure solving the system of equations (Π_{Solve}), two depths of multiplications are required for Item 3 and one extra round to open the value in Item 4. In case $\mathbf{T}$ is full-rank, 3 more rounds are required to compute a solution to the system (see from Item 6 onwards). Finally, two rounds are required to transform the solution to the system into a signature and reveal it (see Item 8). In total, it takes 9 rounds to perform signing assuming one finds a solution to the system of equations in the first try. Assuming a probability of success p of solving the system of equations, we can compute the average round complexity as $6 + \frac{1}{p} \cdot 3$ (in the current protocol, we would have $p \approx 1 - \frac{2}{q}$).

The multiplications performed in this procedure are:

- m matrix multiplications of dimension $k \times (n - o)$ and $(n - o) \times o$.
- m matrix multiplications of dimension $(n - o) \times (n - o)$ and $(n - o) \times k$.
- 2 matrix multiplication of dimension $m \times ko$ and $ko \times ko$.
- 1 matrix multiplication of dimension $m \times m$ and $m \times ko$.
- 1 multiplication of a matrix of dimension $m \times m$ with a vector $\in m$.
- 1 multiplication of a matrix of dimension $ko \times ko$ with a vector $\in ko$.
- 1 matrix multiplication of dimension $ko \times o$ and $o \times (n - o)$.

Verification of inputs: $\Pi_{\mathsf{ABB+CertInp}}$. Looking at the protocol, we see that it requires a depth of two multiplications (see Item 2 and Item 7) and one reveal (see Item 8). In Item 4 coin sampling is called, which can be started in parallel with the first multiplication. This leads to a 4 round protocol.

The multiplications performed in this procedure are: m matrix multiplications of dimension $k \times n$ and $n \times k$. The computational cost of these algorithms is primarily driven by the m multiplications required. Threshold variants of MAYO can be more costly than those of UOV, due to the parameter k, which directly increases the total multiplication cost. For example, at security level 1, MAYO uses $k = 9$, whereas UOV consistently sets $k = 1$.

Acknowledgments. We would like to thank Ward Beullens, Lisa Kohl and Yashvanth Kondi for their helpful discussions and insight.

This paper was prepared in part for information purposes by the Artificial Intelligence Research group of JPMorgan Chase & Co and its affiliates ("JP Morgan"), and is not a product of the Research Department of JP Morgan. JP Morgan makes no representation and warranty whatsoever and disclaims all liability, for the completeness, accuracy or reliability of the information contained herein. This document is not intended as investment research or investment advice, or a recommendation, offer or solicitation for the purchase or sale of any security, financial instrument, financial product or service, or to be used in any way for evaluating the merits of participating in any transaction, and shall not constitute a solicitation under any jurisdiction or to any person, if such solicitation under such jurisdiction or to such person would be unlawful.

References

[ADN06] Almansa, J.F., Damgård, I., Nielsen, J.B.: Simplified threshold RSA with adaptive and proactive security. In: Vaudenay, S. (ed.) EUROCRYPT 2006. LNCS, vol. 4004, pp. 593–611. Springer, Heidelberg (2006). https://doi.org/10.1007/11761679_35

[Adr24] Adrian, D.: Post-quantum cryptography is too damn big. Personal blogpost. (2024). https://dadrian.io/blog/posts/pqcsignatures-2024/

[Ala+24] Alagic, G., et al.: Status Report on the First Round of the Additional Digital Signature Schemes for the NIST Post-Quantum Cryptography Standardization Process. National Institute of Standards and Technology (2024). https://doi.org/10.6028/NIST.IR.8528

[Ara+21] Aranha, D.F., Dalskov, A., Escudero, D., Orlandi, C.: Improved threshold signatures, proactive secret sharing, and input certification from LSS isomorphisms. In: Longa, P., Ràfols, C. (eds.) LATINCRYPT 2021. LNCS, vol. 12912, pp. 382–404. Springer, Cham (2021). https://doi.org/10.1007/978-3-030-88238-9_19

[ASY22] Agrawal, S., Stehlé, D., Yadav, A.: Round-optimal lattice-based threshold signatures, revisited. In: Bojanczyk, M., Merelli, E., Woodruff, D.P. (eds.) ICALP 2022, vol. 229. LIPIcs. Schloss Dagstuhl, July 2022, pp. 8:1–8:20 (2022). https://doi.org/10.4230/LIPIcs.ICALP.2022.8

[Aul+23a] Aulbach, T., Campos, F., Krämer, J., Samardjiska, S., Stöttinger, M.: Separating oil and vinegar with a single trace. Cryptology ePrint Archive, Report 2023/335 (2023). https://eprint.iacr.org/2023/335

[Aul+23b] Aulbach, T., Campos, F., Krämer, J., Samardjiska, S., Stöttinger, M.: Separating oil and vinegar with a single trace side-channel assisted Kipnis-Shamir attack on UOV. In: IACR TCHES 2023.3, pp. 221–245 (2023). https://doi.org/10.46586/tches.v2023.i3.221-245

[Bea92] Beaver, D.: Efficient multiparty protocols using circuit randomization. In: Feigenbaum, J. (ed.) CRYPTO 1991. LNCS, vol. 576, pp. 420–432. Springer, Heidelberg (1992). https://doi.org/10.1007/3-540-46766-1_34

[Beu20] Beullens, W.: Improved Cryptanalysis of UOV and Rainbow. Cryptology ePrint Archive, Report 2020/1343 (2020). https://eprint.iacr.org/2020/1343

[Beu21] Beullens, W.: MAYO: practical post-quantum signatures from oil-and-vinegar maps. Cryptology ePrint Archive, Report 2021/1144 (2021). https://eprint.iacr.org/2021/1144

[Beu+23a] Beullens, W., Campos, F., Celi, S., Hess, B., Kannwischer, M.J.: MAYO. Technical report. National Institute of Standards and Technology (2023). https://csrc.nist.gov/Projects/pqc-dig-sig/round-1-additional-signatures

[Beu+23b] Beullens, W., et al.: UOV - Unbalanced Oil and Vinegar. Technical report. National Institute of Standards and Technology (2023). https://csrc.nist.gov/Projects/pqc-dig-sig/round-1-additional-signatures

[Beu+23c] Beullens, W., et al.: Oil and vinegar: modern parameters and implementations. In: IACR TCHES 2023.3, pp. 321–365 (2023). https://doi.org/10.46586/tches.v2023.i3.321-365

[Beu24] Beullens, W.: Improved cryptanalysis of SNOVA. Cryptology ePrint Archive, Paper 2024/1297 (2024). https://eprint.iacr.org/2024/1297

[BJ18] Blanton, M., Jeong, M.: Improved signature schemes for secure multi-party computation with certified inputs. In: Lopez, J., Zhou, J., Soriano, M. (eds.) ESORICS 2018. Lecture Notes in Computer Science, vol. 11099, pp. 438–460. Springer, Cham (2018). https://doi.org/10.1007/978-3-319-98989-1_22

[BKP13] Bendlin, R., Krehbiel, S., Peikert, C.: How to share a lattice trapdoor: threshold protocols for signatures and (H)IBE. In: Jacobson, M., Locasto, M., Mohassel, P., Safavi-Naini, R. (eds.) ACNS 2013. LNCS, vol. 7954, pp. 218–236. Springer, Heidelberg (2013). https://doi.org/10.1007/978-3-642-38980-1_14

[BMP22] Blokh, C., Makriyannis, N., Peled, U.: Efficient asymmetric threshold ECDSA for MPC-based cold storage. Cryptology ePrint Archive, Paper 2022/1296 (2022). https://eprint.iacr.org/2022/1296

[Bol03] Boldyreva, A.: Threshold signatures, multisignatures and blind signatures based on the gap-Diffie-Hellman-group signature scheme. In: Desmedt, Y.G. (ed.) PKC 2003. LNCS, vol. 2567, pp. 31–46. Springer, Heidelberg (2003). https://doi.org/10.1007/3-540-36288-6_3

[Bon+19] Boneh, D., Boyle, E., Corrigan-Gibbs, H., Gilboa, N., Ishai, Y.: Zero-knowledge proofs on secret-shared data via fully linear PCPs. In: Boldyreva, A., Micciancio, D. (eds.) CRYPTO 2019. LNCS, vol. 11694, pp. 67–97. Springer, Cham (2019). https://doi.org/10.1007/978-3-030-26954-8_3

[Bos+24] Boschini, C., Kaviani, D., Lai, R.W.F., Malavolta, G., Takahashi, A., Tibouchi, M.: Ringtail: practical two-round threshold signatures from learning with errors. cryptology ePrint Archive, Paper 2024/1113 (2024). https://eprint.iacr.org/2024/1113

[Cab+24] Cabarcas, D., Li, P., Verbel, J., Villanueva-Polanco, R.: Improved Attacks for SNOVA by Exploiting Stability under a Group Action. Cryptology ePrint Archive, Paper 2024/1770 (2024). https://eprint.iacr.org/2024/1770

[Can01] Canetti, R.: Universally composable security: a new paradigm for cryptographic protocols. In: 42nd FOCS, pp. 136–145. IEEE Computer Society Press, October 2001. https://doi.org/10.1109/SFCS.2001.959888

[Can+02] Canetti, R., Lindell, Y., Ostrovsky, R., Sahai, A.: Universally composable two-party and multi-party secure computation. Cryptology ePrint Archive, Report 2002/140 (2002). https://eprint.iacr.org/2002/140

[Cas+19] Castagnos, G., Catalano, D., Laguillaumie, F., Savasta, F., Tucker, I.: Two-Party ECDSA from hash proof systems and efficient instantiations. In: Boldyreva, A., Micciancio, D. (eds.) CRYPTO 2019. LNCS, vol. 11694, pp. 191–221. Springer, Cham (2019). https://doi.org/10.1007/978-3-030-26954-8_7

[CDP22] Chatterjee, S., Laxman Das, M.P., Pandit, T.: Revisiting the security of salted UOV signature. In: Isobe, T., Sarkar, S. (eds.) INDOCRYPT 2022, Vol. 13774, pp. 697–719. LNCS. Springer, Cham (2022). https://doi.org/10.1007/978-3-031-22912-1_31

[Che+20] Chen, H., Kim, M., Razenshteyn, I., Rotaru, D., Song, Y., Wagh, S.: Maliciously secure matrix multiplication with applications to private deep learning. In: Moriai, S., Wang, H. (eds.) ASIACRYPT 2020. LNCS, vol. 12493, pp. 31–59. Springer, Cham (2020). https://doi.org/10.1007/978-3-030-64840-4_2

[Cog+24] Cogliati, B., Fouque, P.-A., Goubin, L., Minaud, B.: New security proofs and techniques for hash-and-sign with retry signature schemes. Cryptology ePrint Archive, Paper 2024/609 (2024). https://eprint.iacr.org/2024/609

[CS19] Cozzo, D., Smart, N.P.: Sharing the LUOV: threshold post-quantum signatures. In: Albrecht, M. (ed.) IMACC 2019. LNCS, vol. 11929, pp. 128–153. Springer, Cham (2019). https://doi.org/10.1007/978-3-030-35199-1_7

[Des90] Desmedt, Y.: Abuses in cryptography and how to fight them. In: Goldwasser, S. (ed.) CRYPTO 1988. LNCS, vol. 403, pp. 375–389. Springer, New York (1990). https://doi.org/10.1007/0-387-34799-2_29

[DF90] Desmedt, Y., Frankel, Y.: Threshold cryptosystems. In: Brassard, G. (ed.) CRYPTO 1989. LNCS, vol. 435, pp. 307–315. Springer, New York (1990). https://doi.org/10.1007/0-387-34805-0_28

[DM20] De Feo, L., Meyer, M.: Threshold schemes from isogeny assumptions. In: Kiayias, A., Kohlweiss, M., Wallden, P., Zikas, V. (eds.) PKC 2020. LNCS, vol. 12111, pp. 187–212. Springer, Cham (2020). https://doi.org/10.1007/978-3-030-45388-6_7

[DN07] Damgård, I., Nielsen, J.B.: Scalable and unconditionally secure multiparty computation. In: Menezes, A. (ed.) CRYPTO 2007. LNCS, vol. 4622, pp. 572–590. Springer, Heidelberg (2007). https://doi.org/10.1007/978-3-540-74143-5_32

[Doe+18] Doerner, J., Kondi, Y., Lee, E., Shelat, A.: Secure two-party threshold ECDSA from ECDSA assumptions. In: 2018 IEEE Symposium on Security and Privacy. IEEE Computer Society Press, pp. 980–997, May 2018. https://doi.org/10.1109/SP.2018.00036

[Doe+19] Doerner, J., Kondi, Y., Lee, E., Shelat, A.: Threshold ECDSA from ECDSA assumptions: the multiparty case. In: 2019 IEEE Symposium on Security and Privacy, pp. 1051–1066. IEEE Computer Society Press, May 2019. https://doi.org/10.1109/SP.2019.00024

[Doe+23] Doerner, J., Kondi, Y., Lee, E., Shelat, A.: Threshold ECDSA in three rounds. Cryptology ePrint Archive, Paper 2023/765 (2023). https://eprint.iacr.org/2023/765

[ENP24] Espitau, T., Niot, G., Prest, T.: Flood and submerse: distributed key generation and robust threshold signature from lattices. Cryptology ePrint Archive, Paper 2024/959 (2024). https://eprint.iacr.org/2024/959

[Gar+21] Garillot, F., Kondi, Y., Mohassel, P., Nikolaenko, V.: Threshold Schnorr with stateless deterministic signing from standard assumptions. In: Malkin, T., Peikert, C. (eds.) CRYPTO 2021. LNCS, vol. 12825, pp. 127–156. Springer, Cham (2021). https://doi.org/10.1007/978-3-030-84242-0_6

[Gen+07] Gennaro, R., Jarecki, S., Krawczyk, H., Rabin, T.: Secure distributed key generation for discrete-log based cryptosystems. J. Cryptol. **20**(1), 51–83 (2006). https://doi.org/10.1007/s00145-006-0347-3

[GG19] Gennaro, R., Goldfeder, S.: Fast Multiparty threshold ECDSA with fast trustless setup. Cryptology ePrint Archive, Report 2019/114 (2019). https://eprint.iacr.org/2019/114

[GGN16] Gennaro, R., Goldfeder, S., Narayanan, A.: Threshold optimal DSA/ECDSA signatures and an application to Bitcoin wallet security. Cryptology ePrint Archive, Report 2016/013 (2016). https://eprint.iacr.org/2016/013

[GJ90] Garey, M.R., Johnson, D.S.: Computers and Intractability; A Guide to the Theory of NP-Completeness. W. H. Freeman & Co., USA (1990). ISBN: 0716710455

[Kat23] Katz, J.: Round optimal fully secure distributed key generation. Cryptology ePrint Archive, Paper 2023/1094 (2023). https://eprint.iacr.org/2023/1094

[KG20] Komlo, C., Goldberg, I.: FROST: flexible round-optimized Schnorr threshold signatures. In: Dunkelman, O., Jacobson, Jr., M.J., O'Flynn, C. (eds.) SAC 2020. LNCS, vol. 12804, pp. 34–65. Springer, Cham (2021). https://doi.org/10.1007/978-3-030-81652-0_2

[Kha+22] Khaburzaniya, I., Chalkias, K., Lewi, K., Malvai, H.: Aggregating and thresholdizing hash-based signatures using STARKs. In: Suga, Y., Sakurai, K., Ding, X., Sako, K. ASIACCS 2022, pp. 393–407. ACM Press (2022). https://doi.org/10.1145/3488932.3524128

[Kon+21] Kondi, Y., Magri, B., Orlandi, C., Shlomovits, O.: Refresh When you wake up: proactive threshold wallets with offline devices. In: 2021 IEEE Symposium on Security and Privacy, pp. 608–625. IEEE Computer Society Press, May 2021. https://doi.org/10.1109/SP40001.2021.00067

[KPG99] Kipnis, A., Patarin, J., Goubin, L.: Unbalanced oil and vinegar signature schemes. In: Stern, J. (ed.) EUROCRYPT 1999. LNCS, vol. 1592, pp. 206–222. Springer, Heidelberg (1999). https://doi.org/10.1007/3-540-48910-X_15

[KS98] Kipnis, A., Shamir, A.: Cryptanalysis of the oil and vinegar signature scheme. In: Krawczyk, H. (ed.) CRYPTO 1998. LNCS, vol. 1462, pp. 257–266. Springer, Heidelberg (1998). https://doi.org/10.1007/BFb0055733

[KX22] Kosuge, H., Xagawa, K.: Probabilistic hash-and-sign with retry in the quantum random oracle model. Cryptology ePrint Archive, Paper 2022/1359 (2022). https://eprint.iacr.org/2022/1359

[KX24] Kosuge, H., Xagawa, K.: Probabilistic hash-and-sign with retry in the quantum random oracle model. In: Tang, Q., Teague, V. (eds.) PKC 2024, Part I, vol. 14601. LNCS, pp. 259–288. Springer, Cham (2024). https://doi.org/10.1007/978-3-031-57718-5_9

[Lin20] Yehuda Lindell. Secure Multiparty Computation (MPC). Cryptology ePrint Archive, Report 2020/300. https://eprint.iacr.org/2020/300. 2020

[Lin24] Lindell, Y.: Simple Three-Round Multiparty Schnorr Signing with Full Simulatability. In: CiC 1.1, p. 25 (2024). DOI:https://doi.org/10.62056/a36c0l5vt

[LNR18] Lindell, Y., Nof, A., Ranellucci, S.: Fast secure multiparty ECDSA with practical distributed key generation and applications to cryptocurrency custody. Cryptology ePrint Archive, Report 2018/987 (2018). https://eprint.iacr.org/2018/987

[Mak22] Makriyannis, N.: On the classic protocol for MPC Schnorr signatures. Cryptology ePrint Archive, Paper 2022/1332 (2022). https://eprint.iacr.org/2022/1332

[MI88] Matsumoto, T., Imai, H.: Public quadratic polynomial-tuples for efficient signature-verification and message-encryption. In: Barstow, D., Brauer, W., Brinch Hansen, P., Gries, D., Luckham, D., Moler, C., Pnueli, A., Seegmüller, G., Stoer, J., Wirth, N., Günther, C.G. (eds.) EUROCRYPT 1988. LNCS, vol. 330, pp. 419–453. Springer, Heidelberg (1988). https://doi.org/10.1007/3-540-45961-8_39

[MZ17] Mohassel, P., Zhang, Y.: SecureML: a system for scalable privacy-preserving machine learning. In: 2017 IEEE Symposium on Security and Privacy, pp. 19–38. IEEE Computer Society Press, May 2017. https://doi.org/10.1109/SP.2017.12

[NIS22] NIST Computer Security Division. Post-Quantum Cryptography: Digital Signature Schemes (2022). https://csrc.nist.gov/projects/pqc-dig-sig

[OSS84] Ong, H., Schnorr, C.P., Shamir, A.: Efficient signature schemes based on polynomial equations (preliminary version). In: Blakley, G.R., Chaum, D. (eds.) CRYPTO 1984. LNCS, vol. 196, pp. 37–46. Springer, Heidelberg (1985). https://doi.org/10.1007/3-540-39568-7_4

[Pat00] Patarin, J.: Cryptanalysis of the Matsumoto and Imai public key scheme of Eurocrypt' 88. In: Coppersmith, D. (ed.) CRYPTO 1995. LNCS, vol. 963, pp. 248–261. Springer, Heidelberg (1995). https://doi.org/10.1007/3-540-44750-4_20

[Pat97] Patarin, J.: The Oil and Vinegar signature scheme. In: Dagstuhl Workshop on Cryptography (1997)

[PB23] Peralta, R., Brandão, L.: NIST first call for multiparty threshold schemes. National Institute of Standards and Technology (2023). https://nvlpubs.nist.gov/nistpubs/ir/2023/NIST.IR.8214C.ipd.pdf

[Pin+24] Del Pino, R., Katsumata, S., Maller, M., Mouhartem, F., Prest, T., Saarinen, M-J.O.: Threshold raccoon: practical threshold signatures from standard lattice assumptions. In: Joye, M., Leander, G. (eds.) EUROCRYPT 2024 Part II, vol. 14652. LNCS, pp. 219–248. Springer, Cham (2024). https://doi.org/10.1007/978-3-031-58723-8_8

[PS15] Pointcheval, D., Sanders, O.: Short randomizable signatures. In: Sako, K. (ed.) CT-RSA 2016. LNCS, vol. 9610, pp. 111–126. Springer, Cham (2016). https://doi.org/10.1007/978-3-319-29485-8_7

[Ruf+22] Ruffing, T., Ronge, V., Jin, E., Schneider-Bensch, J., Schröder, D.: ROAST: Robust asynchronous Schnorr threshold signatures. In: Yin, H., Stavrou, A., Cremers, C., Shi, E. ACM CCS 2022, pp. 2551–2564. ACM Press (2022). https://doi.org/10.1145/3548606.3560583

[Sho99] Shoup, V.: Practical threshold signatures. In: Preneel, B. (ed.) EUROCRYPT 2000. LNCS, vol. 1807, pp. 207–220. Springer, Heidelberg (2000). https://doi.org/10.1007/3-540-45539-6_15

[SSH11] Sakumoto, K., Shirai, T., Hiwatari, H.: On provable security of UOV and HFE signature schemes against chosen-message attack. In: Yang, B.-Y. (ed.) PQCrypto 2011. LNCS, vol. 7071, pp. 68–82. Springer, Heidelberg (2011). https://doi.org/10.1007/978-3-642-25405-5_5

[Wan+23] Wang, L.-C., et al.: SNOVA. Technical report. National Institute of Standards and Technology (2023). https://csrc.nist.gov/Projects/pqc-dig-sig/round-1-additional-signatures

[Wes24] Westerbaan, B.: The state of the post-quantum Internet. Cloudflare blogpost (2024). https://blog.cloudflare.com/pq-2024/

[Wik05] Wikström, D.: Universally composable DKG with linear number of exponentiations. In: Blundo, C., Cimato, S. (eds.) SCN 2004. LNCS, vol. 3352, pp. 263–277. Springer, Heidelberg (2005). https://doi.org/10.1007/978-3-540-30598-9_19

[Yao82] Yao, A.C.-C.: Protocols for secure computations (extended abstract). In: 23rd FOCS, pp. 160–164. IEEE Computer Society Press, November 1982. https://doi.org/10.1109/SFCS198238

SoK: On the Physical Security of UOV-Based Signature Schemes

Thomas Aulbach[1(✉)], Fabio Campos[2], and Juliane Krämer[1]

[1] University of Regensburg, Regensburg, Germany
{thomas.aulbach,juliane.kraemer}@ur.de

[2] Bonn-Rhein-Sieg University of Applied Sciences, Sankt Augustin, Germany
campos@sopmac.de

Abstract. Multivariate cryptography currently centres mostly around UOV-based signature schemes: All multivariate round 2 candidates in the selection process for additional digital signatures by NIST are either UOV itself or close variations of it: MAYO, QR-UOV, SNOVA, and UOV. Also schemes which have been in the focus of the multivariate research community, but are broken by now - like Rainbow and LUOV - are based on UOV. Both UOV and the schemes based on it have been frequently analyzed regarding their physical security in the course of the NIST process. However, a comprehensive analysis regarding the physical security of UOV-based signature schemes is missing.

In this work, we want to bridge this gap and create a comprehensive overview of physical attacks on UOV and its variants from the second round of NIST's selection process for additional post-quantum signature schemes, which just started. First, we collect all existing side-channel and fault attacks on UOV-based schemes and transfer them to the current UOV specification. Since UOV was subject to significant changes over the past few years, e.g., adaptions to the expanded secret key, some attacks need to be reassessed. Next, we introduce new physical attacks in order to obtain an overview as complete as possible. We then show how all these attacks would translate to MAYO, QR-UOV, and SNOVA. To improve the resistance of UOV-based signature schemes towards physical attacks, we discuss and introduce dedicated countermeasures. As related result, we observe that certain implementation decisions, like key compression techniques and randomization choices, also have a large impact on the physical security, in particular on the effectiveness of the considered fault attacks. Finally, we provide implementations of UOV and MAYO for the ARM Cortex-M4 architecture that feature first-order masking and protection against selected fault attacks. We benchmark the resulting overhead on a NUCLEO-L4R5ZI board and validate our approach by performing a TVLA on original and protected subroutines, yielding significantly smaller t-values for the latter.

Author list in alphabetical order; see https://www.ams.org/profession/leaders/CultureStatement04.pdf. This work has been supported by the German Federal Ministry of Education and Research (BMBF) under the project SASPIT (ID 16KIS1858). Furthermore, this work was funded by the Deutsche Forschungsgemeinschaft (DFG, German Research Foundation) - project number 50550035. Date of this document: 2025-01-31.

R. Niederhagen and M.-J. O. Saarinen (Eds.): PQCrypto 2025, LNCS 15577, pp. 199–231, 2025.
https://doi.org/10.1007/978-3-031-86599-2_7

Keywords: Multivariate Cryptography · Physical Security · Fault Attacks · Side-channel Analysis · Masking · ARM Cortex-M4 · TVLA

1 Introduction

At the latest since the standards FIPS 203, FIPS 204, and FIPS 205 have been published, post-quantum cryptography can be considered mature enough for practical use. For practical applications, however, not only standardized schemes are interesting, but also other post-quantum schemes which offer useful alternatives, for instance, regarding key sizes or computation times. Depending on the application, schemes that are not (yet) standardized might be therefore also in demand.

A very promising post-quantum family for signature schemes with interesting properties is multivariate cryptography. Two multivariate signature schemes, including Rainbow [17], also advanced to the third round of NIST's standardization process for post-quantum cryptography (PQC).[1] However, powerful attacks against both schemes showed that these two schemes should not be standardized [8,42]. The two attacks, especially the one on Rainbow by Beullens, brought the unbalanced oil and vinegar (UOV) scheme [29] back into the interest of the research community. Although UOV had already been published at the end of the 1990s and is the basis for Rainbow, research concentrated on Rainbow after its publication because it seemed to be more efficient than UOV both in terms of required memory and computation time. This is also why UOV has initially not been submitted to the NIST PQC standardization process. However, although Rainbow is a generalization of the oil-and-vinegar construction underlying UOV, the sweeping attack on Rainbow does not apply to UOV. This makes UOV again a very interesting signature scheme since it withstands cryptanalysis since more than two decades.

UOV in particular and multivariate signature schemes in general feature very small signatures. Short signatures (and fast verification) were also features of signature schemes NIST was explicitly interested in for their call for additional post-quantum signatures.[2] The goal of this process is to diversify the post-quantum signature standards by selecting additional general-purpose signature schemes not based on structured lattices and schemes that are particularly suitable for certain applications. Hence, it was not surprising that ten out of fourty submissions to the call in 2023 have been based on multivariate cryptography.[3] For three of these schemes - 3WISE, DME, and HPPC - rapidly efficient attacks have been found. The remaining seven schemes all rely on the oil-and-vinegar principle, i.e., are UOV-based: MAYO [11], PROV [23], QR-UOV [20], SNOVA [44], TUOV [19], UOV [12], and VOX [35]. Hence, since then, all multivariate

[1] https://csrc.nist.gov/Projects/post-quantum-cryptography/post-quantum-cryptography-standardization/round-3-submissions.

[2] https://csrc.nist.gov/csrc/media/Projects/pqc-dig-sig/documents/call-for-proposals-dig-sig-sept-2022.pdf.

[3] https://csrc.nist.gov/Projects/pqc-dig-sig/round-1-additional-signatures.

signature schemes which are in the focus of the research community are based on the UOV principle. Very recently, on October 25, 2024 NIST announced the 14 schemes to advance to the next round.[4] The share of multivariate signature schemes even increased slightly, since four of the schemes advanced to round 2: MAYO, QR-UOV, SNOVA, and UOV.

When cryptographic schemes are used in practical applications, not only their mathematical security and efficiency, but also their resistance towards physical attacks is important. Hence, post-quantum schemes have been analyzed with respect to their physical security in recent years, and there is also a line of research targeting multivariate cryptography in general and UOV-based signature schemes in particular.

1.1 State of the Art and Related Work

Starting in 2011 [24], UOV-based signature schemes have been analyzed both with respect to passive, i.e., side-channel, and active, i.e., fault attacks. There are results that specifically target UOV [2,21] or another UOV-based scheme [3, 4,25,32,39,41], but also publications that analyze several schemes [24,31,34].

However, by reading these publications, one does not get a comprehensive picture of the state of the art of the physical security of UOV-based signature schemes. This has several reasons: 1) Some of the schemes have received more attention from the research community than others; simply because of their age, but also because of the existence of a mature implementation. To the best of our knowledge, there was no effort yet to study the transferability of all attacks to all UOV-based signature schemes. 2) Some of the attacks [3,32] targeted schemes that have since been proven to be insecure, like LUOV and Rainbow. Also for these attacks, it is often unknown if and how they transfer to other schemes. 3) Both the specifications of the schemes and their implementations have been subject to various changes and optimizations over time, e.g., the method of generating compressed public keys introduced in [37]. Hence, it is not even clear if the older attacks still remain a realistic threat to the current version of the algorithms. 4) Although attacks are usually published with descriptions of countermeasures, there are limited results about implemented countermeasures and their overhead, or physically secure implementations of multivariate schemes in general. This might also be due to the fact that for a long time there were no common reference implementations that could serve as a basis. 5) Moreover, since the recent history of multivariate signatures is characterized by major breaks and fixes, e.g., [8,18,42], the research community focused initially on the mathematical security of the schemes, which is natural and reasonable.

Now, with NIST's process for standardizing additional digital signature schemes commencing the second round, we have the chance to study all remaining UOV-based schemes on the basis of consistent specifications and implementations. Our goal is to advance their resistance against physical attacks by creating an extensive survey of possible attack vectors, implementing countermeasures, and measuring their overhead directly in comparison to existing implementations.

[4] https://csrc.nist.gov/Projects/pqc-dig-sig/round-2-additional-signatures.

1.2 Contribution

In this project, we provide a comprehensive overview on the physical security of today's most relevant UOV-based signature schemes, i.e., the schemes MAYO, QR-UOV, SNOVA, and UOV, that are being analyzed in the second round of NIST's standardization process for additional signature schemes. While we analyze all four schemes in this work, we specifically focus on UOV and MAYO, since they provide the more advanced implementation: The more practical a physical attack is carried out, the greater its relevance. To practically perform a physical attack, however, a target implementation is needed. Therefore, UOV and MAYO can be considered the most relevant signature schemes in the field of multivariate cryptography with respect to physical attacks. They both provide optimized implementations for the ARM Cortex-M4 architecture and both are analyzed several times in the literature, already.

In this work, we provide a complete overview of known side-channel and fault attacks against UOV-based schemes and derive their core attack vectors. We set out to understand if further vulnerabilities exist. In finding new vulnerabilities, we concentrate on side-channel attacks, since so far most attacks are based on faults. We provide a complete overview for all considered schemes regarding their susceptibility towards physical attacks: For all attacks, both known and new, we analyze if and how they can be transferred to all considered schemes. For all attacks, we provide existing and newly developed countermeasures. Moreover, we describe the effect of certain implementation decisions on the physical security of the schemes and derive implementation guidelines from this.

For UOV and MAYO, based on existing optimized M4 implementations, we provide first-order masked implementations for the ARM Cortex-M4 architecture. Additionally, the implementations include protection against the most relevant fault attacks. We benchmark the resulting overhead on a NUCLEO-L4R5ZI board and validate our approach by performing a test vector leakage assessment (TVLA) on original and protected subroutines, yielding significantly smaller t-values for the latter. Our implementation is available to the public at https://github.com/SoK-Psec-UOV-based/code.

1.3 Organization

In Sect. 2, we discuss the notation used in this work, describe the UOV scheme and the main differences between UOV and MAYO, QR-UOV, and SNOVA, and explain why an attack on a UOV-based scheme often leads to full key recovery once a single oil vector is found. In Sects. 3 and 4, we present a comprehensive collection of fault attacks and side-channel attacks, respectively, on UOV-based signature schemes. We present both known and new attacks, and analyze if they can be transferred to the current specifications of UOV, MAYO, QR-UOV, and SNOVA. In Sect. 5, we describe implementation guidelines that we derived from the analysis of the attacks. In Sect. 6, we present implementations of UOV and MAYO that include protection against selected fault attacks from Sect. 3 and countermeasures against all side-channel attacks from Sect. 4, i.e., are first-order masked. In Sect. 7, we conclude this work.

2 Background

2.1 Notation

In this paper we describe physical attacks and countermeasures to existing UOV-based signature schemes, which are all submitted to NIST's call for additional digital signatures for the PQC standardization process. Thus, we deem it reasonable to use exactly the notations and conventions introduced in the specification of the designated signature scheme. E.g., the discussions on UOV follow the notation given in [12], the findings about MAYO follow the notation in [11], etc. This requires the reader to be cautious at time, since the respective specifications might use different names or variables for similar objects. Nevertheless, we think this is the correct way, since using a fixed notation in here, would force the reader to adjust the notation on their own when referring to different schemes.

2.2 UOV

Here, we would like to recall UOV in its current form and the most important properties. We will also link its abstract mathematical description to the steps listed in the pseudo code.

The main objects in multivariate cryptography are multivariate quadratic maps $\mathcal{P} : \mathbb{F}_q^n \to \mathbb{F}_q^m$. In general, it is hard to find a solution $\mathbf{s} \in \mathbb{F}_q^n$ to a given target $\mathbf{t} \in \mathbb{F}_q^m$ such that $\mathcal{P}(\mathbf{s}) = \mathbf{t}$. This task is also known as the MQ Problem. It can be solved in polynomial time in the very under- or overdetermined case, i.e. $m \geq n(n+1)/2$ or $n \geq m(m+1)$, but is believed to be exponentially hard even for large scale quantum computers if $n \sim m$. By installing a secret trapdoor into the public map $\mathcal{P}$, one can render this task efficiently solvable and construct a signature scheme thereof. In UOV this trapdoor is a m-dimensional linear subspace $O \subset \mathbb{F}_q^n$ - the oil space - with the property $\mathcal{P}(\mathbf{o}) = 0$ for all $\mathbf{o} \in O$. The message μ, together with a random $\texttt{salt}$, is mapped to a target value $\mathbf{t}$ in the codomain $\mathbb{F}_q^m$ using a cryptographic hash function $\mathcal{H}$, i.e. $\mathbf{t} = \mathcal{H}(\mu||\texttt{salt})$. Computing a signature boils down to finding a preimage $\mathbf{s} \in \mathbb{F}_q^n$ with $P(\mathbf{s}) = \mathbf{t}$. To this end one can deploy the following method, if knowledge of the oil space is provided. First, one picks a vector $\mathbf{v}$ at random and then solves the equation

$$\mathcal{P}(\mathbf{v} + \mathbf{o}) = \mathcal{P}(\mathbf{v}) + \mathcal{P}(\mathbf{o}) + \mathcal{P}'(\mathbf{v}, \mathbf{o}) = \mathbf{t} \tag{1}$$

for $\mathbf{o} \in O$. The map $\mathcal{P}' : \mathbb{F}_q^n \times \mathbb{F}_q^n \to \mathbb{F}_q^m$ defined by the equation above, is called the differential of $\mathcal{P}$ and is bilinear and symmetric [6]. Viewing the oil vector $\mathbf{o}$ as a linear combination of its m basis vectors given in O ensures $\mathcal{P}(\mathbf{o}) = \mathbf{0}_m$ and shows clearly that

$$\mathcal{P}'(\mathbf{v}, \mathbf{o}) = \mathbf{t} - \mathcal{P}(\mathbf{v}) \tag{2}$$

is a system of m linear equations in m variables. If there exists a solution, it can be computed efficiently, if not, one samples a new $\mathbf{v}$ and tries again. Together, the vinegar and oil vector yield a preimage $\mathbf{s} = \mathbf{v} + \mathbf{o}$ to the target $\mathbf{t}$, which constitutes the core of the signature.

Key Generation. Within key generation we need to generate the m-dimensional oil space O and a multivariate quadratic map $\mathcal{P} : \mathbb{F}_q^n \rightarrow \mathbb{F}_q^m$ that vanishes on O. The map $\mathcal{P}$ is a sequence of m quadratic polynomials $p_1(\mathbf{x}), \ldots, p_m(\mathbf{x})$ in n variables. The linear and constant part of the polynomials is omitted, and the coefficients of the quadratic monomials can be stored in an upper triangular matrix $\mathbf{P}_i$, such that evaluating the polynomial p_i at a value $\mathbf{a}$ can be realized by computing $p_i(\mathbf{a}) = \mathbf{a}^\top \mathbf{P}_i \mathbf{a}$.

The oil space is chosen to be the space spanned by the rows of a matrix $\bar{\mathbf{O}} = (\mathbf{O}^\top \ \mathbf{I}_m)$, where $\mathbf{O} \in \mathbb{F}_q^{(n-m)\times m}$ is sampled uniformly at random. Thus, to guarantee that the quadratic polynomials p_i vanish on O, i.e. $\mathbf{o}^\top \mathbf{P}_i \mathbf{o} = 0$ for all $\mathbf{o} \in O$, one can set the term

$$(\mathbf{O}^\top \ \mathbf{I}_m) \begin{pmatrix} \mathbf{P}_i^{(1)} & \mathbf{P}_i^{(2)} \\ 0 & \mathbf{P}_i^{(3)} \end{pmatrix} \begin{pmatrix} \mathbf{O} \\ \mathbf{I}_m \end{pmatrix} = \mathbf{O}^\top \mathbf{P}_i^{(1)} \mathbf{O} + \mathbf{O}^\top \mathbf{P}_i^{(2)} + \mathbf{P}_i^{(3)}$$

to zero. This is achieved by sampling $\mathbf{P}_i^{(1)} \in \mathbb{F}_q^{(n-m)\times(n-m)}$ (upper triangular) and $\mathbf{P}_i^{(2)} \in \mathbb{F}_q^{(n-m)\times m}$ uniformly at random and setting $\mathbf{P}_i^{(3)}$ accordingly to

$$\mathbf{P}_i^{(3)} = \mathtt{Upper}(-\mathbf{O}^\top \mathbf{P}_i^{(1)} \mathbf{O} - \mathbf{O}^\top \mathbf{P}_i^{(2)}).$$

The described procedure is exactly the key generation algorithm of UOV, which is depicted in Fig. 1. Hereby, $\mathbf{O}$ and $\mathbf{P}_i^{(1)}, \mathbf{P}_i^{(2)}$ can be expanded from a private or public seed, respectively.

UOV.CompactKeyGen() // $csk = (\mathsf{seed}_{\mathsf{sk}}, \mathsf{seed}_{\mathsf{pk}})$

1 : $\mathsf{seed}_{\mathsf{sk}} \leftarrow \{0,1\}^{\mathsf{sk\_seed\_}len}$
2 : $\mathsf{seed}_{\mathsf{pk}} \leftarrow \{0,1\}^{\mathsf{pk\_seed\_}len}$
3 : $\mathbf{O} \leftarrow \mathsf{Expand}_{\mathsf{sk}}(\mathsf{seed}_{\mathsf{sk}})$
4 : $\{\mathbf{P}_i^{(1)}, \mathbf{P}_i^{(2)}\}_{i\in[m]} \leftarrow \mathsf{Expand}_{P}(\mathsf{seed}_{\mathsf{pk}})$
5 : **for** $j = i, \ldots, m$ **do**
6 : $\quad \mathbf{P}_i^{(3)} \leftarrow \mathtt{Upper}(-\mathbf{O}^\top \mathbf{P}_i^{(1)} \mathbf{O} - \mathbf{O}^\top \mathbf{P}_i^{(2)})$
7 : $cpk \leftarrow (\mathsf{seed}_{\mathsf{pk}}, \{\mathbf{P}_i^{(3)}\}_{i\in[m]})$
8 : $csk \leftarrow (\mathsf{seed}_{\mathsf{pk}}, \mathsf{seed}_{\mathsf{sk}})$
9 : **return** (cpk, csk)

Fig. 1. UOV key generation algorithm

Secret Key Expansion. As indicated above, it is necessary to solve Eq. 2 with respect to $\mathbf{o}$ during signing. The i-th component of $\mathcal{P}'(\mathbf{v}, \mathbf{o})$ is computed by $\mathbf{v}^\top(\mathbf{P}_i + \mathbf{P}_i^\top)\mathbf{o}$ and $\mathbf{o}$ is written as a linear combination of its basis vectors in

$\bar{\mathbf{O}}$, where the coefficients $\mathbf{x}$ are the variables we need to solve for. Thus, we can prepare the term $(\mathbf{P}_i + \mathbf{P}_i^\top)\mathbf{o}$ by setting $\mathbf{S}_i = (\mathbf{P}_i^{(1)} + \mathbf{P}_i^{(1)\top})\mathbf{O} + \mathbf{P}_i^{(2)}$ and store it in the expanded secret key *esk*, since it is independent from the message μ. The coefficients in $\mathbf{P}_i^{(1)}$ are necessary to compute $\mathcal{P}(\mathbf{v})$, so they are also added to *esk*. The pseudo code of the secret key expansion is presented in Fig. 2.

$\mathit{UOV.ExpandSK}(\mathit{csk})$ // $\mathit{csk} = (\mathsf{seed_{sk}}, \mathsf{seed_{pk}})$

$\mathbf{O} \leftarrow \mathsf{Expand_{sk}}(\mathsf{seed_{sk}})$

$\{\mathbf{P}_i^{(1)}, \mathbf{P}_i^{(2)}\}_{i\in[m]} \leftarrow \mathsf{Expand}_{\mathcal{P}}(\mathsf{seed_{pk}})$

for $j = i, \ldots, m$ **do**

$\quad \mathbf{S}_i \leftarrow (\mathbf{P}_i^{(1)} + \mathbf{P}_i^{(1)\top})\mathbf{O} + \mathbf{P}_i^{(2)}$

$\mathit{esk} \leftarrow (\mathsf{seed_{sk}}, \mathbf{O}, \{\mathbf{P}_i^{(1)}, \mathbf{S}_i\}_{i\in[m]})$

return *esk*

Fig. 2. Algorithm that expands csk to esk in UOV

Signing. The signing algorithm is shown in Fig. 3. After generating the `salt` and deriving the target value $\mathbf{t}$, the vinegar vector $\mathbf{v}$ is sampled. Note, that the last m entries of $\mathbf{v}$ are set to zero, which enables a more efficient implementation. With $\mathbf{v}$ at hand, one computes the remaining part of $\mathcal{P}'(\mathbf{v}, \mathbf{o})$ in Line 7, which represents the linear part of the system given in Line 10. In order to evaluate $\mathbf{y} = \mathcal{P}(\mathbf{v})$ in Line 9, only the submatrix $\mathbf{P}_i^{(1)}$ is necessary, since the last entries of $\mathbf{v}$ were chosen to be zero. Solving the derived linear system reveals the coefficients $\mathbf{x}$ of the oil vector $\mathbf{o} = \bar{\mathbf{O}}\mathbf{x} = [\mathbf{O}\mathbf{x}, \mathbf{x}]$. Finally, the sum of the vinegar and oil vector yield the signature $\mathbf{s} = [\mathbf{v}, \mathbf{0}_m] + \bar{\mathbf{O}}\mathbf{x}$.

Public Key Expansion and Verification. To verify that the signer really found a preimage $\mathbf{s}$ under the public map $\mathcal{P}$ of the target vector $\mathbf{t}$, one needs to expand the public coefficients in $\mathbf{P}_i^{(1)}$ and $\mathbf{P}_i^{(2)}$ from the seed and check if $\mathcal{P}(\mathbf{s}) = \mathbf{t}$ really holds. We omit the pseudo code of these two functionalities, since we do not focus on them in the main part of this work.

Variants. We have to differentiate between the variants `uov-classic`, `uov-pkc` and `uov-pkc+skc`. In `uov-pkc+skc` the secret key is stored in a compact way *csk*, such that the function *UOV.ExpandSK* is called before signing with *UOV.Sign* and has to be protected as well. In `uov-classic` and `uov-pkc` *UOV.ExpandSK* is part of the key gen, since the secret key is stored in an expanded manner.

One considerable drawback of UOV are its large public keys, due to the amount of coefficients needed to define the public map $\mathcal{P}$. Even in the variants with compressed public keys `uov-pkc+skc` and `uov-pkc`, where a large fraction

$\mathit{UOV.Sign}(esk, \mu)$ // $esk = (\mathtt{seed}_{sk}, \mathbf{O}, \{\mathbf{P}_i^{(1)}, \mathbf{S}_i\}_{i\in[m]})$

$\mathtt{salt} \leftarrow \{0,1\}^{\mathtt{salt\_len}}$
$\mathbf{t} \leftarrow \mathtt{H}(\mu||\mathtt{salt})$ // $\mathbf{t} \in \mathbb{F}_q^m$
for $ctr = 0, \ldots, 255$ **do**
  $\mathbf{v} \leftarrow \mathbf{Expand}_v(\mu||\mathtt{salt}||\mathtt{seed_{sk}}||ctr)$ // $\mathbf{v} \in \mathbb{F}_q^{n-m}$
  $\mathbf{L} \leftarrow \mathbf{0}_{m\times m}$
  for $i = 1, \ldots, m$ **do**
    Set i-th row of $\mathbf{L}$ to $\mathbf{v}^\top \mathbf{S}_i$
  if L is invertible then
    $\mathbf{y} \leftarrow [\mathbf{v}^\top \mathbf{P}_i^{(1)} \mathbf{v}]_{i\in[m]}$ // $\mathbf{y} \in \mathbb{F}_q^m$
    Solve $\mathbf{Lx} = \mathbf{t} - \mathbf{y}$ for $\mathbf{x}$
    $\mathbf{s} \leftarrow [\mathbf{v}, \mathbf{0}_m] + \bar{\mathbf{O}}\mathbf{x}$ // $\mathbf{s} \in \mathbb{F}_q^n$
    $\sigma \leftarrow (\mathbf{s}, \mathtt{salt})$
    return σ
return 0

Fig. 3. Algorithm that signs a message μ in UOV

of the coefficients is expanded from a short seed, the part $\mathbf{P}_i^{(3)}$ still needs to be stored explicitly and contains around $m^3/2$ coefficients in $\mathbb{F}_q$. Here, one factor m comes from the number of polynomials m in the public map $\mathcal{P}$, but the remaining factor $m^2/2$ depends on the dimension of the oil space $dim(O) = m$, which are chosen to be equal in UOV.

2.3 MAYO, QR-UOV and SNOVA

In [7], Beullens presented MAYO, a signature scheme that also employs the oil-and-vinegar principle but reduces the dimension of the oil space from m to o drastically, which in turn reduces the number of coefficients in $\mathbf{P}_i^{(3)}$ to $mo^2/2$ and eventually shrinks down the public key size. The problem is that one can not simply decrease the dimension of the oil space from m to o, with $o \ll m$ and continue as before, since the system $\mathcal{P}'(\mathbf{v}, \mathbf{o}) = \mathbf{t} - \mathcal{P}(\mathbf{v})$ in Eq. (2) becomes a system of m linear equations in o variables and bears no solution with high probability. Thus an adaption to the signing and verification procedure was necessary and the following solution was suggested: The public key map $\mathcal{P}$ is stretched into a larger whipped map $\mathcal{P}^* : \mathbb{F}_q^{kn} \to \mathbb{F}_q^m$, such that it accepts k input vectors $\mathbf{s} \in \mathbb{F}_q^n$. This is realized by setting

$$\mathcal{P}^*(\mathbf{s}_1, \ldots, \mathbf{s}_k) := \sum_{i=1}^{k} \mathbf{E}_{ii}\mathcal{P}(\mathbf{s}_i) + \sum_{1\le i<j\le k} \mathbf{E}_{ij}\mathcal{P}'(\mathbf{s}_i, \mathbf{s}_j), \tag{3}$$

where the matrices $\mathbf{E}_{ij} \in \mathbb{F}_q^{m\times m}$ are fixed system parameters with the property that all their non-trivial linear combinations have rank m. The map $\mathcal{P}^*$ vanishes on the subspace $O^k = \{(\mathbf{o}_1, \ldots, \mathbf{o}_k) | \text{ with } \mathbf{o}_i \in O \text{ for all } i \in [k]\}$ of dimension ko. This gives back some degrees of freedom when looking for a solution in the new domain $\mathbb{F}_q^{kn}$, i.e. the system obtained from

$$\mathcal{P}^*(\mathbf{v}_1 + \mathbf{o}_1, \ldots, \mathbf{v}_k + \mathbf{o}_k) = \mathbf{t} \tag{4}$$

after randomly sampling and inserting $(\mathbf{v}_1, \ldots, \mathbf{v}_k) \in \mathbb{F}_q^{kn}$, is a system of m linear equations in ko variables. Consequently, if the parameters are chosen such that $ko > m$, it possible to sample signatures $\mathbf{s} = (\mathbf{s}_1, \ldots, \mathbf{s}_k) = (\mathbf{v}_1 + \mathbf{o}_1, \ldots, \mathbf{v}_k + \mathbf{o}_k)$ similar as before, despite the small dimension of the initial oil space O.

Another attempt in reducing the public key size of UOV is made by QR-UOV. It is very similar to UOV, except that elements of a quotient ring $\mathbb{F}_q[x]/(f)$ are employed, instead of just finite field elements $\mathbb{F}_q$. Let l be a positive integer and $f \in \mathbb{F}_q[x]$ of degree l. Then any element g of the quotient ring $\mathbb{F}_q[x]/(f)$ uniquely defines a $l \times l$ matrix Φ_g^f over $\mathbb{F}_q$ such that $(1, x, \ldots, x^{l-1}) \cdot \Phi_g^f = (g, xg, \ldots, x^{l-1}g)$. The mapping from g to its polynomial matrix Φ_g^f is an injective ring homomorphism from $\mathbb{F}_q[x]/(f)$ to $\mathbb{F}_q^{l \times l}$ and every element of $\mathcal{A}_f := \{\Phi_g^f \in \mathbb{F}_q^{l \times l} | g, \in \mathbb{F}_q[x]/(f)\}$ can be represented by only l elements in $\mathbb{F}_q$. For the construction of QR-UOV, the central maps F_i and public maps P_i are set to be composed of such matrices. This additional structure allows that not every element of these maps are stored since l^2 entries of Φ_g^f can be represented by just l coefficients of g. The central maps F_i are secret, easily invertible maps, that allow the signer to generate signatures efficiently. Their structure is hidden via the transformation $P_i = S^\top F_i S$.

SNOVA also work with quotient rings, but apply even more structure to the central and public maps. Each component of the central map $F = [F_1, \ldots, F_m] : \mathcal{R}^n \to \mathcal{R}^m$ is defined by

$$F_i = \sum_{\alpha=1}^{l^2} A_\alpha \cdot \left(\sum_{(j,k) \in \Omega} X_j (Q_{\alpha 1} F_{i,jk} Q_{\alpha 1}) X_k \right) \cdot B_\alpha,$$

where the $F_{i,jk}$ are randomly chosen from $\mathcal{R}$, A_α and B_α are invertible elements randomly chosen from $\mathcal{R}$, and $Q_{\alpha 1}, Q_{\alpha 2}$ are invertible matrices randomly chosen from $\mathbb{F}_q[S]$. Here $\mathcal{R}$ is the matrix ring $\mathbb{F}_q^{(l \times l)}$ and $\mathbb{F}_q[S]$ is a commutative symmetric subring of $\mathcal{R}$. Like in UOV, the public matrices are then set to fulfill the equation $P_i = F_i \circ T$ and therefore, are of similar type than the central matrices.

For more details about MAYO, QR-UOV, and SNOVA we refer to the respective specifications given in [11,20,44].

2.4 One Vinegar or One Oil Vector Is (In Many Cases) Sufficient for Complete Key Recovery

With respect to signature schemes, it is always an interesting task to determine the amount of data that is necessary to forge signatures, especially from an adversarial point of view. When the secret key is just a seed, as in MAYO, it might become infeasible to recover this seed with side-channel attacks. But it still is useful to obtain information about the values of the expanded seed. Conversely, in `uov-classic` the secret key is of enormous size and only a fraction of it suffices to forge signatures. However, for UOV-based signature schemes, there is a pretty and common answer to this problem: knowledge of the employed oil space O allows to efficiently generate signatures. Even more, there are algebraic methods, that allow to recover the entire space in polynomial time as soon as one or several (depending on the concrete dimensions) oil vectors $\mathbf{o} \in O$ are found.

Regarding MAYO, it was already clear from the description in [7, Section 4.1] that one oil vector is enough to efficiently recover O. The case for UOV was treated in [2] and [36], where again only a single oil vector is needed, since all existing UOV parameter sets fulfill the equation $n - m \leq 2m$.

In [36], Pebereau also elaborated on the very unbalanced case, i.e. when $n > 3m$. In this scenario, there might be several oil vectors needed for polynomial time key recovery, namely β of them, where β is the smallest integer such that $n - \beta m \leq 2m$ holds. This becomes interesting, since some parameter sets suggested by QR-UOV and SNOVA lie in the very unbalanced case with $n \geq 6m$ or even up to $n \geq 9m$. In these cases, the security of the scheme might already be compromised when one or two oil vectors are leaked, but attackers are only able to forge signatures in polynomial time, when they get their hands on β of them.

However, if it is possible to reveal one oil vector by means of a physical attack, repeating it on several signing procedures will probably leak more of them. Thus, the attack strategy remains the same, even in the very unbalanced case. Most of the time obtaining a vinegar vector $\mathbf{v}$ is equally strong, since the corresponding oil vector $\mathbf{o}$ can be recovered by subtracting it from the signature $\mathbf{s} = \mathbf{v} + \mathbf{o}$. Consequently, every time one of them is used in a computation, it has to be protected against physical attacks.

3 Fault Attacks on UOV-Based Signatures

In this section, we study the vulnerability of UOV-based signature schemes towards fault attacks. We investigate existing fault attacks on UOV-based signature schemes and provide a more complete catalog of vulnerabilities by also presenting new attacks. Our analysis results in a list of functions that need to be protected in order to achieve an implementation that is more resistant to fault attacks.

We first analyze the vulnerability of UOV, as this scheme builds the base for all remaining signature schemes analyzed in this work. Subsequently, we explain how these attacks translate to the MAYO signature scheme and its current Cortex M4 implementation. Finally, we consider the case of the remaining UOV-based signatures, QR-UOV and SNOVA. We expect these rather young schemes to be subject to various algorithmical changes and code modifications in the future, thus the findings of this work can be seen as a starting point towards their physical security and as a general estimation whether the respective scheme might be vulnerable to this kind of attack.

To provide a better overview of the existing, transferred, and new vulnerabilities, we summarize the findings of this section in Table 1.

Table 1. Overview of existing and new fault attacks on UOV, MAYO, QR-UOV, and SNOVA. Regarding the feasibility of the attacks, we refer to the specifications submitted to the NIST call for additional signatures in mid-2023. When there are differences between the three UOV-variants `uov-classic`, `uov-pkc` and `uov-pkc+skc`, deterministic and randomized MAYO or the variants `SNOVA-esk` and `SNOVA-ssk`, we list them individually in the given order. With ✓ we state that an attack is possible, while ✗ means the opposite. By ⋆ we denote that an attack is generally possible, but the technical execution is more difficult than in the initially presented attack.

Attack description	Source	Initially for	Feasible in current version	Target
Fix vinegar vector	[3,4,24]	Rainbow	UOV: ✓	`UOV.Sign Line 4`
	[25,31,41]	UOV	MAYO: ✓	[11] `Alg.8 Line 16,18`
		MAYO	QR-UOV: ✓	[20] `Alg.2 Line 10`
			SNOVA: ✓	[44] `Alg.11 Line 8`
Rowhammer on oil space O	[32]	LUOV	UOV: ✓ | ✓ | ⋆	
			MAYO: ⋆	uncompressed
			QR-UOV: ⋆	secret key in memory
			SNOVA: ✓ | ⋆	
Bit flip on stored secret matrices	[21,24,31]	Rainbow	UOV: ✓ | ✓ | ⋆	
		UOV	MAYO: ✓ | ✗	uncompressed
			QR-UOV: ⋆	secret key in memory
			SNOVA: ✗	
Prevent addition of oil and vinegar	[39]	MAYO	UOV: ✓	`UOV.Sign Line 11`
			MAYO: ✓	[11] `Alg.8 Line 44`
			QR-UOV: ✗	[20] `Alg.2 Line 18`
			SNOVA: ✗	[44] `Alg.11 Line 14`
Disturb linear system setup	This work	UOV	UOV: ✗	`UOV.Sign Line 7`
			MAYO: ✓ | ✗	[11] `Alg.8 Line 22-33`
			QR-UOV: ✗	[20] `Alg.2 Line 11,12`
			SNOVA: ✗	[44] `Alg.11 Line 9,10`

3.1 Existing Attacks

In the following, we discuss fault attacks against UOV-based schemes that are present in the literature. If the attack was initially not developed for UOV itself, we try to give a detailed analysis of its applicability to UOV.

Fault Injection to Fix the Vinegar Vector. There has been a series of works [3,4,25,31,41] studying the effectiveness of an instruction skip in Line 4 of Fig. 3. These works set the number of necessary faulted signatures to $m = n - v$, which lies in the range from several dozens to hundreds, depending on the security level. Using the findings in [2,36] and [30] it is now clear that one faulted signature is enough for efficient key-recovery. This can be obtained by the following observations.

If the instruction skip is applied successfully, it leads to the reusage of the vinegar variables that are still stored in $\mathbf{v}$ from a previous signing process. Denote the unfaulted previous signature by $\mathbf{s}$ and the faulted signature by $\tilde{\mathbf{s}}$. The oil vectors $\mathbf{o}$ and $\tilde{\mathbf{o}}$, which are computed during the respective signature generation and added to the vinegar vector $\mathbf{v}$, are different, but both are elements of the oilspace O. Thus, we have

$$\tilde{\mathbf{s}} - \mathbf{s} = (\mathbf{v} + \tilde{\mathbf{o}}) - (\mathbf{v} - \mathbf{o}) = \tilde{\mathbf{o}} - \mathbf{o} \in O,$$

since O is a linear subspace of $\mathbb{F}_q^n$. With a secret oil vector at hand, full key recovery can be achieved in a matter of seconds.

In [25], the authors present two attacks - an absorption skipping and absorption abort attack - directly on the SHAKE256 function that is used to derive the vinegar vectors. These lead to an predictable output of the sampling and therefore reveal the vinegar vectors $\mathbf{v}_i$. They do not make any assumptions about the memory initialization of the device. Since they present this attack specifically on MAYO, we will resume to this in Sect. 3.3.

RowHammer to Alter a Value in O. In [32], the authors present a Rowhammer attack to cause bit flips in the secret transformation $\mathbf{T}$ in LUOV and show how this can be exploited to recover individual bits of $\mathbf{T}$. Repeated execution of the fault attack leads to partial knowledge of the secret $\mathbf{T}$, one bit for every faulted signature. Once enough key bits of $\mathbf{T}$ are recovered, the attacker can apply algebraic analysis techniques to increase the efficiency of the attack and limit the number of faulted signatures that need to be obtained for a full key recovery.

Briefly summarized, the QuantumHammer attack works as follows. The secret data is stored in the DRAMs in memory cells. There is a certain threshold of the voltage level that determines whether a capacitor represents a binary one or zero. If one manages to activate neighboring rows rapidly, this can cause variations in the voltage level of the victim cells due to induction. When a certain threshold is passed, this results in a bit-flip from 0 to 1 or vice versa. Since the attacker does not know at which entry of the secret transformation $\mathbf{T}$ the bit flip occurred, he needs to apply a bit-tracing algorithm to locate the faulted spot and learn the initial value of the flipped bit. The bit flip in $\mathbf{T}$ causes an error in the last part of the signing algorithm in LUOV, where the (vinegar part of the) signature is finally computed by

$$\begin{pmatrix} s_1 \\ \vdots \\ s_v \end{pmatrix} = \begin{pmatrix} t_{11} & \cdots & t_{1m} \\ \vdots & \ddots & \vdots \\ t_{v1} & \cdots & t_{vm} \end{pmatrix} \times \begin{pmatrix} o_1 \\ \vdots \\ o_m \end{pmatrix} + \begin{pmatrix} v_1 \\ \vdots \\ v_v \end{pmatrix}. \tag{5}$$

Thus, a bit flip of the entry t_{ij} leads to a faulted signature entry $\tilde{s}_i$, where the erroneous entry $\tilde{s}_i$ differs from the correct one s_i by o_j. The bit-tracing algorithm now tries to correct the faulted signature by successively adding the values o_k

for $k \in \{1, \ldots, m\}$ to the entries s_l for $l \in \{1, \ldots, v\}$. Once the signature is corrected, the position (i, j) of the induced bit flip is successfully located. This works particularly well, since the entries t_{ij} in LUOV are binary, while the values o_l are elements of a larger field, depending on the parameter choice, e.g., of $\mathbb{F}_{2^8}$. Therefore, the chances that different bit flips in T, say at position t_{ij} and t_{ik}, cause the same error in s are rather small, since then $o_j = o_k$ needs to hold. For more details, please see [32, Section 3.3].

This attack can be transferred to UOV, since the targeted operation in Eq. (5) similarly appears in the signing algorithm of UOV, see Line 11 of Fig. 3. Here, the oilspace O takes the role of the linear transformation T and they behave equivalently. Since the second block of $\bar{\mathbf{O}} = (\mathbf{O}, \mathbf{I}_m)$ is the identity, the values in $\mathbf{x} \in \mathbb{F}_q^m$ are visible to any attacker as the last m entries of the signature $\mathbf{s}$, analogically to the vector $\mathbf{o}$ in LUOV.

However, when it comes to the bit-tracing algorithm we need to be more careful, since in UOV the entries $t_{i,j}$ are not binary anymore, but elements of $\mathbb{F}_{2^8}$ as well. Let $s_i = \sum_{l=1}^{m} t_{il} \cdot o_l + v_i$ be the entry of the unfaulted signature vector. Introducing a single bit flip to t_{ij} results in an faulted entry $\tilde{s}_i = \sum_{l=1}^{m} t_{il} \cdot o_l + v_i + f_{ij} \cdot o_j$, with $f_{ij} \in \mathbb{F}_{2^8}$ having hamming weight 1. Now, if we have $f_{ij} \cdot o_j = f_{ik} \cdot o_k$, for two different indices $j \neq k$, this implies a bit flip corresponding to f_{ij} results in the same faulted signature entry $\tilde{s}_i$ as a bit flip corresponding to f_{ik} would. The bit-tracing algorithm is still able to correct the faulted signature, but would not be able to decide if the deviation results from f_{ij} or f_{ik} and thus, could not uniquely determine the position of the introduced bit flip.

Bit Flip in Matrices of esk. See [21,24,31] for this attack. It is shown that changing a single coefficient of $\mathbf{F}_i$ leads to reduction of the UOV instance to a smaller one. Recent UOV implementations, including the NIST submission [12], are not working with the central maps $\mathbf{F}_i$ anymore, but include the public matrices $\mathbf{P}_i^{(1)}$ and auxiliary matrices $\mathbf{S}_i = (\mathbf{P}_i^{(1)} + \mathbf{P}_i^{(1)\top})\mathbf{O} + \mathbf{P}_i^{(2)}$ in their secret key. However, this is merely a change in notation, since the former blocks $\mathbf{F}_i^{(1)}$ and $\mathbf{F}_i^{(2)}$ of $\mathbf{F}_i$ were defined just like that. The analysis [21,24,31] can be applied to the new setting accordingly and a single altered coefficient in $\mathbf{P}_i^{(1)}$ or $\mathbf{S}_i$, leads to faulted signature $\mathbf{s}'$, such that $\mathcal{P}(\mathbf{s}')$ and $\mathbf{t}$ indeed deviate in exactly one entry. This difference then allows conclusions about the used oil space O.

Fault Injection to Skip the Addition of the Vinegar and Oil Parts. This fault attack targets the addition in Line 11 of Fig. 3, where the vinegar and oil part are added to receive the signature $\mathbf{s} = \mathbf{v} + \mathbf{o}$. It highly depends on the chosen implementation, but if an attacker is able to exclude the vinegar part by an instruction skip, this is threatening. If there is a way to avoid the contribution of $\mathbf{v}$, this directly reveals $\mathbf{s} = \mathbf{o}$ in the signature, which enables key recovery. Currently, this is implemented via a `memcpy` call that copies $\mathbf{v}$ to $\mathbf{s}$, so this line needs to be protected.

Remark 1. Sampling the vinegar vector $\mathbf{v}$ is randomized by including the `salt` as input to the expand function in Line 4 of Fig. 3. If we would deal with a deterministic approach instead, where the signing procedure generates the same vinegar vector $\mathbf{v}$ and outputs identical signatures when a message is signed twice, an adversary could exploit the faulted signature $\mathbf{s}' = \mathbf{v}$ as follows: Subtracting the un-faulted signature $\mathbf{s}$ of the same message $\mathbf{s} - \mathbf{s}' = \mathbf{v} + \mathbf{O}\mathbf{x} - \mathbf{v} = \mathbf{O}\mathbf{x} = \mathbf{o}$ reveals an oil vector.

A similar strategy that also only works in the deterministic setting, is to disturb the computation of the oil vector during signing. If one is able to enforce the computation of a different solution $\mathbf{x}'$ to the linear system, then this again reveals an oil vector. Subtracting the two signatures $\mathbf{s}' - \mathbf{s} = \mathbf{v} + \mathbf{O}\mathbf{x}' - \mathbf{v} - \mathbf{O}\mathbf{x} = \mathbf{O}(\mathbf{x} - \mathbf{x}')$ would cancel out the identical vinegar values and reveal an non-zero oil vector, since $\mathbf{x}' \neq \mathbf{x}$. A similar strategy is applied by the following fault attack.

3.2 New Attack

In addition to the attacks gathered in the section above, we identified the following spots, where exploits by an adversary are conceivable and countermeasures should be applied.

Fault Injection to Disturb Linear System Setup (Skip the New Assignment of L or Y). Disturbing the linear system $\mathbf{L}\mathbf{x} = \mathbf{t} - \mathbf{y}$ leads to a different solution $\mathbf{x}'$, which might lead to key recovery in the deterministic setting, as explained in Remark 1. Perturbing the values in $\mathbf{L}$ or $\mathbf{y}$ can be achieved by skipping Line 5 of Fig. 3 and some or all of the loop in Line 6–7 or introducing faults to the computation of $\mathbf{y}$ in Line 9, respectively. Hereby, it is important that not a single row of $\mathbf{L}$ remains all zero due to the fault attack. This would imply that the system is not solvable, which results in a second iteration of the signing loop, where $\mathbf{v}$ and $\mathbf{L}$ are refreshed. However, this strategy is only successful when the signature is deterministic and thus, current implementations are not vulnerable.

3.3 Transferability to MAYO

The functionalities of UOV are a subset of those needed to implement MAYO. Therefore, it seems natural to conclude that the listed fault attacks for UOV easily transfer to MAYO. Although this is more or less true, there are some minutiae to bear in mind. 1) The applicability of attacks that target the secret key in memory depends on the format (compressed vs. uncompressed) of the stored keys. MAYO always uses compressed keys, which makes MAYO resistant towards such attacks, although classic UOV is vulnerable. 2) Some attacks depend on the randomization choice of the scheme which might deviate to UOV. More details on these two aspects can be found in Sects. 5.1 and 5.2. 3) While UOV works with only one pair of oil and vinegar vectors, there are k of them in MAYO. Nevertheless, a single known oil vector is enough to perform key recovery in polynomial time. Thus, certain attacks might become technically easier in MAYO, since there are k targets available, while only one of them needs to be recovered.

Fault Injection to Fix One or More Vinegar Vectors. This fault attack can be easily transferred to MAYO. Current implementations clear the vinegar vectors at the end of the signing procedure as a security measure to avoid reusing attacks. However, in MAYO one all-zero vinegar vector will not lead to an unsolvable system in Line 37 of MAYO.Sign. This is due to the fact that multiple matrices $\mathbf{M}_i[j,:] = \mathbf{v}_i^\top \mathbf{L}_j$ contribute to the linear part of the system $\mathbf{A}$. Consequently, having some $\mathbf{v}_i$ set to zero will not necessarily result in a non-invertible system and another iteration of the signing loop. Thus, by inserting an instruction skip or loop abort in Line 16 or Line 18 such that one or more (but not all) vinegar vectors remain zero makes the corresponding oil vector $\mathbf{o}_i$ visible in the signature. Furthermore, the authors of [25] present three attacks on this subroutine, in total. Two of them target the absorption phase of the `shake256` internally and the other one forces the unknown input to be zero. In all cases the attacker can predict the outcome of the sampling process which reveals one or more vinegar vectors. Rightfully predicting randomly sampled intermediate values during the signing phase, by directly attacking the `shake256` function, is disastrous in many cryptographic primitives, as is also shown, e.g., in [27]. Thus, we only consider the latter attack as scheme-specific to MAYO, which should be treated with dedicated countermeasures. Instead of zeroing buffers with sensitive information at the end of signing, overwriting these buffers with random data is suggested in [25]. Countermeasures of the aforementioned attacks are discussed in more detail in Sect. 5.4.

RowHammer to Alter a Value in $\boldsymbol{O}$. In MAYO the secret key only contains a seed $\texttt{seed}_{sk}$. The MAYO.API.sign algorithm (Algorithm 10 in [11]) employs the two functionalities MAYO.ExpandSK (Algorithm 6 in [11]) and MAYO.Sign (Algorithm 8 in [11]) to derive the expanded secret key `esk` from the seed and sign the message using `esk`. The secret oil space $\mathbf{O}$, which is the target of the original fault attack, is therefore not a part of the compressed secret key `csk` Thus, it is not stored in memory permanently and less accessible for bit-flip attempts. Furthermore, the addressed variable is zeroed at the end of the signing procedure as a security measure. This is not depicted in the pseudo code, but realized in the submitted implementations [11]. Thus we do not deem the attack given in [32] to be technically feasible in this scenario.

However, in case an adversary could manage to insert a bit-flip during signing, while $\mathbf{O}$ is stored as part of `esk` in the memory, a similar description as in Sect. 3.1 would apply, since the oil space takes an equivalent role as in UOV.

Bit Flip in Matrices of `esk`. Let $\mathbf{s}'$ be the faulted signature, that is generated when a single bit-flip is applied to either of the matrices $\{\mathbf{P}_i^{(1)}, \mathbf{S}_i\}$ in the expanded secret key, The crucial part of this fault attack against UOV is that $\mathcal{P}(\mathbf{s})$ and $\mathbf{t}$ only deviate in one entry. In contrast, the whipped public map $\mathcal{P}^*(\mathbf{s}_1, ..., \mathbf{s}_k) = \sum_{i=1}^{k} \mathbf{E}_{ii}\mathcal{P}(\mathbf{s}_i) + \sum_{1\leq i<j\leq k} \mathbf{E}_{ij}\mathcal{P}'(\mathbf{s}_i, \mathbf{s}_j)$ in MAYO is of different structure. The $\binom{k}{2}$-many emulsifier maps $\mathbf{E}_{ij}$ and the accumulation of all the transformed terms ensures that $\mathcal{P}^*(\mathbf{s}')$ and $\mathbf{t}$ deviate in most of the entries, even if only a single bit-flip was applied. We confirmed this statement with simula-

tions, where we manually change a single bit in one of the $\mathbf{P}_i^{(1)}$ or $\mathbf{S}_i$. Thus, the introduced fault attack can not be transferred to MAYO, at least not in a straightforward way.

However, for the deterministic variant the situation is different. The bit flips lead to altered solution vectors $\mathbf{x}' = (\mathbf{x}'_1, \ldots, \mathbf{x}'_k)$. This most likely results in an invalid signature $\mathbf{s}' = (\mathbf{s}'_1, \ldots, \mathbf{s}'_k) = (\mathbf{v}_1 + \mathbf{O}\mathbf{x}'_1, \ldots, \mathbf{v}_k + \mathbf{O}\mathbf{x}'_k)$. But if we compare that to the correct signature $\mathbf{s} = (\mathbf{s}_1, \ldots, \mathbf{s}_k) = (\mathbf{v}_1 + \mathbf{O}\mathbf{x}_1, \ldots, \mathbf{v}_k + \mathbf{O}\mathbf{x}_k)$ of the same message, we see that the vinegar part is identical in the deterministic scenario. Consequently, the term $\mathbf{s}_i - \mathbf{s}'_i = \mathbf{O}\mathbf{x}_i + \mathbf{O}\mathbf{x}'_i$ would reveal an oil vector, since $\mathbf{O}\mathbf{x}'_i \in O$.

Fault Injection to Skip the Addition of the Vinegar and Oil Parts. In general, this fault attack also applies to MAYO. In the MAYO signing procedure [11, Alg.2, Line 45] the sum of k pairs of vinegar and oil vectors is computed. In the current implementation this is achieved by adding both components into another variable `s` via `mat_add(vi, Ox, s + i * param_n, ..., 1);`. Regarding the fault attack, this approach is more secure than first copying `vi` to `s`, and then adding `Ox` to it, as it is done in UOV. However, before the actual addition happens, the vinegar part gets reassigned via `vi = Vdec + i * (param_n - param_o);`. If this instruction can be skipped and `vi` remains empty or assigned with a certain constant value, then an oil vector can be recovered with the approach given in Remark 1.

Fault Injection to Disturb Linear System Setup (Skip the New Assignment of A or Y). There are plenty of options to introduce faults during the linear system set up in [11, Alg.2] between Line 22 and 33, which might change the solution vectors $\mathbf{x'}_i$ and therefore also the resulting oil vectors $\mathbf{o'}_i$. In the non-randomized setting this could be exploited, similar to the description given in Remark 1.

3.4 Transferability to QR-UOV and SNOVA

In this section we discuss if and how the fault attacks in Table 1 can be transferred to QR-UOV and SNOVA. Both schemes employ the quotient ring structure, but this does not have a large impact on the mentioned attacks.

Fault Injection to Fix the Vinegar Vector. This attack works analogously for QR-UOV and SNOVA. As described in Sect. 3.1, the crucial part here is that the signature is composed of an oil and a vinegar vector. Then, the repeated usage of two identical vinegar vectors makes them canceling each other out, when those signatures are subtracted from each other. In QR-UOV and SNOVA this last step of mixing the oil and vinegar terms is represented by applying the secret linear transformation $\mathbf{s} = S^{-1}(y_1, \ldots, y_v, y_{v+1}, \ldots, y_n)$ in [20, Alg.2, Line 18] or $\mathbf{sig} = [T](X_0, \ldots, X_{v-1}, \tilde{X}_0, \ldots, \tilde{X}_{o-1})$ in [44, Alg.11, Line 14], where the first v entries represent the vinegar and the last o entries represent the oil variables. Due to the block matrix structure of S and T, with an identity and zero block in the first column, the vinegar variables contribute unaltered to the signature.

RowHammer to Alter a Value in S or T. In general, this attack works as initially described for LUOV or adapted to UOV. However, QR-UOV and the variant SNOVA-ssk use compressed secret keys. Consequently, the linear transformations S and T, which are only part of the expanded secret keys, are not permanently stored in memory at a specific location. Thus, from a technical point of view, the execution of the fault attack becomes way more difficult. The time slot where the fault can be induced successfully is reduced to signing time and furthermore, the resulting bit-flip is not permanent, since the secret key will be expanded again in the next signing procedure. However, regarding SNOVA-esk the attack would work equivalently to the original one on LUOV.

Bit flip in Matrices of `esk`. The transfer of this fault attack is again non-trivial. Considering the notation of QR-UOV and SNOVA, there are now the matrices $F_{i,1}, F_{i,1}$ and $F_i^{11}, F_i^{12}, F_i^{21}$ under attack. It is not the quotient-ring structure that determines if a bit-flip in one of these matrices yields useful information for the attacker, but the structure of the public map. In the verification of QR-UOV, the signature is evaluated with the bare public map $\mathcal{P}$, similar to UOV. Therefore, we again are in the case that $\mathcal{P}(\mathbf{sig}')$ and $\mathbf{t}$ only differ in a single entry, which is exploitable.

SNOVA, in contrast, has the whipping structure of MAYO, as pointed out by Beullens in [9]. In Corollary 2 he states that the SNOVA public map can be written as $\mathcal{P}(\mathbf{U}) = \sum_{j=0}^{l-1} \sum_{k=0}^{l-1} \mathbf{E}_{j,k} \mathcal{B}(\mathbf{u}_j, \mathbf{u}_k)$, where the matrices $\mathbf{E}_{j,k}$ have a block diagonal structure with m identical blocks of size $\mathbb{F}_q^{(l^2 \times l^2)}$ on the diagonal. This goes well with the result of our simulations, where a bit-flip introduced to one of the matrices F_i^{11}, F_i^{12}, or F_i^{21}, caused the vectors $\mathcal{P}(\mathbf{sig})$ and $\mathbf{t}$ to deviate in l^2 entries. Thus, the mentioned fault attack can not be applied to SNOVA, at least not without profound modification.

Fault Injection to Skip the Addition of the Vinegar and Oil Parts. QR-UOV and SNOVA are both randomized schemes. As a result, the only way to mount this attack is to stop the vinegar variables - and only them - from contributing to the signature (see Remark 1).

We analyzed the submitted reference implementation from QR-UOV and came to the conclusion that this is not possible with a first-order fault attack. The signature is computed via `sig->s[i] = Fql_sub(vineger[i], t);`, where the vinegar part `vineger` is not altered or reassigned beforehand and the oil part is encoded in `t`. Skipping this instruction would detain both parts from appearing in `s`.

In SNOVA the case is a little different. They first copy the vinegar entry to the signature `gf16m_clone(signature...[index], X...[index]);` and afterwards add the oil entry to it. However, since this is done entry-wise, aborting the loop or similar strategies would not be successful, as they also prevent the remaining oil entries from contributing.

Thus, both schemes do not seem to be vulnerable regarding that attack. Remarkably, this is not due to the quotient ring structure, but to their current implementation details.

Fault Injection to Disturb Linear System Setup. As concluded in Sect. 3.2, this attack only works in the deterministic setting. Since both QR-UOV and SNOVA do not expand the vinegar variables from a fixed seed, but generate them randomly, the given attack is not feasible.

4 Side-Channel Attacks on UOV-Based Signatures

In this section, we investigate the security of UOV-based signature schemes in terms of side-channel attacks. Similar to the previous section, we first recall and transfer existing attacks to UOV. With the goal of being as exhaustive as possible, we then consider further potential vulnerabilities. The resulting attacks are subsequently adapted to MAYO, QR-UOV, and SNOVA. Table 2 presents an overview of this section.

4.1 Existing Attacks

The following attacks against UOV or a familiar scheme are present in the literature. Both existing attacks target the *UOV.Sign* routine shown in Fig. 3 and focus on subroutines where secret data is multiplied with public values.

Power Analysis of the Evaluation of the Vinegar Vector. The target of this side-channel attack is the computation $\mathbf{y} = [\mathbf{v}^\top \mathbf{P}_i^{(1)} \mathbf{v}]_{i \in [m]}$ given in Line 9 of Fig. 3. The vinegar vector $\mathbf{v}$ is multiplied from both sides to m matrices $\mathbf{P}_i^{(1)}$ containing public values. This marks an evident entrance door for side channel attacks via power analysis. In [2] the authors showed how to exploit this vulnerability with a profiling attack, that gets along with only a single attack trace. In the profiling phase, the entries v_i of $\mathbf{v}$ are set by hand to certain known values. Then, the considered function is called and power traces are gathered - labeled with the respective value in v_i as reference. During the attack phase, the power trace of the execution of $\mathbf{y} = [\mathbf{v}^\top \mathbf{P}_i^{(1)} \mathbf{v}]_{i \in [m]}$ with the unknown (and secret) vector $\mathbf{v}$ is recorded and compared to the reference traces. The attack trace is likely to have the highest correlation to the reference trace where the identical value v_i is used. In this manner, the entries of $\mathbf{v}$ are revealed, which in turn exposes a secret oil vector $\mathbf{o}$ and enables complete secret key recovery.

Table 2. Overview of existing and new side-channel attacks on UOV, MAYO, QR-UOV, and SNOVA. Regarding the feasibility of the attacks, we refer to the specifications submitted to the NIST call for additional signatures in mid-2023. When there is a difference between deterministic and randomized MAYO, we list them individually in the given order. With ✓ we state that an attack is possible. By ⋆ we denote that an attack is generally possible, but the technical execution is more difficult than in the initially presented attack.

Description: Power analysis ...	Source	Initially for	Feasible in	Target
of vinegar evaluation	[2]	UOV	UOV: ✓	`UOV.Sign Line 9`
			MAYO: ✓	[11] `Alg.8 Line 29`
			QR-UOV: ✓	[20] `Alg.2 Line 12`
			SNOVA: ✓	[44] `Alg.8 Line 3,4`
of secret matrix multiplication	[26,34]	Rainbow	UOV: ⋆	`UOV.Sign Line 11`
		UOV	MAYO: ✓ | ⋆	[11] `Alg.8 Line 44`
		MAYO[a]	QR-UOV: ⋆	[20] `Alg.2 Line 18`
			SNOVA: ⋆	[44] `Alg.11 Line 14`
of linear system setup	This work	UOV	UOV: ✓	`UOV.Sign Line 7`
			MAYO: ✓	[11] `Alg.8 Line 27,29`
			QR-UOV: ✓	[20] `Alg.2 Line 11`
			SNOVA: ✓	[44] `Alg.9 Line 3,4,14,26`
of secret key expansion	This work	UOV	UOV: ✓	`UOV.ExpandSK Line 4`
	[26]	MAYO[a]	MAYO: ✓	[11] `Alg.6 Line 17`
			QR-UOV: ✓	[20] `Alg.2 Line 7`
			SNOVA: ✓	[44] `Alg.6 Line 6,7`
during key generation	This work	UOV	UOV: ✓	`UOV.CompactKeyGen Line 6`
			MAYO: ✓	[11] `Alg.5 Line 16`
			QR-UOV: ✓	[20] `Alg.1 Line 5`
			SNOVA: ✓	[44] `Alg.5 Line 5`

[a] Simultaneously to our work, Jendral and Dubrova [26] demonstrated a deep learning assisted power analysis of the corresponding functions in MAYO. Note that their attack is the only side-channel attack considered in this work that was explicitly developed against MAYO. For the others, we analyzed if the attacks against UOV can be translated to MAYO.

Power Analysis of the Linear Subspace Matrix Multiplication. The authors of [34] present a differential power analysis (DPA) on the multiplication of the linear transformation $\mathbf{T}$ with the intermediate vector $\mathbf{x}$, that is the solution to the derived linear system. In our notation here, the transformation $\mathbf{T}$ is replaced by the basis $\bar{\mathbf{O}}$ of the linear subspace O. Therefore, this attack can be seen as a power analysis of the matrix vector multiplication in Line 11 of Fig. 3. The attack takes advantage of the fact that some entries of the vector $\mathbf{x}$ are part of the signature, since they are not altered by the identity block of $\bar{\mathbf{O}}$, resp. T. In more detail, we have $\bar{\mathbf{O}}\mathbf{x} = [\mathbf{O}\mathbf{x}, \mathbf{x}]$ and $\mathbf{s} = [\mathbf{v}, \mathbf{0}_m] + [\mathbf{O}\mathbf{x}, \mathbf{x}]$. Thus, during the computation of $\mathbf{O}\mathbf{x}$, the secret entries in $\mathbf{O}$ are multiplied with known values and are consequently vulnerable to DPA.

The authors in [34] require a few dozen of repeated computations of $\mathbf{Ox}$ to recover the entries in $\mathbf{O}$ by using correlation coefficients. At the time they performed this attack on Rainbow and UOV, these schemes used a deterministic approach. This allowed the authors to make the valid assumption that $\mathbf{x}$ will not change when the same message is signed repeatedly. In the current randomized implementation, the solution vector $\mathbf{x}$ will change with every signing procedure, since every time a new vinegar vector $\mathbf{v}$ is sampled, leading to a completely different linear system $\mathbf{Lx} = \mathbf{t} - \mathbf{y}$.

Hence, the attack will not work in the presented form and needs to be adapted to the new setting. However, we still believe the considered function $\mathbf{Ox}$ needs to be protected, since sensitive data is multiplied with public values, which could be exploited with more evolved analysis methods, like profiling or machine learning techniques[5].

4.2 New Attacks

Power analysis attacks are possible on various other spots of the UOV functionalities. In *UOV.ExpandSK* and *UOV.CompactKeyGen* there is a bulk of matrix multiplications that involve the secret matrix $\mathbf{O}$ and public values stored in $\mathbf{P}_i^{(1)}$ and $\mathbf{P}_i^{(2)}$, which is clearly vulnerable. Regarding the algorithm *UOV.Sign*, we additionally identified the following operation where caution is required.

Power Analysis of the Computation of L. In Line 7 of Fig. 3 the linear part $\mathbf{L}$ of the system of equations in Line 10 is computed. Hereby, the i-th row of $\mathbf{L}$ is given by $\mathbf{v}^\top \mathbf{S}_i$. Both components involved are unknown to an attacker, which makes it harder to mount a successful power analysis attack than in the considered scenarios above, where one component is public. However, the matrices $\mathbf{S}_i$ are part of the expanded secret key, and, consequently, remain constant over various signing procedures with the same secret key. If Hamming weight information about one of the factors and their product is leaked, we have seen that blind side-channel attacks [16,38] can exploit this and reveal information about the considered factors $\mathbf{v}$ and $\mathbf{S}_i$.

Power Analysis of the Computation of S_i During Secret Key Expansion. The multiplication in Line 4 of Fig. 2 could be analyzed similarly to the side-channel attack against Line 9 of Fig. 3. This is also critical and needs to be countered. In the variant `uov-pkc+skc` compressed secret keys are used and the mentioned procedure is part of the signing process. Regarding the other two variants `uov` and `uov-pkc`, where the $\mathbf{S}_i$ are already part of the key, this functionality is attributed to key generation.

Power Analysis of the Computation of $P_i^{(3)}$ During Key Generation. The same holds for the matrix multiplications during key generation, depicted in Line 6 of Fig. 1. If an adversary is able to retrieve side-channel information here, these operations also need to be protected, following the same reasoning.

[5] The recent attack [26] confirms this conjecture.

4.3 Transferability to MAYO, QR-UOV, and SNOVA

The task of theoretically transferring the discussed side-channel attacks to MAYO, QR-UOV, and SNOVA is considerably less complicated than it was for the fault attacks. On one hand this is due to the fact that certain implementation choices, like the utilization of compressed keys, have a smaller impact on the effectiveness of side-channel attacks. On the other hand, also the scheme-specific properties are less critical here, since all four schemes contain the typical UOV-like work flow: Generate the vinegar vector(s), compute the constant and linear part of the system of equations, solve the linear system via Gauss, multiply the solution with the oil space to receive corresponding oil vector(s), and finally add the vinegar and oil part together. Thus, the vulnerable subroutines listed in Table 2 need to be executed some way or the other, and whether the scheme uses elements of the field $\mathbb{F}_{2^4}$ or $\mathbb{F}_{2^8}$ or of a quotient ring $\mathbb{F}_q[x]/(f)$, like QR-UOV and SNOVA, is not decisive for the theoretical applicability of the attack, since they also boil down to multiplications over a huge amount of field elements.

The practical execution of the attack, in contrast, will depend heavily on the chosen implementation. In [10], the MAYO team announced that they will change their specification from a bit- to a nibble-sliced representation for their keys etc. Among other things, they present an efficient implementation of MAYO on the Arm Cortex-M4, where the costly matrix multiplications are based on the Method of the Four Russians. This method deviates from previous approaches and to the best of our knowledge, there are no reported side-channel attacks against such implementations in the literature. To perform such a side-channel analysis could pose some interesting challenges and therefore, provides a charming open research questions.

For the remaining schemes QR-UOV and SNOVA, there are currently no Arm Cortex-M4 implementations available, so a concrete analysis of their side-channel security cannot yet be performed. Nevertheless, we hope Table 2 with the respective code lines can provide a good orientation about the vulnerable functions, which need to be treated with caution.

5 Implementation Guidelines

In this section, we present implementation guidelines and dedicated countermeasures to protect implementations of UOV-based signature schemes against the physical attacks presented in this work.

During our research, we identified several theoretical attack vectors - both existing and new ones - that do not lead to physical attacks in practice since the current UOV and MAYO implementations are not vulnerable against them. However, we realized that the implementation decisions that prevent these attacks do not seem to be motivated by preventing physical attacks, primarily. As an example, the utilization of compressed keys first and foremost serves the purpose of reducing key sizes, but at the same time it prevents fault attacks that alter the secret key in memory (cf. Sects. 3.3 and 5.2). Hence, we do not consider it correct to term these parts of the implementations *countermeasures*, in contrast to concrete modifications of implementations with the aim of making the implementations more resistant towards physical attacks. Still, we consider it important to list also these implementation decisions in this section to emphasize their importance for physical attack security, which is why we term this section *implementation guidelines* instead of *countermeasures*.

5.1 Randomized Signatures

From a physical security point of view, it is desirable to utilize a randomized signature generation process. For the considered UOV implementation this is already the case. In Line 1 of Fig. 3 the `salt` s generated randomly. This `salt` among others) contributes as input to the `Hash` and `Expand` functions that are used to derive the target vector $\mathbf{t} \in \mathbb{F}_q^m$ and the vinegar vector $\mathbf{v} \in \mathbb{F}_q^{n-m}$. Thus, if the same message is signed twice, the generated signatures (and most of the intermediate values) are different. In contrast, the considered MAYO implementation offers both options - random and deterministic - that determine how the `salt` s derived in Line 10 of the signing algorithm. If the signature computation is deterministic, this is beneficial for an attacker. Subtracting signatures of identical messages leads to vinegar parts canceling each other out, possibly revealing non-zero oil vectors, if one of the two latter fault attacks in Table 1 is applied correctly. Thus, we recommend the usage of the randomized version to prevent both of these attacks. Furthermore, this helps to mitigate side-channel analysis with the goal of obtaining the sampled vinegar vectors. If the vinegar vectors vary between different signing processes, it will be much harder to apply differential power analysis methods. Nevertheless, we suggest masking as an additional countermeasure, see Sect. 5.5.

5.2 Compressed Keys

In addition to the obvious advantage of reduced key sizes, the use of compressed keys is also beneficial with respect to physical security. If the secret key only consists of a seed, there are less options to introduce exploitable faults while it is stored in memory. Recently, [21] and [32] showed that bit flips introduced to an uncompressed secret key can lead to serious leakage. Even when the precise spot of occurrence is unknown at first, there are methods to localize the bit flips and use them to achieve full key recovery. Moreover, [32] practically executed the attack on LUOV, emphasizing its relevance for UOV-based schemes.

Using compressed keys prevents both fault attacks described in this work that target the secret key in memory, namely the Rowhammer attack on the secret matrix $\mathbf{O}$ and the one introducing bit flips on the secret matrices.

5.3 Counter RowHammer Fault Attack

However, there are scenarios where key compression techniques are undesirable, e.g., in order to enable a faster signing process. Here, we introduce a method to prevent the RowHammer fault attack on the secret subspace O for such scenarios. To be precise, it is not the secret subspace O which is stored in memory, but a certain basis of it. Right now this basis is represented in standard form, such that the identity part $\mathbf{I}_{m\times m}$ can be omitted and only the remaining $\mathbf{O} \in M_{m\times(n-m)}(\mathbb{F}_q)$ is stored. This method is memory efficient, but the standard form for a given oil space is unique, hence fixed. This enables the bit tracing algorithm used in the RowHammer attack.

Instead one could compute m random - though linearly independent - vectors of O and store this modified basis instead. During signing, we would load the modified basis from memory, compute its standard form and continue signing like usual. Afterwards we again transform the basis to a random one by building random linear combinations. This way, the explicit form of the secret key, i.e., the basis of the subspace O, would change with every signature generation, while the secret information remains the same.

The resulting overhead is obvious. On one hand, the size of the matrix to be stored increases from $M_{m\times(n-m)}(\mathbb{F}_q)$ to $M_{m\times n}(\mathbb{F}_q)$. At first glance, this seems like a considerable drawback, but the fraction of the expanded secret key that is consumed by $\mathbf{O}$ or its enlarged version is rather small compared to the matrices $\mathbf{S}_i$ that are also part of the secret key. Thus, the expanded key size would only increase from 238 to 240 KB in `uov-Ip`.

On the other hand, the effort to compute the standard form at the beginning of the signature generation and the randomized basis at the end, will increase the signing time slightly.

5.4 Modify Vinegar Variable After Usage

The fault attack that leads to re-using or zeroing (most of) the vinegar variables belongs to the most prominent ones in literature, see, e.g., [3,24,31,41]. It leads to valid signatures, since the actual signing process is unaltered by the fault. Only the vinegar variables are forced to values that are either known by the attacker, or have been used before. The part of signing that computes the actual solution to the equation $\mathcal{P}(\mathbf{v}+\mathbf{o}) = \mathbf{t}$ is executed correctly and therefore finds a correct signature. Thus, unlike many fault attacks, it can not be detected by a validity check.

Instead, one actively needs to ensure that the sampled vinegar variables are sound and vary across consecutive signing procedures. To this end, we suggest the following modification. After the sampled vinegar variables are used in Line 7 and 9 of Fig. 3, we add a vector with random values to it, i.e., `v += r`. Since the vinegar vector $\mathbf{v}$ is added to the signature s via `s += v` towards the end of the signing process, the component $\mathbf{r}$ needs to be removed from the derived signature at the end by appending the instruction `s -= r`.

Obviously this countermeasure could be circumvented with two additional instruction skips, which would lead to a third-order fault attack altogether. An attacker who is able to introduce three independent faults, however, could probably attack a signature algorithm in a simpler way and is therefore not considered a relevant scenario in this work. Irrespective of this, depending on how the additional random value $\mathbf{r}$ is chosen, this countermeasure can even be circumvented more easily: When $\mathbf{r}$ is designed to be a new variable with randomly sampled values, the assignment of the random value to the variable $\mathbf{r}$ might be skipped, resulting in $\mathbf{r} = 0$. In this case, the countermeasure would be completely circumvented by a single instruction skip, leading to a second-order fault attack altogether, which can be considered to be realistic [14]. To avoid such second-order fault attack, we instead suggest to not initialize $\mathbf{r}$ with randomly sampled values, but to use already existing intermediate values of the signing procedure and directly add them to $\mathbf{v}$. For instance, we can make use of the unknown entries of the vectors $\mathbf{r} := \mathbf{v}^\top \cdot \mathbf{S}_i$ for any $i \in \{1, \ldots, m\}$, that are used to compose the linear system which is solved during signing.

This countermeasure can be seen as an approach to randomize the data stored in $\mathbf{v}$ after its usage, which is also suggested by [25]. Since $\mathbf{v}$ is added to the signature $\mathbf{s}$ subsequently, this furthermore employs the idea of infective computing [22]. The component $\mathbf{r}$ is a secret error, which needs to be removed finally. If an injected fault skips the addition of this error, the output of the algorithm will be incorrect and can not be exploited by an attacker.

5.5 Masking Against Power Analysis

The listed side-channel attacks in Sect. 4 all follow a similar concept, namely the power analysis of certain matrix vector multiplications, that ultimately boil down to field multiplications in $\mathbb{F}_q$. The field is rather small, e.g., $q \in \{2^4, 2^8\}$ in UOV or $q = 2^4$ in MAYO, and 32-bit processors, like the ARM Cortex-M family, treat multiple field elements at once. Even though this hampers Hamming weight analysis of the secret or vulnerable values, it has been shown that DPAs [34] or profiling attacks [2] are possible.

The most common countermeasure to prevent power analysis attacks is masking. Currently, to the best of our knowledge there are no masked implementations of UOV-based signature schemes available. In this work, we bridge this gap by providing a first masked version of UOV and MAYO. The goal is to protect the vulnerable intermediate values, mainly the oil and vinegar vectors, whenever they are used, and thereby protect against the existing and newly developed attacks in Sect. 4.1 and Sect. 4.2. Since the majority of the utilized functions in signing (and key generation) is linear, they are straightforward to mask. In the following, we provide an overview of the affected lines in the pseudo code and the measures we implemented to mitigate their vulnerability. Therefore, we refer to the pseudocode of UOV, especially the signing algorithm in Fig. 3.

- The original implementation uses `shake256` [1] to generate the vinegar vector $\mathbf{v} \in \mathbb{F}_q^n$. In fact it only samples $n - m$ entries of $\mathbf{v}$, as the last m entries are set to zero. Instead, we propose to use a masked version `masked_shake256` [5] to sample two (additive) shares of these entries, that will be used for computations later on and are combined at the end of the signing procedure.

- *Line 7, compute $\boldsymbol{v}^\top \boldsymbol{S}_i$, the linear part of the system of linear equations:* In this step we compute the coefficients of the linear part of the system of equations that needs to be solved during signing. Hereby, the vinegar vector $\mathbf{v}$ is multiplied with numerous matrices $\mathbf{S}_i$, which are part of the (expanded) secret key and do not change in subsequent signature generations. Each resulting vector represents a row in the matrix $\mathbf{L}$ that constitutes the linear system. The matrices $\mathbf{S}_i$ are defined by $\mathbf{S}_i \leftarrow (\mathbf{P}_i^{(1)} + \mathbf{P}_i^{(1)\top})\mathbf{O} + \mathbf{P}_i^{(2)}$ (see Line 4 of Fig. 2) and contain information about the secret oil space O. Therefore, we split them randomly into two additive shares. Since the function $\mathbf{v}^\top \cdot \mathbf{S}_i$ is linear in both components and the vinegar vector already arrives in two shares, we need to compute it four times, one for each combination of the respective two components.
- *Line 9, compute $\boldsymbol{v}^\top \boldsymbol{P}_i^{(1)} \boldsymbol{v}$, which contributes to the constant part of the system of linear equations:* In [2] the authors perform a profiled side-channel attack against this operation. Since the values in $\mathbf{P}_i^{(1)}$ are public, they can take those matrices as given in the public key and collect profiling traces of this operation for various known values of $\mathbf{v}$. After the profiling phase has finished, only a single attack trace of this operation with the used vinegar vector v is needed to recover its actual value. Thus, masking the vector $\mathbf{v}$ is not an option, since an attacker could just recover the value of both shares with this kind of single trace attack. Instead, we suggest to mask the values given in $\mathbf{P}_i^{(1)}$. To collect meaningful profiling traces it is crucial that an attacker knows the exact value of $\mathbf{P}_i^{(1)}$. By masking the entries of these matrices, we prohibit this strategy and render the collected profiling traces useless. Consequently, we compute $\mathbf{y}_0 = \mathbf{v}^\top \mathbf{P}_{i,0}^{(1)} \mathbf{v}$ and $\mathbf{y}_1 = \mathbf{v}^\top \mathbf{P}_{i,1}^{(1)} \mathbf{v}$ for the two shares $\mathbf{P}_{i,0}^{(1)}$ and $\mathbf{P}_{i,1}^{(1)}$ and continue with the additive shares $\mathbf{y}_0$ and $\mathbf{y}_1$, which contribute to the constant part of the system of linear equations.
- *Line 10, solve $\boldsymbol{L}\boldsymbol{x} = \boldsymbol{t} - \boldsymbol{y}$ for $\boldsymbol{x}$:* At this point we already arrive with two shares $\mathbf{y}_0$ and $\mathbf{y}_1$ of $\mathbf{y}$. Since we do not want an attacker to get track of the value $\mathbf{y}$, we suggest to continue with these two shares and compute two solutions $\mathbf{x}_0$ and $\mathbf{x}_1$ of the linear systems $\mathbf{L}\mathbf{x}_0 = \mathbf{t} - \mathbf{y}_0$ and $\mathbf{L}\mathbf{x}_1 = -\mathbf{y}_1$. Their sum $\mathbf{x} = \mathbf{x}_0 + \mathbf{x}_1$ gives us the coefficients of the oil vector, since $\mathbf{L}\mathbf{x} = \mathbf{L}(\mathbf{x}_0 + \mathbf{x}_1) = \mathbf{L}\mathbf{x}_0 + \mathbf{L}\mathbf{x}_1 = \mathbf{t} - \mathbf{y}_0 - \mathbf{y}_1 = \mathbf{t} - \mathbf{y}$ just like in the original implementation.
- *Line 11, add together vinegar and oil vector:* First, we compute two shares $\mathbf{o}_0$ and $\mathbf{o}_1$ of the oil vector. To this end, we split the oil space randomly into two additive shares $\mathbf{O}_0$ and $\mathbf{O}_1$. Now, we can compute $\mathbf{o}_0 = \mathbf{O}_0\mathbf{x}$ and $\mathbf{o}_1 = \mathbf{O}_1\mathbf{x}$. We do not need to work with the shares of $\mathbf{x}$ anymore, since $\mathbf{x}$ itself is leaked as part of the signature to the public anyway. Finally, to receive the signature $\mathbf{s}$, we add up all the shares $\mathbf{s} = \mathbf{v}_0 + \mathbf{v}_1 + \mathbf{o}_0 + \mathbf{o}_1$.

We implemented these countermeasures as described above and measured their overhead. The practical results are presented in Sect. 6. As one could expect, masking the functions in Line 7 and 9 is responsible for the majority of the total overhead induced by masking UOV. These functions are quite expensive themselves and the vast amount of randombytes that is required to generate the shares of the involved matrices also contributes significantly to the increased number of clock cycles, as detailed in Sect. 6.

6 Practical Results

This section firstly presents the performance evaluation of our protected implementations for UOV and MAYO. As there is currently no Cortex-M4 implementation of QR-UOV and SNOVA publicly available, the practical part of this work focus on UOV and MAYO. In this section, we further provide experimental results in terms of side-channel resistance. For all evaluation purposes, we use existing, unprotected implementations for NIST security level I of both schemes as a basis. More precisely, our implementations are based on the respective optimized UOV (`ov-Ip-pkc/m4f`) and MAYO (`mayo1/m4f`) Cortex-M4 implementation available within the pqm4 [28] library.

To increase compatibility, all changes were applied within the respective signing function itself, i.e. the signature of the function remains unchanged. Note that our findings (cf. Sect. 5) and implemented measures can be easily applied to other parameter sets.

6.1 Performance Results

In this section we present some performance figures of our first-order masked implementation of UOV and MAYO. For benchmarking, we target the ST NUCLEO-L4R5ZI board featuring an Arm Cortex-M4F core with 640 KB of RAM and 2 MB of flash memory. All randomness required for masking is generated using the internal hardware random number generator available on that board. We used the `arm-none-eabi-gcc` compiler (version 13.3.1) with the compiler flags `-O3 -std=gnu99 -mthumb -mcpu=cortex-m4 -mfloat-abi-=hard -mfpu=fpv4-sp-d16` for compilation.

For the targeted parameter set (`ov-Ip`) of UOV, the combined size of the expanded secret key and the expanded public key is 516 KB. Due to the 640 KB of RAM, both expanded keys fit into the RAM. However, in order to obtain the required space for masking within the 640 KB of RAM on the ST NUCLEO-L4R5ZI board, we applied the approach [13,15] of writing the keys to flash memory. Table 3 presents the memory requirements of our protected implementations compared to the existing versions. In the case of UOV, it shows 1) the increase of stack usage during the key generation due to having to cache the keys in RAM before writing them to the flash memory, 2) the additional stack usage when signing due to our implemented masking measures, and 3) the increase of code size required for masking. Whereas in the case of MAYO, the additional memory requirement is significantly lower, as the size of the RAM is sufficient for masking without writing the keys to the flash memory. This is due to having to cache the keys in RAM before writing them to flash.

Table 3. Memory requirements for each implementation. Code, data and BSS size listed are in bytes, stack usage in 2^{10} byte (i.e., KiB).

Scheme	Impl.	Library size			Stack usage		
		Code	Data	BSS	keygen	sign	verify
ov-Ip-pkc	m4f	80 006	0	0	15.2	5.1	2.5
	m4f-flash	80 062	0	0	401.6	5.1	2.5
	masked-m4f-flash	213 076	0	0	401.6	264.4	2.5
MAYO_1	m4f	16 513	8	0	72.7	110.8	430.3
	masked-m4f	17 630	8	0	72.7	217.2	430.3

Table 4 compares the performance of protected and unprotected versions of UOV. Thereby, we differentiate between certain subroutines (cf. Sect. 5) to clarify the cost of each measure. In addition to the masked implementation, we implemented blinding as an alternative protecting method for two suitable and most costly subroutines based on the following approach. The functions $\mathbf{v}^\top\mathbf{S}_i$ and $\mathbf{v}^\top\mathbf{P}_i\mathbf{v}$ are linear with respect to the used matrices, so blinding works in a straightforward way. We multiply them with random values $r_i \in \mathbb{F}_q \backslash \{0\}$ beforehand and nullify its effect by multiplying the result with r_i^{-1}. Note that we use different random values r_i for each of the matrices $\mathbf{S}_i$ and $\mathbf{P}_i$ for $i \in \{1, \ldots, m\}$.

This approach is less powerful than masking every single entry of these matrices, but it still ensures that the values in $\mathbf{S}_i$ do not remain identical over various signing procedures and the values in $\mathbf{P}_i$ are not open to public anymore. Table 4 shows that 1) the masked version is about 5× slower than the unprotected implementation and 2) blinding is in total almost 2× slower than masking.

Table 4. Cortex-M4F cycle counts for our protected implementations in comparison to the optimized unprotected implementation of ov-Ip-pkc. Note that the implementation with blinding only differs from the masked implementation in two subroutines.

Pseudo code	Subroutine	UOV unprotected	[this work] masking	[this work] with blinding
Line 4	Sample vinegar vectors SHAKE256	13 455	132 363	132 363
Line 7	Linear part of system $L = v^\top \cdot S_i$	1 083 775	6 816 989	12 069 951
Line 9	Constant part of system $y = v^\top \cdot P_i \cdot v$	903 390	3 721 735	8 359 110
Line 10	Solve linear system Solve $Lx = t - y$ for x	435 349	872 866	872 866
Line 11	Add oil and vinegar $s = v + Ox$	26 633	109 454	109 454
CM of Sec. 5.4	Modify vinegar after usage $\mathrm{v} = \mathrm{v} + \mathrm{r}$	-	768	768
Total cycle counts for signing		2 478 708	11 840 264	21 916 475

Table 5 compares the performance of protected and unprotected versions of MAYO. Similar to UOV, we present the performance results of each implemented subroutine. The present figures show that the overhead of masking is in total smaller than 2×. Although we followed the same approach for both schemes, the slowdown for UOV is significantly larger compared to MAYO.

Table 5. Cortex-M4F cycle counts for various subroutines within the expanding and signing procedure in comparison to the unprotected implementation of MAYO_1.

Pseudo code	Subroutine	MAYO unprotected	[this work] masking
[11] `Alg.6 Line 17`	Secret key expansion $L_i = (P_i^{(1)} + P_i^{(1)T})O + P_i^{(2)}$	2 165 338	5 343 609
[11] `Alg.8 Line 16`	Sample vinegar vectors & randomizer SHAKE256	40 775	394 917
[11] `Alg.8 Line 27`	Linear part of system $M_i[j,:] = v_i^T L_j$	524 900	1 782 457
[11] `Alg.8 Line 30`	Constant part of system $u = v_i^T P_a^{(1)} v_i$	1 969 234	3 782 901
[11] `Alg.8 Line 38`	Solve linear system Solve $Ax = y$ for x	928 381	1 858 051
[11] `Alg.8 Line 45`	Add vinegar and oil terms $s_i = (v_i + Ox_i) \mid\mid x_i$	105 209	188 488
Total cycle counts for signing		9 122 185	16 783 809

6.2 Side-Channel Evaluation

In this section, we present evaluation results for potential side-channel leakages of an unprotected compared to our masked implementation of UOV. All experiments regarding leakage evaluation were carried out using the ChipWhisperer tool chain [33, 43] in Python (version 3.9.5) and performed on a ChipWhisperer-Lite board with an STM32F405 target board featuring an Arm Cortex-M4 core with 192 KB of RAM and 1 MB of flash memory.

Since all vulnerable subroutines (cf. Table 4), with the exception of SHAKE, boil down to multiplications, we focus our efforts on the most costly function `gfmat_prod` which multiplies a vector $\mathbf{v}$ with matrices $\mathbf{S}_i$. Therefore, our implementation for side-channel evaluation only provides the `gfmat_prod` function and all required subroutines for generating traces. For leakage evaluation, we applied the commonly used Welch's t-test methodology [40]. More precisely, we used the fixed vs. random (FvR) approach. Thereby, we multiply a random vinegar vector with fixed matrices or random matrices, resp. In this case, these matrices represent part of the (extended) secret key.

As shown in Fig. 4a, the unmasked implementation is highly leaking by presenting very high t-values in the range of about $(100, -100)$, confirming the threat induced by the leakages. In contrast, the t-values for the masked implementation depicted in Fig. 4b are all in the required range of $(-4.5, 4.5)$.

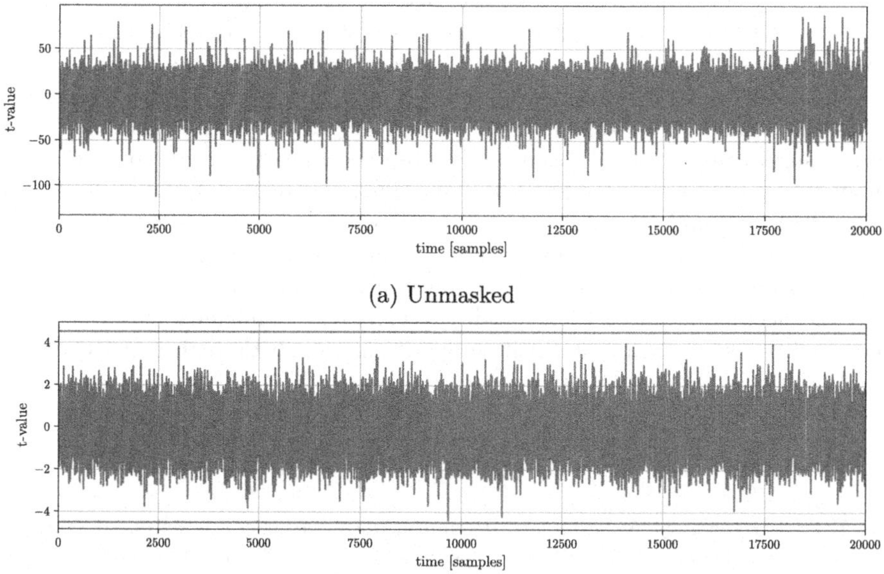

(a) Unmasked

(b) Masked

Fig. 4. Evaluation of the t-test after 10,000 traces for 20 000 samples traced during the computation of the `gfmat_prod` function. The range of the t-values is significantly lower for the masked (b) than for the unmasked version (a). The red lines in (b) indicate the threshold for side-channel leakage. (Color figure online)

7 Conclusion

In this work we conducted an extensive literature review of all existing physical attacks on UOV-based signature schemes and identified further attack vectors. Since all analyzed schemes share a large amount of operations that are contributed to the oil-and-vinegar principle, the theoretical idea behind the attacks transfers really well across the schemes, both for side-channel and fault attacks. Even the utilization of the quotient ring structure in QR-UOV and SNOVA had no impact on the transferability. The technical realization, however, depends highly on the given implementation.

We conclude that certain implementation choices, namely the utilization of compressed keys and employing a randomized signing process, has a positive impact on the resistance against fault attacks. The remaining fault attacks can be covered by dedicated countermeasures, with only a small overhead. Note, that we only covered first-order fault attacks in this work.

However, we see a greater risk with regard to side-channel attacks. In every scheme we analyzed, sensitive values are multiplied with huge amounts of public data, which represents a major gateway for power analysis methods. This observation is confirmed by our TVLA conducted on unprotected multiplication routines of UOV. To this end, we present a first-order masked version of both UOV and MAYO on the basis of their existing optimized Cortex-M4 implementations available within the pqm4 library. The results are supposed to serve as a first assessment of the overhead one can expect when applying masking countermeasures to UOV-based schemes. We observed that the produced overhead is smaller for MAYO than for UOV and identified two reasons for that. First, the amount of random bytes that are necessary to split the matrices into two shares is considerably smaller in MAYO, due to smaller parameters. Second, there are some subroutines in MAYO, i.e., the multiplication with public emulsifier maps and the accumulation of these products, where we concluded masking is not required. Thus, the share of sensitive operations is a little higher in UOV than in MAYO.

References

1. FIPS PUB 202: SHA-3 standard: Permutation-based hash and extendable-output functions. Federal Information Processing Standards Publication 202. National Institute of Standards and Technology, U.S. Department of Commerce (2015)
2. Aulbach, T., Campos, F., Krämer, J., Samardjiska, S., Stöttinger, M.: Separating oil and vinegar with a single trace side-channel assisted Kipnis-Shamir attack on UOV. IACR Trans. Cryptogr. Hardw. Embed. Syst. (2023). https://doi.org/10.46586/tches.v2023.i3.221-245
3. Aulbach, T., Kovats, T., Krämer, J., Marzougui, S.: Recovering rainbow's secret key with a first-order fault attack. In: Progress in Cryptology - AFRICACRYPT 2022: 13th International Conference on Cryptology in Africa. Springer, Cham (2022). https://doi.org/10.1007/978-3-031-17433-9_15
4. Aulbach, T., Marzougui, S., Seifert, J.-P., Ulitzsch, V.Q.: Mayo or may-not: exploring implementation security of the post-quantum signature scheme MAYO against physical attacks. In: Workshop on Fault Detection and Tolerance in Cryptography, FDTC 2024. IEEE (2024). https://doi.org/10.1109/FDTC64268.2024.00012
5. Bertoni, G., Daemen, J., Peeters, M., Van Assche, G.: Building power analysis resistant implementations of Keccak. In: Second SHA-3 Candidate Conference (2010). https://citeseerx.ist.psu.edu/document?repid=rep1&type=pdf&doi=fe3d80a12e34d67ce14d438935302c6ef371901c
6. Beullens, W.: Improved cryptanalysis of UOV and rainbow. In: Canteaut, A., Standaert, F.-X. (eds.) EUROCRYPT 2021. LNCS, vol. 12696, pp. 348–373. Springer, Cham (2021). https://doi.org/10.1007/978-3-030-77870-5_13
7. Beullens, W.: MAYO: practical post-quantum signatures from oil-and-vinegar maps. In: AlTawy, R., Hülsing, A. (eds.) SAC 2021. LNCS, vol. 13203, pp. 355–376. Springer, Cham (2022). https://doi.org/10.1007/978-3-030-99277-4_17
8. Beullens, W.: Breaking rainbow takes a weekend on a laptop. In: Advances in Cryptology - CRYPTO 2022. Springer, Cham (2022). https://doi.org/10.1007/978-3-031-15979-4_16

9. Beullens, W.: Improved cryptanalysis of SNOVA. IACR Cryptol. ePrint Arch. (2024). https://eprint.iacr.org/2024/1297
10. Beullens, W., Campos, F., Celi, S., Hess, B., Kannwischer, M.J.: Nibbling MAYO: optimized implementations for AVX2 and cortex-m4. IACR Trans. Cryptogr. Hardw. Embed. Syst. (2024). https://doi.org/10.46586/tches.v2024.i2.252-275
11. Beullens, W., Campos, F., Celi, S., Hess, B., Kannwischer, M.J.: MAYO. Technical report, National Institute of Standards and Technology (2023). https://csrc.nist.gov/Projects/pqc-dig-sig/round-1-additional-signatures
12. Beullens, W., et al.: UOV. Technical report, National Institute of Standards and Technology (2023). https://csrc.nist.gov/Projects/pqc-dig-sig/round-1-additional-signatures
13. Beullens, W., et al.: Oil and vinegar: modern parameters and implementations. IACR Trans. Cryptogr. Hardw. Embed. Syst. (2023). https://doi.org/10.46586/tches.v2023.i3.321-365
14. Blömer, J., Da Silva, R.G., Günther, P., Krämer, J., Seifert, J.P.: A practical second-order fault attack against a real-world pairing implementation. In: 2014 Workshop on Fault Diagnosis and Tolerance in Cryptography, FDTC 2014. IEEE Computer Society (2014). https://doi.org/10.1109/FDTC.2014.22
15. Chen, M.-S., Chou, T.: Classic McEliece on the ARM cortex-m4. IACR Trans. Cryptogr. Hardw. Embed. Syst. (2021). https://doi.org/10.46586/tches.v2021.i3.125-148
16. Clavier, C., Reynaud, L.: Improved blind side-channel analysis by exploitation of joint distributions of leakages. In: Fischer, W., Homma, N. (eds.) CHES 2017. LNCS, vol. 10529, pp. 24–44. Springer, Cham (2017). https://doi.org/10.1007/978-3-319-66787-4_2
17. Ding, J., et al.: Rainbow. Technical report, National Institute of Standards and Technology (2020). https://csrc.nist.gov/projects/post-quantum-cryptography/round-3-submissions
18. Ding, J., Deaton, J., Vishakha, Yang, B.-Y.: The nested subset differential attack - a practical direct attack against LUOV which forges a signature within 210 minutes. In: Advances in Cryptology - EUROCRYPT 2021. Springer, Cham (2021). https://doi.org/10.1007/978-3-030-77870-5_12
19. Ding, J., et al.: TUOV. Technical report, National Institute of Standards and Technology (2023). https://csrc.nist.gov/Projects/pqc-dig-sig/round-1-additional-signatures
20. Furue, H., et al.: QR-UOV. Technical report, National Institute of Standards and Technology (2023). https://csrc.nist.gov/Projects/pqc-dig-sig/round-1-additional-signatures
21. Furue, H., Kiyomura, Y., Nagasawa, T., Takagi, T.: A new fault attack on UOV multivariate signature scheme. In: Post-Quantum Cryptography - 13th International Workshop, PQCrypto 2022. Springer, Cham (2022). https://doi.org/10.1007/978-3-031-17234-2_7
22. Gierlichs, B., Schmidt, J.-M., Tunstall, M.: Infective computation and dummy rounds: fault protection for block ciphers without check-before-output. In: Hevia, A., Neven, G. (eds.) LATINCRYPT 2012. LNCS, vol. 7533, pp. 305–321. Springer, Heidelberg (2012). https://doi.org/10.1007/978-3-642-33481-8_17
23. Goubin, L., et al.: PROV. Technical report, National Institute of Standards and Technology (2023). https://csrc.nist.gov/Projects/pqc-dig-sig/round-1-additional-signatures

24. Hashimoto, Y., Takagi, T., Sakurai, K.: General fault attacks on multivariate public key cryptosystems. In: Yang, B.-Y. (ed.) PQCrypto 2011. LNCS, vol. 7071, pp. 1–18. Springer, Heidelberg (2011). https://doi.org/10.1007/978-3-642-25405-5_1
25. Jendral, S., Dubrova, E.: MAYO key recovery by fixing vinegar seeds. IACR Cryptol. ePrint Arch. (2024). https://eprint.iacr.org/2024/1550
26. Jendral, S., Dubrova, E.: Single-trace side-channel attacks on MAYO exploiting leaky modular multiplication. IACR Cryptol. ePrint Arch. (2024). https://eprint.iacr.org/2024/1850
27. Jendral, S., Mattsson, J.P., Dubrova, E.: A single-trace fault injection attack on hedged module lattice digital signature algorithm (ML-DSA). In: Workshop on Fault Detection and Tolerance in Cryptography, FDTC 2024. IEEE (2024). https://doi.org/10.1109/FDTC64268.2024.00013
28. Kannwischer, M.J., Rijneveld, J., Schwabe, P., Stoffelen, K.: pqm4: testing and benchmarking NIST PQC on ARM cortex-m4. IACR Cryptol. ePrint Arch. (2019). https://eprint.iacr.org/2019/844
29. Kipnis, A., Patarin, J., Goubin, L.: Unbalanced oil and vinegar signature schemes. In: Stern, J. (ed.) EUROCRYPT 1999. LNCS, vol. 1592, pp. 206–222. Springer, Heidelberg (1999). https://doi.org/10.1007/3-540-48910-X_15
30. Koo, N., Shim, K.-A.: Security analysis of reusing vinegar values in UOV signature scheme. IEEE Access (2024). https://doi.org/10.1109/ACCESS.2024.3409778
31. Krämer, J., Loiero, M.: Fault attacks on UOV and rainbow. In: Polian, I., Stöttinger, M. (eds.) COSADE 2019. LNCS, vol. 11421, pp. 193–214. Springer, Cham (2019). https://doi.org/10.1007/978-3-030-16350-1_11
32. Mus, K., Islam, S., Sunar, B.: Quantumhammer: a practical hybrid attack on the LUOV signature scheme. In: CCS 2020: 2020 ACM SIGSAC Conference on Computer and Communication Security. ACM (2020). https://doi.org/10.1145/3372297.3417272
33. O'Flynn, C., Chen, Z.D.: ChipWhisperer: an open-source platform for hardware embedded security research. In: Prouff, E. (ed.) COSADE 2014. LNCS, vol. 8622, pp. 243–260. Springer, Cham (2014). https://doi.org/10.1007/978-3-319-10175-0_17
34. Park, A., Shim, K.-A., Koo, N., Han, D.-G.: Side-channel attacks on post-quantum signature schemes based on multivariate quadratic equations - rainbow and UOV. IACR Trans. Cryptogr. Hardw. Embed. Syst. (2018). https://doi.org/10.13154/tches.v2018.i3.500-523
35. Patarin, J., et al.: VOX. Technical report, National Institute of Standards and Technology (2023). https://csrc.nist.gov/Projects/pqc-dig-sig/round-1-additional-signatures
36. Pébereau, P.: One vector to rule them all: Key recovery from one vector in UOV schemes. In: Post-Quantum Cryptography - 15th International Workshop, PQCrypto 2024. Springer, Cham (2024). https://doi.org/10.1007/978-3-031-62746-0_5
37. Petzoldt, A., Thomae, E., Bulygin, S., Wolf, C.: Small public keys and fast verification for $\mathcal{M}$ultivariate $\mathcal{Q}$uadratic public key systems. In: Preneel, B., Takagi, T. (eds.) CHES 2011. LNCS, vol. 6917, pp. 475–490. Springer, Heidelberg (2011). https://doi.org/10.1007/978-3-642-23951-9_31
38. Ravi, P., Jap, D., Bhasin, S., Chattopadhyay, A.: Invited paper: machine learning based blind side-channel attacks on PQC-based KEMs - a case study of kyber KEM. In: IEEE/ACM International Conference on Computer Aided Design, ICCAD 2023. IEEE (2023). https://doi.org/10.1109/ICCAD57390.2023.10323721

39. Sayari, O., Marzougui, S., Aulbach, T., Krämer, J., Seifert, J.-P.: HAMAYO: a fault-tolerant reconfigurable hardware implementation of the MAYO signature scheme. In: Constructive Side-Channel Analysis and Secure Design - 15th International Workshop, COSADE 2024. Springer, Cham (2024). https://doi.org/10.1007/978-3-031-57543-3_13
40. Schneider, T., Moradi, A.: Leakage assessment methodology. In: Güneysu, T., Handschuh, H. (eds.) CHES 2015. LNCS, vol. 9293, pp. 495–513. Springer, Heidelberg (2015). https://doi.org/10.1007/978-3-662-48324-4_25
41. Shim, K.-A., Koo, N.: Algebraic fault analysis of UOV and rainbow with the leakage of random vinegar values. IEEE Trans. Inf. Forensics Secur. (2020). https://doi.org/10.1109/TIFS.2020.2969555
42. Tao, C., Petzoldt, A., Ding, J.: Efficient key recovery for all HFE signature variants. In: Malkin, T., Peikert, C. (eds.) CRYPTO 2021. LNCS, vol. 12825, pp. 70–93. Springer, Cham (2021). https://doi.org/10.1007/978-3-030-84242-0_4
43. NewAE Technology. Repository of ChipWhisperer tool chain - commit a9527b5 (2023). https://github.com/newaetech/chipwhisperer
44. Wang, L.-C., et al.: SNOVA. Technical report, National Institute of Standards and Technology (2023). https://csrc.nist.gov/Projects/pqc-dig-sig/round-1-additional-signatures

Shifting Our Knowledge of MQ-Sign Security

Lars Ran[1(✉)] and Monika Trimoska[2]

[1] Radboud Universiteit, Nijmegen, The Netherlands
lran@cs.ru.nl
[2] Eindhoven University of Technology, Eindhoven, The Netherlands
m.trimoska@tue.nl

Abstract. Unbalanced Oil and Vinegar (UOV) is one of the oldest, simplest, and most studied ad-hoc multivariate signature schemes. UOV signature schemes are attractive because they have very small signatures and fast verification. On the downside, they have large public and secret keys. As a result, variations of the traditional UOV scheme are usually developed with the goal to reduce the key sizes. Seven variants of UOV were submitted to the additional call for digital signatures by NIST, prior to which, a variant named MQ-Sign was submitted to the (South) Korean post-quantum cryptography competition (KpqC). MQ-Sign is currently competing in the second round of KpqC with two variants. One of the variants corresponds to the classic description of UOV with certain implementation and parameter choices. In the other variant, called MQ-Sign-LR, a part of the central map is constructed from row shifts of a single matrix. This design makes for smaller secret keys, and in the case where the equivalent keys optimization is used, it also leads to smaller public keys. However, we show in this work that the polynomial systems arising from an algebraic attack have a specific structure that can be exploited. Specifically, we are able to find preimages for d-periodic targets under the public map with a probability of 63% for all security levels. The complexity of finding these preimages, as well as the fraction of d-periodic target increases with d and hence provides a trade-off. We show that for all security levels one can choose $d = \frac{v}{2}$, for v the number of vinegar variables, and reduce the security claim. Our experiments show practical running times for lower d ranging from 6 s to 14 h.

1 Introduction

The quest for cryptographic schemes that are secure even against attackers equipped with a large-scale quantum computer is in full tilt, and a substantial portion of the current focus is on developing secure digital signature schemes. Even though digital signatures are not concerned by the store-now-decrypt-later attack, it is still of great urgency to find practical solutions that replace the

This research has been supported by the Dutch government through the NWO grant OCNW.M.21.193 (ALPaQCa).

R. Niederhagen and M.-J. O. Saarinen (Eds.): PQCrypto 2025, LNCS 15577, pp. 232–252, 2025.
https://doi.org/10.1007/978-3-031-86599-2_8

non-post-quantum signature schemes that are currently deployed. For certain applications, for instance issuing signatures for documents that have a long validity period, replacing the signatures once a quantum computer is available can not bring back confidence in the validity of the signature. Furthermore, many embedded devices are designed to have a long shelf-life and simply replacing the cryptosystem in the future is not a viable option for these use-cases either. This effort is further motivated by the various worldwide standardization initiatives. The additional call for digital signatures by NIST recently came to the start of its second round, where 14 candidates were selected to advance through the selection process [16]. Another initiative that aims at encouraging the development and advancing the field of post-quantum cryptography is the Korean post-quantum Cryptography (KpqC) project [21]. Promoting innovative research and broadening the field being the foremost goal of the KpqC project is also symbolized in the acronym, where the lowercase letters 'p' and 'q' put together resemble the Chinese character for 'door'. Most prominently, the KpqC project is responsible for organizing the KpqC competition that started in 2022, calling for submissions of post-quantum Key Encapsulation Mechanisms (KEMs) and post-quantum digital signatures. The competition is currently moving towards the end of round 2 and the work in this paper analyzes one of the candidates that is competing for the win. An analysis on all round 1 candidates can be found in [7].

Multivariate digital signatures based on the trapdoor construction are an appealing candidate solution because they commonly yield small signatures and fast verification running times. On the other hand, they come with huge public and secret keys. Hence, optimizations of signature schemes that follow this paradigm focus primarily on reducing these sizes. One way to accomplish this is public key compression, a method where the design of the system offers the possibility of having a part of the public map generated from a *seed*. Employing such a method is not always possible, and depends on the concrete construction of the cryptosystem. Another approach is to incorporate an additional structure to the secret/public quadratic maps that allows us to generate them from a smaller input. This second approach also needs a novel design, but moreover, it requires extensive security analysis to ensure that the additional structure does not render the problem of inverting the public maps easier, which would implicitly put in jeopardy the security of the cryptosystem. The latter approach is explored in MQ-Sign, a digital signature scheme that was submitted to the KpqC competition. The initial idea rested on *sparseness*, i.e. having only few nonzero entries in the central map. This design was attacked first in [2] and shortly after in [13], which lead to the idea being abandoned and replaced by a different approach in the round 2 proposal of MQ-Sign. In round 2, a new variant of MQ-Sign, called MQ-Sign-LR, was introduced. This variant uses linear forms to generate a part of the central map, which makes it significantly more compact. In this work, we take a closer look at the underlying structure and the security of this new variant.

Our Contributions. In this work we analyse the security claim of the newly proposed MQ-Sign variant called MQ-Sign-LR. As a first contribution, we give an alternative description of the cyclic systems appearing in the public key of this variant by using row-shift matrices. Then, armed with this reformulation, we observe that we can make quadratic maps coincide by using periodic input. This leads to our discovery of *weak targets*, namely periodic targets, of which we can find preimages faster. Furthermore, we show that we are able to practically find preimages for a substantial subset of them, with running times ranging from 6 s to 14 h. The fact that these weak targets exists and are practically invertible for all security levels of MQ-Sign-LR is already a security concern.

Our second contribution is turning these findings into a universal forgery attack that challenges the security claims for all security levels. More precisely, we show that the class of weak targets is big enough for an attacker to enumerate salts until a weak target is found.

Our third contribution is isolating a hardness assumption, the Shifted MQ problem, $SMQ(n, q)$, underlying this attack, and providing a novel method for solving it. The proposed algorithm is a variant of FXL, whereby care is taken in which variables, or actually linear constraints in this case, are fixed. It turns out that, fixing one linear constraint can lead to two quadratic equations devolving into linear equations, hence simplifying the system considerably. We show that this can be done once per distinct nth root of unity in $\mathbb{F}_q$.

Finally, we back up all our claims by running and documenting an extensive array of experiments.

2 Background

Let $\mathbb{F}_q$ be the finite field of q elements. We use bold letters to denote vectors, e.g. $\mathbf{x}, \mathbf{t}$, and matrices, e.g. $\mathbf{P}, \mathbf{F}$. We write (column) vectors as $\mathbf{a} = (a_1, \ldots, a_n)$ and the entries of a vector $\mathbf{a}$ are denoted by a_i, or, if $\mathbf{a}$ itself has a subscript, e.g. $\mathbf{a}_b$, by $(a_b)_i$. When we use indices in superscript they will always be enclosed in parentheses, for example $\mathbf{P}^{(i)}$.

2.1 Quadratic Forms

Let $p(x_1, \ldots, x_n) = \sum_{1 \leqslant i \leqslant j \leqslant n} \gamma_{ij} x_i x_j$ be a quadratic form over $\mathbb{F}_q$. Then, for fields of odd characteristic, p can be represented by a symmetric matrix $\mathbf{P}$ where $\mathbf{P}_{ij} = \gamma_{ij}/2$ for $i \neq j$, and $\mathbf{P}_{ii} = \gamma_{ii}$. There is a one-to-one correspondence between quadratic forms and symmetric matrices, since for $\mathbf{x} = (x_1, \ldots, x_n)$ it holds that

$$p(x_1, \ldots, x_n) = \mathbf{x}^\top \mathbf{P} \mathbf{x}.$$

With this representation, all operations on quadratic forms naturally transform into operations on matrices since the one-to-one correspondence between quadratic forms and symmetric matrices is actually an isomorphism. Over fields $\mathbb{F}_q$ of even characteristic, this relation does not hold, since for a symmetric matrix

$\mathbf{P}$ we have $(\mathbf{P}_{ij}+\mathbf{P}_{ji})x_ix_j = 2\mathbf{P}_{ij}x_ix_j = 0$. Thus, in even characteristic we associate to p an upper-triangular matrix with coefficients $\mathbf{P}_{ij} = \gamma_{ij}$ for $i \leqslant j$. With this representation, some nice computational properties of the symmetric matrix representation break down, but in practical applications this can be overcome and the upper-triangular representation is used when working with fields of even characteristic. The operation Upper is used to transform any matrix representing a quadratic form to upper-triangular form.

2.2 The UOV Construction

A trapdoor construction is a combination of a function and a trapdoor whereby computing the function is easy for everyone, but inverting it is hard for parties that do not have knowledge on the trapdoor. The oil and vinegar construction, first proposed in [17], is a leading example of such a trapdoor construction. Unfortunately, the initial proposal of this construction was broken one year later in [15]. However, one more year later, Kipnis, Patarin, and Goubin in [14] proposed the Unbalanced Oil and Vinegar construction that is still considered secure to this day.

This construction can be specified as a sequence of m quadratic maps

$$\mathcal{F} = (f^{(1)}, \ldots, f^{(m)}) \in \mathbb{F}_q[x_1, \ldots, x_n]$$

in n variables. However, these maps are of a specific shape, in the sense that not all quadratic monomials are present. This shape can be described by splitting the variables into vinegar variables $(x_1, \ldots, x_v)$ and oil variables $(x_{v+1}, \ldots, x_{v+o})$ where $o = m = n - v$. Then the quadratic maps are given as

$$f^{(k)} = \sum_{\substack{1 \leq i \leq v \\ i \leq j \leq n}} \alpha_{ij}^{(k)} x_i x_j + \sum_i \beta_i^{(k)} x_i + \gamma^{(k)}. \tag{1}$$

Knowing this structure, it is easy to find preimages for any target $\mathbf{t} \in \mathbb{F}_q^m$ by fixing all vinegar variables and solving the remaining linear system. Therefore, we apply an invertible linear map $\mathcal{S}$ to define the public key $\mathcal{P} = \mathcal{F} \circ \mathcal{S}$. This linear transformation hides the special structure of the central map and the security of UOV relies on the assumption that the public map obtained in such a way is indistinguishable from a random quadratic map.

UOV follows the standard signature generation and verification process of a trapdoor-based multivariate signature scheme. In the following, we summarize the two algorithms. For simplicity, we omit the use of the linear transformation of the output, as this is not used in UOV or MQ-Sign.

Signature Generation. To generate a signature for a message M, the signer uses a hash function $H : \{0,1\}^\star \to \mathbb{F}_q^m$ and a salt r to compute the hash value $\mathbf{t} = H(M||r) \in \mathbb{F}_q^m$, and computes recursively $\mathbf{y} = \mathcal{F}^{-1}(\mathbf{t}) \in \mathbb{F}_q^n$, and $\mathbf{z} = \mathcal{S}^{-1}(\mathbf{y})$. The signature of the message M is $\mathbf{z} \in \mathbb{F}_q^n$. Here, $\mathcal{F}^{-1}(\mathbf{t})$ means finding one (of possibly many) preimages of $\mathbf{t}$ under the central map $\mathcal{F}$.

Verification. To check if $\mathbf{z} \in \mathbb{F}_q^n$ is indeed a valid signature for a message M, one computes $\mathbf{t} = H(M||r)$ and $\mathbf{t}' = \mathcal{P}(\mathbf{z}) \in \mathbb{F}_q^m$. If $\mathbf{t}' = \mathbf{t}$ holds, the signature is accepted, otherwise it is rejected.

For cryptographic schemes in the UOV family, the linear and constant parts of Eq. (1) are usually dropped and we work only with quadratic forms. The shape of the quadratic forms that form the central map in upper-triangular form is

$$\mathbf{F}^{(k)} = \begin{pmatrix} \mathbf{F}_1^{(k)} & \mathbf{F}_2^{(k)} \\ \mathbf{0} & \mathbf{0} \end{pmatrix}, \tag{2}$$

where the $\mathbf{F}_1^{(k)}$ are upper-triangular. We use this block matrix notation to distinguish between the so-called vinegar-vinegar part and vinegar-oil part of the secret key. The matrices $\mathbf{F}_1^{(k)}$ hold the coefficients of monomials comprised of two vinegar variables, whereas the matrices $\mathbf{F}_2^{(k)}$ hold the coefficients of the monomials that are a product of one vinegar and one oil variable. Note that the lower-right corner is the zero matrix because there are no oil-oil monomials in the central map. Using this notation the public maps can be computed as

$$\mathbf{P}^{(k)} = \begin{pmatrix} \mathbf{P}_1^{(k)} & \mathbf{P}_2^{(k)} \\ \mathbf{0} & \mathbf{P}_4^{(k)} \end{pmatrix} = \mathcal{S}^T \begin{pmatrix} \mathbf{F}_1^{(k)} & \mathbf{F}_2^{(k)} \\ \mathbf{0} & \mathbf{0} \end{pmatrix} \mathcal{S}. \tag{3}$$

Equivalent Keys. It was shown in [19] that for any instance of a UOV secret key $(\mathcal{F}', \mathcal{S})$, there exists an equivalent secret key $(\mathcal{F}, \mathbf{S})$ with

$$\mathbf{S} = \begin{pmatrix} \mathbf{I}_{v \times v} & \mathbf{S}_1 \\ \mathbf{0}_{m \times v} & \mathbf{I}_{m \times m} \end{pmatrix}. \tag{4}$$

For an attacker, it is not necessary to find the original secret key that was obtained at key generation, i.e. the one that a valid signer is in possession of. The goal is rather to find any of the equivalent keys as they can all be used to forge a signature. Since finding a secret key where $\mathbf{S}$ is of the form as in Eq. (4) seems to be the least computationally intensive, we consider the complexity of this as a baseline for a key recovery attack that aims at finding the secret matrix $\mathbf{S}$. As a consequence, a key of this specific form can be used as part of the specification of the cryptosystem, in which case the matrix $\mathbf{S}$ can be stored using fewer entries. We refer to this as the equivalent-keys optimization, and this optimization is used in most modern instantiations of UOV. Note however that this optimization technique introduces vulnerabilities when we consider physical attacks [1].

2.3 The MQ-Sign Digital Signature Scheme

MQ-Sign is a UOV-based signature scheme, where the main focus is to reduce the size of the public and secret key compared to traditional UOV. In the first-round proposal of MQ-Sign, this was achieved by using sparse polynomials for the quadratic part of the central map. In the central map, we distinguish two main parts: the vinegar-vinegar part, which consists of monomials that contain two vinegar variables, and the vinegar-oil part, comprised of the monomials containing one vinegar variable and one oil variable. There were initially four variations of the scheme: MQ-Sign-SS, MQ-Sign-RS, MQ-Sign-SR and MQ-Sign-RR, where the suffix specifies, for the two parts of the quadratic maps, whether they are defined with sparse or random polynomials.

Three attacks on MQ-Sign were published during the first round of the competition, which eliminated all but the last variant of MQ-Sign, denoted MQ-Sign-RR. This is the most conservative variant as it is built on the UOV trapdoor without any additional structure. The first algebraic attack on MQ-Sign was proposed by Aulbach, Samardjiska, and Trimoska [2], and it exploits the sparseness of the vinegar-oil part of the secret key. The attack also relies on the fact that the map $\mathcal{S}$ is chosen to be given by a matrix of the form as in Eq. (4). Recall that, this typically does not reduce the security of a UOV-based scheme because it was shown in [19] that for any instance of a UOV secret key $(\mathcal{F}', \mathbf{S}')$, there is an equivalent key $(\mathcal{F}, \mathbf{S})$ where $\mathbf{S}$ has the form as in (4). However, coupling this optimization technique with the specific structure of the central map in MQ-Sign yields many linear constraints that allow for a polynomial-time key recovery. The attack was fully implemented, and it was reported to run in 0.6 s for the proposed parameters for security level I, 2.3 s for security level III and 6.9 s for security level V.

Following this, Ikematsu, Jo, and Yasuda proposed another algebraic attack that also targets the MQ-Sign-{S/R}S variants but is not dependent on $\mathbf{S}$ having the equivalent keys structure [13]. These two attacks eliminated both variants where the vinegar-oil part of the secret key is sparse.

Another algebraic attack was proposed in [2] which targets specifically the variant where only the vinegar-vinegar part of the secret key is sparse. This attack is not practical, but shows that the security of MQ-Sign-SR does not meet the required security level and this variant is also removed from the updated submission in round 2.

MQ-Sign advanced to the second round of KpqC and the second-round submission includes the variant corresponding to traditional UOV, MQ-Sign-RR, and a new design that leads to an additional variant called MQ-Sign-LR. This new non-conservative variant of MQ-Sign has smaller secret keys, while maintaining the same signature size as MQ-Sign-RR. This variant reportedly yields better performance for both key generation and signing. Note that since the reduction of the size of the secret key is in the vinegar-vinegar part, when the equivalent-keys optimization is used, this yields a reduction in the public key size as well. This is because when $\mathbf{S}$ is of the form as in Eq. (4), the vinegar-vinegar part of the public key is equal to the vinegar-vinegar part of the secret key. This will be explained in more detail in the following section.

The main difference between the two MQ-Sign variants is in the structure of the vinegar-vinegar part of the central map. In MQ-Sign-LR, the vinegar-vinegar part of the central map is constructed as a product of a circulant matrix where the entries are the vinegar variables $(x_1, \ldots, x_v)$ and a vector whose entries are linear combinations of the vinegar variables. Specifically, the central map is defined as

$$\begin{pmatrix} x_1 & x_2 & \cdots & x_v \\ x_v & x_1 & \cdots & x_{v-1} \\ \cdots & \cdots & \cdots & \cdots \\ x_{v-m+2} & x_{v-m+3} & \cdots & x_{v-m+1} \end{pmatrix} \cdot \begin{pmatrix} L_1 \\ L_2 \\ \cdots \\ L_v \end{pmatrix}, \tag{5}$$

where $L_i = \sum_{j=1}^{v} \gamma_{ij} x_j$, for $i \in \{1, \ldots, v\}$ and each row of the product matrix gives a polynomial in $\mathcal{F}$. As a result, the vinegar-vinegar part of the central map can be represented with v^2 field elements[1], instead of the $\frac{v^2 m}{2}$ field elements that are required in the MQ-Sign-RR variant.

For reference for the rest of the paper, we recall here the parameters of MQ-Sign for all security levels. The parameter choices are the same between the two variants MQ-Sign-LR and MQ-Sign-RR. They are chosen such that the cryptosystem resists all generic attacks againts the UOV family (Table 1).

Table 1. The parameters of MQ-Sign.

Level	q	v	m
I	2^8	72	46
III	2^8	112	72
V	2^8	148	96

2.4 Multivariate System Solving

A problem that comes up naturally in analyzing such UOV-like systems is that of solving multivariate (quadratic) systems. In these problems, one is presented with a system, $\mathcal{F} = (f_1, \ldots, f_m)$, consisting of m equations in n variables over $\mathbb{F}_q$ and one would like to find a solution to the system. In this work, we will only consider such problems with $m \geq n$, also known as (over-)determined systems. Current state-of-the-art algorithms for computing such solutions are, for example, F4 [10], F5 [11], XL, and FXL [8]. All of these algorithms are extensions of the Buchberger algorithm [3]. These algorithms have much the same underlying theory for deriving their asymptotic complexity. We give a simple overview here, focusing on the complexity of XL as this algorithm behaves most predicatively.

The central parameter indicating the complexity is the solving degree d_{solv}. This is the minimum degree d for which the rowspace [6] of the Macaulay matrix of degree d contains the Gröbner basis of the system (w.r.t. the *grevlex* monomial

[1] The submission counts $v(v+m)$ elements, which corresponds to the evaluation costs, but not to the number of stored elements.

order). Computing the solving degree is difficult in general, but it can be upper-bounded by other relevant invariants [6], including the degree of regularity d_{reg} as shown in [20]. Following [4,12], the degree of regularity is defined by

$$d_{reg} = \min\{d \geq 0 \mid (\mathcal{F}^{top})_d = R_d\},$$

where $\mathcal{F}^{top}$ is the top homogenous part of our system, R_d are all monomials of degree d, and $(\mathcal{F}^{top})_d = (\mathcal{F}) \cap R_d$. Now, if $\deg f_i \leq d_{solv}$ for all i, then one obtains the bound

$$d_{solv} \leq d_{reg} + 1.$$

In the case of a semi-regular sequence of quadratic equations, we can actually compute the degree of regularity as the first non-positive coefficient of the Hilbert series

$$\frac{(1-t^2)^m}{(1-t)^n}.$$

However, for structured systems, these estimations may not hold.

Once the solving degree of the system is determined, the complexity of the XL algorithm is given as

$$\mathcal{C}_{XL(n,m,q)} = 3\binom{n+d_{solv}}{d_{solv}}^2 \binom{n+2}{2} \left(\log_2(q)^2 + \log_2(q)\right).$$

This is the cost of applying the block-Wiedemann algorithm on a matrix of size $\binom{n+d_{solv}}{d_{solv}}$, with density $\binom{n+2}{2}$ and a field operation cost of $\left(\log_2(q)^2 + \log_2(q)\right)$.

Then, the FXL algorithm improves on this by fixing g variables first. Choosing the correct g is part of a trade-off and depends on n, m, q. Note that d_{solv} is now generally dependent on g. The complexity of the algorithm is now given by

$$\mathcal{C}_{FXL(n,m,q)} = \min_{g \leq n} q^g \cdot \mathcal{C}_{XL(n-g,m,q)}.$$

3 A Forgery Attack

We show in this section how a forgery attack can be mounted against MQ-Sign-LR. The attack relies on the specific structure arising from the new design, as well as on the use of the equivalent keys optimization. Recall that when this optimization is used, the secret matrix $\mathbf{S}$ is of the form as in Eq. (4), in which case the matrices representing the public and the secret map share a common block. Following the notation in this paper, the common block is the upper-left block that corresponds to the vinegar-vinegar part of the maps. This can be observed from the equation defining the computation of the public key

$$\begin{pmatrix} \mathbf{P}_1^{(k)} & \mathbf{P}_2^{(k)} \\ \mathbf{0} & \mathbf{P}_4^{(k)} \end{pmatrix} = \begin{pmatrix} \mathbf{I} & \mathbf{0} \\ \mathbf{S}_1^\top & \mathbf{I} \end{pmatrix} \begin{pmatrix} \mathbf{F}_1^{(k)} & \mathbf{F}_2^{(k)} \\ \mathbf{0} & \mathbf{0} \end{pmatrix} \begin{pmatrix} \mathbf{I} & \mathbf{S}_1 \\ \mathbf{0} & \mathbf{I} \end{pmatrix},$$

which in upper-triangular matrix form simplifies to

$$\begin{pmatrix} \mathbf{P}_1^{(k)} & \mathbf{P}_2^{(k)} \\ \mathbf{0} & \mathbf{P}_4^{(k)} \end{pmatrix} = \begin{pmatrix} \mathbf{F}_1^{(k)} & (\mathbf{F}_1^{(k)} + \mathbf{F}_1^{(k)\top})\mathbf{S}_1 + \mathbf{F}_2^{(k)} \\ \mathbf{0} & \mathsf{Upper}(\mathbf{S}_1^\top \mathbf{F}_1^{(k)} \mathbf{S}_1 + \mathbf{S}_1^\top \mathbf{F}_2^{(k)}) \end{pmatrix}.$$

In the following, we show how an attacker can forge a signature of a message M, which consists in finding a preimage of $\mathbf{t} = H(M||r)$ under the public map $\mathcal{P}$. We will write in block matrix representation since we are using the specific structure of the upper-left block of the public map. The goal is to find a vector $(\mathbf{x}_v, \mathbf{x}_m) \in \mathbb{F}_q^n$ such that

$$(\mathbf{x}_v \ \mathbf{x}_m) \begin{pmatrix} \mathbf{P}_1^{(k)} & \mathbf{P}_2^{(k)} \\ \mathbf{0} & \mathbf{P}_4^{(k)} \end{pmatrix} \begin{pmatrix} \mathbf{x}_v \\ \mathbf{x}_m \end{pmatrix} = \mathbf{x}_v^T \mathbf{P}_1^{(k)} \mathbf{x}_v + \mathbf{x}_v^T \mathbf{P}_2^{(k)} \mathbf{x}_m + \mathbf{x}_m^T \mathbf{P}_4^{(k)} \mathbf{x}_m = t_k$$

holds for every $k \in \{1, \ldots, m\}$. Note here that $\mathbf{P}_1^{(k)}$ has the same shape as $\mathbf{F}_1^{(k)}$ because of the equivalent keys form of $\mathbf{S}$, and we will use this structure in the attack. Let us denote by $V(\mathbf{t})$ the variety (the set of solutions) of the ideal generated by $\mathcal{P}(\mathbf{x}) = \mathbf{t}$. Since we have m equations in n variables with $n > m$, we can afford to add another $v = n - m$ affine constraints and still expect, heuristically, to have a solution. We use only m (recall that $m < v$) of those to eliminate the non-structured part of this system. Specifically, we assign all variables in $\mathbf{x}_m$ to zero. We are then left with the system

$$\mathbf{x}_v^T \mathbf{P}_1^{(k)} \mathbf{x}_v = t_k \tag{6}$$

that contains only the block $\mathbf{P}_1^{(k)}$, and thus inherits the structure depicted in Eq. (5).

3.1 Quadratic Maps in MQ-Sign-LR

Since our focus is on solving polynomial systems arising from the constraint in Eq. (6), we first take a closer look into the structure of these systems. Recall that the polynomials in this system are obtained as in Eq. (5). Hence, we have the following system of equations

$$\begin{aligned} & x_1 L_1 + x_2 L_2 + \cdots + x_v L_v = t_1, \\ & x_1 L_2 + x_2 L_3 + \cdots + x_v L_1 = t_2, \\ & \cdots \\ & x_1 L_m + x_2 L_{m+1} + \cdots + x_v L_{m-1} = t_m. \end{aligned} \tag{7}$$

Let us denote by σ the mapping that sends L_i to its coordinate vector, i.e.

$$\sigma: \ L_i = \sum_{j=1}^{v} \gamma_{ij} x_j \mapsto \sigma(L_i) = (\gamma_{i1}, \ldots, \gamma_{iv}).$$

When we rewrite the equations from (7) in matrix form we obtain

$$\begin{aligned}
\mathbf{x}_v^\top \mathbf{P}_1^{(1)} \mathbf{x}_v &= t_1, \\
\mathbf{x}_v^\top \mathbf{P}_1^{(2)} \mathbf{x}_v &= t_2, \\
&\dots \\
\mathbf{x}_v^\top \mathbf{P}_1^{(m)} \mathbf{x}_v &= t_m,
\end{aligned}$$

where

$$\mathbf{P}_1^{(1)} = \begin{pmatrix} \sigma(L_1) \\ \sigma(L_2) \\ \dots \\ \sigma(L_v) \end{pmatrix}, \quad \mathbf{P}_1^{(2)} = \begin{pmatrix} \sigma(L_2) \\ \sigma(L_3) \\ \dots \\ \sigma(L_1) \end{pmatrix}, \quad \dots \quad, \quad \mathbf{P}_1^{(m)} = \begin{pmatrix} \sigma(L_m) \\ \sigma(L_{m+1}) \\ \dots \\ \sigma(L_{m-1}) \end{pmatrix}. \tag{8}$$

This is because the i-th row of the matrix contains the coefficients of all monomials containing x_i, which for the k-th polynomial, is exactly given by the coordinates of $L_{i+k \bmod v}$. Note that these matrices are not the canonical representation of the polynomials, as they are not symmetric or upper-triangular. Nevertheless, they are a valid representation of the corresponding polynomials, since we have that the sum of the entry $\{i, j\}$ and the entry $\{j, i\}$ is equal to the coefficient of the monomial $x_i x_j$. We will keep this non-canonical representation, as it facilitates the exposition.

From Eq. (8), it is easy to spot that the matrices representing these quadratic forms are equal up to cyclic row-shifts. Specifically, we have that $\mathbf{P}_1^{(k+1)}$ is obtained from a cyclic upward shift of the rows of $\mathbf{P}_1^{(k)}$. Let us denote by $\mathbf{T}$ the matrix representing the permutation corresponding to a cyclic upward row shift. Then, $\mathbf{T}^i$ represents a cyclic upward row shift by i steps. The system of equations that we aim to solve takes the following form

$$\begin{aligned}
\mathbf{x}_v^\top \mathbf{P}_1^{(1)} \mathbf{x}_v &= t_1, \\
\mathbf{x}_v^\top \mathbf{T} \mathbf{P}_1^{(1)} \mathbf{x}_v &= t_2, \\
&\dots \\
\mathbf{x}_v^\top \mathbf{T}^{m-1} \mathbf{P}_1^{(1)} \mathbf{x}_v &= t_m.
\end{aligned} \tag{9}$$

Since we can now express all equations in terms of $\mathbf{P}_1^{(1)}$, we will write $\mathbf{P} = \mathbf{P}_1^{(1)}$.

3.2 Computing Preimages of Weak Targets

The specific structure of the quadratic maps described in the previous section allows us to find preimages of certain target vectors $\mathbf{t}$ more easily. We will refer to these vectors as weak targets. The reason it is easier to find preimages for these weak targets is that, because of the cyclic structure of the maps, we can construct our input vectors in such a way that they fulfill some constraints by design. To explain this idea, we will start by looking at the homogenous case, i.e. finding preimages of $\mathbf{0}$. The vector $\mathbf{0}$ is indeed one of the weak targets.

We start again from the observation that in the system in Eq. (9), every subsequent matrix $\mathbf{P}_1^{(k)}$ is obtained by a cyclic row-shift of the previous one. Equivalently, we can imagine that we have the same matrix m times, but the permutation is on the $\mathbf{x}_v^\top$ vectors on the left side, performing cyclic shifts on vector entries (a permutation on columns of $\mathbf{x}_v^\top$, since $\mathbf{T}$ acts on the right). It is then evident that for vectors $\mathbf{x}_v$ where all the entries are equal to each other, if $\mathbf{x}_v$ is a solution to the first equation, then $\mathbf{x}_v$ is a solution to the entire system. We generalize this observation to other specific vectors that have a repeating subsequence.

Let us denote by $\sim$ the binary relation on $\mathbb{F}_q^v$ described informally as "$\mathbf{a}$ is equal to $\mathbf{b}$ up to a cyclic right-shift (without loss of generality)". This is indeed an equivalence relation because (i) $\mathbf{a} \sim \mathbf{a}$ by a shift of zero, (ii) if $\mathbf{a}$ is obtained by performing a right-shift of k on $\mathbf{b}$, then $\mathbf{b}$ can be obtained by a right-shift of $v-k$ on $\mathbf{a}$, and (iii) if $\mathbf{a}$ is a k-shift away from $\mathbf{b}$ and $\mathbf{b}$ is an l-shift away from $\mathbf{c}$, then $\mathbf{a}$ is a $((k+l)\text{mod}v)$-shift away from $\mathbf{c}$. We further know that, for a given v, the number and size of such equivalence classes in $\mathbb{F}_q^v$ can be derived by looking at the divisors of v. For each divisor d of v, we have up to q^d equivalence classes of size d. We now make the following observation for the system in Eq. (7). If $\mathbf{x}$ belongs to an equivalence class of size d and $\mathbf{x}$ is a solution to the first d equations in (7), then $\mathbf{x}$ is a solution to the entire system. This observation tells us that the system does not behave like a *random* system and that there are some vectors that are probabilistically more likely to be a solution to the system than others, as they only need to satisfy a subset of the equations. We exploit this by looking for such solutions using the following strategy.

For each divisor d of v, excluding v[2] and taken in ascending order, build a smaller system by taking the first d equations of the initial system in Eq. (7) and replacing the unknown $\mathbf{x}_v = (x_1, \ldots, x_v)$ by

$$\mathbf{x} = (x_1, \ldots, x_d, x_1, \ldots, x_d, \ldots, x_1, \ldots, x_d).$$

This is a quadratic system of d equations in d variables. Denote $\mathbf{x}_d = (x_1, \ldots, x_d)$. To concretely describe the structure, we introduce the matrices

$$\mathbf{J}_{d,n} = (I_d, \ldots, I_d) \in \mathcal{M}^{d \times n}(\mathbb{F}_q)$$

for $d \mid n$. For simplicity, we define $\mathbf{J}_{n,d} = \mathbf{J}_{d,n}^T$. This allows us to write

$$\mathbf{x} = (x_1, \ldots, x_d, x_1, \ldots, x_d, \ldots, x_1, \ldots, x_d) = \mathbf{J}_{n,d}(x_1, \ldots, x_d) = \mathbf{J}_{n,d}\mathbf{x}_d.$$

Also note how this commutes with the cyclic shift matrices

$$\mathbf{T}_n^i \mathbf{J}_{n,d} = \mathbf{J}_{n,d}\mathbf{T}_d^i = \mathbf{J}_{n,d}\mathbf{T}_d^{i \bmod d}.$$

[2] In fact, we also need $d < m$. However, for the systems considered, this holds for all divisors d of v except v itself.

Now let us take a closer look at the equations that we obtain if we look for solutions $\mathbf{x}$ that map to $\mathbf{0}$

$$\begin{aligned} 0 &= \mathbf{x}^\top \mathbf{T}^{i-1}\mathbf{P}\mathbf{x} \\ &= \mathbf{x}_d^\top \mathbf{J}_{d,v}\mathbf{T}^{i-1}\mathbf{P}\mathbf{J}_{v,d}\mathbf{x}_d \\ &= \mathbf{x}_d^\top \mathbf{T}^{i-1}\mathbf{J}_{d,v}\mathbf{P}\mathbf{J}_{v,d}\mathbf{x}_d. \end{aligned} \tag{10}$$

Since these type of equations are central in the rest of this work we will define the following problem to aid the discussion.

Problem 1. SMQ(n, q) (Shifted MQ problem)

Let $\mathbf{P} \in \mathcal{M}^{n\times n}(\mathbb{F}_q)$ be a matrix and let $\mathbf{t} \in \mathbb{F}_q^m$ be a vector. The *Shifted MQ problem* asks to find—if any—a solution $\mathbf{x} \in \mathbb{F}_q^n$ to the following system of equations

$$\mathbf{x}^\top \mathbf{T}^{i-1}\mathbf{P}\mathbf{x} = t_i \quad \text{for all} \quad 1 \le i \le n. \tag{11}$$

Here, $\mathbf{P}$ is called the initial matrix and $\mathbf{t}$ the target vector.

Now, Eq. (10) depicts exactly the shifted MQ problem $SMQ(d, q)$ with initial matrix $\mathbf{J}_{d,v}\mathbf{P}\mathbf{J}_{v,d}$ and target vector $\mathbf{t} = \mathbf{0}$.

Remark 1. With this attack, we are able to find one (or a few) out of many elements in $V(\mathbf{0})$. The secret oil subspace, denoted O, is contained in $V(\mathbf{0})$ and in the case that the obtained vector is part of the oil subspace this would lead to a full key recovery. It is well known from the reconciliation attack [9] that finding the first oil vector is the bottleneck of recovering the secret oil space, and recently it was shown, first in [1] and then in [18], that once we have found the first oil vector, the remaining steps to recover the entire oil space can be done in polynomial time. However, since $V(\mathbf{0})$ is of dimension $n - m$ and O is of dimension m, the probability that the vector we obtain is in O is negligibly small, concretely q^{-n+2m}. Hence, we conclude that this forgery attack does not lead to a key-recovery attack.

Periodic Targets. The reason why the above discussion worked so well is because $\mathbf{0}$ is periodic. In fact, it is even 1-periodic. We can extend the above algorithm to any periodic $\mathbf{t}$. Let $d' \mid v$ with $d' \le m$ and let $\mathbf{t}$ be a d'-periodic vector, in other words $t_i = t_{i+d'}$ for all $1 \le i \le m - d'$. Then for any d with $d' \mid d$ and $d \mid v$ we can apply the same trick and look for d-periodic solutions $\mathbf{x} = (\mathbf{x}_d, \dots, \mathbf{x}_d)$. Building the same equations as above, we obtain the following system of equations

$$\mathbf{x}_d^\top \mathbf{T}^{i-1}\mathbf{J}_{d,v}\mathbf{P}\mathbf{J}_{v,d}\mathbf{x}_d = t_i \quad \text{for all} \quad 1 \le i \le d. \tag{12}$$

This is again the $SMQ(d, q)$ problem with initial matrix $\mathbf{J}_{d',v}\mathbf{P}\mathbf{J}_{v,d'}$, but now with a target vector $\mathbf{t} = (t_1, \dots, t_d)$.

3.3 Forging a Signature

Given that we can find solutions to quite a bit of weak targets, the question is if we can build a signature forgery attack from these findings. In this section, we respond in the affirmative, showing that we can sign any message using this technique, without any knowledge of the secret key. For the MQ-Sign-LR parameter sets, this can be done with a complexity that breaks the security claims for all three levels of security.

Given a message M and a salt r the probability that $\mathbf{t} = H(M||r)$ is d-periodic is quite small. In fact, this probability is given by q^{d-m}. However, as an attacker, we can simply keep on choosing random salts r until we find a hash that is d-periodic. For example, for level I, with $d = v/2 = 36$ and $m = 46$, we only need to resample the salt 2^{80} times on average. Note that the salt is 32 bytes, so for a cryptographic hash function, we will certainly be able to find a good one. Note however that having a d-periodic target is not the only requirement. We also need the corresponding $SMQ(d,q)$ problem to have a solution. In contrast to the signing procedure where the common approach is to resample the chosen values for the v arbitrarily assigned variables, our attack requires that the variables in $\mathbf{x}_m$ are fixed to zero and the rest are chosen as described in the previous section. Let $p_{d,q}$ be the probability that an $SMQ(d,q)$ problem has a solution, and we denote by $\mathcal{C}_{SMQ(d,q)}$ and $\mathcal{C}_H$ the complexity of solving an $SMQ(d,q)$ instance and of computing one hash respectively. We can compute the complexity of forging a signature as

$$\min_{d|v, d<m} p_{d,q}^{-1}(\mathcal{C}_{SMQ(d,q)} + q^{m-d}\mathcal{C}_H). \tag{13}$$

In Sect. 5 we find that, empirically, $p_{d,q}$ is 0.63 and this value is largely independent of d and $q = 2^r$. Furthermore, it turns out that for all parameter sets, the only viable d would be $v/2$. For other d values, the cost of sampling salts would dominate the costs and surpass the security requirement. For this choice of divisor, the amount of salts to generate in the different levels is given in Table 2. This estimation is computed as $q^{m-v/2}$, as the probability of having a $v/2$-periodic hash is $q^{v/2-m}$.

Table 2. The average number of salts to try before finding a $v/2$-periodic hash.

Level	q	v	m	salts
I	2^8	72	46	2^{80}
III	2^8	112	72	2^{128}
V	2^8	148	96	2^{176}

4 Solving the SMQ Problem

As we saw in the last section, the bottleneck of the forgery attack is based on finding solutions to the SMQ problem for random $\mathbf{t}$. In this section, we turn to tacking this problem and perform an initial analysis of our proposed solutions. To use the usual complexity estimates for algorithms in the XL family, we have to find the solving degree. Normally we would assume that our system behaves as a semi-regular system and we would compute the solving degree from that assumption, as explained in the background section. However, given the amount of structure that we observe in the system this seems unlikely. Nevertheless, as we will see in Sect. 5, this assumption still seems to be a good estimator for the solving degree in our experiments. Hence, in this paper, all of the theoretical estimates on the solving degree are done under this counterintuitive assumption. Coupled with extensive experimental work, these estimations are used to show the relevance of the attack, but they should not be used, for instance, for determining security parameters. Indeed, further research is needed to confirm the theoretical findings, or find more precise bounds on the solving degree for instances of the SMQ problem.

4.1 Solving $SMQ(n, q)$ Using FXL

Since the problem at hand consists of a multivariate quadratic system of n equations in n variables, we are going to approach this using a Gröbner basis algorithm. With these parameters, $m \approx n$ and $q = 2^8$, employing a guessing strategy improves the complexity of solving the system. The FXL algorithm [8] is an algorithm that exactly fills that role. The resulting complexities can be found in the left column of Table 3 for several values of n. This is a standard approach and the background section contains further explanations on how these complexities are computed.

Table 3. The theoretical complexity of solving $SMQ(n, 256)$ using FXL with and without improved guessing. The ordinary enumeration due to FXL is denoted by g, whereas the number of guesses made with the improved guessing strategy is denoted by k.

	FXL		Improved guessing FXL	
n	$(g,\, d_{solv})$	$\log_2$ cost	$(k,\, g,\, d_{solv})$	$\log_2$ cost
24	(1, 14)	89	(3, 0, 8)	77
36	(2, 17)	121	(3, 0, 13)	108
56	(3, 24)	174	(1, 1, 26)	171
74	(3, 32)	220	(1, 3, 29)	215

4.2 An Improved Guessing Strategy

Due to the structure of the problem, it turns out that our guessing can be made more effective than usual. Let $\zeta \in \mathbb{F}_q$ be an nth root of unity in $\mathbb{F}_q$. Define the vectors $\mathbf{v}_\zeta, \bar{\mathbf{v}}_\zeta \in \mathbb{F}_q^n$ as $(v_\zeta)_i = \zeta^i$ and $(\bar{v}_\zeta)_i = \zeta^{-i}$. Then we can make the following observation

$$\sum_i \zeta^i \mathbf{T}^i = \bar{\mathbf{v}}_\zeta \mathbf{v}_\zeta^\top.$$

Now we can take and manipulate the following linear equations

$$\begin{aligned}\sum_i \zeta^i t_{i+1} &= \sum_i \zeta^i \mathbf{x}^\top \mathbf{T}^i \mathbf{P}\mathbf{x} \\ &= \mathbf{x}^\top \left(\sum_i \zeta^i \mathbf{T}^i\right) \mathbf{P}\mathbf{x} \\ &= \mathbf{x}^\top \bar{\mathbf{v}}_\zeta \mathbf{v}_\zeta^\top \mathbf{P}\mathbf{x} \\ &= \left(\sum_i \zeta^{-i} x_i\right) \cdot \left(\sum_{i,j} \zeta^i \mathbf{P}_{ij} x_j\right).\end{aligned}$$

Example 1. Pick $\zeta = 1$. Then we get the following equation

$$\sum_i t_i = \left(\sum_i x_i\right) \cdot \left(\sum_i (\mathbf{P}\mathbf{x})_i\right).$$

If we now guess the constraint $\sum_i \zeta^{-i} x_i = \gamma \in \mathbb{F}_q^*$, then we get the linear constraint $\sum_i \zeta^i (\mathbf{P}\mathbf{x})_i = \gamma^{-1} \sum_i \zeta^i t_{i+1}$ for free. To be more precise, using this guess, we were able to turn a quadratic equation into a linear equation. A common technique when we have a linear equation is to trade it to remove one variable. For instance, an equation $\gamma_1 x_1 + \gamma_2 x_2 + \cdots + \gamma_n x_n + \gamma_0 = 0$ is rewritten as $x_1 = -\gamma_1^{-1}(\gamma_2 x_2 + \cdots + \gamma_n x_n + \gamma_0)$ and used to substitute x_1 in the system. Hence, when using k different such roots of unity, we get a system of $n - k$ equations in $n - 2k$ variables using k guesses.

Something interesting happens when $2 \mid n$ in even characteristic. We define the vectors $\mathbf{w}$ and $\bar{\mathbf{w}}$ by

$$(w_\zeta)_i = \begin{cases} \zeta^i & \text{if } i \equiv 0 \mod 2 \\ 0 & \text{if } i \equiv 1 \mod 2 \end{cases} \qquad (\bar{w}_\zeta)_i = \begin{cases} \zeta^{-i} & \text{if } i \equiv 0 \mod 2 \\ 0 & \text{if } i \equiv 1 \mod 2. \end{cases}$$

In that case we have the following observation:

$$\sum_{i \equiv 1 \mod 2} \zeta^i \mathbf{T}^i = \bar{\mathbf{w}}_\zeta \mathbf{v}_\zeta^\top + \bar{\mathbf{v}}_\zeta \mathbf{w}_\zeta^\top. \tag{14}$$

So now if we guess $\mathbf{x}^\top \bar{\mathbf{v}}_\zeta = \gamma \in \mathbb{F}_q^*$ with induced $\mathbf{v}_\zeta^\top \mathbf{P}\mathbf{x} = \beta$ we get:

$$\sum_{i \equiv 1 \mod 2} \zeta^i t_{i+1} = \sum_{i \equiv 1 \mod 2} \zeta^i \mathbf{x}^\top \mathbf{T}^i \mathbf{P}\mathbf{x} \tag{15}$$

$$= \mathbf{x}^\top \left(\bar{\mathbf{w}}_\zeta \mathbf{v}_\zeta^\top + \bar{\mathbf{v}}_\zeta \mathbf{w}_\zeta^\top \right) \mathbf{P}\mathbf{x} \tag{16}$$

$$= \mathbf{x}^\top \bar{\mathbf{w}}_\zeta \mathbf{v}_\zeta^\top \mathbf{P}\mathbf{x} + \mathbf{x}^\top \bar{\mathbf{v}}_\zeta \mathbf{w}_\zeta^\top \mathbf{P}\mathbf{x} \tag{17}$$

$$= \mathbf{x}^\top \bar{\mathbf{w}}_\zeta \beta + \gamma \mathbf{w}_\zeta^\top \mathbf{P}\mathbf{x} \tag{18}$$

And this is a linear constraint again! A consequence is that in this case, we can guess k constraints (up to the amount of distinct nth roots of unity) to obtain a quadratic system of $n - 2k$ equations in $n - 3k$ variables.

Remark 2. One might worry that the guessed constraints and the induced constraints are linearly dependent, or worse yet, inconsistent. However, experiments point out that this is not the case with high probability if $n \gg 3k$ (or $n \gg 2k$ when n or q is odd).

Given the above solving strategy, we want to compute the complexity of solving the remaining system using a Gröbner basis approach. We use again the assumption that the systems (after guessing some variables) behave as semi-regular systems. Since $\mathbb{F}_q$ has at most $\gcd(q-1, n)$ distinct nth roots of unity, we can guess only that many variables in the way described above. Therefore, for some n we would instead like to guess g additional variables for the best trade-off in the FXL algorithm. Then, we can compute the complexity, for even n, as

$$\min_{k \leq \gcd(q-1,n)} q^k \cdot \mathcal{C}_{FXL(n-3k, n-2k, q)}. \tag{19}$$

Here $\mathcal{C}_{FXL(n,m,q)}$ is the cost of FXL over $\mathbb{F}_q$ with m quadratic equations in n variables. The summary of these results can be found in Table 3.

4.3 Complexity of Forging Signatures for MQ-Sign-LR

Now, almost everything is in place to compute the complexity of forging a signature for MQ-Sign-LR. We will assume that $p_{d,q} = 0.63$ as found experimentally in Sect. 5. Furthermore, we will assume that $\mathcal{C}_H \leq 2^{30}$. Generally, for cryptographic hashes, this is a huge overestimation. However, for this attack, picking this bound, makes sure that solving SMQ dominates the complexity. The complexities that result can be found in Table 4. Recall that the solving degree is computed under the assumption that the systems are random enough to use the theory developed for semi-regular systems.

5 Experiments

As we saw in Sect. 3, we are interested in the probability that a random SMQ system has a solution. Furthermore, our analysis on the solving complexity of SMQ is based on some heuristics. Therefore, we also provide experimental evidence backing up our claims.

Table 4. The theoretical complexity of forging MQ-Sign-LR signatures.

Level	q	v	m	$\log_2$ cost
I	256	72	46	108
III	256	112	72	172
V	256	148	96	216

5.1 Probability of SMQ Having a Solution

First, let us consider the probability of a random SMQ system to be solvable. As explained in Sect. 3, when faced with the problem of finding a preimage of a vector $\mathbf{t}$, the setup of the attack does not allow for any choice of the assignment of the variables in $\mathbf{x}_m$. If the corresponding polynomial system does not have a solution, the only option an attacker has is to search for another weak target $\mathbf{t}$. As a result, the probability of an SMQ instance having a solution intervenes in the asymptotic complexity of the attack, and we need to obtain an estimate of this probability.

As the systems are structured, we can not use existing theoretical analysis to derive the probability, and thus we take an experimental approach. We generate and solve many instances of the SMQ problem for different values of n and for q fixed as in the parameters of MQ-Sign. We find empirically that such an SMQ instance has a 0.63 chance to have a solution, independent of $n \geq 3$. The first row in Table 5 shows the number of runs that we performed for a given n, and the second row shows the derived probability, averaged over all runs.

Table 5. Probability of a random $SMQ(n, 256)$ system having a solution.

	5	6	7	8	9	10	11	12
Experiments	10^6	10^6	10^6	10^6	10^5	10^4	10^4	2000
Probability	0.630	0.630	0.631	0.631	0.631	0.623	0.628	0.633

The results were consistent, and we use this empirically obtained probability to calculate the overall complexity of the forgery attack.

5.2 Solving SMQ

Now let us turn to experiments of actually solving SMQ systems. We first aim to confirm our theoretical findings in Sect. 4, focusing on the solving degree of such systems. As we noted before, these systems are not semi-regular. However, we can still use the Hilbert series estimation to predict the degree of regularity of such systems as if they were semi-regular. Recall that this bounds the solving degree of such systems.

Now we do some experimental work to determine if and how far off our estimations are. In these experiments we generate a random SMQ system and solve it using MAGMA's [5] `GroebnerBasis()`. We denote as d_{MAGMA} the highest degree reached in the computation of `GroebnerBasis()`. Following the notation from Sect. 4, the experiment was done for several values of n and k, and in all experiments we set $g = 0$. We chose to limit ourselves to $1 \leq k \leq 3$ and n that are divisors of the different v in MQ-Sign-LR. Note that we still require $k \leq \gcd(n, q-1)$. The results can be found in Table 6.

Table 6. The solving degrees for SMQ instances with different n and k, and $g = 0$. The reported degrees are formatted as d_{MAGMA}/d_{reg}. The degree d_{reg} is computed under the assumption that the systems behave as semi-regular.

n	7	8	9	12	14	16	18	24
$k = 1$	4/4	4/4	5/5	6/6	7/7	7/8	9/9	—
$k = 2$	—	—	4/4	4/4	—	—	7/7	8/9
$k = 3$	—	—	3/3	3/3	—	—	5/5	6/7

Examining Table 6, we see that in all experiments, d_{MAGMA} was equal or lower than the predicted degree of regularity. The lower values can be explained by the extra structure that is present in the system, even after the improved guessing of linear constraints. For example, in these specific cases we found k extra degree falls at degree 3. The propagation of these degree falls might have led to a lower observed degree d_{MAGMA}. It would be interesting to better understand, theoretically, how the actual solving degree behaves. However, practically, these experiments suggest that algorithms for solving these systems have a similar or lower complexity than anticipated. In other words, the proposed attacks might be faster than expected in some instances.

Finally, we turn to solving some instances of weak targets in practice, and we derive average running times[3]. Our experiments include both weak instances that can be solved in practical time on our machine and weak instances of the scale required for mounting a universal forgery attack. For more precise timing estimates, we opted for simulating a single enumeration step of our algorithm by fixing the variables that are supposed to be enumerated to an arbitrary guess. We then account for the enumeration step by multiplying with the corresponding value. Since the enumeration step has predictable complexity, this approach gives us the closest estimate to real running times. Similarly, for practical reasons, the choice of number of variables to enumerate does not necessarily coincide with the choice that yields the optimal trade-off asymptotically.

Again, we use MAGMA's `GroebnerBasis()` to solve the randomly generated instances. For the values of d for which this was infeasible, we report the time for solving a system with higher k and g than optimal. Note that, especially in

[3] All timing experiments were run on an AMD EPYC 7502P.

these cases, being able to pick a lower g would decrease the overall time of the algorithm. Table 7 shows running times for forging signatures having d-periodic hashes, essentially finding preimages of weak targets. We choose d to be a divisor of $v = 72$, so that these experiments correspond exactly to the weak targets of MQ-Sign-LR parameters intended for the first security level. For reference, we also included the fraction of such hashes occurring for the level I parameters. This is an indication of the expected number of times we need to re-salt and hash until we find a weak target. Specifically, the last row contains the period for which it is feasible to perform a universal forgery in time less than the time required to reach the first security level. Interestingly, in the $d = 36$ experiment, the observed degree d_{MAGMA} is equal to 8, which also lines up with the estimated degree of regularity of a semi-regular system with similar parameters.

Table 7. Running times for forging signatures having d-periodic hashes. The last column is the fraction of weak hashes and is computed as q^{m-d} for parameters $q = 2^8$ and $m = 46$. †Expected running time.

	Enumeration		Time		
d	(k, g)	Expected iterations	Single	Full†	Fraction (Level I)
12	(1, 0)	2^7	0.05 s	6.4 s	2^{-272}
18	(2, 0)	2^{15}	1.56 s	14.2 h	2^{-224}
24	(3, 0)	2^{23}	5.94 s	1.6 y	2^{-176}
36	(3, 5)	2^{63}	4.35 h	10^{16} y	2^{-80}

These experiments show that we are able to find preimages of a considerable fraction of weak targets in up to 14.2 h for the parameters of MQ-Sign-LR. For these parameters where it was practical (up to $d = 18$), we were also able to do the full forgery.

6 Countermeasures

The universal forgery attack proposed in this paper has an exponential time complexity. In fact, Table 4 shows how far the current MQ-Sign-LR parameters are from reaching the required security level. Considering only the theoretical complexity of the forgery attack, it might be tempting to increase the parameter choices for all three security levels so that the system reaches the corresponding security requirements. However, this is not a sufficient countermeasure, as we have shown that the system suffers from other vulnerabilities like the many weak targets that we detect in Sect. 3. This means that if MQ-Sign-LR is deployed in real world applications, a verifier can never accept signatures that are build from a weak target, as the preimages of those can be computed in faster running times, sometimes even seconds, as shown in Sect. 5.

The design of the system needs to be modified in such a way that our attack is countered and the existence of weak targets is completely eliminated. Looking at the requirements that we define in Sect. 3 for a vector being a weak target, a straightforward countermeasure for this attack would be to choose parameters such that v is a prime number. Note that it is also possible to adjust the parameter v in such a way that the inverse of the probability of hashing into a weak target surpasses the security threshold. For parameters of the scale of MQ-Sign for instance, it would be enough to take v odd, as even if the greatest divisor is $v/3$, the probability to find a $v/3$-periodic hash is negligibly low. We do not propose this countermeasure because of the same reasons exposed in the previous paragraph. A verifier must never accept such weak targets and hence a different solution that involves substantially changing the specification of the protocol behind the trapdoor construction needs to be developed. This in turn evokes a substantial study on the provable security analysis of the system. We conclude that choosing v prime is the only countermeasure that successfully counters the vulnerabilities found in this work.

Since our attack also relies on the equivalent-keys optimization, excluding its use would protect against this concrete attack. However, further analysis is required to gain confidence in the security of using the cyclic structure of the central map. Indeed, the work in this paper also highlights that the underlying hardness assumptions of MQ-Sign-LR are substantially different than for classic UOV. Furthermore, in this case only the secret key benefits from reduced sizes, whereas for most use cases, it is more advantageous to reduce the public key size.

Acknowledgement. We thank Simona Samardjiska for initial discussions on the attack idea. We thank Magali Bardet for meticulously reviewing our work and for many helpful comments and suggestions.

References

1. Aulbach, T., Campos, F., Krämer, J., Samardjiska, S., Stöttinger, M.: Separating oil and vinegar with a single trace side-channel assisted Kipnis-Shamir attack on UOV. IACR Trans. Cryptogr. Hardw. Embed. Syst. **2023**(3), 221–245 (2023)
2. Aulbach, T., Samardjiska, S., Trimoska, M.: Practical key-recovery attack on MQ-sign and more. In: Saarinen, M.-J., Smith-Tone, D. (eds.) Post-Quantum Cryptography - 15th International Workshop, PQCrypto 2024, Part II, pp. 168–185. Springer, Cham (2024)
3. B.B. Ein algorithmus zum auffinden der basiselemente des restklassenringes nach einem nulldimensionalen polynomideal. Ph.D. thesis, Math. Inst., University of Innsbruck (1965)
4. Bardet, M.: Étude des systèmes algébriques surdéterminés. Applications aux codes correcteurs et à la cryptographie. Theses, Université Pierre et Marie Curie - Paris VI (2004)
5. Bosma, W., Cannon, J., Playoust, C.: The magma algebra system. I. The user language. J. Symbolic Comput. **24**(3-4), 235–265 (1997). Computational algebra and number theory (London, 1993)

6. Caminata, A., Gorla, E.: Solving degree, last fall degree, and related invariants. J. Symb. Comput. **114**, 322–335 (2023)
7. Cottaar, J., et al.: Report on evaluation of KpqC candidates. Cryptology ePrint Archive, Report 2023/1853 (2023)
8. Courtois, N., Klimov, A., Patarin, J., Shamir, A.: Efficient algorithms for solving overdefined systems of multivariate polynomial equations. In: Preneel, B. (ed.) EUROCRYPT 2000. LNCS, vol. 1807, pp. 392–407. Springer, Heidelberg (2000). https://doi.org/10.1007/3-540-45539-6_27
9. Ding, J., Yang, B.-Y., Chen, C.-H.O., Chen, M.-S., Cheng, C.-M.: New differential-algebraic attacks and reparametrization of rainbow. In: Bellovin, S.M., Gennaro, R., Keromytis, A., Yung, M. (eds.) ACNS 2008. LNCS, vol. 5037, pp. 242–257. Springer, Heidelberg (2008). https://doi.org/10.1007/978-3-540-68914-0_15
10. Faugère, J.-C.: A new efficient algorithm for computing gröbner bases (f4). J. Pure Appl. Algebra **139**(1), 61–88 (1999)
11. Faugère, J.C.: A new efficient algorithm for computing gröbner bases without reduction to zero (F5). In: Proceedings of the 2002 International Symposium on Symbolic and Algebraic Computation, ISSAC 2002, pp. 75–83. Association for Computing Machinery, New York (2002)
12. Faugère, J.-C., Bardet, M., Salvy, B.: On the complexity of gröbner basis computation of semi-regular overdetermined algebraic equations (2004)
13. Ikematsu, Y., Jo, H., Yasuda, T.: A security analysis on MQ-Sign. Cryptology ePrint Archive, Paper 2023/581 (2023). https://eprint.iacr.org/2023/581
14. Kipnis, A., Patarin, J., Goubin, L.: Unbalanced oil and vinegar signature schemes. In: Stern, J. (ed.) EUROCRYPT 1999. LNCS, vol. 1592, pp. 206–222. Springer, Heidelberg (1999). https://doi.org/10.1007/3-540-48910-X_15
15. Kipnis, A., Shamir, A.: Cryptanalysis of the oil & vinegar signature scheme. In: Krawczyk, H. (ed.) Advances in Cryptology - CRYPTO'98. Lecture Notes in Computer Science, vol. 1462, pp. 257–266. Springer, Berlin, Heidelberg (1998)
16. NIST. Post-Quantum Cryptography: Additional Digital Signature Schemes. Round 2 Additional Signatures (2024). https://csrc.nist.gov/Projects/pqc-dig-sig/round-2-additional-signatures
17. Patarin, J.: The oil and vinegar signature scheme. Dagstuhl Workshop on Cryptography (1997)
18. Pébereau, P.: One vector to rule them all: Key recovery from one vector in UOV schemes. In: Saarinen, M.-J., Smith-Tone, D. (eds.) Post-Quantum Cryptography - 15th International Workshop. PQCrypto 2024, Part II, pp. 92–108. Springer, Cham (2024)
19. Petzoldt, A.: Selecting and reducing key sizes for multivariate cryptography. Ph.D. thesis, Darmstadt University of Technology, Germany (2013)
20. Salizzoni, F.: An upper bound for the solving degree in terms of the degree of regularity (2023)
21. The KpqC project. Korean post-quantum Cryptography (2022). https://www.kpqc.or.kr/

Lattice-Based Cryptography

Module Learning with Errors with Truncated Matrices

Katharina Boudgoust[1] and Hannah Keller[2(✉)]

[1] CNRS, Univ Montpellier, LIRMM, Montpellier, France
katharina.boudgoust@lirmm.fr
[2] Aarhus University, Aarhus, Denmark
hkeller@cs.au.dk

Abstract. The Module Learning with Errors (MLWE) problem is one of the most commonly used hardness assumption in lattice-based cryptography. In its standard version, a matrix $\mathbf{A}$ is sampled uniformly at random over a quotient ring R_q, as well as noisy linear equations in the form of $\mathbf{As} + \mathbf{e} \bmod q$, where $\mathbf{s}$ is the secret, sampled uniformly at random over R_q, and $\mathbf{e}$ is the error, coming from a Gaussian distribution. Many previous works have focused on variants of MLWE, where the secret and/or the error are sampled from different distributions. Only few works have focused on different distributions for the matrix $\mathbf{A}$. One variant proposed in the literature is to consider matrix distributions, where the low-order bits of a uniform $\mathbf{A}$ are deleted. This seems a natural approach in order to save in bandwidth. We call it *truncated* MLWE.

In this work, we show that the hardness of standard MLWE implies the hardness of truncated MLWE, both for search and decision versions. Prior works only covered the search variant and relied on the (module) NTRU assumption, limitations which we are able to overcome. Overall, we provide two approaches, offering different advantages. The first uses a general Rényi divergence argument, applicable to a wide range of secret/error distributions, but which only works for the search variants of (truncated) MLWE. The second applies to the decision versions, by going through an intermediate variant of MLWE, where additional *hints* on the secret are given to the adversary. However, the reduction makes use of discrete Gaussian distributions.

Keywords: Lattices · Module Learning with Errors · Truncation

1 Introduction

The Module Learning with Errors (MLWE) problem [LS15] is among the most commonly used hardness assumptions in lattice-based cryptography. Besides its strong connection to well-studied, worst-case, structured lattice problems, it also comes with an easy-to-work-with shape in the language of linear algebra. It has shown to be very versatile in its possible applications in cryptography. Informally, MLWE can be seen as noisy linear equations over the quotient $R_q := R/qR$

R. Niederhagen and M.-J. O. Saarinen (Eds.): PQCrypto 2025, LNCS 15577, pp. 255–277, 2025.
https://doi.org/10.1007/978-3-031-86599-2_9

for some ring R and positive integer q. More formally, a sample of MLWE can be described as follows. Sample a *matrix* $\mathbf{A}$ from a distribution $\mathsf{D}_{\mathsf{mat}}$ over R_q, a *secret vector* $\mathbf{s}$ from a distribution $\mathsf{D}_{\mathsf{sec}}$ over R_q and an *error vector* $\mathbf{e}$ from a distribution $\mathsf{D}_{\mathsf{err}}$ over R. Then, compute $\mathbf{b} = \mathbf{A}\mathbf{s} + \mathbf{e} \bmod q$ and output $(\mathbf{A}, \mathbf{b})$. The search variant of MLWE asks to find the secret $\mathbf{s}$, whereas the decision variant asks to distinguish an MLWE sample from an instance of the uniform distribution of matrices and vectors over R_q. Originally, the problem was studied over the special ring $R = \mathbb{Z}$, and termed Learning with Errors (LWE) [Reg05, Reg09]. Later, the problem was generalized to the ring of integers of number fields of higher degrees [LS15]. The original formulation of MLWE, which is connected by a worst-case to average-case reduction to well-studied module lattice problems, sets $\mathsf{D}_{\mathsf{mat}}$ and $\mathsf{D}_{\mathsf{sec}}$ as the uniform distributions over R_q and $\mathsf{D}_{\mathsf{err}}$ as a rounded or discrete Gaussian distribution [Reg05, LS15]. The reduction first made use of quantum algorithms, but was later made classical [Pei09, BLP+13, BJRW20].

Since then, different lines of work studied the hardness of MLWE for different distributions. Regarding variants for the secret distribution, an early result showed that, with only a small loss in the row dimension of $\mathbf{A}$, the secret distribution $\mathsf{D}_{\mathsf{sec}}$ can be set the same as the error distribution $\mathsf{D}_{\mathsf{err}}$ [ACPS09]. This variant is commonly referred to as MLWE in its *Hermite normal form*. Moreover, the hardness of MLWE where the secret is sampled uniformly over a small subset of R_q was established for the degree-1 case in [GKPV10, BLP+13, Mic18] (focusing on the special subset $\{0, 1\}$). It was then generalized to rings of larger degrees [BJRW20, BJRW23] and to *any* secret distribution with enough min-entropy [BD20, BJRW22, LWZW24]. Regarding variants for the error distribution, different results have shown the hardness of MLWE if the error is sampled uniformly over a small subset of $\mathbb{Z}_q$ [DM13, MP13, BCD+16, BLR+18, STA20] and for higher-degree rings R_q [BJRW23]. So far, only few works have studied the hardness of MLWE when the matrix $\mathbf{A}$ does not follow the uniform distribution over R_q. By a rather simple reduction, one can reduce standard MLWE with a uniform matrix to a variant where $\mathbf{A}$ is composed of polynomials which only have binary coefficients.[1] The idea is to compute the bit-decomposition of every coefficient of each polynomial entry in the uniform $\mathbf{A} = \mathsf{bin}(\mathbf{A}) \cdot \mathbf{G}$, where $\mathbf{G}$ is the so-called gadget matrix. A given MLWE instance $(\mathbf{A}, \mathbf{A}\mathbf{s} + \mathbf{e})$ then automatically defines an instance of MLWE with a binary matrix $(\mathsf{bin}(\mathbf{A}), \mathsf{bin}(\mathbf{A})\mathbf{s}' + \mathbf{e})$, where $\mathbf{s}' = \mathbf{G}\mathbf{s}$. If $\mathbf{A}$ was originally an $m \times n$ matrix, $\mathsf{bin}(\mathbf{A})$ is now an $m \times (n \cdot \lceil \log q \rceil)$ matrix. Other works have used matrix distributions $\mathsf{D}_{\mathsf{mat}}$ that are computationally [GKPV10, BD20], statistically [Reg05, GPV08], or Rényi [BLR+18] close to the uniform distribution. In a recent work [JLS24], the study of plain LWE with a sparse matrix was initiated, yielding improved computation and storage efficiency.

[1] Throughout this work, we use the so-called coefficient embedding to identify elements in R_q with polynomials having coefficients in $\mathbb{Z}_q$.

Truncated MLWE. In this work, we study the hardness of MLWE for a different matrix distribution which has been considered in a recent result [JZW+23].[2] The formulation of the problem is rather simple. To sample the matrix, for some small constant c, one samples some matrix $\mathbf{U}$ uniformly at random over R_q, then deletes the c lowest-order bits of every coefficient of each entry in $\mathbf{U}$. We say that the matrix is *truncated* and write $\mathbf{A} = \mathsf{Trunc}(\mathbf{U}, c)$. As before, a sample is given by $(\mathbf{A}, \mathbf{As} + \mathbf{e})$ for some secret $\mathbf{s}$ and error $\mathbf{e}$. Subsequently, we call the variant the *truncated* MLWE problem. Intuitively, the motivation of this variant is to save in bandwidth. Whenever we have to send an MLWE instance $(\mathbf{A}, \mathbf{b})$ (in form of a public key or an encrypted message, for instance), the size of the message to be sent is smaller if we delete the low-order bits of every entry of the matrix. In [JZW+23], a reduction from the module variant of the NTRU problem to the search variant of truncated MLWE (with entropic secret) was proven. As the NTRU assumption [HPS98] and its module version [CPS+20] are seen as less standard than MLWE and the search problem is not enough for many security notions, like standard IND-CPA security of encryption schemes, we would ideally like to show that the hardness of decision truncated MLWE can be reduced from the hardness of standard MLWE. This leaves the following open problem stated by [JZW+23], motivating our work:

> *Does the hardness of standard* MLWE *imply the hardness of search and decision truncated* MLWE*?*

Our Contributions. We answer this research question positively. We show two approaches for how the hardness of standard MLWE implies the hardness of truncated MLWE, both for the search and decision variants. Each of the approaches comes with different advantages. We provide a detailed comparison between our two proofs and the results of [JZW+23] in Sect. 6.

First Approach. In Sect. 4, we reduce the hardness of truncated MLWE from standard MLWE using the Rényi divergence as a measure of distance. The Rényi divergence has been used for tight reductions in lattice-based cryptography since [BLL+15,BLR+18]. The high level idea of Theorem 2 is to view a truncated matrix $\mathbf{A} = \mathsf{Trunc}(\mathbf{U}, c)$ as the difference of the original uniform matrix $\mathbf{U}$ and the deleted low-order bits $\mathbf{N_U}$, i.e., $\mathbf{A} = \mathbf{U} - \mathbf{N_U}$. Then a sample $(\mathsf{Trunc}(\mathbf{U}, c), \mathsf{Trunc}(\mathbf{U}, c)\mathbf{s} + \mathbf{e})$ can be viewed as an instance of standard MLWE given by $(\mathbf{U}, \mathbf{Us} + \mathbf{e}')$, where $\mathbf{e}' = -\mathbf{N_U s} + \mathbf{e}$. Note that $\mathbf{e}'$ currently depends on the secret $\mathbf{s}$ and might thus leak sensitive information about it. By a standard Rényi argument, one can make the distribution of $\mathbf{e}'$ independent of $\mathbf{N_U s}$, as long as the error distribution is sufficiently large. The resulting loss in advantage depends on the ring degree, the size of elements coming from the secret distribution $\mathsf{D_{sec}}$, the number of deleted bits c, the dimensions of the matrix, as well as the error distribution $\mathsf{D_{err}}$. The result generally applies to

[2] In [JZW+23], a more general notion of MLWE with *semiuniform matrices* is introduced. As we are not aware of any concrete applications of their more general notion, we decided to keep the presentation of the problem as simple as possible in our work.

any secret and noise distributions for which MLWE is believed to be hard, as long as we can compute the relevant Rényi divergences, but is restricted to the corresponding search variant of the problems. Recent results have for instance put forward the use of Rényi divergence arguments in combination with sum of bounded uniform distributions [dPKPR24]. In contrast to discrete Gaussian distributions, they are easier to implement and to protect against side-channel attacks. As of today, the only way to use Rényi divergence arguments for decision variants, is to make use of the so-called *public sampleability framework* of [BLR+18]. However, as we argue in Sect. 4.1, this framework only leads to a vacuous reduction in our context, as the Rényi divergence between truncated and non-truncated matrices is exponentially large in their dimensions.

Second Approach. To circumvent this issue, we propose an alternative approach in Sect. 5, covering both the search and decision versions. The main idea is to interpret the information $\mathbf{N}_{\mathbf{U}}\mathbf{s}$ leaked about the secret $\mathbf{s}$ as approximate *hints*. The presence of hints is defining another (already studied) variant of MLWE, whose hardness can be derived from standard MLWE, both for the decision and search variants [MKMS22,KLSS23]. Informally, the type of hints we are considering is $\mathbf{Hs}+\mathbf{f}$, for some hint matrix $\mathbf{H}$ known to the adversary and some noise term $\mathbf{f}$ unknown to the adversary. In the truncated context, we can simply set $\mathbf{H}$ to store the low-order bits of the matrix, i.e., $\mathbf{H}=\mathbf{N}_{\mathbf{U}}$. We recall the formal definition and (a generalized) hardness results of MLWE with hints in Sect. 3.2 and then show a reduction from MLWE with hints to truncated MLWE in Theorem 3. The advantage of now applying this result to the decision variant comes with the drawback that the hardness results of MLWE with hints only apply to a limited set of secret and noise distributions. More precisely, the existing reductions make use of decomposition theorems for discrete Gaussian distributions.

Choice of Rings. All of our results are proven for the class of power-of-two cyclotomic rings. This restriction is mainly due to tighter reductions, as we have a good control over the norm growth after multiplying two elements (interpreted as polynomials) in such rings. It is possible to generalize everything to other fields and rings, incurring some additional reduction losses due to the so-called expansion factor [LM06,RSW18]. As power-of-two cyclotomic rings are the most popular choice, both in theory and in practice, we opted for directly showing the tighter results.

Trivial Setup. We would like to mention that there is a setup of truncated MLWE which makes it trivially easy to solve. Let c be the number of bits we are truncating away from the matrix, i.e., $\mathbf{A}=\mathsf{Trunc}(\mathbf{U},c)=\mathbf{U}-\mathbf{N}_{\mathbf{U}}$. If 2^c is a factor of the modulus q, we know that $(\mathbf{As} \bmod q) \bmod 2^c=\mathbf{0}$ for every MLWE secret $\mathbf{s}$. If additionally the noise $\mathbf{e}$ has infinity norm less than 2^c, it would be easy to solve the truncated MLWE instance. On input $(\mathbf{A},\mathbf{b})$ with $\mathbf{b}=\mathbf{As}+\mathbf{e} \bmod q$, we can simply compute $\mathbf{b} \bmod 2^c$ to recover $\mathbf{e}$. We highlight that our reductions do not allow for this trivial setup. The reduction of Theorem 2 in Sect. 4 requires the resulting error distribution of truncated MLWE to be significantly larger than the shift (that is, $\mathbf{N_U s}$) it is trying to hide. This shift is (among other parameters) determined by 2^c, so the error distribution cannot have infinity norm below 2^c. Similarly, the reduction of Theorem 1 in Sect. 5 requires the resulting error distribution to be significantly (among other parameters) larger than the infinity bound on the hint matrix $\mathbf{N_U}$, which is bounded by 2^c.

2 Preliminaries

2.1 Notations

For any positive integer q, we denote by $\mathbb{Z}_q := \mathbb{Z}/q\mathbb{Z}$ the quotient integer ring. Elements in $\mathbb{Z}$ can be reduced mod q and possess a unique representative in the set $\{0, \ldots, q-1\}$. Column vectors are written in bold lowercase letters $\mathbf{b}$ and matrices in bold uppercase letters $\mathbf{A}$. The transpose operator over vectors and matrices is denoted by $\mathbf{b}^T$ and $\mathbf{A}^T$. The determinant of a matrix $\mathbf{A}$ is denoted by $\det(\mathbf{A})$. For any vector $\mathbf{b}$, we denote by $\|\mathbf{b}\|$ its ℓ_2-norm and by $\|\mathbf{b}\|_\infty$ its infinity norm. For any matrix $\mathbf{A}$, we denote by $\|\mathbf{A}\|_\infty$ the maximum of the infinity norms of its column vectors. For any real number $r \in \mathbb{R}$, the operation $\lfloor r \rceil$ denotes rounding it to the nearest integer (with 0.5 being rounded up). The operation $\lceil r \rceil$ denotes rounding it up to the next integer. We can component-wise extend rounding to vectors and matrices. All logarithms are base 2. By $\mathsf{negl}(\lambda)$ we denote a negligible function in λ, thus it decreases faster towards 0 than the inverse of any polynomial function. The abbreviation PPT stands for probabilistic polynomial-time.

We define a truncation function Trunc which takes as input an element x in $\mathbb{Z}_q$ and a positive integer c, computes and outputs an element in $\mathbb{Z}_q$:

$$\mathsf{Trunc}(x, c) = x - (x \bmod 2^c). \tag{1}$$

Informally, during truncation the c lowest bits of $x \in R_q$ are set to 0. We can naturally extend the truncation function to vectors and matrices over $\mathbb{Z}$ by applying them coefficient-wise and entry-wise, respectively.

Let n be a positive integer. An $n \times n$ symmetric real matrix $\mathbf{M}$ is said to be *positive semidefinite* if $\mathbf{x}^T\mathbf{M}\mathbf{x} \geq 0$ for all $\mathbf{x} \in \mathbb{R}^n$. Moreover, an $n \times n$ matrix $\mathbf{M} = (m_{ij})_{i,j\in\{1,\ldots,n\}}$ is called *diagonally dominant* if $|m_{ii}| \geq \sum_{j\neq i}|m_{ij}|$ for all $i \in \{1, \ldots, n\}$. A symmetric diagonally dominant matrix with real non-negative diagonal entries is positive semidefinite.

2.2 Number Theory

A number field $K = \mathbb{Q}(\zeta)$ of degree d is a finite field extension of the rationals $\mathbb{Q}$ obtained by adjoining an algebraic number ζ. We denote its ring of integers by R. We call K a ν-th cyclotomic number field if ζ is a ν-th primitive root of unity. Its degree is given by $d = \varphi(\nu)$, where φ is Euler's totient function. We say R is a power-of-two cyclotomic, if it is the ring of integers of the ν-th cyclotomic field, where ν can be written as 2^{k+1} for some positive integer k. In that case, $d = 2^k$.

We can identify $K = \mathbb{Q}[X]/\langle \Phi(X) \rangle$, where $\Phi(X)$ is the minimal polynomial of ζ. Every element $x \in K$ can then by written with respect to the basis $\{1, \zeta, \ldots, \zeta^{d-1}\}$, thus $x = \sum_{i=0}^{d-1} x_i \zeta^i$ with $x_i \in \mathbb{Q}$. The isomorphism $\tau \colon K \to \mathbb{Q}^d$ which maps x to its coefficient vector $\tau(x) = (x_0, \ldots, x_{d-1})^T$ is called the coefficient embedding. By restricting τ to R, we obtain an isomorphism between R and $\mathbb{Z}^d$. By associating the norm of an element x in R with the norm of its corresponding $\tau(x) \in \mathbb{Z}^d$, it is possible to equip R with a geometry. With this geometry at hand, we can define norms of vectors and matrices over R, as well as round and truncate elements in R coefficient-wise.

Every product of two ring elements $x \cdot y = z \in R$ can be represented as a matrix vector product over $\mathbb{Z}$, such that $\mathsf{Rot}(x) \cdot \tau(y) = \tau(z) \in \mathbb{Z}^d$. We call $\mathsf{Rot}(x)$ the rotation matrix associated to x in the coefficient embedding. The exact shape of $\mathsf{Rot}(x)$ depends on the number field (and associated ring of integers) we are considering. Throughout the paper, we make use of the fact that for power-of-two cyclotomics, $\mathsf{Rot}(x)$ is nega-cyclic and that $\|\mathsf{Rot}(x)\|_\infty = \|x\|_\infty$. One could move to different fields and rings, at the expenses of the norm of the rotation matrix being larger than the norm of the underlying ring element. The multiplicative factor is sometimes also called expansion factor of K [LM06, RSW18].

2.3 Lattices

Let d be a positive integer. A (full-rank) Euclidean lattice Λ is a discrete subgroup of $\mathbb{R}^d$ and can be represented by some basis vectors $\{\mathbf{b}_1, \ldots, \mathbf{b}_d\} \in \mathbb{R}^d$ s.t. $\Lambda = \{\sum_{i=1}^{d} z_i \mathbf{b}_i \mid z_i \in \mathbb{Z}\}$. Let $\mathbf{B} = (\mathbf{b}_i)_{i \in \{1,\ldots,d\}}$ be the matrix composed of the basis column vectors. The determinant of a lattice is defined as $\det(\Lambda) = \det(\mathbf{B})$. We further define the span of a lattice as $\mathsf{Span}(\Lambda) = \{\sum_{i=1}^{d} r_i \mathbf{b}_i \mid r_i \in \mathbb{R}\}$ and its dual by $\Lambda^* = \{\mathbf{x} \in \mathsf{Span}(\Lambda) \mid \mathbf{x}^T \mathbf{y} \in \mathbb{Z} \ \forall \mathbf{y} \in \Lambda\}$. Every ring of integers R defines a lattice $\Lambda = \{\tau(x) \mid x \in R\}$, using the coefficient embedding.

2.4 Probability Measures

For a finite set S, we denote by $x \leftarrow S$ the process of sampling x uniformly at random over S. For d, and $k_1 \leq k_2$ positive integers, let $\mathbf{U}_{k_1,k_2}$ denote the uniform distribution over $\{k_1, \ldots, k_2 - 1\}^d$, i.e., $\Pr_{\mathbf{x} \leftarrow \mathbf{U}_{k_1,k_2}}[\mathbf{x} = \mathbf{y}] = (1/(k_2 - k_1))^d$ for every $\mathbf{y} \in \{k_1, \ldots, k_2 - 1\}^d$. By using the coefficient embedding $\tau \colon R \to \mathbb{Z}^d$, this can be seen as a distribution over R.

Definition 1. *Let $B, \delta > 0$ and R be a degree d ring of integers. A distribution $\mathcal{D}$ over R is (B, δ)-bounded if*

$$\Pr_{x \leftarrow \mathcal{D}}[\|\tau(x)\|_\infty > B] \leq \delta,$$

where τ is the coefficient embedding of R into $\mathbb{Z}^d$.

Continuous, Rounded and Discrete Gaussian Distributions.

Definition 2 (One-dimensional Gaussian Distribution). *Probability distribution D_{μ,σ^2} with mean $\mu \in \mathbb{R}$ and variance $\sigma^2 \in \mathbb{R}$ samples value $x \in \mathbb{R}$ with probability distribution function*

$$D_{\mu,\sigma^2}(x) := \frac{1}{\sigma\sqrt{2\pi}} \exp(-(x-\mu)^2/(2\sigma^2)).$$

Definition 3 (Multivariate Gaussian Distribution). *Probability distribution $D_{\boldsymbol{\mu},\boldsymbol{\Sigma}}$ with mean $\boldsymbol{\mu} \in \mathbb{R}^d$ and covariance matrix $\boldsymbol{\Sigma} \in \mathbb{R}^{d\times d}$ samples vector $\mathbf{x} \in \mathbb{R}^d$ with probability distribution function*

$$D_{\boldsymbol{\mu},\boldsymbol{\Sigma}}(\mathbf{x}) := \frac{1}{\sqrt{(2\pi)^d \det(\boldsymbol{\Sigma})}} \exp(-(\mathbf{x}-\boldsymbol{\mu})^T \boldsymbol{\Sigma}^{-1} (\mathbf{x}-\boldsymbol{\mu})^T/2).$$

If $\boldsymbol{\Sigma} = \sigma^2 \cdot \mathbf{I}_d$, we call the distribution spherical and simply write $D_{\boldsymbol{\mu},\sigma^2}$. For $\boldsymbol{\mu} = \mathbf{0}$, we might omit it from the notation and simply write $D_{\boldsymbol{\Sigma}}$.

We further define the *rounded* Gaussian distribution $\lfloor D_{\boldsymbol{\mu},\boldsymbol{\Sigma}} \rceil$ over $\mathbb{Z}^d$, where the instance sampled from the continuous Gaussian distribution over $\mathbb{R}^d$ is rounded to the nearest integer.

Definition 4 (Discrete Gaussian Distribution for Lattices). *Probability distribution $D_{\Lambda,\boldsymbol{\mu},\boldsymbol{\Sigma}}$ over a lattice $\Lambda \subseteq \mathbb{R}^d$ with mean $\boldsymbol{\mu} \in \mathbb{R}^d$ and covariance matrix $\boldsymbol{\Sigma} \in \mathbb{R}^{d\times d}$ samples vector $\mathbf{x} \in \Lambda \subseteq \mathbb{R}^d$ in lattice Λ with probability distribution function*

$$D_{\Lambda,\boldsymbol{\mu},\boldsymbol{\Sigma}}(\mathbf{x}) := D_{\boldsymbol{\mu},\boldsymbol{\Sigma}}(\mathbf{x}) / \sum_{\mathbf{y}\in\Lambda} D_{\boldsymbol{\mu},\boldsymbol{\Sigma}}(\mathbf{y}).$$

As for the continuous case, if $\boldsymbol{\Sigma} = \sigma^2 \cdot \mathbf{I}_d$, we simply write $D_{\Lambda,\boldsymbol{\mu},\sigma^2}$. For $\boldsymbol{\mu} = \mathbf{0}$, we might omit it from the notation and simply write $D_{\Lambda,\boldsymbol{\Sigma}}$.

The smoothing parameter of a lattice Λ, denoted by $\eta_\epsilon(\Lambda)$ for some $\epsilon > 0$ and introduced by [MR04], is the smallest $s > 0$ such that $\rho_{1/s}(\Lambda^* \setminus \{\mathbf{0}\}) \leq \epsilon$, where $\rho_\sigma(\mathbf{x}) := \exp(-\pi\|\mathbf{x}\|^2/\sigma^2)$. When ϵ is omitted, it is some unspecified negligible function $\epsilon = \mathsf{negl}(\lambda)$ in the lattice dimension or the security parameter. By specializing [MR04, Lem. 3.2] to the integer lattice $\Lambda = \mathbb{Z}^d$ (which is self-dual), we know that for $\epsilon = 2^{-d}$ it holds $\eta_\epsilon(\Lambda) \leq \sqrt{d}$.

We use the coefficient embedding τ to sample discrete Gaussian distributions over R of degree d. We denote by $\mathbf{s} \leftarrow D_{R^m,\boldsymbol{\mu},\boldsymbol{\Sigma}}$ the process of sampling $\mathbf{s}' \leftarrow D_{\mathbb{Z}^{dm},\boldsymbol{\mu},\boldsymbol{\Sigma}}$ and setting $\mathbf{s} := \tau^{-1}(\mathbf{s}')$.

Lemma 1 (Adapted from [Lyu12, Lem. 4.4]). *Let t, σ be positive reals and R be a degree-d ring of integers. Then D_{R,σ^2} is $(t, 2d\exp(-t^2/2\sigma^2))$-bounded.*

Lemma 2 (Adapted from [MR04, Lem. 4.4]). *Let Λ be an n-dimensional lattice and $\epsilon \in (0,1)$. Then for any $\mathbf{c} \in \mathbb{R}^n$ and $\sigma \geq \eta_\epsilon(\Lambda)$ we have that $\rho_{\mathbf{c},\sigma^2}(\Lambda) := \sum_{\mathbf{x}\in\Lambda} \exp(-\pi\|\mathbf{x}-\mathbf{c}\|^2/\sigma^2)$ is in the range $[1-\epsilon, 1+\epsilon] \cdot \det(\Lambda)^{-1}$.*

The smoothing parameter is relevant when decomposing discrete Gaussians.

Lemma 3 (Decomposition)

1. *Let $\sigma, \delta \in \mathbb{R}$ be two variances and $\Lambda \subset \mathbb{R}^d$ be a lattice. Let $\mathbf{x}_1 \leftarrow D_{\Lambda,\sigma^2}$ and $\mathbf{x}_2 \leftarrow D_{\Lambda,\delta^2}$ with $\sigma, \delta \geq \sqrt{2} \cdot \eta(\Lambda)$. Then, $\mathbf{x} := \mathbf{x}_1 + \mathbf{x}_2$ is statistically close to a zero-centered discrete Gaussian distribution over Λ with covariance $\gamma^2 = \sigma^2 + \delta^2$.*
2. *Let $\Lambda \subset \mathbb{Z}^m$ be a sub-lattice of rank n with basis $\mathbf{L} \in \mathbb{Z}^{m \times n}$. Further, let σ be a positive real, defining $\boldsymbol{\Sigma} = \sigma^2 \mathbf{L}\mathbf{L}^T \in \mathbb{Z}^{m \times m}$, and $\boldsymbol{\Sigma}' \in \mathbb{Z}^{m \times m}$ be a positive semidefinite matrix. Moreover, we assume that the eigenvalues of the matrix $\Gamma = \sigma\sqrt{\mathbf{I}_m - \sigma^2 \mathbf{L}(\boldsymbol{\Sigma} + \boldsymbol{\Sigma}')^{-1}\mathbf{L}^T}$ are greater than or equal to the smoothing parameter $\eta(\mathbb{Z}^m)$. Let $\mathbf{x}_1 \leftarrow D_{\mathbb{Z}^m,\boldsymbol{\Sigma}'}$ and $\mathbf{x}_2 \leftarrow D_{\Lambda,\boldsymbol{\Sigma}}$. Then, $\mathbf{x} := \mathbf{x}_1 + \mathbf{x}_2$ is statistically close to a zero-centered discrete Gaussian distribution over $\mathbb{Z}^m$ with covariance matrix $\boldsymbol{\Sigma} + \boldsymbol{\Sigma}'$.*

Proof. Item 1. This is a special case of [MP13, Thm. 3.3] with $m = 2$ and $\mathbf{z}$ the all-1 vector. Item 2. Proven in [MKMS22, Lem. 1]. □

Measurement of Distribution Closeness. In the following, we recall the definition of the Rényi divergence of some order α. Even though it is technically possible to allow the order to take a real value, we limit ourselves to α being a positive integer throughout the work.

Definition 5 (Rényi Divergence). *For any two probability distributions P and Q defined over $\mathbb{R}$, the Rényi divergence (RD) of order $\alpha > 1$ is defined as*

$$\mathsf{RD}_\alpha(P\|Q) = \mathbb{E}_{x\sim Q}\left(\frac{P(x)}{Q(x)}\right)^{\frac{\alpha}{\alpha-1}}.$$

For discrete distributions with $\mathsf{Supp}(P) \subseteq \mathsf{Supp}(Q)$, this is:

$$\mathsf{RD}_\alpha(P\|Q) = \left(\sum_{x \in \mathsf{Supp}(P)} \frac{P(x)^\alpha}{Q(x)^{\alpha-1}}\right)^{\frac{1}{\alpha-1}}.$$

Lemma 4 (Multiplicativity [LSS14, Lemma 4.1]). *Let $\alpha \in (1, \infty)$. Let P and Q denote distributions of a pair of random variables (Y_1, Y_2). Also, for $i \in \{1, 2\}$ let P_i and Q_i be the marginal distribution of Y_i under P and Q, respectively. Then if Y_1 and Y_2 are independent:*

$$\mathsf{RD}_\alpha(P\|Q) = \mathsf{RD}_\alpha(P_1\|Q_1) \cdot \mathsf{RD}_\alpha(P_2\|Q_2).$$

Lemma 5 (Probability Preservation [LSS14, Lemma 4.1]). *Let $\alpha \in (1, \infty)$ and $E \subseteq \mathsf{Supp}(Q)$ be an arbitrary event. Then:*

$$Q(E) \geq P(E)^{\frac{\alpha}{\alpha-1}} / \mathsf{RD}_\alpha(P\|Q).$$

Lemma 6 (Data Processing Inequality [vEH14, **Theorem 9**]**).** *Let $\alpha \in (1, \infty)$. For any function f, where P^f (respectively Q^f) denotes the distribution of $f(y)$ induced by sampling $y \leftarrow P$ (respectively $y \leftarrow Q$):*

$$\mathsf{RD}_\alpha(P^f \| Q^f) \leq \mathsf{RD}_\alpha(P \| Q).$$

Lemma 7 ([Mir17, **Prop. 7**]). *For mean $\mu \in \mathbb{R}$, variance $\sigma^2 \in \mathbb{R}$ and order $\alpha > 1$ it holds*

$$\mathsf{RD}_\alpha(D_{\sigma^2} \| D_{\mu,\sigma^2}) = \mathsf{RD}_\alpha(D_{\mu,\sigma^2} \| D_{\sigma^2}) = \exp(\alpha\mu^2/(2\sigma^2)).$$

The following lemma generalizes a result on the Rényi divergence of discrete Gaussians from [LSS14] to arbitrary orders. We specialize it to spherical discrete Gaussians for simplicity of presentation.

Lemma 8 (Adapted from [LSS14, **Lem. 4.2**]**).** *Let α be a positive integer, $\boldsymbol{\mu_1}, \boldsymbol{\mu_2} \in \mathbb{R}^d$ and σ be a positive real. Further, let $\Lambda \subset \mathbb{Z}^d$ be a lattice. If $\boldsymbol{\mu_1}, \boldsymbol{\mu_2} \in \Lambda$, let $\epsilon = 0$. Otherwise, fix $\epsilon \in (0,1)$ and assume $\sigma \geq \eta_\epsilon(\Lambda)$. For any lattice $\Lambda \in \mathbb{R}^d$:*

$$\mathsf{RD}_\alpha := \mathsf{RD}_\alpha(D_{\Lambda,\boldsymbol{\mu_1},\sigma^2} \| D_{\Lambda,\boldsymbol{\mu_2},\sigma^2}) \leq \left(\frac{1+\epsilon}{1-\epsilon}\right)^{\alpha/(\alpha-1)} \cdot \exp(\alpha\|\boldsymbol{\mu_1} - \boldsymbol{\mu_2}\|^2/(2\sigma^2)).$$

Proof. By definition of discrete Gaussians,

$$D_{\Lambda,\boldsymbol{\mu_1},\sigma^2}(\mathbf{x}) = \frac{\exp(-\|\mathbf{x} - \boldsymbol{\mu_1}\|^2/(2\sigma^2))}{\rho_{\boldsymbol{\mu_1},\sigma^2}(\Lambda)} \quad \text{and}$$
$$D_{\Lambda,\boldsymbol{\mu_2},\sigma^2}(\mathbf{x}) = \frac{\exp(-\|\mathbf{x} - \boldsymbol{\mu_2}\|^2/(2\sigma^2))}{\rho_{\boldsymbol{\mu_2},\sigma^2}(\Lambda)},$$

where $\rho_{\boldsymbol{\mu},\sigma^2}(\Lambda) = \sum_{\mathbf{y}\in\Lambda} \exp(-\|\mathbf{y} - \boldsymbol{\mu_1}\|^2/(2\sigma^2))$ for any $\boldsymbol{\mu} \in \mathbb{R}^d$. We compute

$$\mathsf{RD}_\alpha = \left(\sum_{\mathbf{x}\in\Lambda} \frac{D_{\Lambda,\boldsymbol{\mu_1},\sigma^2}(\mathbf{x})^\alpha}{D_{\Lambda,\boldsymbol{\mu_2},\sigma^2}(\mathbf{x})^{\alpha-1}}\right)^{1/(\alpha-1)} = \frac{\rho_{\boldsymbol{\mu_2},\sigma^2}(\Lambda)}{\rho_{\boldsymbol{\mu_1},\sigma^2}(\Lambda)^{\alpha/(\alpha-1)}}$$
$$\cdot \left(\sum_{\mathbf{x}\in\Lambda} \exp(-\alpha\|\mathbf{x} - \boldsymbol{\mu_1}\|^2/(2\sigma^2) + (\alpha-1)\|\mathbf{x} - \boldsymbol{\mu_2}\|^2/(2\sigma^2))\right)^{1/(\alpha-1)}.$$

We first simplify the right term of the multiplication, then simplify the whole multiplication. Defining $\boldsymbol{c} = \alpha\boldsymbol{\mu_1} - (\alpha-1)\boldsymbol{\mu_2}$ we claim that:

Claim. $\alpha\|\mathbf{x} - \boldsymbol{\mu_1}\|^2 - (\alpha-1)\|\mathbf{x} - \boldsymbol{\mu_2}\|^2 = \|\mathbf{x} - \mathbf{c}\|^2 - \alpha(\alpha-1)\|\boldsymbol{\mu_1} - \boldsymbol{\mu_2}\|^2$.

Proof.

$$\begin{aligned}
&\alpha\|\mathbf{x} - \boldsymbol{\mu_1}\|^2 - (\alpha-1)\|\mathbf{x} - \boldsymbol{\mu_2}\|^2 \\
&= \|\mathbf{x}\|^2 + (\alpha-1)^2\|\boldsymbol{\mu_2}\|^2 + 2(\alpha-1)\langle\mathbf{x}, \boldsymbol{\mu_2}\rangle + \alpha^2\|\boldsymbol{\mu_1}\|^2 - 2\alpha\langle\mathbf{x}, \boldsymbol{\mu_1}\rangle \\
&- 2\alpha\langle(\alpha-1)\boldsymbol{\mu_2}, \boldsymbol{\mu_1}\rangle - (\alpha-1)^2\|\boldsymbol{\mu_2}\|^2 - (\alpha-1)\|\boldsymbol{\mu_2}\|^2 + \alpha\|\boldsymbol{\mu_1}\|^2 \\
&- \alpha^2\|\boldsymbol{\mu_1}\|^2 + 2\alpha\langle(\alpha-1)\boldsymbol{\mu_2}, \boldsymbol{\mu_1}\rangle \\
&= \|\mathbf{x} - \mathbf{c}\|^2 - \alpha(\alpha-1)\|\boldsymbol{\mu_1} - \boldsymbol{\mu_2}\|^2
\end{aligned}$$

■

Hence the right term of the multiplication simplifies as follows:

$$\left(\sum_{\mathbf{x}\in\Lambda} \exp(-\alpha\|\mathbf{x}-\boldsymbol{\mu_1}\|^2/(2\sigma^2)+(\alpha-1)\|\mathbf{x}-\boldsymbol{\mu_2}\|^2/(2\sigma^2))\right)^{1/(\alpha-1)}$$

$$= \exp(\alpha\|\boldsymbol{\mu_1}-\boldsymbol{\mu_2}\|^2/(2\sigma^2)) \cdot \left(\sum_{\mathbf{x}\in\Lambda} \exp(-\|\mathbf{x}-\mathbf{c}\|^2/(2\sigma^2))\right)^{1/(\alpha-1)}$$

$$= \exp(\alpha\|\boldsymbol{\mu_1}-\boldsymbol{\mu_2}\|^2/(2\sigma^2)) \cdot \rho_{\mathbf{c},\sigma^2}(\Lambda)^{1/(\alpha-1)}.$$

Notice that for $\boldsymbol{\mu_1}, \boldsymbol{\mu_2} \in \Lambda$ and thus $\mathbf{c} \in \Lambda$, we have $\rho_{\boldsymbol{\mu_1},\sigma^2}(\Lambda) = \rho_{\boldsymbol{\mu_2},\sigma^2}(\Lambda) = \rho_{\mathbf{c},\sigma^2}(\Lambda)$. From this, we conclude that

$$\frac{\rho_{\boldsymbol{\mu_2},\sigma^2}(\Lambda)}{\rho_{\boldsymbol{\mu_1},\sigma^2}(\Lambda)^{\alpha/(\alpha-1)}} \cdot \rho_{\mathbf{c},\sigma^2}(\Lambda)^{1/(\alpha-1)} = 1.$$

As a result, we get $\mathsf{RD}_\alpha = \exp(\alpha\|\boldsymbol{\mu_1}-\boldsymbol{\mu_2}\|^2/(2\sigma^2))$.

Otherwise, we can use the assumption that $\sigma \geq \eta_\epsilon(\Lambda)$ and apply Lemma 2, fixing $\epsilon \in (0,1)$, from which we know that for any $\boldsymbol{z} \in \mathbb{R}^n$, $\rho_{\boldsymbol{z},\sigma^2}(\Lambda)$ is in the range $[1-\epsilon, 1+\epsilon] \cdot \det(\Lambda)^{-1}$. Applying this to the sums in the expression for RD_α gives the claimed interval for RD_α. □

3 Module Learning with Errors and Variants

We first introduce in Sect. 3.1 the definition of truncated Module Learning with Errors, from which standard LWE [Reg05] and MLWE [LS15] can be obtained as special cases. In Sect. 3.2, we recall the definition of MLWE with hints on the secret and prove that its hardness can be reduced from standard MLWE.

3.1 Truncated Module Learning with Errors

Truncated MLWE as we define it has a matrix $\mathbf{A} \in R_q^{m\times n}$ whose entries are truncated, where Trunc is defined in Eq. 1. The only existing similar definition in the literature is given in [JZW+23], where truncation can be seen as a special case of semiuniform distributions.

Definition 6 (Truncated MLWE Problem). *Let R be a degree-d ring of integers. Let q, m, n and c be positive integers. Further let $\mathsf{D}_{\mathsf{err}}$ and $\mathsf{D}_{\mathsf{sec}}$ be distributions over R. The (non-interactive) experiments of the search and decision versions of truncated* MLWE *are defined in Fig. 1. For an adversary $\mathcal{A}$ trying to solve the* Trunc-MLWE *problem, the respective advantage is defined as*

$$\mathsf{Adv}^{\mathsf{S\text{-}Trunc\text{-}MLWE}}_{q,m,n,\mathsf{D}_{\mathsf{sec}},\mathsf{D}_{\mathsf{err}},c}(\mathcal{A}) = \Pr[\mathsf{S\text{-}Trunc\text{-}MLWE}^c_{q,m,n,\mathsf{D}_{\mathsf{sec}},\mathsf{D}_{\mathsf{err}}}(\mathcal{A}) = 1],$$

and

$$\mathsf{Adv}^{\mathsf{D\text{-}Trunc\text{-}MLWE}}_{q,m,n,\mathsf{D}_{\mathsf{sec}},\mathsf{D}_{\mathsf{err}},c}(\mathcal{A}) = \Pr[\mathsf{D\text{-}Trunc\text{-}MLWE}^c_{q,m,n,\mathsf{D}_{\mathsf{sec}},\mathsf{D}_{\mathsf{err}}}(\mathcal{A}) = 1] - \frac{1}{2}.$$

$\mathsf{S\text{-}Trunc\text{-}MLWE}^{c}_{q,m,n,\mathsf{D_{sec}},\mathsf{D_{err}}}(\mathcal{A})$

$\mathbf{U} \leftarrow R_q^{m\times n}$
$\mathbf{A} = \mathsf{Trunc}(\mathbf{U}, c)$
$\mathbf{s} \leftarrow \mathsf{D}_{\mathsf{sec}}^{n}$
$\mathbf{e} \leftarrow \mathsf{D}_{\mathsf{err}}^{m}$
$\mathbf{b} := \mathbf{A}\mathbf{s} + \mathbf{e} \bmod q$
$\mathbf{s}' \leftarrow \mathcal{A}(\mathbf{A}, \mathbf{b})$
return $\mathbf{s} = \mathbf{s}'$

$\mathsf{D\text{-}Trunc\text{-}MLWE}^{c}_{q,m,n,\mathsf{D_{sec}},\mathsf{D_{err}}}(\mathcal{A})$

$\mathbf{U} \leftarrow R_q^{m\times n}$
$\mathbf{A} = \mathsf{Trunc}(\mathbf{U}, c)$
$b \leftarrow \{0, 1\}$
if $b = 0$:
  $\mathbf{s} \leftarrow \mathsf{D}_{\mathsf{sec}}^{n}$
  $\mathbf{e} \leftarrow \mathsf{D}_{\mathsf{err}}^{m}$
  $\mathbf{b} := \mathbf{A}\mathbf{s} + \mathbf{e} \bmod q$
else :
  $\mathbf{b} \leftarrow R_q^{m}$
$b' \leftarrow \mathcal{A}(\mathbf{A}, \mathbf{b})$
return $b = b'$

Fig. 1. The experiments for S-Trunc-MLWE and D-Trunc-MLWE.

If no bits are truncated from the matrix, i.e., $c = 0$, we recover the standard MLWE problem [LS15] and simply write $\mathsf{S\text{-}MLWE}_{q,m,n,\mathsf{D_{sec}},\mathsf{D_{err}}}$ and respectively $\mathsf{D\text{-}MLWE}_{q,m,n,\mathsf{D_{sec}},\mathsf{D_{err}}}$. If additionally the ring is of degree 1, i.e., $R = \mathbb{Z}$, we recover the standard LWE problem [Reg05].

3.2 Module Learning with Errors with Hints

In the following, we define a variant of the Module Learning with Errors problem, where some approximate hints on the MLWE secret $\mathbf{s}$ are additionally given to the adversary, denoted by Hint-MLWE. Concretely, a hint is of the form $(\mathbf{H}, \mathbf{h})$, with $\mathbf{h} = \mathbf{H}\mathbf{s} + \mathbf{f}$, where $\mathbf{H}$ is the *hint matrix* of bounded infinity norm and $\mathbf{f}$ the *hint noise* coming from some distribution $\mathsf{D_{noi}}$ over R. Note that $\mathbf{h}$ is in general not taken modulo q.

Different variants of MLWE with hints have been proposed in the literature before. Sometimes, $\mathbf{H}$ is honestly sampled from some distribution [KLSS23]. Other times, it is chosen by the adversary. Here, the adversary either has to choose before seeing the MLWE matrix $\mathbf{A}$, or after having seen it as in [PS24]. In our case, we require the latter case, as we later in Sect. 5 use Hint-MLWE, where the hint matrix stores the low-order bits of $\mathbf{A}$.

Definition 7 (MLWE with Hints Problem). *Let R be a degree-d ring of integers. Let q, m, n, B and ℓ be positive integers. Further let $\mathsf{D_{err}}$, $\mathsf{D_{sec}}$ and $\mathsf{D_{noi}}$ be distributions over R. The (interactive) experiments of the search and decision versions of* MLWE *with hints are defined in Fig. 2. For an adversary $\mathcal{A}$ trying to solve the* Hint-MLWE *problem, the respective advantage is defined as*

$$\mathsf{Adv}^{\mathsf{S\text{-}Hint\text{-}MLWE}}_{q,m,n,\mathsf{D_{sec}},\mathsf{D_{err}},\mathsf{D_{noi}},B,\ell}(\mathcal{A}) = \Pr[\mathsf{S\text{-}Hint\text{-}MLWE}^{\mathsf{D_{noi}},B,\ell}_{q,m,n,\mathsf{D_{sec}},\mathsf{D_{err}}}(\mathcal{A}) = 1],$$

and

$$\text{Adv}^{\text{D-Hint-MLWE}}_{q,m,n,\mathsf{D}_{\text{sec}},\mathsf{D}_{\text{err}},\mathsf{D}_{\text{noi}},B,\ell}(\mathcal{A}) = \Pr[\text{D-Hint-MLWE}^{\mathsf{D}_{\text{noi}},B,\ell}_{q,m,n,\mathsf{D}_{\text{sec}},\mathsf{D}_{\text{err}}}(\mathcal{A}) = 1] - \frac{1}{2}.$$

S-Hint-MLWE$^{\mathsf{D}_{\text{noi}},B,\ell}_{q,m,n,\mathsf{D}_{\text{sec}},\mathsf{D}_{\text{err}}}(\mathcal{A})$

1 : $\mathbf{A} \leftarrow \mathbb{Z}_q^{m \times n}$
2 : $\mathbb{Z}^{\ell \times n} \ni \mathbf{H} \leftarrow \mathcal{A}(\mathbf{A})$
3 : if $\|\mathbf{H}\|_\infty > B$
4 :   return $\bot$
5 : $\mathbf{s} \leftarrow \mathsf{D}_{\text{sec}}^n$
6 : $\mathbf{e} \leftarrow \mathsf{D}_{\text{err}}^m$
7 : $\mathbf{b} := \mathbf{As} + \mathbf{e} \bmod q$
8 : $\mathbf{f} \leftarrow \mathsf{D}_{\text{noi}}^\ell$
9 : $\mathbf{h} := \mathbf{Hs} + \mathbf{f} \bmod q$
10 : $\mathbf{s}' \leftarrow \mathcal{A}(\mathbf{b}, \mathbf{h})$
11 : return $\mathbf{s} = \mathbf{s}'$

D-Hint-MLWE$^{\mathsf{D}_{\text{noi}},B,\ell}_{q,m,n,\mathsf{D}_{\text{sec}},\mathsf{D}_{\text{err}}}(\mathcal{A})$

1 : $\mathbf{A} \leftarrow \mathbb{Z}_q^{m \times n}$
2 : $\mathbb{Z}^{\ell \times n} \ni \mathbf{H} \leftarrow \mathcal{A}(\mathbf{A})$
3 : if $\|\mathbf{H}\|_\infty > B$
4 :   return $\bot$
5 : $\mathbf{s} \leftarrow \mathsf{D}_{\text{sec}}^n$
6 : $b \leftarrow \{0,1\}$
7 : if $b = 0$:
8 : $\mathbf{e} \leftarrow \mathsf{D}_{\text{err}}^m$
9 : $\mathbf{b} := \mathbf{As} + \mathbf{e} \bmod q$
10 : else :
11 : $\mathbf{b} \leftarrow \mathbb{Z}_q^m$
12 : $\mathbf{f} \leftarrow \mathsf{D}_{\text{noi}}^\ell$
13 : $\mathbf{h} := \mathbf{Hs} + \mathbf{f} \bmod q$
14 : $b' \leftarrow \mathcal{A}(\mathbf{b}, \mathbf{h})$
15 : return $b = b'$

Fig. 2. The experiments for S-Hint-MLWE and D-Hint-MLWE.

The hardness of Hint-MLWE can be reduced from the hardness of the standard MLWE problem in the case of discrete Gaussian secret and hint noise distributions. This has been proven in the case of RLWE (that is, the special case of MLWE with rank $n = 1$). Our result generalizes their proof to higher ranks, whereas the proof strategy closely follows their original proof. Note that as in the original proof, we restrict the result to power-of-two cyclotomics. This is mainly due to the fact that we bound the infinity norm of Rot($\mathbf{H}$) through the infinity norm of the hint matrix $\mathbf{H}$. One could generalize it to other fields and rings, at the expense of looser norm bounds, determined by the so-called expansion factor [LM06,RSW18].

Theorem 1 (Adapted from [MKMS22, Thm. 1]). *Let R be a power-of-two cyclotomic ring of degree d. Let q, m, n, B and ℓ be positive integers and σ, δ be positive reals such that $\sigma\sqrt{1 - \sigma^2 B^2 d^2 n(\ell + 2)/\delta^2} \geq \sqrt{d(n+\ell)}$. By D_{err} we denote an arbitrary distribution over R. We set $\mathsf{D}_{\text{sec}} = D_{R,\sigma^2}$, $\mathsf{D}'_{\text{sec}} = D_{R,\delta^2}$ and $\mathsf{D}_{\text{noi}} = D_{R,\delta^2}$. Then, there is a reduction from the problem $\text{MLWE}_{q,m,n,\mathsf{D}_{\text{sec}},\mathsf{D}_{\text{err}}}$ to Hint-MLWE$^{\mathsf{D}_{\text{noi}},B,\ell}_{q,m,n,\mathsf{D}'_{\text{sec}},\mathsf{D}_{\text{err}}}$. More concretely, assuming that there exists an adversary $\mathcal{A}$ against Hint-MLWE with advantage Adv, we can construct an adversary $\mathcal{B}$*

against MLWE *with advantage at least* Adv. *The reduction works for both, the search and the decision variants of the problem.*

As example parameters, we can set $\delta^2 \geq 2\sigma^2 B^2 d^2 n(\ell+2)$ and $\sigma \geq \sqrt{2d(n+\ell)}$. When setting $n = 1$, we recover the original result [MKMS22, Thm. 1]. When setting $d = 1$, we obtain the result for plain LWE.

Proof. We detail out the proof in the case of the corresponding decision variants. The proof for the search variants works analogously. Let $\mathcal{A}$ be an adversary against D-Hint-MLWE with advantage Adv. We now construct a reduction $\mathcal{B}$ against D-MLWE with advantage at least Adv.

In the D-MLWE experiment, $\mathcal{A}$ is given as input $(\mathbf{A}, \mathbf{b}) \in R_q^{m\times n} \times R_q^m$. The reduction now forwards $\mathbf{A}$ as input to the adversary $\mathcal{A}$, who responds with a hint matrix $\mathbf{H} \in R^{\ell \times n}$ such that $\|\mathbf{H}\|_\infty := \|\tau(\mathbf{H})\|_\infty \leq B$.

The matrix $\mathbf{H}$ defines the matrix $\mathsf{Rot}(\mathbf{H}) \in \mathbb{Z}^{d\ell\times dn}$, where every coefficient in $\mathbf{H}$ is replaced by its corresponding multiplication matrix. The matrix $\mathsf{Rot}(\mathbf{H})$ defines a lattice Λ in $R^{d(n+\ell)}$, given as $\Lambda = \{(\tau(\mathbf{s}), -\mathsf{Rot}(\mathbf{H})\tau(\mathbf{s}))^T \mid \mathbf{s} \in R^n\}$, where τ denotes the coefficient embedding. Every element in Λ can be written as $\mathbf{L}\cdot\tau(\mathbf{s})$ with $\mathbf{L} = (\mathbf{I}_{dn}, -\mathsf{Rot}(\mathbf{H}))^T \in \mathbb{Z}^{d(n+\ell)\times dn}$. By the properties of discrete Gaussians, if $\mathbf{s} \leftarrow \mathsf{D}_{\mathsf{sec}}^n = D_{R^n,\sigma^2}$ (i.e., $\tau(\mathbf{s}) \leftarrow D_{\mathbb{Z}^{dn},\sigma^2}$), then $\mathbf{L}\cdot\tau(\mathbf{s}) \sim D_{\Lambda,\boldsymbol{\Sigma}}$, where $\boldsymbol{\Sigma} = \sigma^2 \mathbf{L}\mathbf{L}^T \in \mathbb{Z}^{d(n+\ell)\times d(n+\ell)}$. We further set $\boldsymbol{\Sigma}' = \delta^2 \mathbf{I}_{d(n+\ell)} - \boldsymbol{\Sigma}$. As we later use $\boldsymbol{\Sigma}'$ as the covariance matrix of a discrete Gaussian distribution, we have to make sure that it is positive semi-definite.

Claim. Assume $\delta \geq \sigma B d\sqrt{n(\ell+2)}$, then the matrix $\boldsymbol{\Sigma}'$ is positive semi-definite.

Proof (Claim). Note that $\boldsymbol{\Sigma}$ is symmetric over $\mathbb{Z}$, thus $\boldsymbol{\Sigma}' = \delta^2 \mathbf{I}_{n+\ell} - \boldsymbol{\Sigma}$ is symmetric over $\mathbb{Z}$ as well. Let us recall the concrete forms of $\boldsymbol{\Sigma}$ and $\boldsymbol{\Sigma}'$ given by

$$\boldsymbol{\Sigma} = \sigma^2 \begin{pmatrix} \mathbf{I}_{dn} & -\mathsf{Rot}(\mathbf{H})^T \\ -\mathsf{Rot}(\mathbf{H}) & \mathsf{Rot}(\mathbf{H})\mathsf{Rot}(\mathbf{H})^T \end{pmatrix},$$

and

$$\boldsymbol{\Sigma}' = \begin{pmatrix} (\delta^2-\sigma^2)\mathbf{I}_{dn} & \sigma^2\mathsf{Rot}(\mathbf{H})^T \\ \sigma^2\mathsf{Rot}(\mathbf{H}) & \delta^2\mathbf{I}_{d\ell} - \sigma^2\mathsf{Rot}(\mathbf{H})\mathsf{Rot}(\mathbf{H})^T \end{pmatrix}.$$

The first dn diagonals of $\boldsymbol{\Sigma}'$ are given by $\delta^2 - \sigma^2$, the last $d\ell$ diagonals are given by $\delta^2 - \sigma^2\|\mathbf{h}_i\|^2$, where $\mathbf{h}_i$ is the i-th row of $\mathsf{Rot}(\mathbf{H})$ for $i \in \{1,\ldots,d\ell\}$. Note that $\|\mathbf{h}_i\|^2 \leq ndB^2$, as we are working over a power-of-two cyclotomic ring. Thus, assuming

$$\delta \geq \sigma B\sqrt{nd}, \tag{2}$$

the diagonal entries of $\boldsymbol{\Sigma}'$ are non-negative. In this case, it is enough to show that $\boldsymbol{\Sigma}'$ is diagonally dominant. By construction, $\|\boldsymbol{\Sigma}\|_\infty \leq \sigma^2 ndB^2$. We write $\boldsymbol{\Sigma}' = (\boldsymbol{\Sigma}'_{ij})_{ij}$ with $i,j \in \{1,\ldots,d(n+\ell)\}$. On the one side, the absolute values of the entries on the diagonal can be lower bounded as $|\boldsymbol{\Sigma}'_{ii}| \geq \delta^2 - \sigma^2 ndB^2$

for $i \in \{1, \ldots, d(n+\ell)\}$. On the other side, the sum of the absolute values of the entries off the diagonal can be upper bounded as

$$\sum_{j \neq i} |\boldsymbol{\Sigma}'_{ij}| \leq \max\left\{\sigma^2 dnB + \sigma^2 d^2 \ell n B^2, \sigma^2 d\ell B\right\} \leq \sigma^2 B^2 d^2 n(\ell+1),$$

where we used that B, d, ℓ are positive integers. Overall $\boldsymbol{\Sigma}'$ is diagonally dominant if

$$\delta \geq \sigma B d\sqrt{n(\ell+2)}. \tag{3}$$

■

The reduction $\mathcal{B}$ continues as follows. They sample $(\mathbf{s}', \mathbf{f}') \leftarrow D_{R^{n+\ell}, \boldsymbol{\Sigma}'}$ (i.e., $(\tau(\mathbf{s}'), \tau(\mathbf{f}')) \leftarrow D_{\mathbb{Z}^{d(n+\ell)}, \boldsymbol{\Sigma}'}$) and set $\mathbf{b}' = \mathbf{b} + \mathbf{A}\mathbf{s}'$ and $\mathbf{h} = \mathbf{H}\mathbf{s}' + \mathbf{f}'$. They then forward $(\mathbf{b}', \mathbf{h})$ to the adversary $\mathcal{A}$. On the output bit b by $\mathcal{A}$, the reduction also outputs b as their answer. We now analyze the advantage of $\mathcal{B}$, assuming that $\mathcal{A}$ has advantage Adv.

Case 1) Assume that $(\mathbf{A}, \mathbf{b})$ is given as $\mathbf{b} = \mathbf{A}\mathbf{s} + \mathbf{e}$. Thus, $\mathbf{b}' = \mathbf{A}(\mathbf{s} + \mathbf{s}') + \mathbf{e}$. Set $\mathbf{f} = -\mathbf{H}\mathbf{s} + \mathbf{f}'$. Note that the values $\mathbf{s}$ and $\mathbf{f}$ are not known to the reduction $\mathcal{B}$, but only needed to argue that $(\mathbf{b}', \mathbf{h})$ has the right distribution. Then, $(\mathbf{s}+\mathbf{s}', \mathbf{f}) = (\mathbf{s}+\mathbf{s}', -\mathbf{H}\mathbf{s}+\mathbf{f}') = (\mathbf{s}, -\mathbf{H}\mathbf{s}) + (\mathbf{s}', \mathbf{f}')$, with $(\mathbf{s}, -\mathbf{H}\mathbf{s}) \sim D_{R^{n+\ell}, \boldsymbol{\Sigma}}$ and $(\mathbf{s}', \mathbf{f}') \sim D_{R^{n+\ell}, \boldsymbol{\Sigma}'}$. By Lemma 3 Item 2, this implies that $(\mathbf{s}+\mathbf{s}', \mathbf{f}) \sim D_{R^{n+\ell}, \delta^2}$ as long as the eigenvalues of $\boldsymbol{\Gamma} = \sigma\sqrt{\mathbf{I}_{d(n+\ell)} - \sigma^2 \mathbf{L}\mathbf{L}^T/\delta^2}$ are above the smoothing parameter of $\mathbb{Z}^{d(n+\ell)}$. To lower bound the eigenvalues of $\boldsymbol{\Gamma}$, it suffices to upper bound the eigenvalues of $\mathbf{L}\mathbf{L}^T$. To do so, we use a known result of spectral theory: It states that the eigenvalues of $\mathbf{L}\mathbf{L}^T$ can be upper bounded by the sum of the absolute values of any of its row. The latter can be upper bounded by $B^2 d^2 n(\ell+2)$, implying the condition

$$\sigma\sqrt{1 - \sigma^2 B^2 d^2 n(\ell+2)/\delta^2} \geq \eta(\mathbb{Z}^{d(n+\ell)}). \tag{4}$$

Note that Eq. 4 subsumes Eqs. 3 and 2. Moreover, $\eta(\mathbb{Z}^{d(n+\ell)}) \leq \sqrt{d(n+\ell)}$ and thus the condition of the theorem statement fulfills the above conditions. It yields $\mathbf{H}(\mathbf{s}+\mathbf{s}') + \mathbf{f} = \mathbf{H}(\mathbf{s}+\mathbf{s}') - \mathbf{H}\mathbf{s} + \mathbf{f}' = \mathbf{H}\mathbf{s}' + \mathbf{f}'$ and thus $(\mathbf{b}', \mathbf{h})$ is distributed correctly.

Case 2) Assuming $(\mathbf{A}, \mathbf{b})$ comes from the uniform distribution, so does $(\mathbf{A}, \mathbf{b}')$. With the same argumentation as above, $\mathbf{h}$ has the correct distribution and hence $(\mathbf{b}', \mathbf{h})$ is a valid input to $\mathcal{A}$, concluding the proof. □

4 Hardness of Truncated MLWE Using Rényi Divergence

We begin with our first approach to reduce the hardness of $\mathsf{Trunc\text{-}MLWE}$ from standard MLWE, using the Rényi divergence. Note that the results only apply to the respective search variants.

Theorem 2. *Let R be a power-of-two cyclotomic ring of degree d. Further, let α, q, m, n, η and c be positive integers and δ be a positive real. Further, let $\mathsf{D}_{\mathsf{sec}}$, $\mathsf{D}_{\mathsf{err}}$ and $\mathsf{D}'_{\mathsf{err}}$ be distributions over R such that $\mathsf{D}_{\mathsf{sec}}$ is (η, δ)-bounded (Definition 1). Then, there is a reduction from the problem $\mathsf{S\text{-}MLWE}_{q,m,n,\mathsf{D}_{\mathsf{sec}},\mathsf{D}'_{\mathsf{err}}}$ to the problem $\mathsf{S\text{-}Trunc\text{-}MLWE}^c_{q,m,n,\mathsf{D}_{\mathsf{sec}},\mathsf{D}_{\mathsf{err}}}$. More concretely, assuming there exists an adversary $\mathcal{A}$ against $\mathsf{S\text{-}Trunc\text{-}MLWE}$ with advantage Adv, we can transform them into an adversary against $\mathsf{S\text{-}MLWE}$ with advantage Adv' such that*

$$(\mathsf{Adv} - \delta^n)^{\frac{\alpha}{\alpha-1}} \leq \mathsf{Adv}' \cdot \mathsf{RD}_\alpha(\mathsf{D}_{\mathsf{err}} + \vec{\mu} \| \mathsf{D}'_{\mathsf{err}})^m,$$

where $\vec{\mu} = (\mu, \ldots, \mu) \in \mathbb{Z}^d \cong R$, with $\mu = d \cdot 2^c \cdot n \cdot \eta$.

The reduction loss is reflected by replacing the error distribution $\mathsf{D}_{\mathsf{err}}$ by a wider distribution $\mathsf{D}'_{\mathsf{err}}$. How much wider the distribution has to be is impacted by the ring degree d, the number of truncated bits c, the bound on secrets η and the rank n of the MLWE problem.

Proof. Let $\mathcal{A}$ be an adversary against $\mathsf{S\text{-}Trunc\text{-}MLWE}$, whose experiment is defined in Fig. 1. On input $(\mathbf{A}, \mathbf{b})$, the adversary $\mathcal{A}$ outputs a guess $\mathbf{s}'$ and wins the experiment if the guess was correct. Below, we argue the theorem via a series of intermediate hybrids, each specifying the distribution of the input $(\mathbf{A}, \mathbf{b})$ given to $\mathcal{A}$.

H_0: Sample $(\mathbf{A}, \mathbf{b})$ as specified in the $\mathsf{S\text{-}Trunc\text{-}MLWE}$ game in Fig. 1. Thus, $\mathbf{A} = \mathsf{Trunc}(\mathbf{U}, c)$ with $\mathbf{U} \leftarrow R_q^{m \times n}$. Moreover, $\mathbf{b} = \mathbf{A}\mathbf{s} + \mathbf{e} \bmod q$, with $\mathbf{s} \leftarrow \mathsf{D}^n_{\mathsf{sec}}$ and $\mathbf{e} \leftarrow \mathsf{D}^m_{\mathsf{err}}$.

H_1: We now sample $\mathbf{A}$ as in H_0, but change how $\mathbf{b}$ is defined. First, we sample $\mathbf{f} \leftarrow (\mathsf{D}'_{\mathsf{err}})^m$ and then we set $\mathbf{b} = \mathbf{U}\mathbf{s} + \mathbf{f} \bmod q$.

H_2: Now, $\mathbf{b}$ is sampled as in H_1. However, we modify the input $\mathbf{A}$ by setting it to $\mathbf{A} := \mathbf{U}$. In other words, $(\mathbf{A}, \mathbf{b})$ corresponds to an instance of $\mathsf{S\text{-}MLWE}$ (without truncation).

From H_0 to H_1: First, we use that $\mathsf{D}_{\mathsf{sec}}$ is (η, δ)-bounded, to condition on the event of $\|\mathbf{s}\|_\infty \leq \eta$ implying

$$\begin{aligned}
\mathsf{Adv} &= \Pr[\mathbf{s} \leftarrow \mathcal{A}(\mathbf{A}, \mathbf{b}) \mid (\mathbf{A}, \mathbf{b}) \sim \mathsf{H}_0] \\
&= \Pr[\mathbf{s} \leftarrow \mathcal{A}(\mathbf{A}, \mathbf{b}) \mid (\mathbf{A}, \mathbf{b}) \sim \mathsf{H}_0 \wedge \|\mathbf{s}\|_\infty \leq \eta] \cdot \Pr[\|\mathbf{s}\|_\infty \leq \eta] \\
&\quad + \Pr[\mathbf{s} \leftarrow \mathcal{A}(\mathbf{A}, \mathbf{b}) \mid (\mathbf{A}, \mathbf{b}) \sim \mathsf{H}_0 \wedge \|\mathbf{s}\|_\infty > \eta] \cdot \Pr[\|\mathbf{s}\|_\infty > \eta] \\
&\leq \Pr[\mathbf{s} \leftarrow \mathcal{A}(\mathbf{A}, \mathbf{b}) \mid (\mathbf{A}, \mathbf{b}) \sim \mathsf{H}_0 \wedge \|\mathbf{s}\|_\infty \leq \eta] + \delta^n.
\end{aligned}$$

Second, we use the probability preservation property of the Rényi divergence from Lemma 5 to argue

$$\begin{aligned}
&\Pr[\mathbf{s} \leftarrow \mathcal{A}(\mathbf{A}, \mathbf{b}) \mid (\mathbf{A}, \mathbf{b}) \sim \mathsf{H}_0 \wedge \|\mathbf{s}\|_\infty \leq \eta]^{\frac{\alpha}{\alpha-1}} \\
&\leq \Pr[\mathbf{s} \leftarrow \mathcal{A}(\mathbf{A}, \mathbf{b}) \mid (\mathbf{A}, \mathbf{b}) \sim \mathsf{H}_1 \wedge \|\mathbf{s}\|_\infty \leq \eta] \cdot \mathsf{RD}_\alpha(\mathsf{H}_0 \| \mathsf{H}_1).
\end{aligned}$$

Note that the only difference between the two hybrids is how $\mathbf{b}$ is defined. In H_0, $\mathbf{b} = \mathbf{A}\mathbf{s} + \mathbf{e} = (\mathbf{U} - \mathbf{N_U})\mathbf{s} + \mathbf{e} = \mathbf{U}\mathbf{s} + (\mathbf{e} - \mathbf{N_U}\mathbf{s})$, where $\mathbf{N_U} = \mathbf{U} \bmod 2^c$. In H_1, $\mathbf{b} = \mathbf{U}\mathbf{s} + \mathbf{f}$. By the data processing inequality from Lemma 6, consider the function $f(y) = (\mathbf{A}, \mathbf{A}\mathbf{s} + y)$, where $\mathbf{N}_\mathbf{U}\mathbf{s}$ serves as a fixed parameter for the distributions and the function; however, only the first distribution uses $\mathbf{N}_\mathbf{U}\mathbf{s}$, subtracting it from every sample. This yields:

$$\begin{aligned}\mathsf{RD}_\alpha(\mathsf{H}_0\|\mathsf{H}_1) &\leq \mathsf{RD}_\alpha(\mathbf{e} - \mathbf{N}_\mathbf{U}\mathbf{s}\|\mathbf{f}) \\ &\leq \mathsf{RD}_\alpha(\mathsf{D}_{\mathsf{err}} + \vec{\mu}\|\mathsf{D}'_{\mathsf{err}})^m.\end{aligned}$$

where $\|-\mathbf{N}_\mathbf{U}\mathbf{s}\|_\infty \leq d \cdot 2^c \cdot n \cdot \eta = \mu$. Note that here we are using the properties of power-of-two cyclotomics. When generalizing to other rings, the bound would be looser by the so-called expansion factor [LM06, RSW18]. Overall,

$$(\mathsf{Adv} - \delta^n)^{\frac{\alpha}{\alpha-1}} \leq \Pr[\mathbf{s} \leftarrow \mathcal{A}(\mathbf{A}, \mathbf{b}) \mid (\mathbf{A}, \mathbf{b}) \sim \mathsf{H}_1] \cdot \mathsf{RD}_\alpha(\mathsf{D}_{\mathsf{err}} + \vec{\mu}\|\mathsf{D}'_{\mathsf{err}})^m.$$

From H_1 to H_2: We observe that the only difference between H_1 and H_2 is that the c least significant bits of $\mathbf{U}$ are removed in H_1, but not in H_2. Removing the low-order bits only results in less information being transmitted, so the advantage of an adversary in H_1 cannot be greater than that of an adversary in H_2:

$$\Pr[\mathbf{s} \leftarrow \mathcal{A}(\mathbf{A}, \mathbf{b}) \mid (\mathbf{A}, \mathbf{b}) \sim \mathsf{H}_1] \leq \Pr[\mathbf{s} \leftarrow \mathcal{A}(\mathbf{A}, \mathbf{b}) \mid (\mathbf{A}, \mathbf{b}) \sim \mathsf{H}_2].$$

The proof concludes by observing that H_2 is equivalent to an instance of the problem $\mathsf{S\text{-}MLWE}_{q,m,n,\mathsf{D}_{\mathsf{sec}},\mathsf{D}'_{\mathsf{err}}}$. □

Theorem 2 applies to any secret and error distributions as long as the secrets are of bounded infinity norm and the Rényi divergences are well-defined and small enough. We now provide example corollaries for bounded uniform, rounded and discrete Gaussian distributions.

Corollary 1. *Let R be a power-of-two cyclotomic ring of degree d. Further, let α, q, m, n, η and c be positive integers. We set $\mathsf{D}_{\mathsf{sec}} = \mathbf{U}_{0,\eta+1}$ and $\mathsf{D}_{\mathsf{err}} = \mathbf{U}_{0,k}$ and $\mathsf{D}'_{\mathsf{err}} = \mathbf{U}_{0,k+\mu}$, where $\mu = d \cdot n \cdot 2^c \cdot \eta$. Then, for any adversary $\mathcal{A}$ it holds*

$$\mathsf{Adv}^{\mathsf{S\text{-}Trunc\text{-}MLWE}}_{q,m,n,\mathsf{D}_{\mathsf{sec}},\mathsf{D}_{\mathsf{err}},c}(\mathcal{A})^{\frac{\alpha}{\alpha-1}} \leq \mathsf{Adv}^{\mathsf{S\text{-}MLWE}}_{q,m,n,\mathsf{D}_{\mathsf{sec}},\mathsf{D}'_{\mathsf{err}}}(\mathcal{A}) \cdot \left(\frac{k+\mu}{k}\right)^{d \cdot m}.$$

Here, it is very clear that the resulting error distribution $\mathsf{D}'_{\mathsf{err}}$ has infinity norm larger than 2^c, avoiding the trivial setup mentioned in the introduction.

Remark 1. In order to bound the reduction loss, one has to make sure that k is large enough. For instance, when $k \geq d^2mn$, the loss is bounded above by

$$\left(\frac{k+\mu}{k}\right)^{d \cdot m} = \left(1 + \frac{\mu}{k}\right)^{d \cdot m} \leq \left(1 + \frac{\eta \cdot 2^c}{dm}\right)^{dm} \leq e^{\eta \cdot 2^c},$$

which is constant for η and c being constants.

Proof. We observe that $\mathsf{D}_{\mathsf{sec}} = \mathbf{U}_{0,\eta+1}$ is $(\eta, 0)$-bounded. We now provide a concrete value for the Rényi divergence from Theorem 2. We observe that $\mathsf{D}_{\mathsf{err}} + \vec{\mu} = \mathbf{U}_{0,k} + \vec{\mu} = \mathbf{U}_{\mu,k+\mu}$ and $\mathsf{Supp}(\mathsf{D}_{\mathsf{err}} + \vec{\mu}) = \mathsf{Supp}(\mathbf{U}_{\mu,k+\mu}) = \{\mu, \ldots, \mu + k - 1\}^d \subset \{0, \ldots, \mu + k - 1\}^d = \mathsf{Supp}(\mathbf{U}_{0,k+\mu}) = \mathsf{Supp}(\mathsf{D}'_{\mathsf{err}})$, implying a well-defined Rényi divergence.

$$\begin{aligned}\mathsf{RD}_\alpha(\mathsf{D}_{\mathsf{err}} + \vec{\mu} \| \mathsf{D}'_{\mathsf{err}}) &= \left(\sum_{x \in \mathsf{Supp}(\mathbf{U}_{\mu,k+\mu})} \frac{\mathbf{U}_{\mu,k+\mu}(x)^\alpha}{\mathbf{U}_{0,k+\mu}(x)^{\alpha-1}} \right)^{1/(\alpha-1)} \\ &= \left((k)^d \cdot \frac{(1/(k))^{d\alpha}}{(1/(k+\mu))^{d(\alpha-1)}} \right)^{1/(\alpha-1)} = \left(\frac{k+\mu}{k} \right)^d .\end{aligned}$$

□

Corollary 2. *Let R be a power-of-two cyclotomic ring of degree d. Further, let α, q, m, n, η and c be positive integers and $\mathsf{D}_{\mathsf{sec}}$ be any (η, δ)-bounded distribution over R. We set $\mathsf{D}_{\mathsf{err}} = \mathsf{D}'_{\mathsf{err}} = \lfloor D_{\sigma^2} \rceil$ over R (via coefficient embedding τ) for positive real σ. Then, for any adversary $\mathcal{A}$ it holds*

$$\left(\mathsf{Adv}^{\mathsf{S\text{-}Trunc\text{-}MLWE}}_{q,m,n,\mathsf{D}_{\mathsf{sec}},\mathsf{D}_{\mathsf{err}},c}(\mathcal{A}) - \delta^n \right)^{\frac{\alpha}{\alpha-1}} \leq \mathsf{Adv}^{\mathsf{S\text{-}MLWE}}_{q,m,n,\mathsf{D}_{\mathsf{sec}},\mathsf{D}'_{\mathsf{err}}}(\mathcal{A}) \cdot \exp\left(\frac{\alpha d m \mu^2}{2\sigma^2} \right),$$

where $\mu = d \cdot n \cdot 2^c \cdot \eta$.

Proof. We provide a concrete value for the Rényi divergence in Theorem 2. We use Lemma 6 with $f(\mathbf{x}) = \lfloor \mathbf{x} \rceil$ and $\vec{\mu} \in \mathbb{Z}^d$ to argue that

$$\mathsf{RD}_\alpha(\mathsf{D}_{\mathsf{err}} + \vec{\mu} \| \mathsf{D}'_{\mathsf{err}}) = \mathsf{RD}_\alpha(\lfloor D_{\mu,\sigma^2} \rceil \| \lfloor D_{\sigma^2} \rceil) \leq \mathsf{RD}_\alpha(D_{\mu,\sigma^2} \| D_{\sigma^2}).$$

By Lemma 7 it yields

$$\mathsf{RD}_\alpha(D_{\mu,\sigma^2} \| D_{\sigma^2}) \leq \exp\left(\frac{\alpha d \mu^2}{2\sigma^2} \right).$$

Thus, overall

$$\mathsf{RD}_\alpha(\mathsf{D}_{\mathsf{err}} + \mu \| \mathsf{D}'_{\mathsf{err}})^m = \exp\left(\frac{m \alpha d \mu^2}{2\sigma^2} \right),$$

concluding the proof. □

Corollary 3. *Let R be a power-of-two cyclotomic ring of degree d. Further, let α, q, m, n, η and c be positive integers and $\mathsf{D}_{\mathsf{sec}}$ be any (η, δ)-bounded distribution over R. We set $\mathsf{D}_{\mathsf{err}} = \mathsf{D}'_{\mathsf{err}} = D_{R,\sigma^2}$ for positive real σ. Then, for any adversary $\mathcal{A}$ it holds*

$$\left(\mathsf{Adv}^{\mathsf{S\text{-}Trunc\text{-}MLWE}}_{q,m,n,\mathsf{D}_{\mathsf{sec}},\mathsf{D}_{\mathsf{err}},c}(\mathcal{A}) - \delta^n \right)^{\frac{\alpha}{\alpha-1}} \leq \mathsf{Adv}^{\mathsf{S\text{-}MLWE}}_{q,m,n,\mathsf{D}_{\mathsf{sec}},\mathsf{D}'_{\mathsf{err}}}(\mathcal{A}) \cdot \exp\left(\frac{\alpha d m \mu^2}{2\sigma^2} \right),$$

where $\mu = d \cdot n \cdot 2^c \cdot \eta$.

Proof. As before, we provide concrete values for the two corresponding Rényi divergences in Theorem 2. We observe that

$$\mathsf{RD}_\alpha(\mathsf{D}_{\mathsf{err}} + \vec{\mu} \| \mathsf{D}'_{\mathsf{err}})^m = \mathsf{RD}_\alpha(D_{R,\vec{\mu},\sigma^2} \| D_{R,\sigma^2})^m = \mathsf{RD}_\alpha(D_{R^m,\boldsymbol{\mu},\sigma^2} \| D_{R^m,\sigma^2}).$$

where $\boldsymbol{\mu} = (\vec{\mu}, \ldots, \vec{\mu})^T \in R^m$. By applying Lemma 8 and noticing that $\boldsymbol{\mu} \in \mathbb{Z}^{md}$ and therefore $\epsilon = 0$, we can argue that

$$\mathsf{RD}_\alpha(D_{R^m,\boldsymbol{\mu},\sigma^2} \| D_{R^m,\sigma^2}) \leq \left(\frac{1+\epsilon}{1-\epsilon}\right)^{\alpha/\alpha-1} \cdot e^{\alpha\|\boldsymbol{\mu}\|^2/(2\sigma^2)} = e^{\alpha d m \mu^2/(2\sigma^2)},$$

with $\|\boldsymbol{\mu}\| = md\mu^2$, concluding the proof. □

4.1 Public Sampleability Does Not Help Here

As of today, the only way to use the Rényi divergence for decision problems is to use the public sampleability framework from [BLR+18, Sec. 4]. We argue below that, even though the truncated MLWE problem can be expressed as a publicly sampleable problem, it does not lead to meaningful results. Intuitively, the problem is that truncated and uniform matrices are not Rényi close, which would be needed.

More formally, we observe that truncated MLWE fits well into the public sampleable setting: given $(\mathbf{A}, \mathbf{b})$, one can easily sample fresh samples by drawing new MLWE secret and errors. A very similar setting was used in [BLR+18, Sec. 4.2]. However, the loss in the advantage depends on the Rényi divergence between the standard way to sample $\mathbf{A}$ (i.e. uniformly over R_q) and the truncated way to sample it (i.e. cutting the c lowest order bits off). Unfortunately, their Rényi divergence is given by 2^{cdmn}, which is exponential in the product of ring degree and matrix dimensions, which is usually linear proportional to the security parameter. Given this big loss, the reduction becomes vacuous.

5 Hardness of Truncated Module LWE Using Hints

We continue with our second approach to reduce the hardness of Trunc-MLWE from standard MLWE, going through the intermediate Hint-MLWE problem (cf. Sect. 3.2). The result now applies to both search and decision variants, but requires a decomposition property for the error/noise distributions.

The following theorem establishes a reduction from Hint-MLWE to Trunc-MLWE.

Theorem 3. *Let R be a ring of integers of degree d, and let q, m, n, B and c be positive integers such that $B = 2^c$. Moreover, let $\mathsf{D}_{\mathsf{sec}}, \mathsf{D}_{\mathsf{err}}, \mathsf{D}'_{\mathsf{err}}$ and $\mathsf{D}_{\mathsf{noi}}$ be distributions over R such that $(\mathsf{D}'_{\mathsf{err}})^m$ is statistically close to $(\mathsf{D}_{\mathsf{err}})^m + (\mathsf{D}_{\mathsf{noi}})^m$. Then, there is a reduction from the problem $\mathsf{Hint\text{-}MLWE}^{\mathsf{D}_{\mathsf{noi}},B,m}_{q,m,n,\mathsf{D}_{\mathsf{sec}},\mathsf{D}_{\mathsf{err}}}$ to the problem $\mathsf{Trunc\text{-}MLWE}^{c}_{q,m,n,\mathsf{D}_{\mathsf{sec}},\mathsf{D}'_{\mathsf{err}}}$. More concretely, assuming that there exists an adversary $\mathcal{A}$ against Trunc-MLWE with advantage Adv, we can construct an adversary $\mathcal{B}$ against Hint-MLWE with advantage at least Adv. The reduction works for both, the search and the decision variants of the problems.*

Proof. We detail out the proof in the case of the corresponding decision variants. The proof for the search variants works analogously. Let $\mathcal{A}$ be an adversary against $\mathsf{Trunc\text{-}MLWE}$ with advantage Adv. We now construct a reduction $\mathcal{B}$ against $\mathsf{Hint\text{-}MLWE}$ with advantage at least Adv.

In the $\mathsf{Hint\text{-}MLWE}$ experiment, $\mathcal{B}$ is given as input $\mathbf{A}$, sampled uniformly at random from $R_q^{m\times n}$. The reduction $\mathcal{B}$ now outputs $\mathbf{H} := -(\mathbf{A} \bmod 2^c) \in R_q^{m\times n}$ as hint matrix. Upon receiving $(\mathbf{b}, \mathbf{h}) \in R_q^m \times R_q^m$, the reduction $\mathcal{B}$ sets $\mathbf{t} := (\mathbf{b}+\mathbf{h})^T \in R_q^m$ as well as $\mathbf{B} := (\mathbf{A}+\mathbf{H})^T \in R_q^{m\times n}$. Then, they provide $(\mathbf{B}, \mathbf{t})$ as input to $\mathcal{A}$. Let b' be the guess of $\mathcal{A}$, then $\mathcal{B}$ forwards b' as their guess.

First, we observe that $\|\mathbf{H}\|_\infty \leq 2^c = B$, hence $\mathbf{H}$ is a valid hint matrix for $\mathsf{Hint\text{-}MLWE}$, as specified in the $\mathsf{Hint\text{-}MLWE}$ experiment in Fig. 2. Further, we see that $\mathbf{A}+\mathbf{H} = \mathbf{A} - (\mathbf{A} \bmod 2^c) = \mathsf{Trunc}(\mathbf{A}, c)$. Hence, $\mathbf{B}$ has the correct distribution as specified in the $\mathsf{Trunc\text{-}MLWE}$ experiment in Fig. 1.

Case 1: If $b = 0$ in the $\mathsf{Hint\text{-}MLWE}$ experiment, then $\mathbf{b} = \mathbf{A}\mathbf{s}+\mathbf{e} \bmod q$ and $\mathbf{h} = \mathbf{H}\mathbf{s} + \mathbf{f}''$ for some $\mathbf{s} \leftarrow \mathsf{D}_{\mathsf{sec}}^n$, $\mathbf{e} \leftarrow \mathsf{D}_{\mathsf{err}}^m$ and $\mathbf{f}'' \leftarrow \mathsf{D}_{\mathsf{noi}}^m$. Hence, $\mathbf{t} = \mathbf{A}\mathbf{s}+\mathbf{e}+\mathbf{h} = (\mathbf{A}+\mathbf{H})\mathbf{s}+\mathbf{e}+\mathbf{f} = \mathsf{Trunc}(\mathbf{A}, c)\mathbf{s}+\mathbf{e}+\mathbf{f}$. Note that $(\mathbf{e}+\mathbf{f})^T$ is statistically close to some $\mathbf{g} \leftarrow (\mathsf{D}'_{\mathsf{err}})^m$. Overall, $(\mathbf{B}, \mathbf{t})$ is statistically close to the input distribution in case of $b = 0$ in $\mathsf{Trunc\text{-}MLWE}$.

Case 2: If $b = 1$ in the $\mathsf{Hint\text{-}MLWE}$ experiment, then $\mathbf{b} \leftarrow R_q^m$ and $\mathbf{h}$ and $\mathbf{f}'$ are chosen independently of $\mathbf{b}$. Thus, $\mathbf{t}$ is also distributed uniformly at random over R_q^m and hence $(\mathbf{B}, \mathbf{t})$ corresponds to the input distribution in case of $b = 1$ in $\mathsf{Trunc\text{-}MLWE}$.

If $\mathcal{A}$ succeeds to guess correctly (i.e., $b' = b$) with probability Adv in the experiment of $\mathsf{Trunc\text{-}MLWE}$, then $\mathcal{B}$ succeeds to guess correctly in the game of $\mathsf{Hint\text{-}MLWE}$ with probability at least Adv as well. □

The following corollary instantiates the above theorem with discrete Gaussian distributions over power-of-two cyclotomic rings and combines it with Theorem 1 to provide the complete reduction from MLWE to $\mathsf{Trunc\text{-}MLWE}$.

Corollary 4. *Let R be a power-of-two cyclotomic ring of degree d. Further, let q, m, n and c be positive integers. Moreover, let γ, δ and σ be positive reals such that $\sigma \geq \sqrt{2d(n+m)}$, $\delta \geq \sigma 2^c d\sqrt{2n(m+2)}$, and $\sigma^2 + \delta^2 = \gamma^2$. We set $\mathsf{D}_{\mathsf{sec}} = \mathsf{D}_{\mathsf{err}} = D_{R,\sigma^2}$, $\mathsf{D}'_{\mathsf{sec}} = D_{R,\delta^2}$ and $\mathsf{D}'_{\mathsf{err}} = D_{R,\gamma^2}$. Then, there is a reduction from $\mathsf{MLWE}_{q,m,n,\mathsf{D}_{\mathsf{sec}},\mathsf{D}_{\mathsf{err}}}$ to the problem $\mathsf{Trunc\text{-}MLWE}^c_{q,m,n,\mathsf{D}'_{\mathsf{sec}},\mathsf{D}'_{\mathsf{err}}}$.*

Proof. Note that $(D_{R,\sigma^2})^m = D_{R^m,\sigma^2}$ for every positive real σ. The corollary follows by Lemma 3 Item 1 with $\Lambda = R^m$ and noting that $\eta(R^m) \leq \sqrt{dm}$, thus $\sigma, \delta \geq \sqrt{2} \cdot \eta(R^m)$. Moreover, we instantiate Theorem 1 with $\ell = m$ and MLWE noise distributed as D_{R,σ^2}. □

6 Comparison

As explained in the introduction, our work closes an open problem left open by [JZW+23], by providing a reduction from standard MLWE to the truncated problem in its decision variant. Their work only provides a reduction from the less standard module variant of NTRU, denoted by MNTRU, and is limited to the search versions. In total, we describe two approaches. The two different reductions in Theorem 2 and Theorem 3 come with different advantages and disadvantages, as detailed out in the following and summarized in Table 1.

Table 1. Comparison of [JZW+23] with our two results to prove the hardness of Trunc-MLWE. Entropic distributions denote any distribution with enough min-entropy. Rényi-close denotes the fact that the (shifted) starting and ending error distribution have to be Rényi-close.

Result	Assumption	Variant	Secret	Error
[JZW+23]	MNTRU	Search	Entropic	Gaussian
Theorem 2	MLWE	Search	Bounded	Rényi-close
Theorem 3	MLWE	Decision	Gaussian	Gaussian

Note that all reductions, including [JZW+23] and ours, preserve the ring degree d, the modulus q, as well as the MLWE dimensions m and n.

The reduction of [JZW+23] works for any secret distribution which has enough min-entropy, what we denote by an *entropic* distribution. Thus, it also covers secret distributions which have large infinity norm. Both the distribution of the starting MNTRU problem and the final error distribution of truncated MLWE are assumed to be discrete Gaussians.

The most important positive aspect of the reduction in Theorem 2 using the Rényi divergence (Sect. 4) is its flexibility in terms of considered secret and error distributions. In particular, the reduction preserves the secret distribution $\mathsf{D}_{\mathsf{sec}}$, which can be any (η, δ)-bounded distribution over R. Moreover, it can be instantiated with various error distributions, as long as their corresponding Rényi divergences are defined and small. Of course, only error distributions for which the starting MLWE problem is hard are useful. Corollaries 1, 2 and 3 give three concrete examples for bounded uniform, rounded Gaussian, and discrete Gaussian, but these are by far not the only ones possible. On the other hand, the reduction is limited to the search variants, as the public sampleability result in Sect. 4.1 is vacuous.

The biggest advantage of the reduction in Theorem 3 using hints (Sect. 5) is that it works for the decision variant, which is needed when using it in the context of IND-CPA secure public-key encryption schemes, for example to compressed public keys. However, both Theorems 1 and 3 make use of the decomposition theorems of discrete Gaussians. Thus, our overall result in Corollary 4 is limited to discrete Gaussians secret and error distributions. Furthermore, the reduction significantly increases the width of the discrete Gaussian secret distribution.

Finally, we concretely compare the parameter conditions of our results for the case of discrete Gaussians, as summarized in Table 2. For simplicity, we set the starting secret distribution to $\mathsf{D}_{\mathsf{sec}} = D_{R,\beta^2}$ for some positive real β. By Lemma 1, the distribution $\mathsf{D}_{\mathsf{sec}} = D_{R,\beta^2}$ is then $(\sqrt{d}\beta, \mathsf{negl}(\lambda)[d])$-bounded. Then, both Corollary 3 and Corollary 4 reduce $\mathsf{MLWE}_{q,m,n,D_{R,\beta^2},D_{R,\sigma^2}}$ to the problem $\mathsf{Trunc\text{-}MLWE}^c_{q,m,D_{R,\delta^2},D_{R,\gamma^2}}$. One can observe that the loss in the ring degree d parameter is larger in the first result (left column) than in the second result (right column). The opposite effect can be observed for the matrix dimension m. Overall, the second reduction sets more constraints than the first. The latter is thus preferable in the case of large degrees and small dimension m, as one observes in practice.

Table 2. Parameter comparison between the two different reductions from MLWE to Trunc-MLWE for discrete Gaussian secret and error distributions.

	S-Trunc-MLWE (Corollary 3 & RD_α)	D-Trunc-MLWE (Corollary 4)
β	> 0	$= \sigma$
σ	$\geq \beta d^2 2^c n \sqrt{\alpha m}$	$\geq \sqrt{2d(n+m)}$
δ	$= \beta$	$\geq \sigma 2^c d \sqrt{2n(m+2)}$
γ	$= \sigma$	$= \sqrt{\sigma^2 + \delta^2}$

References

[ACPS09] Applebaum, B., Cash, D., Peikert, C., Sahai, A.: Fast cryptographic primitives and circular-secure encryption based on hard learning problems. In: Halevi, S. (ed.) CRYPTO 2009. LNCS, vol. 5677, pp. 595–618. Springer, Heidelberg (2009). https://doi.org/10.1007/978-3-642-03356-8_35

[BCD+16] Bos, J.W., et al.: Frodo: take off the ring! Practical, quantum-secure key exchange from LWE. In: Weippl, E.R., Katzenbeisser, S., Kruegel, C., Myers, A.C., Halevi, S. (eds.) ACM CCS 2016, pp. 1006–1018. ACM Press (2016)

[BD20] Brakerski, Z., Döttling, N.: Hardness of LWE on general entropic distributions. In: Canteaut, A., Ishai, Y. (eds.) EUROCRYPT 2020. LNCS, vol. 12106, pp. 551–575. Springer, Cham (2020). https://doi.org/10.1007/978-3-030-45724-2_19

[BJRW20] Boudgoust, K., Jeudy, C., Roux-Langlois, A., Wen, W.: Towards classical hardness of module-LWE: the linear rank case. In: Moriai, S., Wang, H. (eds.) ASIACRYPT 2020. LNCS, vol. 12492, pp. 289–317. Springer, Cham (2020). https://doi.org/10.1007/978-3-030-64834-3_10

[BJRW22] Boudgoust, K., Jeudy, C., Roux-Langlois, A., Wen, W.: Entropic hardness of module-LWE from module-NTRU. In: Isobe, T., Sarkar, S. (eds.) INDOCRYPT 2022. LNCS, vol. 13774, pp. 78–99. Springer, Cham (2022)

[BJRW23] Boudgoust, K., Jeudy, C., Roux-Langlois, A., Wen, W.: On the hardness of module learning with errors with short distributions. J. Cryptol. **36**(1), 1 (2023)

[BLL+15] Bai, S., Langlois, A., Lepoint, T., Stehlé, D., Steinfeld, R.: Improved security proofs in lattice-based cryptography: using the Rényi divergence rather than the statistical distance. In: Iwata, T., Cheon, J.H. (eds.) ASIACRYPT 2015. LNCS, vol. 9452, pp. 3–24. Springer, Heidelberg (2015). https://doi.org/10.1007/978-3-662-48797-6_1

[BLP+13] Brakerski, Z., Langlois, A., Peikert, C., Regev, O., Stehlé, D.: Classical hardness of learning with errors. In: Boneh, D., Roughgarden, T., Feigenbaum, J. (eds.) 45th ACM STOC, pp. 575–584. ACM Press (2013)

[BLR+18] Bai, S., Lepoint, T., Roux-Langlois, A., Sakzad, A., Stehlé, D., Steinfeld, R.: Improved security proofs in lattice-based cryptography: using the Rényi divergence rather than the statistical distance. J. Cryptol. **31**(2), 610–640 (2018)

[CPS+20] Chuengsatiansup, C., Prest, T., Stehlé, D., Wallet, A., Xagawa, K.: ModFalcon: compact signatures based on module-NTRU lattices. In: Sun, H.-M., Shieh, S.-P., Gu, G., Ateniese, G. (eds.) ASIACCS 2020, pp. 853–866. ACM Press (2020)

[DM13] Döttling, N., Müller-Quade, J.: Lossy codes and a new variant of the learning-with-errors problem. In: Johansson, T., Nguyen, P.Q. (eds.) EUROCRYPT 2013. LNCS, vol. 7881, pp. 18–34. Springer, Heidelberg (2013). https://doi.org/10.1007/978-3-642-38348-9_2

[dPKPR24] del Pino, R., Katsumata, S., Prest, T., Rossi, M.: Raccoon: a masking-friendly signature proven in the probing model. In: CRYPTO (1). Lecture Notes in Computer Science, vol. 14920, pp. 409–444. Springer, Cham (2024)

[GKPV10] Goldwasser, S., Kalai, Y.T., Peikert, C., Vaikuntanathan, V.: Robustness of the learning with errors assumption. In: Yao, A.C.-C. (ed.) ICS 2010, pp. 230–240. Tsinghua University Press (2010)

[GPV08] Gentry, C., Peikert, C., Vaikuntanathan, V.: Trapdoors for hard lattices and new cryptographic constructions. In: Ladner, R.E., Dwork, C. (eds.) 40th ACM STOC, pp. 197–206. ACM Press (2008)

[HPS98] Hoffstein, J., Pipher, J., Silverman, J.H.: NTRU: a ring-based public key cryptosystem. In: Buhler, J.P. (ed.) ANTS 1998. LNCS, vol. 1423, pp. 267–288. Springer, Heidelberg (1998). https://doi.org/10.1007/BFb0054868

[JLS24] Jain, A., Lin, H., Saha, S.: A systematic study of sparse LWE. In: CRYPTO 2024, Part III. LNCS, pp. 210–245 (2024)

[JZW+23] Jia, W., Zhang, J., Wang, B., et al.: Hardness of module-LWE with semi-uniform seeds from module-NTRU. IET Inf. Secur. **2023** (2023)

[KLSS23] Kim, D., Lee, D., Seo, J., Song, Y.: Toward practical lattice-based proof of knowledge from hint-MLWE. In: CRYPTO (5). Lecture Notes in Computer Science, vol. 14085, pp. 549–580. Springer, Cham (2023)

[LM06] Lyubashevsky, V., Micciancio, D.: Generalized compact knapsacks are collision resistant. In: Bugliesi, M., Preneel, B., Sassone, V., Wegener, I. (eds.) ICALP 2006. LNCS, vol. 4052, pp. 144–155. Springer, Heidelberg (2006). https://doi.org/10.1007/11787006_13

[LS15] Langlois, A., Stehlé, D.: Worst-case to average-case reductions for module lattices. Des. Codes Cryptogr. **75**(3), 565–599 (2015)

[LSS14] Langlois, A., Stehlé, D., Steinfeld, R.: GGHLite: more efficient multilinear maps from ideal lattices. In: Nguyen, P.Q., Oswald, E. (eds.) EUROCRYPT 2014. LNCS, vol. 8441, pp. 239–256. Springer, Heidelberg (2014). https://doi.org/10.1007/978-3-642-55220-5_14

[LWZW24] Lin, H., Wang, M., Zhuang, J., Wang, Y.: Hardness of entropic module-LWE. Theor. Comput. Sci. **999**, 114553 (2024)

[Lyu12] Lyubashevsky, V.: Lattice signatures without trapdoors. In: Pointcheval, D., Johansson, T. (eds.) EUROCRYPT 2012. LNCS, vol. 7237, pp. 738–755. Springer, Heidelberg (2012). https://doi.org/10.1007/978-3-642-29011-4_43

[Mic18] Micciancio, D.: On the hardness of learning with errors with binary secrets. Theory Comput. **14**(1), 1–17 (2018)

[Mir17] Mironov, I.: Rényi differential privacy. In: IEEE Computer Security Foundations Symposium (2017)

[MKMS22] Mera, J.M.B., Karmakar, A., Marc, T., Soleimanian, A.: Efficient lattice-based inner-product functional encryption. In: PKC 2022, Part II. LNCS, pp. 163–193. Springer, Heidelberg (2022)

[MP13] Micciancio, D., Peikert, C.: Hardness of SIS and LWE with small parameters. In: Canetti, R., Garay, J.A. (eds.) CRYPTO 2013. LNCS, vol. 8042, pp. 21–39. Springer, Heidelberg (2013). https://doi.org/10.1007/978-3-642-40041-4_2

[MR04] Micciancio, D., Regev, O.: Worst-case to average-case reductions based on gaussian measures. In: 45th Annual IEEE Symposium on Foundations of Computer Science, pp. 372–381 (2004)

[Pei09] Peikert, C.: Public-key cryptosystems from the worst-case shortest vector problem: extended abstract. In: Mitzenmacher, M. (ed.) 41st ACM STOC, pp. 333–342. ACM Press (2009)

[PS24] Passelègue, A., Stehlé, D.: Low communication threshold fully homomorphic encryption. To appear in ASIACRYPT (2024)

[Reg05] Regev, O.: On lattices, learning with errors, random linear codes, and cryptography. In: Gabow, H.N., Fagin, R. (eds.) 37th ACM STOC, pp. 84–93. ACM Press (2005)

[Reg09] Regev, O.: On lattices, learning with errors, random linear codes, and cryptography. J. ACM **56**(6), 34:1–34:40 (2009)

[RSW18] Rosca, M., Stehlé, D., Wallet, A.: On the ring-LWE and polynomial-LWE problems. In: Nielsen, J.B., Rijmen, V. (eds.) EUROCRYPT 2018. LNCS, vol. 10820, pp. 146–173. Springer, Cham (2018). https://doi.org/10.1007/978-3-319-78381-9_6

[STA20] Sun, C., Tibouchi, M., Abe, M.: Revisiting the hardness of binary error LWE. In: Liu, J.K., Cui, H. (eds.) ACISP 2020. LNCS, vol. 12248, pp. 425–444. Springer, Cham (2020). https://doi.org/10.1007/978-3-030-55304-3_22

[vEH14] van Erven, T., Harremos, P.: Rényi divergence and Kullback-Leibler divergence. IEEE Trans. Inf. Theory **60**(7), 3797–3820 (2014)

Lattice-Based Sanitizable Signature Schemes: Chameleon Hash Functions and More

Sebastian Clermont[1(✉)], Samed Düzlü[2], Christian Janson[1], Laurens Porzenheim[3], and Patrick Struck[4]

[1] Technische Universität Darmstadt, Darmstadt, Germany
sebastian.clermont@tu-darmstadt.de, christian.janson@cryptoplexity.de
[2] Universität Regensburg, Regensburg, Germany
samed.duzlu@ur.de
[3] Universität Paderborn, Paderborn, Germany
laurens.porzenheim@uni-paderborn.de
[4] Universität Konstanz, Konstanz, Germany
patrick.struck@uni-konstanz.de

Abstract. Sanitizable Signature Schemes (SSS) enable a designated party, the sanitizer, to modify predefined parts of a signed message without invalidating the signature, making them useful for applications like pseudonymization and redaction. Since their introduction by Ateniese et al. (ESORICS'05), several classical SSS constructions have been proposed, but none have been instantiated from quantum-resistant assumptions. In this work, we develop the first quantum-secure sanitizable signature schemes based on lattice assumptions. Our primary focus is on SSS constructions that rely on chameleon hash functions (CHFs), a key component for enabling the controlled modification of messages. While lattice-based CHFs exist, they do not meet the required security guarantees for SSS, becoming insecure under adversarial access to an adapt oracle. To address this, we construct a novel lattice-based CHF that achieves collision resistance even in such settings, called full collision resistance. However, our CHF lacks the *uniqueness* property, a limitation we show to be inherent in lattice-based CHFs. As a result, our SSS constructions initially fall short of achieving the critical security property of accountability. To overcome this, we apply a transformation based on verifiable ring signatures (VRS), for which we present the first lattice-based instantiation. Additionally, we provide a comprehensive analysis of existing classical SSS constructions, explore their potential for post-quantum instantiations, and present new attacks on previously assumed secure SSS schemes. Our work closes the gap in constructing quantum-secure SSS and lays the groundwork for further research into advanced cryptographic primitives based on lattice assumptions.

This work was funded by the German Federal Ministry of Education and Research (BMBF) under reference 16KISQ074, the German Research Foundation (DFG) – SFB 1119 – 236615297, the Ministry of Culture and Science of the State of North Rhine-Westphalia, and the Hector Foundation II.

R. Niederhagen and M.-J. O. Saarinen (Eds.): PQCrypto 2025, LNCS 15577, pp. 278–311, 2025.
https://doi.org/10.1007/978-3-031-86599-2_10

1 Introduction

In modern cryptography, the digital signature scheme is an essential primitive that enjoys ubiquitous usage. However, depending on the use case, one might need more advanced signature schemes which come with additional functionality. These advanced variants usually build upon their base versions, offering strong security guarantees for their specialized functionality and alleviating the need for ad-hoc constructions. Advanced signature-based primitives include sanitizable signatures, ring signatures, group signatures, threshold signatures, and more.

The main focus of this paper are sanitizable signature schemes (SSS). They can be applied, for instance, to pseudonymize sensitive data, like patient names in medical records, while maintaining the authenticity. Sanitizable signature schemes allow the signer of a message to partially delegate signature rights to a semi-trusted third party, the sanitizer. This sanitizer may modify predefined parts of the message without invalidating the signature. In a sanitizable signature scheme, the message is divided into blocks, among which the sanitizer can modify exactly the *admissible blocks*. In contrast, all other blocks, the *immutable blocks*, cannot be modified by the sanitizer without invalidating the signature. The signer defines which blocks are admissible during the signing operation. Another use-case of sanitizable signature schemes are classified documents. SSS constructions allow the signing of such documents (by the signer) such that a censor (the sanitizer) can redact certain parts, depending on which parts should not be made public.

Sanitizable signature schemes were first introduced in Ateniese et al.'s seminal work [2]. Since then, many more works on sanitizable signature schemes have been published, covering new constructions focusing on different, sometimes novel, security notions. Current literature contains only two constructions that exclusively use basic primitives [11,19], one construction is based on group signatures [10], two are based on ring signatures [13,27], one is based on signatures with rerandomizable keys [20], while all others, [2,5,9,14,27], make use of so-called *chameleon hash functions* (CHFs) [25].

Chameleon hash functions are families of hash functions with public and secret keys. In contrast to regular hash functions, their input consists of not just the message, but also an auxiliary random value. The public key of a chameleon hash function defines a collision-resistant function mapping pairs (μ, r) to some hash value h, where μ is the message and r is a randomly chosen auxiliary value. With the corresponding secret key, however, one can then *adapt* the message to a new μ', by finding a suitable auxiliary value r' such that the pair (μ', r') evaluates to the original digest h, i.e., find a collision. Besides weak collision resistance, where the adversary only receives the public key, chameleon hash functions can support stronger forms of collision resistance, where an adapt oracle is available to the adversary. Apart from SSS, chameleon hash functions are a widely used building block in other cryptographic schemes. For example, they can transform a non-adaptively secure signature scheme to an existentially unforgeable one [34].

The gist of constructing a SSS from a CHF is a simple hash-then-adapt approach. In this approach, the admissible blocks are hashed using the CHF with a public key generated by the sanitizer and then signed by the signer using a regular signature scheme. The sanitizer can thus modify the message without altering the hash value, retaining the original signature's validity. More advanced constructions of SSS have been developed over the years, some of which attain additional security properties and explore alternative approaches.

Given the general transition to post-quantum cryptography, analyzing which advanced primitives can also be constructed from quantum-hard assumptions is crucial. While there are positive results for various advanced primitives, sanitizable signatures from quantum-hard assumptions have yet to be considered.

1.1 Our Contribution

We close the aforementioned gap by developing post-quantum secure sanitizable signatures from lattices. Our main focus is on constructions based on chameleon hash functions. While lattice-based CHFs exist [16,28], we observe that they cannot be used to instantiate existing SSS constructions. The reason is that they do not achieve the necessary security guarantees. Thus, we develop a new chameleon hash function inspired by the one given in [28]. Our construction achieves collision resistance even against adversaries with access to an adapt oracle that provides collision to the adversary—for SSS constructions this is necessary since sanitized signatures are effectively that. This is our first contribution as we believe this strongly secure CHF can be of independent interest.

However, this construction is not sufficient to already instantiate the SSS constructions. The reason is that it lacks another property called *uniqueness*. When a chameleon hash has uniqueness, it is hard to come up with two different auxiliary values r, r' that both map some message μ to the same digest h. Unfortunately, the lack of the uniqueness property seems not to be a flaw of our specific construction but a more general problem of lattice-based CHFs. The absence of this property implies that the SSS constructions lack crucial security properties like unforgeability and accountability. However, there is a generic transform [13] which turns such a SSS (which they call weakly-secure) into a secure SSS. This transform requires another advanced signature, called verifiable ring signature (VRS), i.e., a variant of a ring signature that allows to prove or deny ownership of a signature at a later point. Thus, as our second contribution, we develop a lattice-based VRS scheme. To do that, we first design a generic construction of a VRS scheme using a so-called linking indistinguishable tag and a non-interactive zero-knowledge proof. Then, we instantiate that generic construction with lattice-based constructions.

With these contributions (illustrated in Fig. 1), we close the aforementioned gap by giving multiple post-quantum sanitizable signatures from lattices.

As additional contributions, we give an attack against an SSS construction [9], breaking the accountability, i.e., an attack that allows the signer to blame the sanitizer for messages of its own choosing. Furthermore, we revisit the SSS constructions that do not rely on chameleon hash functions. We show that for some of them, the necessary building blocks are readily available in the lattice-based literature, meaning they can easily be instantiated as well. Finally, we show additional implications between the security notions, which also show some additional security properties for some SSS construction—in particular, security properties that were developed after some of the older SSS constructions.

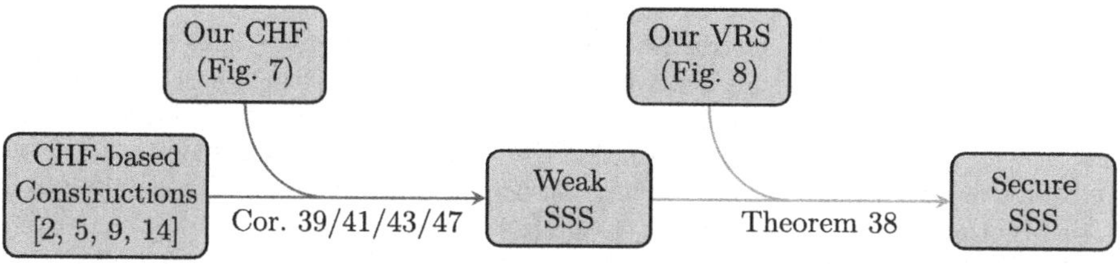

Fig. 1. Overview of our main results. Instantiating the SSS constructions given in [2, 5,9,14] with our new lattice-based chameleon hash function results in weak sanitizable signatures. The transformation from [13]—using these weak sanitizable signatures and our new verifiable ring signature scheme—then yields secure sanitizable signatures.

1.2 Related Work

Current literature provides a variety of constructions of sanitizable signature schemes. Two of them, [11,19], require standard assumptions only. Some of them, [10,13,20] provide constructions based on other advanced signatures. The work [27] by Lai et al. contains two constructions: one based on accountable ring signatures and another one based on chameleon hash functions. Finally, many more constructions based on chameleon hash functions exist, [2,5,9,13,14]. Besides the different primitives they use, the various works have distinct goals regarding the security notions they achieve. The achieved security properties can be seen in Table 1. Another construction is due to Klonowski and Lauks [24]. Later, however, Canard and Jambert [15] showed it to lack accountability.

Constructions of chameleon hash functions based on lattices are very rare. Cash et al. [16] came forward with the first construction based on a trapdoor in the Ajtai hash function. This chameleon hash function achieves merely a weak form of collision-resistance. Only recently, a new lattice-based construction was brought forward by Li and Liu [28]. They use one-time tags, making the hash function not applicable to known generic constructions of SSS. However, we use and improve their ideas to construct our novel chameleon hash function.

Due to the missing uniqueness of our CHF, we apply the transform introduced in [13] to increase the security of the instantiations from weak SSS to strong SSS. The transform relies on verifiable ring signatures (VRS). In [13], it is stated that other ring signatures with extended functionality, such as linkable ring signatures, imply VRS. However, we were not able to verify that claim.

[33] present (among others) a notion of ring signatures equivalent to VRS, called claimable and repudiable ring signatures. They also show how to construct

Table 1. Overview of our results. The table provides an overview of the SSS constructions that use chameleon hash functions: ACMT05 [2], BCD+17 [5], CDK+17 [14], and BFF+09 [9]. The entries with the color blue are the results of the instantiations of the respective constructions with our chameleon hash function defined in Sect. 3.1. The entries with the color orange are the results after using our verifiable ring signature defined in Sect. 3.2 to apply a transform as described in [13] to ensure unforgeability as well as signer and sanitizer accountability. The various symbols represent: the instantiation achieves the notion (✓), the construction does not achieve the notion (✗), the instantiation does not achieve a notion that the construction otherwise could achieve (✦), the instantiation has not been analyzed with respect to the notion (?), and there is no lattice-based instantiation due to missing building blocks (❍). Note that some notions contradict each other, consequently it is impossible to come up with a construction achieving all notions (cf. the full version of this paper).

	Chameleon Hash Function based Sanitizable Signatures				
	ACMT05 [2]	LZCS16-1 [27]	BCD+17 [5]	CDK+17 [14]	BFF+09 [9]
Unforgeability	✓	❍|✓	✦|✓	✦|✓	✓
Signer Accountability	✓	❍|✓	✦|✓	✓	✗|✓
Sanitizer Accountability	?|✓	❍|✓	✦|✓	✦|✓	✓
NIPA	✗	✗	✗	✗	✗
Immutability	✓	❍	✓	✓	✓
Transparency	✓	❍	✓	✓	✓
Privacy	✓	❍	✓	✓	✓
Unlinkability	✗	✗	✗	✗	✗
Invisibility	?	?	✓	✓	?

such a ring signature. However that requires verifiable random functions, which can be difficult to construct (e.g., [18]) or use (non-interactive) proofs in their construction. Furthermore, the construction of [33] requires a proof over statements including the VRF, i.e., proofs over proofs, which is why we opted for a more direct approach for constructing a VRS.

2 Background

We define some notation. By $x \leftarrow y$ we define deterministic assignment of y to x. If S is some set, we denote by $x \leftarrow\$ S$ sampling a uniform value x from S. Overloading notation, if A is some probabilistic polynomial-time (*ppt*) or quantum polynomial time (*qpt*) algorithm, we denote by $y \leftarrow\$ A(x)$ assigning the random output of $A(x)$ to y. The statement of the kind "for all $y \leftarrow\$ A(x)$" means for all y that can be output by the randomized algorithm A on input

x. We denote column vectors by lowercase bold-face letters $\mathbf{a}$, while row-vectors are denoted as $\mathbf{a}^t$. Matrices $\mathbf{A}$ are denoted in uppercase. By $\|\mathbf{x}\|$ we denote the Euclidian norm of $\mathbf{x}$. If we want to query the random oracle on some input x, we denote it by $y \leftarrow \mathcal{RO}(x)$. We will often assume security parameters and public parameters as implicit inputs to algorithms and omit them for readability.

Signature schemes as well as public key encryption schemes follow the commonly established syntax and notation. The security analysis under the presence of quantum adversary takes place in the Q1 security model, allowing local quantum computer access to adversaries, but only classical access to oracles including the random oracle. We will formalize less ubiquitous primitives in this section.

2.1 Chameleon Hash Function

First, we introduce chameleon hash functions, which we will later build from lattices as one of our core contributions in this paper.

Definition 1 (Chameleon Hash Function). *A chameleon hash function* CH *consists of four ppt algorithms* $\mathsf{CH} = (\mathsf{CKGen}, \mathsf{CHash}, \mathsf{CHashCheck}, \mathsf{CAdapt})$.

$(\mathsf{pk}_{\mathsf{ch}}, \mathsf{sk}_{\mathsf{ch}}) \leftarrow\$ \mathsf{CKGen}(1^\lambda)$: *The key generation algorithm* CKGen *takes as input the security parameter* 1^λ *and outputs a private-public key pair.*

$(h, r) \leftarrow\$ \mathsf{CHash}(\mathsf{pk}_{\mathsf{ch}}, \mu)$: *The algorithm* CHash *takes as input a public key* $\mathsf{pk}_{\mathsf{ch}}$ *and a message* μ. *It outputs a hash* h *and randomness* r, *under the given public key* $\mathsf{pk}_{\mathsf{ch}}$.

$b \leftarrow \mathsf{CHashCheck}(\mathsf{pk}_{\mathsf{ch}}, h, \mu, r)$: *Given a public key* $\mathsf{pk}_{\mathsf{ch}}$, *a hash value* h, *a message* μ, *and randomness* r, *the deterministic algorithm* $\mathsf{CHashCheck}$ *outputs a boolean value* $b \in \{0, 1\}$, *indicating whether the hash* h *is valid under* $\mathsf{pk}_{\mathsf{ch}}$ *or not.*

$r' \leftarrow\$ \mathsf{CAdapt}(\mathsf{sk}_{\mathsf{ch}}, h, \mu, r, \mu')$: *The algorithm* CAdapt *takes as input the secret key* $\mathsf{sk}_{\mathsf{ch}}$, *a hash* h, *a message* μ, *randomness* r, *and a new message* μ'. *It then outputs new randomness* r', *such that* $1 \leftarrow \mathsf{CHashCheck}(\mathsf{pk}_{\mathsf{ch}}, h, \mu', r')$.

Definition 2 (Correctness of a Chameleon Hash Function). *A chameleon hash function* CH *is correct, iff*

$$\forall \lambda, \forall (\mathsf{pk}_{\mathsf{ch}}, \mathsf{sk}_{\mathsf{ch}}) \leftarrow\$ \mathsf{CKGen}(1^\lambda), \forall \mu, \mu' \in \mathcal{M},$$
$$\forall (h, r) \leftarrow\$ \mathsf{CHash}(\mathsf{pk}_{\mathsf{ch}}, \mu), \forall r' \leftarrow\$ \mathsf{CAdapt}(\mathsf{sk}_{\mathsf{ch}}, h, \mu, r, \mu') :$$
$$\mathsf{CHashCheck}(\mathsf{pk}_{\mathsf{ch}}, h, \mu, r) = \mathsf{CHashCheck}(\mathsf{pk}_{\mathsf{ch}}, h, \mu', r') = 1$$

For security we require that the chameleon hash function is collision-resistant, even in the presence of a collision oracle. Furthermore, we require that it hard to distinguish whether a hash randomness pair (h, r) was output by CH or CAdapt. We model the security games in Figs. 2, 3.

Definition 3. *We say that a chameleon hash function* CH *is fully collision-resistant, if there exists a negligible function* $\mathsf{negl}(\lambda)$ *such that for all qpt adversaries* $\mathcal{A}$ *we have that* $\Pr[\mathsf{f\text{-}CR}_{\Pi,\mathcal{A}}(1^\lambda) = 1] \leq \mathsf{negl}(\lambda)$.

$\mathsf{f\text{-}CR}_{\mathsf{CH},\mathcal{A}}(1^\lambda)$	$\mathsf{Adapt}\mathcal{O}(\mathsf{sk_{ch}},\cdot,\cdot,\cdot,\cdot)$ with (h,μ,r,μ')
$\mathcal{Q} \leftarrow \emptyset$	**if** $\mathsf{CHashCheck}(\mathsf{pk_{ch}},h,\mu,r)=0$
$(\mathsf{pk_{ch}},\mathsf{sk_{ch}}) \leftarrow\!\$\ \mathsf{CKGen}(1^\lambda)$	**return** $\perp$
$(h,\mu,r,\mu',r') \leftarrow\!\$\ \mathcal{A}^{\mathsf{Adapt}\mathcal{O}}(\mathsf{pk_{ch}})$	$r' \leftarrow\!\$\ \mathsf{CAdapt}(\mathsf{sk_{ch}},h,\mu,r,\mu')$
return $\big(\mathsf{CHashCheck}(\mathsf{pk_{ch}},h,\mu,r)=1$	$\mathcal{Q} \leftarrow \mathcal{Q} \cup \{(h,\mu),(h,\mu')\}$
$\wedge\ \mathsf{CHashCheck}(\mathsf{pk_{ch}},h,\mu',r')=1$	**return** r'
$\wedge\ \mu \neq \mu' \wedge (h,\mu) \notin \mathcal{Q}\big)$	

Fig. 2. f-CR security game.

There exist other, weaker notions of collision-resistance of a chameleon hash function, called standard, enhanced, and weak collision-resistance. For definitions and comparisons, see [17]. However, we only concern ourselves with the strongest version, which implies the others.

$\mathsf{CHIndist}_{\Pi,\mathcal{A},b}(\lambda)$	$\mathsf{HashOrAdapt}\mathcal{O}_b(\mathsf{sk_{ch}},\cdot,\cdot)$ with (μ,μ')
$(\mathsf{pk_{ch}},\mathsf{sk_{ch}}) \leftarrow\!\$\ \mathsf{CKGen}(1^\lambda)$	$(h,r) \leftarrow\!\$\ \mathsf{CHash}(\mathsf{pk_{ch}},\mu)$
$b' \leftarrow\!\$\ \mathcal{A}^{\mathsf{HashOrAdapt}\mathcal{O}_b,\mathsf{Adapt}\mathcal{O}}(\mathsf{pk_{ch}})$	$(h',r') \leftarrow\!\$\ \mathsf{CHash}(\mathsf{pk_{ch}},\mu')$
return b'	$r'' \leftarrow\!\$\ \mathsf{CAdapt}(\mathsf{sk_{ch}},h',\mu',r',\mu)$
	if $b=0$ **return** (h,r)
	if $b=1$ **return** (h',r'')

Fig. 3. CH Indistinguishability game.

Definition 4. *We say that a chameleon hash function* CH *is indistinguishable, if there exists a negligible function* $\mathsf{negl}(\lambda)$, *such that for all qpt adversaries* $\mathcal{A}$ *we have that* $|\Pr[\mathsf{CHIndist}_{\mathsf{CH},\mathcal{A},0}(\lambda)=1]-\Pr[\mathsf{CHIndist}_{\mathsf{CH},\mathcal{A},1}(\lambda)=1]| \leq \mathsf{negl}(\lambda)$.

2.2 Lattices

Next, we cover various relevant definitions and results for lattices.

Definition 5. *An* n*-dimensional lattice* Λ *is a discrete, additive subgroup of* $\mathbb{R}^n$.

Definition 6. *In the short integer solution (SIS) problem* $\mathsf{SIS}_{n,m,q,\beta}$ *a qpt adversary* $\mathcal{A}$ *is given a uniformly random* $\mathbf{A} \in \mathbb{Z}_q^{n\times m}$ *and is asked to compute a* $\mathbf{x} \in \mathbb{Z}^m$ *such that* $\mathbf{Ax}=\mathbf{0}$ *and* $0 < \|\mathbf{x}\| \leq \beta$.

We define the advantage of a qpt adversary $\mathcal{A}$ *against* $\mathsf{SIS}_{n,m,q,\beta}$ *as*

$$\mathsf{SIS}_{n,m,q,\beta}(\mathcal{A}) := \Pr[\mathbf{Ax}=\mathbf{0} \mod q, 0<\|\mathbf{x}\|\leq\beta : \mathbf{A} \leftarrow\!\$\ \mathbb{Z}_q^{n\times m}, \mathbf{x} \leftarrow\!\$\ \mathcal{A}(\mathbf{A})].$$

Definition 7. *Define the multidimensional Gaussian function with Gaussian parameter s and center $\mathbf{c}$ as $\rho_{s,\mathbf{c}}(\mathbf{x}) = \exp(-\|\mathbf{x}-\mathbf{c}\|/s)$. Then, we define the discrete Gaussian distribution over lattice Λ with Gaussian parameter s and center $\mathbf{c}$ as $D_{\Lambda,s,\mathbf{c}}(\mathbf{x}) = \frac{\rho_{s,\mathbf{c}}(\mathbf{x})}{\rho_{s,\mathbf{c}}(\Lambda)}$.*

To construct our chameleon hash, we need a lattice-based trapdoor. We use so-called G-trapdoors.

Definition 8 ([32]). *Let $\mathbf{G} \in \mathbb{Z}_q^{n\times w}$ be a so-called gadget matrix, for which SIS is easy. Define a G-trapdoor for a matrix $\mathbf{A} \in \mathbb{Z}_q^{n\times m}$ to be some matrix $\mathbf{R} \in \mathbb{Z}_q^{m\times w}$ such that $\mathbf{AR} = \mathbf{G} \mod q$.*

We denote the quality of a G-trapdoor by its spectral norm $s_1(\mathbf{R})$. Note that if one has a trapdoor $\mathbf{R}$ for $\mathbf{A}$, then $[\mathbf{R}^t, \mathbf{0}_{w\times k}]^t \in \mathbb{Z}_q^{m+k\times w}$ is a trapdoor for $[\mathbf{A}|\mathbf{B}]$ for any $\mathbf{B} \in \mathbb{Z}_q^{n\times k}$, where $\mathbf{0}_{a\times b}$ is the all-zero matrix of dimension $a \times b$.

With a G-trapdoor, we can invert matrix-vector multiplication of the trapdoored matrix $\mathbf{A}$, where the inverted preimage has a certain (conditioned) Gaussian distribution.

Theorem 9 ([32]). *There exists a ppt algorithm $\mathsf{TrapGen}(1^n, 1^m, q)$ that, given any integers $n \geq 1$, $q \geq 2$, and sufficiently large $m = \mathcal{O}(n \log q)$, outputs a matrix $\mathbf{A} \in \mathbb{Z}_q^{n\times m}$ and a G-trapdoor $\mathbf{R}$ for $\mathbf{A}$, such that the distribution of $\mathbf{A}$ is negligibly far from uniform. Moreover, there exists a ppt algorithm $\mathsf{PreSample}(\mathbf{A}, \mathbf{R}, \mathbf{u}, s)$ that, given some $\mathbf{A} \in \mathbb{Z}_q^{n\times m}$, some G-trapdoor $\mathbf{R} \in \mathbb{Z}_q^{m\times w}$ for $\mathbf{A}$ with $s_1(\mathbf{R}) \in \mathcal{O}(\sqrt{n \log q})$, some $\mathbf{u} \in \mathbb{Z}_q^n$ and large enough $s = \mathcal{O}(\sqrt{n \log q})$, samples from a distribution that is within negligible statistical distance from $D_{\Lambda_{\mathbf{u}}^{\perp}(\mathbf{A}), s\cdot\omega(\sqrt{\log n})}$. Furthermore, the distribution of sampling $\mathbf{x} \leftarrow\!\$\, D_{\mathbb{Z}_{q,s}^m}$, setting $\mathbf{y} = \mathbf{Ax}$, and outputting $(\mathbf{x}, \mathbf{y})$ is statistically indistinguishable from the distribution of choosing $\mathbf{y}' \leftarrow\!\$\, \mathbb{Z}_q^n$, computing $\mathbf{x}' \leftarrow\!\$\, \mathsf{PreSample}(\mathbf{A}, \mathbf{R}, \mathbf{y}, s)$, and outputting $(\mathbf{x}', \mathbf{y}')$.*

If $\mathbf{R}$ is a trapdoor for $\mathbf{A}$, we sometimes write $\mathsf{PreSample}([\mathbf{A}\ \mathbf{B}], \mathbf{R}, \mathbf{u}, s)$ instead of $\mathsf{PreSample}([\mathbf{A}\ \mathbf{B}], [\mathbf{R}^t\ \mathbf{0}^t]^t, \mathbf{u}, s)$, since $\mathbf{R}$ can be extended to a trapdoor for $[\mathbf{A}\ \mathbf{B}]$ for any $\mathbf{B}$, as noted above.

2.3 Trapdoor Commitment Scheme

A trapdoor commitment scheme is a commitment scheme that is (computationally) binding and hiding, but if someone is in possession of a trapdoor to the public parameters, then one can break binding. We model that by introducing an additional ppt algorithm Equiv that equivocates a commitment c to any message μ' with the help of the trapdoor.

Definition 10. *A trapdoor commitment scheme consists of four ppt algorithms* (TdGen, Com, $\mathsf{ComCheck}$, Equiv).

(pp, td) $\leftarrow\!\$\, \mathsf{TdGen}(1^\lambda)$: *On input a security parameter 1^λ, the algorithm outputs public parameters* pp *and a trapdoor* td.

$(c,d) \leftarrow\$ \mathsf{Com}(\mathsf{pp},\mu)$: *On input some* pp *and a message* μ, *the algorithm outputs a commitment* c *and an opening value* d.

$b \leftarrow \mathsf{ComCheck}(\mathsf{pp},\mu,c,d)$: *On input some* pp, *a message* μ, *a commitment* c *and an opening value* d, *the algorithm outputs a bit* b.

$d' \leftarrow\$ \mathsf{Equiv}(\mathsf{pp},\mathsf{td},c,\mu')$: *On input some* pp, *a trapdoor* td, *a commitment* c *and a message* μ', *the algorithm outputs some opening value* d'.

A trapdoor commitment scheme is correct, iff

$$\forall\lambda, \forall(\mathsf{pp},\mathsf{td}) \leftarrow\$ \mathsf{TdGen}(1^\lambda), \forall\mu,\mu',\in\mathcal{M},$$
$$\forall(c,d) \leftarrow\$ \mathsf{Com}(\mathsf{pp},\mu), \forall d' \leftarrow\$ \mathsf{Equiv}(\mathsf{pp},\mathsf{td},c,\mu'),$$
$$\mathsf{ComCheck}(\mathsf{pp},\mu,c,d) = \mathsf{ComCheck}(\mathsf{pp},\mu',c,d') = 1.$$

We need two security notions for a trapdoor commitment scheme. One is the typical binding, which states that an adversary cannot open a commitment to two different messages. The other security notion is called *distributional equivalence of equivocation.* This requires that, for fixed pp and μ, the joint distribution of a commitment and an opening value is computationally indistinguishable when either committing to the message or committing to 0 and equivocating to the message. We model these security games in Fig. 4.

$\mathsf{Bind}_{\Pi,\mathcal{A}}(\lambda)$	$\mathsf{DEE}_{\Pi,\mathcal{A},b}(\lambda)$
$(\mathsf{pp},\mathsf{td}) \leftarrow\$ \mathsf{TdGen}(1^\lambda)$	$(\mathsf{pp},\mathsf{td}) \leftarrow\$ \mathsf{TdGen}(1^\lambda)$
$(c,\mu,d,\mu',d') \leftarrow\$ \mathcal{A}(\mathsf{pp})$	$\mu \leftarrow\$ \mathcal{A}(\mathsf{pp})$
if $\mathsf{ComCheck}(\mathsf{pp},\mu,c,d) = 1$	$(c_0,d_0) \leftarrow\$ \mathsf{Com}(\mathsf{pp},\mu)$
$\quad\wedge\ \mathsf{ComCheck}(\mathsf{pp},\mu',c,d') = 1$	$c_1 \leftarrow\$ \mathsf{Com}(\mathsf{pp},0)$
$\quad\wedge\ \mu \neq \mu'$	$d_1 \leftarrow\$ \mathsf{Equiv}(\mathsf{pp},\mathsf{td},c_1,\mu)$
$\quad$ **return** 1	$b' \leftarrow\$ \mathcal{A}(c_b,d_b)$
return 0	**return** b'

Fig. 4. Trapdoor commitment security games. DEE is distributional equivalence of equivocation.

Definition 11. *We say that a commitment scheme* Π *is computationally binding, if there exists a negligible function* negl *such that for all qpt adversaries* $\mathcal{A}$ *it holds that* $\Pr[\mathsf{Bind}_{\Pi,\mathcal{A}}(\lambda)] \leq \mathsf{negl}(\lambda)$.

Definition 12. *We say that a commitment scheme* Π *has distributional equivalence of equivocation (DEE), if there exists a negligible function* negl *such that for all qpt adversaries* $\mathcal{A}$ *it holds that*

$$|\Pr[\mathsf{DEE}_{\Pi,\mathcal{A},0}(\lambda) = 1] - \Pr[\mathsf{DEE}_{\Pi,\mathcal{A},1}(\lambda) = 1]| \leq \mathsf{negl}(\lambda).$$

It is possible to adapt known lattice-based commitment schemes such as Ajtai [1] or BDLOP [4] to be trapdoor commitment schemes by replacing their uniform generation of matrices by $\mathsf{TrapGen}$. Then, one uses $\mathsf{PreSample}$ to construct Equiv, and due to the properties mentioned in Theorem 9 we can show DEE.

Note that we did not define the typical notion of a hiding commitment scheme as we do not need it explicitly for our construction. However, hiding is implied by DEE, since in the DEE security game c_1 is generated by committing to 0. If the commitment scheme was not hiding, the adversary could get information about b by c_b alone. Note that binding trapdoor commitment schemes with DEE are strongly related to collision-resistant preimage-sampleable functions [21].

2.4 Linking Indistinguishable Tag

To later construct the VRS we need so-called *linking indistinguishable tags* (LIT) [6,7]. This is a secret key tagging scheme like a MAC, except that there exists an additional linking algorithm. With this, it is possible to detect if the same person tagged the same message twice. Additionally, there exists a function f that computes a public key from a secret key. While this is not used for the LIT itself, it is useful when using LITs to construct other schemes. For security we require that it is hard to trick the linking algorithm as well as unforgeability similar to a MAC, but also that apart from linking, it is hard to decide which person created a tag. Also it should be hard to compute a secret key from a public key and tags.

Definition 13. *A linking indistinguishable tag scheme consists of a function f and the following ppt algorithms:*

$sk \leftarrow\$ \mathsf{KGen}(1^\lambda)$*: On input a security parameter 1^λ, it outputs a secret sk.*
$t \leftarrow\$ \mathsf{Tag}(sk, \mu)$*: On input a secret key sk and a message μ, it outputs a tag t.*
$b \leftarrow \mathsf{Vrfy}(sk, \mu, t)$*: On input a secret key sk, a message μ and a tag t, it outputs a bit b.*
$b \leftarrow \mathsf{Link}(\mu, t_0, t_1)$*: On input a message μ and two tags t_0, t_1, it outputs a bit b.*

We require that a LIT is correct. This is the case if

$$\forall \lambda, \forall sk \leftarrow\$ \mathsf{KGen}(1^\lambda), \forall \mu, \forall t_0, t_1 \leftarrow\$ \mathsf{Tag}(sk, \mu) :$$
$$\mathsf{Vrfy}(sk, \mu, t_0) = \mathsf{Link}(\mu, t_0, t_1) = 1.$$

For the security model, we use the one from [7], with one change improving the security. We use the same games for tag-indistinguishability, non-invertability, linkability, and unforgeability. However, as can be seen in Fig. 5, when defining the oracles, we no longer return a previously computed tag if a message has been previously queried. Instead, the adversary gets a fresh tag every time it queries the oracle.

Definition 14. *A LIT Π has tag-indistinguishability, if there exists a negligible function* negl *such that for all ppt adversaries $\mathcal{A}$ it holds that*

$$\mathsf{Adv}_{\Pi,\mathcal{A}}^{LIT Anon}(\lambda) := \left|\Pr[\mathsf{Anon}_{\Pi,\mathcal{A},0}^{\mathsf{LIT}}(\lambda) = 1] - \Pr[\mathsf{Anon}_{\Pi,\mathcal{A},1}^{\mathsf{LIT}}(\lambda) = 1]\right| \leq \mathsf{negl}(\lambda).$$

$$\begin{array}{l}
\underline{\mathsf{Anon}^{\mathsf{LIT}}_{\Pi,\mathcal{A},b}(\lambda)}\\
\mathcal{Q} \leftarrow \emptyset\\
sk_0, sk_1 \leftarrow\!\!\$\ \mathsf{KGen}(1^\lambda)\\
pk_i \leftarrow f(sk_i), i \in \{0,1\}\\
\mu^* \leftarrow\!\!\$\ \mathcal{A}^{\mathsf{Tag}\mathcal{O}}(pk_0, pk_1)\\
t^* \leftarrow\!\!\$\ \mathsf{Tag}(sk_b, \mu^*)\\
b' \leftarrow\!\!\$\ \mathcal{A}^{\mathsf{Tag}\mathcal{O}}(t^*)\\
\textbf{if } (\mu^*, \cdot) \in \mathcal{Q}\\
\quad \textbf{return } 0\\
\textbf{return } b'
\end{array}$$

$$\begin{array}{l}
\underline{\mathsf{Linkable}^{\mathsf{LIT}}_{\Pi,\mathcal{A}}(\lambda)}\\
(sk_0, sk_1, \mu, t_0, t_1) \leftarrow\!\!\$\ \mathcal{A}(1^\lambda)\\
\textbf{if } f(sk_0) \neq f(sk_1)\\
\quad \textbf{return } 0\\
\textbf{if } \exists i \in \{0,1\} :\ \mathsf{Vrfy}(sk_i, \mu, t_i) = 0\\
\quad \textbf{return } 0\\
\textbf{if } \mathsf{Link}(\mu, t_0, t_1) = 0\\
\quad \textbf{return } 1\\
\textbf{return } 0
\end{array}$$

$$\begin{array}{l}
\underline{\mathsf{Tag}\mathcal{O}(\{sk_j\}_j, \cdot, \cdot) \text{ with } (i, \mu)}\\
t \leftarrow\!\!\$\ \mathsf{Tag}(sk_i, \mu)\\
\mathcal{Q} \leftarrow \mathcal{Q} \cup \{(\mu, t)\}\\
\textbf{return } t
\end{array}$$

$$\begin{array}{l}
\underline{\mathsf{Invert}^{\mathsf{LIT}}_{\Pi,\mathcal{A}}(\lambda)}\\
sk \leftarrow\!\!\$\ \mathsf{KGen}(1^\lambda)\\
pk_0 \leftarrow f(sk_0)\\
sk' \leftarrow\!\!\$\ \mathcal{A}^{\mathsf{Tag}\mathcal{O}}(pk_0)\\
\textbf{if } pk = f(sk')\\
\quad \textbf{return } 1\\
\textbf{return } 0
\end{array}$$

$$\begin{array}{l}
\underline{\mathsf{Forge}^{\mathsf{LIT}}_{\Pi,\mathcal{A}}(\lambda)}\\
\mathcal{Q} \leftarrow \emptyset\\
sk_0 \leftarrow\!\!\$\ \mathsf{KGen}(1^\lambda), pk_0 \leftarrow f(sk)\\
(sk^*, \mu, t^*) \leftarrow\!\!\$\ \mathcal{A}^{\mathsf{Tag}\mathcal{O}}(pk_0)\\
\textbf{if } \mathsf{Vrfy}(sk^*, \mu, t^*) = 0\\
\quad \textbf{return } 0.\\
\textbf{if } \exists\ (\mu, t) \in \mathcal{Q} : \mathsf{Link}(\mu, t, t^*) = 1\\
\quad \textbf{return } 1\\
\textbf{return } 0
\end{array}$$

Fig. 5. LIT security games.

Definition 15. *A LIT Π has linkability if there exists a negligible function* negl *such that for all ppt adversaries $\mathcal{A}$ it holds that*

$$\Pr[\mathsf{Linkable}^{\mathsf{LIT}}_{\Pi,\mathcal{A}}(\lambda) = 1] \leq \mathsf{negl}(\lambda).$$

Definition 16. *A LIT Π is unforgeable, if there exists a negligible function* negl *such that for all ppt adversaries $\mathcal{A}$ it holds that*

$$\Pr[\mathsf{Forge}^{\mathsf{LIT}}_{\Pi,\mathcal{A}}(\lambda) = 1] \leq \mathsf{negl}(\lambda).$$

Definition 17. *A LIT Π has non-invertability, if there exists a negligible function* negl *such that for all ppt adversaries $\mathcal{A}$ it holds that*

$$\Pr[\mathsf{Invert}^{\mathsf{LIT}}_{\Pi,\mathcal{A}}(\lambda) = 1] \leq \mathsf{negl}(\lambda).$$

Due to the aforementioned change in security model, the construction of a LIT from [7] is not secure in the new model. This is because if this construction tags the same message twice, the adversary receives two *learning with errors* (LWE) samples with the same $\mathbf{A}$. To remedy this, we propose a construction similar to that of [7], that instead of relying on LWE uses *learning with rounding* (LWR) [3]. Due to this, tagging becomes deterministic and linking becomes an equality check. Thus, naturally there is only one tag for each message under a secret key. Therefore, with the LWR-based LIT the security model of [7] and our new one look the same for an adversary, which is why we can then do the same reductions as for the LWE-based LIT of [7] to show that the deterministic LIT is secure if LWR is hard. Thus, the following lemma follows directly from [7].

Lemma 18. *There exists a LIT that has tag-indistinguishability, linkability, unforgeability, and invertability if decisional LWR and search LWR are hard.*

For the formal proof, we refer to the full version of this paper.

2.5 Non-interactive Zero-Knowledge Proof

We model non-interactive zero-knowledge proof systems in the random oracle model as in [7].

Definition 19 (NIZK). *A non-interactive proof system (NIZK) for a relation* $\mathfrak{R}$ *in the random oracle model is defined as a triple* $\Pi_{\mathsf{NIZK}} = (\mathsf{Setup}, \mathsf{P}, \mathsf{V})$ *of ppt algorithms:*

$\mathsf{crs} \leftarrow\!\!\$\, \mathsf{Setup}(1^\lambda)$: *On input* 1^λ *the setup algorithm outputs a common reference string* crs.

$\pi \leftarrow\!\!\$\, \mathsf{P}^{\mathcal{RO}}(\mathsf{crs}, x, w, \mu)$: *On input a common reference string* crs, *an instance* x, *witness* w, *and a message* μ, *and given oracle access to the random oracle* $\mathcal{RO}$, *the prover outputs a proof* π.

$b \leftarrow \mathsf{V}^{\mathcal{RO}}(\mathsf{crs}, x, \mu, \pi)$: *On input a common reference string* crs, *a statement* x, *a message* μ, *and a proof* π, *and given oracle access to the random oracle* $\mathcal{RO}$, *the verifier outputs a bit* b.

To simplify notation, we sometimes omit the random oracle $\mathcal{RO}$, *but assume implicitly that the prover and verifier have access to it. We say that the NIZK is* correct, *if for all* $(x, w) \in \mathfrak{R}$ *and* $m \in \{0,1\}^*$, *we have that*

$$\Pr[\mathsf{V}(\mathsf{crs}, x, m, \mathsf{P}(\mathsf{crs}, x, w, m)) : \mathsf{crs} \leftarrow\!\!\$\, \mathsf{Setup}(1^\lambda)] = 1.$$

The message in the above definition is not necessary for a NIZK itself, but since the NIZK we use uses the Fiat-Shamir heuristic, we want to be able make the proof dependent on a message. For a relation $\mathfrak{R}$, we define $L_{\mathfrak{R}} = \{x \mid \exists w : (x, w) \in \mathfrak{R}\}$ as the language of $\mathfrak{R}$. We define a shorthand notation to quickly show what relation we want to prove.

Definition 20. *We denote the generation of a proof* $\pi \leftarrow\!\!\$\, \mathsf{P}(\mathsf{crs}, x, w, \mu)$ *by*

$$\pi \leftarrow\!\!\$\, \mathsf{NIZK}\{x; w; \mathfrak{R}(x, w)\}(\mu),$$

where P *is from a non-interactive proof system* Π_{NIZK} *for the relation* $\mathfrak{R}$.

For security, we use the standard notions of zero-knowledge and straight-line extractability.

Definition 21 (Zero-Knowledge). *A NIZK Π is* zero-knowledge *if there exists a simulator* Sim *consisting of three ppt algorithms* $\mathsf{Sim} = (\mathsf{Sim.Setup}, \mathsf{Sim}.\mathcal{RO}, \mathsf{Sim.Sim})$ *such that for all ppt $\mathcal{A}$ there exists a negligible function* negl *such that,*

$$\left| \begin{array}{l} \Pr[\mathcal{A}^{\mathsf{P}\mathcal{O},\mathcal{RO}}(1^\lambda, \mathsf{crs}) = 1 : \mathsf{crs} \leftarrow\!\$\, \mathsf{Setup}(1^\lambda)] \\ - \Pr[\mathcal{A}^{\mathsf{Sim.Sim},\mathsf{Sim}.\mathcal{RO}}(1^\lambda, \mathsf{crs}) = 1 : \mathsf{crs} \leftarrow\!\$\, \mathsf{Sim.Setup}(1^\lambda)] \end{array} \right| \le \mathsf{negl}(\lambda)$$

where $\mathcal{RO}$ denotes a random oracle and $\mathsf{P}\mathcal{O}$, queried on input (x, w, μ), returns $\mathsf{P}(\mathsf{crs}, x, w, \mu)$. The oracle $\mathsf{Sim}(x, w, \mu)$ checks if $(x, w) \in \mathfrak{R}$ and if so, returns $\mathsf{Sim.Sim}(x, \mu)$. We assume that Sim *is stateful, i.e., it implicitly keeps state between invocations of* Sim.Setup, $\mathsf{Sim}.\mathcal{RO}$, *and* Sim.Sim.

Definition 22 (Straight-line extractability). *Let $\Pi = (\mathsf{Setup}, \mathsf{P}, \mathsf{V})$ be a NIZK. We say that Π is a* straight-line extractable proof of knowledge *if there are ppt algorithms $\mathsf{Ext}_0, \mathsf{Ext}_1$ such that for all ppt $\mathcal{A}_0, \mathcal{A}_1$, there exist negligible functions $\mathsf{negl}_0, \mathsf{negl}_1$ such that*

$$\left| \begin{array}{l} \Pr[\mathcal{A}_0(1^\lambda, \mathsf{crs}) = 1 : \mathsf{crs} \leftarrow\!\$\, \mathsf{Setup}(1^\lambda)] \\ - \Pr[\mathcal{A}_0(1^\lambda, \mathsf{crs}) = 1 : (\mathsf{crs}, \mathsf{td}) \leftarrow\!\$\, \mathsf{Ext}_0(1^\lambda)] \end{array} \right| \le \mathsf{negl}_0(\lambda)$$

and

$$\Pr\left[\begin{array}{l} \mathsf{V}^{\mathcal{RO}}(\mathsf{crs}, x, m, \pi) = 1 \\ \wedge\ (x, w) \notin \mathfrak{R} \end{array} : \begin{array}{l} (\mathsf{crs}, \mathsf{td}) \leftarrow\!\$\, \mathsf{Ext}_0(1^\lambda), \\ (x, m, \pi) \leftarrow\!\$\, \mathcal{A}_1(1^\lambda, \mathsf{crs}), \\ w \leftarrow \mathsf{Ext}_1(\mathsf{td}, x, m, \pi) \end{array} \right] \le \mathsf{negl}_1(\lambda)$$

In the random oracle model, Ext_1 gets the list of random oracle queries that $\mathcal{A}$ made as additional input.

2.6 Verifiable Ring Signature

A verifiable ring signature (VRS) is a standard ring signature with an additional functionality. At any point after creating a signature, a signer can output a proof showing that in fact it created the signature. On the other hand, people who did not sign the signature, but are part of the ring, can show that they did *not* create the signature. We formalize this by adding two ppt algorithms Prove and Judge to the standard ring signature model.

Definition 23. *A verifiable ring signature consists of five ppt algorithms* (Setup, KGen, Sign, Vrfy, Link).

$\mathsf{pp} \leftarrow\!\$\, \mathsf{Setup}(1^\lambda)$: *On input a security parameter 1^λ, the setup algorithm outputs public parameters* pp.

$(sk, pk) \leftarrow\!\$\, \mathsf{KGen}(\mathsf{pp})$: *On input public parameters* pp, *the key generation algorithm outputs a secret, public key pair (sk, pk).*

$\sigma \leftarrow\!\!\$\,\mathsf{Sign}(sk, R, \mu)$: *On input a secret key sk, a ring* $R = \{pk_i\}_i$ *and a message* μ*, the signing algorithm outputs a signature* σ*.*

$b \leftarrow \mathsf{Vrfy}(R, \mu, \sigma)$: *On input a ring R, a message* μ *and a signature* σ*, the verifying algorithm outputs a bit b.*

$\pi \leftarrow\!\!\$\,\mathsf{Prove}(sk, R, \mu, \sigma)$: *On input a secret key sk, a ring R, a message* μ*, and a signature* σ*, the prove algorithm outputs a proof* π*.*

$b \leftarrow \mathsf{Judge}(pk, R, \mu, \sigma, \pi)$: *On input a public key pk, a ring R, a message* μ*, a signature* σ*, and a proof* π*, the judging algorithm outputs a bit b.*

For security, we require strong unforgeability and anonymity of a ring signature, but now the adversary also has an oracle generating proofs with the Prove algorithm. Additionally we require *accountability*, which means that it is hard for an adversary to create a signature, where Judge thinks it did not create it. Furthermore we require *non-seizability*, which means that is hard for an adversary to create a signature, where Judge attributes the signature to an honest user. To model this, we use the security model of [13]. The definition of the games can be found in Fig. 6.

Definition 24. *We say that a VRS* Π *is strongly unforgeable, if there exists a negligible function* negl *such that for all qpt adversaries* $\mathcal{A}$ *and all* $\ell \in \mathsf{poly}(\lambda)$ *it holds that*

$$\Pr[\mathsf{Forge}^{\ell}_{\Pi,\mathcal{A}}(\lambda) = 1] \leq \mathsf{negl}(\lambda).$$

Definition 25. *We say that a VRS* Π *is anonymous, if there exists a negligible function* negl *such that for all qpt adversaries* $\mathcal{A}$ *it holds that*

$$\left|\Pr[\mathsf{Anon}^{0}_{\Pi,\mathcal{A}}(\lambda) = 1] - \Pr[\mathsf{Anon}^{1}_{\Pi,\mathcal{A}}(\lambda) = 1]\right| \leq \mathsf{negl}(\lambda).$$

Definition 26. *We say that a VRS* Π *is strongly accountable, if there exists a negligible function* negl *such that for all qpt adversaries* $\mathcal{A}$ *and all* $\ell \in \mathsf{poly}(\lambda)$ *it holds that*

$$\Pr[\mathsf{Acc}^{\ell}_{\Pi,\mathcal{A}}(\lambda) = 1] \leq \mathsf{negl}(\lambda).$$

Definition 27. *We say that a VRS* Π *is strongly non-seizable, if there exists a negligible function* negl *such that for all qpt adversaries* $\mathcal{A}$ *it holds that*

$$\Pr[\mathsf{Seiz}_{\Pi,\mathcal{A}}(\lambda) = 1] \leq \mathsf{negl}(\lambda).$$

3 New Lattice Constructions

3.1 A Fully Collision-Resistant Chameleon Hash Function

We now want to construct our new chameleon hash to later use it when instantiating SSS constructions. Since the security notion that [28] achieves is close to our target security, full collision-resistance, we take their construction as a starting point. The idea of their random oracle model construction is to first generate a trapdoored matrix $\mathbf{A}$ in the setup. To hash a message μ, they query

$\mathsf{Sign}\mathcal{O}(\{sk_i\}_i, \cdot, \cdot, \cdot)$ with (j, R, μ)

$\sigma \leftarrow\!\!\$\ \mathsf{Sign}(sk_j, R, \mu)$
$\mathcal{Q}_{\mathsf{Sign}} \leftarrow \mathcal{Q}_{\mathsf{Sign}} \cup \{\mu, \sigma\}$
return σ

$\mathsf{Prove}\mathcal{O}(\{sk_i\}_i, \cdot, \cdot, \cdot, \cdot)$ with (j, R, μ, σ)

if $pk_i \in R \wedge (\mu, \sigma) \notin \mathcal{Q}_{\mathsf{LoR}}$
  return $\mathsf{Prove}(sk_j, R, \mu, \sigma)$
else
  return $\perp$

$\mathsf{LoRSign}\mathcal{O}_b(sk_0, sk_1, \cdot, \cdot)$ with (R, μ)

if $\{pk_0, pk_1\} \subseteq R$
  $\sigma \leftarrow\!\!\$\ \mathsf{Sign}(sk_b, R, \mu)$
  $\mathcal{Q}_{\mathsf{LoR}} \leftarrow \mathcal{Q}_{\mathsf{LoR}} \cup \{\mu, \sigma\}$
  return σ
else
  return $\perp$

$\mathsf{Forge}^{\ell}_{\Pi,\mathcal{A}}(\lambda)$

$\mathcal{Q}_{\mathsf{Sign}} \leftarrow \emptyset$, $\mathsf{pp} \leftarrow\!\!\$\ \mathsf{Setup}(1^\lambda)$
$\forall i \in [\ell], (sk_i, pk_i) \leftarrow\!\!\$\ \mathsf{KGen}(\mathsf{pp})$
$(R^*, \mu^*, \sigma^*) \leftarrow\!\!\$\ \mathcal{A}^{\mathsf{Sign}\mathcal{O},\mathsf{Prove}\mathcal{O}}(\{pk_i\}_{i\in[\ell]})$
$b_0 \leftarrow \mathsf{Vrfy}(R^*, \mu^*, \sigma^*)$
$b_1 \leftarrow R^* \subseteq \{pk_i\}_{i\in[\ell]}$
$b_2 \leftarrow (\mu^*, \sigma^*) \notin \mathcal{Q}_{\mathsf{Sign}}$
return $b_0 \wedge b_1 \wedge b_2$

$\mathsf{Anon}^{b}_{\Pi,\mathcal{A}}(\lambda)$

$\mathcal{Q}_{\mathsf{LoR}} \leftarrow \emptyset$, $\mathsf{pp} \leftarrow\!\!\$\ \mathsf{Setup}(1^\lambda)$
$(sk_0, pk_0) \leftarrow\!\!\$\ \mathsf{KGen}(\mathsf{pp})$
$(sk_1, pk_1) \leftarrow\!\!\$\ \mathsf{KGen}(\mathsf{pp})$
$b' \leftarrow\!\!\$\ \mathcal{A}^{\mathsf{Sign}\mathcal{O},\mathsf{Prove}\mathcal{O},\mathsf{LoRSign}\mathcal{O}}(pk_0, pk_1)$
return b'

$\mathsf{Acc}^{\ell}_{\Pi,\mathcal{A}}(\lambda)$

$\mathcal{Q}_{\mathsf{Sign}} \leftarrow \emptyset$, $\mathsf{pp} \leftarrow\!\!\$\ \mathsf{Setup}(1^\lambda)$
$\forall i \in [\ell], (sk_i, pk_i) \leftarrow\!\!\$\ \mathsf{KGen}(\mathsf{pp})$
$(pk^*, R^*, \mu^*, \sigma^*, \pi^*) \leftarrow\!\!\$\ \mathcal{A}^{\mathsf{Sign}\mathcal{O},\mathsf{Prove}\mathcal{O}}(\{pk_i\}_{i\in[\ell]})$
$b_0 \leftarrow \mathsf{Vrfy}(R^*, \mu^*, \sigma^*)$
$b_1 \leftarrow (\mathsf{Judge}(pk^*, R^*, \mu^*, \sigma^*, \pi^*) = 0)$
$b_2 \leftarrow R^* \subseteq \{pk_i\}_{i\in[\ell]} \cup \{pk^*\}$
$b_3 \leftarrow (\mu^*, \sigma^*) \notin \mathcal{Q}_{\mathsf{Sign}}$
return $b_0 \wedge b_1 \wedge b_2 \wedge b_3$

$\mathsf{Seiz}_{\Pi,\mathcal{A}}(\lambda)$

$\mathcal{Q}_{\mathsf{Sign}} \leftarrow \emptyset$, $\mathsf{pp} \leftarrow\!\!\$\ \mathsf{Setup}(1^\lambda)$
$(sk_0, pk_0) \leftarrow\!\!\$\ \mathsf{KGen}(\mathsf{pp})$
$(R^*, \mu^*, \sigma^*) \leftarrow\!\!\$\ \mathcal{A}^{\mathsf{Sign}\mathcal{O},\mathsf{Prove}\mathcal{O}}(pk_0)$
$\pi^* \leftarrow\!\!\$\ \mathsf{Prove}(sk_0, R^*, \mu^*, \sigma^*)$
$b_0 \leftarrow \mathsf{Vrfy}(R^*, \mu^*, \sigma^*)$
$b_1 \leftarrow (\mathsf{Judge}(pk_0, R^*, \mu^*, \sigma^*, \pi^*) \neq 0)$
$b_2 \leftarrow (\mu^*, \sigma^*) \notin \mathcal{Q}_{\mathsf{Sign}}$
return $b_0 \wedge b_1 \wedge b_2$

Fig. 6. VRS security games and oracles.

the random oracle on μ and some other values to get another matrix $\mathbf{A}_h$ and choose a small Gaussian value $\mathbf{e}$. Then, they use the well known Ajtai hash function to compute $[\mathbf{A}|\mathbf{A}_h]\mathbf{e} = \mathbf{h}$, which is their hash value. To adapt a message, they use the trapdoor to compute some short $\mathbf{e}'$ such that $[\mathbf{A}|\mathbf{A}_h']\mathbf{e}' = \mathbf{h}$ for some different $\mathbf{A}_h'$ also output by the random oracle. The issue with this idea is that to show security they need to assume having a unique tag τ each time a new $\mathbf{h}$ is created, which they use as additional input to the random oracle. While this is no problem in their application of redactable blockchains, the constructions of SSS that we look at require the chameleon hash to be tag-free. If we simply removed the tag from their construction, their construction would not be fully collision-resistant. An adversary could query the adapt oracle for a collision $[\mathbf{A}|\mathbf{A}_h]\mathbf{e} = [\mathbf{A}|\mathbf{A}'_h]\mathbf{e}'$ and return $(2\mathbf{e}, 2\mathbf{e}')$ as a new collision which wins the security game.

The problem with this approach is that $\mathbf{e}$ can be freely chosen by the adversary without any restrictions. Therefore, the idea for our construction is to use the construction of [28] without tags and to additionally bind $\mathbf{e}$ with a commitment scheme to prohibit this attack. In fact, a commitment scheme is not sufficient, as we then would not be able to implement the CAdapt algorithm correctly. Instead, we use a trapdoor commitment scheme and its DEE property.

We can now construct our chameleon hash function. For this, let $n, q > 1$, $m = \mathcal{O}(n \log q)$, $s = \mathcal{O}(\sqrt{n \log q})$ large enough, and $\beta = s \cdot \sqrt{2m}$. Let $\Pi_{\mathsf{Com}} = (\mathsf{TdGen}, \mathsf{Com}, \mathsf{ComCheck}, \mathsf{Equiv})$ be a trapdoor commitment scheme. Let the random oracle $\mathcal{RO} : \{0,1\}^* \to \mathbb{Z}_q^{n \times m}$. We then construct our chameleon hash function as seen in Fig. 7.

$\mathsf{CKGen}(1^\lambda)$

$(\mathbf{A}, \mathsf{td}) \leftarrow\!\!\$\ \mathsf{TrapGen}(n, m, q, s)$
$(\mathsf{pp}, \mathsf{td}_{\mathsf{Com}}) \leftarrow\!\!\$\ \mathsf{TdGen}(1^\lambda)$
$\mathsf{pk}_{\mathsf{ch}} \leftarrow (\mathbf{A}, \mathsf{pp})$
$\mathsf{sk}_{\mathsf{ch}} \leftarrow (\mathsf{td}, \mathsf{td}_{\mathsf{Com}})$
return $(\mathsf{pk}_{\mathsf{ch}}, \mathsf{sk}_{\mathsf{ch}})$

$\mathsf{CHash}(\mathsf{pk}_{\mathsf{ch}}, \mu)$

$z \leftarrow\!\!\$\ \{0,1\}^\lambda$
$\mathbf{e} \leftarrow\!\!\$\ D_{\mathbb{Z}^{2m}, s}$
$(c, d) \leftarrow\!\!\$\ \mathsf{Com}(\mathsf{pp}, \mathbf{e})$
$\mathbf{B} \leftarrow \mathcal{RO}(\mu, z, c)$
$\mathbf{h} \leftarrow \left[\mathbf{A}\ \mathbf{B}\right] \mathbf{e}$
$h \leftarrow \mathbf{h}, r \leftarrow (z, \mathbf{e}, c, d)$
return (h, r)

$\mathsf{CHashCheck}(\mathsf{pk}_{\mathsf{ch}}, h, \mu, r)$

Parse $(z, \mathbf{e} = (\mathbf{e}_1^t, \mathbf{e}_2^t)^t, c, d) \leftarrow r$
with $\mathbf{e}_2 \in \mathbb{Z}_q^m$, and $\mathbf{h} \leftarrow h$
$\mathbf{B} \leftarrow \mathcal{RO}(\mu, z, c)$
if $\mathbf{h} = \left[\mathbf{A}\ \mathbf{B}\right] \mathbf{e}$
$\wedge\ \mathsf{ComCheck}(\mathsf{pp}, \mathbf{e}, c, d) = 1$
$\wedge\ \|\mathbf{e}\| \leq \beta \wedge \mathbf{e}_2 \neq \mathbf{0}$
return 1
return 0

$\mathsf{CAdapt}(\mathsf{sk}_{\mathsf{ch}}, h, \mu, r, \mu')$

$\mathbf{h} \leftarrow h$
if $\mathsf{CHashCheck}(\mathsf{pk}_{\mathsf{ch}}, h, \mu, r) = 0$
return $\perp$
$z' \leftarrow\!\!\$\ \{0,1\}^\lambda$
$c' \leftarrow\!\!\$\ \mathsf{Com}(\mathsf{pp}, 0)$
$\mathbf{B} \leftarrow \mathcal{RO}(\mu', z', c')$
$\mathbf{e}' \leftarrow\!\!\$\ \mathsf{PreSample}(\left[\mathbf{A}\ \mathbf{B}\right], \mathsf{td}, \mathbf{h}, s)$
$d' \leftarrow\!\!\$\ \mathsf{Equiv}(\mathsf{pp}, \mathsf{td}_{\mathsf{Com}}, c', \mathbf{e}')$
$r' \leftarrow (z', \mathbf{e}', c', d')$
return r'

Fig. 7. Lattice-based fully-collision-resistant chameleon hash function.

Note that we require $\mathbf{e}_2 \neq \mathbf{0}$ for security to hold (which we show in the full version of this paper).

Theorem 28. *If the commitment scheme has DEE, then the chameleon hash function construction given in Fig. 7 has indistinguishability.*

Proof. Let D_{CHash} be the distribution of $(\mathbf{h}, r = (z, \mathbf{e}, c, d) \leftarrow\$ \mathsf{CHash}(\mathsf{pk}_{\mathsf{ch}}, \mu))$ and let D_{CAdapt} be the distribution of $(\mathbf{h}', r'' = (z'', \mathbf{e}'', c'', d''))$, where $(\mathbf{h}', r') \leftarrow\$ \mathsf{CHash}(\mathsf{pk}_{\mathsf{ch}}, \mu'), r'' \leftarrow\$ \mathsf{CAdapt}(\mathsf{sk}_{\mathsf{ch}}, \mathbf{h}', \mu', r', \mu)$ for some μ, μ'. Then we can easily see the marginal distributions of $\mathbf{h}$ and $\mathbf{h}'$ are statistically close to uniformly random, which we formally prove in the full version of this paper. Furthermore, z, z'' are uniform by definition. For $\mathbf{e}, \mathbf{e}''$ we know that their distribution is statistically indistinguishable due to Theorem 9. Finally, by the DEE property of the commitment scheme we know that $(c, d), (c'', d'')$ are computationally indistinguishable. □

Lemma 29. *The construction given in Fig. 7 does* not *have uniqueness (as defined in the full version of this paper).*

This can be shown by the following attack. Since the adversary in the uniqueness game can choose the public key, it can generate a public key honestly together with a trapdoor. Then, it can just hash some message μ to (h, r) and use the CAdapt algorithm with input $(\mathsf{sk}_{\mathsf{ch}}, h, \mu, r, \mu)$ to get some new $r' = (z', \mathbf{e}', c', d')$ for the same message μ. While it is possible to derandomize z', c', d', such that $z = z', c = c', d = d'$ (for the same μ and $\mathbf{e}$) with the help of a PRF, by design, $\mathbf{e}' \neq \mathbf{e}$ with overwhelming probability, since the output distribution of $\mathsf{PreSample}$ is a (conditioned) discrete Gaussian. We expect it is necessary that in order to construct a chameleon hash function with uniqueness, one needs to use another building block than $\mathsf{PreSample}$.

Theorem 30. *If $\mathsf{SIS}_{n,m,q,\beta'}$ is hard, where $\beta' = 2s' \cdot (\sqrt{n} + \sqrt{m} + t + 1) \cdot s\sqrt{2m}$ with $t \geq 0$ and $s' = \omega(\sqrt{\log m})$, and if Π is a computationally binding trapdoor commitment scheme that has DEE, the construction* CH *given in Fig. 7 is fully collision-resistant in the random oracle model.*

The idea of the proof is as follows. First, we take an adversary $\mathcal{A}$ against the full collision-resistance of the construction. Then, we define an alternative security game for $\mathcal{A}$ to play in, in which we do not generate a trapdoor for $\mathbf{A}$ and forget the trapdoor for the commitment scheme. Instead, when answering a CAdapt query, we use the random oracle to program a trapdoor into the $\mathbf{B}$ we generate during it. However, when we answer a random oracle query, we do not program a trapdoor into $\mathbf{B}$. Then, we want to construct an adversary $\mathcal{B}$ against SIS that simulates $\mathcal{A}$ in the alternative security game. If $\mathcal{A}$ wins this game by outputting a valid collision (h, μ, r, μ', r'), there are multiple cases that can happen. First, for $(h, \mu, r = (z, \mathbf{e}, c, d))$ we look at $\mathbf{B} \leftarrow \mathcal{RO}(\mu, z, c)$. If $\mathbf{B}$ was generated without a trapdoor, we are fine and can use it to extract an SIS solution. However, we need a second part to do that. In the case that $(h, \mu') \notin \mathcal{Q}$, we hope that $\mathbf{B}' \leftarrow \mathcal{RO}(\mu', z', c')$, where $r' = (z', \mathbf{e}', c', d')$, was generated without a trapdoor as well. In the other case, i.e., $(h, \mu') \in \mathcal{Q}$, we can argue that there must exist a candidate $(h, \hat{\mu}, \hat{r} = (\hat{z}, \hat{\mathbf{e}}, \hat{c}, \hat{d}))$. For this candidate, we hope that $\hat{\mathbf{B}} \leftarrow \mathcal{RO}(\hat{\mu}, \hat{z}, \hat{c})$ was generated without a trapdoor as well. Finally, if $\mathbf{B}$ was generated without trapdoor and either $\mathbf{B}'$ or $\hat{\mathbf{B}}$ was generated without trapdoor (in the respective case), we can extract an SIS solution. We will later formally define this as the event Free. If, on the other hand, we have $\neg\mathsf{Free}$, we can instead break the binding of the commitment scheme. This is because with the commitment scheme we bind $\mathbf{e}$ to some $\mathbf{B}$ and therefore to some h. If $\neg\mathsf{Free}$ and thus one of the $\mathbf{B}$ has a trapdoor in it, the adversary used some $\mathbf{B}$ with two different $\mathbf{e}, \mathbf{e}'$. A full, formal version of this proof can be found in the full version of this paper.

Since we argued before that a lattice-based trapdoor commitment scheme with the required properties exist, we get the following corollary.

Corollary 31. *There exists a construction of a chameleon hash function that is f-CR secure, if SIS is hard.*

The fully-collision-resistant chameleon hash function based on lattice assumptions we constructed here, will be applied to instantiate various SSS constructions in Sect. 5.

3.2 A Generic Verifiable Ring Signature Construction, Instantiated with Lattices

Let $\mathsf{LIT} = (\mathsf{LIT.KGen}, \mathsf{Tag}, \mathsf{LIT.Vrfy}, \mathsf{Link}, f)$ $\mathsf{NIZK} = (\mathsf{NIZK.Setup}, \mathsf{P}, \mathsf{V})$ respectively be a LIT and NIZK for the relations required in our construction of a VRS, which can be found in Fig. 8.

Theorem 32. *If the LIT has non-invertability and if the NIZK is straight-line extractable and zero-knowledge, then the VRS construction has strong unforgeability.*

Proof. Let $\ell \in \mathsf{poly}(\lambda)$ and let $\mathcal{A}$ be a *qpt* adversary against the strong unforgeability of the VRS construction. We construct an adversary $\mathcal{B}$ against the non-invertability of the LIT. On input a pk, $\mathcal{B}$ first samples ℓ keys $sk_i \leftarrow\$ \mathsf{LIT.KGen}(1^\lambda)$ and sets $pk_i \leftarrow f(sk_i)$. Then, it guesses a $k \leftarrow\$ [\ell]$ and replaces the kth public key $pk_k \leftarrow pk$. $\mathcal{B}$ then simulates $\mathcal{A}$ as in the strong unforgeability game, except for the following two changes.

- When $\mathcal{A}$ makes a query (i, R, μ) to its Sign oracle with $i = k$, $\mathcal{B}$ generates the tag with $t_{\mathsf{Sign}} \leftarrow\$ \mathsf{Tag}\mathcal{O}((R, \mu, r_{\mathsf{Sign}}))$, where $r_{\mathsf{Sign}} \leftarrow\$ \{0,1\}^\lambda$ as in the construction. The proof π is generated with the simulator of the NIZK.
- When $\mathcal{A}$ makes a query (i, R, μ, σ) to its $\mathsf{Prove}\mathcal{O}$ oracle with $i = k$, and if $pk \in R$ and $\mathsf{Vrfy}(R, \mu, \sigma) = 1$, and where $\sigma = (r_{\mathsf{Sign}}, t_{\mathsf{Sign}}, \pi_{\mathsf{Sign}})$, then $\mathcal{B}$ generates the tag with $t_{\mathsf{Prove}} \leftarrow\$ \mathsf{Tag}\mathcal{O}((R, \mu, r_{\mathsf{Sign}}))$. The proof is generated with the simulator of the NIZK.

$\mathsf{Setup}(1^\lambda)$

$\mathsf{pp} \leftarrow\!\!\$\ \mathsf{NIZK.Setup}(1^\lambda)$
return pp

$\mathsf{KGen}(\mathsf{pp})$

$sk \leftarrow\!\!\$\ \mathsf{LIT.KGen}(1^\lambda)$
$pk \leftarrow f(sk)$
return (sk, pk)

$\mathsf{Sign}(sk, R, \mu)$

if $f(sk) \notin R$
  return $\bot$
$r_{\mathsf{Sign}} \leftarrow\!\!\$\ \{0,1\}^\lambda$
$t_{\mathsf{Sign}} \leftarrow\!\!\$\ \mathsf{Tag}(sk, (R, \mu, r_{\mathsf{Sign}}))$
$\pi_{\mathsf{Sign}} \leftarrow\!\!\$\ \mathsf{NIZK}\{(R, \mu, r_{\mathsf{Sign}}, t_{\mathsf{Sign}});$
  $(sk, pk);$
  $f(sk) = pk, pk \in R,$
  $\mathsf{LIT.Vrfy}(sk, (R, \mu, r_{\mathsf{Sign}}), t_{\mathsf{Sign}}) = 1\}$
$\sigma \leftarrow (r_{\mathsf{Sign}}, t_{\mathsf{Sign}}, \pi_{\mathsf{Sign}})$
return σ

$\mathsf{Vrfy}(R, \mu, \sigma)$

return $\mathsf{V}(\mathsf{crs}, (R, \mu, r_{\mathsf{Sign}}, t_{\mathsf{Sign}}), \pi_{\mathsf{Sign}}) = 1$

$\mathsf{Prove}(sk, R, \mu, \sigma)$

if $f(sk) \notin R \vee \mathsf{Vrfy}(R, \mu, \sigma) = 0$
  return $\bot$
$t_{\mathsf{Prove}} \leftarrow\!\!\$\ \mathsf{Tag}(sk, (R, \mu, r_{\mathsf{Sign}}))$
$\pi_{\mathsf{Prove}} \leftarrow\!\!\$\ \mathsf{NIZK}\{(pk, R, \mu, r_{\mathsf{Sign}}, t_{\mathsf{Prove}}); sk;$
  $f(sk) = pk,$
  $\mathsf{LIT.Vrfy}(sk, (R, \mu, r_{\mathsf{Sign}})) = 1\}$
$\pi \leftarrow (t_{\mathsf{Prove}}, \pi_{\mathsf{Prove}})$
return π

$\mathsf{Judge}(pk, R, \mu, \sigma, \pi_{\mathsf{Prove}})$

if $\mathsf{V}(\mathsf{crs}, (pk, R, \mu, r_{\mathsf{Sign}}, t_{\mathsf{Prove}}), \pi_{\mathsf{Prove}}) = 0$
  $\vee\ \mathsf{Vrfy}(R, \mu, \sigma) = 0$
  return $\bot$
if $pk \notin R$
  return 0
return $\mathsf{Link}((R, \mu), t_{\mathsf{Sign}}, t_{\mathsf{Prove}})$

Fig. 8. Generic VRS construction.

After $\mathcal{A}$ has output a forgery $(R^*, \mu^*, \sigma^* = (r^*_{\mathsf{Sign}}, t^*_{\mathsf{Sign}}, \pi^*_{\mathsf{Sign}}))$, if $b_0 \wedge b_1 \wedge b_2$ is true, $\mathcal{B}$ uses the straight-line extractor of the NIZK to extract (sk^*, pk^*) from π^*_{Sign}. If $pk = pk^*$, $\mathcal{B}$ outputs sk^*.

By the definition of the non-invertability game and the zero-knowledgeness of the NIZK, $\mathcal{A}$ is perfectly simulated. Since b_0 and b_2 are true, we know that the straight-line extractability is successful and therefore that $f(sk^*) = pk^*$ and that $pk^* \in R^*$. Then, since b_1 is true, there exists a $j \in [\ell]$ such that $pk^* = pk_j$. If $j = k$, we therefore have $f(sk^*) = pk_k = pk^*$, thus sk^* is a valid solution for the invertability game, and we have

$$\Pr[\mathsf{Inv}_{\mathsf{LIT},\mathcal{B}}(\lambda) = 1] = \frac{1}{\ell}\Pr[\mathsf{Forge}^{\ell}_{\Pi,\mathcal{A}}(\lambda) = 1].$$

□

Theorem 33. *If the LIT has tag-indistinguishability and if the NIZK is zero-knowledge, then the VRS construction has anonymity.*

Proof. Let $\mathcal{A}$ be an adversary against the anonymity of the VRS. We first define an alternative security game and then construct an adversary against the tag-indistinguishability of the LIT. The alternative security game Game_1^b for $b \in \{0,1\}$ works like $\mathsf{Anon}_{\Pi,\mathcal{A}}^b(\lambda)$, except that during the oracle calls to $\mathsf{Sign}\mathcal{O}, \mathsf{Prove}\mathcal{O}, \mathsf{LoRSign}\mathcal{O}$, the pi_{Sign} and π_{Prove} are generated with the zero-knowledge simulator of the NIZK. We know that these games only differ negligibly by the zero-knowledge property of the NIZK. Then, we construct an adversary $\mathcal{B}$ against the tag-indistinguishability of the LIT. On input $(\hat{pk}_0, \hat{pk}_1)$, $\mathcal{B}$ simulates $\mathcal{A}$ in Game_1, except for the following changes.

- Instead of generating pk_0, pk_1, $\mathcal{B}$ instead sets $pk_0 \leftarrow \hat{pk}_0, pk_1 \leftarrow \hat{pk}_1$.
- Whenever $\mathcal{B}$ needs to compute a tag on a message $(R, \mu, r_{\mathsf{Sign}})$ to answer an oracle query of $\mathcal{A}$, $\mathcal{B}$ instead queries its own tag oracle on input $(R, \mu, r_{\mathsf{Sign}})$.

Then, after $\mathcal{A}$ outputs a bit $\hat{b}$, $\mathcal{B}$ outputs $\hat{b}$. We know that by the definition of Game_1 and of the tag-indistinguishability game that if $b = 0$ (or $b = 1$) then $\mathcal{A}$ is simulated as in Game_1^0 (or Game_1^1, respectively). Thus, we know that

$$\begin{aligned} &\left|\Pr[\mathsf{Anon}_{\Pi,\mathcal{A}}^0(\lambda) = 1] - \Pr[\mathsf{Anon}_{\Pi,\mathcal{A}}^1(\lambda) = 1]\right| \\ = &\left|\Pr[\mathsf{Anon}_{\mathsf{LIT},\mathcal{B},0}^{\mathsf{LIT}}(\lambda) = 1] - \Pr[\mathsf{Anon}_{\mathsf{LIT},\mathcal{B},1}^{\mathsf{LIT}}(\lambda) = 1]\right|, \end{aligned}$$

which concludes the proof. □

Theorem 34. *If the LIT has non-invertability and linkability and if the NIZK is straight-line extractable and zero-knowledge, then the VRS construction has accountability.*

Proof. Let $\ell \in \mathsf{poly}(\lambda)$ and let $\mathcal{A}$ be a *qpt* adversary against the accountability of the VRS construction. We define a series of games Game_i, in which $\mathcal{A}$ is simulated.

Game_0 is the same as $\mathsf{Acc}_{\Pi,\mathcal{A}}^{\ell}(\lambda)$. Define the event Win_0 to be the event that $b_0 \wedge b_1 \wedge b_2 \wedge b_3$ is true.

Game_1 is the same as Game_0, except that after $\mathcal{A}$ outputs a forgery $(pk^*, R^*, \mu^*, \sigma^*, \pi^*)$ with $\sigma^* = (r_{\mathsf{Sign}}^*, t_{\mathsf{Sign}}^*, \pi_{\mathsf{Sign}}^*)$ and $\pi^* = (t_{\mathsf{Prove}}^*, \pi_{\mathsf{Prove}}^*)$ and $b_0 \wedge b_1 \wedge b_2 \wedge b_3$ being true, the game uses the straight-line extractor of the NIZK to extract $(sk_{\mathsf{Sign}}^*, pk_{\mathsf{Sign}}^*)$ from π_{Sign}^* and sk_{Prove}^* from π_{Prove}^*. Define the event Win_1 to be the event that Win_0 is true and that both extractions are successful. Then we know by the straight-line extractability of the NIZK that

$$\Pr[\mathsf{Win}_0] \leq \Pr[\mathsf{Win}_1] + \mathsf{negl}(\lambda).$$

Thus, in Game_1 we always successfully extract if $\mathcal{A}$ wins Game_0.

Game_2 is the same game as Game_1, except that we always have $pk^* \in R^*$, i.e., we define Win_2 as $\mathsf{Win}_1 \wedge pk^* \in R^*$. We can show that the probabilities of Win_1 and Win_2 only differ negligibly by using the strong unforgeability of the VRS. Since b_0 and b_3 are true, (R^*, μ^*, σ^*) forms a valid forgery in the strong unforgeability game against the VRS. The input and oracles of $\mathcal{A}$ match in the two games. Thus, since we require non-invertability and linkability, we can construct an adversary $\mathcal{C}$ as in the proof of Theorem 32. Thus, we know that

$$\Pr[\mathsf{Win}_1] \leq \frac{1}{\ell} \Pr[\mathsf{Win}_2].$$

Game_3 is the same as Game_2, except that the extracted pk^*_{Sign} is always equal to pk^*, i.e., we define Win_3 as $\mathsf{Win}_2 \wedge pk^*_{\mathsf{Sign}} = pk^*$. Again we can use the strong unforgeability of the VRS to show that Game_2 and Game_3 differ negligibly. With the same argument as in Game_2, we can argue that

$$\Pr[\mathsf{Win}_2] \leq \frac{1}{\ell} \Pr[\mathsf{Win}_3].$$

We can now construct an adversary $\mathcal{B}$ against the linkability of the LIT. $\mathcal{B}$ simulates $\mathcal{A}$ as in Game_3, i.e., we assume that $\mathcal{A}$ wins, the extraction is successful, $pk^* \in R^*$, and the extracted $pk^*_{\mathsf{Sign}} = pk^*$. Then, $\mathcal{B}$ returns $(sk^*_{\mathsf{Sign}}, sk^*_{\mathsf{Prove}}, (R^*, \mu^*, r^*_{\mathsf{Sign}}), t^*_{\mathsf{Sign}}, t^*_{\mathsf{Prove}})$ to its challenger. To argue that $\mathcal{B}$ wins the linkability game, we need to show that

1. $f(sk^*_{\mathsf{Sign}}) = f(sk^*)$
2. $\mathsf{LIT.Vrfy}(sk^*_{\mathsf{Sign}}, (R^*, \mu^*, r^*_{\mathsf{Sign}}), t^*_{\mathsf{Sign}}) = \mathsf{LIT.Vrfy}(sk^*, (R^*, \mu^*, r^*_{\mathsf{Sign}}), t^*_{\mathsf{Prove}}) = 1$
3. $\mathsf{Link}((R^*, \mu^*, r^*_{\mathsf{Sign}}), t^*_{\mathsf{Sign}}, t^*_{\mathsf{Prove}}) = 0$.

Condition (2) follows immediately from the successful extraction, while this fact together with the assumption that $pk^*_{\mathsf{Sign}} = pk^*$ implies (1). For condition (3), we know that since b_1 is true, the judge outputs 0. Due to $pk^* \in R^*$, we know that this only happens if condition (3) is true. Thus, we know that if $\mathcal{A}$ wins Game_3, then $\mathcal{B}$ wins the linkability game. Therefore, we have that

$$\Pr[\mathsf{Acc}^{\ell}_{\Pi,\mathcal{A}}(\lambda) = 1] \leq \frac{1}{\ell^2} \Pr[\mathsf{Linkable}^{\mathsf{LIT}}_{\mathsf{LIT},\mathcal{B}}(\lambda) = 1] + \mathsf{negl}(\lambda),$$

and the VRS is accountable[1].

Theorem 35. *If the LIT is unforgeable, and if the NIZK is straight-line extractable and zero-knowledge, then the VRS construction has non-seizability.*

Proof. Let $\mathcal{A}$ be a *qpt* adversary against the accountability of the VRS construction. We construct an adversary $\mathcal{B}$ against the unforgeability of the LIT. On input pk, $\mathcal{B}$ simulates $\mathcal{A}$ as in the non-seizability game, except that $\mathcal{B}$ sets $pk_0 \leftarrow pk$, and except for the following two changes.

- When $\mathcal{A}$ makes a query (i, R, μ) to its Sign oracle with $i = k$, $\mathcal{B}$ generates the tag with $t_{\mathsf{Sign}} \leftarrow\$ \mathsf{Tag}\mathcal{O}((R, \mu, r_{\mathsf{Sign}}))$, where $r_{\mathsf{Sign}} \leftarrow\$ \{0,1\}^\lambda$ as in the construction. The proof π is generated with the simulator of the NIZK.
- When $\mathcal{A}$ makes a query (i, R, μ, σ) to its $\mathsf{Prove}\mathcal{O}$ oracle with $i = k$, and if $pk \in R$ and $\mathsf{Vrfy}(R, \mu, \sigma) = 1$, and where $\sigma = (r_{\mathsf{Sign}}, t_{\mathsf{Sign}}, \pi_{\mathsf{Sign}})$, then $\mathcal{B}$ generates the tag with $t_{\mathsf{Prove}} \leftarrow\$ \mathsf{Tag}\mathcal{O}((R, \mu, r_{\mathsf{Sign}}))$. The proof is generated with the simulator of the NIZK.

[1] It is possible to reduce the multiplicative loss from $1/\ell^2$ to $1/\ell$ by going from Game_1 to Game_3 directly.

When $\mathcal{A}$ outputs a forgery $(R^*, mu^*, \sigma^* = (r^*_{\mathsf{Sign}}, t^*_{\mathsf{Sign}}, \pi^*_{\mathsf{Sign}}))$ and if $b_0 \wedge b_1 \wedge b_2 \wedge b_3$ is true, $\mathcal{B}$ uses the straight-line extractor of the NIZK to extract (sk^*, pk^*) from π^*_{Sign}. Then, $\mathcal{B}$ queries $t^*_{\mathsf{Prove}} \leftarrow\$ \mathsf{Tag}\mathcal{O}((R^*, \mu^*, r^*_{\mathsf{Sign}}))$ and uses the simulator to create π^*_{Prove} to define $\pi^* = (t^*_{\mathsf{Prove}}, \pi^*_{\mathsf{Prove}})$. Afterwards, $\mathcal{B}$ outputs $(sk^*, (R^*, \mu^*, r^*_{\mathsf{Sign}}), t^*_{\mathsf{Sign}})$.

By definition of the non-invertability game of the LIT and the zero-knowledge of the NIZK, we know that $\mathcal{A}$ is perfectly simulated. Since b_1 is true, $pk_0 \in R^*$. Furthermore, we know that $\mathsf{Judge}(pk_0, R^*, \mu^*, \sigma^*, \pi^*_{\mathsf{Prove}}) = \perp$ if either $\mathsf{NIZK.Vrfy}(\mathsf{crs}, (pk_0, R^*, t^*_{\mathsf{Prove}}), \mu^*, \pi^*_{\mathsf{Prove}}) = 0$ or $\mathsf{Vrfy}(R^*, \mu^*, \sigma^*) = 0$. However, the former case does not happen due to the correctness of the NIZK, while the latter is not true due to b_0 being true. Thus, $\mathsf{Judge}(pk_0, R^*, \mu^*, \sigma^*, \pi^*_{\mathsf{Prove}}) = 1$, and $\mathsf{Link}((R^*, \mu^*), t^*_{\mathsf{Sign}}, t^*_{\mathsf{Prove}}) = 1$. Due to this and b_0 being true, we know that $\mathcal{B}$ wins the unforgeability game and we have

$$\Pr[\mathsf{Forge}^{\mathsf{LIT}}_{\mathsf{LIT},\mathcal{B}}(\lambda) = 1] = \Pr[\mathsf{Seiz}_{\Pi,\mathcal{A}}(\lambda) = 1].$$

□

We now want to instantiate the generic construction with lattice-based building blocks. For the LIT, we can use the one described in Lemma 18. The NIZK need not only be lattice-based, but also be able to prove the statements we need. We use the NIZK from [31] made straight-line extractable with Katsumata's transform [23] as seen in [7,8]. We need to able to prove that

1. $f(sk) = pk$
2. $pk \in R$
3. $\mathsf{LIT}, \mathsf{Vrfy}(sk, (R, \mu, r_{\mathsf{Sign}}), t_{\mathsf{Sign}}) = 1$.

Since $R, \mu, r_{\mathsf{Sign}}$ are public, we can use the argument from [7] to show that we can prove (1) and (3) with the NIZK. For (2), in our use case of SSS the ring R will only consist of two public keys. Thus, it is sufficient if we prove (2) by creating an OR-proof over the condition in (1). If one wants to use the VRS with more than two parties, it is advisable to prove (2) by using accumulators (e.g. [29]) or one-out-of-many proofs (e.g. [30]) to be more efficient.

4 Sanitizable Signature Schemes

We now move on to defining sanitizable signature schemes in this section before providing instantiations in the next section.

The definition for sanitizable signature schemes is an extension of regular signature schemes. Due to the addition of the sanitizer, extra operations for generating keys for the sanitizer as well as sanitization itself are required.

Definition 36. *A sanitizable signature scheme* SSS *is a tuple of seven probabilistic polynomial-time algorithms* $\mathsf{SSS} = (\mathsf{KGen}_{\mathsf{Sig}}, \mathsf{KGen}_{\mathsf{San}}, \mathsf{Sign}, \mathsf{Sanit}, \mathsf{Vrfy}, \mathsf{Proof}, \mathsf{Judge})$ *defined as follows:*

$(pk_{\mathsf{Sig}}, sk_{\mathsf{Sig}}) \leftarrow\$ \mathsf{KGen}_{\mathsf{Sig}}(1^\lambda)$: *The algorithm takes the security parameter as input and outputs a signer key pair* $(pk_{\mathsf{Sig}}, sk_{\mathsf{Sig}})$.

$(pk_{\mathsf{San}}, sk_{\mathsf{San}}) \leftarrow\$ \mathsf{KGen}_{\mathsf{San}}(1^\lambda)$: *The algorithm takes the security parameter as input and outputs a sanitizer key pair* $(pk_{\mathsf{San}}, sk_{\mathsf{San}})$.

$\sigma \leftarrow\$ \mathsf{Sign}(\mu, sk_{\mathsf{Sig}}, pk_{\mathsf{San}}, \mathrm{ADM})$: *On input of a message* μ *in the message space* $\mathcal{M}$, *signer secret key* sk_{Sig}, *a sanitizer public key* sk_{San}, *as well as the admissible sanitization rights* ADM, *the algorithm outputs a signature* σ *or an error message* $\perp$. ADM *contains the indices of block that are admissible for modification. Furthermore, we assume that* ADM *is always valid with regards to the input message.* $\mathrm{ADM}_0 \cap \mathrm{ADM}_1$ *denotes the intersection of admissible blocks.*

$(\mu', \sigma') \leftarrow\$ \mathsf{Sanit}(\mu, \mathrm{MOD}, \sigma, sk_{\mathsf{San}}, pk_{\mathsf{Sig}})$: *On input of a message* μ, *a signature* σ, *a sanitizer secret key* sk_{San}, *a signer public key* pk_{Sig}, *as well as the modification instructions* MOD. *The algorithm outputs the modified message* m' *along with the corresponding sanitized signature* σ' *or an error message* $\perp$. *We model* MOD *as a function which takes the old message as input and outputs the modified message* $m' \leftarrow \mathrm{MOD}(m)$. *We write* $\mathrm{MOD}(\mathrm{ADM}) \rightarrow \top/\perp$ *to check if the intended modifications are allowed or not.*

$d \leftarrow \mathsf{Vrfy}(\mu, \sigma, pk_{\mathsf{Sig}}, pk_{\mathsf{San}})$: *On input of a message* μ, *a signature* σ, *a signer public key* pk_{Sig}, *and a sanitizer public key* pk_{San}, *the algorithm outputs a decision bit* $d \in \{\top, \perp\}$.

$\pi \leftarrow\$ \mathsf{Proof}(\mu, \sigma, \{(\mu_i, \sigma_i)\}_{i=1}^{k}, sk_{\mathsf{Sig}}, pk_{\mathsf{Sig}}, pk_{\mathsf{San}})$: *On input of a message* μ, *a signature* σ, *a set of additional message-signature pairs* $\{(\mu_i, \sigma_i)\}_{i=1}^{k}$, *signer secret key* sk_{Sig} *and public key* pk_{Sig}, *and the sanitizer public key* pk_{San}, *the algorithm outputs a proof* $\pi \in \{0,1\}^*$ *or an error message* $\perp$.

$d \leftarrow \mathsf{Judge}(\mu, \sigma, pk_{\mathsf{Sig}}, pk_{\mathsf{San}}, \pi)$: *On input of a message* μ, *a signature* σ, *a signer public key* pk_{Sig}, *a sanitizer public key* pk_{San}, *and a proof* π, *the algorithm outputs a bit determining who generated the signature, i.e.,* $d \in \{\mathsf{Sig}, \mathsf{San}\}$, *or returns an error message* $\perp$.

We follow the correctness definition of Brzuska et al. [9,10] as well as subsequent works that require that genuinely signed or sanitized messages are accepted, and a genuinely generated proof by the signer will lead the judge to determine the accountable party correctly. The formal definition can be found in the full version of this paper.

4.1 Security Notions

Here we briefly describe the intuition for each of the usual security properties for sanitizable signature schemes. Observe that most of these properties were stated in [9,10,12,14]. Furthermore, some later papers like [26] consider "stronger" versions of the security properties while others like [10,20,27] introduce slightly weaker versions. In this work, we will adhere to the basic notions for security.

In the following list we will state all possible security notions for sanitizable signature schemes and give a brief and informal intuition on what they achieve. Formal definitions for all notions can be found in the full version of this paper.

Unforgeability. No efficient adversary should be able to produce valid message-signature pairs that it has not seen before.

Immutability. A malicious sanitizer should not be able to modify blocks that the signer has not set to be admissible for modification.

Signer Accountability. A signer must not be able to craft a valid message-signature pair and a proof, such that the Judge algorithm will output San.

Sanitizer Accountability. A sanitizer must not be able to craft a valid message-signature pair such that honest proofs generated by the signer will lead to the Judge algorithm outputting Sig.

Accountability. Both sanitizer- and signer accountability hold.

Non-Interactive Public Accountability. Given a valid pair of message and signature, a third party can correctly determine who created the signature with no additional information.

Transparency. Detecting if a signature has been sanitized must be hard.

Privacy. Given a sanitized message, it must be hard to recover any information about the original message's content before being sanitized.

Unlinkability. Two different sanitized messages cannot be identified as belonging to the same initial message.

Invisibility. It must be hard to detect which parts of the message may be modified by the sanitizer.

In the literature, there exist several varieties of each of these properties, the use of which we try to limit in this paper for improved readability. To this end, we refer to the notion formally known as "proof-restricted transparency" simply as "transparency". Definitions for strong/weak variants can be found in the full version of this paper.

4.2 Signer Accountability

For the main body we limit ourselves to the formal definition of signer accountability, as we later show a new attack on this notion in Theorem 46 for one of the constructions examined as part of this work.

Definition 37 (Signer-Accountability). *A sanitizable signature scheme* SSS *is (strongly) signer-accountable, if for all qpt adversaries* $\mathcal{A}$*, the advantage in winning the game* $\mathsf{Exp}^{\mathsf{(s)sig\text{-}acc}}_{\mathsf{SSS},\mathcal{A}}(\lambda)$ *as described in Fig. 9, defined as*

$$\mathsf{Adv}^{(s)sig\text{-}acc}_{\mathsf{SSS},\mathcal{A}}(\lambda) := \Pr\left[\mathsf{Exp}^{\mathsf{(s)sig\text{-}acc}}_{\mathsf{SSS},\mathcal{A}}(\lambda) = 1\right]$$

is negligible in the security parameter λ*.*

5 Lattice-Based Instantiations with CH

This section is devoted to the instantiation of the various SSS constructions with the chameleon hash function. We explain the results of utilizing the chameleon

$\mathsf{Exp}^{\mathsf{(s)sig\text{-}acc}}_{\mathsf{SSS},\mathcal{A}}(\lambda)$

$(pk_{\mathsf{San}}, sk_{\mathsf{San}}) \leftarrow\$ \mathsf{KGen}_{\mathsf{San}}(1^{\lambda})$
$\mathcal{Q}_{\mathsf{San}} \leftarrow \emptyset$
$(pk^*_{\mathsf{Sig}}, \pi^*, \mu^*, \sigma^*) \leftarrow\$ \mathcal{A}^{\mathsf{Sanit}\mathcal{O}}(pk_{\mathsf{San}})$
if $(*, \mu^*, \sigma^*, pk^*_{\mathsf{Sig}}) \notin \mathcal{Q}_{\mathsf{San}}$
  $\wedge\, \mathsf{Vrfy}(\mu^*, \sigma^*, pk^*_{\mathsf{Sig}}, pk_{\mathsf{San}}) = \top$
  $\wedge\, \mathsf{Judge}(\mu^*, \sigma^*, pk^*_{\mathsf{Sig}}, pk_{\mathsf{San}}, \pi^*) = \mathsf{San}$
  return 1
else return 0

$\mathsf{Sanit}\mathcal{O}(sk_{\mathsf{San}}, \cdot, \cdot, \cdot, \cdot)$ **with** $(\mu, \mathrm{MOD}, \sigma, pk_{\mathsf{Sig}})$

$(\mu', \sigma') \leftarrow\$ \mathsf{Sanit}(\mu, \mathrm{MOD}, \sigma, sk_{\mathsf{San}}, pk_{\mathsf{Sig}})$
$\mathcal{Q}_{\mathsf{San}} \leftarrow \mathcal{Q}_{\mathsf{San}} \cup \{(\mu, \mu', \sigma', pk_{\mathsf{Sig}})\}$
return (μ', σ')

Fig. 9. Game based security definition for signer accountability. Inclusion of the gray box yields strong signer accountability (Color figure online)

hash function we constructed in Sect. 3.1 first. Due to the missing uniqueness of the chameleon hash function, the resulting sanitizable signature schemes lack important security features like unforgeability and accountability.[2] Luckily, we can employ the transform by [13]. This transform takes a sanitizable signature scheme, which does not necessarily satisfy unforgeability, and a verifiable ring signature (VRS) to a sanitizable signature scheme that satisfies unforgeability and full accountability. In the present case, we make use of the VRS constructed in Sect. 3.2, to increase the security guarantees of the lattice-based SSSs.

Before we iterate through the collection of SSS constructions using chameleon hash functions, we explain the transform to ensure unforgeability and accountability from [13].

Theorem 38. *For a sanitizable signature scheme* SSS_2 *resulting from applying the transformation explained in [13, Fig. 5] to a sanitizable signature scheme* SSS_1 *and a verifiable ring signature* VRS, *the following implications hold: If* SSS_1 *is weakly immutable, then* SSS_2 *is immutable. If* SSS_1 *is weakly unlinkable, and* VRS *is strongly unforgeable, then* SSS_2 *is unlinkable. If* SSS_1 *is strongly invisible then* SSS_2 *is strongly invisible. If* VRS *is strongly accountable, then* SSS_2 *is strongly signer accountable. If* VRS *is strongly non-seizable, then* SSS_2 *is strongly sanitizer accountable. If* VRS *is anonymous and* SSS_1 *is strongly transparent, then* SSS_2 *is strongly transparent.*

Finally, we note that standard instantiations of PRFs and PRGs are used in the protocols, without further specification. Post-quantum secure variants are given, for instance, in [22].

[2] Only in [2], sanitizer accountability has not been defined and has neither been attacked nor proven.

5.1 The ACMT05 Construction

The work by Ateniese et al. [2] marked the beginning of sanitizable signatures and gave the first construction of such. This first construction makes use of only two building blocks, a secure digital signature scheme Σ and a chameleon hash function CH which is strongly unforgeable. While the strongly unforgeable notion is not defined explicitly, we inferred that full collision-resistance and indistinguishability is sufficient.

The sanitizable signature scheme in [2] is stated to be *indistinguishable*, *unforgeable*, and satisfy *identical distribution of sanitized and original signatures*, [2, Section 4.4]. By the general relations between the notions, we have the following results.

Corollary 39. *The construction by Ateniese et al. in [2] instantiated using a DSS from* $\{\mathsf{Dilithium}, \mathsf{Falcon}\}$ *and the chameleon hash function constructed in Fig. 7 satisfies unforgeability, signer accountability, immutability, transparency, and privacy.*

We note that sanitizer accountability and invisibility have been developed after the publication of the work by Ateniese et al. The corresponding construction has not been analyzed regarding this notion. Here, we take the easy road and apply Theorem 38, to additionally achieve sanitizer accountability.

Corollary 40. *Using the transform from Theorem 38 and combining the verifiable ring signature given in Fig. 8 with the construction by Ateniese et al. in [2] as instantiated in Corollary 39, we obtain a sanitizable signature that satisfies unforgeability, signer accountability, sanitizer accountability, immutability, transparency, and privacy.*

5.2 The LZCS16-1 Construction

Recall that [27] gives two constructions. One is based on accountable ring signatures, (cf. the full version of this paper) while the other uses rerandomizable tagging schemes which are constructed from tag-based trapdoor functions and double-trapdoor chameleon hash functions. While tag-based trapdoor functions are merely weaker versions of chameleon hash functions, and thus, can be instantiated from our lattice-based chameleon hash function given in Fig. 7, it is not clear whether double-trapdoor chameleon hash functions can be instantiated from lattices. Thus, as of now, the construction by Lai et al. using chameleon hash functions, cannot be instantiated from known lattice constructions.

5.3 The BCD$^+$17 Construction

The construction by Beck et al. [5] uses a regular digital signature scheme, a *labeled* PKE, and a secure chameleon hash function, by which they mean indistinguishable, unique, and standard collision-resistant. Further, the sanitizable signature construction requires a PRG and a PRF.

As labeled PKEs are non-standard, we present a brief account including how to construct them from regular PKEs. In the construction, the labeled PKE provides strong invisibility of the sanitizable signature scheme, in which the signer public key is used as a label to prevent re-use of ciphertexts from different signer public keys. Further details including full definitions and proofs of the following can be found in the full version of this paper.

Labeled PKEs from Regular PKEs. A *labeled PKE* (we refer to the full version of this paper) consists of a triple $(\mathsf{KGen}_\tau, \mathsf{Enc}_\tau, \mathsf{Dec}_\tau)$, closely resembling the properties of regular PKEs. The key generation algorithm KGen_τ creates a key pair (pk, sk). The probabilistic encryption algorithm Enc_τ additionally requires a label $\tau \in \{0,1\}^n$, where the length n of the label depends on the security parameter λ. The decryption algorithm Dec_τ additionally requires the label τ. The (perfect) correctness of a labeled PKE is defined as $\mathsf{Enc}_\tau(sk, \mathsf{Dec}_\tau(pk, \mu, \tau), \tau) = \mu$ whenever $(pk, sk) \leftarrow\$ \mathsf{KGen}_\tau$ is honestly generated.

We explain now, how IND-CCA secure PKEs can be transformed to IND-CCA secure labeled PKEs with the proof provided in the full version of this paper. Given a PKE $\Pi = (\mathsf{KGen}, \mathsf{Enc}, \mathsf{Dec})$, we define a labeled PKE $\Pi_\tau = (\mathsf{KGen}_\tau, \mathsf{Enc}_\tau, \mathsf{Dec}_\tau)$ as follows. First, we note that for any label set $\{0,1\}^n$ we can concatenate a label τ and a message μ as $\tau\|\mu$ so that both, the label and the message can be recovered from $\tau\|\mu$ by either projecting to the first n bits or removing them. Then, $\mathsf{KGen}_\tau = \mathsf{KGen}$ and $\mathsf{Enc}_\tau(pk, \mu, \tau) \leftarrow \mathsf{Enc}(pk, \tau\|\mu)$. Finally, the decryption Dec_τ on input (sk, c, τ) first runs $\mathsf{Dec}(sk, c)$ to get $\tau'\|\mu'$. Then, Dec_τ checks if τ' coincides with the input label τ. If so, Dec_τ returns μ'. Otherwise, it returns $\perp$.

Instantiation of the SSS Construction. The uniqueness, which our construction in Sect. 3.1 does not achieve, is required for unforgeability, signer accountability, and sanitizer accountability. So that we have the following result that follows from [5, Theorem 1] and the construction given in Sect. 3.1.

Corollary 41. *The SSS construction by Beck et al. [5] instantiated with a signature scheme among {Dilithium, Falcon}, the PKE Kyber, and the chameleon hash function given in Fig. 7, satisfies immutability, transparency, privacy, and strong invisibility.*

The missing unforgeability and signer and sanitizer accountability are added via the transform Theorem 38.

Corollary 42. *The transform in Theorem 38 applied with the VRS given in Fig. 8 to the construction by Beck in [5] as instantiated in Corollary 41, satisfies unforgeability, signer accountability, sanitizer accountability, immutability, transparency, privacy, and strong invisibility.*

5.4 The CDK$^+$17 Construction

In [14], Camenisch et al. introduce a new notion called chameleon hash function with ephemeral trapdoors (CHET). They show how to generically construct CHET from chameleon hash functions such that the required security properties carry over. Thus, it is sufficient to have a chameleon hash function with the required properties. In total, the requirements are a correct, indistinguishable, unique, and standard collision-resistant chameleon hash function, a secure DSS, an IND-CPA secure PKE, PRGs, and PRFs, and an indistinguishable and standard collision-resistant CHET.

In their construction, Camenisch et al. use the uniqueness of the CHF in the proof of unforgeability and sanitizer accountability. Hence, from [14, Theorem 3] and taking into account the missing uniqueness, we get the following.

Corollary 43. *The construction by Camenish et al. in [14] instantiated using a DSS from {Dilithium, Falcon}, the PKE Kyber, the chameleon hash function given in Fig. 7, which is used twice, for the chameleon hash function and the CHET, satisfies signer accountability, immutability, transparency, privacy, and invisibility.*

To ensure unforgeability and sanitizer accountability, we apply Theorem 38.

Corollary 44. *The transform in Theorem 38 applied with the VRS given in Fig. 8 to the construction by Camenisch et al. in [14] as instantiated in Corollary 43, satisfies unforgeability, signer accountability, sanitizer accountability, immutability, transparency, privacy, and invisibility.*

5.5 The BFF$^+$09 Construction

Brzuska et al. [9] give a SSS construction that relies on a chameleon hash function but—unlike the constructions in [5] and [14]—they do not require the chameleon hash function to satisfy the uniqueness property. It therefore is an interesting candidate to be instantiated using the new construction in Sect. 3.1, without the need for the transform in Theorem 38. However, it turns out that an error in the security proof makes the signer accountability of the construction vulnerable to a generic attack. Therefore, this section is structured differently than the prior ones. First, we show that the security formalization of tagged chameleon hashes is unachievable and needs to be replaced in the construction by the tagged version of full collision resistance. Afterwards, we present the attack on signer accountability, which works irrespectively of the underlying building blocks. Still, the construction by Brzuska et al. can be instantiated with the chameleon hash function we constructed, merely missing the signer accountability. To achieve signer accountability as well, we can apply the transform in Theorem 38.

Idea of the Construction. We begin with a short description of the construction given in [9]. The full construction can be found in the full version of this paper. First, the message is divided into blocks. Admissible blocks are hashed using a tagged chameleon hash function. The signer computes the tag as the output of a pseudorandom function with a random input value and provides this random input as proof for the accountability. It then signs the output of the tagged chameleon hash function. The sanitizer can use its private key to find collisions on the chameleon hash function, however it chooses the tag randomly. While this ensures sanitizer accountability, we show that signer-accountability for this construction is unachievable, contrary to the claim in [9]. Indeed, there are two distinct errors in the presentation of [9]. First, the notion of *collision-resistance under random-tagging attacks*, which is a strong version of collision-resistance for chameleon hash functions, is too strong and in fact, cannot be achieved by any chameleon hash function. The reason is the oracle being too strong and the winning condition too weak. We present the generic attack here in detail. Second, the claimed signer-accountability does not hold independently of the chameleon hash function's security properties. We present an outline of the generic attack at the end of this section and the detailed proof in the full version of this paper.

Infeasibility of Random Tagging. To show security, Brzuska et al. [9] rely on different properties for the different SSS security notions. For signer accountability, they rely on the *collision-resistance under random-tagging attacks* of the used chameleon hash function. This security notion was developed along with the SSS construction and we describe it in Fig. 10.

$\mathsf{RndTag}^{\mathsf{CH}}_{\mathcal{A}}(\lambda)$

$(pk, sk) \leftarrow\$ \mathsf{CKGen}(1^\lambda)$
$(\mathrm{TAG}, \mu, r, \mathrm{TAG}', \mu', r') \leftarrow\$ \mathcal{A}^{\mathsf{Adapt}\mathcal{O}}(pk)$
$\textbf{return } 1 \textbf{ if } (\mathrm{TAG}, \mu) \neq (\mathrm{TAG}', \mu')$
$\wedge\ \mathsf{CH}(pk, \mathrm{TAG}, \mu, r) = \mathsf{CH}(pk, \mathrm{TAG}', \mu', r')$
$\wedge\ \{(\mathrm{TAG}, \mu), (\mathrm{TAG}', \mu')\} \neq \{(\mathrm{TAG}_i, \mu_i), (\mathrm{TAG}'_i, \mu'_i)\}$, for all $i = 1, \ldots, q$
$\wedge\ \{(\mathrm{TAG}, \mu), (\mathrm{TAG}', \mu')\} \neq \{(\mathrm{TAG}'_i, \mu'_i), (\mathrm{TAG}'_j, \mu'_j)\}$, for all $i, j = 1, \ldots, q$

$\mathsf{Adapt}\mathcal{O}(sk, \mathrm{TAG}_i, \mu_i, r_i, \mu'_i)$

$\mathrm{TAG}'_i \leftarrow\$ \{0, 1\}^{2n}$
$r'_i \leftarrow\$ \mathsf{CAdapt}(sk, \mathrm{TAG}_i, \mu_i, r_i, \mathrm{TAG}'_i, \mu'_i)$
Store $(\mathrm{TAG}_i, \mu_i), (\mathrm{TAG}'_i, \mu'_i)$
$\textbf{return } (\mathrm{TAG}'_i, r'_i)$

Fig. 10. Collision-resistance under random-tagging attacks from [9].

To exclude trivial wins, the game numbers the adversary's queries and stores them as (TAG_i, μ_i) and $(\mathrm{TAG}'_i, \mu'_i)$, for $i = 1, \ldots, q$. An adversary wins, if it can output a non-trivial collision $\mathsf{CH}(pk, \mathrm{TAG}, \mu, r) = \mathsf{CH}(pk, \mathrm{TAG}', \mu', r')$ with

$$\begin{aligned} &\{(\mathrm{TAG}, \mu), (\mathrm{TAG}', \mu')\} \neq \{(\mathrm{TAG}_i, \mu_i), (\mathrm{TAG}'_i, \mu'_i)\} \text{ for all } i, \\ \text{and} \quad &\{(\mathrm{TAG}, \mu), (\mathrm{TAG}', \mu')\} \neq \{(\mathrm{TAG}'_i, \mu'_i), (\mathrm{TAG}'_j, \mu'_j)\} \text{ for all } i, j. \end{aligned}$$

The former condition prevents the adversary to output a collision that it obtains from a single query to its oracle $\mathsf{Adapt}\mathcal{O}$. The latter prevents the adversary trivial transitive collisions: By querying the oracle $\mathsf{Adapt}\mathcal{O}$ twice on the same input for different target messages, as depicted on the left of Fig. 11.

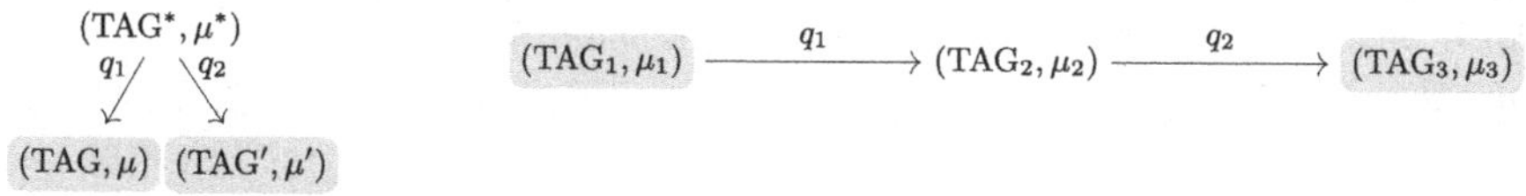

Fig. 11. Left: a trivial collision that is excluded in the security game. Right: a trivial collision that composes a generic attack on the security notion.

It turns out, that the two excluded types of trivial collisions do not suffice. In fact, the adversary can make an arbitrary query to the oracle $\mathsf{Adapt}\mathcal{O}$ and then make a second query on the response of the first query. Then, all three tuples collide, but the first and third as output, are not defined as a trivial win. This is depicted on the right of Fig. 11. In conclusion, *no* chameleon hash function can satisfy this security notion as stated in the theorem below.

Theorem 45. *Collision-resistance under random-tagging attacks is unachievable for any chameleon hash function.*

Proof. The attack idea is depicted in Fig. 11. Given a public key pk we define the attacker against collision-resistance under random-tagging attacks as follows: First, the adversary picks distinct messages μ_1, μ_2, and μ_3. Further it generates TAG_1 and r_1. Then, the adversary makes two queries to the oracle: first, query $(\mathrm{TAG}_1, \mu_1, r_1, \mu_2)$ to receive (TAG_2, r_2), second, $(\mathrm{TAG}_2, \mu_2, r_2, \mu_3)$ to receive (TAG_3, r_3). Thus, we have a collision of the hash values of $(pk, \mathrm{TAG}_1, \mu_1, r_1)$ and $(pk, \mathrm{TAG}_3, \mu_3, r_3)$, the definition of the oracle. The adversary returning $(\mathrm{TAG}_1, \mu_1, r_1)$ and $(\mathrm{TAG}_3, \mu_3, r_3)$ wins the game. Indeed, the collision is valid, as (TAG_1, μ_1) was never an output (hence the collision is not of the second form), and (TAG_1, μ_1) and (TAG_3, μ_3) were not part of the same query. $\square$

Signer-Accountability. Theorem 45 leaves a gap in the construction of [9] as no instantiation achieves signer accountability. A natural question that arises is whether the construction is secure if one strengthens the requirements towards the underlying chameleon hash function by excluding the transitivity attack that we described above. Here, we answer this question in the negative by providing a generic attack against the signer accountability.

We show that a signer can put the blame on a message to the sanitizer even though the sanitizer did not sanitize to this message. On a high-level, the attack works as follows. The signer prepares an arbitrary message containing two blocks $\mu_1 \| \mu_2$ such that only the second one is admissible. It then lets the sanitizer change the message to $\mu_1 \| \mu_2^*$. Finally, the adversary can create a signature on the message $\mu_1^* \| \mu_2^*$ by replacing the first message block. When questioned about the message $\mu_1^* \| \mu_2$ created by the signer, the judge will blame the sanitizer. This is stated formally in the following theorem, the proof is given in the full version of this paper.

Theorem 46. *There is an efficient adversary $\mathcal{A}$ that breaks signer accountability of the* BFF$^+$09 *construction with probability* 1*, using a single query to* $\mathsf{Sanit}\mathcal{O}$.

Instantiations. Finally, we want to apply our constructions in Sect. 3 to the construction by Brzuska et al. To account for the unachievable security notion for tagged chameleon hash functions, we refer to the full version of this paper for the notion of f-CR tagged chameleon hash functions, which can be constructed from a f-CRCHash as in Fig. 7. As uniqueness of the CHF is not required, we get the following result.

Corollary 47. *The construction by Brzuska et al. in [9] instantiated using a DSS from* {Dilithium, Falcon} *and the tagged chameleon hash function deduced from the chameleon hash in Fig. 7 as explained in the full version of this paper satisfies unforgeability, sanitizer accountability, immutability, transparency, and privacy.*

This follows from [9, Theorem 5.3], again noting that signer accountability does not hold. Using Theorem 38, we can increase the security to cover signer accountability.

Corollary 48. *The transform in Theorem 38 applied with the VRS given in Fig. 8 to the construction by Brzuska et al. in [9] as instantiated in Corollary 47, satisfies unforgeability, signer accountability, sanitizer accountability, immutability, transparency, and privacy.*

5.6 General Observations

Unfortunately, the efficiency of the proposed instantiations may be suboptimal for any real world use cases. For example, the signature of the construction of [14] instantiated securely with our building blocks and the transform of [13] contains an encryption of a chameleon hash trapdoor, i.e. an encryption of a G-trapdoor $\mathbf{R}$ for each message block. On the positive side, we do not impose inefficient requirements such as a superpolynomial modulus and the reduction losses are not substantial.

Corollary 49. *There exists an SSS construction that has unforgeability, signer accountability, sanitizer accountability, immutability, transparency, privacy, and invisibility in the random oracle model, if LWE and LWR and SIS with polynomial modulus are hard.*

Furthermore, we expect our building blocks and thus the generic constructions of SSS to carry over to ring or module lattices in a straightforward fashion.

An additional drawback is the necessary inclusion of the transform of [13] for many SSS constructions, which incurs the cost of a NIZK. However, a secure construction without this transformation requires uniqueness of the chameleon hash function, which seems highly non-trivial for lattice-based constructions. Previous non lattice-based constructions used bijections to ensure that only one auxiliary value exists, thus even with a trapdoor an adversary cannot find a second auxiliary value to break uniqueness. Lattice-based trapdoored functions, especially ones used in conjunction with PreSample, have many different preimages for each image by design, which leads us to believe that a chameleon hash achieving uniqueness requires a fundamentally different approach to trapdoor its hash function.

References

1. Ajtai, M.: Generating hard instances of lattice problems (extended abstract). In: 28th ACM STOC, pp. 99–108. ACM Press, May 1996. https://doi.org/10.1145/237814.237838
2. Ateniese, G., Chou, D.H., de Medeiros, B., Tsudik, G.: Sanitizable signatures. In: di Vimercati, S.C., Syverson, P., Gollmann, D. (eds.) ESORICS 2005. LNCS, vol. 3679, pp. 159–177. Springer, Heidelberg (2005). https://doi.org/10.1007/11555827_10
3. Banerjee, A., Peikert, C., Rosen, A.: Pseudorandom functions and lattices. In: Pointcheval, D., Johansson, T. (eds.) EUROCRYPT 2012. LNCS, vol. 7237, pp. 719–737. Springer, Heidelberg (2012). https://doi.org/10.1007/978-3-642-29011-4_42
4. Baum, C., Damgård, I., Lyubashevsky, V., Oechsner, S., Peikert, C.: More efficient commitments from structured lattice assumptions. In: Catalano, D., De Prisco, R. (eds.) SCN 2018. LNCS, vol. 11035, pp. 368–385. Springer, Cham (2018). https://doi.org/10.1007/978-3-319-98113-0_20
5. Beck, M.T., et al.: Practical strongly invisible and strongly accountable sanitizable signatures. In: Pieprzyk, J., Suriadi, S. (eds.) ACISP 2017. LNCS, vol. 10342, pp. 437–452. Springer, Cham (2017). https://doi.org/10.1007/978-3-319-60055-0_23
6. Bernhard, D., Fuchsbauer, G., Ghadafi, E., Smart, N.P., Warinschi, B.: Anonymous attestation with user-controlled linkability. Int. J. Inf. Sec. **12**(3), 219–249 (2013). https://doi.org/10.1007/S10207-013-0191-Z
7. Blömer, J., Bobolz, J., Porzenheim, L.: A generic construction of an anonymous reputation system and instantiations from lattices. In: Guo, J., Steinfeld, R. (eds.) ASIACRYPT 2023. LNCS, vol. 14439, pp. 418–452. Springer, Singapore (2023). https://doi.org/10.1007/978-981-99-8724-5_13

8. Bootle, J., Lyubashevsky, V., Nguyen, N.K., Sorniotti, A.: A framework for practical anonymous credentials from lattices. In: Guo, J., Steinfeld, R. (eds.) ASIACRYPT 2023. LNCS, vol. 14439, pp. 384–417. Springer, Singapore (2023). https://doi.org/10.1007/978-3-031-38545-2_13
9. Brzuska, C., et al.: Security of sanitizable signatures revisited. In: Jarecki, S., Tsudik, G. (eds.) PKC 2009. LNCS, vol. 5443, pp. 317–336. Springer, Heidelberg (2009). https://doi.org/10.1007/978-3-642-00468-1_18
10. Brzuska, C., Fischlin, M., Lehmann, A., Schröder, D.: Unlinkability of sanitizable signatures. In: Nguyen, P.Q., Pointcheval, D. (eds.) PKC 2010. LNCS, vol. 6056, pp. 444–461. Springer, Heidelberg (2010). https://doi.org/10.1007/978-3-642-13013-7_26
11. Brzuska, C., Fischlin, M., Lehmann, A., Schröder, D.: Sanitizable signatures: how to partially delegate control for authenticated data. In: BIOSIG 2009. Gesellschaft für Informatik e.V., Bonn, pp. 117–128 (2009). ISBN 978-3-88579-249-1
12. Brzuska, C., Pöhls, H.C., Samelin, K.: Non-interactive public accountability for sanitizable signatures. In: De Capitani di Vimercati, S., Mitchell, C. (eds.) EuroPKI 2012. LNCS, vol. 7868, pp. 178–193. Springer, Heidelberg (2013). https://doi.org/10.1007/978-3-642-40012-4_12
13. Bultel, X., Lafourcade, P., Lai, R.W.F., Malavolta, G., Schröder, D., Thyagarajan, S.A.K.: Efficient invisible and unlinkable sanitizable signatures. In: Lin, D., Sako, K. (eds.) PKC 2019. LNCS, vol. 11442, pp. 159–189. Springer, Cham (2019). https://doi.org/10.1007/978-3-030-17253-4_6
14. Camenisch, J., Derler, D., Krenn, S., Pöhls, H.C., Samelin, K., Slamanig, D.: Chameleon-hashes with ephemeral trapdoors. In: Fehr, S. (ed.) PKC 2017. LNCS, vol. 10175, pp. 152–182. Springer, Heidelberg (2017). https://doi.org/10.1007/978-3-662-54388-7_6
15. Canard, S., Jambert, A.: On extended sanitizable signature schemes. In: Pieprzyk, J. (ed.) CT-RSA 2010. LNCS, vol. 5985, pp. 179–194. Springer, Heidelberg (2010). https://doi.org/10.1007/978-3-642-11925-5_13
16. Cash, D., Hofheinz, D., Kiltz, E., Peikert, C.: Bonsai trees, or how to delegate a lattice basis. In: Gilbert, H. (ed.) EUROCRYPT 2010. LNCS, vol. 6110, pp. 523–552. Springer, Heidelberg (2010). https://doi.org/10.1007/978-3-642-13190-5_27
17. Derler, D., Samelin, K., Slamanig, D.: Bringing order to chaos: the case of collision-resistant Chameleon-Hashes. In: Kiayias, A., Kohlweiss, M., Wallden, P., Zikas, V. (eds.) PKC 2020. LNCS, vol. 12110, pp. 462–492. Springer, Cham (2020). https://doi.org/10.1007/978-3-030-45374-9_16
18. Esgin, M.F., Steinfeld, R., Liu, D., Ruj, S.: Efficient hybrid exact/relaxed lattice proofs and applications to rounding and VRFs. In: Handschuh, H., Lysyanskaya, A. (eds.) CRYPTO 2023. LNCS, vol. 14085, pp. 484–517. Springer, Cham (2023). https://doi.org/10.1007/978-3-031-38554-4_16
19. Fischlin, M., Harasser, P.: Invisible sanitizable signatures and public-key encryption are equivalent. In: Preneel, B., Vercauteren, F. (eds.) ACNS 2018. LNCS, vol. 10892, pp. 202–220. Springer, Cham (2018). https://doi.org/10.1007/978-3-319-93387-0_11
20. Fleischhacker, N., Krupp, J., Malavolta, G., Schneider, J., Schröder, D., Simkin, M.: Efficient unlinkable sanitizable signatures from signatures with re-randomizable keys. In: Cheng, C.-M., Chung, K.-M., Persiano, G., Yang, B.-Y. (eds.) PKC 2016. LNCS, vol. 9614, pp. 301–330. Springer, Heidelberg (2016). https://doi.org/10.1007/978-3-662-49384-7_12

21. Gentry, C., Peikert, C., Vaikuntanathan, V.: Trapdoors for hard lattices and new cryptographic constructions. In: Ladner, R.E., Dwork, C. (eds.) 40th ACM STOC, pp. 197–206. ACM Press, May 2008. https://doi.org/10.1145/1374376.1374407
22. Janson, C., Struck, P.: Sponge-based authenticated encryption: security against quantum attackers. In: Handschuh, H., Lysyanskaya, A. (eds.) CRYPTO 2023. LNCS, vol. 14085, pp. 230–259. Springer, Cham (2023). https://doi.org/10.1007/978-3-031-17234-2_12
23. Katsumata, S.: A new simple technique to bootstrap various lattice zero-knowledge proofs to QROM secure NIZKs. In: Malkin, T., Peikert, C. (eds.) CRYPTO 2021. LNCS, vol. 12826, pp. 580–610. Springer, Cham (2021). https://doi.org/10.1007/978-3-030-84245-1_20
24. Klonowski, M., Lauks, A.: Extended sanitizable signatures. In: Rhee, M.S., Lee, B. (eds.) ICISC 2006. LNCS, vol. 4296, pp. 343–355. Springer, Heidelberg (2006). https://doi.org/10.1007/11927587_28
25. Krawczyk, H., Rabin, T.: Chameleon Signatures. In: NDSS 2000. The Internet Society, February 2000
26. Krenn, S., Samelin, K., Sommer, D.: Stronger security for sanitizable signatures. In: Garcia-Alfaro, J., Navarro-Arribas, G., Aldini, A., Martinelli, F., Suri, N. (eds.) DPM/QASA -2015. LNCS, vol. 9481, pp. 100–117. Springer, Cham (2016). https://doi.org/10.1007/978-3-319-29883-2_7
27. Lai, R.W.F., Zhang, T., Chow, S.S.M., Schröder, D.: Efficient sanitizable signatures without random oracles. In: Askoxylakis, I., Ioannidis, S., Katsikas, S., Meadows, C. (eds.) ESORICS 2016. LNCS, vol. 9878, pp. 363–380. Springer, Cham (2016). https://doi.org/10.1007/978-3-319-45744-4_18
28. Li, Y., Liu, S.: Tagged chameleon hash from lattices and application to redactable blockchain. In: Tang, Q., Teague, V. (eds.) PKC 2024. LNCS, vol. 14603, pp. 288–320. Springer, Cham (2024). https://doi.org/10.1007/978-3-031-57725-3_10
29. Libert, B., Ling, S., Nguyen, K., Wang, H.: Zero-knowledge arguments for lattice-based accumulators: logarithmic-size ring signatures and group signatures without trapdoors. In: Fischlin, M., Coron, J.-S. (eds.) EUROCRYPT 2016. LNCS, vol. 9666, pp. 1–31. Springer, Heidelberg (2016). https://doi.org/10.1007/978-3-662-49896-5_1
30. Lyubashevsky, V., Nguyen, N.K.: BLOOM: bimodal lattice one-out-of-many proofs and applications. In: Tang, Q., Teague, V. (eds.) PKC 2024. LNCS, vol. 14603, pp. 95–125. Springer, Cham (2024). https://doi.org/10.1007/978-3-031-22972-5_4
31. Lyubashevsky, V., Nguyen, N.K., Plançon, M.: Lattice-based zero-knowledge proofs and applications: shorter, simpler, and more general. In: Dodis, Y., Shrimpton, T. (eds.) CRYPTO 2022. LNCS, vol. 13508, pp. 71– 101. Springer, Cham (2022). https://doi.org/10.1007/978-3-031-15979-4_3
32. Micciancio, D., Peikert, C.: Trapdoors for lattices: simpler, tighter, faster, smaller. In: Pointcheval, D., Johansson, T. (eds.) EUROCRYPT 2012. LNCS, vol. 7237, pp. 700–718. Springer, Heidelberg (2012). https://doi.org/10.1007/978-3-642-29011-4_41
33. Park, S., Sealfon, A.: It wasn't Me! In: Boldyreva, A., Micciancio, D. (eds.) CRYPTO 2019. LNCS, vol. 11694, pp. 159–190. Springer, Cham (2019). https://doi.org/10.1007/978-3-030-26954-8_6
34. Shamir, A., Tauman, Y.: Improved online/offline signature schemes. In: Kilian, J. (ed.) CRYPTO 2001. LNCS, vol. 2139, pp. 355–367. Springer, Heidelberg (2001). https://doi.org/10.1007/3-540-44647-8_21

Giant Does NOT Mean Strong: Cryptanalysis of BQTRU

Ali Raya[1(✉)], Vikas Kumar[2], Aditi Kar Gangopadhyay[2], and Sugata Gangopadhyay[1]

[1] Department of Computer Science and Engineering, Indian Institute of Technology Roorkee, Roorkee 247667, Uttarakhand, India
{ali_r,sugata.gangopadhyay}@cs.iitr.ac.in
[2] Department of Mathematics, Indian Institute of Technology Roorkee, Roorkee 247667, Uttarakhand, India
{v_kumar,aditi.gangopadhyay}@ma.iitr.ac.in

Abstract. NTRU-like constructions are among the most studied lattice-based schemes. The freedom of design of NTRU resulted in many variants in literature motivated by faster computations or more resistance against lattice attacks by changing the underlying algebra. To the best of our knowledge, BQTRU (DCC 2017), a noncommutative NTRU-like cryptosystem, is the fastest claimed variant of NTRU built over the quaternion algebra of the bivariate ring of polynomials. The key generation and the encryption of BQTRU are claimed to be 16/7 times faster than standard NTRU for equivalent levels of security. For key recovery attacks, the authors claim that retrieving a decryption key is equivalent to solving the Shortest Vector Problem (SVP) in expanded Euclidean lattices of giant dimensions. This work disproves this claim and proposes practical key and message recovery attacks that break the moderate parameter sets of BQTRU estimated to achieve 2^{92} message security and 2^{166} key security on a standard desktop within less than two core weeks. Furthermore, our analysis shows that the proposed parameter set for the highest security level claiming 2^{212} message security and 2^{396} key security can barely achieve 2^{82} message security and 2^{125} key security. Our work not only provides cryptanalysis for BQTRU but also demonstrates the potential of extending Gentry's attack to other rings beyond the cyclotomic polynomial ring.

Keywords: Post-quantum cryptography · Lattice · NTRU · BQTRU · Quaternion algebra

1 Introduction

NTRU [19] is one of the initial and extensively studied lattice-based post-quantum cryptosystems. It is known for its efficiency, low memory requirements, and long cryptanalytic history. Its design flexibility allows the construction of new schemes with different algebras. NTRU proposals [10,23] that proceeded

R. Niederhagen and M.-J. O. Saarinen (Eds.): PQCrypto 2025, LNCS 15577, pp. 312–348, 2025.
https://doi.org/10.1007/978-3-031-86599-2_11

to the final round of NIST's post-quantum standardization process are built over commutative rings of polynomials. However, there is also growing interest in utilizing noncommutative algebras within the NTRU framework motivated by improved performance or resistance against some attacks. Recently, Raya et al. [37,38] and Kumar et al. [28,29] designed variants of NTRU over the group rings of the noncommutative groups. The quaternion algebra has also been investigated in the context of designing noncommutative NTRU-like cryptosystems. QTRU [34] is built upon the quaternion algebra of the ring of polynomials. It is claimed to be more resistant to lattice attacks than NTRU, with a performance trade-off of 4 times slower than NTRU for equivalent security levels. Ling and Mendelsohn [32] theoretically introduced an IND-CPA secure variant of NTRU using quaternion algebra of bounded discriminant.

BQTRU [5] is a noncommutative variant of NTRU built upon the quaternion algebra of the bivariate ring of polynomials. The scheme's security is claimed to be based on hard problems in hybrid lattices rather than the usual Euclidean lattices. Hybrid lattices are algebraic objects that provide a way to combine two mainstream post-quantum families, lattice-based and code-based cryptography. Hence, they can be used to build cryptosystems whose security relies upon hard problems in lattices and codes.

BQTRU is a timely advancement of a series of works beginning with GB-NTRU [9] that uses a *hidden ideal* of a bivariate ring of polynomials for key construction and decryption. Although deciphering is more costly, GB-NTRU claimed to improve the encryption costs compared to NTRU. Boschini et al. [8] showed that GB-NTRU can be interpreted as a cryptosystem over hybrid lattices combining Euclidean and Hamming distances. GB-NTRU was shown to be vulnerable to some algebraic attacks on messages [8]. In the same work [8], NTWO was proposed as a modification to address the vulnerabilities of GB-NTRU. Similarly to GB-NTRU, the decryption process of NTWO is costly as it involves solving a hard lattice problem. Consequently, NTWO failed to provide a practical alternative to NTRU but introduced an interesting application of hybrid lattices as a proof-of-concept. The advertised attractive feature of NTWO is its enhanced key security, which makes lattice-based key attacks almost infeasible. According to the authors, the secret key is the shortest vector in the hybrid lattice and, hence, cannot be recovered by usual lattice reduction algorithms. One can map the secret to the short vector of purely Euclidean lattice but with such an extended dimension where the complexity of lattice reduction algorithms is too high to be practical.

Motivation Behind Cryptanalysis. BQTRU is the blend of NTWO and QTRU. The authors claim that it inherits the amplified key security due to its hybrid lattice structure, and the quaternion algebra makes the decryption possible, which was a bottleneck in the previous designs. It is claimed to be the fastest variant of NTRU in the literature, with key generation and encryption being 16/7 times faster compared to NTRU. Additionally, the noncommutativity of BQTRU could be an extra advantage from a security standpoint, as some attacks could exploit the commutative structure. For instance, Kim and Lee [25] and Bai et al. [6] demonstrated attacks on the NTRU Learning Problem [36, Section 4.4.4] by leveraging the commutativity to recover the secret key, as discussed and motivated in [29,37].

Despite these promising features and theoretical soundness, BQTRU has a few shortcomings. The lack of robust security analysis and implementation raises concerns about its practical suitability, prompting us to delve into its security and implementation aspects. Our study identified technical weaknesses that render the cryptosystem susceptible to attacks. We successfully compromised the keys and messages for the proposed moderate-level security parameters and proved that the highest-level security parameters do not provide the claimed security. Interestingly, we discovered that the specific structure of the chosen quaternion algebra, intended to improve performance, actually weakens the security of the cryptosystem. Therefore, our work highlights the significance of addressing new security vulnerabilities arising from changing the underlying algebra for fast multiplications. In brief, this work provides a perspective to generalize Gentry's dimension reduction attack [17] on NTRU-composite over the commutative ring of polynomials $R' = \mathbb{Z}[x]/\langle x^N - 1\rangle$ (N composite) to the noncommutative algebra of quaternions. Gentry's approach is based on the Chinese Remainder Theorem (CRT) that factors the ring R' into polynomial rings of smaller degrees. Here, we provide a different frame of view to look for the possibilities of dimension reduction in a particular algebraic structure using the matrix representations and *folding* them to reduce dimensions. We find our method easy to implement, and the concept of dealing with matrices may extend its applicability to other algebras.

1.1 Technical Overview

Simply put, a parameter set that achieves a certain security level λ for a specific construction indicates that an adversary requires at least 2^λ operations to break the scheme using the best-known attacks. Lattice attacks are the most successful attacks against NTRU-like constructions. In the first proposal of NTRU introduced over the truncated polynomial ring $\mathbb{Z}[x]/\langle x^N - 1\rangle$ for prime N and modulus q, the public key is calculated as $h = f^{-1} * g \pmod q$ for ternary polynomials f and g with f being invertible modulo q. Key recovery attack against NTRU is mapped into finding the vector $(\boldsymbol{f}, \boldsymbol{g})$ associated with the private key or its rotations in the lattice Λ_{CS} [13], also referred to as Coppersmith and Shamir lattice, generated by the basis matrix $\begin{pmatrix} I_N & \mathcal{H} \\ 0_N & qI_N \end{pmatrix}$, where $\mathcal{H}$ is a circulant matrix constructed from h; the i–th row of $\mathcal{H}$ is calculated as $x^i * h \mod (x^N - 1)$, for $i = 0, 1, \ldots, N-1$.

For BQTRU, the public key is calculated as $h = f^{-1} * g + v \pmod q$, where f, g, and v are sampled from the quaternion algebra of the bivariate ring of polynomials denoted by $\mathbb{A}$ (as detailed in Sect. 3) with the following conditions:

- f, g are ternary elements (i.e., small in Euclidean norm), and f is invertible modulo q and a *private ideal* of $\mathbb{A}$.

- v has just a small number of non-zero coefficients with respect to the Lagrange basis (i.e., small in Hamming weight).

Since v does not need to have small coefficients as in f, g, the authors claim that any search attack to retrieve the decryption key (f, g, v) is extremely costly and much harder than that for the original NTRU. Additionally, lattice attacks are not as efficient as NTRU key recovery attacks since the problem of finding the decryption key is mapped into finding short vectors in expanded Euclidean lattices of extremely large dimensions.

This work disproves this claim and shows that getting a possible decryption key in BQTRU is much easier than the original NTRU for equivalent dimensions. Our key recovery attack involves two main steps: ① guessing step, ② lattice reduction step. We show that according to the procedure of the proposed key generation in BQTRU, guessing **the positions** of the non-zero coefficients of v (with respect to Lagrange basis) is enough to correctly retrieve v. After retrieving v correctly, one can compute $s = h - v \pmod q$ and proceed using lattice reduction attacks against Euclidean lattices to find a short vector $(\boldsymbol{f}, \boldsymbol{g})$ as in the case of the original NTRU. It may look like finding a decryption key is at least as hard as that for the original NTRU in the same dimension, as the attacker needs to guess the positions of nonzero elements before proceeding with the lattice reduction. However, the lattice $\mathcal{L}_{CS}$ associated with BQTRU, is generated from the basis

$$\mathcal{B}_{CS} = \begin{pmatrix} I_N & \mathcal{S} \\ 0_N & qI_N \end{pmatrix} \tag{1}$$

where $N = 4n^2$ for quaternion algebras of the bivariate ring of polynomials, and $\mathcal{S}$ is the matrix corresponding to s that has a special structure:

$$\mathcal{S} = \begin{pmatrix} S_0 & S_1 & S_2 & S_3 \\ S_1 & S_0 & S_3 & S_2 \\ S_2 & -S_3 & S_0 & -S_1 \\ -S_3 & S_2 & -S_1 & S_0 \end{pmatrix}. \tag{2}$$

Our dimension reduction method, which we call *folding*, exploits the structure of $\mathcal{S}$, and define a map from $\mathcal{S}$ to a matrix of half the dimension given by

$$\phi(\mathcal{S}) \longrightarrow \begin{pmatrix} S_0 + S_1 & S_2 + S_3 \\ S_2 - S_3 & S_0 - S_1 \end{pmatrix} \tag{3}$$

that preserves the matrix addition and multiplication. Therefore, instead of looking for the short vector $(\boldsymbol{f}, \boldsymbol{g}) \in \mathcal{L}_{CS}$, we look for its image in the lattice $\mathcal{L}_{CS,\phi}$ generated by the basis

$$\mathcal{B}_{CS,\phi} = \begin{pmatrix} I_{N/2} & \phi(\mathcal{S}) \\ 0_{N/2} & qI_{N/2} \end{pmatrix}. \tag{4}$$

Finding this image in $\mathcal{L}_{CS,\phi}$ is much easier for a lattice reduction algorithm like BKZ [39] as the dimension of the lattice is reduced by a factor of 2, while the norm of the target vector (on average) does not increase. Overall, combining the costs of the guessing step and the lattice reduction step is more beneficial for attacking the cryptosystem and retrieving the decryption key. Furthermore, the idea of key *folding* attack is extended to the message recovery attack against the lattice generated from BQTRU's ciphertext. This work proves the efficiency of our folding attack theoretically and cross-validates the results experimentally.

1.2 Our Work

Implementation of BQTRU. We provide an implementation of BQTRU for a better understanding of the practical aspects of the cryptosystem. Our findings identify some issues related to the key generation process proposed in the original work, as well as some other problems related to the decryption failure and possible alternative keys.

Efficient Key and Message Recovery Attacks. We propose an efficient key and message recovery attack against BQTRU. For a key recovery attack, instead of considering only the authors' search cost or the proposed lattice reduction in expanded lattices, we consider a combined approach that searches for some values of the key before converting the key retrieval attack into reducing a structured lattice of lower dimension that is further susceptible to dimension reduction attacks. For message recovery attacks, similarly, we show that one can benefit from the structure of the underlying ring to launch an attack in a lattice of smaller dimensions compared to the original NTRU. Using our approach, we estimate that the proposed parameter sets of BQTRU achieve much lower security levels than claimed, as shown in Fig. 1 and Table 4. Further, this work experimentally breaks the moderate parameter set of claimed key security 2^{166} and message security 2^{92} just in less than 12 core days (on average) for key and message attacks on a standard desktop.

How NOT to Fix BQTRU. We provide our attempts to fix the BQTRU cryptosystem against the proposed attacks, especially the key recovery attack. These attempts originated from the trials to change the key generation process to make the guessing part harder for an attacker. However, we managed to show that an extension of the proposed attack can be applied even against the new proposal. We consider these attempts unsuccessful and advise against using them in future efforts to fix BQTRU.

Our artifacts for the experiment with a detailed documentation can be accessed at https://github.com/The-Isogeniest/BQTRU_Cryptanalysis.

1.3 Road Map

Section 2 introduces the preliminaries and notations and briefly discusses the lattice attacks on NTRU-like constructions. Section 3 describes BQTRU and its relation to hybrid lattices. Section 4 is about the security claims by authors of BQTRU regarding keys and messages. In Sect. 5, we propose our key and message attacks, while Sect. 6 experimentally verifies the correctness of our attacks along

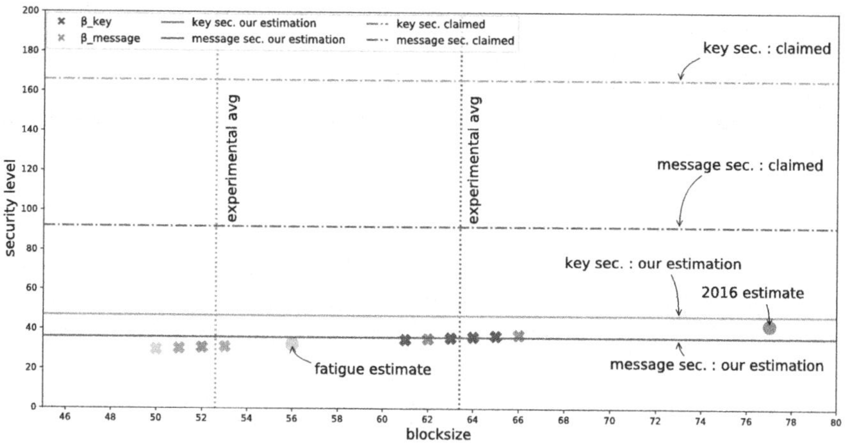

Fig. 1. The claimed vs. our estimation of the security level for the moderate parameter set of BQTRU ($n = 7$ and $q = 113$). The original proposal of BQTRU estimates the key security to be greater than 2^{166}−bit and the message security to be 2^{92}−bit. On the other hand, our estimation shows that the key security and the message security provide no more than 2^{47} and 2^{37}−bit security level and hence can be broken on a standard desktop within 2 core weeks, approximately. Although the experimentally obtained blocksizes for the key attack are lower than for the message attack, our *worst-case* estimate for the key security is higher than the message as the key attack involves guessing and lattice reduction, whereas the message is straightforwardly based on lattice reduction.

with a cost analysis. Section 7 gives a few of our unsuccessful attempts to fix BQTRU. We conclude our work in Sect. 8.

2 Preliminaries

2.1 Notations

- $\mathbb{Z}, \mathbb{R}$ denote the set of integers and real numbers, respectively.
- For a positive integer q, $\mathbb{Z}_q$ is the ring of integers modulo q, and $\mathbb{Z}_q^\star$ is the group of units, i.e., group of invertible elements in $\mathbb{Z}_q$.
- For a set A, $|A|$ is the cardinality of A, and $a \xleftarrow{\$} A$ denotes sampling an element a uniformly at random from A.
- For any ring R and a positive integer m, $R^m = \{(a_1, a_2, \ldots, a_m) : a_i \in R\}$, and $M_m(R)$ denotes the ring of $m \times m$ matrices with entries from R.
- The symbols $*$ and $\star$, respectively, denote the multiplication of elements of the underlying algebraic structure and the multiplication of their associated vectors. The underlying algebras should be clear from the context. Further, $\star$ is also used to denote matrix multiplication.
- The symbol $\otimes$ denotes the Kronecker product of matrices.

- For a vector $\boldsymbol{v} = (v_1, v_2, \ldots, v_m) \in \mathbb{R}^m$, the Euclidean norm of $\boldsymbol{v}$ is defined as $||\boldsymbol{v}|| = \sqrt{\sum_{i=1}^{m} v_i^2}$, and for a vector $\boldsymbol{v} = (v_1, v_2, \ldots, v_m) \in \mathbb{Z}_q^m$, the Hamming norm of $\boldsymbol{v}$ is defined as $||\boldsymbol{v}||_H = |\{i : v_i \neq 0\}|$.
- $A \cong B$ denotes that two algebraic structures A and B are isomorphic to each other.

2.2 Lattices: Definitions and Reductions

Definition 1 (Lattice). *Let B be a $d \times m$ matrix with d linearly independent rows $\{\boldsymbol{b}_0, \boldsymbol{b}_1, \ldots, \boldsymbol{b}_{d-1}\} \subset \mathbb{R}^m$. The lattice generated by B is defined as*

$$\mathcal{L}_B = \mathbb{Z}^d B = \left\{ \sum_{i=0}^{d-1} \gamma_i \boldsymbol{b}_i : \gamma_i \in \mathbb{Z} \right\}. \tag{5}$$

The matrix B is called the basis matrix for the lattice $\mathcal{L}_B$. Here, d, i.e., the number of linearly independent rows in the basis matrix, is called the *rank*, and m is called the *dimension* of $\mathcal{L}_B$. The lattice is referred to as *full-rank* if $d = m$. If $\boldsymbol{b}_i \in \mathbb{Z}^m$, we call the lattice to be an *integral lattice.* For this work, we consider full-rank integral lattices. The volume of a lattice $\mathcal{L}_B$ defined by a basis matrix B is given by $vol(\mathcal{L}_B) = \sqrt{|det(BB^{Tr})|}$, and it is independent of the choice of basis. For $i \in \{0, 1, \ldots, d-1\}$, define π_i to be the projection on the space orthogonal to the span of $\{\boldsymbol{b}_0, \ldots \boldsymbol{b}_{i-1}\}$, and denote Gram-Schmidt basis as $\{\boldsymbol{b}_0^\star, \boldsymbol{b}_1^\star, \ldots \boldsymbol{b}_{d-1}^\star\}$, where $\boldsymbol{b}_i^\star = \pi_i(\boldsymbol{b}_i)$. We refer to the lattice generated from $\{\pi_\ell(\boldsymbol{b}_\ell), \ldots, \pi_\ell(\boldsymbol{b}_{r-1})\}$ as the projected sublattice and denote it by $\mathcal{L}_{B[\ell,r)}$. We refer to the lengths of $||\boldsymbol{b}_i^\star||$ for $i \in \{0, 1, \ldots, d-1\}$ as the profile of the basis B.

Definition 2 ($q-$ary lattice). *A lattice of dimension d is called $q-$ary lattice if $q\mathbb{Z}^d \subset \mathcal{L}_B$ for some $q > 0$.*

Definition 3 (Minimum length). *The minimum length $\lambda_1(\mathcal{L})$ of a lattice $\mathcal{L}$ is defined as the length of its shortest nonzero vector, i.e., $\lambda_1(\mathcal{L}) = \min_{\boldsymbol{v} \in \mathcal{L}-\{0\}} ||\boldsymbol{v}||$.*

Definition 4 (Gaussian heuristics). *Given a random $d-$dimensional lattice $\mathcal{L}_B$ defined by basis B, Gaussian heuristic estimates that the expected length of the shortest nonzero vector in $\mathcal{L}_B$ is*

$$\lambda_1(\mathcal{L}_B) \approx \sqrt{\frac{d}{2\pi e}} vol(\mathcal{L}_B)^{\frac{1}{d}}. \tag{6}$$

Definition 5 (Hard lattice problems). *Let $\mathcal{L}_B \subset \mathbb{R}^d$ be a full-rank lattice defined by the basis B.*

1. *Shortest Vector Problem (SVP): Find a nonzero vector $\boldsymbol{v} \in \mathcal{L}_B$ such that $||\boldsymbol{v}|| = \lambda_1(\mathcal{L}_B)$.*
2. *Closest Vector Problem (CVP): Find a vector $\boldsymbol{v} \in \mathcal{L}_B$ closest to the given target vector $\boldsymbol{t} \in \mathbb{R}^d$, i.e., $||\boldsymbol{v} - \boldsymbol{t}|| \leq ||\boldsymbol{w} - \boldsymbol{t}||$ for all $\boldsymbol{w} \in \mathcal{L}_B$. Further, when $||\boldsymbol{v} - \boldsymbol{t}|| < \alpha\lambda_1(\mathcal{L}_B)$ for some $\alpha < 1$, the problem is referred to as the Bounded Distance Decoding (BDD) problem.*

The Kannan embedding technique [24] transforms the problem of solving the Closest Vector Problem (CVP) in a $d-$dimensional lattice into solving the Shortest Vector Problem (SVP) in a $(d+1)-$dimensional lattice. For instance, finding the closest vector in the lattice $\mathcal{L}_B$ (generated by basis B) to the target vector $\boldsymbol{t} \in \mathbb{R}^d$ can be converted into solving the SVP in the lattice generated by the basis

$$B' = \begin{pmatrix} B & 0 \\ \boldsymbol{t} & u \end{pmatrix} \tag{7}$$

where $u \in \mathbb{R}$ is the embedding factor (usually 1).

2.3 Lattice Reduction

There are infinitely many bases to define a lattice of dimension ≥2. From the attacker's perspective, some bases are more friendly to launch lattice attacks against the public key and, therefore, described as *'good'* basis. Compared to *'bad'* basis, good ones are defined with a set of reasonably short and almost orthogonal vectors. Given a publicly available bad basis, a lattice reduction algorithm tries to find a good basis that defines the same lattice. LLL [31] is a famous example of a polynomial-time basis reduction algorithm that produces a reasonably reduced good basis for low dimensions. Although LLL runs in polynomial time, the quality of the reduced basis degrades as the dimension of the lattice increases. BKZ [39] can be thought of as a generalization of LLL that considers an additional parameter: the blocksize or β.

Definition 6 (BKZ). *A basis $B = \{\boldsymbol{b}_0, \boldsymbol{b}_1, \dots, \boldsymbol{b}_{d-1}\}$ is called BKZ$-\beta$ reduced if*

$$\|\boldsymbol{b}_\kappa^\star\| = \lambda_1(\mathcal{L}_{B[\kappa:min(\kappa+\beta,d))}) \quad \textit{for all} \quad \kappa = 0, \dots, d-1.$$

For each $\kappa \in \{0, 1, \dots, d-1\}$, the BKZ algorithm calls internally an SVP oracle to find the shortest vector in the projected sublattice $\mathcal{L}_{B[\kappa:min(\kappa+\beta,d))}$. Repeating this process for all the indices is called a BKZ tour, and the algorithm keeps on applying tours until the condition is satisfied for all the positions. The most expensive part of generating the BKZ$-\beta$ reduced basis is due to calling the SVP oracle while the number of the tours is polynomially bounded. Enumeration [16, 35] and Sieving [7,18] are commonly used techniques in the oracle. Although the memory requirements for enumeration are polynomial, the running time is super-exponential in the blocksize β. On the other hand, memory and time requirements for sieving are both exponential in β.

Several improvements have been introduced to BKZ, resulting in BKZ2.0 [12] and progressive BKZ [4]. Progressive BKZ reduces the running time in practice while instead of running many tours for a blocksize β, the algorithm applies a few tours for increasing blocksizes up to β. Generally, the quality of a BKZ$-\beta$ reduced basis is measured by a quantity called the root Hermite factor.

Definition 7 (Root Hermite factor). *For a d−dimensional lattice $\mathcal{L}_B$, the root Hermite factor is defined as*

$$\delta_\beta = \left(\|\boldsymbol{b}_1\| / vol(\mathcal{L}_B)^{1/d} \right)^{1/d}. \tag{8}$$

For a small blocksize β, the root Hermite factor can be computed experimentally, while Chen [11] showed that for reasonably large $\beta > 50$, δ_β can be estimated as

$$\delta_\beta = \left(\frac{\beta}{2\pi e} (\pi\beta)^{\frac{1}{\beta}} \right)^{\frac{1}{2(\beta-1)}}. \tag{9}$$

This leads to the Geometry Series Assumption(GSA) that heuristically estimates the profile for a BKZ−β reduced basis.

Definition 8 (Geometry Series Assumption). *Let $B = \{\boldsymbol{b}_0, \boldsymbol{b}_1, \ldots, \boldsymbol{b}_{d-1}\}$ be a BKZ−β reduced basis, then the GSA estimates that $\|\boldsymbol{b}_i^\star\| \approx \delta_\beta{}^{-2} \|\boldsymbol{b}_{i-1}^\star\|$.*

The accuracy of the GSA is observed for sufficiently large blocksizes ($\beta > 50$ and $\beta \ll d$) when BKZ is applied to random lattices.

2.4 Lattice Attack Against NTRU-Like Constructions

Since its introduction in 1998, several versions of NTRU have emerged in the literature. NTRU is now recognized as a hard problem in cryptography rather than a unique cryptosystem that can be extended to different algebraic structures. The NTRU design and the problem can be outlined as:

Definition 9 (NTRU). *Let N be a prime, q be a positive integer, and $f, g \in \mathbb{Z}[x]/\langle x^N - 1\rangle$ be two polynomials with small coefficients (mostly ternary) such that f is invertible modulo q. The pair (f, g) forms the secret key and $h = f^{-1} * g \pmod q \in \mathbb{Z}_q[x]/\langle x^N - 1\rangle$ is the public key. The NTRU problem asks to find the private key or its rotations $(x^i * f, x^i * g)$.*

As discussed earlier, the most renowned technique to attack the NTRU problem is to solve SVP in the $2N$−dimensional lattice Λ_{CS} generated by the basis

$$\mathcal{M}_{CS} = \begin{pmatrix} I_N & \mathcal{H} \\ 0_N & qI_N \end{pmatrix}, \tag{10}$$

since the vector $(\boldsymbol{f}, \boldsymbol{g})$ associated with the private key (f, g) or its rotations are the shortest vectors in the lattice Λ_{CS} with high probability.

Gentry Attack. The selection of N as prime is crucial to NTRU construction over the ring $\mathbb{Z}_q[x]/\langle x^N - 1\rangle$. For example, Silverman [40] proposed a variant of NTRU where N was selected to be a power of 2 to enable Fast Fourier Transformations (FFTs) for fast polynomial multiplications. However, Gentry [17] used the Chinese Remainder Theorem (CRT) to demonstrate that for composite values of N, the ring $\mathbb{Z}_q[x]/\langle x^N - 1\rangle$ can be factored into polynomial rings with smaller degree such that the coefficients of the polynomials under this factoring map do not grow much. In particular, for even N, we have the following isomorphism:

$$\frac{\mathbb{Z}_q[x]}{\langle x^N - 1\rangle} \to \frac{\mathbb{Z}_q[x]}{\langle x^{N/2} - 1\rangle} \times \frac{\mathbb{Z}_q[x]}{\langle x^{N/2} + 1\rangle} : \quad u \to (u_0 + u_1, u_0 - u_1)$$

for every $u = (u_0, u_1) \in \mathbb{Z}_q[x]/\langle x^N - 1\rangle$. Consequently, the secret vector $(\boldsymbol{f}, \boldsymbol{g}) \in \Lambda_{CS}$ is mapped to the short vectors $(\boldsymbol{f}_0 + \boldsymbol{f}_1, \boldsymbol{g}_0 + \boldsymbol{g}_1) \in \Lambda_{CS}^+$ and $(\boldsymbol{f}_0 - \boldsymbol{f}_1, \boldsymbol{g}_0 - \boldsymbol{g}_1) \in \Lambda_{CS}^-$, where Λ_{CS}^+ and Λ_{CS}^- are the N-dimensional lattices generated by the matrices

$$\mathcal{M}_{CS}^+ = \begin{pmatrix} I_{N/2} & \mathcal{H}^+ \\ 0_{N/2} & qI_{N/2} \end{pmatrix} \quad \text{and} \quad \mathcal{M}_{CS}^- = \begin{pmatrix} I_{N/2} & \mathcal{H}^- \\ 0_{N/2} & qI_{N/2} \end{pmatrix}. \tag{11}$$

Here, $\mathcal{H}^+$ is the matrix representation of the image of the public key $h_0 + h_1 \in \mathbb{Z}_q[x]/\langle x^{N/2} - 1\rangle$ whose i-th row is defined by $x^i * (h_0 + h_1) \bmod (x^{N/2} - 1)$ and $\mathcal{H}^-$ is the matrix representation of $h_0 - h_1 \in \mathbb{Z}_q[x]/\langle x^{N/2} + 1\rangle$ whose i-th row is defined by $x^i * (h_0 - h_1) \bmod (x^{N/2} + 1)$. This way, Gentry exploited the special structure of the underlying algebra to reduce the dimension of the lattice to be attacked by half.

Different Perspective. We look at Gentry's dimension reduction from the perspective of matrices. For even N, the matrix of the public key h is of a particular form

$$\mathcal{H} = \begin{pmatrix} H_0 & H_1 \\ H_1 & H_0 \end{pmatrix} \in M_N(\mathbb{Z}_q). \tag{12}$$

The effect of the Chinese Remainder Theorem in Gentry's method can be captured in the matrix ring homomorphisms $\mathcal{H} \to \mathcal{H}^+ = H_0 + H_1$ and $\mathcal{H} \to \mathcal{H}^- = H_0 - H_1 \in M_{N/2}(\mathbb{Z}_q)$. These homomorphisms allow mapping the public key equation $\boldsymbol{f} \star \mathcal{H} = \boldsymbol{g} \pmod q$ to $(\boldsymbol{f}_0 + \boldsymbol{f}_1) \star \mathcal{H}^+ = \boldsymbol{g}_0 + \boldsymbol{g}_1 \pmod q$ and $(\boldsymbol{f}_0 - \boldsymbol{f}_1) \star \mathcal{H}^- = \boldsymbol{g}_0 - \boldsymbol{g}_1 \pmod q$. As a result, the vectors $(\boldsymbol{f}_0 + \boldsymbol{f}_1, \boldsymbol{g}_0 + \boldsymbol{g}_1) \in \Lambda_{CS}^+$ and $(\boldsymbol{f}_0 - \boldsymbol{f}_1, \boldsymbol{g}_0 - \boldsymbol{g}_1) \in \Lambda_{CS}^-$, which is the same scenario as for Gentry.

We find our description of Gentry's attack in terms of matrices suitable to those algebras whose matrix representations possess special structures and can be reduced homomorphically; however, it is difficult to define algebra linked to the matrices of reduced dimensions. We believe that our approach extends the possible applicability of Gentry's attack to different rings. In this work, we demonstrate an application of our dimension reduction technique based on matrices on BQTRU, which is built over the quaternion algebra of a bivariate ring of polynomials.

3 BQTRU

In this section, we give a detailed description of BQTRU and its relation to the hybrid lattices. For more insights, we refer the readers to [5].

Definition 10 (Quaternion algebra). *[5, Definition 1] The quaternion algebra $\mathbb{A}$ over a field $\mathbb{F}$ is a 4-dimensional vector space generated with basis $1, i, j$, and k, defined as*

$$\left(\frac{a,b}{\mathbb{F}}\right) = \{f_0 + f_1 i + f_2 j + f_3 k : f_i \in \mathbb{F}\}. \tag{13}$$

where a, b are two nonzero elements of $\mathbb{F}$. The bilinear multiplication is defined by the conditions that 1 is the unity element and

$$i^2 = a, j^2 = b, ij = -ji = k. \tag{14}$$

Consequently,

$$k^2 = -ab, jk = -kj = -ib, ki = -ik = -ja. \tag{15}$$

For an element $f = f_0 + f_1 i + f_2 j + f_3 k \in \mathbb{A}$, the conjugate of f is given by $\bar{f} = f_0 - f_1 i - f_2 j - f_3 k$, and norm of f is $N(f) = f * \bar{f} = \bar{f} * f = f_0^2 - af_1^2 - bf_2^2 + abf_3^2$. A quaternion f is invertible if and only if $N(f)$ is nonzero, and in that case, the inverse of f is given by $f^{-1} = N(f)^{-1} * \bar{f}$. A quaternion with norm 1 is called a unit quaternion. It is known that for any field $\mathbb{F}$, the quaternion algebra $\left(\frac{1,1}{\mathbb{F}}\right) \cong M_2(\mathbb{F})$ [33], where the isomorphism $\psi : \left(\frac{1,1}{\mathbb{F}}\right) \to M_2(\mathbb{F})$ is given by

$$\psi(f_0 + f_1 i + f_2 j + f_3 k) = \begin{pmatrix} f_0 + f_1 & f_2 + f_3 \\ f_2 - f_3 & f_0 - f_1 \end{pmatrix}. \tag{16}$$

In general, the quaternion algebra $\mathbb{A}$ can be defined over any commutative ring with unity R, i.e., $\mathbb{A} = \left(\frac{a,b}{R}\right)$ where a, b are nonzero elements of the ring R. For the rings R, considered in this paper, we have $\left(\frac{a,b}{R}\right) \cong M_2(R)$ with the same isomorphism as defined in (16).

Setup. The parameters (n, p, q) are chosen such that n, p, and q are primes with $p \ll q$, and let $d_f, d_g, d_r, d_m \approx \lfloor n^2/7 \rfloor$, where $\lfloor \cdot \rfloor$ is the greatest integer function. Let $\mathcal{T}(d_1, d_2)$ be a subset of R consisting of ternary elements with d_1 coefficients equal to 1, d_2 coefficients equal to -1, other coefficients equal to 0. Define $L = \mathcal{T}(d_f, d_f)$. BQTRU operates on the quaternion algebras of the bivariate ring of polynomials

$$\mathbb{A} = \left(\frac{1,1}{R}\right), \quad \mathbb{A}_p = \left(\frac{1,1}{R_p}\right), \quad \text{and} \quad \mathbb{A}_q = \left(\frac{1,1}{R_q}\right),$$

where,

$$R = \frac{\mathbb{Z}[x,y]}{\langle x^n - 1, y^n - 1 \rangle}, \quad R_p = \frac{\mathbb{Z}_p[x,y]}{\langle x^n - 1, y^n - 1 \rangle}, \quad \text{and} \quad R_q = \frac{\mathbb{Z}_q[x,y]}{\langle x^n - 1, y^n - 1 \rangle}.$$

Every element $v(x,y) = v_0 + v_1x + \ldots + v_{n-1}x^{n-1} + v_ny + v_{n+1}yx + \ldots + v_{2n-1}yx^{n-1} + \ldots + v_{n^2-n}y^{n-1} + v_{n^2-n+1}y^{n-1}x + \ldots + v_{n^2-1}y^{n-1}x^{n-1} \in R$ can be uniquely mapped to its coefficient vector

$$\boldsymbol{v} = (v_0, v_1, \ldots, v_{n^2-1}) \in \mathbb{Z}^{n^2}.$$

Therefore, considering the monomial basis, R is isomorphic to $\mathbb{Z}^{n^2}$ as an additive module over $\mathbb{Z}$. Similarly, $\mathbb{A} \cong \mathbb{Z}^{4n^2}$ as every quaternion $f = f_0 + f_1i + f_2j + f_3k \in \mathbb{A}$ can be mapped uniquely to its coefficient vector

$$\boldsymbol{f} = (\boldsymbol{f}_0, \boldsymbol{f}_1, \boldsymbol{f}_2, \boldsymbol{f}_3) \in \mathbb{Z}^{4n^2},$$

where $\boldsymbol{f}_i \in \mathbb{Z}^{n^2}$ is the coefficient vector of f_i for $i = 0, 1, 2, 3$. For two quaternions $f, g \in \mathbb{A}$, the coefficient vectors of $f + g$ and $f * g$ are denoted by $\boldsymbol{f} + \boldsymbol{g}$ and $\boldsymbol{f} \star \boldsymbol{g}$, respectively.

In addition, n is chosen such that $n | q - 1$ so that $\mathbb{Z}_q$ contains the nth roots of unity. Let $E = \{(a,b) \in \mathbb{Z}_q \times \mathbb{Z}_q : a^n = b^n = 1\}$, then $|E| = n^2$. The ring R_q is an n^2−dimensional vector space over the field $\mathbb{Z}_q$ with Lagrange basis $\{\lambda_{a,b}(x,y) : (a,b) \in E\}$, where $\lambda_{a,b}(x,y)$ are the Lagrange interpolants given by

$$\lambda_{a,b}(x,y) = \frac{ab(x^n - 1)(y^n - 1)}{n^2(x-a)(y-b)}. \tag{17}$$

Every polynomial $f(x,y) \in R_q$ can be expressed uniquely as the linear combination of Lagrange basis as

$$f(x,y) = \sum_{(a,b)\in E} f(a,b)\lambda_{a,b}(x,y). \tag{18}$$

Let T be a non-empty subset of E and Q_q be the ideal of R_q consisting of all polynomials vanishing outside T. The ideal Q_q is also a vector subspace of R_q generated by the basis elements corresponding to $T \cap E$. The set T is chosen to be small for cryptographic purposes, particularly to facilitate correct decryption. Without loss of generality, assume that T consists of the first $|T|$ elements of E. As an ideal, Q_q can be generated by a polynomial

$$\sigma(x,y) = \sum_{i=1}^{|T|} q_i \lambda_{a_i,b_i}(x,y), \tag{19}$$

where q_i are randomly chosen nonzero elements in $\mathbb{Z}_q$. Let $Q = \langle q, \sigma(x,y)\rangle_R$ be the ideal of R and $J = Q + Qi + Qj + Qk = \langle q, \sigma(x,y)\rangle_{\mathbb{A}}$ be the ideal of $\mathbb{A}$. The ideal J is called the *private ideal* and is used for key generation and decryption. Since Q is an ideal of R and hence an additive subgroup. Therefore, Q can be viewed as an n^2−dimensional lattice $\mathcal{L}_Q$ in $\mathbb{Z}^{n^2}$. Similarly, $\mathbb{A} \cong \mathbb{Z}^{n^2} + \mathbb{Z}^{n^2}i + \mathbb{Z}^{n^2}j + \mathbb{Z}^{n^2}k \cong \mathbb{Z}^{4n^2}$ and the ideal J can be viewed as a $4n^2$−dimensional lattice in $\mathbb{Z}^{4n^2}$. This lattice is called *private lattice* and is denoted by $\mathcal{L}_{private}$.

We discuss the method given in [5] to construct the generator matrix D' of the lattice $\mathcal{L}_Q$. First, consider a matrix L whose rows are the coefficients vectors of the Lagrange interpolants $\{\lambda_{a_i,b_i}(x,y) : i = 1,2,\ldots,|T|\}$. Since the row rank of a matrix is equal to the column rank, suppose that $i_1, i_2, \ldots, i_{|T|}$ columns in L are linearly independent. Let $\{j_1, j_2, \ldots, j_{n^2-|T|}\} = \{1,2,\ldots,n^2\}\backslash\{i_1, i_2, \ldots, i_{|T|}\}$. Then the matrix D' whose rows are the coefficient vectors of Lagrange interpolants $\{\lambda_{a_i,b_i}(x,y)\}_{i=1}^{|T|}$ and $qe_{j_1}, qe_{j_2}, \ldots, e_{j_{n^2-|T|}}$ forms a basis of $\mathcal{L}_Q$ with a high probability. Further, since $J \cong Q^4$, the private lattice $\mathcal{L}_{private}$ is generated by the basis matrix

$$\mathcal{B}_{private} = \begin{pmatrix} D' & 0 & 0 & 0 \\ 0 & D' & 0 & 0 \\ 0 & 0 & D' & 0 \\ 0 & 0 & 0 & D' \end{pmatrix}. \tag{20}$$

Key Generation. Two quaternions $f = f_0 + f_1 i + f_2 j + f_3 k$ and $g = g_0 + g_1 i + g_2 j + g_3 k$ are randomly chosen such that $f_0 \in \mathcal{T}(d_f + 1, d_f)$, $f_i \in L$ for $i = 1,2,3$, and $g_i \in L$, for $i = 0,1,2,3$. Since f_i, g_i are ternary polynomials, therefore, the Euclidean norm of coefficients vectors $\boldsymbol{f} = (\boldsymbol{f}_0, \boldsymbol{f}_1, \boldsymbol{f}_2, \boldsymbol{f}_3)$ and $\boldsymbol{g} = (\boldsymbol{g}_0, \boldsymbol{g}_1, \boldsymbol{g}_2, \boldsymbol{g}_3)$ is small. Further, f and g are chosen to be invertible in $\mathbb{A}$ modulo the private ideal J, i.e., there are elements $f^{-1}, g^{-1} \in \mathbb{A}$ such that

$$f * f^{-1} = f^{-1} * f = 1 \,(\text{mod } J), \quad g * g^{-1} = g^{-1} * g = 1 \ (\text{mod } J).$$

Additionally, f must also be invertible in $\mathbb{A}_p$, i.e., there is an element $f_p^{-1} \in \mathbb{A}_p$ such that $f * f_p^{-1} = f_p^{-1} * f = 1(\text{ mod } p)$. For f and g to be invertible in $\mathbb{A}/J$, their norms $N(f), N(g)$ must be invertible in R/Q. Similarly, for f to be invertible in $\mathbb{A}_p$, $N(f)$ must be invertible in R_p. Here, we describe the technique given in [5] to generate such f and g. First, randomly choose $g = g_0 + g_1 i + g_2 j + g_3 k$ where $g_i \in L$ and define the set

$$T = \cap_{i=0}^{3}\{(a,b) \in E : g_i(a,b) = 0\}.$$

If T is empty, choose another g. Then, randomly choose f such that $f_{set} = \{(a,b) \in E : N(f)(a,b) = 0\} \subseteq T$. This gives the required f and g since $N(f), N(g)$ are invertible in R/Q if and only if the roots of $N(f), N(g)$ in E are also contained in T. However, this method has some issues, which we will discuss later. Finally, to construct the public key, a quaternion $w \in \mathbb{L}_q = \left(\frac{1,1}{\mathbb{Z}_q}\right)$ is chosen such that w is invertible in $\mathbb{L}_q$, and the public key is computed as

$$h = f^{-1} * g + v \,(\text{mod } q) \tag{21}$$

where $v = w * \sigma \pmod{q}$ is kept private. The above-discussed key generation process (as given on [5, Page 11]) is compiled in Algorithm 1.

Algorithm 1: Key generation

Input: Public parameters: n, q, p
Output: Public Key: $h \in \mathbb{A}_q$
Private key: $f, g, v \in \mathbb{A}$

1 **for** $i \leftarrow 0$ *to* 3 **do** $g_i \xleftarrow{\$} L$
2 $g \leftarrow g_0 + g_1 i + g_2 j + g_3 k$
3 $T \leftarrow \cap_{i=0}^{3}\{(a,b) \in E : g_i(a,b) = 0\}$
4 **if** T *is empty* **then** go to step 2
5 **for** $(a_i, b_i) \in T$ **do** $q_i \xleftarrow{\$} \mathbb{Z}_q^\star$
6 $\sigma \leftarrow \sum_{(a_i,b_i)\in T} q_i \lambda_{a_i,b_i}(x,y)$
7 $w \xleftarrow{\$} \mathbb{L}_q^\star$ /* $\mathbb{L}_q^\star :=$ set of invertible elements in $\mathbb{L}_q$ */
8 $v \leftarrow w * \sigma \pmod{q}$
9 $f_0 \xleftarrow{\$} \mathcal{T}(d_f + 1, d_f)$
10 **for** $i \leftarrow 1$ *to* 3 **do** $f_i \xleftarrow{\$} L$
11 $f \leftarrow f_0 + f_1 i + f_2 j + f_3 k$
12 $f_{set} \leftarrow \{(a,b) \in E : N(f)(a,b) = 0\}$
13 **if** $f_{set} \subseteq T$ **then**
14 **return** Public Key: $h = f^{-1} * g + v \pmod{q}$
15 Private key: f, g, v
16 **else** go to step 9

Encryption. To encrypt a message $m = m_0 + m_1 i + m_2 j + m_3 k$ where $m_i \in L$, a random quaternion $r = r_0 + r_1 i + r_2 j + r_3 k \in \mathbb{A}$ is chosen such that $r_i \in L$. Then, the ciphertext is given by $c = ph * r + m \pmod{q}$.

Decryption. In order to decrypt c, first compute $a = f * c \pmod{q}$. Then, find the closest vector to $\boldsymbol{a}$ in the private lattice $\mathcal{L}_{private}$, call it $\boldsymbol{b}$, and let $v = a - b$. The receiver then recovers the message by $m = f_p^{-1} * v \pmod{p}$.

Correctness of Decryption. We have $f * f^{-1} = f^{-1} * f = 1 + \alpha * \sigma \pmod{q}$, for some $\alpha \in \mathbb{A}$. Therefore,

$$\begin{aligned} f * h &= (f * f^{-1}) * g + f * v \pmod{q} \\ &= g + \alpha * \sigma * g + f * v \pmod{q} \\ &= g + \gamma \pmod{q} \end{aligned}$$

where $\gamma = \alpha * \sigma * g + f * v \pmod{q}$. Receiver on computing $a = f * c \pmod{q}$ gets

$$\begin{aligned} f * c &= f * (ph * r + m) \pmod{q} \\ &= pg * r + p\gamma * r + f * m \pmod{q} \\ &= pg * r + f * m + (p\gamma * r + \varepsilon q) \\ &= pg * r + f * m + b \end{aligned}$$

where $\varepsilon \in \mathbb{A}$ and $b = (p\alpha * g * r + pf * w * r) * \sigma + \varepsilon q \in J$. The element b is unknown to the receiver and must be found to decrypt the ciphertext. Since f, g, r, and m are ternary polynomials, therefore, the norm of vector $\boldsymbol{pg} \star \ \boldsymbol{r} + \boldsymbol{f} \star \boldsymbol{m}$ is small compared to norm of $\boldsymbol{b} \in \mathcal{L}_{private}$. Hence, the vector $\boldsymbol{b} \in \mathcal{L}_{private}$ is closest to $\boldsymbol{f} \star \boldsymbol{c}$ that the receiver recovers by solving 4 instances of CVP in n^2–dimensional lattice $\mathcal{L}_Q$. Subtracting $\boldsymbol{b}$ from $\boldsymbol{f} \star \boldsymbol{c}$ gives $\boldsymbol{pg} \star \ \boldsymbol{r} + \boldsymbol{f} \star \boldsymbol{m}$. Therefore, for the correct choice of parameters, $\boldsymbol{m}$ can be recovered similarly to NTRU as $\boldsymbol{m} = \boldsymbol{f}_p^{-1} \star (\boldsymbol{pg} \star \ \boldsymbol{r} + \boldsymbol{f} \star \boldsymbol{m}) \pmod p$. For more details, refer to [5].

4 Claimed Security

4.1 Key Security

Lemma 1. *[5, Lemma 1] Let $\rho : \mathbb{A}_q \to (\mathbb{L}_q)^{n^2}$ be a map defined as*

$$\rho(f) = (f(a_1, b_1), f(a_2, b_2), \ldots, f(a_{n^2}, b_{n^2})), \tag{22}$$

where $(a_i, b_i) \in E$ and $\mathbb{L}_q = \left(\frac{1,1}{\mathbb{Z}_q}\right)$ is the quaternion algebra over $\mathbb{Z}_q$. Then, the following properties hold

$$\rho(f + g) = \rho(f) + \rho(g) \qquad \text{and} \qquad \rho(f * g) = \rho(f) * \rho(g), \tag{23}$$

where

$$\rho(f) * \rho(g) = (f(a_1, b_1) * g(a_1, b_1), \ldots, f(a_{n^2}, b_{n^2}) * g(a_{n^2}, b_{n^2})).$$

For an element $f = f_0 + f_1 i + f_2 j + f_3 k \in \mathbb{A}_q$, $\rho(f) = \rho(f_0) + \rho(f_1)i + \rho(f_2)j + \rho(f_3)k$ and the associated vector is given by

$$\boldsymbol{\rho}(\boldsymbol{f}\,) = (\rho(f_0), \rho(f_1), \rho(f_2), \rho(f_3)) \in \mathbb{Z}_q^{4n^2}.$$

Further, every quaternion $f = f_0 + f_1 i + f_2 j + f_3 k \in \mathbb{A}$ is associated with its unique matrix representations

$$\mathcal{F} = \begin{pmatrix} F_0 & F_1 & F_2 & F_3 \\ F_1 & F_0 & F_3 & F_2 \\ F_2 & -F_3 & F_0 & -F_1 \\ -F_3 & F_2 & -F_1 & F_0 \end{pmatrix}, \quad \tilde{\mathcal{F}} = \begin{pmatrix} F_0 & F_1 & F_2 & F_3 \\ F_1 & F_0 & -F_3 & -F_2 \\ F_2 & F_3 & F_0 & F_1 \\ -F_3 & -F_2 & F_1 & F_0 \end{pmatrix} \in M_{4n^2}(\mathbb{Z}), \tag{24}$$

where $F_i \in M_{n^2}(\mathbb{Z})$ is the matrix representation of $f_i \in R$, such that for every $g \in \mathbb{A}$,

$$\boldsymbol{f} \star \boldsymbol{g} = \boldsymbol{f} \star \mathcal{G} = \boldsymbol{g} \star \tilde{\mathcal{F}}, \tag{25}$$

where $\mathcal{G}$ is the matrix representation of quaternion g. We refer the readers to Appendices A, B for more details on the matrix representations of elements in the ring R and the quaternion algebra $\mathbb{A}$.

Theorem 1. *[5, Proposition 1] Suppose that f, g, γ, and h are the private and public BQTRU keys with a quaternion $u \in \mathbb{A}$ such that*

$$f * h = g + \gamma + qu. \tag{26}$$

Then, the vector $(\boldsymbol{g}, \boldsymbol{f}, -\boldsymbol{\rho}(\gamma))$ belongs to the BQTRU lattice $\mathcal{L}_{BQTRU}$ generated by the basis matrix

$$\mathcal{B}_{BQTRU} = \begin{pmatrix} qI_{4n^2} & 0 & 0 \\ \mathcal{H} & I_{4n^2} & 0 \\ \mathcal{D} & 0 & I_{4n^2} \end{pmatrix} \tag{27}$$

where, $\mathcal{H}$ is the matrix representation of h, and

$$\mathcal{D} = \begin{pmatrix} D & 0 & 0 & 0 \\ 0 & D & 0 & 0 \\ 0 & 0 & D & 0 \\ 0 & 0 & 0 & D \end{pmatrix} \tag{28}$$

with $D \in M_{n^2}(\mathbb{Z})$ is a matrix whose rows are the coefficient vectors of the Lagrange interpolants $\lambda_{a,b}(x, y)$ for $(a, b) \in E$.

Since $\boldsymbol{g}, \boldsymbol{f}$ are ternary vectors, they have small Euclidean norms. And, γ is the linear combination of $\lambda_{a,b}$'s for $(a, b) \in T$ with $|T|$ small. Thus, the Hamming norm of $\boldsymbol{\rho}(\gamma)$ is small. Consequently, the hybrid norm of the vector $(\boldsymbol{g}, \boldsymbol{f}, -\boldsymbol{\rho}(\gamma)) \in \mathbb{Z}^{4n^2} \times \mathbb{Z}^{4n^2} \times \mathbb{Z}_q^{4n^2}$ defined as

$$||(\boldsymbol{g}, \boldsymbol{f}, -\boldsymbol{\rho}(\gamma))||_{Hyb} = ||(\boldsymbol{g}, \boldsymbol{f})|| + ||\boldsymbol{\rho}(\gamma)||_H \tag{29}$$

is also small. In fact, $(\boldsymbol{g}, \boldsymbol{f}, -\boldsymbol{\rho}(\gamma))$ is most likely one of the shortest vectors in the hybrid lattice $\mathcal{L}_{BQTRU}$ [5, Theorem 4]. Therefore, the usual lattice reduction algorithms cannot find this short vector in hybrid metric. However, authors in [5] show that the security of the key can be related to finding short vectors in higher dimensional Euclidean lattices by expanding the hybrid lattice.

An attacker can select a subset $\{b_0, b_1, \ldots, b_\ell\} \subseteq \mathbb{Z}_q$ such that every element $a \in \mathbb{Z}_q$ can be expressed as $a = \sum_{i=0}^{\ell} a_i b_i$ where $(a_0, a_1, \ldots, a_\ell)$ is a vector with small Euclidean norm. In particular, one can choose $\{b_0, b_1, \ldots, b_\ell\} = \{1, 2, \ldots, 2^\ell\}$ where $2^\ell \le q < 2^{\ell+1}$ then for every $a \in \mathbb{Z}_q$, $(a_0, a_1, \ldots, a_\ell)$ is a binary vector. Then, expand the BQTRU lattice $\mathcal{L}_{BQTRU}$ to the Euclidean lattice $\mathcal{L}_{exp}$ generated by the rows of the matrix

$$\mathcal{B}_{exp} = \begin{pmatrix} qI_{4n^2} & 0 & 0 \\ \mathcal{H} & I_{4n^2} & 0 \\ \mathcal{D}_{exp} & 0 & I_{4(\ell+1)n^2} \end{pmatrix} \tag{30}$$

where

$$\mathcal{D}_{exp} = \begin{pmatrix} \boldsymbol{b} \otimes D & 0 & 0 & 0 \\ 0 & \boldsymbol{b} \otimes D & 0 & 0 \\ 0 & 0 & \boldsymbol{b} \otimes D & 0 \\ 0 & 0 & 0 & \boldsymbol{b} \otimes D \end{pmatrix}, \quad \boldsymbol{b} = (b_0, b_1, \ldots, b_\ell)^{Tr}. \tag{31}$$

It can be shown that the image of the private vector $(\boldsymbol{g}, \boldsymbol{f}, -\boldsymbol{\rho}(\gamma))$ is one of the shortest vectors in the expanded lattice with high probability [5, Proposition 3]. Therefore, the problem of finding the private key is equivalent to solving SVP in a lattice of dimension $(4\ell + 12)n^2$, which is very large. E.g. for $n = 7$, the dimension of the expanded lattice is approximately 2036. Therefore, the authors claim that the hybrid structure of BQTRU thwarts lattice attacks on key for the proposed parameters.

Alternatively, a brute-force search for the key can be performed. As per the BQTRU authors, an attacker first needs to guess the polynomial $\sigma(x, y) = \sum_{i=1}^{|T|} q_i \lambda_{a_i,b_i}(x, y)$ that is a generator for the ideal $Q = \langle q, \sigma \rangle_R$. Since $|T| \leq n$ is unknown to the attacker, the worst-case cost of searching for σ is

$$\sum_{i=1}^{n} (q-1)^i \binom{n^2}{i}. \tag{32}$$

Then, for each choice of σ, the attacker searches for all the quaternions $f = f_0 + f_1 i + f_2 j + f_3 k \in \mathbb{A}$ where $f_i \in L$ such that $f * h \pmod{J}$ is small ternary quaternion. The possible number of such f is roughly

$$|L| = \binom{n^2}{d_f}^4 \binom{n^2 - d_f}{d_f}^4. \tag{33}$$

In fact, a meet-in-the-middle search [20] is possible on the ternary vector. Further, since $\rho(\gamma) = \rho(f * v)$ where $v = w * \sigma$, the attacker needs to search for $w \in \mathbb{A}_q^\star$ (space of invertible quaternions in $\mathbb{A}_q$) in order to find $\rho(\gamma)$. Hence, the size of the search space is approximately

$$\binom{key}{security} = |\mathbb{A}_q^\star| \binom{n^2}{d_f}^2 \binom{n^2 - d_f}{d_f}^2 \sum_{i=1}^{n} (q-1)^i \binom{n^2}{i}, \tag{34}$$

that amounts to 2^{166} and 2^{396} for the moderate and highest level security parameters, respectively (see Table 4).

4.2 Message Security

The authors discuss the search attack on messages without any mention of the possibility of lattice attacks. As per them, the message can be deciphered by randomly searching for a ternary $r = r_0 + r_1 i + r_2 j + r_3 k \in \mathbb{A}$ where $r_i \in L$ such that $c - ph * r \pmod{q}$ is ternary quaternion. The size of the search space following the meet-in-the-middle strategy is

$$\binom{message}{security} = \binom{n^2}{d_r}^2 \binom{n^2 - d_r}{d_r}^2 = \frac{(n^2!)^2}{(d_r!)^4 (n^2 - 2d_r)!^2}. \tag{35}$$

This results in 2^{92} and 2^{212} message security achieved for the proposed moderate and highest level security parameters, respectively (see Table 4).

5 Our Attack

5.1 On the Proposed Key Generation

As discussed above, the authors estimated the key security based on the combinatorial search solely since, according to them, the lattice attacks on the keys are not feasible. However, they neglected the possibility of combining both kinds of attacks. We propose a hybrid attack that involves searching for the low Hamming weight part of the key and then applying lattice reduction techniques on the remaining Euclidean part.

For a quick revision, the private keys are ternary vectors f, g, both are invertible modulo $J = \langle q, \sigma \rangle_{\mathbb{A}}$. The set $T = \cap_{i=0}^{3}\{(a,b) \in E : g_i(a,b) = 0\}$ is non-empty, and $f_{set} = \{(a,b) \in E : N(f)(a,b) = 0\} \subseteq T$ to ensure the invertibility of f modulo J. We have

$$f * f^{-1} = f^{-1} * f = 1 + \alpha * \sigma \,(\mathrm{mod}\, q) \tag{36}$$

for some $\alpha \in \mathbb{A}$. An attacker first tries to guess the indices of elements of T in E. In simple words, if $E = \{(a_i, b_i) : i = 1, 2, \ldots, n^2\}$ then guess the set $I = \{i : (a_i, b_i) \in T\} \subset \{1, 2, \ldots, n^2\}$ where $|I| = |T| \leq n$. For the correct guess of I and using the relation

$$h = f^{-1} * g + v \,(\mathrm{mod}\, q),$$

one can compute

$$h(a_i, b_i) = v(a_i, b_i) \quad \text{for} \quad i \in I, \tag{37}$$

as $g(a,b) = 0$ for $(a,b) \in T$. Since $v = w * \sigma \,(\mathrm{mod}\, q) \in J \,(\mathrm{mod}\, q) = \langle \sigma \rangle_{\mathbb{A}}$, therefore v is completely determined by its evaluation over the set T. Let

$$s = h - v \,(\mathrm{mod}\, q) = f^{-1} * g \,(\mathrm{mod}\, q)$$

and $\mathcal{S}$ be the matrix representation of s. Then,

$$\begin{aligned} f * s &= (f * f^{-1}) * g \,(\mathrm{mod}\, q) \\ &= (1 + \alpha * \sigma) * g \,(\mathrm{mod}\, q) = g \,(\mathrm{mod}\, q) \\ &= g + qu \quad \text{for some} \quad u \in \mathbb{A} \end{aligned}$$

since $\sigma * g = 0 \,(\mathrm{mod}\, q)$ as $\sigma \in J$ (mod q) and g vanishes on T. Equivalently, $\boldsymbol{f} \star \mathcal{S} = \boldsymbol{g} + q\boldsymbol{u}$. Therefore, the private key $(\boldsymbol{f}, \boldsymbol{g})$ can be recovered by solving SVP in $8n^2$–dimensional Euclidean lattice $\mathcal{L}_{CS}$ generated by the matrix

$$\mathcal{B}_{CS} = \begin{pmatrix} I_{4n^2} & \mathcal{S} \\ 0 & qI_{4n^2} \end{pmatrix}. \tag{38}$$

It is worth noting that the matrix $\mathcal{S}$ has a specific structure, as shown in Eq. (24). We will now discuss how this structure can be exploited to reduce the dimension of the lattice based on the idea introduced by Gentry [17]. We demonstrate that the matrices associated with the elements of quaternion algebra can be *homomorphically folded*, which will reduce the dimension of the lattice to be attacked by half. This thereby disproves the conjecture that BQTRU is safe against Gentry's attack.

Using $\boldsymbol{f} \star \mathcal{S} = \boldsymbol{g} + q\boldsymbol{u}$, we get the following set of equations:

$$\left.\begin{array}{l} \boldsymbol{f}_0 \star S_0 + \boldsymbol{f}_1 \star S_1 + \boldsymbol{f}_2 \star S_2 - \boldsymbol{f}_3 \star S_3 - q\boldsymbol{u}_0 = \boldsymbol{g}_0 \\ \boldsymbol{f}_0 \star S_1 + \boldsymbol{f}_1 \star S_0 - \boldsymbol{f}_2 \star S_3 + \boldsymbol{f}_3 \star S_2 - q\boldsymbol{u}_1 = \boldsymbol{g}_1 \\ \boldsymbol{f}_0 \star S_2 + \boldsymbol{f}_1 \star S_3 + \boldsymbol{f}_2 \star S_0 - \boldsymbol{f}_3 \star S_1 - q\boldsymbol{u}_2 = \boldsymbol{g}_2 \\ \boldsymbol{f}_0 \star S_3 + \boldsymbol{f}_1 \star S_2 - \boldsymbol{f}_2 \star S_1 + \boldsymbol{f}_3 \star S_0 - q\boldsymbol{u}_3 = \boldsymbol{g}_3 \end{array}\right\} \quad (39)$$

Lemma 2 (Key folding). *The map* $\phi : \{\mathcal{F} : f \in \mathbb{A}\} \to M_{2n^2}(\mathbb{Z})$ *defined as*

$$\phi(\mathcal{F}) = \begin{pmatrix} F_0 + F_1 & F_2 + F_3 \\ F_2 - F_3 & F_0 - F_1 \end{pmatrix} \quad (40)$$

is a matrix ring homomorphism, i.e., $\phi(\mathcal{F} + \mathcal{G}) = \phi(\mathcal{F}) + \phi(\mathcal{G})$ *and* $\phi(\mathcal{F} \star \mathcal{G}) = \phi(\mathcal{F}) \star \phi(\mathcal{G})$ *for all* $f, g \in \mathbb{A}$.

Proof. See Appendix C. □

To simplify notations, for every quaternion $f = f_0 + f_1 i + f_2 j + f_3 k \in \mathbb{A}$, we denote by

$$\phi_1(\boldsymbol{f}) = (\boldsymbol{f}_0 + \boldsymbol{f}_1, \boldsymbol{f}_2 + \boldsymbol{f}_3) \quad \text{and} \quad \phi_2(\boldsymbol{f}) = (\boldsymbol{f}_2 - \boldsymbol{f}_3, \boldsymbol{f}_0 - \boldsymbol{f}_1). \quad (41)$$

Then, Lemma 2 and equation set (39) give

$$(\phi_1(\boldsymbol{f}), \phi_1(\boldsymbol{u})) \star \mathcal{B}_{CS,\phi} = (\phi_1(\boldsymbol{f}), \phi_1(\boldsymbol{g})), \quad (\phi_2(\boldsymbol{f}), \phi_2(\boldsymbol{u})) \star \mathcal{B}_{CS,\phi} = (\phi_2(\boldsymbol{f}), \phi_2(\boldsymbol{g}))$$

where

$$\mathcal{B}_{CS,\phi} = \begin{pmatrix} I_{2n^2} & \phi(\mathcal{S}) \\ 0 & qI_{2n^2} \end{pmatrix} \quad (42)$$

generates a $4n^2$–dimensional lattice that we call $\mathcal{L}_{CS,\phi}$. The Gaussian heuristic estimates the expected length of the shortest vector in the lattice $\mathcal{L}_{CS,\phi}$ to be

$$gh(\mathcal{L}_{CS,\phi}) = \sqrt{\frac{4n^2}{2\pi e}}\, |det(\mathcal{B}_{CS,\phi})|^{\frac{1}{4n^2}} = \sqrt{\frac{2qn^2}{\pi e}}. \quad (43)$$

Whereas the images of the private key belonging to the lattice $\mathcal{L}_{CS,\phi}$ have norms

$$||(\phi_1(\boldsymbol{f}), \phi_1(\boldsymbol{g}))|| \approx ||(\phi_2(\boldsymbol{f}), \phi_2(\boldsymbol{g}))|| \leq \sqrt{2}||(\boldsymbol{f}, \boldsymbol{g})|| = \sqrt{\frac{32n^2}{7}}. \quad (44)$$

Since q is taken to be approximately $24n^2/7$, therefore, for the recommended parameters of BQTRU, the vectors $(\phi_1(\boldsymbol{f}), \phi_1(\boldsymbol{g}))$ and $(\phi_2(\boldsymbol{f}), \phi_2(\boldsymbol{g}))$ are $O(1/n)$ shorter than estimated by the Gaussian heuristics. Thus, we expect them to be the shortest vectors in the lattice $\mathcal{L}_{CS,\phi}$ with high probability. This proves that attacking the key is equivalent to searching for the indices of elements of set T in set E times the cost of solving SVP in a $4n^2$–dimensional lattice. We discuss the concrete cost analysis of our attack in Sect. 6.

Alternative Keys. In case the lattice reduction algorithms do not return the exact images of the private keys in the lattice $\mathcal{L}_{CS,\phi}$, we provide an alternative way to handle such situations.

Theorem 2 (Lift-back). *Let the vectors* $(\boldsymbol{x}, \boldsymbol{y}) = (\boldsymbol{x}_0, \boldsymbol{x}_1, \boldsymbol{y}_0, \boldsymbol{y}_1)$ *and* $(\boldsymbol{w}, \boldsymbol{z}) = (\boldsymbol{w}_0, \boldsymbol{w}_1, \boldsymbol{z}_0, \boldsymbol{z}_1)$ *belonging to the lattice* $\mathcal{L}_{CS,\phi}$. *Then the vector*

$$lift(\boldsymbol{x}, \boldsymbol{y}, \boldsymbol{w}, \boldsymbol{z}) = (\boldsymbol{x}_0+\boldsymbol{w}_1, \boldsymbol{x}_0-\boldsymbol{w}_1, \boldsymbol{x}_1+\boldsymbol{w}_0, \boldsymbol{x}_1-\boldsymbol{w}_0, \boldsymbol{y}_0+\boldsymbol{z}_1, \boldsymbol{y}_0-\boldsymbol{z}_1, \boldsymbol{y}_1+\boldsymbol{z}_0, \boldsymbol{y}_1-\boldsymbol{z}_0)$$

belongs to the lattice $\mathcal{L}_{CS}$.

Proof. Let $\boldsymbol{a} = (\boldsymbol{a}_0, \boldsymbol{a}_1), \boldsymbol{b} = (\boldsymbol{b}_0, \boldsymbol{b}_1) \in \mathbb{Z}^{2n^2}$ be such that

$$(\boldsymbol{x}, \boldsymbol{a}) \star \mathcal{B}_{CS,\phi} = (\boldsymbol{x}, \boldsymbol{y}) \quad \text{and} \quad (\boldsymbol{w}, \boldsymbol{b}) \star \mathcal{B}_{CS,\phi} = (\boldsymbol{w}, \boldsymbol{z}). \tag{45}$$

From (45), we get

$$\left.\begin{aligned} \boldsymbol{x}_0 \star (H_0 + H_1) + \boldsymbol{x}_1 \star (H_2 - H_3) + q\boldsymbol{a}_0 &= \boldsymbol{y}_0 \\ \boldsymbol{x}_0 \star (H_2 + H_3) + \boldsymbol{x}_1 \star (H_0 - H_1) + q\boldsymbol{a}_1 &= \boldsymbol{y}_1 \\ \boldsymbol{w}_0 \star (H_0 + H_1) + \boldsymbol{w}_1 \star (H_2 - H_3) + q\boldsymbol{b}_0 &= \boldsymbol{z}_0 \\ \boldsymbol{w}_0 \star (H_2 + H_3) + \boldsymbol{w}_1 \star (H_0 - H_1) + q\boldsymbol{b}_1 &= \boldsymbol{z}_1 \end{aligned}\right\} \tag{46}$$

Using (46), one can show that

$$lift(\boldsymbol{x}, \boldsymbol{a}, \boldsymbol{w}, \boldsymbol{b}) \star \mathcal{B}_{CS} = lift(\boldsymbol{x}, \boldsymbol{y}, \boldsymbol{w}, \boldsymbol{z}).$$

This proves our claim. □

Moreover,

$$||\, lift(\boldsymbol{x}, \boldsymbol{y}, \boldsymbol{w}, \boldsymbol{z})|| \leq 2\sqrt{||(\boldsymbol{x}, \boldsymbol{y})||^2 + ||(\boldsymbol{w}, \boldsymbol{z})||^2}. \tag{47}$$

Therefore, if one is able to find two short enough vectors in the lattice $\mathcal{L}_{CS,\phi}$, then their *lift-back* can serve as a possible decryption key with high probability. The same is reflected in our experiments.

Similar to NTRU, all the rotations of the private key of BQTRU are also potential decryption keys.

Definition 11 (Rotations). *For an element* $f = f_0 + f_1 i + f_2 j + f_3 k \in \mathbb{A}$ *where* $f_i \in \frac{\mathbb{Z}[x,y]}{\langle x^n-1, y^n-1\rangle}$, *the* $4n^2$ *rotations of* f *are given by*

$$x^a y^b * f * \delta = (x^a y^b * f_0)\delta + (x^a y^b * f_1)(i\delta) + (x^a y^b * f_2)(j\delta) + (x^a y^b * f_3)(k\delta)$$

where $\delta \in \{1, i, j, k\}$ *and* $a, b \in \{0, 1, \ldots, n-1\}$.

It is clear that if f, g, and $h \in \mathbb{A}$ are such that $f * h = g \pmod q$. Then, $(x^a y^b * f * \delta) * h = (x^a y^b * g * \delta) \pmod q$, for all $\delta \in \{1, i, j, k\}$ and $a, b \in \{0, 1, \ldots, n-1\}$. Therefore, all the rotations of the private key belong to the lattice $\mathcal{L}_{CS}$ and, by definition, have the same norm as the private key. Hence, their images in the lattice $\mathcal{L}_{CS,\phi}$ are also short vectors with high probability. This increases the chances of an attacker to find suitable short vectors in lower dimensional lattices and lift them back to the original lattice to check for their eligibility as a decryption key.

5.2 On Messages

The ciphertext $c = c_0 + c_1 i + c_2 j + c_3 k$ for a message $m = m_0 + m_1 i + m_2 j + m_3 k$ is computed as

$$c = ph * r + m \pmod q \tag{48}$$

where $r = r_0 + r_1 i + r_2 j + r_3 k \in \mathbb{A}$ such that each r_i is chosen randomly from L. Using Eq. (24), we get

$$\boldsymbol{c} = p\ \boldsymbol{r} \star \tilde{\mathcal{H}} + \boldsymbol{m} + q\boldsymbol{u} \quad \text{for some} \quad u \in \mathbb{A}. \tag{49}$$

This gives us the following set of equations:

$$\left.\begin{array}{l} p(\ \boldsymbol{r}_0 \star H_0 + \ \boldsymbol{r}_1 \star H_1 + \ \boldsymbol{r}_2 \star H_2 - \ \boldsymbol{r}_3 \star H_3) + \boldsymbol{m}_0 + q\boldsymbol{u}_0 = \boldsymbol{c}_0 \\ p(\ \boldsymbol{r}_0 \star H_1 + \ \boldsymbol{r}_1 \star H_0 + \ \boldsymbol{r}_2 \star H_3 - \ \boldsymbol{r}_3 \star H_2) + \boldsymbol{m}_1 + q\boldsymbol{u}_1 = \boldsymbol{c}_1 \\ p(\ \boldsymbol{r}_0 \star H_2 - \ \boldsymbol{r}_1 \star H_3 + \ \boldsymbol{r}_2 \star H_0 + \ \boldsymbol{r}_3 \star H_1) + \boldsymbol{m}_2 + q\boldsymbol{u}_2 = \boldsymbol{c}_2 \\ p(\ \boldsymbol{r}_0 \star H_3 - \ \boldsymbol{r}_1 \star H_2 + \ \boldsymbol{r}_2 \star H_1 + \ \boldsymbol{r}_3 \star H_0) + \boldsymbol{m}_3 + q\boldsymbol{u}_3 = \boldsymbol{c}_3 \end{array}\right\} \tag{50}$$

Lemma 3 (Message folding). *The map* $\tilde{\phi} : \{\tilde{\mathcal{F}} : f \in \mathbb{A}\} \to M_{2n^2}(\mathbb{Z})$ *defined as*

$$\tilde{\phi}(\tilde{\mathcal{F}}) = \begin{pmatrix} F_0 + F_1 & F_2 - F_3 \\ F_2 + F_3 & F_0 - F_1 \end{pmatrix} \tag{51}$$

is a matrix ring homomorphism.

Proof. Similar to the proof of Lemma 2. □

Further, for every quaternion $f = f_0 + f_1 i + f_2 j + f_3 k \in \mathbb{A}$, we denote by

$$\tilde{\phi}_1(\boldsymbol{f}) = (\boldsymbol{f}_0 + \boldsymbol{f}_1, \boldsymbol{f}_2 - \boldsymbol{f}_3) \quad \text{and} \quad \tilde{\phi}_2(\boldsymbol{f}) = (\boldsymbol{f}_2 + \boldsymbol{f}_3, \boldsymbol{f}_0 - \boldsymbol{f}_1). \tag{52}$$

Then, Lemma 3 and equation set (50) give

$$(0, \tilde{\phi}_1(\boldsymbol{c})) = (\tilde{\phi}_1(\ \boldsymbol{r}), \tilde{\phi}_1(\boldsymbol{u})) \star \mathcal{B}_{CS,\tilde{\phi}} + (-\tilde{\phi}_1(\ \boldsymbol{r}), \tilde{\phi}_1(\boldsymbol{m})),$$
$$(0, \tilde{\phi}_2(\boldsymbol{c})) = (\tilde{\phi}_2(\ \boldsymbol{r}), \tilde{\phi}_2(\boldsymbol{u})) \star \mathcal{B}_{CS,\tilde{\phi}} + (-\tilde{\phi}_2(\ \boldsymbol{r}), \tilde{\phi}_2(\boldsymbol{m}))$$

where

$$\mathcal{B}_{CS,\tilde{\phi}} = \begin{pmatrix} I_{2n^2} & \tilde{\phi}(\tilde{\mathcal{H}}) \\ 0 & qI_{2n^2} \end{pmatrix} \tag{53}$$

generates a $4n^2$-dimensional lattice that we call $\mathcal{L}_{CS,\tilde{\phi}}$. Since $\boldsymbol{r}, \boldsymbol{m}$ are ternary vectors with many zeros, therefore, $(-\tilde{\phi}_1(\ \boldsymbol{r}), \tilde{\phi}_1(\boldsymbol{m}))$, $(-\tilde{\phi}_2(\ \boldsymbol{r}), \tilde{\phi}_2(\boldsymbol{m}))$ take values from the set $\{0, \pm 1, \pm 2\}$ with majority of 0 s, ±1 s and a few ±2 s. Therefore, we expect with a high probability that the vectors

$$(\tilde{\phi}_1(\ \boldsymbol{r}), \tilde{\phi}_1(\boldsymbol{u})) \star \mathcal{B}_{CS,\tilde{\phi}} \quad \text{and} \quad (\tilde{\phi}_2(\ \boldsymbol{r}), \tilde{\phi}_2(\boldsymbol{u})) \star \mathcal{B}_{CS,\tilde{\phi}}$$

in the lattice $\mathcal{L}_{CS,\tilde{\phi}}$ are closest to the targets $(0, \tilde{\phi}_1(\boldsymbol{c}))$ and $(0, \tilde{\phi}_2(\boldsymbol{c}))$, respectively. Thus, the message can be recovered by solving CVP in $4n^2$-dimensional lattice $\mathcal{L}_{CS,\tilde{\phi}}$.

5.3 Other Related Issues

Small Values of q. Since $d_f, d_r, d_g, d_m \approx n^2/7$ and p is fixed to be 3, the value of q required to avoid decryption failure is $q \geq 72n^2/7$. One can choose smaller values of q, allowing negligible decryption failure to only an extent that does not pose any security threat [21]. For instance, a cryptosystem achieving security level 2^λ should not have the probability of decryption failure higher than $2^{-\lambda}$. However, the proposed parameters $(n, q, p) = (7, 113, 3), (11, 199, 3)$ claiming to achieve moderate and highest security levels allow approximately 2^{-10} and 2^{-22} decryption failure rate, respectively, which are far away from the requirements.

Low Cardinality of T. The greater the size of set T, the better security against combinatorial search. However, our experiments indicate that for the suggested parameters, the size of set T is quite small when g is randomly selected. In almost all the cases, we found that $|T| = 1$ or 2, which benefits the attacker.

Weak Instances. In experiments, we encountered some instances where for a wrong guess of T, say $T' \neq T$, and corresponding v', the lattice generated by the matrix

$$\mathcal{B}'_{CS} = \begin{pmatrix} I_{4n^2} & \mathcal{H}' \\ 0 & qI_{4n^2} \end{pmatrix}$$

where $\mathcal{H}'$ is matrix of $h' = h - v' \pmod q$, contains short vector (f', g'). This gives a potential decryption key as $f' * (h - v') = g' \pmod q$. Therefore, for a ciphertext $c = ph * r + m \pmod q$, $f' * c = pg' * m + f' * m + pf' * r * v' + \epsilon' q$, for some $\epsilon' \in \mathbb{A}$. Now, decrypt in a similar way as for BQTRU but with the private lattice corresponding to T'. Therefore, these weak instances are beneficial to an adversary when $|T'| < |T|$.

6 Cost Analysis and Experimental Verification

Besides the proposed parameter sets in the original paper, we consider another set of parameters that provides no decryption failure in the same dimension and a toy parameter set with decryption failure for reference comparison in Table 1.

Table 1. Original and decryption-free BQTRU parameter sets (n, q, d_f, d_g, d_r) in equivalent dimensions.

Security tag	No Decryption failure	Decryption failure	
Toy	$(5, 241, 3, 3, 3)$	$(5, 71, 3, 3, 3)$	
Moderate	$(7, 547, 7, 6, 6)$	$(7, 113, 7, 6, 6)$	} original parameters
Highest	$(11, 1277, 17, 17, 13)$	$(11, 199, 17, 17, 13)$	} original parameters

As per the claimed security estimation for key and message attack (Eqs. (34), (35)), the decryption-free parameter sets have higher key security and equivalent message security compared to the original BQTRU parameter sets in the same dimension. Later, our analysis shows that they are easier to attack than the original parameter sets.

Key Recovery Attack. We first guess the positions of the low Hamming weight vector $\boldsymbol{v}$ with respect to the Lagrange basis. Then, for each guess, we attempt to find a short vector in the lattice $\mathcal{L}_{CS}$ constructed based on the guessed $\boldsymbol{v}$. If the positions are guessed correctly, the vector $(\boldsymbol{f}, \boldsymbol{g})$ or its rotations (as in Definition 11) lie in the lattice $\mathcal{L}_{CS}$.

The cost of guessing is related to the cardinality of the set T. In BQTRU's paper, the authors state that $|T| \leq n$ is needed for successful decryption. Therefore, in the worst case, the attacker has to try $\sum_{i=1}^{n} \binom{n^2}{i}$ different guesses for the nonzero positions of $\boldsymbol{v}$. Since the lattice $\mathcal{L}_{CS}$ is vulnerable to the folding attack introduced in Subsect. 5.1, the attacker constructs the folded lattice and runs a lattice reduction algorithm, such as the *progressive* BKZ, in a specific range where β is expected to successfully retrieve the secret key $(\boldsymbol{f}, \boldsymbol{g})$. The lattice reduction cost is estimated based on the blocksize needed to find the two short vectors $(\phi_1(\boldsymbol{f}), \phi_1(\boldsymbol{g}))$ and $(\phi_2(\boldsymbol{f}), \phi_2(\boldsymbol{g}))$ as summarized in Fig. 2. Consequently, the total cost of the key attack is calculated as *the guessing cost* $\times$ *lattice reduction cost.*

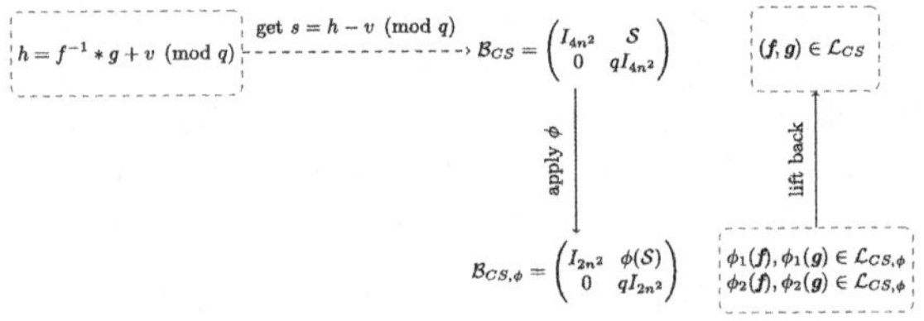

Fig. 2. Key recovery attack against BQTRU lattice; instead of reducing a lattice of dimension $8n^2$ to find a short vector $(\boldsymbol{f}, \boldsymbol{g})$, we map the problem into reducing a lattice of dimension $4n^2$ to find two short vectors $(\phi_1(\boldsymbol{f}), \phi_1(\boldsymbol{g})), (\phi_2(\boldsymbol{f}), \phi_2(\boldsymbol{g}))$ of the same norm (on average) as $(\boldsymbol{f}, \boldsymbol{g})$.

Message Recovery Attack. The message recovery attack, as discussed in Subsect. 5.2, is relatively straightforward. The complexity of recovering the message is determined by the effort required to solve the Closest Vector Problem (CVP) for the lattice $\mathcal{L}_{CS,\tilde{\phi}}$ with respect to two distinct target vectors, namely $(0, \tilde{\phi_1}(\boldsymbol{c}))$ and $(0, \tilde{\phi_2}(\boldsymbol{c}))$. To assess the difficulty of solving the CVP involved in the message attack, we employ the embedding technique (Eq. 5) to transform the CVP into the Shortest Vector Problem (SVP). Consequently, the attack cost depends on the blocksize required to identify the shortest vectors in the two lattices generated from the basis $\mathcal{B}_{CS,\phi_1}$ and $\mathcal{B}_{CS,\phi_2}$, as summarized in Fig. 3.

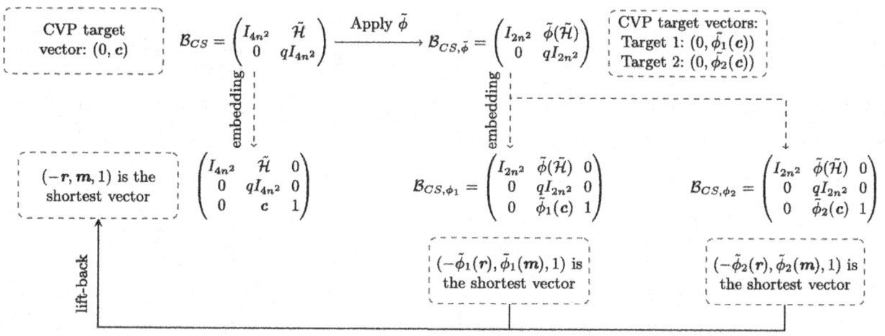

Fig. 3. Message recovery attack against BQTRU lattice; instead of reducing a lattice of dimension $8n^2$ to find a short vector $(-\ r, m, 1)$, we map the problem into reducing two lattices of dimension $4n^2 + 1$ to find two short vectors $(-\tilde{\phi}_1(\ r), \tilde{\phi}_1(m), 1)$ and $(-\tilde{\phi}_2(\ r), \tilde{\phi}_2(m), 1)$ of the same norm (on average) as $(-\ r, m, 1)$.

Estimating β. The literature has introduced several works [3,26] that estimate the blocksize needed for BKZ to recover an unusually short vector (that serves as a decryption key) in lattices. The *2016-estimate* is a well-regarded estimate that suggests that, under the GSA, the BKZ algorithm can find a short vector v in a random $d-$dimensional lattice $\mathcal{L}_B$ if the following condition is met:

$$\sqrt{\beta/d}\ ||v\,|| < \delta_\beta{}^{2\beta-d-1} \cdot det(\mathcal{L}_B)^{1/d}, \tag{54}$$

where δ represents the root Hermite factor. Having the inequality satisfied (for some β) indicates that the BKZ algorithm has potentially identified the projection of the unusually short vector v in the projected sublattice $\mathcal{L}_{B[d-\beta:d)}$ that can be lifted to the vector $v \in \mathcal{L}_B$ and serve as a decryption key. A simple analysis shows that higher values of β are needed to satisfy the inequality (54) when the dimension of the lattice d or the *lattice gap*, defined as $\frac{||v\,||}{gh(\mathcal{L})}$, increases.

The NTRU *Fatigue-estimate* [15] is the state-of-art estimate for NTRU-like lattices. The estimate itself is a refinement of the *2016-estimator* and the probabilistic estimate [14] that allows for describing the profile of a reduced basis even using a few tours of progressive BKZ. The *Fatigue-estimator* incorporates the ZGSA (instead of GSA) as a more accurate description of the profile as well.

Definition 12 (ZGSA). *[15, Heuristic 2.8] Let B be a basis of a $2d-$dimensional $q-$ary lattice $\mathcal{L}_B$ with d $q-$vectors. After BKZ$-\beta$ reduction, the profile of the reduced basis (for $s = \frac{1}{2} + \frac{ln(q)}{ln(\delta_\beta)}$) has the following shape:*

$$||b_i^\star|| = \begin{cases} q, & if\ i \leq d-s \\ \sqrt{q}\cdot\delta_\beta^{2d-1-2i}, & if\ \ d-s < i < d+s \\ 1, & if\ \ i \geq d+s \end{cases} \tag{55}$$

The *Fatigue-estimate*[1] gives a better prediction for the blocksize in both the lattices $\mathcal{L}_{CS}$ and $\mathcal{L}_{CS,\phi}$ as the two lattices are NTRU-like lattices.

Although our attack reduces the dimension of the lattices by half, the blocksize and, hence, the reduction cost depends not only on the dimension but also on the lattice gap. Therefore, to prove the effectiveness of our attack, we need to demonstrate that the blocksize required to find $(\phi_1(\boldsymbol{f}), \phi_1(\boldsymbol{g})), (\phi_2(\boldsymbol{f}), \phi_2\boldsymbol{g})) \in \mathcal{L}_{CS,\phi}$ is much smaller than that needed for finding $(\boldsymbol{f}, \boldsymbol{g}) \in \mathcal{L}_{CS}$.

The secret key $(\boldsymbol{f}, \boldsymbol{g}) \in \mathbb{Z}^{8n^2}$ consists of ternary coefficients, with approximately $8n^2/7$ of the coefficients equal to 1 and -1 each, and the rest being 0. When estimating β using the *Fatigue-estimator*, we consider the coefficients of $(\boldsymbol{f}, \boldsymbol{g})$ to follow a discrete Gaussian distribution with mean $\mu = 0$ and variance $\sigma^2 = 2/7$. Using the fact that if X and Y are two independent and identically distributed discrete Gaussian random variables with mean μ and variance σ^2, then $X + Y$ is a discrete Gaussian random variable with mean 2μ and variance $2\sigma^2$, we get that the coefficients of $(\phi_1(\boldsymbol{f}), \phi_1(\boldsymbol{g}))$ and $(\phi_2(\boldsymbol{f}), \phi_2(\boldsymbol{g}))$ take values from the set $\{-2, -1, 0, 1, 2\}$ following a discrete Gaussian distribution with mean $\mu' = 0$ and variance $\sigma'^2 = 2\sigma^2 = 4/7$. This gives

$$||(\phi_1(\boldsymbol{f}), \phi_1(\boldsymbol{g}))|| \approx ||(\phi_2(\boldsymbol{f}), \phi_2(\boldsymbol{g}))|| \approx \sqrt{4n^2\,\sigma'^2} = 2n\sigma' = ||(\boldsymbol{f}, \boldsymbol{g})||. \quad (56)$$

We experimentally also verified that (56) holds with minor deviations while Eq. (44) gives an upper bound on the norm.

One can check that any β that satisfies the inequality (54) for the lattice $\mathcal{L}_{CS}$ of dimension $8n^2$ also satisfies it for the lattice $\mathcal{L}_{CS,\phi}$ of dimension $4n^2$ for the same norm $||\boldsymbol{v}|| = 2n\sigma'$. Therefore, *2016-estimator* results in smaller values of β for $\mathcal{L}_{CS,\phi}$ compared to $\mathcal{L}_{CS}$. A more precise description of the blocksize estimation for the concrete parameters (with and without decryption failure) based on the *Fatigue* and *2016-estimator* is given in Table 2. The noticeable difference in the blocksizes before and after dimension reduction clearly shows the benefit of our folding.

Experimental Verification. For experimental verification, we apply our key and message attack against the parameter sets of BQTRU. We run progressive BKZ and identify the smallest blocksize needed to retrieve the decryption key and the message with enumeration as an SVP oracle. We depend on FPyLLL [43] as a Python wrapper to FPLLL [42]. Timed results[2] have been measured on a system running Linux (Ubuntu 22.04.2 LTS) with 13th Gen Intel(R) Core(TM) i7-13700 equipped with 16 physical cores @ 800 MHZ (min) and 32 GB RAM; each core can run up to 2 threads on parallel.

[1] We refer to the estimator proposed in [15] as the *Fatigue-estimate*-the estimator functions whether the NTRU cryptosystem is constructed over the non-overstretched or overstretched regime. The estimate gives a better prediction for the blocksize for the key attack as the lattice is an NTRU-like lattice.

[2] Other devices have also been used to run different experiments, as detailed on the GitHub link. We are reporting only the blocksize β for the other results; the time required is an orthogonal question.

Table 2. Blocksize estimation using *2016-estimate* and *Fatigue-estimate* for retrieving a short vector that represents a key/message in BQTRU lattices of dimension $8n^2$ without folding versus $4n^2$ with folding attack; the estimators predicts lower blocksizes when our folding reduction is applied.

	Parameters	No folding		Folding	
	(n, q, d_f, d_g, d_r)	$\beta_{Fatigue}$	β_{2016}	$\beta_{Fatigue}$	β_{2016}
Decryption Failure	$(5, 71, 3, 3, 3)$	52	72	3	–
	$(7, 113, 7, 6, 6)$	145	166	56	77
	$(11, 199, 17, 17, 13)$	421	456	204	224
	$(13, 677, 24, 24, 24)$	529	562	250	268
	$(17, 919, 41, 41, 41)$	960	1014	469	493
No Decryption Failure	$(5, 241, 3, 3, 3)$	20	39	2	–
	$(7, 547, 7, 6, 6)$	101	115	18	–
	$(11, 1277, 17, 17, 13)$	320	340	137	152
	$(13, 1847, 24, 24, 24)$	465	490	210	225
	$(17, 3061, 41, 41, 41)$	840	879	395	414

Trivial Short Vectors. As in NTRU lattice, BQTRU key recovery lattice $\mathcal{L}_{CS}$ contains trivial short vectors like $(\mathbf{1}^{4n^2}, \mathbf{0}^{4n^2})$ that does not help in the decryption process. After applying our folding reduction, the images of these vectors also lie in the lattice $\mathcal{L}_{CS,\phi}$. To avoid these useless vectors, one can project against using the so-called *short vector hints* [14]. However, the cost of retrieving the decryption key may increase as the volume of the lattice to be reduced decreases [27, Theorem 5.6]. In our experiment, we ignore these vectors automatically, considering only the invertible short vectors as possible decryption keys.

Effect of Rotations. Similarly to NTRU, the BQTRU key-recovery lattice does not contain only the decryption key but also other 'rotations' with respect to the underlying structure. While in NTRU, these rotations are cyclic rotations, for BQTRU, these rotations are slightly different (given by Definition 11) but maintain the same norm as the decryption key. Additionally, the number of these rotations is similar to the NTRU lattice and equal $d/2$ where d is the lattice dimension. The effect of these rotations is reflected as lower values of β that are needed to recover the secret key. *Fatigue-estimate* takes into consideration the probabilities of finding one of these rotations, and hence the expected β is smaller compared to the *2016-estimate* that considers only the lattice volume and vector projection. Experimentally, one can also notice that the blocksize required for retrieving the key is smaller than that needed to retrieve messages for roughly the same dimension and lattice volume. See Table 3.

Table 3. Blocksize required to retrieve the key/message verified experimentally against BQTRU parameter sets. The blocksizes are averaged over at least 50 trials except for $\beta > 60$ where only 10 trials have been executed.

	Parameters	No folding		Folding	
	(n, q, d_f, d_g, d_r)	β_{Key}	$\beta_{Message}$	β_{Key}	$\beta_{Message}$
Decryption Failure	$(5, 71, 3, 3, 3)$	27	56	2.5	7.3
	$(7, 113, 7, 6, 6)$	–	–	52.6	63.4
No Decryption Failure	$(5, 241, 3, 3, 3)$	4.4	17.9	2	2.3
	$(7, 547, 7, 6, 6)$	–	–	7	18.1

From Table 3, we can see the efficiency of our folding attack. When a decryption failure is allowed, for $n = 5$, the blocksize required to retrieve the key and message drop from 27 and 56 (when no folding is applied) to just 2.5 and 7.3 on average (when folding is used). Furthermore, for $n = 7$, the estimated blocksize to retrieve the key and the message with no folding is greater than 100, which is higher than the record β that ever has been reached experimentally for NTRU-like lattice [27]. However, with our folding attack, we can retrieve the key and the message with average blocksize 52.6 and 63.4, respectively, for the parameters with decryption failure and just 7 and 18.1 for the no decryption failure parameter sets.

Revised Security Estimation. Following our experimental findings and discussion on the estimated blocksize to find the decryption key or the message, we find that the *Fatigue estimate* serves as a good estimator for the blocksize required to retrieve the decryption key, and the *2016-estimate* serves as a conservative estimator for the blocksize needed to retrieve the message (for larger blocksize $\beta > 50$).

As stated earlier, the cost of the lattice reduction using an algorithm like BKZ is heavily determined by the SVP oracles: Enumeration and sieving. Recent advances [2,27] suggest that sieving can outperform enumeration starting from $\beta > 65$. The literature has introduced different models to estimate the security based on the blocksize β. The proposed models have different elementary operations of measurements. In enumeration, the unit is the number of nodes visited during enumeration, which costs approximately 100 CPU cycles, while in sieving, the unit is an operation on a word-sized integer that costs about 1 CPU cycle. One can refer to [1] for a detailed discussion of these models. By analyzing the different models, it is observed that the security level increases almost by $1-$bit every $2-4$ blocksizes (a relation that does not need to be linear).

For the parameter sets with $n > 7$, the estimated blocksize to get the decryption key or the message is greater than 65; therefore, we rely on the sieving as an SVP oracle. The conservative cost of BKZ with the sieving model, which is widely used to estimate security in many schemes, is given by $2^{0.292\beta+o(\beta)}$ (classically) [7] and $2^{0.265\beta+o(\beta)}$ (quantumly) [30]. However, we rely on the sieving model that gives the highest classical security estimation of $2^{0.368\beta}$ (according to survey [1]) in favor of BQTRU construction. For $n = 7$, we report our experimental findings as an accurate description of the security level. For key lattice, the average β to retrieve the vector is approximately 52.6 compared to 63.4 for the message recovery attack; however, guessing v also contributes to the total cost of the key recovery attack. Similarly to sieving, if we consider the enumeration model that gives the highest security estimation that is $2^{0.000784\beta^2+0.366\beta-0.9+\log_2(8d)}$ (classically), then the lattice reduction part of the key and the message contributes 31 and 36−bit, respectively. The guessing part for v in the key attack contributes at maximum by 26−bit security when the set $|T|$ cardinality is maximal. Overall, the key security is estimated to be 47−bit versus 36−bit for the message security. Experimentally, the key attack is much more successful than estimated as the cardinality of T is coming to be smaller than the maximum possible value n for most of the generated keys as in Algorithm 1. On our system, it takes almost 12 core days (on average) to retrieve the key and the message for the moderate parameter sets. Consequently, we can summarize our security estimation (in favor of BQTRU construction) as in Table 4.

Table 4. Revised security levels for proposed BQTRU parameter sets. The key security estimation is calculated as the cost of guessing v (that is $\sum_{i=1}^{n}\binom{n^2}{i}$) times the lattice reduction cost, while the message security cost is due to the lattice reduction only.

claimed security tag	parameters	key sec.		message sec.	
		claimed	our estimate	claimed	our estimate
Moderate	$(7, 113, 7, 6, 6)$	>166	**47**	92	**36**
Highest	$(11, 199, 17, 17, 13)$	>396	**125**	212	**82**

7 Failed Attempts to Fix BQTRU

7.1 Modifying the Key Generation

Our attack on the key works for the following reasons. Guessing the set $I = \{i : (a_i, b_i) \in T\}$ is enough to completely determine v. Further, since $\sigma * g = 0 \pmod q$ gives $f * (h - v) = g \pmod q$. Therefore, for the correct v, one can overcome the hybrid nature of the associated lattice by searching for the private key as a short vector in an $8n^2$−dimensional q−ary lattice $\mathcal{L}_{CS}$ that can be further subjected to a dimension reduction by half. Moreover, the low cardinality of T also favors the adversary.

To avoid the above-discussed scenarios, we modified the key generation as follows:

Algorithm 2: Modified key generation

Input: `Public parameters:` n, q, p
Output: `Public Key:` $h \in \mathbb{A}_q$
`Private key:` $f, g, v \in \mathbb{A}$

1 $f_0 \xleftarrow{\$} \mathcal{T}(d_f+1, d_f)$
2 **for** $i \leftarrow 1$ *to* 3 **do** $f_i \xleftarrow{\$} L$
3 $f \leftarrow f_0 + f_1 i + f_2 j + f_3 k$
4 $f_{set} \leftarrow \{(a,b) \in E : N(f)(a,b) = 0\}$
5 **if** $|f_{set}| \geq n$ *or* f_{set} *is empty* **then** `go to step 1`
6 $T \leftarrow f_{set}$
7 **while** $|T| < n$ **do**
8 $\quad (a,b) \xleftarrow{\$} E \backslash T$
9 $\quad T = T \cup \{(a,b)\}$
10 **for** $(a_i, b_i) \in T$ **do** $q_i \xleftarrow{\$} \mathbb{Z}_q^\star$
11 $\sigma \leftarrow \sum_{(a_i,b_i)\in T} q_i \lambda_{a_i,b_i}(x,y)$
12 **for** $i \leftarrow 0$ *to* 3 **do** $g_i \xleftarrow{\$} L$
13 $g \leftarrow g_0 + g_1 i + g_2 j + g_3 k$
14 **if** $\sigma * g = 0 \pmod q$ *or* $g_{set} \leftarrow \{(a,b) \in E : g(a,b) = 0\} \subseteq T$ **then**
15 $\quad$ `go to step 12`
16 $w \xleftarrow{\$} \mathbb{L}_q^\star$
17 $v \leftarrow w * \sigma \pmod q$
18 **return** `Public Key:` $h = f^{-1} * g + v \pmod q$, `Private key:` f, g, v

Since f_{set} is a proper subset of T and $g_{set} \not\subseteq T$, the equation $h(a,b) \neq v(a,b) \pmod q$ for at least some of the $(a,b) \in T$. Therefore, Algorithm 2 returns keys such that guessing the set I is not enough to determine v. Moreover, since f_{set} is non-empty, $f * f^{-1} = 1 + \alpha * \sigma \pmod q$ for some nonzero $\alpha \in \mathbb{A}$, and $\sigma * g \neq 0 \pmod q$. Therefore, even for the correct v, $f * (h - v) \neq g \pmod q$. Hence, (f, g) cannot be recovered as a short vector in the $q-$ary lattice $\mathcal{L}_{CS}$.

Intuitively, this approach seems to thwart our key attack. However, we demonstrate that a similar hybrid attack is feasible on the modified key generation. The only change is that we now need to solve SVP in a lattice with a smaller determinant, making the problem slightly harder. Suppose the attacker can correctly guess the set I, then, he can construct the $4n^2 \times 4n^2$ matrix

$$\mathcal{B}_{private} = \begin{pmatrix} D' & 0 & 0 & 0 \\ 0 & D' & 0 & 0 \\ 0 & 0 & D' & 0 \\ 0 & 0 & 0 & D' \end{pmatrix}$$

generating the private lattice $\mathcal{L}_{private}$ corresponding to the ideal $J \cong Q^4 \subseteq \mathbb{A}$ where D' is $n^2 \times n^2$ generator matrix for the lattice $\mathcal{L}_Q$ corresponding to the ideal $Q \subseteq R$. We have,

$$\begin{aligned} f * h &= (f * f^{-1}) * g + v \,(\mathrm{mod}\, q) \\ &= (1 + \alpha * \sigma) * g + f * v \,(\mathrm{mod}\, q) \\ &= g + (\alpha * g + f * w) * \sigma \,(\mathrm{mod}\, q) \\ &= g + (\alpha * g + f * w) * \sigma + qu \quad \text{for some} \quad u \in \mathbb{A} \\ &= g + \gamma \end{aligned}$$

where, $\gamma = (\alpha * g + f * w) * \sigma + qu \in J$. Therefore, there exists some $\boldsymbol{u} \in \mathbb{Z}^{4n^2}$ such that $\boldsymbol{\gamma} = \boldsymbol{u} \star \mathcal{B}_{private}$. As a result,

$$(\boldsymbol{f}, -\boldsymbol{u}) \star \mathcal{B}_{CS}^{new} = (\boldsymbol{f}, \boldsymbol{g}), \tag{57}$$

where,

$$\mathcal{B}_{CS}^{new} = \begin{pmatrix} I_{4n^2} & \mathcal{H} \\ 0 & \mathcal{B}_{private} \end{pmatrix}. \tag{58}$$

Consequently, the private key can be recovered by solving SVP in $8n^2$–dimensional lattice $\mathcal{L}_{CS}^{new}$ generated by the matrix $\mathcal{B}_{CS}^{new}$. Further, a similar dimension reduction as for our attack on the original key generation is possible for the lattice $\mathcal{L}_{CS}^{new}$. Recovering the private key for the modified key generation is also equivalent to solving SVP in a $4n^2$–dimensional lattice $\mathcal{L}_{CS,\phi}^{new}$ generated by the matrix

$$\mathcal{B}_{CS,\phi}^{new} = \begin{pmatrix} I_{2n^2} & \phi(\mathcal{H}) \\ 0 & \mathcal{B}_{private,\phi} \end{pmatrix}, \tag{59}$$

where $\mathcal{B}_{private,\phi} = \begin{pmatrix} D' & 0 \\ 0 & D' \end{pmatrix}$. However, since

$$det(\mathcal{B}_{CS,\phi}^{new}) = det(D')^2 = q^{2(n^2-|T|)} < q^{2n^2} = det(\mathcal{B}_{CS,\phi}).$$

Therefore, solving SVP in the lattice $\mathcal{L}_{CS,\phi}^{new}$ is costlier than $\mathcal{L}_{CS,\phi}$ as reflected in our experiments. For instance, for the parameter set with $n = 7$ and $q = 547$, the average blocksize to find a decryption key increases from 7 (for the old key generation process, Algorithm 1) to 9 (for the modified key generation, Algorithm 2). Similarly for $n = 7$ and $q = 113$, the average blocksize increases from 52.6 to 56. This increment makes the key attack slightly higher but does not thwart the practicality of our folding technique.

7.2 Updating Parameters

The other straightforward way to avoid potential attacks is by increasing the parameter size. For example, one could allow for a larger set T to increase the search cost. However, as discussed in [5], and also experimentally observed, that $|T| \leq n$ is essential for successful decryption. Another possible attempt could be to increase the value of n, which will increase both the search and the lattice reduction cost. We searched for the BQTRU parameter set achieving the first level, i.e., 128-bit security, as suggested by NIST, that allows for no more than 2^{-128} decryption failure probability. Considering our key and message attack, $n = 17$ with $q = 919$ is the smallest prime that reaches the desired requirements. However, the issue with BQTRU is that the receiver needs to solve CVP in an n^2–dimensional ($n^2 = 289$, for $n = 17$) lattice to decrypt. Even with the best algorithms for solving CVP in this dimension, the cost of decryption is prohibitively high, making it impractical as a cryptosystem.

8 Concluding Remarks

The proposal of building a cryptosystem based on the hardness of two prominent post-quantum families (lattice and code-based) is undoubtedly interesting. BQTRU has been introduced as a possibly practical scheme after a few attempts to build such construction based on the hardness of solving the SVP in hybrid lattices. In principle, choosing quaternion algebra was a smart choice to make the decryption practical by mapping the problem of solving CVP in a $4n^2$–dimensional private lattice to 4 instances of CVP in an n^2–dimensional lattice. Further, fast multiplication methods [41] that enable faster multiplication in quaternion algebra defined over $\left(\frac{1,1}{R}\right)$ was an additional reason for the authors of BQTRU to consider their construction. Our analysis indicates that the same reason that allowed for faster multiplication and feasible decryption in the chosen structure made the construction susceptible to a dimension folding attack.

This work demonstrates the effectiveness of the proposed attack both theoretically and experimentally. Consequently, we were able to compromise the moderate BQTRU parameter set and show that higher parameter sets offer much lower security levels than claimed. Further, our few attempts to fix BQTRU in its current form show the possibility of extending our folding attack to the modified key generation or that the scheme is yielding an impractical construction for secure parameter sets. As a result, creating a secure yet practical cryptosystem based on the hardness of the SVP in a hybrid lattice remains an open research problem. One future direction is to explore different structures that are not vulnerable to folding attacks or to build a trapdoor that enables solving the CVP easily in the decryption process for the party possessing the trapdoor information.

A Group Rings

For a ring R and a finite group $G = \{g_i : i = 1, 2, \ldots, n\}$ of order n, the group ring of G over R is the set of formal sums

$$RG = \left\{ a = \sum_{i=1}^{n} \alpha_{g_i} g_i : \alpha_{g_i} \in R \text{ for } i = 1, 2, \ldots, n \right\}, \tag{60}$$

that forms a ring under the following operations: let $a = \sum_{i=1}^{n} \alpha_{g_i} g_i$ and $b = \sum_{i=1}^{n} \beta_{g_i} g_i$ in RG then the sum of a and b is defined as:

$$a + b = \sum_{i=1}^{n} \alpha_{g_i} g_i + \sum_{i=1}^{n} \beta_{g_i} g_i = \sum_{i=1}^{n} (\alpha_{g_i} + \beta_{g_i}) g_i , \tag{61}$$

and the product of a and b as:

$$a * b = \left(\sum_{i=1}^{n} \alpha_{g_i} g_i \right) * \left(\sum_{i=1}^{n} \beta_{g_i} g_i \right) = \sum_{i=1}^{n} \gamma_{g_i} g_i , \tag{62}$$

where

$$\gamma_{g_k} = \sum_{g_i g_j = g_k} \alpha_{g_i} \beta_{g_j} = \sum_{i=1}^{n} \alpha_{g_i} \beta_{g_i^{-1} g_k} = \sum_{i=1}^{n} \alpha_{g_k g_i^{-1}} \beta_{g_i} . \tag{63}$$

For each element $a = \sum_{i=1}^{n} \alpha_{g_i} g_i \in RG$, we associate a unique coefficient vector $\boldsymbol{a} = (\alpha_{g_1}, \alpha_{g_2}, \ldots, \alpha_{g_n})$. We use a and $\boldsymbol{a}$ interchangeably to refer to an element of group ring RG. In vector notation

$$\boldsymbol{a} + \boldsymbol{b} = (\alpha_{g_1} + \beta_{g_1}, \alpha_{g_2} + \beta_{g_2}, \ldots, \alpha_{g_n} + \beta_{g_n}), \quad \boldsymbol{a} \star \boldsymbol{b} = (\gamma_{g_1}, \gamma_{g_2}, \ldots, \gamma_{g_n})$$

where γ_{g_i}, for $i = 1, 2, \ldots, n$, are given by (63), denote coordinatewise addition and the convolutional product of two vectors $\boldsymbol{a}, \boldsymbol{b} \in RG$, respectively. Using Eq. (63), we have

$$\boldsymbol{a} \star \boldsymbol{b} = (\alpha_{g_1}, \alpha_{g_2}, \ldots, \alpha_{g_n}) \star \begin{pmatrix} \beta_{g_1^{-1} g_1} & \beta_{g_1^{-1} g_2} & \cdots\cdots & \beta_{g_1^{-1} g_n} \\ \beta_{g_2^{-1} g_1} & \beta_{g_2^{-1} g_2} & \cdots\cdots & \beta_{g_2^{-1} g_n} \\ \vdots & \vdots & \ddots & \vdots \\ \beta_{g_n^{-1} g_1} & \beta_{g_n^{-1} g_2} & \cdots\cdots & \beta_{g_n^{-1} g_n} \end{pmatrix} \tag{64}$$

$$(\boldsymbol{a} \star \boldsymbol{b})^{Tr} = \begin{pmatrix} \alpha_{g_1 g_1^{-1}} & \alpha_{g_1 g_2^{-1}} & \cdots\cdots & \alpha_{g_1 g_n^{-1}} \\ \alpha_{g_2 g_1^{-1}} & \alpha_{g_2 g_2^{-1}} & \cdots\cdots & \alpha_{g_2 g_n^{-1}} \\ \vdots & \vdots & \ddots & \vdots \\ \alpha_{g_n g_1^{-1}} & \alpha_{g_n g_2^{-1}} & \cdots\cdots & \alpha_{g_n g_n^{-1}} \end{pmatrix} \star \begin{pmatrix} \beta_{g_1} \\ \beta_{g_2} \\ \vdots \\ \beta_{g_n} \end{pmatrix} . \tag{65}$$

Definition 13 (RG-matrices). *[22] For an element $\boldsymbol{a} = (\alpha_{g_1}, \alpha_{g_2}, \ldots, \alpha_{g_n}) \in RG$, define the RG−matrices of $\boldsymbol{a}$ in $M_n(R)$ as follows:*

$$A = \begin{pmatrix} \alpha_{g_1^{-1} g_1} & \alpha_{g_1^{-1} g_2} & \cdots\cdots & \alpha_{g_1^{-1} g_n} \\ \alpha_{g_2^{-1} g_1} & \alpha_{g_2^{-1} g_2} & \cdots\cdots & \alpha_{g_2^{-1} g_n} \\ \vdots & \vdots & \ddots & \vdots \\ \alpha_{g_n^{-1} g_1} & \alpha_{g_n^{-1} g_2} & \cdots\cdots & \alpha_{g_n^{-1} g_n} \end{pmatrix}, \quad A' = \begin{pmatrix} \alpha_{g_1 g_1^{-1}} & \alpha_{g_1 g_2^{-1}} & \cdots\cdots & \alpha_{g_1 g_n^{-1}} \\ \alpha_{g_2 g_1^{-1}} & \alpha_{g_2 g_2^{-1}} & \cdots\cdots & \alpha_{g_2 g_n^{-1}} \\ \vdots & \vdots & \ddots & \vdots \\ \alpha_{g_n g_1^{-1}} & \alpha_{g_n g_2^{-1}} & \cdots\cdots & \alpha_{g_n g_n^{-1}} \end{pmatrix} .$$

Lemma 4. *For* $\boldsymbol{a} = (\alpha_{g_1}, \alpha_{g_2}, \ldots, \alpha_{g_n}), \boldsymbol{b} = (\beta_{g_1}, \beta_{g_2}, \ldots, \beta_{g_n}) \in RG$, *the following hold:*

$$\boldsymbol{a} \star \boldsymbol{b} = \boldsymbol{a} \star B \quad \text{and} \quad (\boldsymbol{a} \star \boldsymbol{b})^{Tr} = A' \star \boldsymbol{b}^{Tr}. \tag{66}$$

Further, if G *is abelian group then* $\quad \boldsymbol{a} \star \boldsymbol{b} = \boldsymbol{b} \star A$.

Proof. The first part of the proof immediately follows from Eqs. (64) and (65). The other part follows from the observation that if G is an abelian group, then $A = (A')^{Tr}$. □

Theorem 3. *[22, Theorem 1] The mapping* $\tau : RG \rightarrow M_n(R)$ *defined as* $\tau(\boldsymbol{a}) = A$ *is a ring homomorphism, i.e.,* $\tau(\boldsymbol{a} + \boldsymbol{b}) = A + B$ *and* $\tau(\boldsymbol{a} \star \boldsymbol{b}) = A \star B$, *where* $+, \star$ *denote the usual matrix addition and multiplication, respectively.*

Example 1. Let $G = \langle x, y : x^n = 1, y^n = 1, xy = yx \rangle$ be a group of order n^2, then $R = \mathbb{Z}[x, y]/\langle x^n - 1, y^n - 1 \rangle \cong \mathbb{Z}G$. We can express every element of ring R as

$$v(x, y) = v_0(x) + y v_1(x) + y^2 v_2(x) + \ldots + y^{n-1} v_{n-1}(x),$$

where each $v_i(x) \in \mathbb{Z}[x]/\langle x^n - 1 \rangle$. Then, the coefficient vector of $v(x, y)$ is $\boldsymbol{v} = (\boldsymbol{v}_0, \boldsymbol{v}_1, \ldots, \boldsymbol{v}_{n-1}) \in \mathbb{Z}^{n^2}$, where $\boldsymbol{v}_i \in \mathbb{Z}^n$ is the coefficient vector of $v_i(x)$, and the matrix representation of $\boldsymbol{v}$ has the form

$$V = \begin{pmatrix} V_0 & V_1 & \ldots & V_{n-1} \\ V_{n-1} & V_0 & \ldots & V_{n-2} \\ \vdots & \vdots & \ddots & \vdots \\ V_1 & V_2 & \ldots & V_0 \end{pmatrix} \in M_{n^2}(\mathbb{Z}), \tag{67}$$

where $V_i \in M_n(\mathbb{Z})$ is the matrix representation of $\boldsymbol{v}_i$ and $V' = V^{Tr}$.

B Multiplication in $\mathbb{A} = \left(\frac{1,1}{R}\right)$

For two quaternions, $f = f_0 + f_1 i + f_2 j + f_3 k, g = g_0 + g_1 i + g_2 j + g_3 k \in \mathbb{A}$, consider the product

$$\begin{aligned} f * g =& (f_0 g_0 + f_1 g_1 + f_2 g_2 - f_3 g_3) + (f_1 g_0 + f_0 g_1 + f_3 g_2 - f_2 g_3) i \\ &+ (f_2 g_0 - f_3 g_1 + f_0 g_2 + f_1 g_3) j + (f_3 g_0 - f_2 g_1 + f_1 g_2 + f_0 g_3) k \end{aligned} \tag{68}$$

Using Lemma 4, the coefficient vector of the product $f * g$ is given by

$$\boldsymbol{f} \star \boldsymbol{g} = (\boldsymbol{f}_0, \boldsymbol{f}_1, \boldsymbol{f}_2, \boldsymbol{f}_3) \star \begin{pmatrix} G_0 & G_1 & G_2 & G_3 \\ G_1 & G_0 & G_3 & G_2 \\ G_2 & -G_3 & G_0 & -G_1 \\ -G_3 & G_2 & -G_1 & G_0 \end{pmatrix}, \tag{69}$$

$$(\boldsymbol{f} \star \boldsymbol{g})^{Tr} = \begin{pmatrix} F_0' & F_1' & F_2' & -F_3' \\ F_1' & F_0' & F_3' & -F_2' \\ F_2' & -F_3' & F_0' & F_1' \\ F_3' & -F_2' & F_1' & F_0 \end{pmatrix} \star \begin{pmatrix} \boldsymbol{g}_0^{Tr} \\ \boldsymbol{g}_1^{Tr} \\ \boldsymbol{g}_2^{Tr} \\ \boldsymbol{g}_3^{Tr} \end{pmatrix}. \tag{70}$$

where $G_i, F_i' \in M_{n^2}(\mathbb{Z})$ are the matrix representations of g_i, f_i as defined in Eq. (67), respectively.

Definition 14 (Quaternion matrices). *For a quaternion* $f = f_0 + f_1 i + f_2 j + f_3 k \in \mathbb{A}$, *define the matrix representations of* f *in* $M_{4n^2}(\mathbb{Z})$ *as follows:*

$$\mathcal{F} = \begin{pmatrix} F_0 & F_1 & F_2 & F_3 \\ F_1 & F_0 & F_3 & F_2 \\ F_2 & -F_3 & F_0 & -F_1 \\ -F_3 & F_2 & -F_1 & F_0 \end{pmatrix}, \quad \mathcal{F}' = \begin{pmatrix} F_0' & F_1' & F_2' & -F_3' \\ F_1' & F_0' & F_3' & -F_2' \\ F_2' & -F_3' & F_0' & F_1' \\ F_3' & -F_2' & F_1' & F_0 \end{pmatrix}. \tag{71}$$

where $F_i, F_i' \in M_{n^2}(\mathbb{Z})$ *are the matrix representations of* f_i *as defined in Eq. (67).*

Lemma 5. *For two quaternions* $f = f_0 + f_1 i + f_2 j + f_3 k, g = g_0 + g_1 i + g_2 j + g_3 k \in \mathbb{A}$, *the following hold:*

$$\boldsymbol{f} \star \boldsymbol{g} = \boldsymbol{f} \star \mathcal{G} \quad \text{and} \quad (\boldsymbol{f} \star \boldsymbol{g})^{Tr} = \mathcal{F}' \star \boldsymbol{b}^{Tr}. \tag{72}$$

Further, if $\tilde{\mathcal{F}} = (\mathcal{F}')^{Tr}$ *then* $\quad \boldsymbol{f} \star \boldsymbol{g} = \boldsymbol{g} \star \tilde{\mathcal{F}}$.

Proof. The proof immediately follows from Eqs. (69) and (70). □

Note: We would like to point out that in [5], the matrix representation of the quaternions in $\mathbb{A}$ is incorrect due to the wrong multiplication in [5, Equation 16].

C Proof of Lemma 2

Let $\mathcal{F}$ and $\mathcal{G}$ be matrices of elements f and $g \in \mathbb{A}$, respectively. Then,

$$\begin{aligned} \phi(\mathcal{F} + \mathcal{G}) &= \phi \begin{pmatrix} F_0 + G_0 & F_1 + G_1 & F_2 + G_2 & F_3 + G_3 \\ F_1 + G_1 & F_0 + G_0 & F_3 + G_3 & F_2 + G_2 \\ F_2 + G_2 & -F_3 - G_3 & F_0 + G_0 & -F_1 - G_1 \\ -F_3 - G_3 & F_2 + G_2 & -F_1 - G_1 & F_0 + G_0 \end{pmatrix} \\ &= \begin{pmatrix} F_0 + G_0 + F_1 + G_1 & F_2 + G_2 + F_3 + G_3 \\ F_2 + G_2 - F_3 - G_3 & F_0 + G_0 - F_1 - G_1 \end{pmatrix} \\ &= \phi(\mathcal{F}) + \phi(\mathcal{G}). \end{aligned}$$

Similarly, one can verify that $\phi(\mathcal{F} \star \mathcal{G}) = \phi(\mathcal{F}) \star \phi(\mathcal{G})$. Therefore, ϕ is a matrix ring homomorphism.

References

1. Albrecht, M.R., et al.: Estimate all the LWE, NTRU schemes! In: Catalano, D., De Prisco, R. (eds.) SCN 2018. LNCS, vol. 11035, pp. 351–367. Springer, Cham (2018). https://doi.org/10.1007/978-3-319-98113-0_19
2. Albrecht, M.R., Ducas, L., Herold, G., Kirshanova, E., Postlethwaite, E.W., Stevens, M.: The general sieve kernel and new records in lattice reduction. In: Ishai, Y., Rijmen, V. (eds.) EUROCRYPT 2019. LNCS, vol. 11477, pp. 717–746. Springer, Cham (2019). https://doi.org/10.1007/978-3-030-17656-3_25

3. Alkim, E., Ducas, L., Pöppelmann, T., Schwabe, P.: Post-quantum key Exchange—a new hope. In: 25th USENIX Security Symposium (USENIX Security 16), pp. 327–343 (2016). https://www.usenix.org/system/files/conference/usenixsecurity16/sec16_paper_alkim.pdf
4. Aono, Y., Wang, Y., Hayashi, T., Takagi, T.: Improved progressive BKZ algorithms and their precise cost estimation by sharp simulator. In: Fischlin, M., Coron, J.-S. (eds.) EUROCRYPT 2016. LNCS, vol. 9665, pp. 789–819. Springer, Heidelberg (2016). https://doi.org/10.1007/978-3-662-49890-3_30
5. Bagheri, K., Sadeghi, M.R., Panario, D.: A non-commutative cryptosystem based on quaternion algebras. Des. Codes Crypt. **86** (2018). https://doi.org/10.1007/s10623-017-0451-4
6. Bai, S., Jangir, H., Ngo, T., Youmans, W.: An algebraic algorithm for breaking NTRU with multiple keys. Des. Codes Crypt., 1–24 (2024). https://doi.org/10.1007/s10623-024-01473-z
7. Becker, A., Ducas, L., Gama, N., Laarhoven, T.: New directions in nearest neighbor searching with applications to lattice sieving. In: Proceedings of the Twenty-Seventh Annual ACM-SIAM Symposium on Discrete Algorithms, pp. 10–24. SIAM (2016). https://doi.org/10.1137/1.9781611974331.ch2
8. Boschini, C., Orsini, E., Traverso, C.: Between codes and lattices: hybrid lattices and the NTWO cryptosystem. In: Proceedings Effective Methods Algebraic Geometry (2015). http://people.cs.bris.ac.uk/~cseao/papr/MEGA2015.pdf
9. Caboara, M., Caruso, F., Traverso, C.: Gröbner bases for public key cryptography. In: Proceedings of the International Symposium on Symbolic and Algebraic Computation, ISSAC, pp. 315–324 (2008).https://doi.org/10.1145/1390768.1390811
10. Chen, C., et al.: PQC round-3 candidate: NTRU. Technical report. NTRU Cryptosystems Technical Report No. 11, Version 2, March 2001 (2019). https://ntru.org/f/ntru-20190330.pdf
11. Chen, Y.: Réduction de réseau et sécurité concrète du chiffrement complètement homomorphe. Ph.D. thesis, l'Université Paris Diderot (2013). http://www.theses.fr/2013PA077242
12. Chen, Y., Nguyen, P.Q.: BKZ 2.0: better lattice security estimates. In: Lee, D.H., Wang, X. (eds.) ASIACRYPT 2011. LNCS, vol. 7073, pp. 1–20. Springer, Heidelberg (2011). https://doi.org/10.1007/978-3-642-25385-0_1
13. Coppersmith, D., Shamir, A.: Lattice attacks on NTRU. In: Fumy, W. (ed.) EUROCRYPT 1997. LNCS, vol. 1233, pp. 52–61. Springer, Heidelberg (1997). https://doi.org/10.1007/3-540-69053-0_5
14. Dachman-Soled, D., Ducas, L., Gong, H., Rossi, M.: LWE with side information: attacks and concrete security estimation. In: Micciancio, D., Ristenpart, T. (eds.) CRYPTO 2020. LNCS, vol. 12171, pp. 329–358. Springer, Cham (2020). https://doi.org/10.1007/978-3-030-56880-1_12
15. Ducas, L., van Woerden, W.: NTRU fatigue: how stretched is overstretched? Cryptology ePrint Archive, Paper 2021/999 (2021). https://eprint.iacr.org/2021/999
16. Fincke, U., Pohst, M.: Improved methods for calculating vectors of short length in a lattice, including a complexity analysis. Math. Comput. **44**(170), 463–471 (1985)
17. Gentry, C.: Key recovery and message attacks on NTRU-composite. In: Pfitzmann, B. (ed.) EUROCRYPT 2001. LNCS, vol. 2045, pp. 182–194. Springer, Heidelberg (2001). https://doi.org/10.1007/3-540-44987-6_12
18. Herold, G., Kirshanova, E., Laarhoven, T.: Speed-ups and time–memory trade-offs for tuple lattice sieving. In: Abdalla, M., Dahab, R. (eds.) PKC 2018. LNCS, vol. 10769, pp. 407–436. Springer, Cham (2018). https://doi.org/10.1007/978-3-319-76578-5_14

19. Hoffstein, J., Pipher, J., Silverman, J.H.: NTRU: a ring-based public key cryptosystem. In: Buhler, J.P. (ed.) ANTS 1998. LNCS, vol. 1423, pp. 267–288. Springer, Heidelberg (1998). https://doi.org/10.1007/BFb0054868
20. Hoffstein, J., Silverman, J.H., Whyte, W.: Meet-in-the-middle attack on an NTRU private key. Technical report, NTRU Cryptosystems, July 2006. Report (2006). https://ntru.org/f/tr/tr004v2.pdf
21. Howgrave-Graham, N., et al.: The impact of decryption failures on the security of NTRU encryption. In: Boneh, D. (ed.) CRYPTO 2003. LNCS, vol. 2729, pp. 226–246. Springer, Heidelberg (2003). https://doi.org/10.1007/978-3-540-45146-4_14
22. Hurley, T.: Group rings and rings of matrices. Int. J. Pure Appl. Math. **31**, 319–335 (2006). https://www.researchgate.net/publication/228928727_Group_rings_and_rings_of_matrices
23. Hülsing, A., Rijneveld, J., Schanck, J., Schwabe, P.: High-speed key encapsulation from NTRU. In: Fischer, W., Homma, N. (eds.) CHES 2017. LNCS, vol. 10529, pp. 232–252. Springer, Cham (2017). https://doi.org/10.1007/978-3-319-66787-4_12
24. Kannan, R.: Improved algorithms for integer programming and related lattice problems. In: Proceedings of the Fifteenth Annual ACM Symposium on Theory of Computing, pp. 193–206 (1983). https://doi.org/10.1145/800061.808749
25. Kim, J., Lee, C.: A polynomial time algorithm for breaking NTRU encryption with multiple keys. Des. Codes Crypt., 1–11 (2023). https://doi.org/10.1007/s10623-023-01233-5
26. Kirchner, P., Fouque, P.-A.: Revisiting lattice attacks on overstretched NTRU parameters. In: Coron, J.-S., Nielsen, J.B. (eds.) EUROCRYPT 2017. LNCS, vol. 10210, pp. 3–26. Springer, Cham (2017). https://doi.org/10.1007/978-3-319-56620-7_1
27. Kirshanova, E., May, A., Nowakowski, J.: New NTRU records with improved lattice bases. In: Johansson, T., Smith-Tone, D. (eds.) PQCrypto 2023. LNCS, vol. 14154, pp. 167–195. Springer, Cham (2023). https://doi.org/10.1007/978-3-031-40003-2_7
28. Kumar, V., Das, R., Gangopadhyay, A.K.: GR-NTRU: Dihedral group over ring of Eisenstein integers. J. Inf. Secur. Appl. **83**, 103795 (2024). https://doi.org/10.1016/j.jisa.2024.103795
29. Kumar, V., Raya, A., Gangopadhyay, A.K., Gangopadhyay, S., Hussain, M.T.: An efficient noncommutative NTRU from semidirect product. Cryptology ePrint Archive, Paper 2024/1721 (2024). https://eprint.iacr.org/2024/1721
30. Laarhoven, T.: Search problems in cryptography: from fingerprinting to lattice sieving. Ph.D thesis, Eindhoven University of Technology (2015). https://research.tue.nl/en/publications/search-problems-in-cryptography-from-fingerprinting-to-lattice-si
31. Lenstra, A.K., Lenstra, H.W., Lovász, L.: Factoring polynomials with rational coefficients. Mathematische Annalen **261**, 515–534 (1982). https://doi.org/10.1007/BF01457454
32. Ling, C., Mendelsohn, A.: NTRU in quaternion algebras of bounded discriminant. In: Johansson, T., Smith-Tone, D. (eds.) PQCrypto 2023. LNCS, vol. 14154, pp. 256–290. Springer, Cham (2023). https://doi.org/10.1007/978-3-031-40003-2_10
33. Maclachlan, C., Reid, A.W.: Arithmetic hyperbolic 3-manifolds and orbifolds. In: The Arithmetic of Hyperbolic 3-Manifolds. Graduate Texts in Mathematics, vol. 219, pp. 275–304. Springer, New York (2003). https://doi.org/10.1007/978-1-4757-6720-9_10

34. Malekian, E., Zakerolhosseini, A., Mashatan, A.: QTRU : a lattice attack resistant version of NTRU PKCS based on quaternion algebra. IACR Cryptology ePrint Archive **386** (2009). https://eprint.iacr.org/2009/386
35. Micciancio, D., Walter, M.: Fast lattice point enumeration with minimal overhead. In: Proceedings of the Twenty-Sixth Annual ACM-SIAM Symposium on Discrete Algorithms, pp. 276–294. SIAM (2014)https://doi.org/10.1137/1.9781611973730.21
36. Peikert, C.: A decade of lattice cryptography. Found. Trends® Theor. Comput. Sci. **10**(4), 283–424 (2016). https://doi.org/10.1561/0400000074
37. Raya, A., Kumar, V., Gangopadhyay, S.: DiTRU: a resurrection of NTRU over Dihedral group. In: Vaudenay, S., Petit, C. (eds.) AFRICACRYPT 2024. LNCS, vol. 14861, pp. 349–375. Springer, Cham (2024). https://doi.org/10.1007/978-3-031-64381-1_16
38. Raya, A., Kumar, V., Gangopadhyay, S., Gangopadhyay, A.K.: Results on the key space of group-ring NTRU: the case of the dihedral group. In: Regazzoni, F., Mazumdar, B., Parameswaran, S. (eds.) SPACE 2023. LNCS, vol. 14412, pp. 1–19. Springer, Cham (2024). https://doi.org/10.1007/978-3-031-51583-5_1
39. Schnorr, C.P.: A hierarchy of polynomial time lattice basis reduction algorithms. Theoret. Comput. Sci. **53**(2–3), 201–224 (1987). https://doi.org/10.1016/0304-3975(87)90064-8
40. Silverman, J.: Wraps, gaps, and lattice constants. Technical report, NTRU Cryptosystems Technical Report No. 11, Version 2, March 2001. Report (2001). https://ntru.org/f/tr/tr011v2.pdf
41. Strassen, V.: Gaussian elimination is not optimal. Numerische mathematik **13**(4), 354–356 (1969). https://doi.org/10.1007/BF02165411
42. The FPLLL development team: FPLLL, a lattice reduction library, Version: 5.4.4 (2023). https://github.com/fplll/fplll
43. The FPLLL development team: FPYLLL, a Python wraper for the FPLLL lattice reduction library, Version: 0.5.9 (2023). https://github.com/fplll/fpylll

Batch Anonymous MAC Tokens from Lattices

Yingfei Yan[1], Sherman S. M. Chow[2], Lucien K. L. Ng[3], Harry W. H. Wong[2], Yongjun Zhao[4], and Baocang Wang[1(✉)]

[1] State Key Laboratory of Integrated Service Networks, Xidian University, Xi'an, China
yanxi@stu.xidian.edu.cn, bcwang@xidian.edu.cn
[2] Department of Information Engineering, Chinese University of Hong Kong, Shatin, N.T., Hong Kong SAR, China
{sherman,whwong}@ie.cuhk.edu.hk
[3] School of Cybersecurity and Privacy, Georgia Institute of Technology, Atlanta, GA 30332, USA
kng68@gatech.edu
[4] Independent Researcher, Shanghai, China

Abstract. Solutions for DDoS protection employed by content delivery networks often burden honest users, especially those using privacy-enhancing tools like VPNs, by forcing them to solve many CAPTCHAs. Helping users avoid repeated CAPTCHAs, anonymous tokens (ATs) now offer a practical alternative to traditional anonymous credentials (ACs). Evolution of ATs, driven by IETF standardization, introduced features like the private metadata bit (Crypto '20, Eurocrypt '22), which encrypts challenge results for verifiers, preventing automated CAPTCHA solver. Regrettably, recent designs overlooked the original goal (PoPETS '18) of batch-issuing tokens along with efficient batch proofs for validation. Moreover, most solutions lack post-quantum security, except a direct adaptation from ACs (ePrint '23) that lacks private metadata support. Adopting lattice-based cryptography in existing AT designs is non-trivial, as they often employ intricate algebraic structures to ensure efficiency. Notably, a lattice-based AT in the keyed-verification setting that supports both batch proofs and private metadata bit remains absent.

For the first time, we propose a batch anonymous MAC token system from lattices, integrating techniques from verifiable oblivious pseudorandom function (PKC '21) and practical zero-knowledge proof (Crypto '22). Extending this design, our AT system supports public metadata (Eurocrypt '22, FC '22, PoPETS '25) with minimal computational overhead. In practice, our AT is only 432 bytes with optimized parameters.

Keywords: anonymous tokens · anonymous MAC tokens · batch proof · keyed verification · private metadata · lattice · IETF · implementations

R. Niederhagen and M.-J. O. Saarinen (Eds.): PQCrypto 2025, LNCS 15577, pp. 349–384, 2025.
https://doi.org/10.1007/978-3-031-86599-2_12

1 Introduction

Spurred by the continued growth of content delivery networks (CDNs), control over internet content delivery has become somewhat more centralized nowadays. However, in their efforts to mitigate malicious traffic, including large-scale attacks such as distributed denial-of-services (DDoS) attacks, CDNs often inadvertently block or restrict legitimate traffic originating from shared IP addresses. Expectedly, privacy-conscious users relying on tools like the onion router (Tor), virtual private networks (VPNs), and the invisible internet project (I2P) are repeatedly targeted by "completely automated public Turing test to tell computers and humans apart" (CAPTCHAs), discouraging privacy-preserving tools. Responding to this, Privacy Pass introduces anonymous tokens (ATs) [20], a lightweight and efficient alternative to traditional anonymous credentials, enabling users to bypass future CAPTCHAs after completing a single verification. Modeled in Fig. 1, the AT workflow outlines the client and issuer interaction. A client initiates the token request process by querying the issuer with a *tag*, which helps the verifier detect token reuse, along with optional public metadata. Necessary for privacy, the tag for each token is a client-chosen random value hidden from the issuer, while any metadata (*e.g.*, a validity period [42]) must remain minimal to ensure a sufficiently large anonymity set and avoid identification.

Completing CAPTCHA challenges allows the client to obtain tokens embedding a private *metadata bit*: a covert bit conveying challenge results to verifiers. Hiding this bit from clients is crucial to discreetly identify potentially malicious clients without alerting them and to deter automated CAPTCHA solver training, though clients can still independently verify token validity, such as confirming they were correctly created using the secret key of the issuer for the hidden tag. Once issued, these tokens can be redeemed with the verifier, who validates token authenticity using a secret key and ensures no tag values have been reused. With keyed verification resembling message authentication codes (MACs), we refer to these as *anonymous MAC tokens* (AMTs), which authenticate the metadata bit and public metadata while restricting validation to authorized parties and mitigating vulnerabilities, such as those identified by Chase *et al.* [14], where adversaries exploit verification results to infer private metadata (see Sect. 1.2).

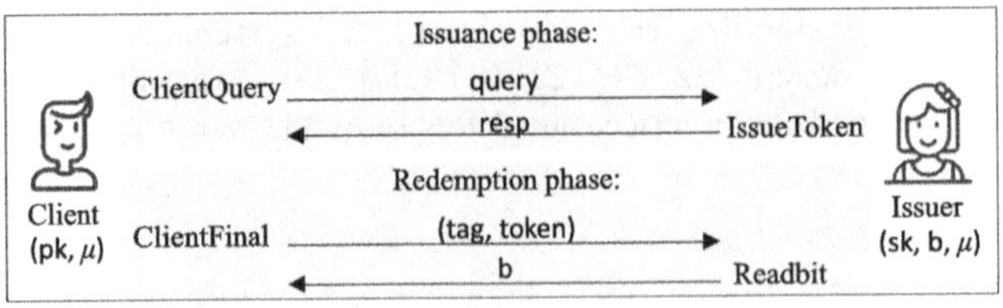

Fig. 1. Workflow of anonymous token

Table 1. Comparison with related works

	Keyed Ver.	Batch Proof	Private Bit	Public Data	Rd.	Basis
[DGS+18] [20]	✓	✓	×	×	2	DL
[KLOR20] [28]	✓	✓	✓	×	2	DDH
[BLOR22] [11]	×	×	✓	×	3	DL
[SS22] [42]	✓	✓	✓	✓	2	Pairings
[PWFW23] [38]	×	✓	×	×	2	Lattice+Hash
[CDV23] [14]	✓	×	✓	✓	2	DL
[CDH23] [19]	×	×	×	×	2	"Generic"
[Orrù24] [37]	✓	×	×	×	2	DL
[AYY25] [4]	×	×	×	✓	2	RSA
BLAST	✓	✓	✓	✓	2	Lattice

1.1 Post-quantum Token Issuance with Batch Proving

Yet, Privacy Pass [20] relies on the discrete-logarithm (DL) assumption, which is vulnerable to quantum attacks. Years later, AT constructions with private metadata [28] and public metadata [42] were introduced, relying on decisional-Diffie-Hellman (DDH) and pairing-based assumptions, respectively, but still lacked quantum security. For all this progress, no scheme has achieved both quantum security and efficient batch issuance—a key feature of the original AT [20] missing from many recent proposals [4,14,19,37].

The batch feature benefits both the issuer and the client: clients can obtain multiple tokens at once (avoiding the need to solve a CAPTCHA for every resource visit), and the issuer can efficiently handle bulk requests, reducing overhead. Considering the state of affairs and the importance of these features, we present *BLAST*, a cryptographic protocol that enables efficient batch issuance of lattice-based anonymous and secure tokens. *BLAST* is a keyed-verification ("Keyed Ver." in Table 1) scheme that supports two-round issuance, batch proofs, private metadata bit, and public metadata. Its security relies on a hashed version of the module learning with errors (LWE) assumption, with commitments in our instantiation relying on the module short integer solution (MSIS) assumption. By leveraging advances in lattice-based blind signatures [12], *BLAST* achieves a compact token size of 432 bytes. Our batch proof incurs only a slight increase in running time and proof size compared to single-issuance proofs. These benefits stem from integrating Albrecht *et al.*'s VOPRF [2] with Lyubashevsky*et al.*'s zero-knowledge proofs [33]. Tables 1 and 2 highlight our improvements.

1.2 Prior Constructions

The common approach [11,14,28,42] to incorporating a private metadata bit b involves the issuer generating two secret keys, sk_0 and sk_1, and using sk_b to create a pre-token. The issuer also provides a non-interactive zero-knowledge (NIZK) proof for a disjunctive statement (an "OR proof") that one of the secret keys was

Table 2. Comparing post-quantum secure blind signatures and anonymous tokens

Protocol	NIZKs	Token Size
Ours (Keyed verification with private metadata bit)	Lattice	432 B
Blind signature (Keyed verification) [12]	Lattice	48 B
Blind signature [27]	Lattice	40.47 kB
Dilithium-based anonymous token [38]	STARK	1∼40 kB
Anonymous credential [5]	Lattice	80 kB

used. The design challenge lies in hiding from clients which key was used for the tag they chose while still enabling verifiers to uniquely identify the key associated with each token. In constructions using oblivious pseudorandom functions (OPRFs), their deterministic nature poses a hindrance. A trivial extension of OPRFs would allow an adversarial client, by querying two tokens with the same tag, to determine if their private bits are identical.

Kreuter *et al.* [28] thus build *randomized* ATs from signatures using a two-part issuing key, one for deterministic tag signing and one for the randomized component. They are also the first to consider including a private metadata bit.

However, Chase *et al.* [14] demonstrate that an adversary can still exploit algebraic relationships between tokens with different tags to craft a new token that is valid only if both tokens share the same private bit. This attack relies on the adversarial client holding an initial token with a known private metadata bit and maliciously forming a tag for a new token request. To mitigate this vulnerability, they propose building AT with private bit using algebraic message authentication codes (MACs), which allow the issuer to contribute randomness to the tag and prevent such exploitation.

Including *public metadata*, such as the expiry date for natural revocation or geographic data for contact tracing, has also been studied [4,44] and considered by IETF standardization [40]. Silde and Strand [42] consider public verification of both private and public metadata. This broadens applications, such as know-your-customer use cases, but with a slight overhead in verification.

Batch queries are vital for user experiences in AT systems, as they avoid repeated challenges that would disrupt usability. Davidson *et al.* [20] proposed a batch proof [25] for the discrete logarithm equality problem to enable batch queries in Privacy Pass, with similar proofs adopted by Kreuter *et al.* [28]. Silde and Strand [42] achieved batch revocation of expired or invalid tokens.

A recent preprint [38] presents a lattice-based Privacy Pass with rate-limiting, built on a Dilithium signature variant optimized for ZK scalable transparent argument of knowledge (STARK) over arithmetic intermediate representation [10]. As its lattice-based AC origin, it does not support private metadata.

Rate-limiting, suggested in an IETF draft [24], was later generalized by Chu *et al.* [19] into a solution relying on a trusted intermediary. In this model, the client provides a key-blinding signature [19] to the intermediary, who knows the client's identity and enforces rate limits while generating an anonymous token linked to the signature. Table 1 marks this construction as "generic" though no lattice-based key-blinding signature scheme is currently known.

1.3 Protocol Overview

A core component of AMT [20] is a VOPRF [26], where an issuer holding a secret key $\mathbf{s}$ evaluates a pseudorandom function $F(\mathbf{s}, x)$ obliviously on input x provided by a client. Verifiability assures the client that the output $F(\mathbf{s}, x)$ is computed correctly, without revealing $\mathbf{s}$. We adopt the construction by Albrecht *et al.* [2]: $F(\mathbf{s}, x) = \lceil \langle f(x), \mathbf{s} \rangle \rfloor_{p_1}$, where $f\colon \{0,1\}^* \to \mathcal{R}_q^n$ [8] maps to a lattice module over the modular polynomial ring $\mathcal{R}_q := \mathbb{Z}_q[X]/(X^d + 1)$ and $\lceil \cdot \rfloor_{p_1}$ retains the high $\log p_1$ bits of its input for a small power of two p_1.

The issuer publishes an LWE instance $\mathbf{t}^\top = \mathbf{s}^\top \mathbf{A} + \mathbf{e}^\top$ as a commitment to the secret key $\mathbf{s}$, where $\mathbf{e}$ is a low-norm polynomial vector and $\mathbf{A}$ is a random square polynomial matrix. The client hides the input x, which is the tag (tag) in our AT scheme, by sampling a short random vector $\mathbf{x}$, computing $\mathbf{c} := \mathbf{A}\mathbf{x} + \mathbf{e}_2 + f(x)$, and providing NIZK for the computation. Upon receiving $\mathbf{c}$, the issuer computes an LWE sample $h := \langle \mathbf{s}, \mathbf{c} \rangle + e_3$ using her secret key $\mathbf{s}$ and proves that h is formed using $\mathbf{s}$ embedded in the public key $\mathbf{t}$. The client then unblinds h using $\langle \mathbf{t}, \mathbf{x} \rangle$:

$$v := \lceil h - \langle \mathbf{t}, \mathbf{x} \rangle \rfloor_{p_1} = \lceil \langle \mathbf{s}, f(x) \rangle + \langle \mathbf{s}, \mathbf{e}_2 \rangle + e_3 - \langle \mathbf{e}, \mathbf{x} \rangle \rfloor_{p_1} = \lceil \langle \mathbf{s}, f(x) \rangle \rfloor_{p_1}. \quad (1)$$

Rounding modulo p_1 removes the last three terms since they are small errors.

Assuming the hardness of a hashed version of module LWE (MLWE) problems [12], $\mathbf{A}\mathbf{x} + \mathbf{e}_2$ and $\lceil \langle \mathbf{s}, f(x) \rangle \rfloor_{p_1}$ can be modeled as (V)OPRF values. The former can hide the tag during token issuance. The latter can be used as a token.

Private Metadata Bit. Securely certifying a private metadata bit b leverages the pseudorandomness of the VOPRF. We introduce two secrets $\mathbf{s}_0, \mathbf{s}_1 \in \mathcal{R}_q^n$ to both the issuer and verifier (beyond the "base" secret key $\mathbf{s}$). Specifically, the issuer computes $h = \langle \mathbf{s}, \mathbf{c} \rangle + e_3 + \langle \mathbf{s}_\mathsf{b}, \mathbf{b} \rangle$, where $\mathbf{b} \in \mathcal{R}_q^n$ comes from the public parameter, and proves that $\mathsf{b} \in \{0, 1\}$. Unblinding similarly leads to $v = \lceil \langle \mathbf{s}, f(\mathsf{tag}) \rangle + \langle \mathbf{s}_\mathsf{b}, \mathbf{b} \rangle \rfloor_{p_1}$. The verifier returns b such that $\lceil \langle \mathbf{s}, f(\mathsf{tag}) \rangle + \langle \mathbf{s}_\mathsf{b}, \mathbf{b} \rangle \rfloor_{p_1} - v = 0$. We use $\langle \mathbf{s}_\mathsf{b}, \mathbf{b} \rangle$ but not $\mathbf{s}_\mathsf{b}$ for compatibility with known NIZK.

Bit Flipping Attack and Unforgeability. Meanwhile, the term $\langle \mathbf{s}, f(\mathsf{tag}) \rangle$ is solely determined by the client. By requesting a token with the same tag, a possibly different commitment $\mathbf{c}$, and a private metadata bit different from b, *i.e.*, a new token $v' = \lceil \langle \mathbf{s}, f(\mathsf{tag}) \rangle + \langle \mathbf{s}_{1-\mathsf{b}}, \mathbf{b} \rangle \rfloor_{p_1}$, a malicious client can use $v - v' \approx \langle \mathbf{s}_\mathsf{b} - \mathbf{s}_{1-\mathsf{b}}, \mathbf{b} \rangle$ to maul other tokens via flipping its private metadata bit b.

To prevent such attacks, we adopt the following modification [12]. We replace $f(x)$ of the PRF [8] by a hash function $\mathsf{H}_1\colon \{0,1\}^* \to \mathcal{R}_q^n$ and embed another hash function $\mathsf{G}\colon \{0,1\}^* \to \{0,1\}^{2\lambda}$ into it, both modeled as random oracles. Our commitment becomes $\mathbf{c} := \mathbf{A}\mathbf{x} + \mathbf{e}_2 + \mathsf{H}_1(\mathsf{tag}, \rho)$ for $\rho := \mathsf{G}(\mathbf{x}, \mathbf{e}_2)$. The collision resistance of the hash functions ensures that $\mathbf{c}$ is uniquely tied to $\mathsf{H}_1(\mathsf{tag}, \rho)$. The issuer is required to reject token requests for reused $\mathbf{c}$, preventing malicious clients from obtaining the same VOPRF value with a flipped private bit. Non-repeating VOPRF values extend the unforgeability to our private metadata bit.

Unlinkability. It is also essential to prevent the issuer from embedding a unique secret in place of $\mathbf{s}_0$ or $\mathbf{s}_1$ to break unlinkability. Hence, the issuer commits to both $\mathbf{s}_0$ and $\mathbf{s}_1$ by publishing $\{\mathbf{t}_b^\top = \mathbf{s}_b^\top \mathbf{A} + \mathbf{e}_b^\top\}_{b \in \{0,1\}}$. During issuance, the issuer proves the embedded $\mathbf{s}_\mathsf{b}$ matches one of the commitments. To align with the dimension of $\mathbf{s}_\mathsf{b}$, we select a public vector $\mathbf{b} \in \mathcal{R}_q^n$ and compute $h = \langle \mathbf{s}, \mathbf{c} \rangle + e_3 + \langle \mathbf{s}_\mathsf{b}, \mathbf{b} \rangle$. In our security proof, unlinkability again relies on the pseudorandomness of $\mathbf{Ax} + \mathbf{e}_2$ in $\mathbf{c}$. It hides $\mathsf{H}_1(\mathsf{tag}, \rho)$ in $\mathbf{c}$ and allows us to replace $\mathbf{c}$ by a PRF value that is unrelated to tag or ρ. To recover the valid token, we use the knowledge extractor to extract the secret keys $(\mathbf{s}, \mathbf{s}_0, \mathbf{s}_1)$ from the issuer's proof. We can then compute $v := \lceil \langle \mathbf{s}, \mathsf{H}_1(\mathsf{tag}, \rho) \rangle + \langle \mathbf{s}_\mathsf{b}, \mathbf{b} \rangle \rfloor_{p_1}$ directly. Thus, the query $\mathbf{c}$ is independent of the token (v, ρ), guaranteeing unlinkability.

For our construction, a technical challenge is about how the issuer proves the correctness of h without revealing private bit b using an efficient NIZK proof. To this end, we introduce a 2-bit secret vector $\nu \in \{0,1\}^2$, where the b-th position is 1 and the other is 0, to select one of $\mathbf{t}_0$ and $\mathbf{t}_1$ in the proof via $(\nu^\top [\mathbf{t}_0 | \mathbf{t}_1])^\top = \mathbf{s}_\mathsf{b}^\top \mathbf{A} + \mathbf{e}_\mathsf{b}^\top$. We can then construct the proof by transforming the above relation into linear or quadratic relations over the witness $(\mathbf{s}, \mathbf{s}_0, \mathbf{s}_1)$ and applying the recent technique [33] for proving general linear/quadratic relations.

Batch Issuance. The proof naturally extends to N issuance instances sharing the same private bit by replacing the single element h with a vector. For a batch involving different private bits, we express $h_i = e_{3,i} + \langle \mathbf{s}, \mathbf{c}_i \rangle + \langle \mathbf{s}_0, \mathbf{b} \rangle (1 - \mathsf{b}_i) + \langle \mathbf{s}_1, \mathbf{b} \rangle \mathsf{b}_i$ for each i, yielding a quadratic equation in $(\mathbf{s}, \mathbf{s}_0, \mathbf{s}_1, \mathsf{b})$. As exactly one of b_i and $(1 - \mathsf{b}_i)$ is zero, the computation remains the same. We then introduce a binary vector $\vec{\mathsf{b}} \in \{0,1\}^N$ to prove the relationships between N sets of h_i and the corresponding public keys $\mathbf{t}$ and private keys $(\mathbf{s}, \mathbf{s}_0, \mathbf{s}_1)$.

Public Metadata. Our protocol seamlessly supports extensions to include public metadata μ with an additional hash function $\mathsf{H}_3 \colon \{0,1\}^* \to \mathcal{R}_q^n$, mapping μ to an n-dimensional vector over $\mathcal{R}_q$. Specifically, the issuer computes $h = \langle \mathbf{s}, \mathbf{c} + \mathsf{H}_3(\mu) \rangle + \langle \mathbf{s}_\mathsf{b}, \mathbf{b} \rangle + e_3$, *i.e.*, adding $\mathsf{H}_3(\mu)$ to $\mathbf{c}$. Intuitively, this simple addition is safeguarded by the proof that $\mathbf{c}$ is well-formed, ensuring that clients cannot manipulate $\mathsf{H}_3(\mu)$ by exploiting malformed $\mathbf{c}$. The resulting token becomes $v_\mathsf{b} = \lceil \langle \mathbf{s}, \mathsf{H}_1(\mathsf{tag}, \rho) + \mathsf{H}_3(\mu) \rangle + \langle \mathbf{s}_\mathsf{b}, \mathbf{b} \rangle \rfloor_{p_1}$. The verifier computes $\{u_b = \lceil \langle \mathbf{s}, \mathsf{H}_1(\mathsf{tag}, \rho) + \mathsf{H}_3(\mu) \rangle + \langle \mathbf{s}_b, \mathbf{b} \rangle \rfloor_{p_1}\}_{b \in \{0,1\}}$ and recovers the private bit b if $u_\mathsf{b} = v$.

Prototype. We implemented our AT protocol in C++ and benchmarked its performance. Analytically, our token size is $2d \log p_1 + 2\lambda$ and is the same as the keyed-verification blind signature size [12]. However, our implementation trades the token size for better overall overhead. We instantiate G with a larger ρ, resulting in larger tokens. However, this design choice enables more efficient NIZK proofs, thereby addressing the primary bottleneck in both computation and communication. With completeness optimization and parameter tuning, our prototype demonstrates the practicality of our design, as summarized in Table 2, which compares post-quantum secure blind signatures and anonymous tokens.

2 Preliminaries

Sampling an element x uniformly at random from a finite set S or according to the distribution $\mathcal{D}$ is denoted by $x \xleftarrow{\$} S$ or $x \leftarrow \mathcal{D}$, respectively. $[N]$ is $\{1, \ldots, N\}$ for an integer N. For security parameter λ, negl denotes a negligible function.

For an integer q, let $\mathbb{Z}_q$ be the ring of integers modulo q and $\vec{v} \in \mathbb{Z}_q^m$ be a vector over $\mathbb{Z}_q$. All vectors are column vectors by default. The ℓ_2-norm of $\vec{v}$ is $\|\vec{v}\| := \sqrt{\sum_{i=1}^{m} v_i^2}$. $|S|$ is the size of set S. Concatenation is denoted by $\|$.

Let rings $\mathcal{R} := \mathbb{Z}[X]/(X^d + 1)$ and $\mathcal{R}_q := \mathbb{Z}_q[X]/(X^d + 1)$, where d is a power of two. Let $\mathsf{Inv}\colon \mathcal{R}_q \to \mathcal{R}_q$ denote the automorphism where $\mathsf{Inv}(X) = X^{-1}$ (which appears in our NIZK proof). Denote $\mathcal{D}_s^n$ as a discrete Gaussian distribution on $\mathcal{R}^n$ with standard deviation s and $\mathcal{B}_\eta$ as a centered binomial distribution on $\mathbb{Z}$ with parameter η. (Also see Appendix B.)

We use lower-case letters (*e.g.*, v) for elements in $\mathcal{R}$ or $\mathcal{R}_q$, bold lower-case (*e.g.*, $\mathbf{v}$) for vectors, and bold upper-case (*e.g.*, $\mathbf{A}$) for matrices over $\mathcal{R}$ or $\mathcal{R}_q$.

2.1 Anonymous (MAC) Tokens

Definition 1 ([14]). *An anonymous token protocol* AT *with a private metadata bit and optional public metadata is defined by the following components.*

- $\mathsf{AT.Gen}(1^\lambda) \to (\mathsf{pp})$: *On input of the security parameter* 1^λ, *it returns the public parameter* pp, *which includes a common reference string* crs *and the description of a tag space* $\mathcal{T}$. *All other algorithms take* pp *implicitly.*
- $\mathsf{AT.KeyGen}(\mathsf{pp}) \to (\mathsf{sk}, \mathsf{pk})$: *On input of the public parameter* pp, *it outputs a signing key* sk *and a public key* pk.
- $\langle \mathsf{AT.Client}(\mathsf{pk}, \mu), \mathsf{AT.Issuer}(\mathsf{sk}, \mathsf{b}, \mu) \rangle \to (\mathsf{tag}, \sigma)$: *An interactive protocol for verifiably issuing tokens can be specified by three algorithms. The common inputs include the issuer public key* pk *and, optionally, the public metadata* μ. *The issuer possesses two secret inputs: a signing key and a private bit* b. *The client maintains a secret state,* st. *The protocol concludes with the client outputting a token* (tag, σ), *where* tag *is a random tag in the tag space* $\mathcal{T}$.
  - $\mathsf{AT.ClientQuery}(\mathsf{pk}, \mu) \to (\mathsf{query}, \mathsf{st})$,
  - $\mathsf{AT.IssueToken}(\mathsf{sk}, \mathsf{b}, \mu, \mathsf{query}) \to (\mathsf{resp})$,
  - $\mathsf{AT.ClientFinal}(\mathsf{pk}, \mathsf{resp}, \mathsf{st}) \to (\mathsf{tag}, \sigma)$ *(or* $\perp$ *for invalid* σ*).*
- $\mathsf{AT.Readbit}(\mathsf{sk}, \mu, \mathsf{tag}, \sigma) \to \mathsf{b}/\perp$: *Given the issuer's signing key* sk, *the token* (tag, σ), *and optionally public metadata* μ, *it returns a private bit* b *or* $\perp$ *for invalid* (tag, σ).

Definition 2 (Completeness). AT *is complete if, for any honest client and issuer, valid tag* $\mathsf{tag} \in \mathcal{T}$, *public metadata* μ, *and private metadata* $\mathsf{b} \in \{0, 1\}$,

$$\Pr\left[\mathsf{b}' = \mathsf{b} \;\middle|\; \begin{array}{l} \mathsf{pp} \leftarrow \mathsf{AT.Gen}(1^\lambda), (\mathsf{sk}, \mathsf{pk}) \leftarrow \mathsf{AT.KeyGen}(\mathsf{pp}), \\ (\mathsf{tag}, \sigma) \leftarrow \langle \mathsf{AT.Client}(\mathsf{pk}, \mu), \mathsf{AT.Issue}(\mathsf{sk}, \mathsf{b}, \mu) \rangle, \\ \mathsf{b}' \leftarrow \mathsf{AT.Readbit}(\mathsf{sk}, \mu, \mathsf{tag}, \sigma). \end{array}\right] \geq 1 - \mathsf{negl}(\lambda).$$

Game $\mathsf{OMUF}_{\mathsf{AT},\mathcal{A},\ell}(1^\lambda)$

1. $\mathsf{AT.Gen}(1^\lambda) \to (\mathsf{pp})$.
2. $\mathsf{AT.KeyGen}(\mathsf{pp}) \to (\mathsf{pk}, \mathsf{sk})$.
3. $\{\mathsf{b}, \mu, (\mathsf{tag}_i, \sigma_i)\}_{i\in[\ell+1]} \leftarrow \mathcal{A}^{\mathcal{O}_{\mathsf{Issue}}, \mathcal{O}_{\mathsf{Readbit}}}(\mathsf{pp}, \mathsf{pk})$.
4. If $|\{\mathsf{tag}_i\}_{i\in[\ell+1]}| < \ell + 1$, return $\perp$.
5. If $\mathsf{b} \notin \{0, 1\}$, return $\perp$.
6. If $\exists i \in [\ell + 1]$, $\mathsf{AT.Readbit}(\mathsf{sk}, \mu, \mathsf{tag}_i, \sigma_i) \neq \mathsf{b}$, return $\perp$.
7. Return 1.

Fig. 2. One-more unforgeability game

AT is secure if it satisfies *unforgeability*, *unlinkability*, and *privacy of the metadata bit*. Unforgeability requires that an adversary cannot create valid tokens with private (or any public) metadata different from all the tokens it received.

Definition 3 (One-more Unforgeability). AT *is one-more unforgeable if, for any PPT adversary $\mathcal{A}$ against the unforgeability game in Fig. 2, and any $\ell \geq 0$,*

$$\mathsf{Adv}_{\mathcal{A}}^{\mathsf{OMUF}} = \Pr[\mathsf{OMUF}_{\mathsf{AT},\mathcal{A},\ell}(1^\lambda) = 1] \leq \mathsf{negl}(\lambda),$$

where the oracles are defined as follows.

- $\mathcal{O}_{\mathsf{Issue}}(b, \mu, \mathsf{query})$*: It maintains a counter $\mathcal{Q}_{\mathsf{query}}$, initially* 0*. If $\mathcal{Q}_{\mathsf{query}} \leq \ell$, it returns* $\mathsf{AT.IssueToken}(\mathsf{sk}, \mathsf{b}, \mu, \mathsf{query})$ *and increments $\mathcal{Q}_{\mathsf{query}}$; $\perp$ otherwise.*
- $\mathcal{O}_{\mathsf{Readbit}}(\mu, \mathsf{tag}, \sigma)$*: It returns* $\mathsf{AT.Readbit}(\mathsf{sk}, \mu, \mathsf{tag}, \sigma)$.

Unlinkability ensures that a malicious issuer cannot link a redeemed token to its issuing session, even after maliciously setting up the public key.

Definition 4 (Unlinkability). *An anonymous token protocol* AT *is unlinkable if, for any PPT adversary $\mathcal{A}$ against the unlinkability game* $\mathsf{Unlink}_{\mathsf{AT},\mathcal{A},\ell}(1^\lambda)$*:*

$$\mathsf{Adv}_{\mathcal{A}}^{\mathsf{Unlink}}(\lambda) := \left|\Pr[\mathsf{Unlink}_{\mathsf{AT},\mathcal{A},\ell}(1^\lambda) = 1] - \frac{2}{\ell}\right| \leq \mathsf{negl}(\lambda),$$

where the oracles are defined as follows.

- $\mathcal{O}_{\mathsf{Query}}(i, \mu_i)$*: It maintains a list of queries $\mathcal{Q}_{\mathsf{query}}$, which is shared with $\mathcal{O}_{\mathsf{Final}}$. If $i \notin \mathcal{Q}_{\mathsf{query}}$, it stores i in $\mathcal{Q}_{\mathsf{query}}$ via $\mathcal{Q}_{\mathsf{query}} := \mathcal{Q}_{\mathsf{query}} \cup \{i\}$, and returns* $\mathsf{AT.ClientQuery}(\mathsf{pk}, \mu_i)$*. Otherwise, it returns $\perp$.*
- $\mathcal{O}_{\mathsf{Final}}(i, \mathsf{resp})$*: It maintains a list of queries $\mathcal{Q}_{\mathsf{final}}$, which is shared with $\mathcal{O}_{\mathsf{Query}}$. If $i \in \mathcal{Q}_{\mathsf{final}}$ or $i \notin \mathcal{Q}_{\mathsf{Query}}$, it returns $\perp$. Otherwise, it updates $\mathcal{Q}_{\mathsf{final}} := \mathcal{Q}_{\mathsf{final}} \cup \{i\}$ and returns* $\mathsf{out}_i \leftarrow \mathsf{AT.ClientFinal}(\mathsf{pk}, \mathsf{resp}, \mathsf{st}_i)$.

Unlinkability game $\mathsf{Unlink}_{\mathsf{AT},\mathcal{A},\ell}(1^\lambda)$ in Fig. 3 follows prior work [14]. We let the adversary receive token request queries from clients and choose to obtain the tokens resulting from a subset of those requests. For the remaining requests, the

Game $\mathsf{Unlink}_{\mathsf{AT},\mathcal{A},\ell}(1^\lambda)$

1. $\mathsf{AT.Gen}(1^\lambda) \rightarrow (\mathsf{pp})$.
2. $(\mathsf{pk}, \mathsf{state}_1) \leftarrow \mathcal{A}_1(\mathsf{pp})$.
3. $\mathcal{Q} := \varnothing$, $\mathcal{Q}_{\mathsf{query}} := \varnothing$, $\mathcal{Q}_{\mathsf{final}} := \varnothing$.
4. $(\mathcal{Q}, \{\mathsf{resp}_i\}_{i\in\mathcal{Q}}, \mathsf{state}_2) \leftarrow \mathcal{A}_2^{\mathcal{O}_{\mathsf{Query}}, \mathcal{O}_{\mathsf{Final}}}(\mathsf{state}_1)$.
5. If $\mathcal{Q} \not\subseteq \mathcal{Q}_{\mathsf{query}} \setminus \mathcal{Q}_{\mathsf{final}}$, return $\perp$.
6. If $|\mathcal{Q}| < \ell$, return $\perp$.
7. For all $i \in \mathcal{Q}$, $\mathsf{out}_i \leftarrow \mathsf{AT.ClientFinal}(\mathsf{pk}, \mathsf{resp}_i, \mathsf{st}_i)$; If $\exists \mathsf{out}_i = \perp$, return $\perp$.
8. If $|\{\mu_i : i \in \mathcal{Q}\}| > 1$, return $\perp$.
9. $j \leftarrow \mathcal{Q}$.
10. Pick a permutation $\phi \xleftarrow{\$} S_{\mathcal{Q}}$.
11. $j^* \leftarrow \mathcal{A}_3(\mathsf{state}_2, \mathsf{out}_j, \{\mathsf{out}_{\phi(i)}\}_{i\in\mathcal{Q}})$.
12. Return $j^* \stackrel{?}{=} j$.

Fig. 3. Unlinkability game

adversary is required to return a response to the blinded token request. After all tokens are issued, the challenger permutes them, selects one, and asks the adversary to identify it. As noted [14], in the private metadata bit setting, the issuer can reduce the search-space size to $\ell/2$ by embedding a private bit. Hence, the adversary's advantage is defined over $2/\ell$. Also, note that the definition can degenerate to cover AT without public metadata by setting $\mu_i = \epsilon$ for all i.

Metadata privacy ensures no clients can deduce the metadata bit b chosen by the issuer when embedding b in a token, even with oracle access to check token validity, but without an oracle to extract the bit after the challenge is issued [11].

Definition 5 (Privacy of Metadata Bit). AT *ensures that the private metadata bit remains confidential if, for any PPT adversary* $\mathcal{A}$ *in the* $\mathsf{PMB}^{\mathsf{b}}_{\mathsf{AT},\mathcal{A}}$ *game,*

$$\mathsf{Adv}^{\mathsf{PMB}}_{\mathcal{A}}(\lambda) := (|\Pr[\mathsf{PMB}^0_{\mathsf{AT},\mathcal{A}}(1^\lambda) = 1] - \Pr[\mathsf{PMB}^1_{\mathsf{AT},\mathcal{A}}(1^\lambda) = 1]|) \leq \mathsf{negl}(\lambda),$$

where $\mathsf{PMB}^{\mathsf{b}}_{\mathsf{AT},\mathcal{A}}$ *is defined in Fig. 4 and the oracles are defined as follows.*

- $\mathcal{O}_{\mathsf{Issue}}(\mathsf{b}, \mu, \mathsf{query})$*: It returns* $\mathsf{resp} \leftarrow \mathsf{AT.IssueToken}(\mathsf{sk}, \mathsf{b}, \mu, \mathsf{query})$.
- $\mathcal{O}_{\mathsf{Readbit}}(\mu, \mathsf{tag}, \sigma)$*: If* $\mu = \mu^*$*, returns* $\perp$*; otherwise,* $\mathsf{AT.Readbit}(\mathsf{sk}, \mu, \mathsf{tag}, \sigma)$.
- $\mathcal{O}_{\mathsf{Chal}}(\mu, \mathsf{query})$*: If* $\mu = \epsilon$*, returns* $\perp$*. If* $\mu^* = \epsilon$*, it sets* $\mu^* := \mu$*, and returns* $\mathsf{resp} \leftarrow \mathsf{AT.IssueToken}(\mathsf{sk}, \mathsf{b}^*, \mu^*, \mathsf{query})$*. Otherwise, it returns* $\perp$.
- $\mathcal{O}_{\mathsf{Valid}}(\mu, \mathsf{tag}, \sigma)$*: It returns* 1 *if and only if* $(\mathsf{AT.Readbit}(\mathsf{sk}, \mu, \mathsf{tag}, \sigma) \neq \perp)$.

To adapt the private metadata bit security game for AT without public metadata, we ignore the μ component in all queries and exclude it from the internal action of all oracles, except that $\mathcal{O}_{\mathsf{Chal}}$ sets $\mu^* := 1$ to signify a challenge has been issued. Correspondingly, $\mathcal{O}_{\mathsf{Readbit}}$ returns $\perp$ if $\mu^* = 1$.

Game $\mathsf{PMB}^{\mathsf{b}^*}_{\mathsf{AT},\mathcal{A}}(1^\lambda)$

1. $\mu^* := \epsilon$.
2. $\mathsf{AT.Gen}(1^\lambda) \to (\mathsf{pp})$.
3. $\mathsf{AT.KeyGen}(\mathsf{pp}) \to (\mathsf{pk}, \mathsf{sk})$.
4. return $\mathcal{A}^{\mathcal{O}_{\mathsf{Issue}}, \mathcal{O}_{\mathsf{Readbit}}, \mathcal{O}_{\mathsf{Chal}}, \mathcal{O}_{\mathsf{Valid}}}(\mathsf{pp}, \mathsf{pk})$.

Fig. 4. Privacy of metadata bit game

2.2 Lattice Backgrounds

Security of our AT scheme relies on the module learning with errors (LWE) problem for module lattices [29] and its variant, the hashed module LWE [12].

Definition 6 ($\mathsf{MLWE}_{q,m,n,\chi}$). *Let $q, m, n > 0$ be integers, and let χ be an error distribution over $\mathcal{R}$. For a secret $\mathbf{s} \in \mathcal{R}_q^n$, the* module-LWE problem *is to distinguish whether the given arbitrarily many samples come from one of the following:*

- *the distribution $(\mathbf{A}, \mathbf{A}\mathbf{s} + \mathbf{e})$, where $\mathbf{A} \leftarrow \mathcal{R}_q^{m \times n}$ and the error is $\mathbf{e} \leftarrow \chi^m$,*
- *or the uniform distribution $(\mathbf{A}, \mathbf{b})$, where $(\mathbf{A}, \mathbf{b}) \leftarrow \mathcal{R}_q^{m \times \lambda} \times \mathcal{R}_q^m$.*

Definition 7 ($\mathsf{HMLWE}_{q,n,\chi}$). *Let $q, n, \lambda > 0$ be integers, and let χ be an error distribution over $\mathcal{R}$. Let $\mathsf{H}_1 \colon \{0,1\}^* \to \mathcal{R}_q^n$ be a hash function mapping to $\mathcal{R}_q^n$, and $\mathsf{H}_2 \colon \{0,1\}^* \to \chi$ be a hash function mapping to χ. For a secret $\mathbf{s} \in \mathcal{R}_q^n$ and a bit string $k \xleftarrow{\$} \{0,1\}^\lambda$, the* hashed MLWE problem *is to distinguish whether the given arbitrarily many queries $\mu \in \{0,1\}^*$ come from one of the following:*

- *the oracle $\mathcal{O}^{\mathbf{s},k}_{HMLWE}$ output $\langle \mathbf{a}, \mathbf{s} \rangle + \mathbf{e}$, where $\mathbf{a} := \mathsf{H}_1(\mu)$ and $\mathbf{e} := \mathsf{H}_2(k, \mu)$,*
- *or a randomly sampled string $\mathbf{b} \leftarrow \mathcal{R}_q^n$.*

We recall the framework of Lyubashevsky *et al.* [33]. In this proof system, witnesses are split into two parts: the short vector $\mathbf{m}_1 \in \mathcal{R}_q^{m_1}$ and the vector $\mathbf{m}_2 \in \mathcal{R}_q^{m_2}$. For the committed [33] messages $(\mathbf{m}_1, \mathbf{m}_2) \in \mathcal{R}_q^{m_1+m_2}$ (refer to Appendix C for details), the framework enables proving:

1. Quadratic relations: For public triples $(\mathbf{D}_2, \mathbf{d}_1, d_0) \in \mathcal{R}_q^{(m_1+m_2)\times(m_1+m_2)} \times \mathcal{R}_q^{(m_1+m_2)} \times \mathcal{R}_q$,
$$(\mathbf{m}_1 \| \mathbf{m}_2)^\top \mathbf{D}_2 (\mathbf{m}_1 \| \mathbf{m}_2) + \mathbf{d}_1^\top (\mathbf{m}_1 \| \mathbf{m}_2) + d_0 = 0.$$
2. Shortness in the ℓ_2 norm: For public bound B and public triples $(\mathbf{D}_1, \mathbf{D}_2, \mathbf{v}) \in \mathcal{R}_q^{m_1 \times m_1} \times \mathcal{R}_q^{m_1 \times m_2} \times \mathcal{R}_q^{m_1}$,
$$\|\mathbf{D}_1 \mathbf{m}_1 + \mathbf{D}_2 \mathbf{m}_2 + \mathbf{v}\| \le B.$$

We transform the relations in our proposed scheme into the above quadratic or shortness relation and then apply this framework. The overall proof size is linear in the number of witnesses $(\mathbf{m}_1, \mathbf{m}_2)$. However, the proof size is influenced not only by the commitment to the witnesses but also by other components like the challenge values, the proof of opening, and additional auxiliary information. Moreover, the size of $\mathbf{m}_1$ is also compressed in the commitment, so adding more witnesses does not significantly increase the proof size. In most instances, the proof size remains dozens of kilobytes [32,33].

3 Our Short Anonymous Token with Private Bit

3.1 Our Construction

We describe below our anonymous token with private bit construction under the MLWE assumption from any public key encryption scheme PKE that is indistinguishable under chosen-plaintext attacks (IND-CPA) and two NIZK instances Π_1 and Π_2 for specific relations to be defined. The key generation algorithm KeyGen is essentially that of the blind signature scheme of Beullens *et al.* [12]. The client randomly picks a tag in ClientQuery and sends a commitment of it with proof to the issuer. The issuer then computes a pre-token for the blinded tag using IssueToken and returns it. The client subsequently unblinds the pre-token via ClientFinal to obtain a valid token for the original tag. In this basic construction, the optional public metadata μ is set to the empty string ϵ.

- $\mathsf{Gen}(1^\lambda)$:
  1. Given security parameter λ, the tag space is $\mathcal{T} = \{0,1\}^{2\lambda}$.
  2. Pick integers n, q, d, η_r and η_e that meet the implied requirements below.
  3. Define the ring $\mathcal{R}_q := \mathbb{Z}_q[X]/(X^d + 1)$ such that the $\mathsf{MLWE}_{q,n,n,\eta_r}$ and $\mathsf{MLWE}_{q,1,n,\eta_e}$ assumptions holds.
  4. Define a small power of two p_1 constrained by d and λ via security proof.
  5. Define three hash functions $\mathsf{G}\colon \{0,1\}^* \to \{0,1\}^{2\lambda}$, $\mathsf{H}_1\colon \{0,1\}^* \to \mathcal{R}_q^n$, and $\mathsf{H}_2\colon \{0,1\}^* \to \mathcal{B}_{\eta_e}^d$.
  6. Run $\Pi_1.\mathsf{Setup}(1^\lambda)$ and $\Pi_2.\mathsf{Setup}(1^\lambda)$ to obtain pp_1 and pp_2, the public parameters of two NIZK proof instances for relations R_1 and R_2 below.
  7. Sample $\mathbf{A} \xleftarrow{\$} \mathcal{R}_q^{n\times n}, \mathbf{b} \xleftarrow{\$} \mathcal{R}_q^n$ and pk_e uniformly from the public key space of PKE.
  8. Output $\mathsf{pp} := (n, q, d, p_1, \eta_r, \eta_e, \mathcal{T}, \mathsf{G}, \mathsf{H}_1, \mathsf{H}_2, \mathsf{pp}_1, \mathsf{pp}_2, \mathbf{A}, \mathbf{b}, \mathsf{pk}_e)$.
- $\mathsf{KeyGen}(\mathsf{pp})$:
  1. Sample $(\mathbf{s}, \mathbf{e}) \leftarrow (\mathcal{B}_{\eta_r}^d)^n \times (\mathcal{B}_{\eta_r}^d)^n$, $k \xleftarrow{\$} \{0,1\}^{2\lambda}$, $(\mathbf{s}_0, \mathbf{s}_1) \xleftarrow{\$} \mathcal{R}_q^n \times \mathcal{R}_q^n$, and $(\mathbf{e}_0, \mathbf{e}_1) \leftarrow (\mathcal{B}_{\eta_r}^d)^n \times (\mathcal{B}_{\eta_r}^d)^n$.
  2. Compute $\mathbf{t}^\top := \mathbf{s}^\top\mathbf{A} + \mathbf{e}^\top$, $\mathbf{t}_0^\top := \mathbf{s}_0^\top\mathbf{A} + \mathbf{e}_0^\top$, and $\mathbf{t}_1^\top := \mathbf{s}_1^\top\mathbf{A} + \mathbf{e}_1^\top$.
  3. Output $\mathsf{pk} := (\mathbf{t}, \mathbf{t}_0, \mathbf{t}_1)$ and $\mathsf{sk} := (\mathbf{s}, \mathbf{s}_0, \mathbf{s}_1, k)$.
- Issuance protocol between $\mathsf{Client}(\mathsf{pk})$ and $\mathsf{Issuer}(\mathsf{sk}, \mathsf{b})$:
  $\mathsf{AT.ClientQuery}(\mathsf{pk} = (\mathbf{t}, \mathbf{t}_0, \mathbf{t}_1))$:
  1. Sample $\mathsf{tag} \xleftarrow{\$} \mathcal{T}$.
  2. Sample $\mathbf{x}, \mathbf{e}_2 \leftarrow (\mathcal{B}_{\eta_r}^d)^n$, and compute $\rho := \mathsf{G}(\mathbf{x}, \mathbf{e}_2)$.
  3. Compute a ciphertext $\mathsf{ct} := \mathsf{PKE.Enc}(\mathsf{pk}_e, (\mathbf{x}, \mathsf{tag}))$.
  4. Compute the blinded message $\mathbf{c} := \mathbf{A}\mathbf{x} + \mathbf{e}_2 + \mathsf{H}_1(\mathsf{tag}, \rho)$.

5. Generate proof π_1 for relation R_1 defined below for the computations of ρ, ct, $\mathbf{c}$, and that $\|\mathbf{e}_2\| \le \beta_r$ and $\|\mathbf{x}\| \le \beta_r$.
6. Return $\mathsf{query} := (\mathbf{c}, \mathsf{ct}, \pi_1)$ (to send) and $\mathsf{st} := (\mathbf{c}, \mathbf{x}, \mathsf{tag}, \rho)$ (kept private).

$\mathsf{AT.IssueToken}(\mathsf{sk} = (\mathbf{s}, \mathbf{s}_0, \mathbf{s}_1, k), \mathsf{b}, \mathsf{query} = (\mathbf{c}, \mathsf{ct}, \pi_1))$:
1. Return $\perp$ if $\mathbf{c}$ appeared in some prior query.
2. Return $\perp$ if $\Pi_1.\mathsf{Verify}(\mathsf{pp}_1, \pi_1, (\mathsf{pk}_e, \mathbf{A}, \mathsf{ct}, \mathbf{c})) = 0$.
3. $e_3 := \mathsf{H}_2(k, \mathbf{c})$.
4. $h := \langle \mathbf{s}, \mathbf{c} \rangle + e_3 + \langle \mathbf{s}_\mathsf{b}, \mathbf{b} \rangle$.
5. Generate proof π_2 for relation R_2 defined below for using a correct secret key in computing $h = \langle \mathbf{s}, \mathbf{c} \rangle + e_3 + \langle \mathbf{s}_\mathsf{b}, \mathbf{b} \rangle$.
6. Return $\mathsf{resp} := (h, \pi_2)$.

$\mathsf{AT.ClientFinal}(\mathsf{pk} = (\mathbf{t}, \mathbf{t}_0, \mathbf{t}_1), \mathsf{resp} = (h, \pi_2), \mathsf{st} = (\mathbf{c}, \mathbf{x}, \mathsf{tag}, \rho))$:
1. Return $\perp$ if $\Pi_2.\mathsf{Verify}(\mathsf{pp}_2, \pi_2, (h, \mathbf{A}, \mathbf{c}, \mathbf{t}, \mathbf{t}_0, \mathbf{t}_1)) = 0$.
2. $v := \mathsf{Comp}_q(h - \langle \mathbf{t}, \mathbf{x} \rangle, p_1)$.
3. Return $(\mathsf{tag}, \sigma := (\rho, v))$.

– $\mathsf{AT.Readbit}(\mathsf{sk} = (\mathbf{s}, \mathbf{s}_0, \mathbf{s}_1, k), \mathsf{tag}, \sigma = (\rho, v))$:
1. Compute $\mathsf{h} := \mathsf{H}_1(\mathsf{tag}, \rho)$.
2. $u := \mathsf{Comp}_q(\langle \mathbf{s}, \mathsf{h} \rangle + \langle \mathbf{s}_\mathsf{b}, \mathbf{b} \rangle, p_1)$.
3. Output b if $u - v = 0$; $\perp$ otherwise.

R_1 states that the ciphertext ct is encrypted with pk_e using $(\mathbf{x}, \mathsf{tag})$, the commitment $\mathbf{c}$ is well-formed, and the secret vectors $\mathbf{x}$ and $\mathbf{e}_2$ are of small norm. R_2 states that the issuer correctly computes the issued token h using the private key associated with $\mathbf{t}$, embedding the private bit b into h using the secret $\mathbf{s}_\mathsf{b}$.

$$R_1 = \left\{ \begin{array}{c|l} & \mathsf{ct} = \mathsf{Enc}(\mathsf{pk}_e, (\mathbf{x}, \mathsf{tag})); \\ (\mathsf{pk}_e, \mathbf{A}, \mathsf{ct}, \mathbf{c}); & \rho := \mathsf{G}(\mathbf{x}, \mathbf{e}_2); \\ (\mathbf{x}, \mathbf{e}_2, \mathsf{tag}, \rho) & \mathbf{c} = \mathbf{A}\mathbf{x} + \mathbf{e}_2 + \mathsf{H}_1(\mathsf{tag}, \rho); \\ & \|\mathbf{e}_2\| \le \beta_r, \|\mathbf{x}\| \le \beta_r. \end{array} \right\}.$$

$$R_2 = \left\{ \begin{array}{c|l} & h = \langle \mathbf{s}, \mathbf{c} \rangle + e_3 + \langle \mathbf{s}_\mathsf{b}, \mathbf{b} \rangle; \\ & \mathbf{t}^\top = \mathbf{s}^\top \mathbf{A} + \mathbf{e}^\top; \\ (h, \mathbf{A}, \mathbf{c}, \mathbf{t}, \mathbf{t}_0, \mathbf{t}_1); & (\nu^\top [\mathbf{t}_0 | \mathbf{t}_1])^\top = \mathbf{s}_\mathsf{b}^\top \mathbf{A} + \mathbf{e}_\mathsf{b}^\top; \\ (\nu, \mathbf{s}, \mathbf{e}, e_3, \mathbf{s}_\mathsf{b}, \mathbf{e}_\mathsf{b}) & \nu \in \{0,1\}^2, \|\nu\| = 1, \|\mathbf{s}\| \le \beta_r; \\ & \|\mathbf{e}\| \le \beta_r, \|e_3\| \le \beta_e, \|\mathbf{e}_\mathsf{b}\| \le \beta_r. \end{array} \right\}.$$

We also employ compression algorithm [13] to reduce the token size:

$$\mathsf{Comp}_q(x, p_1) = \lceil x \rfloor_{p_1} = \lceil \frac{p_1}{q} \cdot x \rfloor \bmod p_1$$

Adding Public Metadata. To integrate μ into the issuer's response, we introduce the hash function $\mathsf{H}_3 \colon \{0,1\}^* \to \mathcal{R}_q^n$ that maps μ into a vector $\mathsf{H}_3(\mu) \in \mathcal{R}_q^n$. Specifically, the issuer now computes $h = \langle \mathbf{s}, \mathbf{c} + \mathsf{H}_3(\mu) \rangle + \langle \mathbf{s}_\mathsf{b}, \mathbf{b} \rangle + e_3$. In the verification phase, the verifier derives the values $u_b = \langle \mathbf{s}, \mathsf{H}_1(\mathsf{tag}, \rho) + \mathsf{H}_3(\mu) \rangle + \langle \mathbf{s}_\mathsf{b}, \mathbf{b} \rangle$ based on μ. These values are used in verification to confirm token validity and retrieve the private bit. This approach supports public metadata without increasing the token or proof size and requires only simple hash operations.

3.2 Security

We discuss the completeness and the three security properties.

Theorem 1 (Completeness). *Let $q, p_1, d, \eta_r, \eta_e$ be integers where $d \log p_1 > \lambda$ and $q > 2p_1(2d\eta_r^2 + \eta_e + 1)$. The protocol* AT *in Sect. 3.1 is correct if the NIZK arguments Π_1 and Π_2 satisfy completeness.*

Proofs π_1 and π_2 pass the verification with overwhelming probability. So, we focus on analyzing the correctness of the response (v_0, v_1). Specifically, we aim to show that for the correct private bit b, the conditions $v = \mathsf{Comp}_q(\langle \mathbf{s}, \mathsf{H}_1(\mathsf{tag}, \rho)\rangle + \langle \mathbf{s}_\mathsf{b}, \mathbf{b}\rangle, p_1)$ hold with overwhelming probability.

As the response from $\mathsf{IssueToken}$ is $h = \langle \mathbf{s}, \mathbf{c}\rangle + e_3 + \langle \mathbf{s}_\mathsf{b}, \mathbf{b}\rangle = e_3 + \langle \mathbf{s}, \mathbf{Ax}\rangle + \langle \mathbf{s}, \mathbf{e}_2\rangle + \langle \mathbf{s}, \mathsf{H}_1(\mathsf{tag}, \rho)\rangle + \langle \mathbf{s}_\mathsf{b}, \mathbf{b}\rangle$ and the public key $\mathbf{t}^\top = \mathbf{s}^\top \mathbf{A} + \mathbf{e}^\top$, the token derived by $\mathsf{ClientFinal}$ is $v = \mathsf{Comp}_q(h - \langle \mathbf{t}, \mathbf{x}\rangle, p_1) = \lceil \frac{p_1}{q}(\langle \mathbf{s}, \mathsf{H}_1(\mathsf{tag}, \rho)\rangle + \langle \mathbf{s}_\mathsf{b}, \mathbf{b}\rangle + \langle \mathbf{s}, \mathbf{e}_2\rangle + e_3 - \langle \mathbf{e}, \mathbf{x}\rangle)\rfloor \bmod p_1$, which is expected to equal $\mathsf{Comp}_q(\langle \mathbf{s}, \mathsf{H}_1(\mathsf{tag}, \rho)\rangle + \langle \mathbf{s}_\mathsf{b}, \mathbf{b}\rangle, p_1) = \lceil \frac{p_1}{q}(\langle \mathbf{s}, \mathsf{H}_1(\mathsf{tag}, \rho)\rangle + \langle \mathbf{s}_\mathsf{b}, \mathbf{b}\rangle)\rfloor \bmod p_1$. To verify this, we examine the effect of error terms introduced by the compression operation.

Let $e' = \langle \mathbf{s}, \mathbf{e}_2\rangle + e_3 - \langle \mathbf{e}, \mathbf{x}\rangle$. If the infinity norm $\|e'\|_\infty \leq (2d\eta_r^2 + \eta_e) \leq \lceil \frac{q}{2p_1} \rfloor$, the error term does not affect the high $\log p_1$ bits. So we can set $q > 2p_1(2d\eta_r^2 + \eta_e + 1)$ and this establishes that $v = \mathsf{Comp}_q(\langle \mathbf{s}, \mathsf{H}_1(\mathsf{tag}, \rho)\rangle + \langle \mathbf{s}_\mathsf{b}, \mathbf{b}\rangle, p_1)$ as desired.

Theorem 2 (One-More Unforgeability). *Let $q, p_1, d, \eta_r, \eta_e$ be integers as defined in the protocol* AT *in Sect. 3.1. The protocol* AT *is one more unforgeable, assuming* PKE *is correct, the NIZK argument Π_1 satisfies knowledge soundness, Π_2 is zero knowledge, the hash functions $\mathsf{H}_1, \mathsf{H}_2, \mathsf{G}$ are collision-resistant, and the hashed MLWE problem $\mathsf{HMLWE}_{q,n,\eta_e}$ is hard.*

Proof. We prove the one-more unforgeability via a series of games. Suppose that $\mathcal{A}$ queries $\mathcal{O}_{\mathsf{Issue}}$ oracle Q_i times and $\mathcal{O}_{\mathsf{Readbit}}$ oracle Q_r times. We assume $f_\mathbf{A}(\mathsf{tag}, \mathbf{x}, \mathbf{e}_2) = \mathbf{Ax} + \mathbf{e}_2 + \mathsf{H}_1(\mathsf{tag}, \mathsf{G}(\mathbf{x}, \mathbf{e}_2))$ is collision-resistant. At the beginning, the challenger initializes a list $\mathcal{Q}_{\mathsf{Issue}} = \varnothing$.

- **Game** 0. This is the real one-more unforgeability game.
- **Game** 1. The game is identical to **Game** 0, except that pk_e is replaced with a real encryption key from $(\mathsf{pk}_e, \mathsf{sk}_e) \leftarrow \mathsf{PKE.KeyGen}(1^\lambda)$.
- **Game** 2. The game is the same as **Game** 1, except when answering an $\mathcal{O}_{\mathsf{Issue}}$ query, the challenger replaces π_2 with a simulated proof. We have

$$|\Pr[G_2] - \Pr[G_1]| \leq Q_i \mathsf{Adv}_{\Pi_2}^{\mathrm{ZK}}.$$

- **Game** 3. In this game, when the adversary makes a query $(\mathbf{c}, \mathsf{ct}, \pi_1)$, the challenger uses sk_e to decrypt $(\mathbf{x}, \mathsf{tag}) := \mathsf{PKE.Dec}(\mathsf{sk}_e, \mathsf{ct})$ and extracts $(\mathbf{x}, \mathbf{e}_2, \mathsf{tag})$ by computing $\mathbf{e}_2 = \mathbf{c} - \mathbf{Ax} - \mathsf{H}_1(\mathsf{tag}, \mathsf{G}(\mathbf{x}, \mathbf{e}_2))$. If $\mathbf{e}_2 \notin (\mathcal{B}_{\eta_r}^d)^n$, it returns $\perp$. The challenger updates $\mathcal{Q}_{\mathsf{Issue}} := \mathcal{Q}_{\mathsf{Issue}} \cup \{(\mathsf{tag}, \mathbf{x}, \mathbf{e}_2, \mathbf{c}, h, \mathsf{b})\}$. All the above are deterministic procedures, except Dec, which works over a probabilistically generated ciphertext ct. This requires PKE to be correct.

$$|\Pr[G_3] - \Pr[G_2]| \leq Q_i \mathsf{Adv}_{\mathsf{PKE}}^{\mathrm{Correctness}}.$$

- **Game** 4. The challenger aborts if $\rho = \mathsf{G}(\mathbf{x}, \mathbf{e}_2)$ exists in $\mathcal{O}_\mathsf{G}$ but $(\mathbf{x}', \mathbf{e}_2')$ extracted from $\mathsf{query} = (\mathbf{c}, \mathsf{ct}, \pi_1)$ is "fresh." Similarly, the challenger aborts if $\mathsf{H}_1(\mathsf{tag}, \rho)$ exists in $\mathcal{O}_{\mathsf{H}_1}$ but $(\mathsf{tag}', \rho' = \mathsf{G}(\mathbf{x}', \mathbf{e}_2'))$ extracted from $\mathsf{query} = (\mathbf{c}, \mathsf{ct}, \pi_1)$ is "fresh." Aborting means the adversary found a collision of G or H_1, which happens with negligible probability.
- **Game** 5. The challenger aborts if before its updating $\mathcal{Q}_\mathsf{Issue}$, (tag, ρ) exists in $\mathcal{Q}_\mathsf{Issue}$. **Game** 5 is indistinguishable from **Game** 4 because if $(\mathsf{tag}, \rho = \mathsf{G}(\mathbf{x}, \mathbf{e}_2))$ exists in a previous query, the issuer must have seen $\mathbf{c} = \mathbf{A}\mathbf{x} + \mathbf{e}_2 + \mathsf{H}_1(\mathsf{tag}, \rho)$ and should abort from the issuance.
- **Game** 6. The game is identical to **Game** 5 except for the way to sample e_3. The challenger replaces $e_3 = \mathsf{H}_2(k, \mathbf{c})$ by $\mathsf{H}_2'(k, \mathsf{tag}, \mathsf{G}(\mathbf{x}, \mathbf{e}_2))$ and aborts if $\mathbf{c}$ was queried but $(\mathsf{tag}, \mathbf{x}, \mathbf{e}_2)$ is "fresh," where $\mathsf{H}_2' \colon \{0,1\}^* \to (\mathcal{B}^d_{\eta_e})^n$. Noticing this change means the adversary found a collision of $f_\mathbf{A}$, which happens with negligible probability.
- **Game** 7. In this game, the challenger changes the issuer's responses and the verification condition.
It answers any $\mathcal{O}_\mathsf{Issue}$ query by $h = \langle \mathbf{t}, \mathbf{x} \rangle + \mathcal{O}^{\mathbf{s},k}_\mathsf{HMLWE}(\mathsf{tag}, \mathsf{G}(\mathbf{x}, \mathbf{e}_2)) + \langle \mathbf{s}_\mathsf{b}, \mathbf{b} \rangle$. For a query $(\mathsf{tag}, (v, \rho))$ to $\mathcal{O}_\mathsf{Readbit}$, the challenger returns b if there exist $\mathsf{b} \in \{0,1\}$ such that $v = \mathsf{Comp}_q(\mathcal{O}^{\mathbf{s},k}_\mathsf{HMLWE}(\mathsf{tag}, \rho) + \langle \mathbf{s}_\mathsf{b}, \mathbf{b} \rangle, p_1)$; or returns $\perp$ otherwise. Notice that this v is close to the v' in **Game** 6, namely,

$$\begin{aligned} v &= \mathsf{Comp}_q(h - \langle \mathbf{t}, \mathbf{x} \rangle, p_1) \\ &= \lceil \underbrace{\langle \mathbf{s}, \mathsf{H}_1(\mathsf{tag}, \mathsf{G}(\mathbf{x}, \mathbf{e}_2)) \rangle + \mathsf{H}_2'(k, \mathsf{tag}, \mathsf{G}(\mathbf{x}, \mathbf{e}_2))}_{\mathcal{O}^{\mathbf{s},k}_\mathsf{HMLWE}(\mathsf{tag}, \mathsf{G}(\mathbf{x}, \mathbf{e}_2))} + \langle \mathbf{s}_\mathsf{b}, \mathbf{b} \rangle \rfloor_{p_1}. \end{aligned}$$

$$\begin{aligned} v' &= \lceil \langle \mathbf{s}, \mathbf{c} \rangle + \mathsf{H}_2'(k, \mathsf{tag}, \mathsf{G}(\mathbf{x}, \mathbf{e}_2)) + \langle \mathbf{s}_\mathsf{b}, \mathbf{b} \rangle - \langle \mathbf{t}, \mathbf{x} \rangle \rfloor_{p_1} \\ &= \lceil \langle \mathbf{s}, \mathsf{H}_1(\mathsf{tag}, \mathsf{G}(\mathbf{x}, \mathbf{e}_2)) \rangle + \langle \mathbf{s}_\mathsf{b}, \mathbf{b} \rangle + \underbrace{\mathsf{H}_2'(k, \mathsf{tag}, \mathsf{G}(\mathbf{x}, \mathbf{e}_2)) + \langle \mathbf{s}, \mathbf{e}_2 \rangle - \langle \mathbf{e}, \mathbf{x} \rangle}_{\text{error terms in } \mathbf{Game}\ 6} \rfloor_{p_1}. \end{aligned}$$

The error term $\langle \mathbf{s}, \mathbf{e}_2 \rangle - \langle \mathbf{e}, \mathbf{x} \rangle$ is removed from v' in **Game** 6. With the correctness of the rounding, **Game** 6 and **Game** 7 are indistinguishable.
- **Game** 8. The challenger replaces $\mathcal{O}^{\mathbf{s},k}_\mathsf{HMLWE}$ by a random oracle $\mathcal{O}_\mathcal{R}$. If the adversary can distinguish **Game** 7 and **Game** 8, we can construct a distinguisher to solve $\mathsf{HMLWE}_{q,n,\eta_e}$ [12].
- **Game** 9. Upon a query $(\mathbf{c}, \mathsf{b})$, the challenger replaces h by $\mathcal{O}_\mathcal{R}(\mathsf{tag}, \rho) + \langle \mathbf{t}, \mathbf{x} \rangle$ in this game. Upon an $\mathcal{O}_\mathsf{Readbit}$ query (tag, ρ, v), it searches for (tag, ρ) in the issued responses $\mathcal{Q}_\mathsf{Issue}$ and returns b if $v = \mathsf{Comp}_q(\mathcal{O}_\mathcal{R}(\mathsf{tag}, \rho), p_1)$. It returns $\perp$ if it fails to find an entry associated with (tag, ρ) in $\mathcal{O}_\mathsf{Readbit}$. Since $\mathcal{O}_\mathcal{R}(\mathsf{tag}, \rho)$ is only queried once, $\mathcal{O}_\mathcal{R}(\mathsf{tag}, \rho) + \langle \mathbf{s}_\mathsf{b}, \mathbf{b} \rangle$ and $\mathcal{O}_\mathcal{R}(\mathsf{tag}, \rho)$ are indistinguishable, so do **Game** 8 and **Game** 9.

In the final game, the valid v (accepted by the challenger) is uniquely determined by $\mathcal{O}_\mathcal{R}(\mathsf{tag}, \rho)$. Also, the adversary can only query $\mathcal{O}_\mathcal{R}$ through $\mathcal{O}_\mathsf{Issue}$. Since the adversary has only submitted ℓ queries to $\mathcal{O}_\mathsf{Issue}$, there are at most ℓ valid tuples $(\mathsf{b}, \mathsf{tag}, \sigma = (v, \rho))$, except that with negligible probability, the adversary correctly guesses an output of $\mathcal{O}_\mathcal{R}$ on an unseen input. Therefore, the probability of winning **Game** 10 is negligible. Since the increase of the adversary's advantage of each game transition is negligible, the adversary has a negligible probability of winning **Game** 0, *i.e.*, the one-more unforgeability game.

Theorem 3 (Unlinkability). *Let $q, p_1, d, \eta_r, \eta_e$ be integers as defined in the protocol* AT *in Sect. 3.1. The protocol* AT *is unlinkable if the public key encryption PKE is IND-CPA, the NIZK argument Π_1 satisfies zero knowledge, Π_2 is knowledge soundness, and the $\mathsf{MLWE}_{q,n,n,\eta_r}$ problems is hard.*

Proof. We prove the unlinkability via a series of games. Suppose that $\mathcal{A}$ queries $\mathcal{O}_{\mathsf{Query}}$ oracle Q_q times and $\mathcal{O}_{\mathsf{Final}}$ oracle Q_f times.

- **Game** 0. The game is a real unlinkability game.
- **Game** 1. In this game, the challenger simulates the random oracle and uses the simulator of Π_1 to answer the $\mathcal{O}_{\mathsf{Query}}$ query. This game is indistinguishable from **Game** 0 as Π_1 satisfies zero knowledge.

$$\Pr[G_1] - \Pr[G_0] \le Q_q \mathsf{Adv}_{\Pi_1}^{\mathrm{ZK}}.$$

- **Game** 2. The game is identical to **Game** 1 except that the challenger encrypts a dummy message to generate ct when answering the $\mathcal{O}_{\mathsf{Query}}$ query.

$$\Pr[G_2] - \Pr[G_1] \le Q_q \mathsf{Adv}_{\mathsf{PKE}}^{\mathrm{CPA}}.$$

- **Game** 3. The challenger's goal in this game is to learn the secret keys $(\mathbf{s}, \mathbf{s}_0, \mathbf{s}_1)$ from Π_2. When the adversary queries $\mathcal{O}_{\mathsf{Final}}$ the challenger runs the extractor of Π_2 to extract $(\mathbf{s}, \mathbf{s}_{\mathsf{b}}, \mathsf{b})$ and store $(\mathbf{s}, \mathbf{s}_{\mathsf{b}})$. It aborts if $\mathbf{t}^\top \not\approx \mathbf{s}^\top \mathbf{A}$. To learn $\mathbf{s}_{1-\mathsf{b}}$, the challenger tries to extract this key when the adversary further queries $\mathcal{O}_{\mathsf{Final}}$. For each query, the challenger uses the previously stored secret key $\mathbf{s}_{\mathsf{b}}$ to compute $h' = \langle \mathbf{s}, \mathbf{c} \rangle + \langle \mathbf{s}_{\mathsf{b}}, \mathbf{b} \rangle$ and compares it with the queried h. If $\|h - h'\|_\infty \ge \eta_e$, which means the adversary uses the secret key $\mathbf{s}_{1-\mathsf{b}}$ to generate the query h, the challenger then runs the extractor of Π_2 to extract the second secret key $\mathbf{s}_{1-\mathsf{b}}$. Since the adversary at most makes Q_q queries to $\mathcal{O}_{\mathsf{Query}}$, we have

$$\Pr[G_3] - \Pr[G_2] \le Q_q \mathsf{Adv}_{\Pi_2}^{\mathrm{KS}}.$$

- **Game** 4. In this game, the challenger uses the extracted secret keys to answer queries to $\mathcal{O}_{\mathsf{Final}}$. For each query, the challenger first extracts the private b: Similar to the same trick in **Game** 3, the challenger checks the norm of $h - \langle \mathbf{s}, \mathbf{c} \rangle - \langle \mathbf{s}_{\mathsf{b}}, \mathbf{b} \rangle$ to obtain the private bit b. (If the challenger has not obtained $\mathbf{s}_{\mathsf{b}}$ in **Game** 3, it runs the same step in **Game** 3 to extract $\mathbf{s}_{\mathsf{b}}$ from h.) Then, it computes and returns $v = \mathsf{Comp}(\langle \mathbf{s}, \mathsf{H}_1(\mathsf{tag}, \rho) \rangle + \langle \mathbf{s}_{\mathsf{b}}, \mathbf{b} \rangle, p_1)$. Since only the error terms disappear in v, the distinguishing probability is negligible.
- **Game** 5. The challenger sets $\mathbf{c}$ as a uniformly random value. To answer a query to $\mathcal{O}_{\mathsf{Final}}$, the challenger identifies $\mathsf{b} \in \{0,1\}$ such that $h - \langle \mathbf{s}, \mathbf{c} \rangle - \langle \mathbf{s}_{\mathsf{b}}, \mathbf{b} \rangle$ has small norm, and then returns $v = \mathsf{Comp}(\langle \mathbf{s}, \mathsf{H}_1(\mathsf{tag}, \rho) \rangle + \langle \mathbf{s}_{\mathsf{b}}, \mathbf{b} \rangle, p_1)$. If no such b is found, the challenger returns $\perp$.
  If the adversary can distinguish **Game** 4 and **Game** 5, we can construct a distinguisher to solve the $\mathsf{MLWE}_{q,n,n,\eta_r}$ problem of $\mathbf{c} = \mathbf{A}\mathbf{x} + \mathbf{e}_2$ and $\mathbf{c} \leftarrow \mathcal{R}_q^n$.

$$\Pr[G_5] - \Pr[G_4] \le Q_q \mathsf{Adv}^{\mathsf{MLWE}_{q,n,n,\eta_r}}.$$

In **Game** 5, the queries $\mathsf{query} = (\mathbf{c}, \mathsf{ct}, \pi_1)$ produced by $\mathcal{O}_{\mathsf{Query}}$ are dummy and unrelated to (tag, ρ), the adversary has zero advantage on linking a token query to a token. Since the distinguishing probability of each game transition is negligible, the adversary's advantage in winning the real unlinkability game (*i.e.*, **Game** 0) is negligible.

Theorem 4 (Privacy of PMB). *Let $q, p_1, d, \eta_r, \eta_e$ be integers as defined in the protocol* AT *in Sect. 3.1. The protocol* AT *satisfies the privacy of the private metadata bit (PMB), assuming* PKE *is correct, the NIZK argument Π_1 satisfies knowledge soundness, Π_2 is zero knowledge, the hash functions $\mathsf{H}_1, \mathsf{H}_2, \mathsf{G}$ are collision-resistant, and the $\mathsf{MLWE}_{q,1,n,\eta_e}$ problem is hard.*

Proof. The security proof is similar to the proof of one-more unforgeability. As the challenger progressively replaces responses from $\mathcal{O}_{\mathsf{Issue}}$ with samples from a uniform random distribution, and finally removes b from the responses, adversaries cannot distinguish between these scenarios during protocol execution.

We start from the real $\mathsf{PMB}^{\mathsf{b}^*}_{\mathsf{AT},\mathcal{A}}(1^\lambda)$ game **Game** 0.

- **Game** 1. The challenger replaces pk_e with a real encryption key in this game. In detail, the challenger runs $(\mathsf{pk}_e, \mathsf{sk}_e) \leftarrow \mathsf{PKE.KeyGen}(1^\lambda)$, embeds pk_e into the public parameter pp, then sets up the adversary with input $\mathsf{pk} \leftarrow \mathsf{AT.KeyGen}(\mathsf{pp})$.
- **Game** 2. For an issuing query $\mathsf{query} = (\mathsf{b}, \mathbf{c}, \mathsf{ct}, \pi_1)$, the challenger decrypts $(\mathbf{x}, \mathsf{tag}) := \mathsf{Dec}(\mathsf{sk}_e, \mathsf{ct})$ and updates $\mathcal{Q}_{\mathsf{Issue}} := \mathcal{Q}_{\mathsf{Issue}} \cup \{(\mathsf{tag}, \mathbf{x}, \mathbf{e}_2, \mathbf{c}, h, \mathsf{b})\}$, where $\mathbf{e}_2 = \mathbf{c} - \mathbf{A}\mathbf{x} - \mathsf{H}_1(\mathsf{tag}, \mathsf{G}(\mathbf{x}, \mathbf{e}_2))$. For the query $(\mathbf{c}, \mathsf{ct}, \pi_1)$ to $\mathcal{O}_{\mathsf{Chal}}$, the challenger decrypts $(\mathbf{x}, \mathsf{tag})$, and stores the query in $\mathcal{Q}_{\mathsf{Issue}} := \mathcal{Q}_{\mathsf{Issue}} \cup \{(\mathsf{tag}, \mathbf{x}, \mathbf{e}_2, \mathbf{c}, h, \mathsf{b}^*)\}$. (Note that this b^* is a game parameter.) **Game** 1 and **Game** 2 are indistinguishable as the encryption PKE is correct.
- **Game** 3. The game aborts if the adversary finds the collision of one of the hash functions $\mathsf{H}_1, \mathsf{H}_2$, and G, which happens with a negligible probability. This is the same as the hybrid **Game** 4–6 in the security proof of Theorem 2.
- **Game** 4. In this game, the challenger replaces π_2 with a simulated proof in $\mathcal{O}_{\mathsf{Chal}}$. **Game** 3 and **Game** 4 are indistinguishable as the proof Π_2 is zero knowledge.
- **Game** 5. The challenger answers $h = \langle \mathbf{t}, \mathbf{x} \rangle + \mathcal{O}^{\mathbf{s},k}_{\mathsf{HMLWE}}(\mathsf{tag}, \mathsf{G}(\mathbf{x}, \mathbf{e}_2)) + \langle \mathbf{s}_{\mathsf{b}}, \mathbf{b} \rangle$, in the $\mathcal{O}_{\mathsf{Chal}}$ challenge query. Note that $\mathcal{O}_{\mathsf{Issue}}$ remains unchanged. The challenger answers $\mathcal{O}_{\mathsf{Readbit}}$ as in the original game. For the query $(\mathsf{tag}, (\rho, v))$ to $\mathcal{O}_{\mathsf{Valid}}$, it returns 1 iff $\mathcal{O}_{\mathsf{Readbit}}(\mathsf{tag}, (\rho, v)) \neq \perp$. When $\mathcal{O}_{\mathsf{Readbit}}(\cdot) = \perp$, which means the adversary queried an invalid token or a response from the challenge oracle $\mathcal{O}_{\mathsf{Chal}}$, the oracle $\mathcal{O}_{\mathsf{Valid}}$ returns 1 iff $v = \mathsf{Comp}_q(\mathcal{O}^{\mathbf{s},k}_{\mathsf{HMLWE}}(\mathsf{tag}, \rho) + \langle \mathbf{s}_{\mathsf{b}}, \mathbf{b} \rangle, p_1)$ and returns $\perp$ otherwise.
- **Game** 6. This game replaces $\mathcal{O}^{\mathbf{s},k}_{\mathsf{HMLWE}}$ by a random oracle $\mathcal{O}_{\mathcal{R}}$ in the $\mathcal{O}_{\mathsf{Chal}}$ oracle. When $\mathcal{O}_{\mathsf{Readbit}}(\cdot) = \perp$, $\mathcal{O}_{\mathsf{Valid}}(\mathsf{tag}, (\rho, v))$ returns 1 if and only if $v = \mathsf{Comp}_q(\mathcal{O}_{\mathcal{R}}(\mathsf{tag}, \rho) + \langle \mathbf{s}_{\mathsf{b}}, \mathbf{b} \rangle, p_1)$. Distinguishing this game from the prior one is equivalent to breaking $\mathsf{HMLWE}_{q,n,\eta_e}$ problem.

- **Game** 7. We remove $\langle \mathbf{s}_{\mathsf{b}}, \mathbf{b}\rangle$ from $h := \mathcal{O}_{\mathcal{R}}(\mathsf{tag}, \rho) + \langle \mathbf{t}, \mathbf{x}\rangle$ in the $\mathcal{O}_{\mathsf{Chal}}$ query. When $\mathcal{O}_{\mathsf{Readbit}}(\cdot) = \perp$, $\mathcal{O}_{\mathsf{Valid}}(\mathsf{tag}, (\rho, v))$ returns 1 if and only if $v = \mathsf{Comp}_q(\mathcal{O}_{\mathcal{R}}(\mathsf{tag}, \rho), p_1)$. If this equation does not pass or the challenger cannot identify such an entry, it returns $\perp$. Because $\mathcal{O}^{\mathbf{s},k}_{\mathsf{HMLWE}}(\mathsf{tag}, \rho)$ is always queried with the same b, these changes are indistinguishable.

In the final game, the adversary has no advantage of guessing b^* correctly because the response from the challenge oracle is entirely independent of b^*. Since the advantage change in each game transition is negligible, the adversary's advantage of correctly guess b^* in the PMB game, *i.e.*, **Game** 0, is also negligible.

3.3 Batching Issuance

When a client submits multiple queries at once, individually proving that each response is well-formed requires the issuer to commit to the same witness $(\mathbf{s}, \mathbf{s}_0, \mathbf{s}_1)$ and prove the knowledge of its opening repeatedly across separate invocations of π_2. Consequently, the total response size scales linearly with the number of queries, N. To eliminate this redundancy, we introduce a batch proof mechanism that allows the issuer to commit to the secret keys $(\mathbf{s}, \mathbf{s}_0, \mathbf{s}_1)$ once, thereby collectively establishing the well-formedness of all N responses $(h_1, \ldots, h_N)$.

When the issuer assigns different private bits $\{\mathsf{b}_i\}_{i\in[N]}$ for each issue, the proof must conceal all N bits simultaneously. In this case, a single batch issuance involves both secret keys $\mathbf{s}_0$ and $\mathbf{s}_1$. Each response h_i is expressed as: $h_i = e_{3,i} + \langle \mathbf{s}, \mathbf{c}_i\rangle + \langle \mathbf{s}_0, \mathbf{b}\rangle(1 - \mathsf{b}_i) + \langle \mathbf{s}_1, \mathbf{b}\rangle \mathsf{b}_i$, which is a quadratic equation in $(\mathbf{s}, \mathbf{s}_0, \mathbf{s}_1, \mathsf{b}_i)$. This formulation restructures the equation without altering the computation, as either b_i or $(1-\mathsf{b}_i)$ will always be zero. In the batch proof, we can then introduce a binary vector $\vec{\mathsf{b}} \in \{0,1\}^N$ to collectively prove the relationships between all N responses $(h_1, \ldots, h_N)$ and the public keys $\mathbf{t}$ and secret keys $(\mathbf{s}, \mathbf{s}_0, \mathbf{s}_1)$.

Below, we present the algorithm for batch issuing.

$\mathsf{AT.IssueToken}(\mathsf{sk}, \vec{\mathsf{b}}, \mathsf{query} = (\mathbf{C}, \mathsf{ct}, \pi_{1,1}, \ldots, \pi_{1,N}))$:

1. Split $\mathbf{C}$ into $(\mathbf{c}_1, \ldots, \mathbf{c}_N)$.
2. Return $\perp$ if $\exists i \in [N]$ such that $\mathbf{c}_i$ appeared in some prior query.
3. Return $\perp$ if $\exists i \in [N]$ such that $\Pi_1.\mathsf{Verify}(\mathsf{pp}, \pi_{1,i}, (\mathsf{pk}, \mathsf{ct}, \mathbf{c}_i)) = 0$.
4. Compute $\mathbf{e}_3^\top := (\mathsf{H}_2(k, \mathbf{c}_1), \ldots, \mathsf{H}_2(k, \mathbf{c}_N))$.
5. $\mathbf{h} := \mathbf{s}^\top \mathbf{C} + \langle \mathbf{s}_0, \mathbf{b}\rangle(\mathbf{1}_N - \vec{\mathsf{b}}) + \langle \mathbf{s}_1, \mathbf{b}\rangle \vec{\mathsf{b}} + \mathbf{e}_3$.
6. Generate proof π_{Batch} for relation R_2^{Batch}.
7. Send out $\mathsf{resp} := (\mathbf{h}, \pi_{\mathsf{Batch}})$.

Relation R_2^{Batch} is adapted to batch queries.

$$R_2^{\mathsf{Batch}} = \left\{ \begin{array}{l|l} & \mathbf{h} = \mathbf{s}^\top \mathbf{C} + \langle \mathbf{s}_0, \mathbf{b} \rangle (\mathbf{1}_N - \vec{\mathsf{b}}) + \langle \mathbf{s}_1, \mathbf{b} \rangle \vec{\mathsf{b}} + \mathbf{e}_3; \\ (\mathbf{h}, \mathbf{A}, \mathbf{C}, & \mathbf{t}^\top = \mathbf{s}^\top \mathbf{A} + \mathbf{e}^\top; \\ \ \mathbf{t}, \mathbf{t}_0, \mathbf{t}_1); & \mathbf{t}_0^\top = \mathbf{s}_0^\top \mathbf{A} + \mathbf{e}_0^\top; \mathbf{t}_1^\top = \mathbf{s}_1^\top \mathbf{A} + \mathbf{e}_1^\top; \\ (\vec{\mathsf{b}}, \mathbf{s}, \mathbf{e}, \mathbf{e}_3 & \vec{\mathsf{b}} \in \{0,1\}^N, \|\vec{\mathsf{b}}\| = N, \|\mathbf{s}\| \le \beta_r; \\ \ \mathbf{s}_0, \mathbf{s}_1, \mathbf{e}_0, \mathbf{e}_1) & \|\mathbf{e}\| \le \beta_r, \|\mathbf{e}_3\| \le \sqrt{N}\beta_e, \|\mathbf{s}_0\| \le \beta_r; \\ & \|\mathbf{s}_1\| \le \beta_r, \|\mathbf{e}_0\| \le \beta_r, \|\mathbf{e}_1\| \le \beta_r. \end{array} \right\}.$$

This batch relation involves three types of witnesses: the issuer's secret keys $(\mathbf{s}, \mathbf{e}, \mathbf{s}_0, \mathbf{s}_1)$, a vector of error terms $\mathbf{e}_3 = (e_{3,1}, \ldots, e_{3,N})^\top \in (\mathcal{B}^d_{\eta_e})^N$ for token generation, and a binary vector $\vec{\mathsf{b}}$ encoding N private bits. While the secret keys remain constant regardless of batch size N, both $\mathbf{e}_3$ and $\vec{\mathsf{b}}$ grow linearly with N. The binary nature of $\vec{\mathsf{b}}$ allows efficient embedding as polynomial coefficients, incurring a minimal overhead to the proof size. In contrast, $\mathbf{e}_3$ requires distinct entries for each token in $\mathbf{h}$, preventing further batching. It is thus the dominant factor in the proof size of π_{Batch}. Table 4 analyzes the concrete sizes at different N.

4 Concrete Instantiation

We suggest an instantiation for practical deployment, using:

- Lattice-based hash functions [30] for G and H_1, and SHAKE-256 for H_2,
- Regev's encryption [39] (with CRYSTALS-Kyber's optimization [7]) under the MLWE assumption for PKE, and
- Lyubashevsky's framework for the NIZK [33].

Encryption. We recall Regev's public-key encryption scheme as follows. In the implementation, we will apply CRYSTALS-Kyber for better efficiency.

- $\mathsf{KeyGen}(1^\lambda)$: On input 1^λ, it samples a matrix $\mathbf{C} \leftarrow \mathcal{R}_p^{k_1 \times k_2}$ and two short matrices $\mathbf{S} \leftarrow \mathcal{D}_s^{k_2 \times k_3}$ and $\mathbf{E} \leftarrow \mathcal{D}_s^{k_1 \times k_3}$ uniformly at random. At last, it outputs the public key $\mathsf{pk} := (\mathbf{C}, \mathbf{D} := \mathbf{CS} + \mathbf{E})$ and the secret key $\mathsf{sk} := \mathbf{S}$.
- $\mathsf{Enc}(\mathbf{m}, \mathsf{pk})$: On inputs of the encryption key $\mathsf{pk} = \mathbf{D}$ and the message $\mathbf{m} \in \{0,1\}^{k_3 d}$, it samples $\mathbf{r} \leftarrow \chi^{k_1}, \mathbf{e}_a \leftarrow \chi^{k_2}, \mathbf{e}_b \leftarrow \chi^{k_3}$ from an error distribution χ and outputs $\mathsf{ct} := (\mathbf{u}, \mathbf{v})$:

$$\mathbf{u} := \mathbf{C}^\top \mathbf{r} + \mathbf{e}_a, \qquad \mathbf{v} := \mathbf{D}^\top \mathbf{r} + \mathbf{e}_b + \lfloor \frac{q}{2} \rceil \mathbf{m}.$$

- $\mathsf{Dec}(\mathsf{sk}, \mathsf{ct})$: On inputs of the secret key $\mathsf{sk} = \mathbf{S}$ and the ciphertext $\mathsf{ct} = (\mathbf{u}, \mathbf{v})$, it computes $\mathbf{m}' := \mathbf{v} - \mathbf{S}^\top \mathbf{u}$. Decode $\mathbf{m}$ according to $\mathbf{m}'$ and outputs $\mathbf{m}$.

Hash Function. Π_1 proves the hash function evaluation, which requires knowing its inner operations. Instead of using general hash functions, we use a relaxed programmable hash function from lattices [30] as follows.

- $\mathsf{H.Gen}(1^\lambda) \to \mathsf{hk}$: On input 1^λ, it defines the input length ℓ and samples $\mathbf{h}_j \xleftarrow{\$} \mathcal{R}_q^k$ for $j \in [\ell+1]$. Return the hash key $\mathsf{hk} := \{\mathbf{h}_j\}_{j\in[\ell+1]}$.
- $\mathsf{H.Eval}(\mathsf{hk}, x = \{x_1, \ldots, x_\ell\}) \to \mathbf{z}$: Return $\mathbf{z} := \mathbf{h}_0 + \sum_{j=1}^{\ell}(2x_j - 1)\mathbf{h}_j$.

For H_1, we set $\mathbf{z}_{\mathsf{H}_1} \in \mathcal{R}_q^n$ to align with the length of the commitment $\mathbf{c}$. For G, we set $\mathbf{z}_{\mathsf{G}} \in \mathcal{R}_p^2$ for simplicity.

NIZK for Relation R_1. The relation R_1 ensures the client encrypts the tuple $(\mathbf{x}, \mathsf{tag})$ and computes the commitment $\mathbf{c} = \mathbf{A}\mathbf{x}+\mathbf{e}_2+\mathsf{H}_1(\mathsf{tag}, \mathsf{G}(\mathbf{x}, \mathbf{e}_2))$ correctly. The last term $\mathsf{H}_1(\mathsf{tag}, \mathsf{G}(\mathbf{x}, \mathbf{e}_2))$ requires proving the evaluations of the hash $\rho = \mathsf{G}(\mathbf{x}, \mathbf{e}_2)$ and $\mathsf{h} = \mathsf{H}_1(\mathsf{tag}, \rho)$. The soundness of the proof guarantees that the client uses the correct $(\mathbf{x}, \mathbf{e}_2, \mathsf{tag})$ when requesting a token.

The encryption scheme is instantiated using Regev's encryption, where $\mathsf{pk}_e = (\mathbf{C}, \mathbf{D})$, $\mathsf{ct} = (\mathbf{u}, \mathbf{v})$, and the encryption randomness is $(\mathbf{r}, \mathbf{e}_a, \mathbf{e}_b)$. The evaluations of hash functions $\mathsf{H}_1.\mathsf{Eval}$ and $\mathsf{G.Eval}$ are $\mathsf{hk}^{\mathsf{G}} = \{\mathbf{h}_j^{\mathsf{G}}\}_{j\in[0,\ell_{\mathsf{G}}]}$ and $\mathsf{hk}^{\mathsf{H}_1} = \{\mathbf{h}_j^{\mathsf{H}_1}\}_{j\in[0,\ell_{\mathsf{H}_1}]}$, where $\ell_{\mathsf{G}} = 2nd\log\eta_r$ and $\ell_{\mathsf{H}_1} = \lambda + 2d\log p$ are the input length of G and H_1, respectively.

$$R_1 = \left\{ \begin{array}{l|l} & \mathsf{ct} = \mathsf{PKE.Enc}(\mathsf{pk}_e, \mathbf{m}'); \\ (\mathsf{pk}_e, \mathbf{A}, \mathsf{ct}, \mathbf{c}, & \mathbf{m}' = (\mathbf{x}, \mathsf{tag}) \in \{0,1\}^{k_3 d}; \\ \mathsf{hk}^{\mathsf{G}}, \mathsf{hk}^{\mathsf{H}_1}); & \rho = \mathsf{G.Eval}(\mathsf{hk}^{\mathsf{G}}, \mathbf{x}, \mathbf{e}_2); \\ (\mathbf{x}, \mathbf{e}_2, \mathsf{tag}, \rho) & \mathbf{c} = \mathbf{A}\mathbf{x} + \mathbf{e}_2 + \mathsf{H}_1.\mathsf{Eval}(\mathsf{hk}^{\mathsf{H}_1}, \mathsf{tag}, \rho); \\ & \|\mathbf{e}_2\| \le \beta_r, \|\mathbf{x}\| \le \beta_r. \end{array} \right\}.$$

To manage the overflow that occurs when computations exceed modulus p, we introduce vectors $(\mathbf{v}_0, \mathbf{v}_1) \in \mathcal{R}_q^{k_2+k_3}$ below to capture these extra components:

$$\begin{bmatrix} \mathbf{v}_0 \\ \mathbf{v}_1 \end{bmatrix} := p^{-1}\left(\begin{bmatrix} \mathbf{C}^\top & \mathbf{0}_{k_2\times k_3} \\ \mathbf{D}^\top & \lfloor \frac{p}{2} \rceil \mathbf{I}_{k_3} \end{bmatrix} \begin{bmatrix} \mathbf{r} \\ \mathbf{m}' \end{bmatrix} + \begin{bmatrix} \mathbf{e}_a \\ \mathbf{e}_b \end{bmatrix} - \begin{bmatrix} \mathbf{u} \\ \mathbf{v} \end{bmatrix} \right).$$

Since the encryption algorithm operates over $\mathcal{R}_p$, any operations involving matrix and vector multiplication exceeding p are eliminated modulo p. However, we will use a larger modulus q, where any excess beyond p is retained. The vector $(\mathbf{v}_0, \mathbf{v}_1)$ thus stores these overflow components. Therefore, each component of $(\mathbf{v}_0, \mathbf{v}_1)$ does not exceed $\eta_1 dp/2$, where η_1 is the infinite norm of $\mathbf{r}$. Thus, $\|(\mathbf{v}_0, \mathbf{v}_1)\|_\infty \le B_v = \sqrt{(\eta_1 k_2 d/2)^2 k_2 d + (\eta_1 k_3 d/2)^2 k_3 d}$.

To prove R_1, we employ a general strategy [33] to transform the relations into quadratic functions. The full proof is provided in Appendix D. Specifically, define the witness $w = (\mathbf{m}_1, \mathbf{m}_2) \in \mathcal{R}_q^{2n+2\lambda/d+4+k_1+k_2+k_3} \times \mathcal{R}_q^{n+2}$, where

$$\mathbf{m}_1 := (\mathbf{x}\|a_1\|\mathbf{e}_2\|a_2\|\mathsf{tag}\|\mathbf{r}\|a_3\|\mathbf{e}_a\|\mathbf{e}_b\|a_4), \qquad \mathbf{m}_2 := (\mathsf{h}\|\rho)$$

and commit them via ABDLOP commitment [33] (Appendix C).

Recall $\mathsf{Inv}\colon \mathcal{R}_q \to \mathcal{R}_q$ is an automorphism where $\mathsf{Inv}(X) = X^{-1}$. We define $(7+2n+k_2+k_3)$ quadratic functions mapping the witness w to an $\mathcal{R}_q$ element:

$$\begin{aligned}
F_1(w) &= \mathsf{Inv}(\mathbf{1}_{2\lambda/d} - \mathsf{tag})^\top(\mathsf{tag}); \\
F_2(w) &= \mathsf{Inv}(\mathbf{x}\|a_1)^\top(\mathbf{x}\|a_1) - \beta_r^2; \\
F_3(w) &= \mathsf{Inv}(\mathbf{e}_2\|a_2)^\top(\mathbf{e}_2\|a_2) - \beta_r^2; \\
F_4(w) &= \mathsf{Inv}(\mathbf{r}\|a_3)^\top(\mathbf{r}\|a_3) - \beta_v^2; \\
F_5(w) &= \mathsf{Inv}(\mathbf{e}_a\|\mathbf{e}_b\|a_4)^\top(\mathbf{e}_a\|\mathbf{e}_b\|a_4) - \beta_e^2; \\
F_{i+5}(w) &= h_{0,i}^{\mathsf{G}} + h_i^{\mathsf{G}\top}(2(\vec{\mathbf{x}}\|\vec{\mathbf{e}}_1) - \mathbf{1}_{\ell_\mathsf{G}}) - \hat{\mathbf{e}}_i^\top\rho, && \forall i \in [2]; \\
F_{i+7}(w) &= h_{0,i}^{\mathsf{H}_1} + h_i^{\mathsf{H}_1\top}(2(\mathsf{tag}\|\vec{\rho}) - \mathbf{1}_{\ell_{\mathsf{H}_1}}) - \hat{\mathbf{e}}_i^\top\mathsf{h}, && \forall i \in [n]; \\
F_{i+7+n}(w) &= \mathbf{a}_i^\top\mathbf{x} + \hat{\mathbf{e}}_i^\top(\mathbf{e}_2 + \mathsf{h}) - c_i, && \forall i \in [n]; \\
F_{i+7+2n}(w) &= \mathbf{c}_i^\top\mathbf{r} + \hat{\mathbf{e}}_i^\top\mathbf{e}_a - pv_{0,i} - u_i, && \forall i \in [k_2]; \\
F_{i+7+2n+k_2}(w) &= \mathbf{d}_i^\top\mathbf{r} + \hat{\mathbf{e}}_i^\top(\mathbf{e}_b + \lfloor\tfrac{p}{2}\rceil(\vec{\mathbf{x}}\|\mathsf{tag}))) - pv_{1,i} - v_i, && \forall i \in [k_3];
\end{aligned}$$

to describe the above relations, where c_i, u_i, v_i denotes the i-th entry of $\mathbf{c}, \mathbf{u}$, and $\mathbf{v}$, $h_i^{\mathsf{G}}, h_i^{\mathsf{H}_1}$ is the i-th row of the matrices $[\mathbf{h}_1^{\mathsf{G}}|\cdots]$ and $[\mathbf{h}_1^{\mathsf{H}_1}|\cdots]$ $\mathbf{a}_i, \mathbf{c}_i, \mathbf{d}_i$ is the i-th row of matrices $\mathbf{A}, \mathbf{C}^\top$, and $\mathbf{D}^\top$, $\hat{\mathbf{e}}_i$ is a unit vector $\hat{e}_i$ with its i-th entry being 1, and $\mathbf{1}_{2\lambda/d}$ is a full-one vector of length $2\lambda/d$, $\vec{\mathbf{x}}$ and $\vec{\mathbf{e}_2}$ denotes the binary string of $\mathbf{x}$ and $\mathbf{e}_2$.

We choose a set of challenges $(\gamma_1, \ldots, \gamma_{7+2n+k_2+k_3})$ from $\mathcal{R}_q$ and apply linear combinations of the functions above to batch them together. To achieve one-shot soundness, we select challenges τ to prove the well-formedness of the batched functions in parallel. Then, for $j \in [1, \tau]$, denote f_j as the function

$$f_j := \sum_{i=1}^{7+2n+k_2+k_3} \gamma_{j,i} F_i. \tag{2}$$

NIZK for Relation R_2. Relation R_2 requires the issuer proving that $h = \langle \mathbf{s}, \mathbf{c}\rangle + e_3 + \langle \mathbf{s}_\mathsf{b}, \mathbf{b}\rangle$ is constructed using the correct private key $(\mathbf{s}, \mathbf{s}_\mathsf{b})$ for the private bit b. The issuer must prove that $\mathbf{s}, \mathbf{s}_\mathsf{b}$ are the secret keys corresponding to the public commitment $\mathbf{t} = \mathbf{A}^\top\mathbf{s} + \mathbf{e}, \mathbf{t}_\mathsf{b} = \mathbf{A}^\top\mathbf{s}_\mathsf{b} + \mathbf{e}_\mathsf{b}$ without revealing b. We introduce a 2-bit secret vector ν to select $\mathbf{t}_\mathsf{b}$, where the b-th position is set to 1 and the other is 0. Thus, we have $\nu^\top[\mathbf{t}_0|\mathbf{t}_1] = \mathbf{t}_\mathsf{b}$. The issuer accomplishes it by proving

$$\nu^\top[\mathbf{t}_0|\mathbf{t}_1] = \mathbf{A}^\top\mathbf{s}_\mathsf{b} + \mathbf{e}_\mathsf{b}.$$

As in the prior work [12], the evaluation of the error term $e_3 = \mathsf{H}_2(k, \mathbf{c})$ is not involved in the proof π_2. The issuer only proves that $e_3 \in \mathcal{B}_{\eta_e}^d$ by proving $\|e_3\| \leq \beta_r^2$. Define the witness $\mathbf{m}_1 := (\nu\|\mathbf{s}\|a_1\|\mathbf{e}\|a_2\|\mathbf{s}_\mathsf{b}\|a_3\|\mathbf{e}_\mathsf{b}\|a_4\|e_3\|a_5) \in \mathcal{R}_q^{4n+7}$. Accordingly, for each quadratic constraint, we define $2n+8$ functions $G_1, \ldots, G_{2n+8}$:

$$G_1(w) = \mathbf{c}^\top \mathbf{s} + \mathbf{b}^\top \mathbf{s}_{\mathsf{b}} + e_3 - h;$$
$$G_{i+1}(w) = \mathbf{a}_i^\top \mathbf{s} + \hat{\mathbf{e}}_i^\top \mathbf{e} - t_i, \quad \forall i \in [1, n];$$
$$G_{i+1+n}(w) = \mathbf{a}_i^\top \mathbf{s}_{\mathsf{b}} + \hat{\mathbf{e}}_i^\top \mathbf{e}_{\mathsf{b}} - [t_{0,i} | t_{1,i}]\nu, \quad \forall i \in [1, n]$$
$$G_{2n+2}(w) = \mathsf{Inv}(\mathbf{s}\|a_1)^\top (\mathbf{s}\|a_1) - \beta_r^2; \quad G_{2n+3}(w) = \mathsf{Inv}(\mathbf{e}\|a_2)^\top (\mathbf{e}\|a_2) - \beta_r^2;$$
$$G_{2n+4}(w) = \mathsf{Inv}(\mathbf{s}_{\mathsf{b}}\|a_3)^\top (\mathbf{s}_{\mathsf{b}}\|a_3) - \beta_r^2; \quad G_{2n+5}(w) = \mathsf{Inv}(\mathbf{e}_{\mathsf{b}}\|a_4)^\top (\mathbf{e}_{\mathsf{b}}\|a_4) - \beta_r^2;$$
$$G_{2n+6}(w) = \mathsf{Inv}(e_3\|a_5)^\top (e_3\|a_5) - \beta_e^2; \quad G_{2n+7}(w) = \mathsf{Inv}(\nu)^\top (\mathbf{1}_2 - \nu);$$
$$G_{2n+8}(w) = \mathsf{Inv}(\nu)^\top (\nu) - 1;$$

where $\mathbf{a}_i$ is the i-th column of matrix $\mathbf{A}$; $t_i, t_{0,i}, t_{1,i}$ denotes the i-th entry of $\mathbf{t}, \mathbf{t}_0$ and $\mathbf{t}_1$; $\hat{\mathbf{e}}_i$ is a unit vector with its i-th entry being 1. Challenge values $\gamma_{1,1}, \ldots, \gamma_{\tau,2n+8}$ are then selected to provide a one-shot proof for R_2 through a batch combination of these functions. Refer to Appendix E for the full proof.

NIZK for the Batch Relation R_{Batch}**.** To equip our protocol with batch capability, we apply the method above [33] for proving R_{Batch}. Here, a binary vector $\vec{\mathsf{b}}$ represents the private bits across multiple queries. Since the protocol and proofs operate over polynomials, we embed $\vec{\mathsf{b}}$ as coefficients in a polynomial over $\mathcal{R}_q$. Consequently, when $N < d$, $\vec{\mathsf{b}}$ is compressed into a single polynomial, further reducing proof size while maintaining protocol integrity.

5 Implementations

5.1 Concrete Efficiency

We propose specific parameters to instantiate anonymous tokens with a targeted 128-bit classical security level. These parameters are chosen to ensure security against computational lattice-based hard problems for each primitive, as well as soundness and zero-knowledge properties for the proofs.

Specifically, we set $\lambda = 128$. Assuming the adversary accesses the oracles up to 2^{32} times, this incurs 32 bits of security loss. As a result, the underlying lattice problems must achieve a hardness level of 160 bits. To analyze the hardness of the MLWE and MSIS problems (defined in Appendix C), we use the LWE estimator [3] and the techniques of Ducas *et al.* [22], respectively.[1] We set $q > 2p_1(2d\eta_r^2 + \eta_e + 1)$ and $d \log p_2 > \lambda$ to guarantee the correctness of the entire protocol. The encryption parameters align with Kyber encryption [7].

For the proof Π_1 and Π_2, we choose the module $q = 68,719,468,801 \approx 2^{36}$ and the parallel repetition time $\tau = 4$ to ensure that $q^{-\tau}$ and $q^{-d/2}$ are less than 2^{-128}. Then, we select the standard deviations y_1, y_2, y_3, and y_4 for the discrete Gaussian distributions to ensure the overall rejection time is approximately 4 to 5. Table 3 lists the specific parameters and distributions. (See Appendix B for the detailed probability distributions).

We evaluated our protocol on a laptop equipped with an Intel i5-1135G7 2.40 GHz processor and 16 GB of RAM. The source code is publicly available [46].

---

[1] The former is available at https://bitbucket.org/malb/lwe-estimator.

Table 4 presents the component sizes and execution times of our protocol. Essentially, we trade increased token size for reduced overall communication costs. Recall that our token complexity, $d\lceil \log p_1 \rceil + 2\lambda$, matches that of the keyed-verification blind signature [12]. Their instantiation [12] assumes the existence of a hash function that provides a small ρ (specifically, 2λ bits) for compact NIZK proofs of its correctness.

However, specialized and efficient proofs for hash function evaluation within lattice-based cryptography are rare, compelling existing approaches to rely on generic proof systems that may not offer optimal efficiency for lattice-specific applications. To address this, we instantiate $\mathsf{G}(\cdot)$ by a lattice-based hash function [30] defined over $\mathcal{R}_p^2$, with a size of $2d\lceil \log p \rceil = 384$ bytes. While G has a larger ρ, it facilitates smaller NIZK proofs. Developing a more efficient G would immediately enhance the performance of our protocol.

Table 3. Parameters

Variables	Explanation	Value
λ	Security Parameter	128
d	Degree of Polynomials	128
p	Encryption Module	3329
k_1, k_2	Height, Weight of $\mathbf{C}$	4, 4
k_3	# of Ciphertexts	$4n+2$
η_1	Param. of Binomial Dist. of $\mathbf{r}$	3
η_2	Param. of Binomial Dist. of $\mathbf{e}_a$, $\mathbf{e}_b$	2
η_r, η_e	Param. of Binomial Dist. of $\mathbf{s}, \mathbf{x}$ and e_3	7
q	System Module	$\approx 2^{36}$
n	Matrix $\mathbf{A}$'s Dimension	13
p_1	Compress Constant	2^3
Proof Π_1 and Π_2		
τ	Repetition Time	4
n_1	Height of Commitment Matrix $\mathbf{E}_1$	4
m_2	Length of Masking Vector $\mathbf{r}_1$	13
$\mathcal{D}_{s_r}$	Distribution of $\mathbf{r}_1$ (Appendix C)	$\mathcal{B}_7$
y_1, y_2	Standard Deviation of $\mathbf{y}_1$, $\mathbf{y}_2$	6664, 5140
y_3, y_4	Standard Deviation of $\mathbf{y}_3$, $\mathbf{y}_4$	2887, 1120801
Security Estimates		
$\epsilon^1_{\mathsf{MSIS}}$	Hardness of MSIS in Π_1	$2^{512.5}$
$\epsilon^2_{\mathsf{MSIS}}$	Hardness of MSIS in Π_2 and Π_{Batch}	$2^{235.9}$
$\epsilon^1_{\mathsf{MLWE}}, \epsilon^*_{\mathsf{MLWE}}$	Hardness of MLWE in Π_1, AT	$2^{169.7}$
$\epsilon^2_{\mathsf{MLWE}}$	Hardness of MLWE in Π_2	$2^{169.5}$

Table 4. Benchmark results (Statistics over 20 executions)

Rd.	Algorithm	Component	Times (ms)			Sizes (kB)	
			mean	min.	max.	item	
	KeyGen		22.41	19.92	25.36	pk	23.41
						sk	2.43
1	ClientQuery	Total (with Π_1)	4503	394.6	21041	Query (with π_1)	60.92
		Proof Π_1	4488	380.7	20894	Proof π_1 only	42.95
2	IssueToken	Single issuing	1998.2	1282.8	3178	Response (with π_2)	31.54
		Single proof Π_2	1854.2	1149.8	3034.2	Proof π_2 only	24.68
		Batch proof	2992.4	1348.4	4093	$N = 10$	34.04
						$N = 50$	44.62
3	ClientFinal		98.77	90.44	125.3	Token (without tag)	432 B
						tag	32 B
	Readbit		6.642	5.745	9.053		

5.2 Further Optimization

Our protocol can be further optimized for efficiency and size in several ways:

1. Apply Dilithium's optimization [22] to the ABDOLP commitments [33] in the proof system by truncating the last few bits of the commitment vectors and proof values and using the MakeHint and UseHint algorithms to convey a small amount of carry information.
2. Use binomial rejection sampling [21], which supports selecting a discrete Gaussian distribution with smaller variance, thereby reducing the size of the proof values.
3. Utilize AVX2 instructions [34,41] to accelerate NTT multiplication operations, reducing runtime.

6 Conclusion

This paper presents a lattice-based anonymous token scheme that achieves both post-quantum security and efficient batch issuance. By integrating verifiable oblivious pseudorandom functions with recent advances in lattice-based zero-knowledge proofs, our construction achieves a token size of 432 bytes. Comparable to recent keyed-verification blind signatures, our scheme offers additional features such as batch proofs and a private metadata bit, showcasing the efficiency potential of lattice-based techniques in privacy-preserving protocols.

Addressing challenges of efficient token issuance, this work is particularly relevant in light of the IETF's proposal for a batched token issuance protocol[2], which aims to enhance token issuance by allowing multiple tokens to be

[2] https://www.ietf.org/archive/id/draft-ietf-privacypass-batched-tokens-01.html.

issued in a single request. The keyed-verification approach strengthens privacy by restricting validation to authorized entities, thus mitigating inference-based attacks while maintaining the lightweight nature.

Future work may focus on further optimizing the proof size and adapting the protocol to support additional use cases, as outlined in the appendix.

Acknowledgment. We thank Baishun Sun for his assistance with the implementations. We would also like to express our gratitude to the program co-chairs, Ruben Niederhagen and Markku-Juhani O. Saarinen, and the program committee, for their support and comment throughout the process. Yan and Wang are supported by the National Natural Science Foundation of China (Grant No. 62272362, 12441104) and the Youth Innovation Team of Shaanxi Universities. Chow is supported in part by the General Research Fund (CUHK 14210621) from the Research Grant Council, Hong Kong, Direct Grant (4055238), and Strategic Impact Enhancement Fund (3135517) from Chinese University of Hong Kong.

A Further Potential Applications

Keyed-verification anonymous tokens are well-suited for scenarios where the token issuer has a vested interest in verifying issued tokens, as well as for relay settings that facilitate delegated verification. For instance, in access control encryption [45] (where the objective is to eliminate subliminal channels created by the client rather than maintaining a single private metadata bit from the issuer), the issuer can manage permissions and revocation by issuing tokens, while intermediary entities like sanitizers can serve as verifiers. Another application is (updatable) anonymous credentials with reputation [18,35]. Our token could replace BBS+ signatures [6]. However, we need to accommodate additional hidden data, much like how BBS+ extends the original BBS signatures.

Single-tag certification is applicable in various scenarios, notably in anonymous payment systems. In layer-2 cryptocurrency systems such as LDSP [36]—a payment system collectively maintained by merchants who also receive the issued tokens—our anonymous tokens with public metadata can substitute partially blind signatures [17] in LDSP with certain adaptations. Firstly, the keyed-verification setting requires non-issuing recipients to communicate with the issuer immediately, unlike the delayed clearing process in the original LDSP design. Secondly, LDSP employs a distributed issuing process, necessitating the participation of all (of a small group of) distributed issuers for any token issuance.

Anonymous identity-based key issuing [23,43] also only certifies a single field, which is the user identity. In a privacy-preserving architecture designed to eliminate key escrow in identity-based encryption (IBE) [15,16], the system comprises an identity-certifying authority (ICA) that oversees and certifies user identities. Upon receiving anonymous proof from the ICA, the key generation center engages in an anonymous private key issuing protocol based on the certified hidden identity. To adapt our lattice-based construction to this framework, we need to instantiate it with a commitment scheme that is efficiently compatible with the associated IBE scheme for the issuance of IBE secret keys for hidden identities.

B Probability Distributions

Discrete Gaussian Distribution. In lattice-based cryptography, secret vectors are often sampled from a discrete Gaussian distribution. Rejection sampling is often used to ensure signatures or proofs are indistinguishable from this distribution.

Definition 8. *$\mathcal{D}^n_{\mathbf{x},s}(\mathbf{z})$ below defines the discrete Gaussian distribution on $\mathcal{R}^n$ centered around $\mathbf{x} \in \mathcal{R}^n$ with standard deviation $s > 0$:*

$$\mathcal{D}^n_{\mathbf{x},s}(\mathbf{z}) = \frac{e^{-\|\mathbf{z}-\mathbf{x}\|^2/2\,s^2}}{\sum_{\mathbf{z}' \in \mathcal{R}^n} e^{-\|\mathbf{z}'\|^2/2\,s^2}}.$$

For $\mathbf{x} = 0$, we use $\mathcal{D}^n_s$ for short.

Centered Binomial Distribution. Practical applications often use a substitute for the discrete Gaussian distribution. In our protocol, secret and noise vectors are sampled from a centered binomial distribution $\mathcal{B}_\eta$ instead, defined as:

$$\mathcal{B}_\eta = \left\{ \sum_{i=1}^{\eta} (a_i - b_i) \colon a_i, b_i \in \{0, 1\} \right\}.$$

Its standard deviation is $\sqrt{\eta/2}$. For a degree-$(d-1)$ polynomial $x \leftarrow \mathcal{B}^d_\eta \subset \mathcal{R}$, the Euclidean norm, or ℓ^2-norm $||x|| \leq \eta\sqrt{d}$. We write $\mathcal{B}$ for short if $\eta = 1$.

C ABDLOP Commitment and Proving Its Opening

We recall the ABDLOP commitment scheme [33], which is a combination of the Ajtai commitment [1] and BDLOP commitment [9] schemes.

$\mathsf{Setup}(1^\lambda) \to \mathsf{pp}$: Take the security parameter 1^λ as input and output the public parameters $\mathsf{pp} = (q, n_1, m_1, m_2, n_2, \mathcal{D}_{s_e})$, where $\mathcal{D}_{s_e}$ is the distribution of $\mathbf{e}$.

$\mathsf{KeyGen}(\mathsf{pp}) \to \mathsf{ck}$: Take the public parameters pp as input and output the commitment key ck. In detail, it samples the matrices $\mathbf{E}_1 \leftarrow \mathcal{R}_q^{n_1 \times m_1}, \mathbf{E}_2 \leftarrow \mathcal{R}_q^{n_1 \times m_2}, \mathbf{F}_1 \leftarrow \mathcal{R}_q^{n_2 \times m_2}$ uniformly at random and $\mathsf{ck} := (\mathbf{E}_1, \mathbf{E}_2, \mathbf{F}_1)$.

$\mathsf{Com}(\mathsf{ck}, (\mathbf{m}_1, \mathbf{m}_2), \mathbf{e}) \to c$: Take the commitment key ck, the commitment messages $\mathbf{m}_1 \in \mathcal{R}_q^{m_1}, \mathbf{m}_2 \in \mathcal{R}_q^{n_2}$, and the randomness $\mathbf{r}_1 \leftarrow \mathcal{D}_{s_r}^{m_2}$ as inputs and output a commitment c such that

$$c := \begin{bmatrix} \mathbf{t}_A \\ \mathbf{t}_B \end{bmatrix} = \begin{bmatrix} \mathbf{E}_1 \\ \mathbf{0} \end{bmatrix} \mathbf{m}_1 + \begin{bmatrix} \mathbf{E}_2 \\ \mathbf{F}_1 \end{bmatrix} \mathbf{r}_1 + \begin{bmatrix} \mathbf{0} \\ \mathbf{m}_2 \end{bmatrix}.$$

$\mathsf{Open}(\mathsf{ck}, c, (\mathbf{m}_1, \mathbf{m}_2), \mathbf{e}) \to b$: Output $b = 1$ if and only if

$$c = \begin{bmatrix} \mathbf{E}_1 \\ \mathbf{0} \end{bmatrix} \mathbf{m}_1 + \begin{bmatrix} \mathbf{E}_2 \\ \mathbf{F}_1 \end{bmatrix} \mathbf{r}_1 + \begin{bmatrix} \mathbf{0} \\ \mathbf{m}_2 \end{bmatrix};$$

otherwise, it outputs $b = 0$.

Here, we recall the challenge space [33]. Define $\mathcal{S}_\kappa = \{x \in \mathcal{R}_q : \|x\|_\infty \leq \kappa\}$. Fix $\eta > 0$ and a power-of-two k, then the challenge space is:

$$\mathcal{C} = \left\{ c \in \mathcal{S}_\kappa : \mathsf{Inv}(c) = c, \sqrt[2k]{\|c^{2k}\|_1} \leq \eta \right\}.$$

Then, we write $\bar{\mathcal{C}}$ for a subtractive subset $\bar{\mathcal{C}} := \{c - c' : (c, c' \in \mathcal{C}) \wedge (c \neq c')\}$. We set $\kappa = 2$ and $\eta = 59$ to implement the challenge space.

$\mathsf{Rej}(\vec{z}, \vec{v}, s)$
$u \leftarrow [0, 1)$
If $u > \frac{1}{M} \cdot \exp\left(\frac{-2\langle \vec{z}, \vec{v} \rangle + \|\vec{v}\|^2}{2s^2}\right)$, return 0 (*reject*)
Else return 1 (*accept*)

Fig. 5. Rejection sampling

Proving an opening of the commitment is to prove the knowledge of a triple $(\mathbf{m}_1, \mathbf{m}_2, \mathbf{e})$, where the prover calls the rejection sampling algorithm [31] (described as in Fig. 5) to ensure zero-knowledge. Like most previous work in lattice-based proofs, we recall the definition of a relaxed opening as follows.

Definition 9. *A relaxed opening of the ABDLOP commitment* $(\mathbf{t}_A, \mathbf{t}_B)$ *is a tuple* $(\mathbf{m}_1, \mathbf{m}_2, \mathbf{e}, c)$ *which satisfies:*

$$\mathbf{E}_1\mathbf{m}_1 + \mathbf{E}_2\mathbf{r}_1 = \mathbf{t}_A, \mathbf{E}_2\mathbf{r}_1 + \mathbf{m}_2 = \mathbf{t}_B, \quad c \in \bar{\mathcal{C}}, \|c\mathbf{m}_1\| \leq B_1, \|c\mathbf{r}_1\| \leq B_2.$$

Definition 10. **($\mathsf{MSIS}_{q,\kappa,m,B}$)** *Let* $q, \kappa, m > 0$ *be integers, and* B *be a real number with* $0 < B < q$. *Given* $\mathbf{A} \leftarrow \mathcal{R}_q^{\kappa \times m}$, *the* module-SIS problem *is to find a short solution* $\mathbf{z} \in \mathcal{R}_q^m$ *such that* $\mathbf{Ax} = \mathbf{0}$ *and* $0 < \|\mathbf{x}\| \leqslant B$.

The following lemma shows the above commitment scheme is computationally binding and computationally hiding.

Lemma 1. **([33]).** *The ABDLOP commitment scheme is computationally binding under the assumption that* $\mathsf{MSIS}_{q,n_1,m_1+m_2,B}$ *is hard for the bound* $B = 4\eta\sqrt{B_1^2 + B_2^2}$, *where* $\|c\mathbf{m}_1\| \leq B_1, \|c\mathbf{r}_1\| \leq B_2$. *It is computationally hiding under the assumption that* $\mathsf{MLWE}_{q,n_1+n_2,m_2,s_r}$ *is hard.*

D NIZK Proof Π_1

Here, we describe the full proof for the relation R_1. Its security refers to [33].

Let $m = 2\lambda/d$ and $m_1 = 2n + 2\lambda/d + 4 + k_1 + k_2 + k_3$. Let vectors $w = (\mathbf{m}_1, \mathbf{m}_2) \in \mathcal{R}_q^{m_1+n+2}$, where $\mathbf{m}_1$ and $\mathbf{m}_2$ are defined in Section 4. Define a vector $\mathbf{g} = (g_1, \ldots, g_\tau)$ for masking f_j. By linear combination with a tuple of challenge values $(\mu_1, \ldots, \mu_\tau)$, we compile these functions into one:

$$f := \sum_{j=1}^{\tau} \mu_j (g_j + f_j). \tag{3}$$

We define message $\mathbf{m} := (\mathbf{m}_1 \| \mathsf{Inv}(\mathbf{m}_1) \| (\mathbf{m}_2 \| \mathbf{g} \| \mathbf{y}_3 \| \mathbf{y}_4) \| \mathsf{Inv}(\mathbf{m}_2 \| \mathbf{g} \| \mathbf{y}_3 \| \mathbf{y}_4)) \in \mathcal{R}_q^{2m_1+2(n+\tau+512/d)}$. The quadratic Eq. (3) can be written as $\mathbf{m}^\top \mathbf{D}_2 \mathbf{m} + \mathbf{d}_1^\top \mathbf{m} + d_0$. In detail, we set $\mathbf{d}_{2,2}$ to be the second-row block of $\mathbf{D}_2$, and define:

$$\mathbf{D}_2 := \begin{bmatrix} \mathbf{0} \\ \mathbf{d}_{2,2} \\ \mathbf{0} \\ \mathbf{0} \end{bmatrix}, \quad \mathbf{d}_{2,2}^\top := \begin{bmatrix} \sum_{j=1}^{\tau} \mu_j (\gamma_{j,2}) \mathbf{I}_{n+1} & \mathbf{0}_{m_1-n-1} & \\ \mathbf{0}_{n+1} & \sum_{j=1}^{\tau} \mu_j (\gamma_{j,3}) \mathbf{I}_{n+1} & \mathbf{0} \\ \mathbf{0}_{2n+2} & \sum_{j=1}^{\tau} \mu_j (\gamma_{j,1}) \mathbf{I}_{2\lambda/d} & \mathbf{0} \\ \mathbf{0}_{2n+m+2} & \sum_{j=1}^{\tau} \mu_j (\gamma_{j,3}) \mathbf{I}_{k_1+1} & \mathbf{0} \\ & \mathbf{0} & \\ \mathbf{0}_{m_1-k_2-k_3-1} & \sum_{j=1}^{\tau} \mu_j (\gamma_{j,4}) \mathbf{I}_{k_2+k_3+1} & \mathbf{0} \\ & \mathbf{0} & \end{bmatrix}, \tag{4}$$

$$\mathbf{d}_1 := \mathbf{d}_{1,0} + \mathbf{d}_{1,1} + \mathbf{d}_{1,2}, \tag{5}$$

$$\mathbf{d}_{1,0} := \begin{bmatrix} \sum_{j=1}^{\tau} \mu_j \sum_{i=1}^{n} \gamma_{j,i+7+n} \mathbf{a}_i + \sum_{i=1}^{2} \gamma_{j,i+5} 2h_{i,H}^{\mathsf{G}} \\ 0 \\ \sum_{j=1}^{\tau} \mu_j \sum_{i=1}^{n} \gamma_{j,i+7+n} \hat{\mathbf{e}}_i + \sum_{i=1}^{2} \gamma_{j,i+5} 2h_{i,L}^{\mathsf{G}} \\ 0 \\ \sum_{j=1}^{\tau} \mu_j (\gamma_{j,1} \mathbf{1}_{2\lambda/d} + \sum_{i=1}^{n} \gamma_{j,i+7} 2h_{i,H}^{\mathsf{H}_1} + \sum_{i=1}^{k_3} \gamma_{j,i+5} \lfloor \frac{p}{2} \rceil \hat{e}_i) \\ \sum_{j=1}^{\tau} \mu_j (\sum_{i=1}^{k_2} \gamma_{j,i+7+2n} \mathbf{c}_i + \sum_{i=1}^{k_3} \gamma_{j,i+7+2n+k_2} \mathbf{d}_i) \\ 0 \\ \sum_{j=1}^{\tau} \mu_j \sum_{i=1}^{k_2} \gamma_{j,i+7+2n} \hat{\mathbf{e}}_i \\ \sum_{j=1}^{\tau} \mu_j \sum_{i=1}^{k_3} \gamma_{j,i+7+2n+k_2} \hat{\mathbf{e}}_i \\ \mathbf{0}_{m_1+1} \\ \sum_{j=1}^{\tau} \mu_j (\sum_{i=1}^{n} (\gamma_{j,i+7+n} + \gamma_{j,7+i}) \hat{\mathbf{e}}_i \\ \sum_{j=1}^{\tau} \mu_j \sum_{i=1}^{n} \gamma_{j,i+7} 2h_{i,L}^{\mathsf{H}_1} \\ \sum_{j=1}^{\tau} \mu_j \sum_{i=1}^{512} \gamma_{j,i+n+k_2+k_3+5} \hat{\mathbf{e}}_i \\ \vec{\mu} \\ \mathbf{0}_{n+\tau+512/d} \end{bmatrix},$$

$$\mathbf{d}_{1,1} := \begin{bmatrix} \sum_{j=1}^{\tau} \mu_j \sum_{i=1}^{256} \gamma_{j,i+7+2n+k_2+k_3} \mathsf{Inv}(R_{0,j}) \\ \mathbf{0}_{m_1+2(n+\tau+512/d)} \end{bmatrix},$$

$$\mathbf{d}_{1,2} := \begin{bmatrix} \mathbf{0}_{2(n+1)+m+k_1} \\ \sum_{j=1}^{\tau} \mu_j \sum_{i=1}^{256} \gamma_{j,i+7+2n+k_2+k_3+256} \mathsf{Inv}(R_{1,j}) \\ \mathbf{0}_{m_1+2(n+\tau+512/d)} \end{bmatrix},$$

$$\begin{aligned} d_0 := -\sum_{j=1}^{\tau} \mu_j \Big(& h_j + \sum_{i=1}^{n} \gamma_{j,i+7+n} c_i + (\gamma_{j,2} + \gamma_{j,3}) \beta_r^2 + \gamma_{j,4} \beta_v^2 + \gamma_{j,5} \beta_e^2 \\ & + \sum_{i=1}^{k_2} \gamma_{j,i+7+2n} u_i + \sum_{i=1}^{k_3} \gamma_{j,i+7+2n+k_2} v_i + \sum_{i=1}^{256} \gamma_{j,i+7+2n+k_2+k_3} z_{3,i} \\ & + \gamma_{j,i+2n+k_2+k_3+263} z_{4,i} \Big). \end{aligned} \tag{6}$$

Define matrix $\mathbf{F}_y$ and vectors $\mathbf{y}$, $\mathbf{t}_y$ and $\mathbf{z}$:

$$\mathbf{F}_y := \begin{bmatrix} \mathbf{F}_1 \\ \mathbf{F}_g \\ \mathbf{F}_3 \\ \mathbf{F}_4 \end{bmatrix}, \mathbf{y} := \begin{bmatrix} \mathbf{y}_1 \\ \mathsf{Inv}(\mathbf{y}_1) \\ -\mathbf{F}_y \mathbf{y}_2 \\ -\mathsf{Inv}(\mathbf{F}_y \mathbf{y}_2) \end{bmatrix}, \mathbf{t}_y := \begin{bmatrix} \mathbf{t}_F \\ \mathbf{t}_g \\ \mathbf{t}_3 \\ \mathbf{t}_4 \end{bmatrix}, \mathbf{z} := \begin{bmatrix} \mathbf{z}_1 \\ \mathsf{Inv}(\mathbf{z}_1) \\ c\mathbf{t}_y - \mathbf{F}_y \mathbf{z}_2 \\ \mathsf{Inv}(c\mathbf{t}_y - \mathbf{F}_y \mathbf{z}_2) \end{bmatrix}. \tag{7}$$

Now, we describe the full proof, which is non-interactive. For simplicity, we add the number of rounds each time we apply the Fiat-Shamir transform.

$\mathsf{Setup}(1^\lambda)$: On input of λ in unary, choose real numbers s_e, y_1, y_2, y_3, y_4, sample matrices $\mathbf{E}_1 \in \mathcal{R}_q^{n_1 \times m_1}$, $\mathbf{E}_2 \in \mathcal{R}_q^{n_1 \times m_2}$, $\mathbf{F}_1 \in \mathcal{R}_q^{n \times m_2}$, $\mathbf{F}_g \in \mathcal{R}_q^{\tau \times m_2}$, $\mathbf{F}_3 \in \mathcal{R}_q^{(256/d) \times m_2}$, $\mathbf{F}_4 \in \mathcal{R}_q^{(256/d) \times m_2}$, $\mathbf{F}_5 \in \mathcal{R}_q^{3 \times m_2}$, and vector $\mathbf{f}_g \in \mathcal{R}_q^{m_2}$, and define hash functions $\mathsf{H}_1 \colon \{0,1\}^* \to \mathcal{B}^{256 \times (m_1+k_2+k_3)d}$, $\mathsf{H}_2 \colon \{0,1\}^* \to \mathbb{Z}_q^{\tau \times (7+2n+k_2+k_3)}$, $\mathsf{H}_3 \colon \{0,1\}^* \to \mathcal{R}_q^{\tau}$, and $\mathsf{H}_4 \colon \{0,1\}^* \to \mathcal{C}$. Output $\mathsf{crs} := (s_e, y_1, y_2, y_3, y_4, \mathbf{E}_1, \mathbf{E}_2, \mathbf{F}_1, \mathbf{F}_g, \mathbf{F}_3, \mathbf{F}_4, \mathbf{f}_g)$ and the statement $x := (\mathbf{D}, \mathbf{C}, \mathbf{A}, (\mathbf{u}, \mathbf{v}), \mathbf{c}, \mathsf{hk}^{\mathsf{H}_1}, \mathsf{hk}^{\mathsf{G}})$.

$\mathsf{Prove}(\mathsf{crs}, x, w)$: Prover $\mathcal{P}$ performs the following given witness $w = (\mathbf{m}_1, \mathbf{m}_2)$:

1. First round:
   - Sample $\mathbf{r}_1 \leftarrow \mathcal{D}_{s_r}^{m_2}$, and compute $\begin{bmatrix} \mathbf{t}_E \\ \mathbf{t}_F \end{bmatrix} = \begin{bmatrix} \mathbf{E}_1 \\ \mathbf{0} \end{bmatrix} \mathbf{m}_1 + \begin{bmatrix} \mathbf{E}_2 \\ \mathbf{F}_1 \end{bmatrix} \mathbf{r}_1 + \begin{bmatrix} \mathbf{0} \\ \mathbf{m}_2 \end{bmatrix}$.
   - Sample $\mathbf{y}_1 \leftarrow \mathcal{D}_{y_1}^{m_1}$ and $\mathbf{y}_2 \leftarrow \mathcal{D}_{y_2}^{m_2}$ and set $\mathbf{w} := \mathbf{E}_1\mathbf{y}_1 + \mathbf{E}_2\mathbf{y}_2$.
   - Sample $\mathbf{g} \xleftarrow{\$} \{x \in \mathcal{R}_q \colon x_0 = 0\}^{\tau}$ and compute $\mathbf{t}_g := \mathbf{F}_g\mathbf{r}_1 + \mathbf{g}$.
   - Sample $\mathbf{y}_3 \leftarrow \mathcal{D}_{y_3}^{256/d}, \mathbf{y}_4 \leftarrow \mathcal{D}_{y_4}^{256/d}$.
   - Compute $\mathbf{t}_3 := \mathbf{F}_3\mathbf{r}_1 + \mathbf{y}_3, \mathbf{t}_4 := \mathbf{F}_4\mathbf{r}_1 + \mathbf{y}_4$.
2. Second round:
   - Define the commitment $\alpha_1 := (\mathbf{t}_3, \mathbf{t}_4, \mathbf{t}_g, \mathbf{t}_E, \mathbf{t}_F, \mathbf{w})$.
   - Derive the challenge $R = (R_0, R_1) := \mathsf{H}_1(\mathsf{crs}, x, \alpha_1)$.
   - Denote $\mathbf{v}' = (\mathbf{v}_0, \mathbf{v}_1)$.
   - Compute $\vec{z}_3 := R_0\vec{m}_1 + \vec{y}_3$ and $\vec{z}_4 := R_1\vec{v}' + \vec{y}_4$.
   - Run rejection sampling $\mathsf{Rej}(\vec{z}_3, R_0\vec{m}, y_3)$ and $\mathsf{Rej}(\vec{z}_4, R_1\vec{v}', y_4)$.
3. Third round:
   - Define the second response $\alpha_2 := (\vec{z}_3, \vec{z}_4)$.
   - Compute the challenge $\Gamma := [\gamma_{j,i}]_{j \in [\tau], i \in [7+2n+k_2+k_3]} = \mathsf{H}_2(\mathsf{crs}, x, \alpha_1, \alpha_2)$.
   - Compute $h_j := g_j + f_j, \forall j \in [1, \tau]$ with f_j defined in Eq. (2).
4. Fourth round:
   - Define the third response $\alpha_3 := \mathbf{h} = (h_1, \ldots, h_\tau)$.
   - Generate the challenges $\boldsymbol{\mu} = (\mu_1, \ldots, \mu_\tau) := \mathsf{H}_3(\mathsf{crs}, x, \alpha_1, \alpha_2, \alpha_3)$.
   - Compute $f := \sum_{j=1}^{\tau} \mu_j h_j$.
   - Define $\mathbf{D}_2$, $\mathbf{d}_1$, d_0 as in Eqs. (4) to (6).
   - Define $\mathbf{y}$ as in Eq. (7).
   - Compute the garbage term $g_1 := \mathbf{m}^\top \mathbf{D}_2 \mathbf{y} + \mathbf{y}^\top \mathbf{D}_2 \mathbf{m} + \mathbf{d}_1^\top \mathbf{y}$ and its commitment $t := \mathbf{f}_g^\top \mathbf{r}_1 + g_1$.
   - Set $v := \mathbf{y}^\top \mathbf{D}_2 \mathbf{y} + \mathbf{f}_g^\top \mathbf{y}_2$.
5. Fifth round:
   - Define the fourth response $\alpha_4 := (t, v)$.
   - Derive $c := \mathsf{H}_4(\mathsf{crs}, x, \alpha_1, \alpha_2, \alpha_3, \alpha_4)$.
   - Upon challenge c, compute $\mathbf{z}_1 = c\mathbf{m}_1 + \mathbf{y}_1$ and $\mathbf{z}_2 = c\mathbf{r}_1 + \mathbf{y}_2$ and run rejection sampling $\mathsf{Rej}(\mathbf{z}_1, c\mathbf{m}_1, y_1)$ and $\mathsf{Rej}(\mathbf{z}_2, c\mathbf{e}, y_2)$ respectively.
   - Output the proof $\pi_{\mathsf{ct}} := (\alpha_1, \alpha_2, \alpha_3, \alpha_4, \mathbf{z}_1, \mathbf{z}_2)$.

$\mathsf{Verify}(\mathsf{crs}, x, \pi_{\mathsf{ct}})$:

- Parse $\pi_{\mathsf{ct}} := (\mathbf{t}_3, \mathbf{t}_4, \mathbf{t}_g, \mathbf{t}_E, \mathbf{t}_F, \mathbf{w}, \vec{z}_3, \vec{z}_4, \mathbf{h}, t, v, \mathbf{z}_1, \mathbf{z}_2)$.
- Set $\alpha_1 := (\mathbf{t}_3, \mathbf{t}_4, \mathbf{t}_g, \mathbf{t}_E, \mathbf{t}_F, \mathbf{w})$, $\alpha_2 := (\vec{z}_3, \vec{z}_4)$, $\alpha_3 := \mathbf{h}$ and $\alpha_4 := (t, v)$.
- Generate four hash values: $R := \mathsf{H}_1(\mathsf{crs}, x, \alpha_1)$, $\Gamma := \mathsf{H}_2(\mathsf{crs}, x, \alpha_1, \alpha_2)$, $\boldsymbol{\mu} := \mathsf{H}_3(\mathsf{crs}, x, \alpha_1, \alpha_2, \alpha_3)$, and $c := \mathsf{H}_4(\mathsf{crs}, x, \alpha_1, \alpha_2, \alpha_3, \alpha_4)$.
- Define $\mathbf{z}$ as in Eq. (7) and compute $\mathbf{D}_2, \mathbf{d}_1, d_0$ as above.
- Accept if and only if all of the following hold:
  - $\|\mathbf{z}_1\| \leq B_1$, $\|\mathbf{z}_2\| \leq B_2$, $\|\mathbf{z}_3\| \leq B_3$, $\|\mathbf{z}_4\|_\infty \leq B_4$;
  - $\mathbf{E}_1\mathbf{z}_1 + \mathbf{E}_2\mathbf{z}_2 = \mathbf{w} + c\mathbf{t}_E$;
  - $\mathbf{z}^\top \mathbf{D}_2 \mathbf{z} + c\mathbf{d}_1^\top \mathbf{z} + c^2 d_0 - (ct - \mathbf{f}_g^\top \mathbf{z}_2) = v$;
  - constant coefficients of $h_1, \ldots, h_\tau$ are 0s.

E NIZK Proof Π_2

This section describes the full proof for the relation R_2. Let vector $w = \mathbf{m}_1 \in \mathcal{R}_q^{m_1}$, where $m_1 = 4n+7$ for short. For $\mathbf{m} := (\mathbf{m}_1 \| \mathsf{Inv}(\mathbf{m}_1) \| (\mathbf{g} \| \mathbf{y}_3) \| \mathsf{Inv}(\mathbf{g} \| \mathbf{y}_3)) \in \mathcal{R}^{2m_1 + 2\cdot(\tau+2)}$, define $\mathbf{D}_2, \mathbf{d}_1$, and d_0 as follows.

$$\mathbf{D}_2 := \begin{bmatrix} \mathbf{0} \\ \mathbf{d}_{2,2} \\ \mathbf{0} \\ \mathbf{0} \end{bmatrix}, \mathbf{d}_{2,2}^\top := \begin{bmatrix} \sum_{j=1}^{\tau} \mu_j(\gamma_{j,2n+8} - \gamma_{j,2n+7}) & \mathbf{0} \\ 0 & \sum_{j=1}^{\tau} \mu_j(\gamma_{j,2n+2})\mathbf{I}_{n+1}\ \mathbf{0} \\ \mathbf{0}_{n+2} & \sum_{j=1}^{\tau} \mu_j(\gamma_{j,2n+3})\mathbf{I}_{n+1}\ \mathbf{0} \\ \mathbf{0}_{2n+3} & \sum_{j=1}^{\tau} \mu_j(\gamma_{j,2n+4})\mathbf{I}_{n+1}\ \mathbf{0} \\ \mathbf{0}_{3n+4} & \sum_{j=1}^{\tau} \mu_j(\gamma_{j,2n+5})\mathbf{I}_{n+1}\ \mathbf{0} \\ & \mathbf{0} \end{bmatrix}, \quad (8)$$

$$\mathbf{d}_1 := \begin{bmatrix} \sum_{j=1}^{\tau} \mu_j(\gamma_{j,2n+7}\mathbf{1}_2 - \sum_{i=1}^{n}\gamma_{j,i+1+n}t_i) \\ \sum_{j=1}^{\tau} \mu_j \sum_{i=1}^{n}(\gamma_{j,i+1}\mathbf{a}_i + \gamma_{j,1}\mathbf{c}) \\ 0 \\ \sum_{j=1}^{\tau} \mu_j \sum_{i=1}^{n} \gamma_{j,i+1}\hat{\mathbf{e}}_i \\ 0 \\ \sum_{j=1}^{\tau} \mu_j \sum_{i=1}^{n}(\gamma_{j,i+1+n}\mathbf{a}_i + \gamma_{j,1}\mathbf{b}) \\ 0 \\ \sum_{j=1}^{\tau} \mu_j \sum_{i=1}^{n} \gamma_{j,i+1+n}\hat{\mathbf{e}}_i \\ 0 \\ \sum_{j=1}^{\tau} \mu_j\gamma_{j,1} \\ \sum_{j=1}^{\tau} \mu_j\gamma_{j,1} \\ \mathbf{0} \\ \vec{\mu} \\ \mathbf{0}_{\tau+2} \end{bmatrix} + \begin{bmatrix} \sum_{j=1}^{\tau} \mu_j \sum_{i=1}^{256} \gamma_{j,i+n+5}\mathsf{Inv}(R_j) \\ \mathbf{0}_{m_1+2(\tau+2)} \end{bmatrix}, \quad (9)$$

$$d_0 := -\sum_{j=1}^{\tau} \mu_j(h_j + \gamma_{j,1}h + \sum_{i=1}^{n} \gamma_{j,i+1}t_i + \sum_{i=1}^{4} \gamma_{j,i+2n+1}\beta_r^2 + \gamma_{j,2n+6}\beta_e^2 + \gamma_{j,2n+8} + \sum_{i=1}^{256} \gamma_{j,n+4+i}z_{3,i}). \quad (10)$$

Define matrix $\mathbf{F}_y$ and vectors $\mathbf{y}$, $\mathbf{t}_y$, and $\mathbf{z}$:

$$\mathbf{F}_y := \begin{bmatrix}\mathbf{F}_g\\ \mathbf{F}_3\end{bmatrix}, \mathbf{t}_y := \begin{bmatrix}\mathbf{t}_g\\ \mathbf{t}_3\end{bmatrix}, \mathbf{y} := \begin{bmatrix}\mathbf{y}_1\\ \mathsf{Inv}(\mathbf{y}_1)\\ -\mathbf{F}_y\mathbf{y}_2\\ -\mathsf{Inv}(\mathbf{F}_y\mathbf{y}_2)\end{bmatrix}, \mathbf{z} := \begin{bmatrix}\mathbf{z}_1\\ \mathsf{Inv}(\mathbf{z}_1)\\ c\mathbf{t}_y - \mathbf{F}_y\mathbf{z}_2\\ \mathsf{Inv}(\mathbf{t}_y - \mathbf{F}_y\mathbf{z}_2)\end{bmatrix}. \quad (11)$$

Below, we describe the non-interactive proof from the Fiat–Shamir transformation. The verification is consistent with that in Appendix D and is omitted.

$\mathsf{Setup}(1^\lambda)$: On input of λ in unary, choose real numbers s_e, y_1, y_2, y_3, sample matrices $\mathbf{E}_1 \in \mathcal{R}_q^{n_1\times m_1}$, $\mathbf{E}_2 \in \mathcal{R}_q^{n_1\times m_2}$, $\mathbf{F}_g \in \mathcal{R}_q^{\tau\times m_2}$, $\mathbf{F}_3 \in \mathcal{R}_q^{(256/d)\times m_2}$, $\mathbf{F}_4 \in \mathcal{R}_q^{2\times m_2}$, and vector $\mathbf{f}_g \in \mathcal{R}_q^{m_2}$, and define hash functions $\mathsf{H}_1\colon \{0,1\}^* \to \mathcal{B}^{256\times m_1 d}$, $\mathsf{H}_2\colon \{0,1\}^* \to \mathbb{Z}_q^{\tau\times(2n+264)}$, $\mathsf{H}_3\colon \{0,1\}^* \to \mathcal{R}_q^\tau$, $\mathsf{H}_4\colon \{0,1\}^* \to \mathcal{C}$. Output $\mathsf{crs} := (s_e, y_1, y_2, y_3, \mathbf{E}_1, \mathbf{E}_2, \mathbf{F}_g, \mathbf{F}_3, \mathbf{F}_4, \mathbf{f}_g)$ and the statement $x := (h, \mathbf{t}, \mathbf{t}_0, \mathbf{t}_1, \mathbf{c}, \mathbf{b}, \mathbf{A})$.

$\mathsf{Prove}(\mathsf{crs}, x, w = \mathbf{m}_1 := (\nu\|\mathbf{s}\|a_1\|\mathbf{e}\|a_2\|\mathbf{s}_\mathsf{b}\|a_3\|\mathbf{e}_\mathsf{b}\|a_4\|e_3\|a_5) \in \mathcal{R}_q^{4n+7})$:

1. First round:
   - Sample $\mathbf{r}_1 \leftarrow \mathcal{D}_{s_r}^{m_2}$ and compute the commitment $\mathbf{t}_E = \mathbf{E}_1\mathbf{m}_1 + \mathbf{E}_2\mathbf{r}_1$.
   - Sample $\mathbf{y}_1 \leftarrow \mathcal{D}_{y_1}^{m_1}$ and $\mathbf{y}_2 \leftarrow \mathcal{D}_{y_2}^{m_2}$ and set $\mathbf{w} := \mathbf{E}_1\mathbf{y}_1 + \mathbf{E}_2\mathbf{y}_2$.
   - Sample $\mathbf{g} \xleftarrow{\$} \{x \in \mathcal{R}_q\colon x_0 = 0\}^\tau$ and compute $\mathbf{t}_g := \mathbf{F}_g\mathbf{r}_1 + \mathbf{g}$.
   - Sample $\mathbf{y}_3 \leftarrow \mathcal{D}_{y_3}^{256/d}$ and compute $\mathbf{t}_3 := \mathbf{F}_3\mathbf{r}_1 + \mathbf{y}_3$.
2. Second round:
   - Define $\alpha_1 := (\mathbf{t}_3, \mathbf{t}_g, \mathbf{t}_E, \mathbf{w})$, derive challenge $R := \mathsf{H}_1(\mathsf{crs}, x, \alpha_1)$.
   - Compute $\vec{z}_3 := R\vec{m}_1 + \vec{y}_3$ and run rejection sampling $\mathsf{Rej}(\vec{z}_3, R\vec{m}_1, y_3)$.
3. Third round:
   - Define $\alpha_2 := \vec{z}_3$ and compute the challenge $\Gamma := [\gamma_{j,i}]_{j\in[\tau], i\in[2n+264]} = \mathsf{H}_2(\mathsf{crs}, x, \alpha_1, \alpha_2)$.
   - Compute $h_j := g_j + f_j, \forall j \in [1,\tau]$ with f_j defined as $f_j := \sum_{i=1}^{n+4} \gamma_{j,i} G_i$.
4. Fourth round:
   - Define $\alpha_3 := \mathbf{h} = (h_1, \ldots, h_\tau)$.
   - Generate the challenges $\boldsymbol{\mu} = (\mu_1, \ldots, \mu_\tau) := \mathsf{H}_3(\mathsf{crs}, x, \alpha_1, \alpha_2, \alpha_3)$.
   - Compute $f := \sum_{j=1}^{\tau} \mu_j h_j$.
   - Define $\mathbf{D}_2$, $\mathbf{d}_1$, and d_0 as in Eqs. (8) to (10).
   - Define $\mathbf{y}$ as in Eq. (11).
   - Compute the garbage term $g_1 := \mathbf{m}^\top\mathbf{D}_2\mathbf{y} + \mathbf{y}^\top\mathbf{D}_2\mathbf{m} + \mathbf{d}_1^\top\mathbf{y}$ and the commitment $t := \mathbf{f}_g^\top\mathbf{r}_1 + g_1$.
   - Set $v := \mathbf{y}^\top\mathbf{D}_2\mathbf{y} + \mathbf{f}_g^\top\mathbf{y}_2$.
5. Fifth round:
   - Define $\alpha_4 := (t, v)$ and $c := \mathsf{H}_4(\mathsf{crs}, x, \alpha_1, \alpha_2, \alpha_3, \alpha_4)$.
   - Upon challenge c, compute $\mathbf{z}_1 = c\mathbf{m}_1 + \mathbf{y}_1$ and $\mathbf{z}_2 = c\mathbf{r}_1 + \mathbf{y}_2$ and run rejection sampling $\mathsf{Rej}(\mathbf{z}_1, c\mathbf{m}_1, y_1)$ and $\mathsf{Rej}(\mathbf{z}_2, c\mathbf{r}_1, y_2)$, respectively.
   - Output the proof $\pi_{\mathsf{ct}} := (\alpha_1, \alpha_2, \alpha_3, \alpha_4, \mathbf{z}_1, \mathbf{z}_2)$.

F Batching

We first define the following before describing the batch-proof protocol. Let the witness $w = \mathbf{m}_1 := (\vec{\mathsf{b}}\|\mathbf{s}\|a_0\|\mathbf{e}\|a_1\|\mathbf{s}_0\|a_2\|\mathbf{e}_0\|a_3\|\mathbf{s}_1\|a_4\|\mathbf{e}_1\|a_5\|\mathbf{e}_3\|a_6) \in \mathcal{R}_q^{m_1}$, where $m_1 = 6n+7+N$. Define $N+3n+9$ functions $E_1, \ldots, E_{N+3n+9}$ as follows:

$$
\begin{aligned}
&\forall i \in [1, N], E_i = \mathbf{s}^\top \mathbf{c}_i + \mathsf{Inv}(\mathbf{s}_0)^\top \mathbf{b}(1-\mathsf{b}_i) + \mathsf{Inv}(\mathbf{s}_1)^\top \mathbf{b}\mathsf{b}_i + \hat{\mathbf{e}}_i^\top \mathbf{e}_3 - \mathbf{h}_i;\\
&\forall i \in [1, n],\ E_{i+N} = \mathbf{a}_i^\top \mathbf{s}_0 + \hat{\mathbf{e}}_i^\top \mathbf{e}_0 - t_{0,i};\ E_{i+n+N} = \mathbf{a}_i^\top \mathbf{s}_1 + \hat{\mathbf{e}}_i^\top \mathbf{e}_1 - t_{1,i};\\
&\forall i \in [1, n],\ E_{i+2n+N} = \mathbf{a}_i^\top \mathbf{s} + \hat{\mathbf{e}}_i^\top \mathbf{e} - t_i;\\
&\quad E_{1+3n+N} = \mathsf{Inv}(\mathbf{s}\|a_0)^\top (\mathbf{s}\|a_0) - \beta_r^2;\ E_{2+3n+N} = \mathsf{Inv}(\mathbf{s}\|a_1)^\top (\mathbf{s}\|a_1) - \beta_r^2;\\
&\quad E_{3+3n+N} = \mathsf{Inv}(\mathbf{s}_0\|a_0)^\top (\mathbf{s}_0\|a_0) - \beta_r^2;\ E_{4+3n+N} = \mathsf{Inv}(\mathbf{s}_1\|a_1)^\top (\mathbf{s}_1\|a_1) - \beta_r^2;\\
&\quad E_{5+3n+N} = \mathsf{Inv}(\mathbf{e}_0\|a_2)^\top (\mathbf{e}_0\|a_2) - \beta_r^2;\ E_{6+3n+N} = \mathsf{Inv}(\mathbf{e}_1\|a_3)^\top (\mathbf{e}_1\|a_3) - \beta_r^2;\\
&\quad E_{7+3n+N} = \mathsf{Inv}(\mathbf{e}_3\|a_3)^\top (\mathbf{e}_3\|a_3) - N\beta_e^2;\ E_{8+3n+N} = \mathsf{Inv}(\mathbf{1} - \vec{\mathsf{b}})^\top \vec{\mathsf{b}};\\
&\quad E_{9+3n+N} = \mathsf{Inv}(\vec{\mathsf{b}})^\top \vec{\mathsf{b}} - N;
\end{aligned}
$$

where $\mathbf{a}_i, \mathbf{c}_i$ are the i-th column of matrix $\mathbf{A}, \mathbf{C}$; $\mathbf{h}_i, t_i$ denote the i-th entry of $\mathbf{h}, \mathbf{t}$, respectively; $\hat{\mathbf{e}}_i$ is a unit vector $\hat{e}_i$ with its i-th entry being 1.

Define messages: $\mathbf{m} := (\mathbf{m}_1\|\mathsf{Inv}(\mathbf{m}_1)\|(\mathbf{g}\|\mathbf{y}_3)\|\mathsf{Inv}(\mathbf{g}\|\mathbf{y}_3)) \in \mathcal{R}^{2m_1+2\cdot(\tau+2)}$. The quadratic equation can be written as $f := \mathbf{m}^\top \mathbf{D}_2 \mathbf{m} + \mathbf{d}_1^\top \mathbf{m} + d_0$ for the following $\mathbf{D}_2, \mathbf{d}_1, d_0$, where $\tilde{N} = N + 3n$ (as a shorthand used in defining $\mathbf{d}_{2,2}^\top$).

$$
\mathbf{D}_2 := \begin{bmatrix} \mathbf{0} \\ \mathbf{d}_{2,2} \\ \mathbf{0} \\ \mathbf{0} \end{bmatrix}, \mathbf{d}_{2,2}^\top := \begin{bmatrix}
\sum_{j=1}^{\tau} \mu_j(\gamma_{j,\tilde{N}+9} - \gamma_{j,\tilde{N}+8}) & \mathbf{0} & \\
0 & \sum_{j=1}^{\tau} \mu_j \gamma_{j,\tilde{N}+1} \mathbf{I}_{n+1} & \mathbf{0} \\
\mathbf{0}_{n+2} & \sum_{j=1}^{\tau} \mu_j \gamma_{j,\tilde{N}+2} \mathbf{I}_{n+1} & \mathbf{0} \\
\mathbf{0}_{2n+3} & \sum_{j=1}^{\tau} \mu_j \gamma_{j,\tilde{N}+3} \mathbf{I}_{n+1} & \mathbf{0} \\
\mathbf{0}_{3n+4} & \sum_{j=1}^{\tau} \mu_j \gamma_{j,\tilde{N}+4} \mathbf{I}_{n+1} & \mathbf{0} \\
\mathbf{0}_{4n+5} & \sum_{j=1}^{\tau} \mu_j \gamma_{j,\tilde{N}+5} \mathbf{I}_{n+1} & \mathbf{0} \\
\mathbf{0}_{5n+6} & \sum_{j=1}^{\tau} \mu_j \gamma_{j,\tilde{N}+6} \mathbf{I}_{n+1} & \mathbf{0} \\
\mathbf{0}_{6n+7} & \sum_{j=1}^{\tau} \mu_j (\gamma_{j,\tilde{N}+7}) \mathbf{I}_N & \mathbf{0} \\
\sum_{j=1}^{\tau} \mu_j \sum_{i=1}^{N} \gamma_{j,i} \mathbf{b} & \mathbf{0} & \\
-\sum_{j=1}^{\tau} \mu_j \sum_{i=1}^{N} \gamma_{j,i} \mathbf{b} & \mathbf{0} &
\end{bmatrix}, \tag{12}
$$

$$
\mathbf{d}_1 := \begin{bmatrix}
\sum_{j=1}^{\tau} \mu_j \gamma_{j,8+3n+N} \\
\sum_{j=1}^{\tau} \mu_j (\sum_{i=1}^{N} \gamma_{j,i} \mathbf{c}_i + \sum_{i=1}^{n} \gamma_{j,i+N} \mathbf{a}_i) \\
0 \\
\sum_{j=1}^{\tau} \mu_j \sum_{i=1}^{n} \gamma_{j,i+N} \hat{\mathbf{e}}_i \\
0 \\
\sum_{j=1}^{\tau} \mu_j \sum_{i=1}^{n} \gamma_{j,i+n+N} \mathbf{a}_i \\
0 \\
\sum_{j=1}^{\tau} \mu_j \sum_{i=1}^{n} \gamma_{j,i+n+N} \hat{\mathbf{e}}_i \\
0 \\
\sum_{j=1}^{\tau} \mu_j \sum_{i=1}^{n} \gamma_{j,i+2n+N} \mathbf{a}_i \\
0 \\
\sum_{j=1}^{\tau} \mu_j \sum_{i=1}^{n} \gamma_{j,i+2n+N} \hat{\mathbf{e}}_i \\
0 \\
\sum_{j=1}^{\tau} \mu_j \sum_{i=1}^{N} \gamma_{j,i} \hat{\mathbf{e}}_i \\
\mathbf{0}_{m_1+1} \\
\sum_{j=1}^{\tau} \mu_j \sum_{i=1}^{256} \gamma_{j,i+3n+N+8} \hat{\mathbf{e}}_i \\
\vec{\mu} \\
\mathbf{0}_{\tau+2}
\end{bmatrix} + \begin{bmatrix}
\sum_{j=1}^{\tau} \mu_j \sum_{i=1}^{256} \gamma_{j,i+N+n+4} \mathsf{Inv}(R_j) \\
\mathbf{0}_{m_1+2(\tau+2)}
\end{bmatrix}, \tag{13}
$$

$$d_0 := -\sum_{j=1}^{\tau} \mu_j (\sum_{i=1}^{N} \gamma_{j,i}\mathbf{h}_i + \sum_{i=1}^{n} \gamma_{j,N+i} t_i - h_j + \sum_{i=1}^{7} \gamma_{j,N+3n+i}\beta_r^2 + \sum_{i=1}^{n} \gamma_{j,N+n+i} t_{0,i}$$
$$+ \sum_{i=1}^{n} \gamma_{j,N+2n+i} t_{1,i} + \gamma_{j,N+2n+5} N\beta_e^2 + \gamma_{j,N+2n+9} N + \sum_{i=1}^{256} \gamma_{j,2n+5+N+i} z_{3,i}). \tag{14}$$

$\mathsf{Setup}(1^\lambda)$: On input of the security parameter λ in unary, choose real numbers s_e, y_1, y_2, y_3, sample $\mathbf{E}_1 \in \mathcal{R}_q^{n_1 \times m_1}$, $\mathbf{E}_2 \in \mathcal{R}_q^{n_1 \times m_2}$, $\mathbf{F}_g \in \mathcal{R}_q^{\tau \times m_2}$, $\mathbf{F}_3 \in \mathcal{R}_q^{(256/d) \times m_2}$, and $\mathbf{f}_g \in \mathcal{R}_q^{m_2}$. Define hash functions $\mathsf{H}_1 \colon \{0,1\}^* \to \mathcal{B}^{256 \times m_1 d}$, $\mathsf{H}_2 \colon \{0,1\}^* \to \mathbb{Z}_q^{\tau \times (N+3n+9+256)}$, $\mathsf{H}_3 \colon \{0,1\}^* \to \mathcal{R}_q^{\tau}$, and $\mathsf{H}_4 \colon \{0,1\}^* \to \mathcal{C}$. Output $\mathsf{crs} := (\mathbf{E}_1, \mathbf{E}_2, \mathbf{F}_g, \mathbf{F}_3, \mathbf{f}_g)$ and the statement $x := (h, \mathbf{t}, \mathbf{t}_0, \mathbf{t}_1, \mathbf{b}, \mathbf{c}, \mathbf{A})$.

$\mathsf{Prove}(\mathsf{crs}, x, w)$: Given the witness $w = \mathbf{m}_1 := (\vec{\mathsf{b}} \| \mathbf{s} \| a_0 \| \mathbf{e} \| a_1 \| \mathbf{s}_0 \| a_2 \| \mathbf{e}_0 \| a_3 \| \mathbf{s}_1 \| a_4 \| \mathbf{e}_1 \| a_5 \| \mathbf{e}_3 \| a_6) \in \mathcal{R}_q^{m_1}$, prover $\mathcal{P}$ does:

1. First round:
   - Set $\mathbf{m}_1' := (\mathbf{m}_1 \| \mathbf{b})$ and compute the commitment $\mathbf{t}_E = \mathbf{E}_1 \mathbf{m}_1' + \mathbf{E}_2 \mathbf{e}$.
   - Sample $\mathbf{y}_1 \leftarrow \mathcal{D}_{y_1}^{m_1}$ and $\mathbf{y}_2 \leftarrow \mathcal{D}_{y_2}^{m_2}$, and set $\mathbf{w} := \mathbf{E}_1 \mathbf{y}_1 + \mathbf{E}_2 \mathbf{y}_2$.
   - Sample $\mathbf{g} \xleftarrow{\$} \{x \in \mathcal{R}_q \colon x_0 = 0\}^{\tau}$, $\mathbf{r}_1 \leftarrow \mathcal{D}_{s_r}^{m_2}$, and compute $\mathbf{t}_g := \mathbf{F}_g \mathbf{r}_1 + \mathbf{g}$.
   - Sample $\mathbf{y}_3 \leftarrow D_{y_3}^{256/d}$ and compute $\mathbf{t}_3 := \mathbf{F}_3 \mathbf{r}_1 + \mathbf{y}_3$.
2. Second round:
   - Define $\alpha_1 := (\mathbf{t}_3, \mathbf{t}_g, \mathbf{t}_E, \mathbf{w})$, derive challenge $R := \mathsf{H}_1(\mathsf{crs}, x, \alpha_1)$.
   - Compute $\vec{z}_3 := R\vec{m}_1 + \vec{y}_3$ and run rejection sampling $\mathsf{Rej}(\vec{z}_3, R\vec{m}_1, y_3)$.
3. Third round:
   - Define $\alpha_2 := \vec{z}_3$.
   - Derive the challenge $\Gamma = [\gamma_{j,i}]_{j \in [\tau], i \in [N+3n+9+256]}$ from $\mathsf{H}_2(\mathsf{crs}, x, \alpha_1, \alpha_2)$.
   - Compute $h_j := g_j + f_j, \forall j \in [1, \tau]$ where $f_j := \sum_{i=1}^{N+n+4} \gamma_{j,i} E_i$.
4. Fourth round:
   - Define $\alpha_3 := \mathbf{h} = (h_1, \ldots, h_\tau)$.
   - Generate the challenges $\boldsymbol{\mu} = (\mu_1, \ldots, \mu_\tau)$ from $\mathsf{H}_3(\mathsf{crs}, x, \alpha_1, \alpha_2, \alpha_3)$.
   - Compute $f := \sum_{j=1}^{\tau} \mu_j h_j$
   - Define $\mathbf{y}$ as in Eq. (11).
   - Define $\mathbf{D}_2$, $\mathbf{d}_1$, and d_0 as in Eqs. (12) to (14).
   - Compute the garbage term $g_1 := \mathbf{m}^\top \mathbf{D}_2 \mathbf{y} + \mathbf{y}^\top \mathbf{D}_2 \mathbf{m} + \mathbf{d}_1^\top \mathbf{y}$.
   - Compute the commitment $t := \mathbf{f}_g^\top \mathbf{r}_1 + g_1$.
   - Set $v := \mathbf{y}^\top \mathbf{D}_2 \mathbf{y} + \mathbf{f}_g^\top \mathbf{y}_2$.
5. Fifth round:
   - Define $\alpha_4 := (t, v)$ and $c := \mathsf{H}_4(\mathsf{crs}, x, \alpha_1, \alpha_2, \alpha_3, \alpha_4)$.
   - Upon challenge c, compute $\mathbf{z}_1 = c\mathbf{m}_1 + \mathbf{y}_1$ and $\mathbf{z}_2 = c\mathbf{r}_1 + \mathbf{y}_2$ and run rejection sampling $\mathsf{Rej}(\mathbf{z}_1, c\mathbf{m}_1, y_1)$ and $\mathsf{Rej}(\mathbf{z}_2, c\mathbf{r}_1, y_2)$ respectively.
   - Output the proof $\pi_{\mathsf{ct}} := (\alpha_1, \alpha_2, \alpha_3, \alpha_4, \mathbf{z}_1, \mathbf{z}_2)$.

References

1. Ajtai, M.: Generating hard instances of lattice problems (extended abstract). In: Miller, G.L. (ed.) Proceedings of the Twenty-Eighth Annual ACM Symposium on the Theory of Computing, Philadelphia, Pennsylvania, USA, 22-24 May 1996, pp. 99–108. ACM (1996), https://doi.org/10.1145/237814.237838
2. Albrecht, M.R., Davidson, A., Deo, A., Smart, N.P.: Round-optimal verifiable oblivious pseudorandom functions from ideal lattices. In: Garay, J.A. (ed.) PKC 2021. LNCS, vol. 12711, pp. 261–289. Springer, Cham (2021). https://doi.org/10.1007/978-3-030-75248-4_10
3. Albrecht, M.R., Player, R., Scott, S.: On the concrete hardness of learning with errors. J. Math. Cryptol. **9**(3), 169–203 (2015), http://www.degruyter.com/view/j/jmc.2015.9.issue-3/jmc-2015-0016/jmc-2015-0016.xml
4. Amjad, G., Yeo, K., Yung, M.: RSA blind signatures with public metadata. Proc. Priv. Enhancing Technol. **2025**(1), 37–57 (2025). https://doi.org/10.56553/popets-2025-0004
5. Argo, S., Güneysu, T., Jeudy, C., Land, G., Roux-Langlois, A., Sanders, O.: Practical post-quantum signatures for privacy. In: Luo, B., Liao, X., Xu, J., Kirda, E., Lie, D. (eds.) Proceedings of the 2024 on ACM SIGSAC Conference on Computer and Communications Security, CCS 2024, Salt Lake City, UT, USA, 14-18 October 2024, pp. 1523–1537. ACM (2024), https://doi.org/10.1145/3658644.3670297
6. Au, M.H., Susilo, W., Mu, Y., Chow, S.: Constant-size dynamic k-times anonymous authentication. IEEE Syst. J. **7**(2), 249–261 (2013). https://doi.org/10.1109/JSYST.2012.2221931
7. Avanzi, R., et al.: CRYSTALS-Kyber: Algorithm specifications and supporting documentation (2021)
8. Banerjee, A., Peikert, C.: New and improved key-homomorphic pseudorandom functions. In: Garay, J.A., Gennaro, R. (eds.) CRYPTO 2014. LNCS, vol. 8616, pp. 353–370. Springer, Heidelberg (2014). https://doi.org/10.1007/978-3-662-44371-2_20
9. Baum, C., Damgård, I., Lyubashevsky, V., Oechsner, S., Peikert, C.: More efficient commitments from structured lattice assumptions. In: Catalano, D., De Prisco, R. (eds.) SCN 2018. LNCS, vol. 11035, pp. 368–385. Springer, Cham (2018). https://doi.org/10.1007/978-3-319-98113-0_20
10. Ben-Sasson, E., Bentov, I., Horesh, Y., Riabzev, M.: Scalable, transparent, and post-quantum secure computational integrity. IACR Cryptol. ePrint Arch. 2018/046 (2018). http://eprint.iacr.org/2018/046
11. Benhamouda, F., Lepoint, T., Orrù, M., Raykova, M.: Publicly verifiable anonymous tokens with private metadata bit. IACR Cryptol. ePrint Arch. 2022/004 (2022). https://eprint.iacr.org/2022/004
12. Beullens, W., Lyubashevsky, V., Nguyen, N.K., Seiler, G.: Lattice-based blind signatures: short, efficient, and round-optimal. In: Meng, W., Jensen, C.D., Cremers, C., Kirda, E. (eds.) Proceedings of the 2023 ACM SIGSAC Conference on Computer and Communications Security, CCS 2023, Copenhagen, Denmark, 26-30 November 2023, pp. 16–29. ACM (2023), https://doi.org/10.1145/3576915.3616613
13. Bos, J.W., et al.: CRYSTALS - Kyber: a CCA-secure module-lattice-based KEM. In: 2018 IEEE European Symposium on Security and Privacy, EuroS&P 2018, London, United Kingdom, 24-26 April 2018, pp. 353–367. IEEE (2018) .https://doi.org/10.1109/EuroSP.2018.00032

14. Chase, M., Durak, F.B., Vaudenay, S.: Anonymous tokens with stronger metadata bit hiding from algebraic MACs. In: Handschuh, H., Lysyanskaya, A. (eds.) Advances in Cryptology - CRYPTO 2023 - 43rd Annual International Cryptology Conference, CRYPTO 2023, Santa Barbara, CA, USA, 20-24 August 2023, Proceedings, Part II. LNCS, vol. 14082, pp. 418–449. Springer (2023), https://doi.org/10.1007/978-3-031-38545-2_14
15. Chow, S.: Removing escrow from identity-based encryption. In: Jarecki, S., Tsudik, G. (eds.) PKC 2009. LNCS, vol. 5443, pp. 256–276. Springer, Heidelberg (2009). https://doi.org/10.1007/978-3-642-00468-1_15
16. Chow, S.S.M.: New Privacy-Preserving Architectures for Identity-/Attribute-based Encryption. Ph.D. thesis, New York University, USA (2010). https://dl.acm.org/doi/10.5555/2049343
17. Chow, S., Hui, L., Yiu, S.M., Chow, K.P.: Two improved partially blind signature schemes from bilinear pairings. In: Boyd, C., González Nieto, J.M. (eds.) ACISP 2005. LNCS, vol. 3574, pp. 316–328. Springer, Heidelberg (2005). https://doi.org/10.1007/11506157_27
18. Chow, S.S.M., Ma, J.P.K., Yuen, T.H.: Scored anonymous credentials. In: Tibouchi, M., Wang, X. (eds.) Applied Cryptography and Network Security - 21st International Conference, ACNS 2023, Kyoto, Japan, 19-22 June 2023, Proceedings, Part II. LNCS, vol. 13906, pp. 484–515. Springer (2023), https://doi.org/10.1007/978-3-031-33491-7_18
19. Chu, H., Do, K., Hanzlik, L.: On the security of rate-limited Privacy Pass. In: Meng, W., Jensen, C.D., Cremers, C., Kirda, E. (eds.) Proceedings of the 2023 ACM SIGSAC Conference on Computer and Communications Security, CCS 2023, Copenhagen, Denmark, 26-30 November 2023, pp. 2871–2885. ACM (2023), https://doi.org/10.1145/3576915.3616619
20. Davidson, A., Goldberg, I., Sullivan, N., Tankersley, G., Valsorda, F.: Privacy pass: bypassing internet challenges anonymously. Proc. Priv. Enhancing Technol. **2018**(3), 164–180 (2018), https://doi.org/10.1515/popets-2018-0026
21. Ducas, L., Durmus, A., Lepoint, T., Lyubashevsky, V.: Lattice signatures and bimodal gaussians. In: Canetti, R., Garay, J.A. (eds.) CRYPTO 2013. LNCS, vol. 8042, pp. 40–56. Springer, Heidelberg (2013). https://doi.org/10.1007/978-3-642-40041-4_3
22. Ducas, L., Lepoint, T., Lyubashevsky, V., Schwabe, P., Seiler, G., Stehlé, D.: CRYSTALS - Dilithium: Digital signatures from module lattices. IACR Cryptol. ePrint Arch. 2017/633 (2017). http://eprint.iacr.org/2017/633
23. Emura, K., Katsumata, S., Watanabe, Y.: Identity-based encryption with security against the KGC: a formal model and its instantiation from lattices. In: Sako, K., Schneider, S., Ryan, P. (eds.) ESORICS 2019. LNCS, vol. 11736, pp. 113–133. Springer, Cham (2019). https://doi.org/10.1007/978-3-030-29962-0_6
24. Hendrickson, S., Iyengar, J., Pauly, T., Valdez, S., Wood., C.A.: Rate-limited token issuance protocol (2022). https://www.ietf.org/archive/id/draft-ietf-privacypass-rate-limit-tokens-00.txt
25. Henry, R.: Efficient Zero-Knowledge Proofs and Applications. Ph.D. thesis, University of Waterloo, Ontario, Canada (2014). https://hdl.handle.net/10012/8621
26. Jarecki, S., Kiayias, A., Krawczyk, H.: Round-optimal password-protected secret sharing and T-PAKE in the password-only model. In: Sarkar, P., Iwata, T. (eds.) ASIACRYPT 2014. LNCS, vol. 8874, pp. 233–253. Springer, Heidelberg (2014). https://doi.org/10.1007/978-3-662-45608-8_13
27. Jeudy, C., Sanders, O.: Improved lattice blind signatures from recycled entropy (2024). https://eprint.iacr.org/2024/1289

28. Kreuter, B., Lepoint, T., Orrù, M., Raykova, M.: Anonymous tokens with private metadata bit. In: Micciancio, D., Ristenpart, T. (eds.) CRYPTO 2020. LNCS, vol. 12170, pp. 308–336. Springer, Cham (2020). https://doi.org/10.1007/978-3-030-56784-2_11
29. Langlois, A., Stehlé, D.: Worst-case to average-case reductions for module lattices. Des. Codes Cryptogr. **75**(3), 565–599 (2015). https://doi.org/10.1007/s10623-014-9938-4
30. Lu, X., Fan, J., Au, M.H.: Relaxed lattice-based programmable hash functions: New efficient adaptively secure IBEs. IACR Cryptol. ePrint Arch. 2024/1535 (2024). https://eprint.iacr.org/2024/1535
31. Lyubashevsky, V.: Lattice signatures without trapdoors. In: Pointcheval, D., Johansson, T. (eds.) EUROCRYPT 2012. LNCS, vol. 7237, pp. 738–755. Springer, Heidelberg (2012). https://doi.org/10.1007/978-3-642-29011-4_43
32. Lyubashevsky, V., Nguyen, N.K.: BLOOM: bimodal lattice one-out-of-many proofs and applications. In: Agrawal, S., Lin, D. (eds.) Advances in Cryptology - ASIACRYPT 2022 - 28th International Conference on the Theory and Application of Cryptology and Information Security, Taipei, Taiwan, 5-9 December 2022, Proceedings, Part IV. LNCS, vol. 13794, pp. 95–125. Springer (2022). https://doi.org/10.1007/978-3-031-22972-5_4
33. Lyubashevsky, V., Nguyen, N.K., Plançon, M.: Lattice-based zero-knowledge proofs and applications: Shorter, simpler, and more general. In: Dodis, Y., Shrimpton, T. (eds.) Advances in Cryptology - CRYPTO 2022 - 42nd Annual International Cryptology Conference, CRYPTO 2022, Santa Barbara, CA, USA, 15-18 August 2022, Proceedings, Part II. LNCS, vol. 13508, pp. 71–101. Springer (2022). https://doi.org/10.1007/978-3-031-15979-4_3
34. Lyubashevsky, V., Seiler, G., Steuer, P.: The LaZer library: lattice-based zero knowledge and succinct proofs for quantum-safe privacy. In: Luo, B., Liao, X., Xu, J., Kirda, E., Lie, D. (eds.) Proceedings of the 2024 on ACM SIGSAC Conference on Computer and Communications Security, CCS 2024, Salt Lake City, UT, USA, 14-18 October 2024. pp. 3125–3137. ACM (2024). https://doi.org/10.1145/3658644.3690330
35. Ma, J.P.K., Chow, S.S.M.: SMART credentials in the multi-queue of slackness (or Secure management of anonymous reputation traits without global halting). In: 8th IEEE European Symposium on Security and Privacy, EuroS&P 2023, Delft, Netherlands, 3-7 July 2023, pp. 896–912. IEEE (2023). https://doi.org/10.1109/EuroSP57164.2023.00057
36. Ng, L.K.L., Chow, S.S.M., Wong, D.P.H., Woo, A.P.Y.: LDSP: shopping with cryptocurrency privately and quickly under leadership. In: 41st IEEE International Conference on Distributed Computing Systems, ICDCS 2021, Washington DC, USA, 7-10 July 2021. pp. 261–271. IEEE (2021). https://doi.org/10.1109/ICDCS51616.2021.00033
37. Orrù, M.: Revisiting keyed-verification anonymous credentials. IACR Cryptol. ePrint Arch. 2024/1552 (2024). https://eprint.iacr.org/2024/1552
38. Policharla, G., Westerbaan, B., Faz-Hernández, A., Wood, C.A.: Post-quantum Privacy Pass via post-quantum anonymous credentials. IACR Cryptol. ePrint Arch. 2023/414 (2023). https://eprint.iacr.org/2023/414
39. Regev, O.: On lattices, learning with errors, random linear codes, and cryptography. In: Gabow, H.N., Fagin, R. (eds.) Proceedings of the 37th Annual ACM Symposium on Theory of Computing, Baltimore, MD, USA, 22-24 May 2005, pp. 84–93. ACM (2005). https://doi.org/10.1145/1060590.1060603

40. Schwartz, B.M., Salowey, J.A., Wouters, P.: IETF data tracker: Privacy Pass. https://datatracker.ietf.org/wg/privacypass/about
41. Seiler, G.: Faster AVX2 optimized NTT multiplication for ring-LWE lattice cryptography. IACR Cryptol. ePrint Arch. 2018/039 (2018). http://eprint.iacr.org/2018/039
42. Silde, T., Strand, M.: Anonymous tokens with public metadata and applications to private contact tracing. In: Eyal, I., Garay, J.A. (eds.) Financial Cryptography and Data Security - 26th International Conference, FC 2022, Grenada, 2-6 May 2022, Revised Selected Papers. LNCS, vol. 13411, pp. 179–199. Springer (2022). https://doi.org/10.1007/978-3-031-18283-9_9
43. Sui, A.F., et al.: Separable and anonymous identity-based key issuing. In: 11th International Conference on Parallel and Distributed Systems, ICPADS 2005, Fuduoka, Japan, 20-22 July 2005. pp. 275–279. IEEE Computer Society (2005). https://doi.org/10.1109/ICPADS.2005.263
44. Tyagi, N., Celi, S., Ristenpart, T., Sullivan, N., Tessaro, S., Wood, C.A.: A fast and simple partially oblivious PRF, with applications. In: Dunkelman, O., Dziembowski, S. (eds.) Advances in Cryptology - EUROCRYPT 2022 - 41st Annual International Conference on the Theory and Applications of Cryptographic Techniques, Trondheim, Norway, 30 May - 3 June 2022, Proceedings, Part II. LNCS, vol. 13276, pp. 674–705. Springer (2022). https://doi.org/10.1007/978-3-031-07085-3_23
45. Wang, X., Wong, H., Chow, S.: Access control encryption from group encryption. In: Sako, K., Tippenhauer, N.O. (eds.) ACNS 2021. LNCS, vol. 12726, pp. 417–441. Springer, Cham (2021). https://doi.org/10.1007/978-3-030-78372-3_16
46. Yan, Y., Chow, S.S.M., Ng, L.K.L., Wong, H.W.H., Zhao, Y., Wang, B.: Batch anonymous MAC tokens from lattices. https://github.com/YanYingfei/KVAT (2025), source code

Author Index

A
Aikawa, Yusuke I-104
Aragon, Nicolas II-267
Aulbach, Thomas I-199

B
Bambury, Henry II-153
Battagliola, Michele I-129
Benedikt, Barbara Jiabao II-231
Bhasin, Shivam II-294
Borin, Giacomo I-129
Boudgoust, Katharina I-255

C
Caminata, Alessio I-35
Campos, Fabio I-199
Cartor, Ryann I-35
Celi, Sofia I-165
Chakraborty, Anirban II-351
Chatterjee, Ayantika II-351
Chattopadhyay, Anupam II-294
Chaturvedi, Bhuvnesh II-351
Chow, Sherman S. M. I-349
Clermont, Sebastian I-278
Couvreur, Alain I-3

D
Das, Sayan II-294
Di Crescenzo, Giovanni I-129
Düzlü, Samed I-278

E
Escudero, Daniel I-165

F
Furue, Hiroki I-104

G
Gaborit, Philippe II-267
Gangopadhyay, Aditi Kar I-312
Gangopadhyay, Sugata I-312
Godard, Julie II-267
Gu, Dawu II-119

H
Hövelmanns, Kathrin II-325

J
Janson, Christian I-278
Jao, David II-38
Jap, Dirmanto II-294

K
Keller, Hannah I-255
Krämer, Juliane I-199
Kudinov, Mikhail II-325
Kudo, Momonari II-3
Kumar, Vikas I-312

L
Loiseau, Antoine II-267

M
Maillard, Julien II-267
Meneghetti, Alessio I-35, I-129
Mishra, Nimish II-351
Mokrani, Youcef II-38
Mora, Rocco I-35
Mukhopadhyay, Debdeep II-351

N
Ng, Lucien K. L. I-349
Nguyen, Phong Q. II-153
Niot, Guilhem I-165
Nowakowski, Julian I-71
Nuida, Koji II-3

O
Ohashi, Ryo II-3, II-89
Onuki, Hiroshi II-3, II-89

R. Niederhagen and M.-J. O. Saarinen (Eds.): PQCrypto 2025, LNCS 15577, pp. 385–386, 2025.
https://doi.org/10.1007/978-3-031-86599-2

P
Paiva, Thales B. II-294
Pellegrini, Alex I-35, II-176
Persichetti, Edoardo I-129
Porzenheim, Laurens I-278
Pouly, Amaury II-63
Pratihar, Rakhi I-3

R
Ran, Lars I-232
Ravi, Prasanna II-294
Raya, Ali I-312

S
Shen, Yixin II-63
Struck, Patrick I-278
Sui, Han II-195

T
Tanısalı, Nihan I-3
Trimoska, Monika I-232

V
Vorstermans, Marc II-176

W
Wang, Baocang I-349
Wang, Geng II-119
Wong, Harry W. H. I-349
Wu, Wenling II-195

X
Xia, Wenwen II-119

Y
Yan, Yingfei I-349
Yoshizumi, Ryo II-3

Z
Zappatore, Ilaria I-3
Zhang, Mengyuan II-195
Zhao, Yongjun I-349

Made in the USA
Monee, IL
03 May 2026

49438503R00221